BRITISH
LITERARY
MAGAZINES

HISTORICAL GUIDES TO THE WORLD'S PERIODICALS AND NEWSPAPERS

This series provides historically focused narrative and analytical profiles of periodicals and newspapers with accompanying bibliographical data.

Black Journals of the United States
Walter C. Daniel

Mystery, Detective, and Espionage Magazines
Michael L. Cook

American Indian and Alaska Native Newspapers and Periodicals
Daniel F. Littlefield, Jr., and James W. Parins

Children's Periodicals of the United States
R. Gordon Kelly, editor

British Literary Magazines: The Augustan Age and the Age of Johnson, 1698-1788
Alvin Sullivan, editor

British Literary Magazines: The Romantic Age, 1789-1836
Alvin Sullivan, editor

BRITISH LITERARY MAGAZINES

The Victorian and Edwardian Age, 1837–1913

Edited by
Alvin Sullivan

Historical Guides to the World's Periodicals and Newspapers

Greenwood Press
Westport, Connecticut • London, England

Library of Congress Cataloging in Publication Data
(Revised for volume 3)
Main entry under title:

British literary magazines.
  (Historical guides to the world's periodicals and
newspapers)
  Includes bibliographies and indexes.
  Contents: [1] The Augustan age and the age of Johnson,
1698-1788—[2] The romantic age, 1789-1836—[3] The
Victorian and Edwardian Age, 1837-1913.
    1. English periodicals—History. 2. Literature—
Periodicals—History. 3. English literature—Periodicals
—History. I. Sullivan, Alvin. II. Series.
PN5124.L6B74 1983   820′.8   82-21136
ISBN 0-313-22871-X (v. 1 : lib. bdg.)
ISBN 0-313-24335-2 (v. 3 : lib. bdg.)

Library of Congress Catalog Card Number: 82-21136
ISBN: 0-313-24335-2

First published in 1984

Greenwood Press
A division of Congressional Information Service, Inc.
88 Post Road West
Westport, Connecticut 06881

Printed in the United States of America

10 9 8 7 6 5 4 3 2 1

Contents

Preface

British Literary Magazines: The Victorian and Edwardian Age, 1837–1913, continues a four-part reference guide to literary magazines from 1698 to the mid-1980s. The first two parts, published in 1983, are *The Augustan Age and the Age of Johnson, 1698–1788* and *The Romantic Age, 1789–1836*. The present part covers the years from Victoria's accession to the throne until the outbreak of World War I. The fourth part will treat *The Modern Age* from 1914 to 1984. The first two parts profile nearly 200 titles and treat another 183 in appendixes, while this volume provides essays on 90 titles and lists 209 others in appendixes.

For every one hundred or so titles profiled in this part and especially in the next part, another two hundred might easily have been added. The proliferation of magazines and books in the nineteenth century—made possible by such technology as web presses that reduced costs and a universal education act that dramatically increased the reading public—was only a forerunner of the phenomenon of exponential growth in the twentieth century.

Our aim in *The Victorian and Edwardian Age*, as in the preceding two parts, has been to reflect the variety of magazines by selecting representative titles. From the many new "shilling monthlies," we profile both the popular *Sharpe's London Magazine* (and trace its attempts to carve out its slice of a burgeoning lower-middle-class audience for literary entertainment) and the more seriously literary *Cornhill*. Literary movements spawned a number of new magazines; two titles—*Arrow* and *Samhain*—treat, for example, the Irish National Theatre, while others represent the Aesthete and Decadent schools. Some magazines that we include began as organs for political or religious groups but transcended their mission and became literary, such as the *Contemporary Review*, the *New Age*, the *Nineteenth Century*, the *North British Review*, and *St. Martin's Review*. Some avowedly literary magazines have been omitted because their appeal was so narrow that they neither flourished in their own time nor gained prominence in retrospect. Some large-circulation magazines, such as *Harmsworth's*, are excluded in favor of others that better indicate Victorian literary tastes—*Windsor* and *Pearson's*, for example. Other titles only peripherally literary, such as *Vanity Fair*, are featured because of their effect on literary efforts, while others belong here as records of the profession of letters—notably, the *Author* and the *Bookseller*. Copies of two titles that we originally planned to profile—the 1892–1911 *Isis* and the 1907–1914 *Orpheus*, a Theosophical Society journal—were found to be unavailable even at such bastions of culture as the Bodleian and British libraries. Finally, one title remains so important that to attempt a profile seemed futile: the venerable *Times Literary Supplement*, technically not a magazine but practically the archetypal modern review, would require several volumes to trace its contributions to a dozen fields. From the thousands of titles in the nineteenth and twentieth centuries, we have, then, profiled the ones that seem most likely to be cited in literary histories, added several popular titles that reveal the reading taste of the growing Victorian middle class (including that of a growing feminine audience), and listed in Appendixes F,G, and H specialized magazines (foreign, comic, and religious) whose contents attracted a literary audience.

The number of editorial options for the Victorian Age is exacerbated by the pluralism of the period. Of the four periods covered by *British Literary Magazines*, the Romantic Age is the only one adequately subsumed by its rubric— an age when a literary and philosophical movement embraced all the social and political issues of the time. The Victorian and Edwardian rubrics derive only from the rulers who governed over nearly a century of transition, one without a literary or philosophical "frame." (See Appendix E for a chronology of social and literary events.) Much of the century borrowed forms that did not fit substance. Especially in poety, "decayed" romantic forms served as a bulwark against the "new science" of Charles Lyell, Charles Darwin, and later, Sigmund Freud. Prose fiction struggled more vigorously to accommodate realism—as George Eliot advocated in the *Westminster Review*, John Forster in the *Examiner*, and G. H. Lewes in the *Leader*—and by century's end it had yielded to naturalism. Poetry followed contradictory impulses, as the Georgians filled the *Blue Review* and the early symbolists found room in the even more ephemeral *Green Sheaf*.

The "dissociation of sensibilities" that the Modern Age accepted, the growing Victorian reading public usually tried to ignore. For the new industrial lower classes there developed a new genre of "penny dreadfuls," of tawdry subjects produced on cheap paper. Even the new literary magazines that appeared at midcentury appealed largely to a middle class that wanted to be entertained, not confronted with contemporary issues: *Ainsworth's*, *All the Year Round*, the *Cornhill*, *Douglas Jerrold's Shilling Magazine*, *Good Words*, *Hood's*, *Macmillan's*, *Pearson's*, and *Sharpe's London*. They joined the very large number of titles from the Romantic Age that flourished throughout the Victorian period by allotting more space to long fiction and illustrations than to poetry or to political and cultural essays: the *Athenaeum*, *Blackwood's*, *Edinburgh Review*, *Fraser's*, and *Westminster*. Filling their pages frequently were romances dealing with English history, escapist tales, or translations from Alexandre Dumas or George

Sand or other romantics. The reading public rewarded these magazines with phenomenal sales; their most popular novelist, Charles Dickens, reported a circulation of 300,000 for *All the Year Round*, which serialized his *Great Expectations*, Wilkie Collins's *Moonstone*, and Charles Reade's *Hard Cash*. Of course, the number of such popular titles was disproportionate to the number of more overtly literary or artistic magazines that sought a narrower audience: the *Germ*, the *Oxford and Cambridge*, or the *Reader*, for example. But none of these lasted for more than four years, the *Germ* for only six months. The failure of these coterie publications and the success of popular fiction magazines indicate a trend that the twentieth century would confirm. Established magazines like *Macmillan's* and the *Saturday Reivew*, representing the conservative upper class and eschewing popular taste, had folded by 1905 and 1933, respectively. Only a half dozen or so large-circulation, advertisement-supported literary magazines survive in the Modern Age, while the number of subsidized "little magazines" requires a monthly journal of bibliography just to keep track of them.

Christopher Kent, in the introduction that follows, discusses in detail the social forces, technological permutations, and economic policies that produced this phenomenon. The ninety profiles in this volume not only suggest the variety of this long age of transition, but provide details about strong-willed authors and publishers of this period that literary biographies often overlook. The relationships of Richard Bentley, Henry Colburn, and Charles Dickens, for example, are amply discussed by Roger Wallins in his entry on *Bentley's Miscellany*; Dickens's quarrel with the publishers Bradbury and Evans is touched upon in J. Don Vann's essay on *All the Year Round*; and John Murray's quarrel with *Academy* editor Charles Appleton is a subject for Christopher Kent's essay. John Morley's infamous review of Algernon Charles Swinburne's *Poems and Ballads* in the *Saturday Review*, the attacks by the Whiggish *North British* on John Stuart Mill and on the Spasmodics, and James Martineau's attacks on his sister Harriet's literary production in the *Prospective Review*—she refused to speak to him for the rest of her life—all enliven the profiles in this part of *British Literary Magazines*.

Each profile in *British Literary Magazines* focuses on the most important contributions or literary contents of the subject magazine. For a few titles, such as the *English Review*, literary importance may be indicated merely by a listing of contributors: Conrad, Ford, Lawrence, James, Hardy, Tolstoy, Pound. Authors of such profiles can do little more than survey the contents or discuss a few representative issues, and readers are referred to longer studies of these more prominent magazines. For many magazines, however, the profile in this volume will be the first to examine its literary importance directly. Almost all of the titles profiled here have been examined in other works, at least peripherally, a situation that was not the case with the earlier parts of this reference work. However, literary history often focuses on movements of which magazines were only representative, such as socialism and the *New Statesman* or the Metaphysical Society and the *Nineteenth Century*, or on editors who were more important than their magazines, as with Henry Labouchere of *Truth* or Oscar Wilde of

Woman's World. The greatest value of *British Literary Magazines*, then, owes not to the treatment of ephemeral or hard-to-locate magazines (with such exceptions as *The Golden Hynde* or *Wales*) nor the inclusion, in most cases, of new information about them. Readers will find it useful, rather, for its relative thoroughness of contents, its concise histories, its literary focus, and the bibliographic details for each title.

Each profile concludes with sections in which data on Information Sources and Publication History are provided in tabular form. The section on Information Sources gives bibliographic information, index sources, reprint sources, and location sources. The section on Publication History lists title changes and alternative titles, volume and issue data, publisher and place of publication, and editors.

The Information Sources have been supplied by the authors of essays and verified in the *National Union Catalog* and the *British Museum Catalogue of Printed Books* (vols. 184–86), the catalogues of microform reprints by University Microfilms International, Ward's *Finding List of Serials*, the *Wellesley Index to Victorian Periodicals*, Poole's *Index to Periodical Literature*, the *British Union Catalogue of Periodicals*, and the *Union List of Serials*. The last three are frequently unreliable, and where additional information (from Ward's *Findings List* or authors' sources) is given, we have relied on that. If, for example, authors advise that only a partial run may be found at "Xy" though the *ULS* lists a complete run there, we have indicated a partial run. (We cite "British Museum" rather than "British Library," except when the Newspaper Library at Colindale is given as a location.) In most cases, however, for locations we have had to rely on the *BUCOP* and the *ULS* listings. We have also relied extensively on the *BUCOP* to list reprint editions. For reprint microforms, we have also searched the 1982 *Guide to Reprints* and the *Guide to Microforms in Print*; the latter lacks many titles that we found in reprint house catalogues, notably that of University Microfilms International, and should not be regarded as an authoritative source. We have tried to list all the index sources and reprints available, but given the vagaries of publishing history over the centuries, others undoubtedly remain to be discovered. For a more accurate listing of location sources than Ward's, the *BUCOP* and the *ULS*, Richard Fulton is presently preparing a findings list for literary periodicals.

Indexes are listed only if the magazine is completely indexed by author, title, and/or subject, either internally or in a separate publication. Items from some magazines have been included in special indexes. For example, Donald Reiman's *The Romantics Reviewed* includes all reviews of Romantic works published in magazines. Such specialized or partial indexes are not listed, since they usually cover a narrow part of the magazines' contents.

Reprints are listed by date only when the title remains unchanged; the city is London if no other is given. If publishers have given editions, we have listed them with dates. Many editions may be facsimiles, but not described as such.

Most microform editions are by University Microfilms International, and are catalogued in one of two series, Early British Periodicals or English Literary Periodicals. We have identified series and reel numbers from catalogues. When other sources report UMI reprints that we have not found in catalogues, we list only UMI.

Location sources are listed by complete and partial runs and by reprints, when that information is available. If a title is held by ten or more libraries, we report it as "widely available," and users should consult the *Union List of Serials* and *National Union Catalog* for American holdings, the *British Union Catalogue of Periodicals* for holdings in the United Kingdom, and Ward's *Finding List of Serials* for additional locations.

The following information is also helpful for users of this work:

When the magazine being discussed is cited, the citation is given in the text in parentheses by volume and page or by number and page, unless a note specifies another system of citation. When another source is cited, the citation is given in a numbered note at the end of the profile.

When magazines spanned two or more eras, they are assigned to parts of *British Literary Magazines* according to the year in which they began publication:

1698–1788	*The Augustan Age and the Age of Johnson (AAAJ)*
1789–1836	*The Romantic Age (RA)*
1837–1913	*The Victorian and Edwardian Age (VEA)*
1914–1984	*The Modern Age (MA)*

There is only one entry for magazines spanning two or more ages, with the exception of five titles. The longevity of these five and their literary importance call for entries in both the age in which they began publication and the *Modern Age: Blackwood's Edinburgh Magazine (RA, MA), Contemporary Review (VEA, MA), Cornhill Magazine (VEA, MA), Fortnightly Review (VEA, MA),* and *Quarterly Review (RA, MA)*. Appendixes A, B, C, and D, which list the titles included in *The Augustan Age and the Age of Johnson,* in *The Romantic Age,* in *The Victorian and Edwardian Age,* and in *The Modern Age,* will help those who are not certain when a magazine began publication to locate specific profiles.

The inclusion of cross-references within the text provides further access to the profiles. An asterisk following a periodical title mentioned in the text indicates that the periodical has been profiled in *British Literary Magazines.* In some cases a *see* reference to another part of *British Literary Magazines* appears after the asterisk, for example, "*Cornhill Magazine* (see *VEA*)." An asterisk not followed by a *see* reference indicates that the profile appears in this part of *British Literary Magazines.* When a magazine began publication close to the end of an age or is more in spirit with the preceding or the following age, thus making it likely that a reader might look under the wrong age for a profile, there is an entry providing a cross-reference to the proper part of *British Literary Magazines*; for example:

WESTMINSTER REVIEW. See RA.

Finally, when a magazine underwent title changes, cross-references are provided to the title the magazine is discussed under.

Errata

It has been discovered since the publication of *The Romantic Age* volume that incorrect location sources were given for the *Inquirer* (1814–1815). The *Inquirer* is available only at the Bodleian Library; the erroneous other listings are the fault, not of the contributor, Keith Wilson, but of the editor. Also in *The Romantic Age*, the *London Magazine* new series should read volumes 1–10, January 1825–March 1828; and Bertrand Goldgar reports that the *Covent-Garden Journal* has a complete run in America only at the University of Texas, Austin, Library and a partial run at the University of Illinois Library, while in Britain there is a complete run only at the Cambridge University Library and partial runs may be found at the Bodleian Library, British Museum, London Library, and the University of London Library.

The editor welcomes further additions or corrections.

Alvin Sullivan

Introduction

Of no time or place can it be said that periodicals had greater cultural impact than they had on Victorian Britain. The sheer numbers overwhelm—over 50,000 individual titles according to the latest estimate.[1] The greater proportion of these would not be judged literary by most definitions, but one is still left with an astonishing number that carried at least some reviews, reflective prose, poetry, or fiction. Recent scholarship has brought home to us very forcibly that Victorian Britain was above all a journalizing society. But the *locus classicus* of scholarship is still Matthew Arnold's "The Function of Criticism at the Present Time" (1864), which noted the excessive sectarianism, provincialism, and partisanship of Victorian literary periodicals and lamented the absence of any authoritative mainstream or national school of criticism. Current research at once illustrates the point by illuminating many of the journals Arnold had in mind but qualifies his indictment by showing that the diversity generated more light and less heat than Arnold admits.[2] By lifting the veil of anonymity, the work of Walter Houghton and his associates has made plain the existence of a body of professional critics and reviewers whose work appeared in a variety of places. G. H. Lewes, for example, radical and free-thinker though he was, published in the Tory (radical-Romantic wing) *Blackwood's** (see *RA, MA*), the Whiggish *Edinburgh Review** (see *RA*), the smart, establishment intellectual *Saturday Review** and *Pall Mall Gazette*, and the respectable, family-oriented *Cornhill Magazine*,* as well as in the liberal-radical *Westminster Review** (see *RA*), and *Leader.** W. R. Greg, Leslie Stephen, R. H. Hutton, and Arnold himself similarly wrote for a wide spectrum of journals whose conventional sectarian or political labels can be misleading guides to their contents. This diversity enabled writers to target their works by choosing their audiences, though of course the readerships had significant overlaps.

Anonymity was an important factor. It was the general rule in journalism up to the 1860s, when a new generation of magazines—such as *Macmillan's*,* the *Cornhill*, the *Contemporary Review*,* and more self-consciously the *Fortnightly*

*Review** and later the *Nineteenth Century**—began to repudiate the practice. The advantages and disadvantages of anonymity were thoroughly debated during the mid-Victorian years.[3] Its defenders argued that anonymity made it easier for unknown writers to get a start, insuring that articles were more likely to be judged on intrinsic merit than on expectations created by reputation or its absence. It enabled professional men, notably barristers and civil servants, to express their views and supplement their incomes without jeopardizing their professional prospects. (Briefless barristers like Fitzjames Stephen did not wish to advertise the fact that they had so much time on their hands.)

Anonymity gave greater freedom and authority to editors in shaping a journal's identity and giving it a distinctive style or tone. Both John Morley and Leslie Stephen complained of the constraints such a house style could impose on the journalist in the case of the closely edited *Saturday Review*. Yet anonymity could also liberate the journalist, enabling him or her to adopt various personas, to experiment more freely. The golden age of creative anonymity came in the earlier years of *Blackwood's* under John Gibson Lockhart and John Wilson's "Christopher North," and of *Fraser's Magazine** (see *RA*) with its fictitious editor "Oliver Yorke." Thomas Carlyle, whose *Past and Present* first appeared in *Fraser's*, continued to find freedom by using fictitious editors and other intervening figures as personas in the early *Blackwood's/Fraser's* style in many of his later, nonjournalistic works.

Opponents of anonymity, on the other hand, argued that it hindered the emergence of a publicly recognized profession of journalism and encouraged irresponsibility among reviewers who were not publicly accountable by name. Certainly it was more conducive to literary vendettas, as in Fitzjames Stephen's "double reviewing" of Dickens,[4] or E. A. Freeman's journalistic persecution of his fellow historian J. A. Froude. However, the growing trend toward signature owed most, one suspects, to an increasingly liberal-democratic intellectual climate emphasizing openness and individualism in the Millite sense, and to a more sophisticated notion of "public opinion." There was also editorial recognition of the circulation-enhancing advantages of "big name" journalism, most plainly in the case of James Knowles's *Nineteenth Century*, where Gladstone published regularly during his intervals out of office. This publicly set the seal on higher journalism as fully compatible with the status of gentlemen. The famous duels involving the early editors of *Blackwood's* and *Fraser's* stemmed not only from the protective (and irresponsible) aspect of anonymity, but from the gentlemanly code itself, which evolved considerably during the Victorian era to accommodate itself to the widening of the public sphere of life.

The respectability of journalism can be exaggerated, however. While the sort of fashion-scandal journalism exemplified by the *Age*, the *Satirist** (see *RA*), and the early *John Bull** (see *RA*) had effectively died out by the late 1840s, even before the passage of the Obscene Publications Act of 1857, there continued to be a flourishing lower world of journals not to be neglected by the literary scholar or the social historian. Even before the abolition of the so-called taxes on knowledge—the removal of the last penny of the newspaper stamp duty and the advertising tax in 1855, and of the paper duties in 1861—journals such as *Lloyd's Penny Weekly* (1843) and *Reynold's Miscellany* (1847) won massive circulations with their emphasis on sensational crime stories and court reports, and equally sensational novels that must fall under any sociological definition of literature.

The advances in printing technology, notably the web rotary press (introduced by Edward Lloyd in 1856) and hot metal typesetting (1885), also had the greatest impact on periodicals with the largest circulations rather than on literary magazines with more limited circulations; even here, though, some price reduction occurred, the quality shilling magazine of the 1860s being about half the price of its equivalents of the 1830s and 1840s.

Entrepreneurial efforts to expand existing markets and to identify or create new ones ensured that the Victorian periodical press covered the widest spectrum of taste and education, but the profit motive was not the only force at work. Through Charles Knight the Society for the Diffusion of Useful Knowledge launched the illustrated weekly *Penny Magazine* (1832) to provide cheap, "improving" reading to the masses: its circulation briefly exceeded 200,000.[5] Religiously oriented journals like the *Servant's Magazine* (1837), often paid for by concerned employers, could hardly compete in appeal with the unsubsidized, unimproving reading on which servants spent their own pennies.[6] However, the lessening of evangelical distrust of fiction and a growing awareness of its didactic potential saw the emergence of more respectable cheap weekly magazines of wide appeal, such as the *Family Herald* (1842) and *Leisure Hour* (published by the Religious Tract Society, 1852), though here the readership extended firmly into the middle class. These journals were also important as a market for the many forgotten women novelists who specialized in producing innocuous "Sunday reading." Also worth mentioning are the juvenile magazines *Boys of England* (1866), *Boy's Own Paper* (1879), and *Girl's Own Paper* (1880). These and many other journals launched the reading careers of many whose tastes subsequently extended to "higher" literature (and many more whose tastes never changed). Charles Dickens, after all, cut his teeth as a boy on the bloodcurdling sensations of the *Terrific Register*.[7]

Dickens's own connections with magazines are well known, from the first *Sketches by Boz* to his editorship (and substantial ownership) of *Household Words** (1850) and *All the Year Round** (1859). Serial publication in magazines helped to bring him not just his huge readership, but the immediate relationship with them that he closely monitored through the fluctuations of weekly sales, which peaked with his famous Christmas issues. Less familiar is the pioneering role of Captain Frederick Marryat, owner-editor of the *Metropolitan Magazine** (1831) (see *RA*), which was the first magazine to depend almost entirely on the work of a single writer, Marryat himself.[8] Another energetic novelist-entrepreneur was Harrison Ainsworth, who at one time or another owned and edited *Bentley's Miscellany** (1837) and the *New Monthly Magazine** (1814) (see *RA*) as well as *Ainsworth's Magazine** (1842) while cranking out the fictions whose popularity for a while rivaled Dickens's. The man who introduced both Ouida and Mrs. Henry Wood to the Victorian magazine reading public was no mean judge of popular taste. These and other monthly magazines of the 1830s–1850s had sales usually well below 10,000 and did not reach the audiences of the cheaper weeklies, which relied more heavily on fiction, larded with the "slice of life" reportage specialized in by Dickens's young men—talented journalists such as John Hollingshead, Edmund Yates, and G. A. Sala.

The high tide of serial fiction came in the 1860s with the emergence of a new generation of monthlies led by *Macmillan's* (1859) but best exemplified by the *Cornhill* (1860), which initially attained a sale of over 80,000 under the aegis of William Makepeace Thackeray as editor, before falling back to a figure nearer 20,000. The new formula of these magazines was respectable middle-class family reading of the highest quality, a mixture of good serial novels and intelligent, instructive articles on noncontroversial subjects—though usually a vaguely liberal tone prevailed. *Macmillan's* and Anthony Trollope's *St. Paul's** (1867) tended to rather more serious subjects. Of somewhat lower literary quality, appealing perhaps to a less well educated stratum of the middle class, were G. A. Sala's *Temple Bar** (1860), Mrs. Henry Wood's *Argosy* (1865), Mrs. Braddon's *Belgravia** (1866), and Edmund Yates's *Tinsley's Magazine** (1867). These were, as the names of their editors suggest, important vehicles for the sensational novels of the 1860s and 1870s and another major marketplace for women authors who specialized in that genre. A major feature of practically all these journals was their use of woodcut illustrations or plates to accompany their fiction. Illustrations had been used since the 1830s, though not widely, but the work of the artists of the 1860s arguably represents the zenith of the English school of black-and-white illustration.[9] Artists of the calibre of John Millais, Frederick Leighton, Frederick Sandys, and Arthur Boyd Houghton did not find it beneath their dignity to do this sort of work.

The greater immediacy of reader response provided by serial publication entailed a greater sensitivity to the sensibilities, real or imagined, of the readership. This raises the question of censorship.[10] Examples are numerous: Charles Kingsley's abrupt conclusion of *Yeast* at the request of the nervous owner-editor of *Fraser's Magazine* in 1848; Thackeray's apologetic refusals as *Cornhill* editor of works by Mrs. Browning and Anthony Trollope on the grounds that they might just bring a blush to the cheek of one of his readers; Thomas Hardy's troubles with various magazine editors, including Thackeray's successor, Leslie Stephen, in trying to publish his novels as he wrote them, and his acquiescence in such pathetic substitutions as "sentimental" for "amorous," not to mention more severe bowdlerization. Yet it is perhaps unfair to lay too much blame at the door of the magazine editors, who in many cases were subordinate to the commercial nervousness of their publishers. Trollope, if turned down by the evangelical *Good Words** (1860) on account of his clerical portraits, could after all look elsewhere, though his notorious hard-headedness perhaps led him to wonder whether 100,000-plus readers (the journal's impressive circulation) *could* be wrong. How much self-censorship was produced by this climate cannot be estimated, but the breadth of appeal consciously sought by Victorian novelists, and so much a strength of the greatest of them, necessarily had its price. And, after all, there were other forms of commercial censorship as well, not least among them such powerful institutions as Mudie's Select Lending Library and W. H. Smith, the bookseller. The positive contribution of the magazines to the vitality and immediacy of Victorian fiction surely outweighs such negatives.

To move up to the highest intellectual (and social) level, the great pre-Victorian quarterlies still enjoyed considerable prestige, though their circulations were at best static: the *Quarterly Review** (see *RA, MA*) around eight thousand, the *Edinburgh Review* around seven thousand in the 1860s.[11] They comfortably overshadowed their younger rivals by sheer subscriber loyalty and better rates of pay to contributors. A few of the junior quarterlies briefly achieved eminence, notably the *North British Review** (1844) and the *National Review** (1855), but the very rationale of this periodical genre came under challenge in the mid-Victorian period. Most of the junior quarterlies died off and virtually no new ones were founded after about 1860, except the purely academic journals which are now practically the sole adherents to this publication cycle.

The year 1860 saw the beginning of the new generation of quality monthlies, which often carried articles of equivalent intellectual calibre to the quarterlies', often better written as well. But there also emerged the more direct competition of a new generation of self-consciously serious journals, notably the *Fortnightly Review* (1865) and the *Contemporary Review* (1866). The stately quarterly rhythm was undercut by the monthly rhythm, which permitted serialization not only of fiction, for which the quarterly interval was too long, but also of more serious pieces. The *Fortnightly* (which in fact became a monthly after a year and a half) was significant in both respects, being the only heavyweight to publish fiction, particularly George Meredith's, while serializing as well such notable works as Walter Bagehot's *The English Constitution*, Frederic Harrison's *Order and Progress*, and John Morley's *On Compromise*.

The more immediate reader reaction could be equally stimulating to the non-fiction author. The response to Matthew Arnold's *Cornhill Magazine* series, for example, encouraged their evolution into *Culture and Anarchy*. Censorship was a signal of powerful response, and a challenge, too. Works were sometimes terminated before completion: Arnold's *Literature and Dogma* in the *Cornhill* (again the action of the publisher, not Leslie Stephen, whose own *Essays in Freethinking and Plainspeaking*, it goes without saying, appeared elsewhere); John Ruskin's *Unto This Last*, also in the *Cornhill*; and *Munera Pulveris* in *Fraser's*. Ruskin's double rebuff helped to spur him to his later efforts in self-publication: the appearance of the remarkable *Fors Clavigera* (1871–1884) in the form of monthly pamphlets allowed freer rein to his creative eccentricities.[12]

Significant, too, were developments in the area of formal criticism and book reviewing. The quarterlies began, as their names indicate, purely as reviews, each article being, nominally at least, a review of one or more books—what Bagehot referred to as the "essay-like review"—though works under consideration often functioned increasingly as nominal springboards for wider discussion of related matters—hence the "review-like essay." Instances are even known of publication titles being invented by reviewers to fit the requirements of what was in essence an article.[13] The review convention was under strain from the start, but such was its prestige that it was incorporated into the title of practically all serious journals until well into the mid-Victorian period, even by such as had abandoned the fiction of the review-like essay for the straightforward article. The latter gave much greater flexibility to author and editor alike, whether it was submitted or commissioned (itself an important consideration—the review convention always implying the latter.) The less formidable title of "magazine" promised greater flexibility still, and its popularity grew from the mid-Victorian period.

The book review continued to be the most important form of literary response for the published author, since the book itself remained a culturally privileged form of publication even when the original form of publication was serial. Not that journals were not themselves reviewed, for reviews often did review reviews, though usually in a rather perfunctory form. But many authors regularly collected their periodical journalism for republication in more prestigious book form: Matthew Arnold, Walter Pater, Leslie Stephen, J. A. Symonds, R. H. Hutton, Walter Bagehot, John Morley, and W. R. Greg are examples. Republication would sometimes mean recasting in more coherent form essays that were not written with a preconceived plan; Frederic Harrison's *Order and Progress* is a good example. It also meant, before about 1865, public acknowledgment of essays first published anonymously. And it meant a formal invitation of critical consideration in book review form. Formal literary reviewing increasingly became the province of the specialized literary weeklies. Among the earliest of these were the *Literary Gazette** (1817) and the *Athenaeum** (1828; for both, see *RA*). By the early Victorian period the latter had overtaken the former as the leading comprehensive literary journal. Its proprietor, C. W. Dilke, made a strong effort to end the era of puffery associated with William Jerdan and never aspired to the personal power that Jerdan exercised in literary circles by virtue of his editorship and part ownership of the *Gazette*. Dilke was said to have prohibited reviews written by friends of the authors.[14]

Dilke's efforts came at a time when the literary world was going through a phase of organized sociability that was reaching out toward greater professionalism and a stronger sense of corporate solidarity. The proliferation of clubs and societies, from the lofty Athenaeum and Reform down through the Garrick and a myriad of tavern clubs, was a feature of the early Victorian literary scene. Dilke and Jerdan were both part of this movement, which produced various plans for mutual aid societies and institutions to protect and enhance the social and economic position of literary men—publication societies, libraries, insurance societies, dining societies, and so on. But probably the strongest force pressing in this direction was the simple proliferation of journals themselves, for the first time making it possible for a significant number of men (and a few women, such as Harriet Martineau and Eliza Lynn Linton) to make their living by writing alone, unsupported by patronage or the crutch of another occupation.[15]

This greater professionalism was a significant shaping factor, one suspects, in certain long-term developments that have been noticed in Victorian literary criticism—particularly the greater tendency of critics to address the work under review on the author's terms, to try to appreciate and interpret it more than to judge it as if the critic represented some external and national public opinion.[16] Such large generalizations are of course precarious, since destructive criticism and criticism as self-display naturally continued. Indeed, the *Saturday Review*, very soon to rival the *Athenaeum* in circulation and to surpass it in influence, encouraged a style of acidic superiority in its reviewers. The mid-Victorian period saw the emergence or resurgence of other political and general weeklies with strong literary departments. The *Spectator** (1828) (see *RA*) enjoyed a renaissance under R. H. Hutton's editorship, while G. H. Lewes was literary editor of the short-lived *Leader* (1850), to which George Eliot contributed.

Commercial forces continued to exercise their inevitable influence. That most of the senior reviews and magazines were owned by leading publishers created obvious pressures. Thus we find William Blackwood, publisher and editor of *Blackwood's*, giving very careful scrutiny to the reviews of George Eliot's novels in his journal.[17] George Smith, on the other hand, showed unusual scruples in ordering that no books published by his firm of Smith, Elder be reviewed in his *Pall Mall Gazette* (a London evening paper notable for publishing in original serial form Arnold's *Friendship's Garland* and Fitzjames Stephen's *Liberty, Equality, Fraternity*).[18] A major commercial force, especially in the mid-Victorian period, was the *Times*, whose chief literary critic was E. S. Dallas. It could not review many books, but the impact of its reviews was great. As the number of books published annually continued to grow—over four thousand in London alone in the mid-1860s—reviewers had to be increasingly selective about what they reviewed. To be chosen for review at all became a major concern for beginning authors, and the flood of books raised doubts about whether the hard-pressed reviewer could even read, let alone effectively assess, those that were reviewed.[19]

Anonymity remained the common practice in the critical weeklies, but the literary network provided a fair degree of identification for insiders, at least. One aspect of the multiplication of books, reviews, and reviewers was a greater degree of specialization among reviewers, indeed specialization among journalists generally, though here again anonymity somewhat obscures the view. In fact, some journalists maintained that anonymity protected their independent status on the grounds that the professional journalist should properly be a generalist, bringing his professional skill to whatever subject came before him, like the barrister accepting a brief. Signed journalism, they feared, would lead to journalists being locked by public expectation into certain topics, their credibility impaired when they strayed from them. Even worse, it would tempt editors to turn to nonjournalist "experts" with public reputations to undercut them.

Today's literary expert is, *par excellence*, the academic critic, a species that barely existed during the Victorian period, when English literature was regarded as a quite inappropriate subject for the universities—Oxford and Cambridge, at least. Despite this formal neglect, the universities, especially through the Oxford *Literae Humaniores* and modern history courses, succeeded very well in turning out an increasing number of men of letters anxious to shape and inform public taste. The midcentury reforms of the universities made them much more conscious of their duties to the nation as centers of learning, and although their undergraduate clientele remained quite exclusive, they, or at least the more liberal fellows and tutors, sought a wider audience and found it through journalism.

The growing presence of university men in Victorian higher journalism is striking.[20] The *Saturday Review* was an important factor; its trenchant writers were widely known to be recruited from the universities' best young men. Soon it was remarked that undergraduates were modeling their student essays on the *Saturday Review* or the *Spectator*, and by the 1870s higher journalism was thronged with dons.[21] The desire of many of them to make the university into the recognized center of intellectual authority that the nation hitherto lacked found issue in various journalistic projects. University liberals were active in the founding both of *Macmillan's Magazine*, which always retained a strong university connection, especially in its criticism, and of the *Reader** (1863), a self-consciously academic literary weekly, unusual for its signed reviews. The most notable of these magazines was, however, the *Academy*,* its very title invoking and offering to fulfill Arnold's wish that England should have some cultural equivalent to the French Academy. The *Academy* (1869), also a journal of signature, established a new level of academic involvement in criticism and provided a platform for such versatile critics as Andrew Lang and George Saintsbury. Before it fell into commercial and then bohemian hands it was perhaps the true precursor of the *Times Literary Supplement*.

The later career of the *Academy* neatly illustrates two of the main contending styles of literary magazine at the turn of the century. First it was "pepped up" by an American advertising man and aimed squarely at middlebrow suburbia. Then it was bohemianized, ending (or taking) its life as a "little magazine." Bohemia and suburbia were in fact the two prime areas of late Victorian journalistic enterprise. In the latter area George Newnes was perhaps the major force. Having demonstrated his marketing genius and having made a fortune with *Tit-Bits* (1881), the prototypical junk food magazine, Newnes studied American magazines such as *Harper's*, *Scribner's*, and *Century* and devised the ruling formula for successful literary magazines of the 1890s with the *Strand Magazine** (1891).[22] A very liberally illustrated monthly, it challenged the largely moribund 1860s generation with a price of six pence, supported by heavy advertising revenues. It abandoned the serial fiction tradition, publishing only short stories and articles complete in each issue. It soon reached sales of nearly half a million and spawned numerous rivals such as the *Pall Mall** (1893), *Windsor** (1895) and *Royal* (1898) magazines. In such journals the articles were less serious than those of the better 1860s magazines, and they placed considerable emphasis on travel and especially on illustrated celebrity notes and interviews, one of the journals' most popular features. This was not in itself particularly new: the appeal of personality and society journalism had been amply demonstrated since the founding of *Vanity Fair** (1868) and the *World* (1874), but the use of photographs added a new intimacy. The fiction was of high quality and the *Strand* formula created a large demand for the short story, a genre hitherto not very significant, artistically or commercially, in Britain, unlike on the Continent and in the United States. The need was soon filled by writers like Conan Doyle (whose work first appeared in the *Strand*), W. W. Jacobs, and Arthur Morrison.

Bohemia, on the other hand, had the *Yellow Book** (1894), which more than any other English journal evokes an era—*fin de siècle*, decadence, aestheticism, *art nouveau*. Although not unprecedented—the Pre-Raphaelite *Germ** (1850) prefigured its evanescence and the Century Guild's *Hobby Horse** (1886) its visual elegance—it remains the most striking and successful attempt at capturing and projecting an avant garde moment in art and letters—in this case, the world of the Rhymers Club, the New English Art Club, and the Café Royale. Self-advertisement being ever the bohemian *forte*, and *épater le bourgeois* the conventional method, the *Yellow Book*—in printed cloth, published quarterly—was neatly unconventional, but not so much so that W. H. Smith would not stock it.[23]

Bohemia was a highly marketable product by the 1890s, as the success of George du Maurier's novel *Trilby* attests, and the *Yellow Book* was an astute venture. It inspired imitators such as the *Savoy** (1896), launched essentially on the reputation of Aubrey Beardsley, who had been fired by the *Yellow Book*'s nervous publishers in the midst of the Oscar Wilde scandal. By an appropriate irony the imitator was more authentically avant garde than its model: the *Savoy* was of higher literary quality and even went to the perilous extreme of rejecting advertisements. However, W. H. Smith refused to sell it and it lasted only a year.[24] Ephemerality was in fact the main point for many journals of this kind— it was part of their subversiveness. The arch-aesthetic *Dial* (1889), sumptuously printed on *brown* paper—how awful!—flaunted its irregularity with only five issues in eight years. The five issues of the Scots-Celtic revival *Evergreen* (1895) were its predetermined life span: all fresh youth, no dull middle age. The confusion of genres—the periodical posing as a book (or was it the other way round?)—was all part of the deliberate repudiation of the Victorian model. The almost programmatic experimentalism heralded the advent of modernism, as did the increasing popularity of the epithet "new"—the new unionism, the new hedonism, the new drama, the new woman, largely products of the hypostatizing propensities of the new journalism.[25]

It is notable that the two polar, quintessentially nineties journals, the *Strand* and the *Yellow Book*, shared at least one thing—trans-Atlantic inspiration. The

Yellow Book's projector and editor, Henry Harland, was an American. Not just American ideas and energy found a place in nineties literary journals (Frank Harris inevitably comes to mind, by now editing the *Saturday Review*), but American money as well. In the last year of the century Lady Randolph Churchill and "John Oliver Hobbes" (Mrs. Pearl Craigie) established an opulent if short-lived review, the *Anglo Saxon*,* and a longer lived tradition—that of rich American women supporting literature in the form of "little magazines."[26]

The difference between the self-conscious languor and hedonism of the "official" bohemia of the 1890s and the leaner, more kinetic bohemia of the early twentieth century is captured in their journals. The years 1900–1914 and beyond saw the proliferation of little magazines, spiritually closer to the earnest and rather shabby Pre-Raphaelite *Germ* than to the *Yellow Book*. They were manifestoes for literary and artistic movements, often urgently proclaiming the advent of one "ism" or another—futurism, imagism, vorticism, cubism: modernism, in short. The little magazines provided immediate channels of communication within the avant garde, facilitating introduction, identification, and recognition. Their efficiency as a medium is testified to by the increasing proportion of modernists whose first literary appearance would be in their pages, though one may speculate whether such an initiation, with its incentives to preciosity and apartness, was wholly preferable to the traditional apprenticeship in more vulgar journals. Certainly, the number of little journals increased almost geometrically, as did their stridency and dogmatism, especially in the years immediately before World War I. Their proliferation paralleled a wider trend in English public life as home rulers, feminists, Tories, and Laborites all adopted a more militant and confrontational style.

From the mildly eclectic *Open Window** (1910) through the Oxbridge Georgianism of the Middleton Murry–Katherine Mansfield *Rhythm** (1911), one moves to the more programmatic, ardently feminist *Freewoman* (1911), financed by Harriet Shaw Weaver, edited by Dora Marsden, and introducing Rebecca West. This gave way to the more literary *New Freewoman* as the cosmopolitan apostles of imagism took command, with Richard Aldington as literary editor, and Ezra Pound, James Joyce, and T. S. Eliot appearing in its pages; the *Egoist** (1914) (see *MA*) was its successor. Aggressive titles seemed increasingly the order of the day—witness T.W.H. Crosland's *Antidote* (1912)—but it was left to Wyndham Lewis to provide a fitting climax to this trend with *Blast** (see *MA*). The typographical explosion on its puce-colored pages was uncannily timed to go off on 20 June 1914, one week before Sarajevo.

Although the mid-Victorian literary consensus, epitomized by journals like the *Cornhill*, had effectively dissolved by the 1890s, one must always resist the temptation to exaggerate discontinuities. *Blackwood's* survived, even flourished, under shrewd family control to become one of Joseph Conrad's earliest publishers, much to his pleasure. "One was in decent company there and had a good sort of public. There isn't a single club and messroom and man-of-war in the British Seas and Dominions which hasn't its copy of Maga," Conrad remarked.[27] What better audience for Marlow? Despite the commercial acumen with which journalistic entrepreneurs segregated mass readerships (with advertising an increasingly important motivation), and the potential for isolation and sectarian fragmentation in the avant garde, there were journals capable of exerting a centripetal force upon the literary community. The most outstanding was the *English Review** (1908), surely the greatest work of Ford Madox Ford, its founding editor. In the early volumes of this monthly one finds D. H. Lawrence, Wyndham Lewis, Pound, E. M. Forster, W. B. Yeats, Arnold Bennett, John Galsworthy, G. K. Chesterton, Conrad, James, and Hardy—an astonishing feat of editorial prescience and influence. It even opened in the high Victorian manner with a serialized novel, H. G. Wells's *Tono-Bungay*, an ebullient work which deals, among other things, with the commercialization of literary journalism.

Another significant literary force was to be found in the critical weeklies, a genre which showed renewed vigor in the 1890s—W. E. Henley's *Scots Observer** (1888), later *National Observer*, is a good example—but which really flowered in the Edwardian era. These journals embodied the urge to bring politics and culture closer together, against the quietist or escapist temptations of aestheticism, or "decadence." They usually had a distinct flavor: Romantic Tory in Henley's journal, anti-Romantic Tory in the *Commentator* (1910), to which T. E. Hulme contributed, or paranoid Tory in Hilaire Belloc's *Eye Witness* (1911), later *New Witness*. Among the varieties of liberalism were Cambridge Apostolic in the *Independent Review* (1903), with G. M. Trevelyan, Lowes Dickinson, E. M. Forster, and Bertrand Russell; neo-Gladstonian progressive in the *Nation* (1907); guild socialist (the English variety of syndicalism) in A. R. Orage's resuscitated *New Age** (1907); and Shavian-Fabian in the *New Statesman and Nation** (1913). These last three were perhaps the most influential organs of cultural opinion of the time. (The first two were moribund journals renamed and revivified under outstanding editors, H. W. Massingham of the *Nation* and Orage of the *New Age*.). All three journals represented facets of the "new liberalism," and all were concerned with establishing a political and cultural *locus standi* which authorized constructive interventionism by the state without succumbing to economistic Marxism. All paid close attention to literature and the arts, and assumed an important mediating role in interpreting both avant garde and mass culture to their readership of concerned intellectuals. Significantly, they made a point of publishing some poetry in each issue, a valuable tradition maintained to the present day by their survivors and successors.

Arnold Bennett's "Books and Persons" in the *New Age* was widely regarded as the best literary column of its time. Rober Fry was art critic for the *Nation*, Desmond MacCarthy drama critic of the *New Statesman*. J. C. Squire, as literary editor of the *New Statesman*, quickly established a position of authority and respect in literary circles. The weeklies were valuable meeting grounds for the avant garde, the established, and young authors. Orage in particular was acutely sensitive to the nuances of modernism. Certain newspapers of opinion, quality evening and Sunday newspapers like J. A. Spender's *Westminster Gazette* and

J. R. Garvin's *Observer*—which also flourished in these years under benign, loss-absorbing owners content to bask in their prestige—made a liberal contribution to the economy of the literature by employing a large corps of reviewers and columnists. Here were "the *SINEWS*, by gob the Sinooz," as Pound called his small but regular income as a *New Age* contributor.[28]

With the establishment of the "tradition of the new" in the little magazines, the founding of the earnest Edwardian weeklies (not forgetting the *Times Literary Supplement* [1902], whose editor wanted Leslie Stephen but settled for his daughter, Virginia Woolf, who became a *TLS* regular as early as 1905), and the emergence of the first modern academic journals of literary scholarship (such as the *Bulletin of the John Rylands Library* and *Modern Languages Review*), the main features of the landscape of twentieth-century British literary journalism were substantially in place by the outbreak of World War I.

Notes

1. John North, "The Rationale—Why Read Victorian Periodicals?" in J. Don Vann and Rosemary Van Arsdel, eds., *Victorian Periodicals: A Guide to Research* (New York, 1978), p. 4.

2. Walter Houghton, "Periodical Literature and the Articulate Classes," in Joanne Shattock and Michael Wolff, eds., *The Victorian Periodical Press: Samplings and Soundings* (Leicester, England, 1982), p. 11.

3. See Oscar Maurer, Jr., "Anonymity vs. Signature in Victorian Reviewing," *University of Texas Studies in English* 26 (June 1948): 1–27.

4. Christopher C. Dahl, "Fitzjames Stephen, Charles Dickens and Double Reviewing," *Victorian Periodicals Review* 14, no. 2 (Summer 1981): 51–58.

5. Scott Bennett, "Revolutions in Thought: Serial Publication and the Mass Market for Reading," in Shattock and Wolff, p. 236.

6. Louis James, "The Trouble with Betsy: Periodicals and the Common Reader in Mid-Nineteenth Century England," in Shattock and Wolff, p. 355.

7. Roland D. McMaster, "Dickens and the Horrific," *Dalhousie Review* 38 (Spring 1958): 18–28.

8. Malcolm Elwin, *Victorian Wallflowers* (London, 1937), p. 128.

9. See Gleeson White, *English Illustration: The Sixties, 1855–70* (London, 1897).

10. Oscar Maurer, Jr., " 'My Squeamish Public': Some Problems of Victorian Magazine Publishers and Editors," *Studies in Bibliography* 12 (1959): 21–40.

11. Circulation figures are of course problematic; on this problem see Alvar Ellegård, *The Readership of the Periodical Press in Mid-Victorian Britain* (Göteborg, 1957); and Joel H. Wiener, "Circulation and the Stamp Tax," in Vann and Van Arsdel, pp. 149–65. Deriving readership from circulation is even more difficult, though it is safe to assume that Victorian journals had more readers per copy than is common today, the quality journals probably having the highest number. John Morley, as editor of the *Fortnightly Review*, with a circulation of around three thousand in 1873, claimed that this meant about thirty thousand readers—a very high ratio. See Christopher Kent, *Brains and Numbers: Elitism, Comtism and Democracy in Mid-Victorian England* (Toronto, 1978), p. 115.

12. Brian Maidment, "John Ruskin and the Periodical Press," in Shattock and Wolff, p. 56.

13. Houghton, p. 24, n.12.
14. Leslie A. Marchand, *"The Athenaeum": Mirror of Victorian Culture* (Chapel Hill, N.C., 1941), pp. 38–39.
15. [G. H. Lewes], "The Condition of Authors in England, Germany and France," *Fraser's Magazine* 35 (March 1847): 283. ("To periodical literature we owe the possibility of authorship as a profession," Lewes declares.)
16. John Woolford, "Periodicals and the Practice of Literary Criticism, 1855–64," in Shattock and Wolff, p. 125.
17. Gordon Haight, *George Eliot* (London, 1968), p. 278.
18. *Dictionary of National Biography*, Supplement (1901), s.v. "Smith, George."
19. G. B. Burgin, "Some Literary Critics," *Idler* 5 (June 1894):503.
20. George C. Brodrick, *Political Studies* (London, 1879), p. 309.
21. William Beach Thomas, *The Story of the "Spectator" 1828–1928* (London, 1928), p. 74.
22. Reginald Pound, *"The Strand Magazine"* (London, 1966), p. 30.
23. Katherine L. Mix, *A Study in Yellow: "The Yellow Book" and Its Contributors* (Lawrence, Kans., 1960), p. 80.
24. Stanley Weintraub, ed., *"The Savoy": Nineties Experiment* (University Park, Pa., 1966), p. xxxv.
25. Ian Fletcher, "Decadence and the Little Magazines," in *Decadence in the 1890s* (London, 1979), pp. 173–74, 192.
26. Stanley Weintraub, *The London Yankees: Portraits of American Writers and Artists in England 1894–1914* (New York, 1979), pp. 76–78.
27. Ian Watt, *Conrad in the Nineteenth Century* (Berkeley, 1979), p. 131.
28. C. David Heymann, *Ezra Pound: The Last Rower* (New York, 1976), p. 34.

Bibliography of General Works

Altick, Richard D. *The English Common Reader: A Social History of the Mass Reading Public 1800–1900*. Chicago, 1957.

Bourne, H.R. Fox. *English Newspapers: Chapters in the History of Journalism*. 2 vols. London, 1887.

Ellegård, Alvar. *The Readership of the Periodical Press in Mid-Victorian Britain*. Göteborgs Universitets Årsskrift, no. 63. Göteburg, 1957.

Elwin, Malcolm. *Victorian Wallflowers*. London, 1937.

Gross, John. *The Rise and Fall of the Man of Letters*. London, 1969.

Hoffman, Frederick J., Charles Allen, and Carolyn F. Ulrich. *The Little Magazine: A History and a Bibliography*. Princeton, 1947.

Houghton, Walter E., ed. *The Wellesley Index to Victorian Periodicals 1824–1900*. Toronto, 1966–.

James, Louis. *Fiction for the Working Man, 1830–1850*. Oxford, 1963.

Kent, Christopher. "Higher Journalism and the Mid-Victorian Clerisy." *Victorian Studies* 13, no. 2 (December 1969).

Madden, Lionel, and Diana Dixon, eds. *The Nineteenth Century Periodical Press in Britain. A Bibliography of Modern Studies 1901–1971*. Supplement to *Victorian Periodicals Newsletter* 8 (September 1975). Reprinted by Garland Press, New York, 1976.

Shattock, Joanne, and Michael Wolff, eds. *The Victorian Periodical Press: Samplings and Soundings*. Leicester, England, 1982.

Vann, J. Don, and Rosemary T. Van Arsdel, eds. *Victorian Periodicals: A Guide to Research*. New York, 1978.

Wolff, Michael, John S. North, and Dorothy Deering, eds. *The Waterloo Directory of Victorian Periodicals 1824–1900: Phase 1*. Waterloo, Ont., 1976.

Christopher Kent

PROFILES OF BRITISH LITERARY MAGAZINES, 1837–1913

A

ACADEMY, THE

The *Academy* was founded in 1869 by Charles Appleton, an energetic and idealistic young Oxford don who intended it to fill the Arnoldian purposes invoked by its title—to serve as an authoritative intellectual organ to which serious readers could turn for reliable judgments on matters of high culture. Although not a notable scholar himself, Appleton was a serious entrepreneur of scholarship. With his close friend Mark Pattison and a group of other distinguished academic intellectuals, he was a central figure in the Endowment of Research movement. The Endowment aimed at challenging the amateur spirit then characteristic of English university teaching and scholarship by promoting the notion of academic professionalism, particularly through greater emphasis on scholarly research. Like many of this persuasion, Appleton greatly admired Continental, particularly German, scholarship, and the *Academy* was intended to be an English counterpart to the *Litterarisches Centralblatt* and the *Revue Critique*.

University men formed the bulk of the *Academy*'s target audience, and of its contributors. The journal aimed at the niche between the smart Oxbridge levity of the *Saturday Review** and the middlebrow stodginess of the *Athenaeum** (see RA). The first review of the first issue, appropriately, was by Matthew Arnold on Senancour's *Obermann*. Like all the *Academy*'s reviews it was signed—in keeping with the developing trend among more liberal intellectual periodicals. From the start the journal was a *succès d'estime* though, particularly in its early issues, it was rather severely scholarly, carrying a number of lengthy notices of daunting Continental works, such as Mark Pattison's review of a *Geschichte der Klassischen Philologie in den Niederlanden*. This emphasis on erudition soon led to a showdown between Appleton and the publisher, John Murray III, who wanted to dilute the editor's high-minded formula and gain wider circulation. Appleton resisted, and within a year Murray withdrew as publisher, leaving

Appleton the sole owner of the *Academy*. Now fully in control, he did in fact lighten the tone when he began to publish fortnightly in 1871, and more so still in 1874 when he went weekly with a significantly revised subtitle that eliminated the forbidding word "learning," and substituted "review" for the sterner "record." The proud motto, *Inter Silvas academi quaerere verum*, also went, and drama, music, and art criticism and notices first appeared. The price was reduced from six pence to four pence, the journal having received a fresh transfusion of money from the creation of the Academy Company Limited, a group composed largely of Oxford men to whom Appleton sold a partial interest. Their share capital was in the nature of a subsidy, since the journal was still not profitable. Eminent university men (chiefly Oxonians) continued to contribute: the reviews of T. H. Green, Henry Sidgwick, Edward Caird, and Pattison ensured the highest quality coverage of philosophical works, but, in addition, promising young men of letters like George Saintsbury, Edmund Gosse, and Andrew Lang frequently contributed, as did "H. Lawrenny" (Edith J. Simcox), a worshipper of George Eliot and a discerning reviewer of novels. The art criticism by W. M. Rossetti, Sidney Colvin, and J. Comyns Carr was also very influential.

Appleton's health failed toward the end of the 1870s, and the paper was sold to the printer Spottiswoode and Co. in the summer of 1878; they apparently sold it the following year to Henry Villers. A subeditor, Charles E. Doble, became interim editor during Appleton's illness and after his death, until James S. Cotton took over. The journal continued to hold its tone under Appleton's immediate successors: both Doble and Cotton were disciples of the founder and reputable Oxford scholars. There was, however, a noticeable decline in the journal's intellectual cosmopolitanism. Notices of foreign learned literature diminished and reviews of English novels became more numerous. Contributions by Grant Allen (from around 1881) and A. W. Benn (from 1885) ensured that Spencerian rationalism and free thought were well represented. James Shedlock was the respected regular music critic, and Claude Phillips the main art critic, though Cosmo Monkhouse, Amelia F.S. Pattison (Mark Pattison's wife), and the drama critic Frederick Wedmore also contributed.

In *Tono-Bungay* H. G. Wells alludes to the *Academy* under a pseudonym, the *Sacred Grove*, characterizing it as the dignified, worthy, and slightly stuffy "representative organ of British intellectual culture" that is bought up and transformed by a crass patent-medicine promoter. The *Academy* was indeed bought up in 1896 by a rich American patent-drug merchant, John Morgan Richards, to provide a vehicle for the editorial talents of Charles Lewis Hind, who had ingratiated himself with Richards's daughter, "John Oliver Hobbes" (Mrs. Pearl Craigie). Hind was a tactful man and an able talent spotter, but he had no reverence for the old *Academy* tradition. He soon transformed the journal into perhaps the liveliest literary journal in England. He offered contests for readers ("choose appropriate literary mottoes for the various rooms of one's house"), lists of the best-selling books in various English cities (unfortunately discontinued after early 1897), and substantial annual prizes of fifty and one hundred pounds for the best books of the year, awarded to such grateful authors as Joseph Conrad for *Tales of Unrest* and Maurice Hewlett for *Forest Lovers*. The reviews were short and snappy, and usually anonymous. There was Grub Street gossip that appealed to the "insider" instinct and to the book trade. The regular contributors included Arnold Bennett (in a sense Hind's discovery); E. V. Lucas; Wilfred Whitten; two leading *poètes maudits* of the nineties, Lionel Johnson and Francis Thompson; and their friends the Meynells, Alice and Wilfred. This latter coterie of distinguished Catholic writers may have owed something to the considerable influence of Mrs. Craigie, an ardent convert.

In 1902 Richards bought *Literature** from the *Times* newspapers and amalgamated it with the *Academy*. In 1903 W. Teignmouth Shore succeeded Hind as editor. Bennett had already left, and Johnson and Thompson went over to the *Athenaeum* on Hind's departure. The journal had somewhat less snap, and in February 1905 Richards sold his copyright to Sir George Newnes. The journal moved to the *Country Life* offices and was jointly edited by P. A. Graham of *Country Life* and H. H. Child (later of the *Times Literary Supplement*). The new editors seem to have tried to rehabilitate the old *Academy* to some degree. The result was less gossip, less book trade emphasis, and less copy. The contributions were almost all anonymous. The result was not particularly successful, and in May 1907 the paper was sold for 2,000 pounds to Sir Edward Tennant, a very rich liberal M.P. and brother-in-law of Asquith, to indulge the editorial and literary ambitions of another in-law, the minor poet and sometime friend of Oscar Wilde, Lord Alfred Douglas.

Under Douglas the journal certainly became more lively. He patronized a group of young bohemian writers that included Henry Savage and Richard Middleton. Arthur Machen was a frequent contributor; Wilfrid Scawen Blunt and Robert Ross were among those who represented the "higher" bohemia in its pages. Douglas soon hired as his subeditor the irascible, talented, self-proclaimed "jobbing poet," T.W.H. Crosland, whose taste for notoriety met no restraint from Douglas. The *Academy* increasingly courted controversy. High Church views were pushed—Douglas converted to Roman Catholicism in 1911—as were high Tory views. The attacks on the Liberal government and on Asquith finally exceeded the endurance of the *Academy*'s tolerant owner. In September 1908 Sir Edward Tennant gave Douglas the paper, along with 500 pounds cash, thereby relieving himself of a great embarrassment. The *Academy* now continued its hectic course under the unfettered control of Douglas and Crosland, who were the "Wilsford Press" (the name was taken from Tennant's country house, an allusion more probably based on mischief than gratitude). "Bohemian puritanism" was part of their polemical stock-in-trade. Denunciation of hypocrisy proliferated, especially of those who published or distributed "obscene" books, such as W. H. Smith, the *Academy*'s printers, who naturally ceased to print or distribute it. Finally, in 1910, amidst financial disarray and two libel suits, the journal was taken over by the immensely rich Lord Howard de Walden, a major creditor, and Lord Fitzwilliam. They installed two nonentities as editors, and under this direction the *Academy* made a return to respectability and dullness, despite occasional contributions from writers like Hilaire Belloc and Frank Harris. Such was its success that in the summer of 1915 Crosland and Henry Savage bought the title for five pounds and in the midst of World War I attempted unsuccessfully to recapture the spirit of the Douglas years. In 1920 the title was resurrected by Douglas himself in his belligerent weekly, *Plain English*, "with which is incorporated the *Academy*" (10 July 1920–11 February 1922).

Information Sources

BIBLIOGRAPHY

Appleton, J. H., and A. H. Sayce. *Dr. Appleton: His Life and Literary Relics*. London, 1881.
Brown, William Sorley. *The Life and Genius of Thomas W.H. Crosland*. London, 1928.
Freeman, William. *The Life of Lord Alfred Douglas*. London, 1948.
Hansen, Diderik Roll. *"The Academy": 1869–79*. Copenhagen, 1957.
Hind, Charles Lewis. *Naphtali*. London, 1926.
Lucas, E. V. *Reading, Writing and Remembering*. London, 1932.
Miller, Anita. *Arnold Bennett: An Annotated Bibliography 1883–1932*. New York, 1977.
Richards, John Morgan. *With John Bull and Jonathan*. London, 1905.
Savage, Henry. *The Receding Shore*. London, 1933.
———. *Richard Middleton: The Man and His Work*. London, 1922.
Sayce, A. H. *Reminiscences*. London, 1923.
Stephen, Sir Herbert. *The Savile Club*. Edinburgh, 1923.

INDEXES

Annual indexes for 1850, 1851, 1853, and 1854.

REPRINT EDITIONS

Microform: Datamics Inc., New York. Early British Periodicals (UMI), reels 164–183. Harvester Press Microfilm, Hassocks, Sussex, 1979, reels 5–15 of Rare Radical and Labour Periodicals of Great Britain, pt. 2. N. A. Kovach, Los Angeles.

LOCATION SOURCES

American

Widely available.

British

Complete runs: British Museum; Newcastle-upon-Tyne Public Library.
Partial runs: Widely available.

Publication History

MAGAZINE TITLE AND TITLE CHANGES

The Academy: A Monthly Record of Literature, Learning, Science and Art, 9 October 1869; *A Record of Literature, Learning, Science, and Art*, 15 January 1871; *A Weekly Review of Literature, Science, and Art*, 3 January 1874; *A Weekly Review of Literature and Life*, 8 October 1898.
The Academy and Literature, 18 January 1902.
The Academy: A Weekly Review of Literature, Science and Art, 11 March 1905; *A Weekly Review*, 10 August 1908; *With Which Are Incorporated "Literature" and "The English Review,"* 24 October 1908.

The Academy and Literature, 17 December 1910.
The Academy: A Journal of Literature, Art, Finance and Politics, 31 January 1914.
The Academy and Literature, 5 September 1914.

VOLUME AND ISSUE DATA
Volume 1, number 1–volume 90, number 2270, 9 October 1869–18 September 1915; plus three monthly issues October–December 1915, and three additional numbers dated 12 May, 17 June, and July–August 1916.

FREQUENCY OF PUBLICATION
Monthly until 1871; then weekly.

PUBLISHERS
9 October 1869: John Murray, Albemarle Street, London. October 1870: Williams and Norgate, 14 Henrietta Street, Covent Garden, London. 1 January 1874: William Greig Smith (Academy Office), 43 Wellington Street, Strand, London. 1875–August 1878: Robert Scott Walker (Academy Office), 43 Wellington Street, London. 5 July 1880: Henry Villers, 27 Chancery Lane, London. November 1896: Peter G. Andrews, 43 Chancery Lane, London. 14 November 1903: Academy Publishing Co., 43 Chancery Lane. 12 December 1903: Academy Publishing Co., 9 East Harding Street, London, E. C. 11 March 1905: *Country Life*, 20 Tavistock Street, Covent Garden, London. 25 May 1907: H. E. Morgan, 95 Fetter Lane, London. 14 March 1908: Odhams Ltd., 67 Long Acre, London, W. C. 19 September 1908: The Wilsford Press, 63 Lincoln's Inn Fields. 29 April 1911: Odhams Ltd., 67 Long Acre, London, W.C. 6 January 1912: Proprietors, Cannon House, Bream's Buildings, London, E.C. 3 August 1912: Dawson and Sons, Cannon House, Bream's Buildings, London E.C. 24 July 1915: Pomegranate Press, 8 and 9 St. James's Market, Jermyn Street S. W., London.

EDITORS
Charles E.C.B. Appleton, from 9 October 1869. Charles E. Doble, Autumn 1878. James Sutherland Cotton, January 1881. Charles Lewis Hind, 14 November 1896. William F. Teignmouth Shore, 10 October 1903. Peter Anderson Graham and Harold H. Child, February 1905. Lord Alfred Bruce Douglas, 25 May 1907. Cecil H.C.M. Cowper, assisted by E. Ashmead Bartlett, 2 July 1910. Henry Savage and T.W.H. Crosland, 24 July 1915. T.W.H. Crosland, May 1916.

Christopher Kent

ACADEMY AND LITERATURE, THE (1902, 1910, 1914). See ACADEMY, THE

AINSWORTH'S MAGAZINE

In December 1841 the following announcement appeared in London:

NEW PERIODICAL WORKS
Preparing for Publication by Mr. Cunningham.

I

MR. AINSWORTH'S MISCELLANY,
illustrated by George Cruikshank
On the 29th of January, 1842, Price Eighteen pence,
No. I of
AINSWORTH'S MAGAZINE
A Monthly Miscellany of Romance
General Literature, and Art.
Edited by W. Harrison Ainsworth, Esq.
and illustrated with designs on steel and woodcuts by
George Cruikshank.
Containing the Commencement of a new work of fiction by Mr.
Ainsworth, with Two illustrations on Steel by George Cruikshank.
With contributions from the most eminent writers of the day.[1]

Thus, in 1842 the popular novelist William Harrison Ainsworth, author of *Rookwood* and *Jack Sheppard*, joined forces with an equally popular illustrator, George Cruikshank, to publish a new magazine aimed solely at entertainment. It was to be entertainment, as Ainsworth advertised, for the whole "FAMILY: This new periodical...is addressed not to Mothers only, but to Daughters." The periodical would not print any material "in the shape of covert slander, personal attack, or indecent frivolity."[2] The contents of the periodical attest his statement.

Its first issue for February 1842 contained no story or essay that would "bring a blush into the cheek of the young person." A preliminary address by Ainsworth spoke to the aims of the periodical: "Romance, Humorous Incident, Playful Satire,...Travel."[3] The issue contained chapters from Ainsworth's most recent novel, *The Miser's Daughter*, with Cruikshank's drawings; short light essays—some fanciful; equally short tales (one by Thackeray, but signed "Major G. O'G. Gahagan");[4] and the lady's page—more short essays and some verse written by women; and ended with "Our Library Table," five pages (in the first issue) of editorial statement, letters, and verses. Religious, political, economic, and social issues were excluded from the pages. The novels and tales were mainly historical romances, direct descendants from Sir Walter Scott and the Gothic novels. Many of them dealt with English history. These were interspersed with translations of equally romantic tales from such writers as Dumas, George Sand, and Boccaccio.

The tone of the periodical seldom shifted, although with the third number its size and price increased—from eighteen pence to two shillings. The price increased again in July 1842 to two shillings, six pence. Ainsworth's reading of the Victorian taste must have been accurate because the circulation reached a respectable 7,000 during its first year of publication.[5]

Part of its success may be attributed to Ainsworth's reliance upon illustrations for his periodical. Besides Cruikshank, Ainsworth employed the French artist Tony Johannot, who illustrated the initial numbers of *Windsor Castle*, the second of Ainsworth's novels to be published in the periodical; W. Alfred Delamotte, who with Cruikshank continued the illustrations for *Windsor Castle*; and Hablot Knight Browne ("Phiz").

The list of contributors to *Ainsworth's* is not as prominent. Besides Ainsworth himself, the most famous are Thackeray (three articles) and William Francis Ainsworth, William's cousin, a prolific contributor who usually wrote short travel or descriptive articles, many of which were on such subjects as the archaeology and anthropology of Africa, Persia, and Asia Minor. William Maginn contributed the novel *John Manesty* to the journal but died after completing only seven chapters. Other contributors who may be recognized today are Lady Harriette D'Orsay, Mrs. Norton, Edward Kenealy, Thomas Medwin, and Charles Brooks, the "Shirley" of *Punch*.

Although *Ainsworth's Magazine* was the first major periodical founded by Ainsworth, he had experimented with others earlier, and his professional experience reveals itself in the success of *Ainsworth's*. His earlier contributions had appeared in *Bentley's Miscellany*,* the *London Magazine*,* the *Edinburgh Magazine*,* *Fraser's Magazine*,* and the *New Monthly Magazine** (for the latter four, see *RA*), as well as in series of minor publications. He had founded a small periodical entitled the *Bœotian* (20 March 1924–24 April 1824), had edited *Bentley's Miscellany* (March 1839–December 1841), and was editing the *New Monthly Magazine* during some of the same years that he published *Ainsworth's Magazine*.

In October 1843 Ainsworth, probably in need of money, sold the periodical to John Mortimer, his publisher, for 1,000 pounds, but he remained as editor until 7 June 1845. From that point on the periodical declined. Cruikshank had dissolved his partnership with Ainsworth, possibly because of this change of proprietorship and his inability to work with Mortimer.[6] Hablot K. Browne became illustrator-in-chief. Samuel Laman Blanchard, the subeditor of *Ainsworth's Magazine*, a prolific essayist and playwright, and a good friend of Ainsworth, became depressed over the death of his wife and committed suicide on 14 February 1845. Finally, Ainsworth himself became angry with Mortimer and impetuously resigned his editorship: Mortimer had failed to pay Ainsworth his usual monthly honorarium of 60 pounds.[7]

Almost immediately, Ainsworth purchased the *New Monthly* for 2,500 pounds from Henry Colburn. At that time, Ainsworth wrote that he planned to repurchase *Ainsworth's Magazine* and "incorporate it with the *New Monthly*," but when he did buy it back in 1845, he did not follow that plan.[8] An outcome of his purchase of the *New Monthly* was that he took important contributors from *Ainsworth's Magazine* with him.

The repurchased *Ainsworth's Magazine* was less lively. Between 1845 and its demise in December 1854, Ainsworth reissued in the magazine a series of his previously published novels—*Old Saint Paul's, Crichton, Guy Faukes*, and *The Lancashire Witches*—and shorter works such as "Michele Orombello" and "A Night's Adventure in Rome." His one new novel to be published was *James II*.

His cousin, W. Francis Ainsworth, also furnished a translation of Alexander Dumas's *Count of Monte Cristo*. With a few exceptions the list of other contributors is not impressive.

About 1850 the decline in the magazine was noticeable. The illustrations disappeared, and more and more anonymous articles and stories appeared, "indicating that the editor was eager to conceal the names of unknown or inferior contributors."[9] Even Francis Ainsworth stopped contributing, although he continued as subeditor. Ainsworth purchased *Bentley's Miscellany* in October 1854 and finally left his own magazine in December of that year. The *Wellesley Index* ends its discussion of *Ainsworth's Magazine* with a very appropriate quotation from Ainsworth's biographer, S. M. Ellis. His words are a fitting obituary: "In its later days [the magazine] had fallen into the sere and yellow leaf, the contributions were poor, and the brilliant illustrations which distinguished the earlier volumes had long been discontinued. It was a sad end to a once famous magazine."[10]

Notes

1. S. M. Ellis, *William Harrison Ainsworth and His Friends* (London, 1911), 1:431–32.
2. *The Wellesley Index to Victorian Periodicals, 1824–1900*, ed. Walter Houghton (Toronto, 1979), 3:6, n.5.
3. Ellis, 2:4.
4. *Wellesley Index*, 3:13.
5. See Ellis, 2:9, 56–57.
6. Ibid., 2:71, 79.
7. Ibid., 2:111–12.
8. Ibid., 2:113.
9. *Wellesley Index*, 3:10.
10. Ibid., 2:220.

Information Sources

BIBLIOGRAPHY
Ellis, S. M. *William Harrison Ainsworth and His Friends*. 2 vols. London, 1911.
The Wellesley Index to Victorian Periodicals, 1824–1900. Edited by Walter Houghton.
      Vol. 3. Toronto, 1979.
INDEXES
      Wellesley Index 3.
REPRINT EDITIONS
      Microform: English Literary Periodicals (UMI), reels 116–122.
LOCATION SOURCES
      American
            Complete runs: Harvard University Library; University of Illinois Library; Yale
            University Library.
            Partial runs: Widely available.

British
>Complete runs: Bodleian Library; British Museum; Cambridge University Library. Partial runs: Finsburg Public Library; Glasgow University Library; Guildhall Library; Leeds University Library; Liverpool University Library; London University Library; Manchester Public Library; Norwich Public Library; West Ham Public Library.

Publication History

MAGAZINE TITLE AND TITLE CHANGES
>*Ainsworth's Magazine.*

VOLUME AND ISSUE DATA
>Volumes 1–26, February 1842–December 1854.

FREQUENCY OF PUBLICATION
>Monthly.

PUBLISHERS (ALL IN LONDON)
>February 1842–June 1842: Hugh Cunningham. July 1842–October 1843: Hugh Cunningham and John Mortimer. November 1843–October 1945: John Mortimer. November(?) 1845–December 1845: Henry Colburn. January 1846–December 1854: Chapman & Hall.

EDITORS
>William Harrison Ainsworth, February 1842–June 1845. Francis Mahoney and John Mortimer, July–November 1845. William Harrison Ainsworth, December 1845–December 1854.

>*William H. Scheuerle*

ALL THE YEAR ROUND

Charles Dickens, editor of *Household Words** since 1850, became irritated in 1859 at the magazine's publishers (Bradbury and Evans) for their opposition to the circulation of a statement about the novelist's separation from his wife. He determined then to buy their quarter-share in the magazine to go with his own half-share. Negotiations proved unsuccessful and the magazine was sold at auction on 16 May and purchased by Dickens through an agent.[1] He then proceeded to found his new periodical. In a letter to Wilkie Collins, Dickens pondered some two dozen titles, including *Weekly Bells, Once a Week,* the *Forge,* and *Time and Tide.*[2] At the top of the front page of each issue of *Household Words* had appeared the motto " 'Familiar in their Mouths as HOUSEHOLD WORDS'— Shakespeare"; for the new magazine he again went to Shakespeare for a quotation: "The Story of our Lives from Year to Year." From this he derived the title *All the Year Round.* From the beginning the magazine was a remarkable success, eventually reaching a circulation of 300,000, eight times the largest number achieved by *Household Words.*

Each issue, selling for two pence, contained an installment of a novel, a poem or two, three to five articles designed to appeal to a general audience, and occasionally a short story (300 scattered through the 500 issues of the first series). The articles covered a wide span of interests, including history—''King Richard's Warrant for the Execution of Buckingham'' and ''Edward's League with Robert Bruce''; geography—''Hong Kong''; popularized science—''Hair under the Microscope''; anthropology—''England Long, Long Ago''; natural history—''Lizards in Ceylon''; and ghost stories—''The Ghost of Samuel Johnson'' and ''London Ghosts.'' But the crown jewel heading each issue was the weekly installment of a serialized novel. The first issue began with *A Tale of Two Cities*. Appended to the last installment of the novel was the editorial note, ''We purpose always reserving the first place in these pages for a continuous original work of fiction, occupying about the same amount of time in its serial publication as that which is just completed'' (2 [26 November 1859]: 95). The magazine then began the serialization of Wilkie Collins's *The Woman in White*. Dickens's intention was to begin the publication of a new novel as each novel finished its serialization. This plan was frustrated once when *A Day's Ride* by Charles Lever failed to draw an audience and the sale of *All the Year Round* plummeted. Lever was disconsolate. Dickens assured him that the novel was of high quality, ''the best you ever wrote,'' but that it did not fit the mode of publication, serialization: ''For *such a purpose*, it does not do what you and I would have it do,'' lacking ''one strong ground of suspended interest.'' Lever was not to feel that he was to blame, for ''some of the best books ever written would not bear the mode of publication.''[3]

The only remedy to the drop in circulation was for Dickens to use the popularity of his work to increase the readership. He had been planning for his next book, *Great Expectations*, to be published in monthly parts, but a Dickens novel was needed for the magazine. Could he manage to write two novels at once? Thirty-three years earlier he had written *Pickwick Papers* and *Oliver Twist* simultaneously, but he was no longer capable of such a task. Thus *Great Expectations* appeared in the weekly issues of *All the Year Round* rather than in the more common format, for Dickens, of twenty discrete parts. The incident of the difficulty with Lever's serial shows clearly that *All the Year Round* was a journal in which a novel was expected to sustain the circulation.[4]

Dickens's chief assistant was William Henry Wills, who had been his secretary on the *Daily News*, which Dickens edited for three weeks, and subeditor of *Household Words* and *All the Year Round*, of which he was one-quarter owner. In numerous letters Dickens acknowledged the valuable service of Wills, who wrote many articles for the magazine.[5] When Wills retired in 1868 following an accident, all the editorial duties fell on Dickens.[6] Charles Dickens, Jr., was then taken into the office and got on so well that his father made him subeditor and willed his share to the young man, who served as editor until the magazine ceased publication in 1895.

All the Year Round is significant for the novels serialized in its covers. They include Dickens's two novels, Mrs. Gaskell's *A Dark Night's Work*, Bulwer-Lytton's *A Strange Story*, Wilkie Collins's *The Moonstone* and *The Woman in*

White, Charles Reade's *Hard Cash*, and Anthony Trollope's *Is He Popenjoy?*, *The Duke's Children*, and *Mr. Scarborough's Family*. An extra Christmas issue was published each season for the first nine years. These issues were patterned after the earlier spectacularly successful *A Christmas Carol* and were generally well received; "Mrs Lirriper's Lodgings," for example, sold 220,000 copies.[7] The poetry and short stories published in *All the Year Round* are of only slight interest.

Notes

1. For an account of the whole affair, see Edgar Johnson, *Charles Dickens: His Tragedy and Triumph* (New York, 1952), 2:943–46.

2. *Letters of Charles Dickens*, ed. Walter Dexter (London, 1938), 3:90.

3. *Letters*, 3:187. The italics are Dickens's.

4. For a fuller study of this point, see J. A. Sutherland, *Victorian Novelists and Publishers* (Chicago, 1978), pp. 174–78.

5. *Letters*, 3:394–95, 654, for example.

6. Ibid., 3:654.

7. Ibid., 3:395.

Information Sources

BIBLIOGRAPHY

Adrian, Arthur A. *Mark Lemon: First Editor of Punch*. Oxford, 1966.

Al-Ani, T.A.H. "Charles Dickens's Weekly Periodicals: Their Establishment, Conduct, and Development." Master's thesis, University of Leicester, 1971.

Casey, E. M. "Novels in Teaspoonfuls: Serial Novels in *All the Year Round*." Ph.D. dissertation, University of Wisconsin, 1969.

Collins, Philip. "The *All the Year Round* Letter Book." *Victorian Periodicals Newsletter*, no. 10 (1970):23–29.

[D., T. C.] "Victorian Editors and Victorian Delicacy." *Notes & Queries* 187 (1944):251–53.

Fitzgerald, P. H. *Memories of Dickens, with an Account of "Household Words" and "All the Year Round."* Bristol, 1913.

Forster, John. *The Life of Charles Dickens*. Edited by J.W.T. Ley. London, 1928.

Grubb, Gerald G. "Dickens Rejects." *Dickensian* 52 (1956):89–90.

———. "Dickens's Editorial Methods." *Studies in Philology* 40 (1943):79–100.

———."Dickens's Influence as Editor." *Studies in Philology* 42 (1945):811–23.

———. "The Editorial Policies of Charles Dickens." *Publications of the Modern Language Association of America* 58 (1943):1110–24.

Haight, Gordon S. "Dickens and Lewes." *Publications of the Modern Language Association of America* 71 (1956):166–79.

Hopkins, Annette B. "Dickens and Mrs. Gaskell." *Huntington Library Quarterly* 9 (1946):357–85.

Johnson, Edgar. *Charles Dickens: His Tragedy and Triumph*. New York, 1952.

Ley, J.W.T. "National Dickens Library, Later Magazine Articles." *Dickensian* 4 (1908):244–46.

Morley, Malcolm. "*All the Year Round* Plays." *Dickensian* 52 (1956):128–31, 177–80.

Pierpoint, Robert. "The Christmas Numbers of *All the Year Round.*" *Dickensian* 4 (1908):48–49.

Seiter, R. D. "Wilkie Collins as Writer for Charles Dickens's *Household Words* (1850–59) and *All the Year Round* (1859–70)." Ph.D. dissertation, Bowling Green State University, 1970.

Stone, Harry D. "Dickens and the Idea of a Periodical." *Western Humanities Review* 21 (1967):237–56.

Troughton, Marion. "Dickens as Editor." *Contemporary Review* 191 (1957):87–91.

INDEXES

Each volume indexed; volumes 1–20 in volume 20. 1859–1881 in *Poole's Index*.

REPRINT EDITIONS

AMS Press, New York.

Microform: Early British Periodicals (UMI), reels 137–152.

LOCATION SOURCES

American

Widely available.

British

Widely available.

Publication History

MAGAZINE TITLE AND TITLE CHANGES

All the Year Round. A Weekly Journal. Conducted by Charles Dickens. With Which Is Incorporated Household Words.

VOLUME AND ISSUE DATA

Volumes 1–76, 30 April 1859–30 March 1895.

FREQUENCY OF PUBLICATION

Weekly.

PUBLISHER

Chapman & Hall, London.

EDITORS

Charles Dickens, 1859–1870. Charles Dickens, Jr., 1870–1895.

J. Don Vann

ANGLO-SAXON REVIEW

The *Anglo-Saxon Review: A Quarterly Miscellany* was conceived by a woman who, recently widowed, financially insecure, and professionally untrained, wanted something more than the life that her wit, beauty, and high social status guaranteed her: "In a despondent mood, I bemoaned the empty life I was leading at the moment. Lord Curzon tried to console me by saying that a woman alone was a godsend in society, and that I might look forward to a long vista of country-house parties, dinners and balls. Thinking over our conversation later, I found myself wondering if this indeed was all that the remainder of my life held for me. I determined to do something, and cogitating for some time over what it should be, decided finally to start a Review.''[1] During late 1898 and early 1899 this determined woman, Lady Randolph Spencer Churchill, formulated the project that was to be one of the most opulent, most expensive—a guinea an issue— and most frequently satirized periodicals of its time. John Lane, the literary entrepreneur and publisher of the *Yellow Book*, agreed to publish the wonderful magazine: no doubt he appreciated the unique resources Lady Churchill brought to the enterprise. For though she had no experience as a journalist and no properly tested skills as an editor, she was a woman of great energy and fortitude, and she counted among her friends people whom she could call on for assistance and encouragement in all aspects of her yet unformed scheme. Lane suggested that the magazine should appear quarterly and—what was to be one of its most distinctive features—that issues be bound in imitation of various Renaissance folio volumes.[2] The magazine was to be, first, a money-making proposition for publisher and editor; it was to be, second, exclusively available to the wealthy. The first-year subscription list is astonishing for the blood, fortune, and power it represented: of about six hundred individuals and institutions named, there are heads of state, royalty, and some of the wealthiest families of Britain and the United States (no. 4:257–68). An impressive portion of the magazine's contributors were, too, members of the nobility, officers of the Church of England, members of Parliament, titled servants of the crown, and foreign dignitaries. Lady Churchill's project was intended to provide her not with a means of escape from her milieu but with a way of putting it to commercial and cultural use. The *Anglo-Saxon Review* might be viewed as an attempt to approximate in print the experience of a *salon* as described in one of its articles (George Whale, ''The *Salon* in England,'' no. 6 [September 1900]:192–207), where men and women engage in social discourse that is ''their ideal, and their test, of civilisation'' (no. 6:192). It is perhaps significant as an indication of the character of the quarterly and as one of the factors leading to its demise that an article in the final issue, a nostalgic reminiscence of a time when women did not smoke or speak in public, laments the absence in the present day of women who willingly sacrifice their independence to stay at home and serve as presiding geniuses over their *salons* (Sir Algernon West, ''Celebrated Women of Recent Times,'' no. 10 [September 1901]:116–21). By an unexpected turn of historical events, Lady Churchill was to temporarily abandon her monthly *salon*. Though she was to return to it, it was not to survive for long after.

Having decided early how frequently her magazine would appear and its cover design, Lady Churchill turned to the tasks of naming it and determining its editorial stance.[3] Among her devoted advisors during the months preceding publication were her son, Winston, and Mrs. Pearl Craigie, who, like Lady Churchill, was an American-born member of fashionable London society. Mrs. Craigie was also a novelist, dramatist, and essayist who published under the name of John Oliver Hobbes. Winston did not approve of the suggestions that the magazine be named the *Arena* or the *International Quarterly* (cumbrous and unoriginal, according to Winston); and Lady Churchill did not approve of Win-

ston's suggestion that it be named the *World's Cinematograph*. A former lover
of Lady Churchill's, Sir Edgar Vincent, suggested *Anglo-Saxon*, a name that
Winston found "very inappropriate to a Mag de Luxe meant only for the cultivated few." Vincent's suggestion prevailed, however, with the necessary addition of "*Review*": Mrs. Craigie discovered there was already a journal bearing
the shorter name. Winston's objection to the name finally chosen was that it
suggested national limits on what he hoped would be a periodical of cosmopolitan
appeal; and, further, he observed, "There is a falling market as regards Imperialism now." Winston suggested that the magazine take as its purpose "to
preserve a permanent record of the thoughts and aspirations of our times, which
vary as swiftly as light changes on running water, for wiser ages yet unborn."
Lady Churchill was sufficiently persuaded by her son's argument against chau-
vinistic fervor to drop the idea of the motto "Blood is thicker than water."[4] But
she was not so persuaded as to forego an appeal to the cultural values the name
of her magazine proclaimed: "I send the first volume out into the world—an
adventurous pioneer. Yet he bears a name which may sustain him even in the
hardest struggles, and of which he will at all times endeavour to be worthy—a
name under which just laws, high purpose, civilising influence, and a fine language, have been spread to the remotest regions" (The Editor, "Introductory,"
no. 1 [June 1899]:2). Lady Churchill's biographer contends that mother and son
collaborated on the prefatory article of the *Anglo-Saxon Review*.[5]

Each volume of the *Anglo-Saxon Review* consists of about 250 pages of print
and half a dozen engravings of portraits. The format established in the first
volume remained essentially unchanged during the thirty-month life of the periodical. It called for a frontispiece, followed by an article by Cyril Davenport
on the design and historical context of the original binding imitated on the cover.
Each volume concludes with several pages of unsigned "Impressions and Opinions," usually of a political nature, and "Notes on the Portraits" that appear in
the volume. Between the fixed opening and closing pieces there usually appear
about twenty contributions, virtually all of which belie the quarterly's claim to
be a review. The *Anglo-Saxon Review* is, rather, a miscellany (as indicated in
the subtitle) of pieces that fall into several categories. There appear in nearly
every volume, for example, one or two articles based on unpublished or little-
known letters and other personal documents: for example, an essay on the eighteenth-century Lady Mary Montague (C. E. Raimond [pseudonym of Elizabeth
Robins, American novelist], "A Modern Woman," no. 1 [June 1899]:39–65);
"Some Letters of George Canning," by Rev. Canon Raven (no. 3 [December
1899]:45–54); "Some Letters and Other Recollections of Lord Beaconsfield and
Others," by Lady Dorothy Nevill, matriarch of London society (no. 4 [March
1900]:140–54); "Incidents in the War with Napoleon," from unpublished cor-
respondence edited by Lt. Col. E. Stuart Wortley (no. 9 [June 1901]:58–75);
"The American Revolution in the Correspondence of Horace Walpole," by
George Hibbard (no. 9 [June 1901]:92–101); and "Sheridan: Some Unpublished
Letters," by Wilfred Sheridan (no. 10 [September 1901]:227–36). A second

category of contributions, historical articles, is apt to be devoted to military exploits and leaders: for instance, "Thoughts Suggested by Some Old Military Books," by Sir Herbert Maxwell (no. 9 [June 1901]:76–91); "War Correspondence and the Censorship under Elizabeth," by Julian Corbett (no. 10 [September 1901]:54–62); and three biographical essays by Judge O'Connor Morris ("Napoleon," no. 7 [December 1900]:68–85; "Moltke," no. 8 [March 1901]:177–94; and "Nelson," no. 10 [September 1901]:150–72). Among a dozen or so articles on the arts are two engaging readings of paintings by Max Beerbohm—one of Rubens's "The Garden of Love" (no. 6 [September 1900]:213–15), and another of George Morland's "The Visit" (no. 10 [September 1901]:205–11); "A Word More about Verdi," by Bernard Shaw (no. 8 [March 1901]:221–29); and "The Absurdity of the Critics of Music," by Gilbert Burgess (no. 10 [September 1901]:186–92), containing devastating parodies of reviews by critics for the *Times, Pall Mall Gazette, Saturday Review,** and other publications; and four articles by regular contributor Cyril Davenport on ornamental artifacts ("On Cameos," no. 2 [September 1899]:110–23; "Anglo-Saxon Gold and Niello Finger Rings," no. 5 [June 1900]:155–61; "Snuff-Boxes," no. 9 [June 1901]:171–81; and "Brooches," no. 10 [September 1901]:94–103).

Articles about women include a few biographical pieces, some on well-known women (Edith Sichel's article on Madame de Maintenon, "A French Governess," no. 6 [September 1900]:133–49; and John Fyvie's "The Most Gorgeous Blessington," no. 10 [September 1901]:6–23), and an occasional one on the more infamous than famous (Andrew Lang's "Three Seeresses," on women who claimed powers of divination, no. 6 [September 1900]:63–73). A more timely article on women is Lady Jeune's "A Century of Women" (no. 4 [March 1900]:197–209), which argues that women lead happier and fuller lives now than they did a century earlier. There are occasional articles on medicine and science, including "Chinese Doctors and Medical Treatment," by Isabella L. Bishop (no. 3 [December 1899]:211–20), who devoted much of her life to medical missions, and was the first woman admitted to the Royal Geographical Society; and "Signalling to Mars," by Howard Swan (no. 9 [June 1901]:108–18), on the language that might be used to communicate with that planet if, as had been recently speculated, there is intelligent life there. "Signalling to Mars" is rare if not unique among all the articles in *Anglo-Saxon Review* for being humorous, albeit unintentionally so.

There are other articles, variously personal, historical, and anecdotal: "The American Athlete," by Theodore A. Cook (no. 9 [June 1901]:139–55), an indictment of the political and intensely competitive attitude toward sports expressed in the United States; "Angling Reminiscences in England and the Tropics," by Susan, Countess of Malmesbury (no. 4 [March 1900]:19–29); "The Young England Movement," by Walter Sichel (no. 9 [June 1901]:15–28); and "Changes in Parliamentary Speech," by Alfred Lyttelton, M.P. (no. 3 [December 1899]:157–64.).

Nearly every volume of the *Anglo-Saxon Review* contains at least one short story and one poem and often—perhaps as a result of Mrs. Craigie's influence—a drama. Among the short stories are Henry James's "The Great Condition," about the consequences of a young man's unfounded suspicion that the woman he hopes to marry has a secret past (no. 1 [June 1899]:7–38); Stephen Crane's "War Memories," based on the writer's Cuban experiences and included in the collection *Wounds in the Rain* (no. 3 [December 1899]:10–38); George Gissing's "Humplebee," about the victimization of a young working-class man by a social superior (no. 4 [March 1900]:7–18); "The Outcasts," by Henry de Vere Stacpoole, remembered best for his novel, *Blue Lagoon* (no. 3 [December 1899]:204–10); and "The Gift of Pity," by Robert Barr, the Scottish-born and Canadian-educated journalist and novelist who completed Crane's last novel, the Irish romance, *O'Ruddy* (no. 10 [September 1901]:40–53). Among the most interesting short stories published here are two that are, by chance, companion pieces on the theme of the unfortunate consequences of confusing the demands of life and art: "A Miniature Moloch" by novelist Ellen Thorneycroft Fowler concerns a gifted woman novelist who nearly sacrifices her career for love of a despicable snob who disdains women writers (no. 2 [September 1899]:8–20); and "The Unflinching Realist," by H. D. Traill, a more complex and tragic story of a young writer who acquiesces to his fiancée's insistence that he change the ending of a story to satisfy her ignorant and selfish ideas about literature (no. 3 [December 1899]:181–90).

Poems that appear in *Anglo-Saxon Review* include ones by Algernon Charles Swinburne ("The Battle of the Nile," no. 1 [June 1899]:186–87); Stephen Phillips ("A Poet's Prayer," no. 2 [September 1899]:90–91); F. B. Money Coutts ("Angling Days," no. 2 [September 1899]:181–83); Maurice Baring (no. 4 [March 1900]:30–34); and Miss M. A. Curtois ("The Call of Psyche," no. 9 [June 1901]:104–7). Most noteworthy is the number of dramas appearing in this quarterly, beginning with Mrs. Craigie's "Osbern and Ursyne," a three-act verse tragedy that is, according to Edmund Gosse, a "tangled skein of passion"[6] (no. 1 [June 1899]:124–75), and including "The Merciful Soul," by Laurence Alma-Tadema (no. 3 [December 1899]:107–28); "The Likeness of the Night," by Mrs. W. K. Clifford (no. 4 [March 1900]:38–93); "Colour-Blind," by Hamilton Aïdé (no. 5 [June 1900]:130–40); and A. Bernard Miall's translation of Maeterlinck's "Sister Beatrice: A Miracle Play in Three Acts" (no. 6 [September 1900]:90–119).

Except for the first volume, every issue of the *Anglo-Saxon Review* contains at least two and as many as four articles on literature. Many of these articles concern writers of the past: for example; Herbert Paul's "Macaulay and his Critics," in which Macaulay's importance in English literature is equated with Napoleon's in European history (no. 4 [March 1900]:115–32); and Andrew Lang's essay on "Smollett" (no. 9 [June 1901]:123–38). Some articles focus on particular themes or texts: Richard Garnett's "Shelley's Views on Art" (no. 6 [September 1900]:120–32); James F. Fasham's "Some Realities of the *Pil-*

grim's Progress," on local sites that inspired landscape in that text (no. 2 [September 1899]:92–97); Amelia Young's "The Ways of an Old World," on the eighteenth-century London newspaper, the *World* (no. 10 [September 1901]:140–49). Of a few articles on foreign literature, most are on French writers: "La Bruyère," by the Earl of Crew (no. 2 [September 1899):98–109); Mrs. Craigie's "Plays of the Modern French School" (no. 8 [March 1901]:130–35); and two articles by J. C. Bailey, "French Claims in Poetry," arguing for a British appreciation of the characteristics of logic and unity of action (no. 8 [March 1901]:136–47), and "Pierre Ronsard: A Forgotten Laureate," which, though faulting Renaissance non-dramatic writers for not seriously contemplating life, acknowledges a certain nostalgia for that earlier time and for the Romantic period, when "everyone was young," when "poets were, in a sense, children delighting in the prettiness of a world of new toys, and asking for no more" (no. 10 [September 1901]:137). Articles on contemporary British writers include Frederick Wedmore's "A Note on Ruskin," written on the occasion of that writer's death (no. 4 [March 1900]:133–36); Richard Garnett's article on Stephen Phillips's poem, "Paolo and Francesca" (no. 3 [December 1899]:145–53); and Sidney Low's "Some Battlepieces," on examples of literary treatment of military events (no. 3 [December 1899]:231–44). More interesting for its form than its substance is Egerton Castle's "The Spirit of Romance"; by means of an imaginary dialogue between a man and a woman, interspersed with segments of a lengthy essay, the author considers a series of commonplace distinctions between the romance and the novel (no. 7 [December 1900]:23–38). Clearly distinguished literary essays found their way to this magazine: drama critic William Archer's knowledgeable plea for a national repertory theater ("What Can Be Done for the Drama?" no. 4 [March 1900]:223–42); Edmund Gosse's history of biographical forms from Cavendish to the *Dictionary of National Biography* ("The Custom of Biography," no. 8 [March 1901]:195–208); W. H. Mallock's reading of the sinister social and aesthetic consequences of novels with a purpose in the manner of Zola ("The Limitations of Art," no. 5 [June 1900]:141–54); Edward Garnett's comparison of two Russian novelists in their ability to create characters that are individualized as well as ones that are types ("Tolstoi and Turgenieff," no. 6 [September 1900]:150–65); and W. Brook Adam's carefully documented comparison of Scott and Dickens in illustration of the historical move away from heroic ideals and toward demonstrations of craftiness as dominant social forces ("Natural Selection in Literature," no. 2 [September 1899]:158–80).

If history did not prove Lady Churchill right and her son wrong concerning the commercial value of imperialism, history does seem to have conspired to provide her and her magazine with monumental events to validate an exaggerated form of patriotism. Between the second and third issues the Boer War broke out, and between the seventh and eighth, Victoria died. From beginning to end, however, in contributions of all genres, the *Anglo-Saxon Review* insists on the rightness of subjugating foreign cultures to British dominion. Volume 1 begins with a jingoistic "Introductory" (no. 1:1–2), and concludes with "Impressions and Opinions,'' which propounds the virtue as well as the profitability of imperialism (no. 1 [June 1899]:243–54). Even an article on Dreyfus interprets that incident as evidence of England's superiority in politics, government, and industry (S. F. Cornély, "The Case of Dreyfus—A Judicial Error," no. 2 [September 1899]:213–45). Sir Frank Swettenham's narrative essay, "A Mezzotint" (no. 1 [June 1899]:215–24), recounts the unhappy consequences of a sentimental relationship between a servant of the British Empire and a Malay woman: "She would have been wiser to remain in the cool, moonlit jungle, where, at least, she was at home with those of her kind; but the creatures of the forest have not yet learned the danger of giving way to natural instincts" (no. 1:224). J. E. Gorst, whose article Lady Churchill and Winston admired very much, argues imperiously for Europe's responsibility toward Eastern civilizations in teaching them how, among other things, to construct communities ("The Oriental Character," no. 2 [September 1899]:124–38). With the Boer War, the *Anglo-Saxon Review* intensified its defense of British civilization as the moral and political standard of the world: for example, Lionel Phillips's prediction that among the glorious events that will mark Victoria's reign will be the consolidation of the British South African Empire ("Past and Future in South Africa," no. 3 [December 1899]:191–203); Sir Alfred C. Lyall's lament that there is no poet now writing who can and will commemorate the heroic event of the Boer War ("Heroic Poetry," no. 5 [June 1900]:116–29); Arthur Waugh's attack on present-day poets for failing to direct their art toward the service of national life, particularly in its present military struggle ("The Poetry of the South African Campaign," no. 7 [December 1900]:42–58); and—the last article of the last issue of the magazine—William Earl Hodgson's hostile attack against the Liberal party for its opposition to the war in South Africa ("Liberalism," no. 10 [September 1901]:237–46). Typical of the more positive expression of patriotic fervor is the essay by Crimean War veteran Major Arthur Griffith, who looks forward to the time when England's realm will be "only circumscribed by the earth itself," and praises his nation for its "self-sacrificing devotion which has brought all classes and all sections of the Empire into line for the maintenance of British prestige" ("The Crimea and the Cape: Parallel and Contrast," no. 4 [March 1900]:114).

It is hardly surprising that the editor of the *Anglo-Saxon Review* should have agreed to take charge of an American-sponsored hospital ship, the *Maine*, which left England for South Africa in late 1899 and returned in April 1900. During her absence from England, editorial duties were assumed by three men who, during the life of the magazine, assisted Lady Churchill in various ways: journalist William Earl Hodgson, critic Charles Whibley, and—especially—writer and ardent imperialist Sidney Low. Issue number 4 appeared during her absence, and its frontispiece is an engraving of a drawing of her by Sargent. In the fifth issue appears a series of letters written by Lady Churchill in which she traces, in engaging detail, her adventures on ship and in South Africa ("Letters from a Hospital Ship," no. 5 [June 1900]:218–37). Of the many articles on the Boer

War appearing in the *Anglo-Saxon Review*, this one is unique in its realistic detail and non-imperialistic attitude. Lady Churchill describes the medical treatment given the wounded, those "very fine fellows" whose pain turns them into children (no. 5:224). She contemplates the fortunes of war by which ordinary men are transformed into heroes and men of proven gallantry turn cowardly. She is impatient of those in command who are devoted to "the traditions and experiences of in many cases a valueless past" (no. 5:227). She is horrified at how brutally the British treat animals. She is appalled to see social life continuing in all its frivolity at a Capetown hotel as war goes on in Durban. One cannot but wonder if Lady Churchill remembered on this trip the definition of *Anglo-Saxon* with which her "Introductory" concluded: "a name under which just laws, high purpose, civilising influence, and a fine language, have been spread to the remotest corners" (1:2).

Lady Churchill was married to George Cornwallis-West in July 1900. The first and most intense stage of the Boer War ended in the fall of that year, and Victoria died in January 1901. For the nation and for the *Anglo-Saxon*'s editor, one epoch was ending and another beginning. The March 1901 issue of the magazine is unique in that it contains articles by Lady Churchill and Winston, the young, promising politician arguing for the creation of a cavalry force worthy of the Empire ("British Cavalry," no. 8 [March 1901]:240–47). Lady Churchill's article, on the greater variety and beauty of materials for domestic furnishings now available compared to a quarter-century earlier, is a celebration of the new age of Edward ("Decorative Domestic Art," no. 8 [March 1901]:125–29). The age of the "heavy uncomfortable monstrosities" (no. 8:125) of early Victorian domestic art is over: "The dawn of this century finds English decorative art in a healthy and flourishing condition; and, in consequence, the 'House Beautiful,' with all its good influences, is open, a thing of beauty and a joy forever, not only to the eclectic few but also to the Philistines" (no. 8:129).

Already, in late 1900, disagreements between Lady Churchill and John Lane had made it clear that the days of the magazine were numbered. Lady Churchill seems not to have been aware that the *Anglo-Saxon Review* depended on the generosity of friends who were unwilling to continue their support of the quarterly much longer.[7] Lady Churchill gave some thought to changing the magazine to give it more widespread appeal, including turning it into a monthly, and presumably a much less expensive, periodical.[8] Perhaps it occurred to her that the *Anglo-Saxon Review*, like a beautiful house of the present time, might be made available to more than the eclectic few. For whatever reason, she decided not to change her quarterly into something more appropriate for the day. With its tenth beautifully bound issue, the magazine was allowed to end on as imperialistic a note as it had begun: "We have been fighting not for our rights or our claims [in South Africa] alone. We have been fighting for the British Empire. . . . Any Liberal statesman who is incapable of seeing that is incapable of seeing anything" (W. Earl Hodgson, "Liberalism," no. 10 [September 1901]:245–46).

Notes

1. Ralph G. Martin, *Jennie: The Life of Lady Randolph Churchill: The Dramatic Years, 1895–1921* (Englewood Cliffs, N.J., 1971), p. 152.
2. Randolph S. Churchill, *Winston S. Churchill: Companion Volume 1, Part 2: 1896–1900* (Boston, 1967), pp. 991–1023, 1045–46.
3. Martin, pp. 152–57.
4. Churchill, pp. 1003–12.
5. Martin, p. 173.
6. Mrs. Pearl Mary Teresa (Richards) Craigie, *The Life of John Oliver Hobbes: Told in Her Correspondence with Numerous Friends* (London, 1911), p. 151.
7. Martin, pp. 261–62.
8. Ibid., p. 282.

Information Sources

BIBLIOGRAPHY

Churchill, Randolph S. *Winston S. Churchill: Companion Volume 1, Part 2: 1896–1900*. Boston, 1967.

Craigie, Mrs. Pearl Mary Teresa (Richards). *The Life of John Oliver Hobbes: Told in Her Correspondence with Numerous Friends*. London, 1911.

Martin, Ralph G. *Jennie: The Life of Lady Randolph Churchill: The Dramatic Years, 1895–1921*. Englewood Cliffs, N. J., 1971.

INDEXES

Table of contents of each volume.

REPRINT EDITIONS

Microform: Early British Periodicals (UMI), reel 50.

LOCATION SOURCES

American

Widely available

British

Widely available.

Publication History

MAGAZINE TITLE AND TITLE CHANGES

Anglo-Saxon Review: A Quarterly Miscellany.

VOLUME AND ISSUE DATA

Numbers 1–10, June 1899–September 1901.

FREQUENCY OF PUBLICATION

Quarterly.

PUBLISHER

John Lane, London and New York.

EDITOR

Lady Randolph Spencer Churchill.

Carol de Saint Victor

ANTI-JACOBIN REVIEW, THE. See RA

ARROW, THE

The *Arrow*, edited by W.B. Yeats in conjunction with his tenure as a director of the Abbey Theatre, was originally planned as a small monthly designed to "interpret or comment on particular plays, make announcements, wrap up the programme and keep it from being lost, and leave general principles to *Samhain*"* (no. 1). The first number was published on 20 October 1906, and number 2 followed shortly, on 24 November 1906, expanding the magazine's purpose to include Yeats's reactions to critics of the Abbey production. He states, "We started *The Arrow* very largely that we might reply to hostile criticism of the kind we faced in its abundance last winter" (no. 2). Though only five numbers were finally issued at sporadic intervals, the *Arrow* did answer two of the most "hostile criticisms" the Abbey Theatre faced: the riot over J. M. Synge's *The Playboy of the Western World* and the attempt by Dublin Castle to censor G. B. Shaw's *The Shewing-up of Blanco Posnet*. The underlying theme of Yeats's answers and reactions in the *Arrow* is reflected in the epigraph from Wagner he chose to head each issue: "In the Theatre there lies the spiritual seed and kernel of all national poetic and national moral culture. No other branch of Art can ever truly flourish or ever aid in cultivating the people until the Theatre's all-powerful assistance has been completely recognized and guaranteed."

This period of the newly formed Abbey Theatre was perhaps its most productive and at the same time its most turbulent. Lady Gregory, the only other contributor to the *Arrow*, reflects in her autobiography: "Lately I have been looking through some letters of Yeats to me and of mine to him written during that time [1903–1910]. And as I read I marvelled to find how much time and energy was not only used, but as it seems squandered, on the endless affairs of the Abbey Theatre, almost crushing out, as it seems, other interests."[1] As Richard Ellmann notes, Yeats almost ceased activities other than those associated with the Abbey and its quarrels during this time. "Into the dozen or so fairly important quarrels in the theatre movement from 1903 to 1911 he threw himself with something like abandon."[2] The first two issues of the *Arrow* are basically playbills, commenting on individual plays and publishing a list of forthcoming performance dates. The most astringent criticism Yeats delivers involves an "appeal to our audience to endeavor to be seated before the rise of the curtain at 8:15" (no. 2). However, between the November *Arrow* and the third number, for 23 February 1907, J. M. Synge's *Playboy of the Western World* premiered, on 26 January 1907. Henceforth, Yeats's rhetorical tone expands and the last three issues of the magazine become a vehicle, however modest, of vengeance.

The *Arrow* originally announced that the premiere of *Playboy* was to be "Saturday, Dec. 29th, to Saturday, Jan. 5th, 1907." Synge had trouble completing the third act, so the play was postponed until 26 January. The "riot" that ensued is well known, but the third and fourth numbers of the *Arrow* reflect some of the vehemence Yeats and Lady Gregory felt toward the chauvinism and nationalistic mob spirit that erupted over the play. "The failure of the audience to understand this powerful and strange work has been the one serious failure of our movement" (no. 4), Yeats laments, for it was precisely this kind of drama that he and the Abbey Company wished to produce.

In the third number Yeats's contempt "for the old Puritanism, the old bourgeois dislike of power and reality [that] have not changed, even when they are called by some Gaelic name" is barely suppressed. The entire issue is devoted to showing, in Yeats's mind, "how old is the attack and how old the defence" that is "unavoidable when certain crude general ideas and propagandist emotions have taken the place of every other kind of thought" (no. 3). Yeats also republishes "Previous Attacks on Irish Writers of Comedy and Satire" and an article he wrote for *Samhain* in 1905 in which he chastizes the "bourgeois mind" for its inability to apprehend true reality in art, for, he maintains, "all good art is extravagant, vehement, impetuous, shaking the dust of time from its feet, as it were, and beating against the walls of the world" (no. 3). He concludes the issue with his "Opening Speech at the Debate of February 4th, at the Abbey Theatre," in which he states, true to his own sense of integrity, "I would indeed despise myself if for the sake of popularity or of a vague sentiment I were to mar the task I have set my hands to, and to cast the precious things of the soul into the trodden mire" (no. 3).

Number 4, for 1 June 1907, continues the defense of *Playboy* and at the same time defends the Abbey Company's decision to bring the play to London, "to some calm audience," Lady Gregory declares in "An Explanation," one of two articles in the fourth issue. Though not as contemptuous as the previous "replies to hostile criticism," number 4 absolutely confirms that the directors of the Abbey Theatre will not be compromised by "members of parties and societies whose main interests are political" (no. 4). Almost two years passed before the last regular issue of the *Arrow* was published, once again in "reply to hostile criticism."

The *Arrow* for 25 August 1909, the fifth and last number, deals with the attempted censorship of Shaw's one-act play, *The Shewing-up of Blanco Posnet*. The play had already been censored by the Lord Chamberlain in England; Shaw then offered it to the Abbey, since the censor had no jurisdiction over the Irish stage. The intricacies of the fight between the Abbey and Dublin Castle have been expounded upon by Lady Gregory in *Our Irish Theatre*,[3] but the *Arrow* makes clear the grounds upon which Yeats and the Abbey Theatre Company stood. The "Statement by the Directors" begins, "During the last week we have been vehemently urged to withdraw Mr. Shaw's play, which had already been advertised and rehearsed, and have refused to do so" (no. 5). The "objectionable" parts of the play (mainly religious) were published, and Yeats defended artistic vision to the extent of evoking the Bible: "Nearly every one of Blanco Posnet's railings [could] be paralleled from Job" (5). The fight was not in vain;

Lady Gregory describes the reaction of the audience triumphantly: "Then, at the end, there was a tremendous burst of cheering, and we knew we had won."[4]

After this issue, however, the *Arrow*, as such, ceased to be. The final, special issue of 1939 departs from its usual form of replying to hostile criticism and instead commemorates Yeats upon his death. Lennox Robinson edited this special issue, with contributions by Oliver Gogarty, Edmund Dulac, John Masefield, W. S. Turner, Gordon Bottomley, Austin Clarke, Richard Hayes, F. R. Higgins, and William Rothenstein. His intention, successfully fulfilled, was to produce one last "*Arrow* in which some who know him well could write of him and his work from different aspects."

Notes

1. Lady Augusta Gregory, *Seventy Years: Being the Autobiography of Lady Gregory* (Gerrards Cross, Ireland, 1974), p. 411.
2. Richard Ellmann, *Yeats: The Man and the Masks* (Oxford, 1979), p. 176.
3. Lady Augusta Gregory, *Our Irish Theatre* (New York, 1965), pp. 140–68.
4. Ibid., p. 168.

Information Sources

BIBLIOGRAPHY
Ellmann, Richard. *Yeats: The Man and the Masks*. Oxford, 1979.
Gregory, Lady Augusta. *Our Irish Theatre*. New York, 1965.
———. *Seventy Years: Being the Autobiography of Lady Gregory*. Gerrards Cross, Ireland, 1974.
Wade, Allan, ed. *The Letters of W. B. Yeats*. New York, 1955.
Yeats, W. B. *The Autobiography of William Butler Yeats*. New York, 1971.
INDEXES
> *Comprehensive Index to English-Language Little Magazines: 1890–1970*, ser. 1, Millwood, N. Y., 1976.

REPRINT EDITIONS
> Microform: New York Public Library Photographic Service.

LOCATION SOURCES
> *American*
>> Complete runs: Harvard University Library; University of California, Berkeley, Library; University of Wisconsin Library; Yale University Library.
>> Partial runs: Widely available.
> *British*
>> Complete run: British Museum.

Publication History

MAGAZINE TITLES AND TITLE CHANGES
> *The Arrow*.
VOLUME AND ISSUE DATA
> Volume 1, number 1, 20 October 1906; number 2, 24 November 1906; number 3, 23 February 1907; number 4, 1 June 1907; number 5, 25 August 1909. Special Commemoration Number, Summer 1939.

FREQUENCY OF PUBLICATION
  Occasional.
PUBLISHER
  The Abbey Theatre, Dublin.
EDITORS
  W. B. Yeats, 1906–1909. Lennox Robinson, 1939.

Cynthia Waguespack

ART AND POETRY. See GERM, THE

ATHENAEUM. See RA

AUTHOR, THE

The *Author*, the official journal of the Society of Authors, was founded in 1890 by Walter Besant, who had been the principal founder of the Society of Authors seven years earlier.[1] A small group had met in September 1883 to form an association of men and women of letters, provisionally called "The Company of Authors," with two stated objects: "to place . . . upon a recognised basis of justice the relations between author and publisher, and . . . to keep steadily in the public mind questions of copyright—domestic and international—that authors may receive by legislation the rewards to which they are entitled" (55:53). The Society of Authors was incorporated in June 1884, and membership increased rapidly to four hundred by the end of the decade. Soon a regular medium of communication between the committee administering the affairs of the association and the membership was needed. The monthly *Author* was designed to furnish a channel of information. The first number was issued on 15 May 1890.

Besant edited the journal from its inception until his death in 1901. In its early days, the journal bore the impress of Besant's personality. The masthead carried the legend "Conducted by Walter Besant" and, for twenty years after his death, "Founded by Sir Walter Besant." In the beginning, he gathered his friends about him in the enterprise. Alexander P. Watt, his literary agent, who would ultimately be his literary executor, was the publisher for the society of the first volume; after 1893, the publisher for the society was Horace Cox, to one of whose journals, the *Queen*, Besant was a regular contributor. In Besant's time, the greatest amount of space in the *Author* was devoted to a discussion of legal aspects of authorship; reports of specific cases considered infringements by publishers of authors' rights; and related correspondence from authors and—often adversary in tone—from publishers. "The journal," wrote Besant in the first number, "will contain papers, notes, letters, questions, and information on all subjects connected with literature and its profession." Some articles on various aspects of literary property were developed into monographs, which were advertised in the periodical.

After Besant's death on 9 June 1901, the journal was reorganized. Publication was suspended after the July issue and resumed in October, inaugurating a policy of ten numbers in each subsequent volume. The secretary of the society, G. Herbert Thring, succeeded Besant as editor. Bradbury and Agnew replaced Horace Cox as printer. Publication decreased to five issues in 1918; and since 1919 the journal has been issued quarterly. Reflecting changes in the organization and name of the society, the journal carried the title *The Author, Playwright and Composer* from October 1926 to the spring issue in 1949, when the original name, *The Author*, was resumed. Responsibility for the editing of the journal continued to be placed in the office of the secretary of the Society of Authors: Thring was succeeded by Denys Kilham Roberts and M. Elizabeth Barber, in turn. Cecil Rolph Hewitt was listed as editor from 1956 to 1960.[2] Since 1961 Richard Findlater has been editor of the *Author*.

The pages of the *Author* are a record of the history of the Society of Authors. The two original concerns of the association had been stated as the protection of literary property, particularly with reference to the relations between author and publisher, and the promotion and reform of domestic and international copyright legislation. From its beginning and throughout its history, the Society of Authors has constituted a pressure group in the interests of clarification and revision of laws of copyright. On the fiftieth anniversary of the society, the *Author* reviewed the progress of copyright over those years, contrasting the ambiguity of the laws in 1884, when the Society of Authors was incorporated, with the situation following subsequent advances, particularly the revised Berne Convention of 1908 and the British Copyright Act of 1911 (44:35). As a member of the British Copyright Council, the Society of Authors continued to monitor and to take official positions on proposed modification of copyright laws (85:99).

Similarly, the problems arising in connection with the literary rights of authors have continued to be treated in the pages of the *Author*. The secretaries of the association have traditionally been barristers with special competence in contracts, even though, as the *Author* noted in its "Sixty Years' Retrospect," "the changing character of authorship as a profession has now enabled differences and disputes to be settled by friendly discussion more often than by militant methods which had to be employed in the early days" (55:54). The *Author* documents such changes through direct reports and through commentary in editorials and in articles by the secretariat and by contributors. Thus, as the organ of the Society of Authors, the *Author* is a major repository of information about the history of authorship over the past century. The historian of the Society of Authors has recently characterized the journal: "*The Author* not only records events but acts...as a forum for discussion of subjects relating directly to authorship as a business."[3] These articles, many of them written by eminent authors who are members of the society, make the *Author* in itself a literary magazine of continuing importance.

Notes

1. Walter Besant, *Autobiography* (New York, 1902), pp. 215–42.
2. *Who's Who* (1982). Cf. [C. H. Rolph], *Living Twice: An Autobiography* (London, 1974).
3. Victor Bonham-Carter, *Authors by Profession* (London, 1978), p. 9.

Information Sources

BIBLIOGRAPHY

Besant, Walter. "Literature as a Career." In *Essays and Historiettes*. 1903. Reprint. 1970.
Bonham-Carter, Victor. "Eighty Years Ago." *Author* 74 (Summer 1964):21–26.
"The Incorporated Society of Authors, Playwrights, and Composers 1884–1934." Supplement to *Author* 44 (1934).
"The Society of Authors—Sixty Years' Retrospect." *Author, Playwright and Composer* 55 (Summer 1945):53–54.
Sprigge, S. Squire. "Memoir [of Sir Walter Besant]." *Author* 12 (July 1901):21–26.

INDEXES

Each volume indexed, volumes 1–36.

REPRINT EDITIONS

Microform: Microform, Ltd. (Clearwater Publishing).

LOCATION SOURCES

American

Widely available.

British

Complete runs: Bodleian Library; British Museum; Cambridge University Library; National Library of Scotland, Edinburgh.
Partial runs: Bristol Public Library; British Library of Political Science; Edinburgh Public Library; London University Library; Manchester Public Library; St. Bride Printing Library; University College Library; Westminster Public Library.

Publication History

MAGAZINE TITLE AND TITLE CHANGES

The Author, May 1890–July 1926. *The Author, Playwright, and Composer*, October 1926–March 1949. *The Author*, Spring 1949–.

VOLUME AND ISSUE DATA

Volume 1, numbers 1–12, 15 May 1890–15 April 1891; volumes 2–11, numbers 1–12, 1 June 1891–1 May 1901; volume 12, numbers 1–10, 1 June 1901–1 July 1902; volumes 13–27, numbers 1–10, October 1902–July 1917; volumes 28–29, numbers 1–5, October 1917–July 1919; volumes 30–, numbers 1–, October 1919–.

FREQUENCY OF PUBLICATION

Monthly, volumes 1–11; monthly except August and September, volumes 12–27; five issues yearly, volumes 28–29; quarterly, volumes 30–.

PUBLISHER

The Society of Authors.

EDITORS

Walter Besant, May 1890–July 1901. G. Herbert Thring, October 1901–1930.
Denys Kilham Roberts, 1930–1956. Cecil Rolph Hewitt (C. H. Rolph), 1956–
1960. Richard Findlater, 1961–.

Charlotte C. Watkins

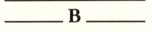

B

BELGRAVIA

Belgravia; A London Magazine was merely one in a series of magazines started or purchased by John Maxwell, an entrepreneur of periodicals ranging from *Halfpenny Journal* and the *Welcome Guest*, penny dreadfuls aimed at the lower classes, to *Temple Bar** and *Belgravia*, well-produced magazines designed for the middle and upper classes.[1] Although owned by Maxwell for eleven years, during that period *Belgravia* was essentially the work of Mary Elizabeth Braddon, a prolific writer of at least eighty novels plus a great quantity of penny dreadful material herself. She was its "conductor," that is, editor, from its founding in 1866 until 1876, when it was sold to Chatto and Windus.

During her years as editor, *Belgravia*, a monthly shilling magazine, was directed to a "genteel, middleclass, lady public, of low to fair education standard."[2] It was accepted by Charles Edward Mudie for his lending library. Its content consisted of biographies, travel accounts, light essays, poetry, and serialized sensational/sentimental novels, many of which were written by Mary Elizabeth Braddon. As she wrote to Edward Bulwer-Lytton, she was "going in for strong sensational stories for 'Belgravia' not because I particularly believe in 'sensation,' but because I think the public shilling can only be extracted by strong measure." The title itself was another "bait for the shillings of Brixton and Bow," as she also told Bulwer-Lytton, when she asked him not to laugh "at the snobbery of the title."[3] The title, it was hoped, would induce the lower middle class to purchase the magazine so that they could move vicariously into a more fashionable world.[4] These devices must have worked, for the circulation reached 18,000 in 1868, according to the Printers' Register, and averaged 15,000 or less.[5] Although not spectacular, this circulation was respectable enough when one remembers William Tinsley's observation that in the middle of the nineteenth century "there were more magazines in the wretched field than were blades of grass to support them."[6]

Before assuming the editorship of *Belgravia*, Mary Elizabeth Braddon had already gained fame as the author of serialized sensation fiction: *Lady Audley's Secret* and *Aurora Floyd*. This type of novel would headline *Belgravia* for the next eleven years as she serialized her own novels in the magazine, some advertised only as "by the author of *Lady Audley's Secret*," others designated by her pseudonym, "Babington White." The titles clearly connote the content: *Colonel Benton's Entanglement, Hostages to Fortune, Loss for Love, Joshua Haggard's Daughter*. Sometimes more than one novel would run simultaneously in the magazine. Without a doubt, Maxwell, who loved Mary Elizabeth Braddon first as a mistress and then as a wife (he married her when his insane wife died in 1874), founded *Belgravia* so that she would have a vehicle for the serialization of her novels.

The second most frequent contributor during those eleven years was George Augustus Sala, a journalist and novelist who contributed articles to *Cornhill Magazine** and numerous other newspapers and periodicals, edited *Temple Bar* (1860–1866), and was a special correspondent of the *Daily Telegraph*, covering the Civil War in the United States, Garibaldi in Italy, and events in France, Russia, and Australia. Sala's articles in *Belgravia* were usually essays—sometimes satirical—whose subjects ranged widely over politics, travel, literature, art, and social commentary. Some such were "Paris Fashions"; "Of the Sensational Literature in Art," which was, in part, a defense of Mary Elizabeth Braddon's type of fiction; "Pre-Raphaelites"; and "Cooking". Other subjects included wills, prisons, architecture, and court and current events. His one serialized story in *Belgravia* during that period was "The Handsome Housekeeper." Few of the other contributors to *Belgravia* during Mary Elizabeth Braddon's editorship are remembered today. Exceptions are W. S. Gilbert and J. S. Le Fanu.

In March 1876 *Belgravia* was sold to Chatto and Windus, then prominent in the field of magazine publishing, and its name was changed to *Belgravia; An Illustrated London Magazine*. The illustrations became an integral part of the magazine, as they depicted sentimental and sensational scenes matching the moods of the story. The illustrators were identified by name, as were more and more authors of stories, poetry, and essays. With this sale, Mary Elizabeth Braddon ceased not only to be its editor but, for many years, a contributor, although her novel *Joshua Haggard's Daughter*, which had begun in *Belgravia* in December 1875, continued to be serialized through December 1876. Her place was taken by such well-known writers as Charles Reade, T. Adolphus Trollope (Anthony's brother), Wilkie Collins, Mark Twain, Ouida, Austin Dobson, A. C. Swinburne, and Bret Harte. Even Thomas Hardy's *The Return of the Native* was serialized in *Belgravia* during 1877–1878. George Sala continued to contribute his essays and stories, but not as frequently as before. The list of contributors was of course enhanced because many of these writers' works were being published in book form by Chatto and Windus. The *Belgravia Annual* was first published in 1876 and soon carried an appendix advertising Chatto and Windus's books.

From approximately 1879 a gradual decline in quality began, in both content and illustrations, although occasionally some good illustrated travel essays appeared, especially ones on country towns in England (1879–1880). By 1883 the decline was reflected in the paucity of illustrations, the increased number of advertisements for Chatto and Windus's books in about every three or four issues, and the numerous novels by relatively unknown writers. A. Conan Doyle ("The Great Keinplatz Experiment"), and Mary Elizabeth Braddon (who appeared again for the first and last time in *Belgravia* since relinquishing the editorship, with a new novel, *Mohawks*, in 1888) were about the only names still recognizable.

With volume 65 for 1888 the journal dropped the word "Illustrated" from its title. Volume 70, 1889, advertised this new title and a new publisher. Its format also changed. It was shorter, published no poetry, and offered no contributors familiar to readers today. Also, as the new title reflects, the illustrations had disappeared.

Another format change occurred in 1890, when *Belgravia* began to run advertisements at the end of each issue for sewing machines, pens, flea powder, "electropathic belts" for "health and strength," cures for corns and asthma, Allan's Anti-fat, Pear soaps, and new books from five new publishers. In all, the advertisements totaled approximately twenty-seven pages. By 1895 the typical story titles were "Story of a Broken Life," "In the Preacher's Heart," and "Only a Woman's Hand". The authors were mainly married women and clergy. *Belgravia* struggled along in this manner, even enlarging its format; but its demise was evident. The last issue was published in June 1899.

Like so many magazines, *Belgravia* was an image of its time. As a recent publication has noted, "It had not been a glorious magazine, but it had offered readers sensational adventures, tolerably harmless chit-chat, and occasional instruction. Its success vouches for its reliability as an index to one level of Victorian taste."[7]

Notes

1. Robert Lee Wolff, *Sensational Victorian* (New York, 1979), p. 80.

2. Alvar Ellegård, "The Readership of the Periodical Press in Mid-Victorian Britain," *Victorian Periodicals Newsletter*, no. 13 (1971):17.

3. Quoted in Wolff, p. 179.

4. Later Swinburne called the name a "damned shopbag sort of title" and added, *"Belgravia* stinks." Ibid.

5. Ellegård, p. 17; Richard D. Altick, *The English Common Reader* (Chicago, 1967), p. 359.

6. Quoted in Altick, p. 359.

7. Daniel Fader and George Bornstein, *British Periodicals of the Eighteenth and Nineteenth Centuries*, microform ed. (Ann Arbor, 1972), pp. 90–91.

Information Sources

BIBLIOGRAPHY

Fader, Daniel, and George Bornstein. *British Periodicals of the Eighteenth and Nineteenth Centuries*. Microform ed. Ann Arbor, 1972.

Wolff, Robert Lee. *Sensational Victorian*. New York, 1979.

INDEXES

1866–1881 in *Poole's Index*.

REPRINT EDITIONS

Microform: Early British Periodicals (UMI), reels 56–70.

LOCATION SOURCES

American

Widely available.

British

Complete runs: British Museum; Liverpool Public Library; National Library of Scotland.

Partial runs: Bodleian Library; Edinburgh Public Library; Edmonton Public Library; London University Library; Manchester Public Library; Roxborough Library (Exeter); Southampton Public Library.

Publication History

MAGAZINE TITLE AND TITLE CHANGES

Belgravia; A London Magazine, 1866–1876. *Belgravia; An Illustrated London Magazine*, 1876–1888. *Belgravia; A London Magazine*, 1888–1899.

VOLUME AND ISSUE DATA

Volumes 1–99, November 1866–June 1899. (Volumes 11–20 also called 2d series 1–10; volumes 21–28 also called 3d series 1–8).

Belgravia Annual, 1876–1889.

FREQUENCY OF PUBLICATION

Monthly.

PUBLISHERS

1866–1876: John Maxwell, Warwick House, Paternoster Row, London, S.E. 1876–1889: Chatto and Windus, Piccadilly, London; Spottiswoode and Co., New Street Square and Parliament Street, London. 1889–1897: F. V. White and Co., 31 Southampton Street, Strand, W.C. London. 1898–1899: May, Wyatt, and Co., 341 Strand, London.

EDITORS

Mary Elizabeth Braddon, November 1866–February 1876. Others unknown.

William H. Scheuerle

BENTLEY'S MISCELLANY

In the third decade of the nineteenth century, Richard Bentley was a successful London printer, in partnership with his older brother Samuel. Not content with just the physical production of someone else's choices, he longed to determine what was printed: to be a publisher. To this end, he left the business he and his brother had built, and by 1830 entered into partnership with Henry Colburn, who had successfully published popular fiction and other books, and was the founder and proprietor of the *New Monthly Magazine** (see *RA*). Bentley and Colburn were both strong-willed individuals—too strong-willed, apparently, for the cooperation necessary in their venture, and the partnership dissolved in 1832. An astute judge of what would sell, Bentley soon became a major force in London publishing. It was perhaps only natural that he should begin thinking of creating a periodical to rival his former partner's *New Monthly*. In particular, Bentley saw a place for an illustrated magazine, more humorous than Colburn's but less vituperative than the successful *Blackwood's** (see *RA*) and *Fraser's** (see *RA*). Originally to be called the *Wits' Miscellany*, it was renamed *Bentley's Miscellany* before the first issue appeared.

Much has been written about Bentley's inability to retain in his employ the talented, creative people necessary to make a monthly publication successful. Certainly, his relationship with his first two editors—Charles Dickens (1837–1839) and William H. Ainsworth (1839–1841)—was stormy. In the first case, at least, the fault was not entirely Bentley's. As his fiction became more popular, Charles Dickens reneged on the terms of his original agreement about the number of novels he had promised to write for the magazine. Bentley gave in to his increasingly temperamental—because so overcommitted—editor until, by mutual consent, Dickens left the *Miscellany* to Ainsworth's guidance.[1] This is not to say that Bentley was completely faultless. He did, for example, reduce Dickens's pay for contributing less than the contracted sixteen pages per issue, even though the editor cut his own work in order to fit in other contributors' fiction and essays. But the two major issues of contention between proprietor and editor were Dickens's claim to be unable to do all he had promised Bentley (while the author-editor nonetheless still had time to work on *Nicholas Nickleby* for Chapman and Hall) and Bentley's desire as publisher to have ultimate control over the material that appeared in the magazine. Not surprisingly, then, in his published statement of resignation Dickens, addressing the magazine as a child, announced with perhaps a touch of bitterness, "You have always been literally 'Bentley's' Miscellany, and never mine" ("Familiar Epistle from a Parent to a Child, Aged Two Years and Two Months," 5[March 1839]:220).

Ainsworth suffered similarly from Richard Bentley's desire to control the content, until he too refused to continue as editor. In December 1841 he resigned, and the editorship remains obscure after that time. Some sources suggest that Albert Smith served for a while; some mention Shirley Brooks; but little evidence for or against either attribution has yet surfaced.[2]

Bentley probably did achieve the greater control over editorial policies that he had wanted but rarely received while Dickens and Ainsworth were editors. Chafing at the behavior of his first editor, Bentley may have been responsible for the magazine's virtual silence on Dickens's work for the remaining years that he owned the magazine. The few comments that did appear were generally unfavorable. A July 1848 discussion of the "Memoir of Sir E. Bulwer Lytton, Bart.," for example, placed Lytton as "the most eminent of our living authors"; Dickens would be mentioned, the writer acknowledged, perhaps deprecatingly, "if you were speaking of comic genius or popularity." Five years later, a reviewer began a discussion of the recently completed *Bleak House* with an appearance of fairness: " 'Bleak House' is, in some respects, the worst of Mr. Dickens' fictions, but, in many more, it is the best." Recognizing merit in some passages of pathos, and acknowledging that some parts of the novel were "more powerful and more tender than anything that Dickens ever wrote," the reviewer nonetheless moved immediately to the obverse reaction: "but the whole is disappointing. . . . The story has not been carefully constructed." In particular, the reviewer objected to Dickens's "tendency to disagreeable exaggeration," to his "unnatural" (that is, unrealistic) characters, and to the "almost entire absence of humour" in the novel.

Although Bentley may have been unable to keep Dickens as editor, no one can dispute his genius at assembling contributions from top creative artists, often anonymously. Because of his own inducements and Dickens's persuasion, the first year's issues contained illustrations by George Cruikshank (to be followed soon after by John Leech); light poetry and short stories by, among others, Francis Mahoney, Samuel Lover, Ainsworth, Thomas Haynes Bayly, George Hogarth (Dickens's father-in-law), William Jerdan, the Reverend Richard Harris Barham, Sheridan Knowles, James Fenimore Cooper, Charles Whitehead, William Thackeray, Theodore Hook, and, of course, Dickens himself; and essays by William Maginn. Two surprises in particular were Maginn, who had written extensively for *Blackwood's* before cofounding and editing *Fraser's*, and Hook, who was the recently appointed editor of Colburn's *New Monthly*, *Bentley's* primary competitor. Maginn's drinking habits had begun to affect both his personal behavior and his professional performance, but his eight essays on Shakespeare, begun in May 1837, were among the finest literary analyses to appear in the *Miscellany* and received strong public approval.

In poetry, humorous and satiric verse dominated in these early years, especially the contributions from "Father Prout" (Francis Mahoney) and "Thomas Ingoldsby" (Richard Barham), whose "Country Legends" were particular favorites of the reading public. The magazine was also a significant means by which Longfellow's poetry reached an English audience.

Nonetheless, *Bentley's Miscellany*'s approximately one hundred pages each issue emphasized fiction. For the first issue, Dickens contributed the "Public Life of Mr. Tulrumble," which Bentley apparently found less humorous than he had hoped from the author of *Pickwick*. But this first issue was a success, and was followed by the even more successful February issue, with a circulation of 6,000, which contained the first installment of "Oliver Twist." Throughout its existence, in fact, *Bentley's* included at least one installment of a serialized novel in most monthly issues, and often overlapped the last installments of one novel with the first installments of the next. Ainsworth's "Jack Sheppard," for example, began early in 1839, before "Oliver Twist" had concluded. Such a procedure was calculated to gain for the new serial the audience that was completing the previous one. Thus, readers of *Bentley's Miscellany* received a constant and heavy dose of serialized fiction.

After Dickens and Ainsworth had left *Bentley's* editorship, Albert Smith became the most serialized novelist in its pages until early 1849. The quality of fiction began a sharp decline, and did not improve even after Ainsworth, having bought the magazine in November 1854, published serially the first of nearly a dozen of his less well known, because less well written, novels.

During the 1840s, however, an important shift occurred in *Bentley's* emphasis that was to become increasingly evident for the remaining two-thirds of its existence. By 1848, the number of reviews, analyses, and critiques of literature and literary figures in its pages had increased significantly. We begin to note among the regular features "Literature of the Month," occasionally called "Literary Notices" or "Popular Books of the Month," reviews which provide readers with brief indications of the contents and quality of biographies, travel books, histories, scientific books, and, of course, fiction and poetry.

In addition, while American literature had often appeared in *Bentley's* pages—in August 1840 "The Fall of the House of Usher" (anonymously); a section from *The Deerslayer* in September 1841; Longfellow's poetry irregularly from the magazine's first year; and Cooper's "Captaine Spite" from late 1846 through early 1848—discussions of American literature appeared more frequently in the late 1840s and early 1850s. Melville's work in particular was highlighted. *Mardi* received a mixed review in April 1849, *Redburn* was preferred in November of that year, and "The Whale" *(Moby Dick)* got high praise in January 1852. William Prescott, George Ticknor, Edward Everett, Longfellow, William Cullen Bryant, Cooper, and George Bancroft were the "American Literary Celebrities" featured in a lengthy June 1853 article.

Surprisingly, *Bentley's* contained very little discussion of American literature during the next fourteen years, while Ainsworth owned the magazine and included many of his own contributions. Not until Bentley had bought the *Miscellany* back from Ainsworth was American literature again discussed to any significant extent. In July 1868, "On Three Contemporary Poets" found Longfellow "deficient in proportion . . . [and] too frequently deficient in fire," and Bryant not "a really good poet," especially because of his "incapacity to write blank verse satisfactorily."

The comments in this discussion reflected another shift evident in *Bentley's* articles. Although *Bentley's* writers initially emphasized the positive in their reviews, they gradually came to be more openly critical of the literature and the authors they were reviewing. "Whatever success may attend Lord John Russell's political manoeuvres, this much is certain with respect to his literary efforts," one reviewer claimed in April 1859: "he is the author of more unreadable books than any other man in the kingdom." And, in his July 1868 article explaining Longfellow's and Bryant's weaknesses, George Smith also found fault with the

Poet Laureate: Tennyson was inferior to Browning "in dramatic power" and to Swinburne "in real lyric fire and fervent feeling." Yet even Swinburne and Browning did not have the "bardic fire" of poets earlier in the century, Smith added, citing Shelley, Byron, Coleridge, and Wordsworth. In addition to omitting any reference to Keats, Smith indicated a further bias, but one which was to prove accurate for half the twentieth century: "It may seem a bold assertion to make—and it is one which will doubtless cause all his indiscreet admirers to rise in arms—but we do not believe that Tennyson's poems will live for a very great length of time." Smith blamed Tennyson's obscurity of communication and frequent "poverty of thought."

Whether negative or positive, however, these analyses, along with literary biographies, were *Bentley's* strongest features during its last two decades. W. J. Clarke, whose pseudonym "Monkshood" was the by-line for many major articles from 1855 through 1859, wrote lengthy discussions of Thomas Macaulay, Thomas De Quincey, William Hazlitt, John Gibson Lockhart, Leigh Hunt, William Gifford, Samuel Coleridge, and other "Essayists and Reviewers," all with grace, good humor, and a keen eye for the particular from which readers could seize on the subject's general qualities. In the early- and mid-sixties, "Monkshood" discussed literary types (among them Harold Skimpole and Mr. Micawber), saying little about the works from which the types received their names, but tracing their development in other literature. Clarke's erudition and broad literary background are evident in both the content and the style of this series of essays.

Between these two series, "Prosings by Monkshood" and the literary types, Clarke reviewed current books or wrote "Retrospective Reviewals" of foreign literature in virtually every issue. And, adding some variety for his readers, his "Mingle-Mangle by Monkshood" provided in-depth analyses of specific literary subjects. In 1859, in two of his most important articles—both because their subjects were widely discussed and because ideas about them were in a state of flux—Clarke agreed with the developing majority view about both historical fiction and didactic fiction (46 [July 1859]:42–51; 46 [August 1859]:135–47). The two articles' lengths exemplify the increasing emphasis on critical discussions of literature that had been evident in *Bentley's Miscellany* for a decade, and that would remain until it merged into Bentley's *Temple Bar** in 1869.

"The value of historical, as well as of other fictions, must be measured," Clarke maintained, "by their power and skill ... rather than by the historical accuracy or importance of the events and persons introduced." Thus, immediately he emphasized the creativity of the author as the primary determinant of the "value" of literature, perhaps a strange word in the normally non-utilitarian universe of artistic endeavor. But Clarke at least implicitly defined "value" for his readers. Well-written historical fiction enabled one to become "familiar with the every-day life of the age and the country in which the scene" occurred, a point also made in other major periodicals of the day. In his discussion, Clarke never lost sight of the efficacy of the imagination to transform "weary, flat, and unprofitable . . . minutiae of historical lore'' into a means of conveying both the essence and the facts of past ages. If the ''history'' in historical fiction were grossly inaccurate, readers would be misled. Historical fiction thus was essential as a ''complement to history'' because the novelist descried ''living human forms beneath the dim formulas of the historian.''

Such a view combined the concept of the creative imagination with an apparently necessary didacticism, and Clarke seemed aware of the inherent danger in that approach. For in the following month's issue he wrote an even longer article stating his opposition to overt didacticism: ''Artistic value is marred by the prominence given to the didactic element:—the characters thereby lose their spontaneity, and want the breath of life; they seem not so much to have sprung into being from the fervent depths of a creative imagination . . . as to have been called into existence for the purpose of embodying certain moral ideas.'' While literature should indeed delight and teach, then, the didactic element ''should be *immanent*, not *transient*.''

Thus, through its thirty-two years of existence, the emphasis of *Bentley's Miscellany* shifted from original literature, which it never eliminated entirely, to literary criticism, which eventually became more interesting than the literature which appeared in its pages. Perhaps best symbolizing this shift was its review of E. S. Dallas's *The Gay Science* in February 1867. The ''gay science'' was criticism, and the reviewer quoted extensively and approvingly from Dallas's text. Agreeing that ''the object of art is pleasure,'' a view writers were to take to extremes over the next thirty years, the reviewer placed that idea in its historical context. Exhibiting the broad range of learning so many other articles in the previous ten years had shown, the reviewer traced the development of criticism from classical antiquity through the Renaissance to contemporary German thought. He looked forward to a ''new era of criticism,'' one of objective criticism during which literary analysis would ''no longer depend . . . upon the mere assertion of individuals, but upon facts, and the knowledge brought by individuals to bear upon any given subject.'' Dallas's book and *Bentley's* lengthy review were looking to the future, past the aestheticism of the coming decades.

Bentley's was ahead of its time in another way as well. Unlike the articles in many contemporary magazines, its articles were clearly written and easy to read; turgid or vapid prose rarely escaped the editorial blue pencil. In this sense, it certainly practiced the techniques that it encouraged among the authors whose work it discussed. In fact, one of its major objections was the obscurity of much contemporary literature. On the one hand, Robert Browning's poetry, for example, expressed ''a lofty moral earnestness, . . . subtle intellect, deep searchings of heart, shrewd experience, genial spirits, aesthetic culture, lyrical expression''; on the other hand, a reader, upon ''the most cursory perusal'' of *Men and Women*, could ''hardly escape a conviction that the poet's penchant for elliptical diction, interjectional dark sayings, *multum in parvo* (and, sometimes, seemingly *minimum in multo*) 'deliverances,' flighty fancies, unkempt similitudes, quaintest conceits, slipshod familiarities, and grotesque exaggerations, is unhealthily on the increase" ("Browning's 'Men and Women,' " 39 [January 1856]:64–65). In fact, a *Bentley's* writer lamented in its final year, such obfuscation was a problem among contemporary poets generally: "Judging by their efforts, many poets of late years would seem to indulge the idea that, until they have produced something the public mind cannot grasp, they have not made out their title to be considered real poets" ("On Three Contemporary Poets," 64 [July 1868]:66).

When he finally merged his *Miscellany* into *Temple Bar*, Richard Bentley may have looked back over the previous three decades with some regret—perhaps at his relationship with some of the people who had worked with him, perhaps at his need to consolidate his literary efforts in an increasingly expensive and competitive world, perhaps even at the decline in quality of the literature that he had published in recent years. But he could be proud that he and William Harrison Ainsworth had provided readers with thirty-two years of literary entertainment that was both informative and well written.

Notes

1. Edgar Johnson, *Charles Dickens: His Tragedy and Triumph* (New York, 1952), 1:179–309 *passim*; L. M. Littlewood, "A Victorian Magazine," *Contemporary Review* 151 (1937):331–39.

2. Smith is listed in *New Cambridge Bibliography of English Literature*, ed. George Watson (Cambridge, England, 1969), vol. 3, col. 1846; Brooks is mentioned by Littlewood, p. 338.

Information Sources

BIBLIOGRAPHY
Axon, W. E. A. *William Harrison Ainsworth. A Memoir*. London, 1902.
Ellis, S. M. *William Harrison Ainsworth and His Friends*. 2 vols. London, 1911.
Johnson, Edgar. *Charles Dickens: His Tragedy and Triumph*. 2 vols. New York, 1952.
INDEXES
> Each volume indexed, except for final volume. *Poole's Index*. *Wellesley Index* 4 (projected).

REPRINT EDITIONS
> Microform: Early British Periodicals (UMI), reels 152–163. NCR Microcard Editions.

LOCATION SOURCES
American
> Widely available.

British
> Complete runs: Aberdeen University Library; Birmingham Public Library; Bodleian Library; British Museum; Cambridge University Library; Edinburgh Public Library; Guildhall Library; Leeds Public Library.
> Partial runs: Widely available.

Publication History

MAGAZINE TITLE AND TITLE CHANGES
Bentley's Miscellany.

VOLUME AND ISSUE DATA
Volumes 1–64, January 1837–December 1868. (Merged into *Temple Bar*.)
FREQUENCY OF PUBLICATION
Monthly.
PUBLISHERS
Volume 1–part of volume 49, January 1837–March 1861: Richard Bentley, New Burlington Street, London. Part of volume 49–volume 63, April 1861–June 1868: Chapman and Hall, 193 Piccadilly, London. Volume 64, July–December 1868: Richard Bentley, New Burlington Street, London; Menzies, Edinburgh; Thomas Murray and Son, Glasgow; M'Glashan and Gill, Dublin. (American edition: Jemima M. Mason, New York, volumes 1–64.)
EDITORS
Charles Dickens, January 1837–February 1839. William Harrison Ainsworth, March 1839–December 1841. Albert Smith, n.d. Shirley Brooks (?), n.d. George Bentley (?), n.d.

Roger P. Wallins

BLACKWOOD'S EDINBURGH MAGAZINE. See RA, MA

BLUE REVIEW, THE

In 1913 the *Blue Review* appeared as a fated supplement to the magazine *Rhythm*,* which John Middleton Murry had begun in 1911 as an undergraduate at Oxford. Like *Rhythm*, the *Blue Review* was an "ambitious, cosmopolitan review [that] betrayed its undergraduate origins."[1] But whereas *Rhythm* had initially acquired solid financial backing, the *Blue Review* was a brief, desperate project. Murry left Oxford in 1912 and shortly thereafter became Katherine Mansfield's lover. She became associate editor of *Rhythm*, and her publisher, Stephen Swift, considered becoming the publisher of the review. But his bankruptcy left Murry and Mansfield financially stranded; *Rhythm* became the *Blue Review* and survived for only three numbers, for May, June, and July 1913.

In addition to suffering financial woes, the *Blue Review* was also caught between the indefatigable idealism of Murry and Mansfield and the reality of its Georgian contributors, who were for the most part mediocre and enervated. The two great exceptions were Mansfield herself, who contributed four stories to the review, and D. H. Lawrence, who contributed a story, "The Soiled Rose," to the first number, and an essay on Thomas Mann to the last: "But Thomas Mann is old—and we are young. Germany does not feel very young to me" (no. 3:206). Also of note is a satirical etching by Max Beerbohm, "A Study in Dubiety," which appears as the frontispiece for the first number.

Otherwise, the reviews of art, music, literature, and drama are generally unimpressive, stilted pieces. J. D. Beresford's essay for the second number—

"Anger and Dismay: A Footnote on the Writings of H. G. Wells"—for example, laboriously debates whether Dickens was more propagandistic than Wells (no. 2:88–96). Murry's essays on literature, particularly on Stendhal and the modern novel, and W. Denis Browne's essays on music, which are critical of Georgian self-indulgence and boredom, are much sharper and more vigorous than most.

While the review articles are merely uneven, the poetry is consistently poor. Virtually all of the poems exhibit the mannerisms, sentimentality, and diluted symbolism against which modernists such as Pound, Eliot, and Lawrence reacted. Even the poetry by recognizable names—Walter De la Mare, Rupert Brooke, W. H. Davies—suffers from these *fin de siècle* symptoms. The fiction of Mansfield and Lawrence nudged the review toward a modernist perspective; the poetry, however, anchored it to the previous century.

In short, the *Blue Review* betrayed contradictory impulses—some Georgian, others "undergraduate," still others modernist. It seems to have lacked political focus as well. Not surprisingly, therefore, Lawrence was at once attracted to the review and scornful of it. To one friend he wrote, "Are you giving any drawings to that scoundrel, the *Blue Review*? 'Scoundrel' is half-affectionate, of course."[2] And it was Lawrence who correctly saw the demise of the review to be a blessing for its coeditors. As Murry tells it, "He had no sympathy with our feeling of depression at the decease of *The Blue Review*; on the contrary, he assured us that it was a good riddance, and he was very insistent that we should seize the opportunity of breaking away from England . . . to live beside him in Italy."[3]

Murry needed to abandon the review for his health; Mansfield needed to give her energies to her remarkable short stories. Of the three "Epilogues" that appeared in the review, one biographer has written, "As virtuoso pieces they are consummately deft (as Katherine knew when she refused to cut 'Violet' by half a page for the *Blue Review*); but put to the test that Lawrence would have applied, they fail: they make us care too little."[4]

The last remark could serve as the epitaph for the *Blue Review*: taken as a whole, it makes us care too little. We should also recognize, however, the courage, ambition, and sheer energy required of Murry and Mansfield simply to keep *Rhythm* and the *Blue Review* afloat for as long as they did. Furthermore, modernist literature has its roots in such uneven, financially troubled magazines, for while their identities were often indistinct, they gave writers like Lawrence an income and an early forum.

Notes

1. Nicholas Joost and Alvin Sullivan, *D. H. Lawrence and "The Dial"* (Carbondale, Ill., 1970), p. 215n.

2. Lawrence to Ernest Collings, 13 May 1913, *The Letters of D. H. Lawrence*, ed. James T. Boulton and George T. Zytaruk (Cambridge, England, 1979), 1:548.

3. John Middleton Murry, *Between Two Worlds: An Autobiography* (New York, 1936), p. 262.

4. Antony Alpers, *Katherine Mansfield: A Biography* (New York, 1953), p. 193.

Information Sources

BIBLIOGRAPHY

Alpers, Antony. *Katherine Mansfield: A Biography*. New York, 1953.

Joost, Nicholas, and Alvin Sullivan. *D. H. Lawrence and "The Dial."* Carbondale, Ill., 1970.

Lawrence, D. H. *The Letters of D. H. Lawrence*. Edited by James T. Boulton and George J. Zytaruk. Cambridge, England, 1979–.

Mansfield, Katherine. *The Letters and Journals of Katherine Mansfield: A Selection*. Edited by C. K. Stead. London, 1977.

Murry, John Middleton. *Between Two Worlds: An Autobiography*. New York, 1936.

INDEXES

> None

REPRINT EDITIONS

> London, 1968.
> Microform: Kraus Reprint.

LOCATION SOURCES

American

> Complete runs: Henry E. Huntington Library; Newberry Library; New York Public Library; Princeton University Library; U.S. Library of Congress; University of Buffalo Library; University of California, Berkeley, Library; University of Michigan Library; University of Minnesota Library.
>
> Partial runs: Ohio State University Library; University of Texas Library; Yale University Library.

British

> Complete runs: British Museum; Leeds Public Library; Manchester Public Library; Victoria and Albert Museum Library.

Publication History

MAGAZINE TITLE AND TITLE CHANGES

> *The Blue Review; Literature, Drama, Art, Music.*

VOLUME AND ISSUE DATA

> Volume 1, numbers 1–3, May–July 1913.

FREQUENCY OF PUBLICATION

> Monthly.

PUBLISHER

> Martin Secker, London.

EDITOR

> John Middleton Murry, with the assistance of Katherine Mansfield and D. H. Lawrence.

Hans Ostrom

BOOKMAN, THE

William Robertson Nicoll planned the *Bookman* in 1886 but other work prevented him from issuing it until 1891. By then he was well known as editor of the *British Weekly* and as literary advisor to the publishers Hodder & Stoughton. Nicoll felt that there was a place for a sixpenny monthly literary journal that would be less costly to produce and more acceptable than a weekly to readers with limited time. He was greatly interested in the history and development of English literature and saw the new publication as a basis for further work in this field.[1] Nicoll was essentially a journalist and a popularizer of literature and this helped his journal to succeed. Such journals as *Literature** and the *Academy,** although more academic in standard, were less successful, and even the famous *Athenaeum** (see *RA*) did not survive long into the twentieth century. Only Nicoll, among his contemporaries, "created a purely literary periodical which proved a commercial success."[2]

The editor claimed in "Ten Years of 'The Bookman' " in the issue for September 1901 that his journal was useful to "Bookbuyers, Bookreaders and Booksellers," and in order to make it popular included many "News Notes" and short paragraphs about authors, publishers, and booksellers. These were curtailed in later issues, and are much criticized by present-day writers as "trash," but are often of interest and value to researchers because they contain facts not always available elsewhere. Book reviews predominated, and a notable feature was a section entitled "The Reader," containing articles on and by well-known authors, as well as general literary subjects. These were as up to date as possible and continued for many years. New authors were specially encouraged by a young authors' page, while other features included literary competitions and lists of new and forthcoming books.

A later writer, inclined to be critical of the magazine, described it as "exclusively devoted to the spirit of belles lettres," and undoubtedly it was, but perhaps this was not necessarily a fault.[3] To the dedicated bookman there is pleasure in browsing over even the many publishers' advertisements that appeared in the magazine and that sometimes contain information of value to bibliographers. Of the first number, an edition of 10,000 copies was quickly sold, to be followed by a further 5,000 and even a third printing. It included "Recollections of the Carlyles and Their Circle" by Francis Espinasse, an article on Kipling by E. Purcell, and a map of Thomas Hardy's Wessex. As noted in "The Majority of the Bookman" for October 1912 (no. 253:43), Nicoll had the help of J. M. Barrie in his early numbers and of the experienced journalists J. A. Spender and H. W. Massingham. Many authors famous at the time were represented, as were many whose reputations have survived well into the present century.

During the first year Nicoll printed contributions by J. M. Barrie, Thomas Hardy, C. H. Herford, A. T. Quiller-Couch, William Watson, and W. B. Yeats. He claimed in the same article cited above that some of Yeats's finest lyrics first appeared in the *Bookman*, and Yeats reviewed Robert Bridges's poetry and wrote on William Morris, while Walter Pater reviewed Oscar Wilde's *The Picture of Dorian Gray*. Although few at first, a notable addition to later issues were the many illustrations, which became a feature of the journal, especially evident in the famous special and supplementary numbers of later years.

In September 1901 Nicoll wrote an article in his journal on "Ten Years of 'The Bookman,' " in which he listed some of the distinguished authors whose work he had printed. In addition to those already mentioned, he named George Saintsbury, Edward Dowden, W. P. Ker, A. C. Swinburne, Andrew Lang, C. K. Shorter, Richard Garnett, G. K. Chesterton, T. E. Page, David Masson, E. K. Chambers, A.E.W. Mason, James Douglas, Thomas Seccombe, and even T. J. Wise. In 1895 advertisements had appeared in the magazine which claimed that "the Bookman is the only monthly magazine entirely devoted to the interests of literature."

Nicoll secured a succession of able assistants, among them Annie Macdonell, who wrote much in the journal. In 1898 Nicoll was joined by J. E. Hodder-Williams, who became assistant editor, and later by Arthur St. John Adcock, who was destined to succeed Nicoll as editor. Although he remained editor-in-chief until his death, Nicoll's many other activities forced him in later years to leave much of the editorial work to his assistant and acting editor, St. John Adcock.

Around the end of the century new contributors included William Archer, William Canton, Conan Doyle, Lionel Johnson, and Alice Meynell. New series were started and some numbers were principally devoted to a literary figure of eminence. There was a Dr. Johnson number, and others on Dickens, Thackeray, and Ruskin. The death of a notable author was the occasion of a symposium from his contemporaries, accompanied by many illustrations. Artists were also represented in such numbers; one was replete with Hugh Thomson's illustrations, while another issue was largely concerned with James McNeill Whistler.

Around 1912 the magazine reached its peak number of illustrations in the enormous Christmas numbers. In December 1912, for two shillings, there were 316 pages and more than 600 illustrations, many in color (actually often surplus plates supplied by publishers from books reviewed).

About this time special "extra numbers" were issued. There was a special Keats-Shelley Memorial Souvenir in connection with matinees at the Haymarket Theatre in June 1912, and in 1913 there appeared what was described as "the first of The Bookman Extra Numbers," a separate publication of 222 pages modeled on the famous Christmas numbers, which sold for five shillings and was devoted solely to Robert Louis Stevenson. It was evidently popular, for an advertisement for it mentioned "10th thousand." A further extra number on Charles Dickens appeared in 1914, with contributions by G. K. Chesterton, F. G. Kitton, B. W. Matz, W. Robertson Nicoll, and Alfred Noyes. The outbreak of war stopped these separate numbers, and they were not resumed when hostilities ceased.

In the early years of the twentieth century some distinguished contributors were added. In 1905 Walter De la Mare first appeared, as did Hilaire Belloc and Arthur Ransome. Edward Thomas reviewed many books, including Richard Jefferies's *The Story of My Heart*. He wrote on "Richard Jefferies and London," while George Saintsbury contributed an article on Henry Fielding for "The

Reader'' section. Walter De la Mare reviewed Hardy's *The Dynasts* and also wrote on William Butler Yeats.

The size of the magazine was reduced during the war years, but there were some special features: a "War Book Supplement," an article on Russian authors, and a contribution from St. John Adcock entitled "For Remembrance," on authors who had died in the war. This was subsequently enlarged and published as a book in at least two editions. The special Christmas numbers continued through the war, but the enlarged spring and autumn issues were not resumed until 1919.

Great efforts were made to extend the range and usefulness of the magazine, and new departments were included on music and drama. The American literary scene was now covered; literary competitions, always a feature, were extended; and even greater efforts were made to encourage new writers. Among new contributors were Harold Child, Walter Jerrold, Arthur Waugh, S.P.B. Mais, H. J. Massingham, Laurence Binyon, Siegfried Sassoon, Rose Macaulay, Somerset Maugham, and Frank Swinnerton.

In October 1921 W. M. Parker wrote in the magazine on the thirty-years' record of the *Bookman*, and he was able to say, "It is doubtful whether any other literary magazine of our day could bring forward so long and catholic a list of remarkable contributors." Two years later Nicoll died and was succeeded as chief editor by St. John Adcock, who had been acting editor for many years. Under his control there was little real change, although the magazine lacked something of the "stimulus of Nicoll's editorial mind."[4] There were, however, still many items of permanent interest, such as those by Major Samuel Butterworth, Roger Ingpen, J. M. Turnbull, and Mrs. G. A. Anderson on Lamb, Hazlitt, Leigh Hunt, and the old *London Magazine** (see *RA*) circle.

Interesting articles included Mary Webb on Jane Austen, G. K. Chesterton on "Magic and Fantasy in Fiction," and "Some Remarks on Ghost Stories," by M. R. James. Opportunities were taken when centenaries occurred; in 1927 John Freeman wrote on William Blake the poet, and Frank Rutter on Blake as an artist. There were articles on Australian, New Zealand, and South African writers. Edmund Blunden wrote on Lafcadio Hearn, Richard Church on Robert Bridges, and Arthur Bryant on Charles II as a man of letters. A section entitled "The Collector" was added dealing with antiquarian books and book sales, backed up by advertisements of dealers in second-hand books.

St. John Adcock died in 1930, and the July issue had tributes from leading men of letters. In these it was said that "to the editor nothing that had its roots in sincere human feeling and in a genuine attempt to widen the limits of literary expression, was outside the province of the journal" (no. 466:238).

The new editor was Hugh Ross Williamson, who set about changing the layout and contents of the journal, bringing it more in line with contemporary taste. Features were added on broadcasting, crossword puzzles, and the gramophone, and articles appeared on contemporary foreign writers and Soviet literature. New contributors to the journal included Geoffrey Grigson, Robert Graves, Edith

Sitwell, Winifred Holtby, and F. R. Leavis; Llewelyn Powys wrote on Lucretius and Sidney Webb on "State Publishing in Russia," and there was a short story by Samuel Beckett.

By 1930 the literary climate was changing, and in 1932 the editor stressed the two most important influences of change: the rapid expansion of the popular press and the introduction of broadcasting. In "Notes at Random" (no. 494:1), he deplored that "a popular press existing on advertisement revenue, which in turn is dependent on a wide circulation, has debased the general level of thought and culture in every department of life." This was reflected in the falling circulation of the *Bookman*.

To counteract this development new sections were added: Collin Brooks on economics, Vernon Barlett on foreign affairs, and C. P. Snow on science, as well as coverage of politics, the theater, the cinema, and religion. Christmas numbers were still enormous; that for 1933 cost six shillings, but for this there were 386 pages, containing much of interest and hundreds of illustrations.

In the spring of 1934 Hugh Ross Williamson left the *Bookman* and became editor of the *Strand Magazine*.* He was succeeded by his younger brother, Reginald Pole Ross Williamson, who made further determined efforts to prolong the life of the journal. However, costs had risen and sales had fallen, until the proprietors decided to get rid of the magazine. The Williamsons attempted to buy it, feeling that it was too good to die, but they failed, and the last number to appear was the Christmas number for December 1934, a sumptuous production with contributions from Arthur Bryant, Geoffrey Grigson, Helen Simpson, James Hilton, William Plomer, A. J. Cronin, T. F. Powys, and C. G. Coulton.[5] Starting in January 1935 the magazine was amalgamated with the *London Mercury*.

Although no longer editor, Hugh Ross Williamson still contributed during the last few months and wrote a valediction, "Last Notes at Random," in the last issue for December 1934 (no. 512:135), in which he said that the "enormous and continually increasing reading public, whose staple diet is the newspaper and the cheap magazine," seek only for these as "narcotics to lessen the strain of living" and ignore the better type of book. This was undoubtedly one of the main causes of the decease of the *Bookman* and was reflected in other popular literary journals of the time.

The popularity of the magazine for much of its life is proved by its longevity. Its object had always been to appeal to the average intelligent reader and to provide a popular account of contemporary literature combined with much about the past, all provided by some of the best writers of the time. In this it succeeded. It was never aimed at a scholarly or academic readership. For this there were other publications, although they were mostly short-lived. The *Bookman* was intended for the lover of books, while including other fields of culture. Few publications can show such a distinguished list of famous names among their contributors. It contained much of value and for many years was acceptable "to the mighty army of conservative readers."[6] Its success was due largely to the ideas of two remarkable men, William Robertson Nicoll, the founder, and J. E. Hodder-Williams, later chief editorial director of the publishers.[7]

Notes

1. John Attenborough, *A Living Memory: Hodder & Stoughton: Publishers 1868–1975* (London, 1975), p. 44.
2. T. H. Darlow, *William Robertson Nicoll: Life and Letters* (London, 1925), p. 102.
3. John Gross, *The Rise and Fall of the Man of Letters* (London, 1973), p. 223.
4. Attenborough, p. 115.
5. Hugh Ross Williamson, *The Walled Garden* (London, 1956), p. 96.
6. Joy Grant, *Harold Monro and the Poetry Bookshop* (London, 1967), p. 136.
7. Letter from Hodder & Stoughton, Ltd., to Claude A. Prance, 22 January 1981.

Information Sources

BIBLIOGRAPHY

Attenborough, John. *A Living Memory: Hodder & Stoughton: Publishers 1868–1975*. London, 1975.
Bookman, The. Various articles, particularly W. Robertson Nicoll, "Ten Years of *The Bookman*," October 1912; W. Robertson Nicoll, "*The Bookman*," September 1917; W. M. Parker, "*The Bookman*: A Thirty Years Record," October 1921.
Darlow, T. H. *William Robertson Nicoll: Life and Letters*. London, 1925.
Gross, John. *The Rise and Fall of the Man of Letters*. London, 1973.
Prance, Claude A. *The Laughing Philosopher*. London, 1976.
Williamson, Hugh Ross. *The Walled Garden*. London, 1956.
INDEXES
Each volume indexed.
REPRINT EDITIONS
Microform: Early British Periodicals (UMI), reels 567–579. N. A. Kovach, Los Angeles, Calif.
LOCATION SOURCES
American
Widely available.
British
Widely available.

Publication History

MAGAZINE TITLE AND TITLE CHANGES
The Bookman. (Merged with *The London Mercury* January 1935–April 1939, and *Life & Letters* May 1939–February 1946.)
VOLUME AND ISSUE DATA
Volumes 1–87, numbers 1–519, October 1891–December 1934.
FREQUENCY OF PUBLICATION
Monthly.

PUBLISHER

Hodder & Stoughton Ltd., 27 Paternoster Row, London E.C./St. Paul's House, Warwick Lane, London (in 1906).

EDITORS

Sir William Robertson Nicoll (editor-in-chief), 1891–1923. Sir J. E. Hodder-Williams (acting assistant editor), 1898–1903. (Most of the editing was actually done by Nicoll's editorial team, including Annie Macdonell and Jane Stoddart.) Arthur St. John Adcock (assistant editor from 1908, editor 1923–1930). Hugh Ross Williamson, 1930–1934. Reginald Pole Ross Williamson, 1934.

Claude A. Prance

BOOKSELLER, THE

In 1858, when he started the *Bookseller*, Joseph Whitaker was the thirty-eight-year-old editor of the *Gentleman's Magazine** (see *AAAJ*). Whitaker served his book trade apprenticeship with John Henry Parker of Oxford. He worked as Parker's London agent, joined J. W. Parker & Co., a prominent theological publisher, and began a number of other ventures, including *Whitaker's Clergyman's Diary,* which prospered for over sixty years. In 1856 Whitaker was appointed editor of the socially prestigious *Gentleman's Magazine,* where he created a basic trade journal that catered to his own needs as editor and bookman. There existed in London at this time various journals serving the major publishing houses, but none which was comprehensive. As early as 1837 a group of publishers who were unhappy with existing trade journals financed the *Publishers' Circular* which, owing to its restricted backing, served a very limited circle. The title page of the initial issue of *The Bookseller; A Handbook of British and Foreign Literature* succinctly expressed Whitaker's needs. The new journal contained "a complete list of all the works issued in the United Kingdom, and the chief works published abroad during the year 1858." The second page of the first issue for January 1858 stated:

This work is intended primarily for the use of BOOKSELLERS and PUBLISHERS furnishing them with a handy book of reference, and doing for the Bookselling trade what *Bradshaw* does for railways, but so conducted that it may be equally useful for the Book-buyer and to the Bookseller. It will be issued on the 23rd of every month, in time for the Trade to order from their monthly parcels.

The opening pages of the January 1858 number contain notices of bankruptcies ("Thos. Taylor, paper-dealer, Birmingham" leads what has become over more than a century a long list), insolvents, dissolutions of partnership, sales by auction, recent sales, and prices realized, followed by "Trade Changes and Gossip."

Joseph Whitaker undoubtedly penned the unsigned editorial statement of aims found in the third issue, for March 1858:

> The Bookseller is published monthly, and is intended to supply the Trade with a complete list of books published or announced during the month, whether issued in Great Britain, the United States of America, or the Continent. This list of books is arranged in classes so that those persons interested in publications of one description may at a glance see what works have been published on the subject. The Bookseller also contains so much of the Gazette as relates to persons connected with the trade, notices of sales by-auction and prices realised, changes in business, law cases, and generally of every matter of interest to the bookseller, including obituary notices of deceased members of the trade. All the principal books of the month are noticed, briefly, but it is believed at sufficient length to convey a very accurate opinion regarding the contents and merits, or assumed merits, of the works noticed.

Whitaker goes on to stress the nature of the reviewing aspect of the Bookseller, whose "notices are to a great extent written for the purpose of conveying information to such persons in the trade as may not have an opportunity of reading the book for themselves, but who may be called upon to give an opinion, or description of the works, to their customers." Over the years, the reviews in the Bookseller have not been its strongest point. Until recently, reviews were unsigned, and few have been distinguished.

The principal importance of the Bookseller throughout its publication lies in its factual accounts of book trade fluctuations, announcements, records of items published, advertisements, obituaries, and gossip. Accordingly, the June 1858 issue notes that "the only remarkable event of the month is the dullness of the book trade, owing to a variety of depressing causes." Four are given: "the warmness of the weather; the unsettled state of political affairs; the unusually early period of the Oxford and Cambridge vacations; and the overspeculativeness of some publishers in the early part of the season." From these it concluded that "the greatest evil of the day is unquestionably the spirit of underselling that prevails"—a subject to which the Bookseller continually returned throughout the nineteenth century. Along with the English Catalogue, the columns of the journal provide, in addition to a record of facts about the book trade, a more or less definitive record of what was published in nineteenth-century Britain. Despite Antonio Panizzi's sterling efforts "to enforce the provision in the copyright law that required copies of all new publications to be deposited" in the British Museum, Richard Altick observes, "relatively little current literature was received."[1] The General Catalogue of Printed Books in the British Museum provides only a partial record of books actually published. For further details regarding publications and dates, the researcher must go to the listings in the Bookseller. Its bibliographical importance as a record of publication cannot be underestimated. Originally, listing was simply comprised of a catalogue of books published under the appropriate classification, with an abbreviated index of authors and titles referring back to the full information in the classified list. This format developed into an alphabetical author, title, and subject listing with the subject forming part of the title. Today there are full details listed on author, title, editor, translator, illustrations, series, price, publication date, publisher, and standard book numbering. The listing appears weekly and is cumulated to form a catalogue of the month's publications. Monthly and annual cumulative listings are also published once a quarter.[2]

A further notable feature of the *Bookseller* has been its obituary sections. The January 1860 number records that "three of the greatest masters, writing the same language and popular in the same land, have been called away from their labours within the brief period of a single month." Admittedly, for an account of the lives of Washington Irving, Thomas De Quincey, and Lord Macaulay it is not necessary to search through the back numbers of the *Bookseller*; however, its obituaries often do provide a record of trade figures who otherwise would pass into total obscurity. In the columns for December 1874, for example, we learn of the death of one William Tunbridge, "assistant of Messrs Hatchard," the famous bookseller's warehouseman and head collector, who "also kept all the collecting cash accounts." Tunbridge worked for Hatchard for half a century and should not be ignored when the definitive history of the shop is written.

Another mine of information found in the *Bookseller* lies in its correspondence, much of which concerns the problems of underselling. For example, an examination of the July to September 1883 issues reveals reaction to Charles Lutwidge Dodgson's insistence that his books be sold by Macmillan's at the price the firm announced. "He insisted," as Morton N. Cohen points out, "that Macmillan notify booksellers that for Lewis Carroll's books, the publisher would in future reduce the discount from [three pence] in the shilling to [two pence] and would no longer supply 'odd books,' that is, twenty-one books for every twenty ordered."[3] Cohen quotes from a 24 July 1883 letter to the *Bookseller* from an unidentified firm of London Booksellers strongly objecting to "the new regime . . . inaugurated by Mr. Lewis Carroll" and recommending a boycott by the book trade of Lewis Carroll's books. Editorials in the *Bookseller* supported Carroll. Macmillan's put pressure on him not to reply publicly. Subsequently published *Bookseller* correspondence reveals both support for Carroll and opposition to his position. Carroll's "books were sold to booksellers and public on very much the terms he himself set, in the face of the continuing discount system practised on almost all other books." The affair may be placed in the context of the *Bookseller*'s continuing attempt to influence the book trade to settle the issue of book discounting. Its correspondence columns and editorials formed part of the pressure leading to the Net Book Agreement of 1899, which, according to Cohen, "eliminated the evil of the discount system altogether."[4]

An indication of the influence and importance of the *Bookseller* in the early decades of the twentieth century, and an assessment of its strengths and weaknesses as a tool of the book trade, may be found in the reports of the committee set up in 1926 to investigate the problems of the British book trade. Three reports were issued in 1928–1929 and published ten years later. Deliberations on "Trade Tools" reported that in 1928 at least five papers "catering for the trade" existed: the *Publishers Circular*; the *Bookseller*; the *Newsagent*; the *Clique*; and the *National Newsagent*. Of these journals, only the *Clique* restricted its circulation to the book trade. The others were available to the public, "and therefore discussion in them of purely trade questions and problems was sometimes inadvisable." The committee decided that, "as the information in them was not necessarily *authoritative* or *official*, booksellers were often ill-informed on vital points connected with their business. A trade paper embodying all the features required for a business tool did not, it was thought, exist." Twelve areas singled out as "of the utmost importance" yet receiving "inadequate treatment" were: (1) "Systematic arrangement of announcements of forthcoming books—with dates as far as possible"; (2) "List of newly published books, with subject index"; (3) "List of second-hand 'wants' and 'offers' "; (4) "Official notices of trade organizations"; (5) Editorials; (6) Correspondence; (7) "Alterations of prices, including de-netting of books"; (8) "Announcements of books offered at remainder prices"; (9) "Travellers' movements"; (10) "Information about books out of print"; (11) "Personal notes"; (12) "Illustrations selected for their value as 'Trade Tools.' "[5]

As a consequence of these findings, in 1928 the *Bookseller* became the "Official Trade Paper." The Whitaker family transferred their journal to the trusteeship of official organizations—the Publishers Association and Associated Booksellers. "G. S. Williams was appointed editor" of what was now called the *Publisher and Bookseller*. "The experiment lasted five years, after which Whitaker's exercised their option and terminated the agreement. The title of the journal reverted to the *Bookseller* and it was edited by Edmond Segrave." Segrave became its fourth editor and the first outside the Whitaker family circle. Editing the *Bookseller* until 1971, he extended its circulation,[6] opened "its columns to trade controversy," and encouraged the whole trade to submit news items. He initiated "features, invariably with a pseudonymous byline," and at the end of each year he published a résumé of the year's events, including a cherished "twice yearly honours list, which did not neglect literature and the book trade."[7] Since Segrave's editorship the masthead of the *Bookseller* has proclaimed its title as "The Organ of the Book Trade." Certainly the range of its contents comprehensively covers the twelve areas cited by the book trade committee of the late 1920s.

The *Bookseller* has come a long way since 1858 and today prospers. The present cover is glossy and the journal is packed with advertisements, letters, articles, news, trade chit-chat, and the indispensable weekly book listings. Segrave wrote in a centenary editorial (3 May 1958) that the *Bookseller* "throughout . . . has chronicled events, controversies . . . disasters, quirks and quiddities of the British book trade." Therein lies its importance. Regrettably, apart from

Whitaker's weekly, monthly, and annual cumulative book listings, no journal index exists. Therefore it is inevitable that much of the fascinating data contained within the *Bookseller*'s pages now lies, thickly bound and seldom used, in library stacks.[8]

Notes

1. Richard Altick, *The English Common Reader* (Chicago, 1957), p. 215.

2. For a comparative analysis of British book listings, see D. Weintraub, *A Comparison of the Weekly Lists of the British National Bibliography, Booksellers and Publishers' Circular and Booksellers' Record* (London, 1960).

3. Morton N. Cohen, "Lewis Carroll and the House of Macmillan," *Browning Institute Studies* 7 (1979):58.

4. Ibid., p. 65.

5. F. D. Sanders, ed., *British Book Trade Organisation: A Report on the Work of the Joint Committee* (London, 1939), pp. 82–83.

6. *Ulrich's International Periodicals Directory*, 21st ed. (New York, 1981), reports a circulation of 18,000.

7. F. A. Mumby and I. Norrie, *Publishing and Bookselling*, 5th ed. (London, 1974), pp. 314, 445–46.

8. Louis Baum, present editor of the *Bookseller*, has been most helpful in providing information about his journal. Sadly, Whitaker's archives were destroyed during the Blitz.

Information Sources

BIBLIOGRAPHY

Bookseller, The. Jubilee Number, 24 January 1908: "Fifty Years of *The Bookseller* and Bookselling. London, 1908."

Bookseller, The. Centenary Number, 3 May 1958. *"The Bookseller*, One Hundred Years." Contains extracts from the journal over a hundred-year period.

Kingsford, R. J. L. *The Publishers Association 1896–1946*. Cambridge, England, 1970.

Mumby, F. A., and I. Norrie. *Publishing and Bookselling*. 5th ed. London, 1974.

Sanders, F. D., ed. *British Book Trade Organisation: A Report on the Work of the Joint Committee*. London, 1939.

INDEXES

None.

REPRINT EDITIONS

UMI.

LOCATION SOURCES

American

Partial runs: Widely available.

British

Complete runs: Bodleian Library; British Museum.

Partial runs: Widely available.

Publication History

MAGAZINE TITLE AND TITLE CHANGES

The Bookseller; a handbook of British and Foreign Literature, January 1858– June 1860. *The Bookseller ... with which is incorporated Bent's literary adver-*

tiser, July 1860–December 1872. *The Bookseller; a newspaper of British* ... *advertiser*, January 1873–December 1908. *The Bookseller; a weekly newspaper* ... *advertiser*, January 1909–December 1921. *Bookseller and stationery trades journal*, January 1922–16 September 1927. *Bookseller; a weekly newspaper* ... *advertiser*, 23 September 1927–30 March 1928. *Publisher and bookseller*, 6 April 1928–29 September 1933. *The Bookseller; The Organ of the Book Trade (Incorporating Bent's Literary Advertiser*, Established 1802), 6 October 1933–.

VOLUME AND ISSUE DATA

Number 1, January 1858–. (Supplements separately paginated and not included in the consecutive numbering of the regular monthly and then weekly issues.)

FREQUENCY OF PUBLICATION

Monthly 1858–1908; weekly 1909–.

PUBLISHERS

January 1858–December 1940; Whitaker's, 17 Warwick Square, Paternoster Row, London/12 Warwick Lane, London, E.C.4. January 1941–December 1978: Whitaker's, 13 Bedford Square, London, W.C.1. January 1979–: Whitaker's, 12 Dyott Street, London, WC1A1DF.

EDITORS

Joseph Whitaker, 1858–1875. Vernon Whitaker, 1875–1895. George Herbert Whitaker, 1895–1928. G. S. Williams, 1928–1933. E. Tucker, J. Whitaker, 1933. Edmond Segrave, 1933–1971. Philothea Thompson, 1971–1976. David Whitaker, 1977–1979. Louis Baum, 1980–.

William Baker

BRITISH AND FOREIGN REVIEW, THE. See RA

BRITISH CRITIC, THE. See RA

BRITISH REVIEW AND NATIONAL OBSERVER, THE. See SCOTS OBSERVER, THE

C

CAMBRIDGE REVIEW, THE

The first appearance of the *Cambridge Review* during the Michaelmas term of 1879 came at the end of considerable journalistic activity at the university. Ever since the late eighteenth century, magazines of various sorts had been appearing at Cambridge. Most were confined to only a few issues, and very few contained material worthy of note. The first university publication in England intended for undergraduates was the *Student** (see *AAAJ*), which appeared at Oxford in 1750, and it preceded any similar effort at Cambridge by twenty-five years. After a few issues the *Student* changed its name to the *Oxford and Cambridge Miscellany*, assumed the patronage of both universities, and published a number of Cambridge contributions. However, the first publication to be produced by Cambridge students *in statu pupillari* was the *Snob*, remembered later for printing Thackeray's earliest work.[1]

There was also an earlier *Cambridge Review* in 1824 that bears an interesting resemblance to its successor. The founders of the modern *Review* appear to have been unaware of its existence until George Parker discovered a mouldering volume in the stacks of the university library and contributed a brief article to the 3 March 1880 issue of the modern *Review* (pp. 70–71). After 1830 the outpouring of undergraduate magazines was fairly steady, but most perished after half a dozen issues. By the late 1870s the university was in the throes of unprecedented educational reform, and it needed a new authority to aid in its modernization. The *Cambridge Review* was born at a propitious moment to provide that authority.

In the inaugural issue of the *Review* for 15 October 1879 the editors set forth their hopes for the new journal. After cautioning their readers not to expect too much or too little from their fledgling magazine, they expressed their intention to produce a publication that would be a fair representative of the life and thought of the university:

It may perhaps seem at first sight that our efforts are on too wide a scale to be successful; that in trying to please all parties we are likely to satisfy none. It may be pointed out that there meet in Cambridge men interested in religion and in philosophy, in literature and in art, in politics and in social science, in out-door sports and evening entertainments. . . . It is to general, not to special interests that we appeal; and it is in the full persuasion that the forming and strengthening of such interests are among the most important objects of University training that we wish to introduce an additional force to assist in developing and sustaining them. [P. 1]

From the beginning the editors were dedicated to maintaining the traditions of old Cambridge in the face of the newer reforms. Parliament might wish to see more specialization at the university, but the *Review* argued strongly in favor of sustaining the wider-based educational experience that had been the traditional foundation of Cambridge training. The *Review* announced that it would not attack authority or mock at youth or slander private character; moreover, it would not leave untouched public evils. The editors appealed to their readers to let them hear

of the last scheme of University reform, and the next men who shall represent us on the waters of Father Thames; of scientific researches and antiquarian explorations; of college debates and Utopias pictured by solitary firesides; of the quips of breakfast table, and, if needs be, of the grumbling at the hall dinner. [P. 1]

The comprehensiveness of the *Cambridge Review* was impressive and pleased almost everyone. The issues during the first year contained notices and short articles on the sports of bicycling, cricket, swimming, and football. There was special coverage of sporting events with Oxford in golf, polo, and racquets, and notice in Lent term of the university whist matches. Receiving the most coverage were river sports: local and special events such as the May races, the C.U.B.C. Meeting, and the University Boat Race. The *Review* also published information of academic interest: schedules of lectures, and meetings of various undergraduate societies such as the Antiquarian, Chess Club, Philological, Religious Equality, and the Union. Under "College Correspondence" were listed the scholarships and fellowships, general college information, and obituaries. The column "University Intelligence" contained the names of freshmen listed by college, the results of the examinations, the university prizes, the Rede lecture, and women's degrees. Under the "University Pulpit" was published the weekly university sermon, and for years various editors of the *Review* were accused of padding the magazine's subscription lists by including an item so obviously of interest to provincial clergymen. In later years, when the sermon was dropped, there was no appreciable decrease in circulation.

Aside from some occasional poetry and the letters to the editors, which for some were the highlight of the magazine, the real intellectual center of the

Cambridge Review was contained in the "Paper Knife" (the book review section) and the articles. It was in these pieces that the breadth and brilliance of the Cambridge mind came into full view. The "Paper Knife" was a catchall feature in which a wide spectrum of literary and scholarly books was subjected to the scrutiny of the university community. Some of the books received only short notices of a few paragraphs; other volumes were reviewed in article-length essays. Among those books considered in 1879–1880 were J. G. M'Kendrick's *Animal Physiology*, the *Cambridge Bible for Schools*, Skeat's *Etymological Dictionary*, Thomas Henry Huxley's *Science Primer*, T. G. Bonney's *Sermons on Some Questions of the Day*, H. Lamb's *Mathematical Theory of Fluids*, Swinburne's *Shakespeare*, and Mark Twain's *A Tramp Abroad*. Although a prominent number of the books reviewed were by Cambridge authors, the list does include a notable selection of important volumes by various writers of the period.

Volume 14 of the *Review*, which covers the 1892–1893 academic year, listed 133 reviews of books, divided into eight categories. There were fifteen works concerned with classical learning, ten works of fiction, nine books on law, eleven on mathematics, sixteen volumes devoted to poetry, five to science, twenty-three on various theological topics, and forty-four sundry books ranging in subject matter from *Documents of the Middle Ages* to a *Shorter Life of Darwin*. This breakdown of books is a fairly representative one from the early period of the *Review*, even though in later issues the number of reviews on scientific books increased and those on theological works decreased. The importance of these reviews cannot be overemphasized. Not only do they represent the broad range of interests that made up the university community, but they reveal the developing intellectual dialectic for which Cambridge became justly famous. These reviews, many of them noteworthy for their length and complexity of analysis, were written not for specialized professional publications but for a university journal of general interest. The fact that a work titled *Hydrostatics and Elementary Hydrokinetics* could be reviewed in the same issue that printed a full-page chart for following the progress of the boats in the Lent term races suggests something of the diversity of the audience to which the publication was aimed.

The articles were divided in the index to the early volumes of the *Review* into the categories of "General" and "Cambridge." The latter dealt with local matters, although many of the "local" matters had national if not international import. The Cambridge essays covered such subjects as "Athletics in Our Public Schools," "Art at the Universities," "Clubs and Cliques," "Duels in Germany," "The Future of College Lectures," "Farming in Iowa," "Furnishing of College Rooms," "James Clerk Maxwell," "Natural Sciences Tripos," "Poor Students," "Social Purity," "Society for the Promotion of Manual Dexterity," "Specialization at Cambridge," "Tripos Fever," and "University Culture." In these essays can be found the history of the affairs of Cambridge of the late Victorian period. The activities of the university were newsworthy and, on occasion, important, for what happened at Cambridge in 1879 or 1885 or 1896 mattered not only to England and her empire but throughout a world in which Britain was still a great power. Cambridge, and Oxford as well, felt this importance and conducted its business as if what happened at the university was significant.

This sense of prominence contributed to the scope of the "General Articles" published in the *Review*. These essays reflect a curious balance among issues in the arts, national and international politics, and current affairs. Essays with titles such as "American Spirit in Literature," "Truth in Art," "Horace's Love of Children," "Life and Work of St. Paul," "Pedantry of George Eliot," and "Renan" compete with "Merchant of Venice at the Lyceum," "Over-education," "On Puns," "School Sports in the Time of Elizabeth," "Philosophy of Afternoon Tea," and "Prehistorical Teetotalers."

Of greater social interest, however, are the number of essays dealing with such topics as "Our Civilization: Is It a Failure," "Economics of Industry," "German Schools," "Hysteria in Politics," "An Essay in Social Criticism," and "Temperance Legislation." The concerns taken up in these pieces reflect a prominent social consciousness and indicate the kinds of problems the journal would pursue in the coming years. The first year's numbers could well serve as models for future volumes; the increase in the number of articles dealing with the sciences is the only substantial alteration in the general contents of the magazine during its first thirty-five years. It is true that before the turn of the century there were more genteel articles which reflected the remnants of the old Cambridge of the mid-nineteenth-century gentleman. The university, as presented in the earlier years of the *Cambridge Review* and in an early anthology of writings from its pages, was a "sweeter" place than in the years before the 1914–1918 war.[2] The concern for the "refinement of sensibility and the dissemination of classical values" that so characterized Victorian Cambridge was still present in those volumes. The "gentlemanly essays, light verse, and much sentimental writing about Cambridge itself" which became such an image of distance and irrelevance by 1914 were still characteristic, if already anachronistic, of a fading world.[3]

The values that were buried, along with the young men who held them, in the trenches of the Western Front were in decline long before the world war delivered the *coup de grâce*. As the editors of *The Cambridge Mind* described it: "The work of men like Frederick Maitland and J. J. Thomson heralded a new and demanding commitment to the highest standards of research and inquiry. And as the University changed again, the *Review* changed with it. Belletristic essays and donnish poetry vanished, leaving the *Review* filled with reviews and discussions, articles and bulletins."[4] The essays and reviews published between 1879 and 1914 reveal an extraordinary intellectual achievement. G. E. Moore wrote about "Naturalism and Agnosticism" (1899), Ludwig Wittgenstein "On Logic, and How Not to Do It" (1913), and Bertrand Russell on "Bergson on Metaphysics and Intuition" (1913). William Morris wrote on "Art Under the Plutocracy" (1883) and Roger Fry on "George Moore and Modern Art" (1893); F. W. Maitland paid homage to an eminent Cambridge historian of a previous generation in an obituary of Lord Acton. Science articles included J. J. Thomson's essay on "The Late Lord Kelvin" (1908), F. W. Aston's "Rutherford and Radioactivity" (1913), and W.C.D. Whetham's (Lord Dampier) "Thomson and the Cambridge School of Experimental Physics" (1903); all of them reveal the great transition that had occurred at the university.

In 1850 the Royal Commission had passed new statutes to widen the curriculum by raising the moral and natural sciences to tripos status and by opening up the fellowships and scholarships to free competition. Fellows were allowed to marry and still retain their positions within the colleges; the poor were encouraged to seek places at what had once been bastions of the rich and privileged; and professional training was supported in an attempt to further the interests of law, medicine, and engineering. One of the immediate results of such reforms was to broaden the intellectual life of undergraduates and through their later careers, that of the outside world. The Cambridge Union produced the orators of "Young England"; private societies, such as the "Apostles," that held together after university life, helped to launch a number of influential journalists, a profession that was becoming the vehicle for many of the brightest men of the age. By the 1880s the "link between the discussions of able university minds, the world of politics, and the world of letters and journalism could hardly be made more evident."[5]

By 1870, the university reforms and the increasing complexity of social, political, and economic life profoundly altered the intellectual atmosphere in Great Britain, a change which naturally affected the role of the university in society. The winds of the moment seemed to favor the training of administrators, civil servants, and members of Parliament who could govern the empire. Oxford became preeminent as a training ground for politicians and administrators, but Cambridge pursued the alternative course. As J.P.C. Roach has noted, "The Cambridge parallel to the Oxford concern with the public service was the development of organized science and the promotion of fundamental scientific research."[6] The growth of science at Cambridge from the time of the report of the Royal Commission was perhaps the greatest achievement of the university since its inception.

The hostilities of August 1914 heralded further drastic change for England and its universities. The *Review* continued to appear during the war, but on a much reduced basis, just as Cambridge itself remained open to students, but with substantially curtailed services. Perhaps the best single description of the conditions at the university at the time is to be found in a letter written to one of his former students by Sir Arthur Quiller-Couch, a fellow of Jesus College and the "Q" of literary fame, which was published in the *Review* for 24 February 1915 under the title "To the Front from the Backs."[7] Sir Arthur recounted the changes that had overtaken the colleges: the nearly empty halls populated only by a few students in uniform; the poor fare at dinner because of the rationing of food; the presence of the Belgian refugees; the hospital sheds on the Clare Cricket Ground; the whole block at King's turned over to house the Red Cross nurses. He likened Cambridge to a garrison town. "Youth had, for once," he wrote, "refused to visit [Cambridge] with autumn, and was busy elsewhere." "Q" concluded by observing that since his generation had made such a mess of the world and then forced the responsibility onto the next, youth could claim more for itself after the war. "You will come back, and those who return to the University will claim for youth a far larger measure of freedom, as they have earned it ten times over." Those who did return altered the university immeasurably, and with it the *Review*. The university has not had another institution that encompassed as much of its life and thought as this journal. The collected volumes of the *Cambridge Review* present a clearer and more comprehensive portrait of the university than any other published source—historical survey, reminiscence, or anthology. Through the years it became a *vade mecum* for generations of undergraduates, as well as an intellectual sparring ground for their mentors. As the age of specialization transformed Victorian into Edwardian and finally into modern Cambridge, the *Review* came more and more to function as a center for the exchange of ideas, a public high table, a "kind of scholarly parlour," the editors of *The Cambridge Mind* have written, "where the human, as well as the professional life of its readers is chronicled: their arrivals and departures noted, their work noticed and their deaths mourned."[8]

Notes

1. The best survey of university periodicals of the eighteenth and nineteenth centuries is still H. C. Marillier, *University Magazines and Their Makers* (London, 1902). See also J.P.C. Roach, "Victorian Universities and the National Intelligentsia," *Victorian Studies* 2 (1959):131–50.

2. *The Book of the "Cambridge Review," 1879–1897* (Cambridge, England, 1898).

3. *The Cambridge Mind: Ninety Years of the "Cambridge Review," 1879–1969*, ed. Eric Homberger, William Janeway, and Simon Schama (Boston, 1970), p. 14.

4. Ibid.

5. Roach, p. 140.

6. Ibid, p. 149.

7. Arthur Quiller-Couch, "To the Front from the Backs," rpt. in Homberger, pp. 31–34.

8. Homberger, p. 17.

Information Sources

BIBLIOGRAPHY

Anon. *The Book of the "Cambridge Review," 1879–1897*. Cambridge, England, 1898.
Homberger, Eric, William Janeway, and Simon Schama, eds. *The Cambridge Mind: Ninety Years of the "Cambridge Review," 1879–1969*. Boston, 1970.

INDEXES

Each volume indexed.

REPRINT EDITIONS

Microform: Kraus Reprint.

LOCATION SOURCES

American

Complete runs: Harvard University Library; Yale University Library.
Partial runs: Widely available.

British

Complete runs: Bodleian Library; British Museum; Cambridge University Library; St. John's College Library; Trinity College Library, Cambridge.

Partial runs: Aberdeen University Library; Birmingham University Library; London University Library; St. Andrews University Library; Sheffield University Library; University of Bristol Library.

Publication History

MAGAZINE TITLE AND TITLE CHANGES

The Cambridge Review: A Journal of University Life and Thought.

VOLUME AND ISSUE DATA

Volumes 1–, numbers 1–, 15 October 1879–.

FREQUENCY OF PUBLICATION

Weekly during Michaelmas, Lent, and May terms (October to June).

PUBLISHER

1879–1914: Elijah Johnson, Trinity Street, Cambridge. 1914–: Unknown.

EDITORS

Term, rotating editorship among students, who have included: E. V. Arnold, 1879–1880. B. Cane, 1886–1887. R. E. Childers, 1882–1883. C. F. Clay, 1885–1886. W. J. Conybeare, 1892–1893. A. B. Cook, 1892. W. J. Corbett, 1888–1889. A.W.W. Dale, 1879–1880, 1882. G. A. Davies, 1891–1892. G. M. Edwards, 1880. H. J. Edwards, 1895–1897. J. Fearnley, 1884. A. Gerstenberg, 1883. I. Gollancz, 1887–1888. G. W. Grant-Wilson, 1890–1891. W. G. Headlam, 1886–1887. W. Hillhouse, 1879–1880. S. M. Leathes, 1886. E. C. Marchant, 1892–1893. R. P. Mahaffy, 1890–1891. F. B. Malin, 1894–1895. J.H.B. Masterman, 1891–1894. T. Morrison, 1884–1885. H. A. Newton, 1882. P. N. Pollock, 1886. W. A. Raleigh, 1883–1884. H. B. Smith, 1883–1884. C. Stevenson, 1889–1890. C. Strachey, 1882. E. M. Sympson, 1882–1883. H.F.W. Tatham, 1886. A. C. Tilley, 1887–1889. E. M. Todhunter, 1890–1891. G. Townsend Warner, 1888. F. B. Westcott, 1880–1881.

Charles L.P. Silet

CAMBRIDGE UNIVERSITY MAGAZINE, THE

Of the three known periodicals that appeared under the title of *Cambridge University Magazine* in the nineteenth century, the one that was published between 1839 and 1843 is by far the most significant.[1] Originally titled *The Symposium, or Dinner Table*, it first appeared in March 1839, and thereafter in May, November, and March of each year, once a term.[2] An editorial statement of intent appeared on the last page of the magazine's first number:

We wish it to be a vehicle through which the Undergraduates, particularly, of this University, may express their opinions on the various subjects of Literature and Politics that may chance to occupy their attention; and it is on this ground solely that we venture to hope it will succeed, by making

it an affair in which all may have a common interest. . . . We depend on
the Undergraduates for support—failing which, our project must fall to
the ground. [1, no. 1:80]

The magazine became what this statement might suggest—an undergraduate
journal that published fiction, poetry, translations, essays on classical, literary,
historical, and political subjects, and somewhat laboured satirical squibs. More
mundanely, it published the texts of tripos examinations and a "University
Intelligence" column in each issue, which provided information about current
university affairs, appointments of graduates, meetings of societies, and degrees
conferred.

The first editor was C. B. Willcox, who had been admitted as a sizar to Trinity
College in October 1838.[3] He appears not to have graduated, but did go on to
produce in 1842 a two-volume edition of the works of Chatterton, published in
Cambridge by W. P. Grant, who was also the publisher of the magazine. Willcox's main contribution to the magazine was a series of articles on "The Poets
of England who have died young." The first of these was a piece on Chatterton
(March 1839), followed by others on Shelley, Keats, Sidney, and Byron. Willcox
was succeeded as editor by Wathen Mark Wilks Call, who had been admitted
to St. John's College as a pensioner in July 1835, readmitted in January 1842,
and graduated in 1843.[4] Apart from Willcox's articles on youthful dead poets,
the most interesting material was Call's series of articles on Poland and his essays
on "The Religion of Poets" and "The Sonnet Writers of England," and a series
by George Brimley on "The Living Dramatists of England."

It is as a showcase for the early work of Brimley and Call that the *Cambridge
University Magazine* is most significant. Both men went on to make important
contributions to the literary life of their times. Brimley, who entered Trinity
College in 1837, stayed on to become college librarian, until his early death in
1857. He contributed to the *Spectator** (see *RA*) and *Fraser's Magazine** (see
RA), as well as a signed essay on Tennyson to the Cambridge essays of 1855.
A collection of his essays was made after his death by W. G. Clark, fellow of
Trinity—and author of two of the university prize poems that appeared in the
Cambridge University Magazine in November 1842.[5] Call became a contributor
to the *Leader*,* *Westminster Review** (see *RA*), *Fortnightly Review*,* and *Theological Review*. His most important work was for the *Westminster*, to which,
after his resignation as an Anglican clergyman, he contributed for nearly thirty
years.[6] He was very much a part of the George Eliot circle; indeed, it was via
Eliot's influence that he became a contributor to the *Westminster Review*. He
also became a minor poet of some repute.[7]

Fortuitously or not, the ending of the *Cambridge University Magazine* seems
to have coincided with the graduation of Call in 1843. Its last issue, which
included a substantial review of Macaulay's *Lays of Ancient Rome*, appeared in
March 1843 as the first number of a third volume which advanced no further.
While not substantially different from many other undergraduate periodicals, its

association with Brimley and Call gives it an interest that it would otherwise certainly lack.

Notes

1. One survived for only two issues in 1835 and the other ran as a weekly in term time between May and December 1886.
2. Walter Graham mistakenly says that the magazine appeared monthly. *English Literary Periodicals* (1930; rpt. New York, 1966), p. 274.
3. Robert Bowes identifies the editor as "Wilcox." *A Catalogue of Books Printed at or Relating to the University Town and County of Cambridge from 1521 to 1893 with Bibliographical and Biographical Notes* (Cambridge, England, 1894), p. 358.
4. *Alumni Cantabrigienses*, comp. J. A. Venn (Cambridge, England, 1940), 1:491.
5. *Dictionary of National Biography*, s. v. "Brimley, George"; *Essays by the Late George Brimley, M.A., Librarian of Trinity College, Cambridge*, ed. William G. Clark (Cambridge, England, 1858).
6. See *The Wellesley Index to Victorian Periodicals, 1824–1900*, ed. Walter E. Houghton (Toronto, 1979), 3:743.
7. His works include *Lyra Hellenica* (Cambridge, England, 1842), *Reverberations* (London, 1849), and *Golden Histories* (London, 1871). See also selections in *The Poets and Poetry of the Century*, vol. 4, ed. Alfred H. Miles (London, 1892).

Information Sources

BIBLIOGRAPHY

Bowes, Robert. *A Catalogue of Books Printed at or Relating to the University Town and County of Cambridge from 1521 to 1893 with Bibliographical and Biographical Notes*. Cambridge, England, 1894.

Graham, Walter. *English Literary Periodicals*. 1930. Reprint. New York, 1966.

INDEXES
None.

REPRINT EDITIONS
Microform: English Literary Periodicals (UMI), reel 110.

LOCATION SOURCES

American

Partial runs: Cornell University Library; Ohio State University Library; Trinity College, Watkinson Library.

British

Complete run: British Museum.

Partial runs: Cambridge University Library; Edinburgh University Library; St. John's (Cambridge) Library.

Publication History

MAGAZINE TITLE AND TITLE CHANGES

The Symposium, or Dinner Table, numbers 1 and 2. *The Symposium, or Cambridge University Magazine*, numbers 3–5. *The Cambridge University Magazine*, numbers 6–13.

VOLUME AND ISSUE DATA
> Volume 1, numbers 1–6; volume 2, numbers 7–12; volume 3, number 1, March
> 1839–March 1843.

FREQUENCY OF PUBLICATION
> Quarterly.

PUBLISHER
> W. P. Grant, Cambridge.

EDITORS
> Charles Bonnycastle Willcox and Wathen Mark Wilks Call.

Keith Wilson

CENTURY GUILD HOBBY HORSE, THE. See HOBBY HORSE,
THE

CHAMBERS'S JOURNAL. See RA

**CHAMBERS'S JOURNAL OF POPULAR LITERATURE,
SCIENCE AND THE ARTS.** See CHAMBERS'S JOURNAL (RA)

CHAMBERS'S LONDON JOURNAL

Chambers's London Journal (1841–1843) was a competitor and imitator of
the successful *Chambers's Edinburgh Journal** (1832–1956) (see *Chambers's
Journal* [*RA*]). Louis James notes that "*Chambers's London Journal*, . . . behind
the name of a fictional 'H. H. Chambers', tried to draw on the popularity of the
publications . . . of the Chambers brothers."[1] There is no mention in two definitive accounts of William and Robert Chambers's publishing activities that
Chambers's London Journal had any connections with them. Indeed, editorial
statements in the *London Journal* went out of the way to disclaim association.[2]
Both magazines appeared weekly with an average of eight pages per issue, were
sold cheaply, and had similar aims. Both dealt with contemporary political and
social questions, especially those related to the changing economic conditions
of the period. Topics range from the Irish question and foreign affairs to prison
and sanitary conditions. The leading article in the first issue of *Chambers's
Edinburgh Journal* speaks of a "grand leading principle" actuating it "to take
advantage of the universal appetite for instruction which at present exists."[3] The
imitator, *Chambers's London Journal*, has as a motto a citation from the Whig
Lord Brougham, to whom a special number was devoted at the end of 1841.
The motto, run on the heading of each number, stresses education: "By Education
men become easy to lead, but difficult to drive—easy to govern, but impossible

to enslave." The opening editorial of the first number, "Our Motto Illustrated," leaves little doubt of the magazine's intentions "to unfold ... the ponderous tomes of history"; "to illustrate the stirring events of the olden time, with the commentaries of travellers and the rhapsodies of poets"; to relate the past "to the state of society in our own time"; "to teach men to think, and to give them matter for reflection"; and to assist "in the great cause of human improvement" (1:1).

The eclectic nature of contributions to *Chambers's London Journal* is revealed by an examination of the index to the first volume. Five subject divisions are indicated. History is subdivided into "Ancient," "Modern," and "Natural." Articles within the first category include descriptions of ancient Egypt, the scientific knowledge of the Egyptians, three pieces on the Persians, and essays on Chinese antiquity. Three contributions on Russia, two on England, and one each on India and America constitute the modern history items. Natural history topics are diverse: there are articles on the natural history of various months, British song birds in the wild and in cages, the antiquity of the earth, formation of coal beds, and the sexual properties of plants. Literature is divided into "Historic" and "Domestic." The former includes three articles on Napoleon and two on America, including "War with America a Blessing to Mankind." The article opposes an idea recommending "the project of encouraging an insurrection of the negros, of placing arms in their hands, supporting them with British troops, and wrapping the Southern States in flames!" (1:7). There are three essays on feminine history, perhaps reflecting an attempt to capture a specific readership. Warren Hastings and French dueling are the subjects of ongoing articles. The second number, for 12 June 1841, leads with an article advocating Jewish emancipation and return to an ancestral homeland in order to create stability in a chaotic Middle East.

More overt literary concerns are reflected under the heading "Domestic Literature." There are various pieces on Robert Burns, "Traits and Sketches of Irish Character," and a series of short fictions of the Bulwer-Lytton "silver-fork" variety entitled "Experiences of Benjamin Truesteel." These include sections on "Distortions of the Female Form—Illustrated" and three articles on "A Fashionable Marriage" concluding in "catastrophe." Surprisingly, abstracts from Sir Walter Scott's *Guy Mannering* and a series of nine "Sketches of Military Life"—a set of tales aimed at army reform—are included in the lengthy listing of "General" contributions. The index includes "Biography & Adventure," with items ranging from two pieces on New Zealand, to an account of an Arab funeral in Cairo, to anecdotes of wolves. A contributors' listing included on the title page of the first volume names Miss Cowper, Miss Reddell, H. H. Chambers, H. S. Chapman, W. Biggar, R. Percival, J. Clark, E. N. Shannon, E. L. Blanchard, John Le Strange, J. H. Fennell, M. P. Haynes, J. Richardson, W. Hughes and an apparently pseudonymous Benjamin Truesteel. Identification of contributors has proved difficult. Very few, if any, contributions were signed during the early runs of the journal and little use was made of initials. Identification becomes easier with the issue for 3 December 1841, which leads with "Glimpses of Women. By the Editor." An essay on Robert Burns is attributed to "W. Biggar"—probably William Biggar, editor of the *Railway Times*—and "A Pithy Paper for Pedestrians" to Leman Blanchard. "Sepulture in London" is by "P. M. Haynes," probably Matthew Priestman Haynes, a "political orator in the reform movement," journalist, and editor of the *Mayo Telegraph* and the *Penny Catholic Magazine*.[4]

Signed contributions in the second volume of *Chambers's London Journal* do not prove to be too helpful in rescuing contributors from total obscurity. Few of the poets (there are sixty-five poems in the second volume compared with thirty-two in the first volume) are found in standard biographical sources. Stories reprinted from *Fraser's Magazine** and *Tait's,** and abridgments from *Ainsworth's Magazine,** the *Dublin University Magazine,** *Metropolitan Magazine,** *Monthly Magazine,** and the *Edinburgh Review** (for the latter four, see *RA*) omit authorship. However, number 46 has extracts from Bulwer-Lytton's *Zanoni*; number 75 contains copious extracts in the form of a notice from Charles Dickens's *Notes of America and the Americans*; and number 63 prints extracts from Lever's *Jack Hinton*. However, many contributions in the second volume, ranging from neo-Shelleyan verses entitled "A Summer's Day-Dream" (no. 57) to a series of "Random Records from the Portfolio of a Deceased Actor" (nos. 45, 48) to two lengthy opening essays on "Milton's 'Comus' " (nos. 62, 64), signed by the editor, Blanchard.

The first editor of *Chambers's London Journal*, Edward Litt (Leman) Blanchard (1820–1889), was a journalist, literary jack-of-all-trades, and dramatist. He wrote farces, burlesques, penny-number novels, and about one hundred pantomimes, including the famous "Babes in the Wood" (with A. Harris and H. Nicholls). A well-known London theater critic for various papers, including the *Daily Telegraph* (from May 1863 to 1889), *Sunday Times*, and *Observer*, he knew Dickens, Leigh Hunt, Edmund Yates, and other distinguished literary figures. His *Life and Reminiscences* provides an insight into the trials and tribulations of a nineteenth-century literary hack.[5] According to Michael R. Booth, Blanchard's diary "is an impressive and sometimes moving account of work done and unhappiness suffered by a nervous, extraordinarily industrious," impoverished, "and often lonely man; it is also the most factual and detailed (though sparse) theatrical memoir of the century."[6]

The primary contributor for eighty-six issues, Blanchard pleaded in a farewell note his "declining health" and the pressure of other work as reasons for relinquishing editorship (no. 87:24). Near the end of the second volume various signs appear pointing toward declining fortunes for the journal. Blanchard's Christmas and end-of-year editorials fail to exude enthusiasm. Frequent requests for advertisements to fill the wrappers of monthly issues and calls for correspondence went largely unheeded. The price, constant from the first number at "three halfpence," was increased at the beginning of the third volume. Colophons for the 14 January and 21 January 1843 issues reveal more editorial changes. The publishers changed from "H. H. Chambers" (who remained printer) to "William Strange," who published the journal for the proprietor. The editor from 21 January 1843 to its demise on 28 October 1843 was George William MacArthur Reynolds, whose "sales in book form and penny instalments undoubtedly were enormous, the aggregate for his scores of romances running into millions." Reynolds became a "hard-hitting political commentator" of mass-circulation weekly newspapers, building "up the pressure which, after the middle of the century, forced the governing class to concede more and more power to the artisan and laborer."[7] A "middle-class man of some interest in the development of cheap fiction," attracted by "the opportunities offered by the new mass audience," Reynolds had "a somewhat paternal attitude" to his public and tried to steer a middle course between "the periodicals devoted exclusively to fiction," such as the *London Journal*, and those exclusively concerned with instruction.[8]

Chambers's London Journal, under Reynolds, appealed to the literate. The first number opened with four and a quarter columns of his "Ottoman History"— a review of an English version shortly to be published of van Hammer's "magnificent" *History of the Ottoman Empire*. A hostile review of Dickens's *Martin Chuzzlewit* followed in which the book is called "a most miserable affair," and Reynolds declares his intention "to devote more attention to literary criticisms than has heretofore been vouchsafed." Reynolds invited publishers and authors to forward works for review. Although his invitation met with a lukewarm response, it illustrates a change in editorial direction. Blanchard had spoken in his valediction of the original objective of *Chambers's London Journal*: "the instruction and amusement of the million" (no. 87:24). Reynolds may have felt he was serving this end by following his review of *Martin Chuzzlewit* with an extract from his own *Master Timothy's Book-case*, which had just been published. Number 88 for 28 January 1843, opens with Reynold's furious onslaught on capital punishment—"The Injustice of the Criminal Law," dependent upon lengthy English citations from Victor Hugo's *Le Dernier jour d'un condamné* (pp. 25–26). Reynolds then begins a tale set in 1287 in the Ottoman Empire which takes up six and a quarter columns (pp. 29–31), followed by unsigned ramblings on "Our Sensations"; a review of a pot-boiler, *Joseph Jenkins*, by James Grant; and five paragraphs on miscellaneous items. A poem, "Morning" (pp. 31–32), signed "S. F. R.," concludes Reynolds's second number.

Thirty-eight issues later *Chambers's London Journal* collapsed—one of Reynolds's failures. As a whole the journal may be viewed as a valiant attempt by Blanchard, in imitation of its far more successful Edinburgh namesake, to gain the weekly middle ground of readership, and as an exercise in self-advertisement by "the most published man of the nineteenth century," George W.M. Reynolds.[9] At its best, *Chambers's London Journal*, with its comprehensive topical coverage, points forward to the liberal weekly journals of the present century, such as the *New Statesman** and the *Guardian Weekly*. Absorption in *Chambers's London Journal* columns has more than intrinsic interest. It provides insight into journalistic ventures of the early 1840s, and the specific concerns of 1842–1843, as well as throwing light upon an undocumented segment of Reynolds's multifarious activities.

Notes

I am grateful to David Lass, cataloguer in English and Classics at Trinity College Library, Dublin, for his assistance with runs of *Chambers's London Journal* in his library.

1. Louis James, *Fiction for the Working Man 1830–1850* (London, 1963), p. 42. Walter Graham identifies the editor as Edward L.L. Blanchard, and his assistant as William Henry Wills. *English Literary Periodicals* (New York, 1930), p. 326. According to the *Dictionary of National Biography* (1973), s.v. Wills, William, after 1846 Wills went for two years to edit *Chambers's Edinburgh Journal*. His name does not appear with those who were associated with *Chambers's London Journal*.

2. See [William Chambers], *Memoir of Robert Chambers with Autobiographical Reminiscences of William Chambers* (Edinburgh, 1872); Sandra M. Cooney, "Publishers for the People—W & R Chambers—The Early Years 1832–1850," Ph.D. dissertation, Ohio State University, 1971; *Chambers's London Journal*, no. 1 (1841):8; no. 33 (1842) :1.

3. *Chambers's Edinburgh Journal*, 1, no. 1.

4. Frederic Boase, *Modern English Biography*, 6 vols. (Truro, 1892–1921), 1:274, 1402.

5. Edward Litt (Leman) Blanchard, *Life and Reminiscences*, ed. C. Scott and G. Howard (London, 1891).

6. Michael R. Booth, *English Plays of the Nineteenth Century: V, Pantomimes, Extravaganzas and Burlesques* (Oxford, 1976), p. 339. See also *Dictionary of National Biography*, s.v. Blanchard, Edward Leman; Boase, 4:425.

7. Richard D. Altick, *The English Common Reader* (Chicago, 1957), pp. 4–5. See also *The Pilgrim Edition of the Letters of Charles Dickens*, ed. G. Storey and K. J. Fielding (Oxford, 1981), 5:603, nn.4, 5.

8. James, p. 41.

9. Reynolds's connection with *Chambers's London Journal* is ignored by his bibliographers, such as Montague Summers in *A Gothic Bibliography* (London, 1940), pp. 146–59, and Donald Kausch, "George W.M. Reynolds: A Bibliography," *Library*, 5th ser. 28, no. 4 (1973):319–26.

Information Sources

BIBLIOGRAPHY

Altick, Richard D. *The English Common Reader*. Chicago, 1957.

Blanchard, Edward Litt (Leman). *Life and Reminiscences*. Edited by C. Scott and G. Howard. London, 1891.

Boase, Frederic. *Modern English Biography*. 6 vols. Truro, 1892–1921.

Dickens, Charles. *The Pilgrim Edition of the Letters of Charles Dickens*. Edited by Kathleen Tillotson. *Volume IV, 1844–1846*. Oxford, 1977. *Volume V, 1847–1849*. Oxford, 1981.

Dictionary of National Biography, s.v. "Blanchard, Edward Leman."

Graham, Walter. *English Literary Periodicals*. New York, 1930.

James, Louis, *Fiction for the Working Man 1830–1850*. London, 1963.

INDEXES
Volumes 1, 2 indexed in each volume.
REPRINT EDITIONS
None.
LOCATION SOURCES
American
Complete run: Harvard University Library.
Partial runs: New York Public Library; University of Illinois Library, Villanova University Library.
British
Complete runs: Bodleian Library; British Museum; Trinity College Library.

Publication History

MAGAZINE TITLE AND TITLE CHANGES
Chambers's London Journal of History, Literature, Poetry, Biography, & Adventure.
VOLUME AND ISSUE DATA
Volume 1, numbers 1–32, Saturday, 5 June–Friday, 31 December 1841. (Number 32 is a separately paginated special number on Lord Brougham issued with number 30 [25 December 1841].) Volume 2, numbers 33–84, Saturday, 8 January–Saturday, 31 December 1842. Volume 3, number 85–127, Saturday, 7 January–Saturday, 28 October 1843.
FREQUENCY OF PUBLICATION
Weekly.
PUBLISHERS
Volumes 1–2, numbers 1–84, 5 June 1841–31 December 1842 (Printed by the Proprietor, H. H. Chambers, Fleet Street, London): W. Strange, Paternoster Row, London; W. Clements, Little Pulteney Street, London; G. Berger, Holywell Street, London; Heywood, Manchester; Watts, Birmingham; Mann, Leeds; Smith, Liverpool; Machen, Dublin; Robinson, Edinburgh; Barnes, Glasgow.
Volume 3, numbers 87–127, 21 January–28 October 1843: William Strange, Paternoster Row, London (Printed by H. H. Chambers, Fleet Street, London).
EDITORS
Edward Litt Blanchard, 5 June 1841–14 January 1843. G.W.M. Reynolds, 21 January–28 October 1843.

William Baker

CHAPBOOK, THE

Two periodicals were published between 1913 and 1925 under the editorship of Harold Monro. Eight issues of the quarterly *Poetry and Drama* appeared in 1913–1914, and forty issues of its successor, the *Chapbook*, between 1919 and 1925. Both magazines represented an expression of Monro's lifelong commitment to support of new directions in poetry, poetic drama, and criticism, and to increasing the audience for this writing.

Immediately prior to establishing *Poetry and Drama*, Monro had edited the *Poetry Review*, the publication of the Poetry Society. His association lasted only a year and ended because Monro had significant philosophical differences with members of the society, but the year was enough to give him some experience in editing a magazine and enough to convince him that an audience for poetry existed. Furthermore, he believed the size of that audience could be much increased if the public were properly approached. In the second issue of *Poetry and Drama* he declared, "A majority of intelligent people still argues that poetry is unpopular; it is one of the objects of *Poetry and Drama* to dispel this illusion." He went on to cite the quantity of weak verse and superficial criticism being circulated, concluding that "the dissatisfaction of the public is the result, not of too much, but too little poetry" (no. 2:126), meaning poetry of real value. Convinced that a potential audience with interest and taste existed, Monro set out to bring audience and artists together.

In 1938 he opened the Poetry Bookshop at 35 Devonshire Street, Theobalds Road. There he established a place where poetry was both printed and sold and where readers assembled at regular intervals to hear poets read their poems in an informal atmosphere designed to promote discussion. In the fourth issue of *Poetry and Drama* Monro anticipated the first anniversary of the Poetry Bookshop:

Official societies for the collective enjoyment or propagation of poetry must always be failures. Here, we have simply a few people gathered together....We make a regular practice of reading poetry aloud and any one who wishes to stroll in and listen may do so....We are absoluteiy certain that the proper values of poetry can only be conveyed through its vocal interpretation by a sympathetic and qualified reader. [No. 1:387]

In March 1913 Monro published the first issue of *Poetry and Drama*, designed to provide poetry, drama, and criticism of the quality Monro believed the public was ready to receive. The magazine was advertised as a continuation of the *Poetry Review* and the first issue contained an account of Monro's disagreement with the Poetry Society. It stated a position that characterized Monro's editorial career: "From the start I absolutely refused compromise to advertisers, su,p-porters, famous people or friends; I insisted on bad verse being called bad verse as often as occasion required" (no. 1:10). Succeeding generations have not always continued to praise what Monro praised and have learned to honor poets whom Monro overlooked or rejected, but, as Joy Grant shows in her life of Monro, he exercised his own best critical judgment without regard for friendship or the opinion of others.

Grant records Monro's concern that at the poetry readings the audience might be more interested in the poet than the poetry.[1] An interesting point is to be noted in the format of the later *Chapbook*. Until the last ten issues, Monro published in each issue a list of the contents with the names of the authors, but the poem or play was printed in the body of the magazine without the author's name. One might guess that Monro wished the writing read without the bias that the reader might attach to a name.

As one might expect, the poets represented in *Poetry and Drama* and the *Chapbook* did not represent a single coterie. In the first issue of *Poetry and Drama*, work by Maurice Hewlett, James Elroy Flecker, and Lascelles Abercrombie appeared. Succeeding issues included contributions by, among others, Emile Verhaeren, Rabindronath Tagore, John Drinkwater, Robert Frost, Robert Bridges, Thomas Hardy, Walter De la Mare, Rupert Brooke, W. H. Davies, Ezra Pound, Amy Lowell, T. Sturge Moore, D. H. Lawrence, and Ernest Rhys. Drama was less fully represented, but the fourth issue presented Lord Dunsany's "The Golden Doom," and the sixth Edward Storer's "Helen."

Articles and criticism ranged widely in subject matter and point of view. The first issue contained an attack on the national anthem. An analysis of the Greek genius by A. Romney Green declared that "Greek literature was produced, not by students and idlers for students and idlers, but by and for the educated working man" (no. 1:21). Leonard Inkster praised Granville-Barker's production of Shakespeare. Rupert Brooke made a scholarly comment on John Webster. Edward Thomas wrote tongue-in-cheek on the effectiveness and popularity of Ella Wheeler Wilcox. He noted: "She says familiar things energetically, for the most part, cheerily, not once but many times. A man who has his Wilcox needs no Shakespeare. The more he reads Wilcox, the less he thinks of Shakespeare" (no. 1:42). The issue contained several reviews, including a favorable one of Monro's *Georgian Poetry 1911–12* and F. S. Flint's thoughtful review of French writers, including Paul Claudel. A list of recent books was a feature of this and succeeding issues.

The issues that followed maintained the pattern: a selection of poems, critical essays, "Chronicles" of other literatures—French, Italian, German, and American—reviews, and annotated lists of recent books. Much of the third issue was devoted to futurism and Filippo Marinetti's "New Futurist Manifesto." Poetry by Paolo Buzzi, Marinetti, and Aldo Palazzeschi [Aldo Giurlani] was included, translated by Harold Monro. In the same issue the choice of Bridges as Laureate was praised with the added comment, "How appalling if the choice had fallen on Kipling." Ford Madox Hueffer wrote on Impressionism in the sixth and seventh issues, as "a frank expression of personality" (no. 6:169ff.). He advised: "Always consider the impressions that you are making upon the mind of the reader, and always consider that the first impression with which you present him will be so strong that it will be all you can ever do to efface it" (no. 6:172). By the seventh and eighth issues the effect of the war made itself felt in comments on the poor quality of war poetry, although an impressive group of poets appeared in the last two issues: Verhaeren, Frost, Pound, Aldington, D. H. Lawrence, Ernest Rhys, Monro himself, Amy Lowell, and Rose Macaulay.

In December 1914 Monro announced the suspension of publication: "The consideration and, indeed, the production of literature require leisure of mind. The suspension of the periodical is designed to last until we have been so fortunate as to regain that leisure'' (no. 8:32). Monro then joined the army; and although he remained for most of the war in England and reasonably close to the Poetry Bookshop, most of his activities were necessarily suspended. The bookshop itself remained open under the management of Alida Klemantaski (later to be Monro's second wife), but the continued publication of a magazine was impossible.

In 1919 Monro announced a successor to *Poetry and Drama* to be published monthly, titled for the first year's issues the *Monthly Chapbook* and from the eleventh issue in January 1920 the *Chapbook*. Its aims were similar to those of its predecessor; its format, at least in intention, more encompassing. Monro designed an ambitious plan which was modified as occasion demanded.

In July 1919 the contents of the number for any one year were projected to include a critical summary of the poetry and drama of the past year, a book of new poems by a single author, a new play, a foreign number chronicle, two books of new poems, an article on drama, a book of songs, an annotated bibliography, and a children's number. Most of these plans were carried out at least once over the history of the magazine, but they were not repeated on the regular cycle Monro originally designed.

Whatever problems were encountered in planning, a survey of the published issues shows a remarkable variety in materials and a high level of interest for the reader. The magazine was attractive. Each issue had a cover design in color and contained woodcuts and pen-and-ink drawings by various artists, most frequently C. Lovat Fraser and Albert Rutherstone. Advertisements for books and bookshops, for the Peasant Shop, for poetry readings and concerts and lectures—not to mention ''Muller's 'Nutrient' '' and the ''Practical Correspondence College''—added an interesting dimension to the magazine. In introductions and informal essays, Monro kept his readers fully informed of his plans, of shifts in publication policy, of the financial condition of the magazine, and of his own continued faith in its *raison d'être*. In all, over the life of the publication, three original plays were published; two issues were devoted entirely to bibliography, one to poems for children, and two to poems set to music. Fourteen issues presented primarily criticism, ranging from general reflections on contemporary trends and philosophical issues in the theory of poetry and drama to specific critiques of English, American, and Continental writers. Eighteen issues were devoted wholly or in large part to poetry, one of them to old broadside ballads. The last six issues contained short stories, poems, essays, and criticism.

Variety also was provided by a range of tone and the occasional introduction of controversy. Some issues were serious and scholarly. The issue for March 1920, for example, contained ''Three Critical Essays on Modern English Poetry.'' The contributors were T. S. Eliot, Aldous Huxley, and F. S. Flint. Eliot's contribution declared, ''The critical genius is inseparable from the creative,'' and maintained that ''the poetic critic is criticising poetry in order to create poetry'' (no. 9:3). Perceiving the subject matter of poetry as the whole of life, Huxley called for a ''dose of astringent criticism'' for the poetry of the time. F. S. Flint praised the poetry of ''H. D.'' In April 1921 a similar issue on

"Poetry in Prose" presented T. S. Eliot again, this time in company with Frederic Manning and Richard Aldington.

As in *Poetry and Drama*, articles explored current literary trends. In November 1920 F. S. Flint criticized Dadaism. At intervals, critics examined—and generally deplored—the current state of poetry, as in the Recorder's comment in January 1923:

> We in the twentieth century are on the tree-tops of the poetic growths represented by the Pre-Raphaelites and the Nineties. In the distance we see the promised land, but between ourselves and it stretches the plain of this machine-made, war-encumbered world. The poets of our day look backward to the great silences and sweet security of the past or turn in horror from the prospect of war and famine, according to their temperament and capacity for intellectual honesty. [No. 33:10]

Not all was solemn, however. Edna St. Vincent Millay's one-act play, "Aria da Capo," was a light-hearted comedy that poked gentle fun at contemporary experimenters. In July 1920 Emmanuel Morgan characterized a number of contemporary authors in "Pins for Wings." He described Henry Van Dyke as "a pulpit slowly waltzing," Alfred Noyes as "Robin Hood singing hymns," and Masters as "a grave-digger thinking it over." Monro himself did not escape. In September 1922 Osbert Sitwell attacked two of Monro's poems in "The Jolly Old Squire, or Way Down in Georgia," a satire on the Georgians. Even in serious moments, touches of humor emerge. In July 1922 the issue was devoted to "Three Questions and About Twenty-Seven Answers." The questions were:

1. Do you think that poetry is a necessity to modern man?
2. What in modern life is the particular function of poetry as distinguished from other kinds of literature?
3. Do you think there is any chance of verse being eventually displaced by prose as narrative poetry apparently is by the novel and ballads already have been by newspaper reports?

Various literary people responded with appropriately discursive thoroughness, but T. S. Eliot shot back:

1. No.
2. Takes up less space.
3. It is up to poets to find something to do in verse which cannot be done in any other form. [No. 27:8]

The issues that contain poems set to music added pleasant balance to issues devoted to bibliography. The one children's issue, though perhaps heavy with advice to be tolerant, obedient, and kind to animals, provided another dimension, as did the one containing reprints of old broadsides and the "Poems Newly Decorated" of September 1919, which coupled illustrations by Fraser, Rupert Lee, and Paul Nash with poetry by Beaumont, Campion, Drayton, and others.

Controversy was never lacking. In addition to critiques of individual authors or groups, a running controversy over the value of American poetry continued through both *Poetry and Drama* and the *Chapbook* and sometimes generated direct response and rebuttal. In March 1914 Louis Untermeyer defended American poets in the "Chronicle"; his remarks were promptly attacked in the July issue. In May 1920 John Gould Fletcher had a series of interesting reflections on "Some Contemporary American Poets." He found in Edward Arlington Robinson the mind of New England, in Robert Frost, the heart. Amy Lowell was two-dimensional. Carl Sandburg could never get beyond the simplest rhythmic forms. Vachel Lindsay was a reformer first, a poet second. Pound had not yet found himself. Alfred Kreymborg "may foreshadow a new field of talent" (no. 11).

Monro himself showed considerable receptivity to American talent. Frost's poems appeared in several issues. Eliot was represented only once as a poet but frequently as a critic. The April 1923 issue was devoted entirely to "New American Poems," and included work by Frost, Witter Bynner, William Carlos Williams, Babette Deutsch, E. E. Cummings, John Gould Fletcher, Jean Untermeyer, Conrad Aiken, Wallace Stevens, Edna St. Vincent Millay, Orrick Jonas, Kreymborg, Marianne Moore, Louis Untermeyer, Louis Grundin, Jean Toomer, and Ridgely Torrance—certainly an eclectic list and less conservative than Monro's selections have sometimes been thought to be.

More than 150 writers contributed work to the two magazines. Many more received critical attention in the essays, chronicles, and bibliographies. Only a few were represented by more than one or two contributions, although their other work in many cases received critical attention. All three of the Sitwells appeared repeatedly, as did Mary Morison Webster, Humbert Wolfe, Anna Wickham, Edna St. Vincent Millay, Charlotte Mew, Aldous Huxley, F. S. Flint, John Gould Fletcher, T. S. Eliot, Camilla Doyle, Walter De la Mare, W. H. Davies, and A.J.C. Brown. Monro himself, in addition to his editorial notes, contributed a play, several poems, and the issue of poems for children.

If the total list is considered, Monro must be judged as far from reactionary. His unwillingness to publish "The Waste Land" and "Prufrock" and his slowness to applaud some of the other innovative work being published have given him a reputation for closed-mindedness that is easily exaggerated. If he seemed to display surprising tolerance for sentimental poets like Mary Morison Webster and Charlotte Mew, he also adhered to his original purpose of introducing to the public new and worthwhile talent. Some of the poetry he published is now almost forgotten, but most of the names from the period that are remembered are represented somewhere in the two magazines.

Throughout its history the *Chapbook*, like all little magazines, experienced financial problems that became increasingly serious as time went on. Initially, the price of the *Chapbook* had been one shilling. After three issues, the price was raised to one shilling, six pence, but was reduced again to one shilling in June 1921 when Monro announced a hiatus in publication. In June 1923 Monro proposed a half-yearly issue. He further proposed to drop criticism and present almost entirely poetry and design. He pointed out that the *Chapbook* enjoyed rent-free offices at the Poetry Bookshop and had to pay neither editorial nor clerical salaries, yet the monthly deficit almost precisely equaled the average monthly payments to contributors. He did not mention that the magazine had survived as long as it had, in part at least, because Monro had a private income and used it in the cause of the poetry to which he was single-heartedly dedicated. He remarked sadly that there seemed no lack of enthusiastic support for the magazine but that the support did not translate into subscriptions. Wider circulation, a benefactor, or cessation of payment to contributors seemed the only long-term solutions. Neither of the first two was forthcoming and Monro refused to publish without paying his contributors. The reduction in issues was an attempt to save the situation.

In 1924 and 1925 he published only one issue each year, but these issues were certainly impressive value for the money. Poetry, critical and familiar essays, short stories, and poems in translation and in the original French, the whole illustrated and bound, sold for six shillings. Publication ceased abruptly at the end of 1925 when Monro's eyesight failed. He lived until 1932 and recovered somewhat from his blindness, but he was unable to resume his work as editor. It seems unlikely that the publication could have continued even without Monro's ill health. Because the decision to stop publication was made after the appearance of the 1925 issue, Monro had no final word for the readers with whom he had always been open about the problems of publication. The only hint of change appeared in the shift from the Poetry Bookshop as publisher to Jonathan Cape at 30 Bedford Square.

The two magazines must be judged successful in terms of their original intention. Designed to give exposure to a wide range of new writers, to offer responsible critical opinion, and so to attract and educate readers, supported by the other activities of the Poetry Bookshop, they fulfilled Monro's stated purpose. As Joy Grant concludes in her excellent biography of Monro, "The part that Monro invented and played was an original one: it may be said with confidence that his vision was unique in his time and that he did more to bring poetry to the public than any other man of his generation."[2]

Notes

1. Joy Grant, *Harold Monro and the Poetry Bookshop* (Berkeley, 1967), p. 80.
2. Ibid., p. 4.

Information Sources

BIBLIOGRAPHY

Grant, Joy. *Harold Monro and the Poetry Bookshop*. Berkeley, 1967.
Hoffman, Frederic J., Charles Allen, and Carolyn Ullrich. *The Little Magazines: A History and a Bibliography*. Princeton, 1947.

INDEXES

None.

REPRINT EDITIONS

The Chapbook, numbers 1–40, in 3 volumes (New York: Kraus Reprint Company, 1976). *Poetry and Drama*, 2 volumes in 1 (New York: Kraus Reprint Company, 1967).

Microform: Kraus Reprint. New York Public Library (*Poetry and Drama*).

LOCATION SOURCES

American

Widely available.

British

Complete runs: Birmingham Public Library; Bodleian Library; British Museum; Cambridge University Library; Leeds Public Library; Liverpool Public Library. Partial runs: Bath Public Library; London University Library; Manchester Public Library; Newport Public Library; Trinity College Library, Dublin; Westminster Public Library.

Publication History

MAGAZINE TITLE AND TITLE CHANGES

Poetry and Drama, 1913–1914. *The Monthly Chapbook*, July–December 1919. *The Chapbook*, 1920–1925.

VOLUME AND ISSUE DATA

Poetry and Drama, numbers 1–8, March 1913–December 1914.

The Monthly Chapbook, numbers 1–6, July-December 1919.

The Chapbook, numbers 7–24, January 1920–June 1921; number 25, February 1922; number 26, May 1922; numbers 27–38, July 1922–June 1923; number 39, 1924; number 40, 1925.

FREQUENCY OF PUBLICATION

Quarterly: *Poetry and Drama*; monthly: *The Monthly Chapbook* and *The Chapbook*, numbers 7–38. (None issued July 1921–January 1922; March, April, June 1922.) One only published in 1924 and 1925.

PUBLISHERS

Numbers 1–39: The Poetry Bookshop, 35 Devonshire Street, Theobald's Road, London, W. C. Number 40: Jonathan Cape, 30 Bedford Square for The Poetry Bookshop.

EDITOR

Harold Monro.

Catharine McCue

CHRISTIAN TEACHER, THE. See PROSPECTIVE REVIEW, THE

CONTEMPORARY REVIEW, THE

The *Contemporary Review*, first published in 1866, was both an organ for the Metaphysical Society and a journal with a major interest in theology.[1] Every number of the magazine was devoted to a philosophic or theological issue. In contrast to the anathemas characteristic of other religious periodicals, it was the review's objective examination of various problems confronting Christianity that comprised its real excellence. Even the most committed opponents of Christianity found their books and ideas respectfully treated, and if the author or text was rejected, it was usually because of faulty scholarship rather than heresy. The policy of providing an open forum for issues of every description was never abandoned, and it was this habit of liberal inquiry that made the *Contemporary Review* unique among the religious periodicals of the day.

Its varied group of contributors included great writers, public figures, religious leaders, and scientists. Among them were Matthew Arnold, Walter Pater, and John Ruskin, as well as William Gladstone, Dean Stanley, Robert Buchanan, Dean Farrar, Herbert Spencer, and Thomas Huxley. These latter wrote for the *Contemporary Review*, usually on a regular basis, and made it into one of the best Victorian journals. It promoted the "best that had been known and thought" in the nineteenth century. However arcane or controversial the material may have been, there were few subjects that were not discussed at length in the *Contemporary Review*.

The literary interests of the magazine are perhaps not as broad or daring as its interests in science, education, poor-relief, or religion, but there is still much material of interest for the advanced student of Victorian literature and poetics. The range of material on poetry, drama, and classical writers found in its pages provides a valuable guide to Victorian taste. The best-established poets were also the favorites of the *Contemporary Review*'s contributors. Tennyson, especially, was praised for the beauty and earnestness of his poetry. Browning was the subject of several flattering review-essays, though his *Sordello* was condemned for its obscurity (4:1–15, 133–48; 13:104–25). The most controversial article in the *Contemporary Review*'s history was probably Robert Buchanan's review of Dante Gabriel Rossetti's poetry. It was published under the title "The Fleshly School of Poetry" in the issue for October 1871, and was closely consonant with Victorian taste in poetry and morals. Buchanan's essay was, as Lionel Stevenson described it, "devastating,"[2] but Rossetti was defended shortly after in an essay by Harry Quilter, though the Quilter essay was signed by Holman Hunt. Quilter defended the poetry of Rossetti with a host of superlative adjectives and noted the "stupid criticism" that had earlier been written against him.[3]

The *Contemporary Review* published an extensive number of articles on religious poetry in general and Victorian religious poetry in specific. The genre was more popular than one might expect after reading the standard accounts of Victorian loss of faith and confidence as manifested in its poetry. Of the great number of religious poets reviewed by the *Contemporary Review*, John Keble was the greatest, and *The Christian Year* easily the greatest specimen of his pious outpourings. W. C. Lake wrote in "Mr. Keble and *The Christian Year*" that Keble's achievement had been to create a "true Eirenicon" (6:337). In contrast, in an 1868 article, "In the Union of Christiandom in Its Home Aspect," Henry Alford wrote that the leaders of the Anglo-Catholic party, while making overtures to Rome, were creating problems within their own church (6:173). Another reviewer, A. Japp, in his 1869 essay, "Religious Poetry and Scientific Criticism," offered thanks for the "quality and worth of her [England's] religious poetry," which served as the one great answer to the growing "positivism" of the time (12:127). In addition to the many essays on individual poets, there is an extensive number of theoretical articles on the function of poetry in an age of growing disbelief in Christianity.

English drama is also well represented in the magazine. Shakespeare was the subject of many articles, as were other leading dramatists of both the medieval and modern periods. Ample attention was given to Greek and Roman dramatists, especially Sophocles and Aeschylus, who were closely examined for the message they might have for an age of diminished belief. Epic literature, in its various representations, was also examined. During the middle years of the *Contemporary Review*'s history, the excavations at Troy were taking place. The magazine examined all the latest findings at Troy with reference to the ultimate question: Was Homer to be trusted as a historian of this age? The ultimate answer was affirmative. Virgil's works and those of other Roman writers were reviewed both as poetry and as historical documents. This fact provides some measure of the abiding interest in classical literature among many of the *Contemporary Review*'s writers; undoubtedly, most of these writers were graduates of Cambridge or Oxford. There was a great amount of attention paid to the importance of education of the poor, non-Anglicans, and women. The first editor, in fact, wrote an essay that called for a review of the education of the clergy, asking that they be better acquainted with the claims of science.

One of the most distinctive features of the *Contemporary Review* is the pervasive attention directed to the Victorian masters of English prose. Charles Lamb and Robert Louis Stevenson were the subjects of several appreciative essays, but the usual emphasis was on the philosophy of the writer and his message for an age of uncertainty.

Among the vast and eclectic collection of articles on English prose writers, John Stuart Mill was the only writer who did not fare well with *Contemporary Review* contributors. The first issue carried a fairly strong condemnation of Mill's philosophy, and the negative response did not really change in the course of several other essays on his work or philosophy. The major objection involved the materialism or positivism of his work, a complaint that is interesting because the *Contemporary Review* was generally sympathetic to many of Mill's ideas on social issues.

Carlyle, perhaps even more curiously, was generally praised in the various articles on his "philosophy," though his admiration of the hero was alien to the usual direction of the magazine's commentary on social issues. Ruskin, Arnold, and John Henry Newman were also subjects of abiding interest to the journal, and in each article the emphasis is invariably on the "religious" philosophy of the writer under discussion. Arnold himself wrote several of his most controversial essays on religious issues and was apparently a great favorite with James Knowles, the second editor of the *Contemporary Review*. Knowles broke one of his few editorial policies—that of not publishing lectures—to accommodate Arnold, and it was Knowles who gave Arnold the forum to answer his growing number of critics.[4]

The various essays on Newman illustrate the essential fairness of the *Contemporary Review*. In spite of his "popery," which the *Contemporary* did not tolerate, he was the subject of several essays which have become standard interpretations of his work in the twentieth century. Newman was regarded as an ally of Arnold in the struggle on behalf of culture, and R. H. Hutton drew lengthy analogies between Newman's efforts and those of Matthew Arnold on behalf of English civilization. Arnold privately admitted this influence, but Hutton was, so far as can be determined, the first to establish the broad range of influences that Arnold derived from his mentor (49:327, 513). F. D. Maurice's review of Newman's *Grammar of Assent* was also one of the most intelligent articles written on the work, and is especially noteworthy because Maurice was an evangelical and an old, vigorous critic of Newman (14:151).[5]

Augustine Birrell's essay, "Dr. Johnson," is important because it refutes modern Johnsonian scholars who contend that the Victorians did not understand or appreciate Dr. Johnson—that he was a "zany" in their eyes.[6] Brief notice might also be made of an appreciative essay on the poetry of Alexander Pope, for the essay contradicted Arnold's celebrated dismissal of his work and the modern assumption that Pope was ignored by Victorian critics.

This habit of detached inquiry into conflicting areas of thought is one of the most attractive features of the journal, but there are several exceptions. James Spedding wrote a series of essays in which he attacked Lord Macaulay's review-essay of Spedding's edition of Francis Bacon's work. A careful reader will notice that Spedding did not really answer the multiple charges that Macaulay had brought against Bacon's life, namely that he accepted bribes; and that Macaulay was dead by the time that Spedding came to write his rebuttal.[7]

Another example that might be noted was E. A. Abbott's essay, "The Early Life of Cardinal Newman." Published shortly after Newman's death and later included in a much larger volume, *The Anglican Career of Cardinal Newman*, it was written, as Abbott admitted, with the express purpose of discrediting

Newman.[8] Yet the *Contemporary Review* also published a rather sharp rebuttal to the Abbott article shortly afterward.

One of the shortcomings of the *Contemporary Review*'s literary concerns is the lack of interest in fiction. *Felix Holt* was the only novel that was actually reviewed at the time of its publication, and George Eliot the only novelist who was the subject of more than one essay. *Felix Holt* was said to lack the "fresh vigour" of *Adam Bede*. On the death of Eliot in 1872 Edward Dowden noted in his essay "George Eliot" that "he [*sic*] has given his gift to men" (20:403). Dickens was praised for the social thought in his work, but little mention was made of his comic style. Wilkie Collins was praised for the complexities of his plots and the effectiveness of his style (53:572). But given the enormous range of other literary interests in the *Contemporary Review*, the general silence on novels is curious.

A clue to the apparent neglect of fiction lies in the correspondence of the editor Henry Alford, where one finds only one novel mentioned in all of his reading—*Uncle Tom's Cabin*.[9] It might also be remarked that an early issue (1866) of the *Contemporary Review* has an article by Alford entitled "Mr. Trollope and the English Clergy," in which Trollope is condemned for his shabby portrait of the English clergy in his recent essays for the *Pall Mall Gazette* (2:240). Yet the author did not mention the Barchester novels, in which the same commentary is made.

The major interests of the *Contemporary Review* were theological and philosophical. Literature was well represented in the numerous articles spread over some forty years of continued operation, but the abiding concern was theology, even in those essays directly concerned with literature. It is worth noting that the major contributors to the *Contemporary Review*, including Arnold, Ruskin, and Pater, among others, invariably contributed work that was religious in theme. Yet there is an urbanity and a controversial aspect to almost every article in the *Contemporary Review*. Arnold summed up a part of his career with the magazine when he wrote to Knowles, "I really *hate* polemics . . . [but] I *thrive* on religious exegesis."[10] The nineteenth-century *Contemporary Review* had a great deal of both. [See also the article on the *Contemporary Review* in *MA*.]

Notes

The author wishes to thank the Faculty Research Committee of the University of Southern Colorado for a grant in support of this project.

1. A. W. Brown, *The Metaphysical Society* (New York, 1973), pp. 174–75.

2. Lionel Stevenson, *The Pre-Raphaelite Poets* (New York, 1974), p. 49.

3. Cf. William Holman Hunt, "The Pre-Raphaelite Brotherhood," *Contemporary Review* 49 (1886):471–88; Harry Quilter claimed authorship for the essay and reprinted it and several of the other essays signed by Hunt as his own in *Preferences in Art, Life, and Literature* (London, 1892).

4. Cf. Matthew Arnold, *Essays, Religious and Mixed*, ed. R. H. Super (Ann Arbor, 1972), p. 383; for Arnold's various contributions to the *Contemporary Review*, see *The Wellesley Index to Victorian Periodicals, 1824–1900*, ed. Walter Houghton (Toronto, 1966), 1:796.

5. For Maurice's attitude toward Newman, see John Griffin, "The Newman-Kingsley Debate: An Essay in Social History," *Faith and Reason* 4 (1978):31ff.

6. B. Bronson, "The Double Tradition of Dr. Johnson," *ELH: A Journal of English Literary History* 18 (1951):90–106.

7. The Spedding essays, three in number, start in the July issue for 1876 and continue through the September issue of the same year; for the accuracy of Macaulay's judgment, see F. H. Anderson, *The Philosophy of Francis Bacon* (Chicago, 1948); also see John Griffin, *The Intellectual Milieu of Lord Macaulay* (Ottawa, 1965).

8. Cf. E. A. Abbott, *The Anglican Career of Cardinal Newman* (London, 1891), p. ix.

9. Henry Alford, *Life, Journal, and Letters*, ed. Fanny Alford (Louisville, Ky., 1966), p. 109.

10. Matthew Arnold, *God and the Bible*, ed. R. H. Super (Ann Arbor, 1970), p. 436.

Information Sources

BIBLIOGRAPHY

Alford, Henry. *Life, Journals, and Letters*. Louisville, Ky., 1966.

Brown, A. W. *The Metaphysical Society*. New York, 1973.

Houghton, Walter, ed. *The Wellesley Index to Victorian Periodicals, 1824–1900*. Vol. 1. Toronto, 1966.

Maddux, Margaret Louise. "Henry Alford and the *Contemporary Review*." Master's thesis, University of Chicago, 1950.

Quilter, Harry. *Preferences in Art, Life, and Literature*. London, 1892.

Stevenson, Lionel. *The Pre-Raphaelite Poets*. New York, 1974.

INDEXES

Volumes 1–41 in *A General Index to the "Contemporary Review," the "Fortnightly Review," and the "Nineteenth Century,"* comp. W. M. Griswold (Bangor, Me., 1882). Indexes to volumes 1–41, rpt. separately (Carrollton Press). 1866–1881 in *Poole's Index*. 1866–1900 in *Wellesley Index* 1.

REPRINT EDITIONS

Microform: Bell & Howell Co., Wooster, Ohio.

LOCATION SOURCES

American

Widely available.

British

Widely available.

Publication History

MAGAZINE TITLE AND TITLE CHANGES

The Contemporary Review.

VOLUME AND ISSUE DATA

Volumes 1–, January 1866–.

FREQUENCY OF PUBLICATION
    Monthly.
PUBLISHERS (ALL IN LONDON)
    Volumes 1–19, January 1866–May 1872: Alexander Strahan. Volumes 20–22,
    June 1872–November 1873: Henry S. King and Co. Volumes 23–27, December
    1873–May 1876: Alexander Strahan. Volume 28, June–November 1876: Henry
    S. King and Co. Volumes 29–41, December 1876–June 1882: Strahan and Co.
    Volumes 42–76, July 1882–December 1899: Isbister and Co. Volumes 77–January
    1900–: Columbus Co. Ltd.
EDITORS
    Henry Alford, January 1866–March 1870. James Thomas Knowles, April 1870–
    January 1877. Alexander Strahan, February 1877–1882 (month uncertain). Percy
    William Bunting, 1882–.

John Griffin

CORNHILL MAGAZINE, THE

George M. Smith, writing forty years after the founding of the *Cornhill Magazine* in 1860, said, "The existing magazines were few, and when not high-priced were narrow in literary range, and it seemed to me that a shilling magazine which contained, in addition to other first-class literary matter, a serial novel by Thackeray must command a large sale" (n.s. 10:4). Having secured Thackeray's agreement to supply a novel, on extremely generous terms, Smith began to cast about for an editor. He approached Tom Hughes, who had already agreed to edit a similar magazine for Macmillan's. After many other names had been suggested and judged to be unsatisfactory, it finally occurred to Smith to hire Thackeray himself. Thackeray agreed on the condition that he would have only editorial duties and that Smith would take care of all the business arrangements for the magazine.

Smith then "set to work with energy to make the undertaking a success" by securing "the most brilliant contributors" with payments "lavish almost to the point of recklessness. No pains and no cost were spared to make the new magazine the best periodical yet known to English literature" (n.s. 10:6). Smith's hunch about the attraction of such a journal was correct: the public flocked to a magazine that gave a serial installment of a novel, short stories, poetry, and articles for the amount of money they had formerly paid for a serial part of a novel alone.

In the first issue the reader received for his shilling not only an installment of a novel by Thackeray, *Lovel the Widower*, and essays by the best writers of the day, including G. H. Lewes, but also an installment of Anthony Trollope's *Framley Parsonage* and Thackeray's *Roundabout Papers*. Contributors to subsequent issues included G.A.H. Sala, Elizabeth Gaskell, John Ruskin, Fitzjames Stephen, Charles Lever, and Anne Ritchie.

Editors of Victorian magazines were well attuned to public taste and generally anxious to avoid publishing any material that might offend. Thackeray was no exception. During his tenure as editor he published two of Trollope's novels but rejected a story on the basis that it was too risqué, much to Trollope's dismay.[1] Thackeray, always uneasy in the editorial chair, resigned after two years but continued to contribute to the magazine.[2] He was succeeded by an editorial committee composed of Smith, Frederick Greenwood, Lewes, and, later, Edward Dutton Cook. The editorial policy remained consistent until 1871. Novels published in this period included Thackeray's *Denis Duval*, Mrs. Gaskell's *Cousin Phyllis* and *Wives and Daughters*, Trollope's *Small House at Allington* and *The Claverings*, George Eliot's *Romola*, Wilkie Collins's *Armadale*, Charles Reade's *Put Yourself in His Place*, and George Meredith's *Adventures of Harry Richmond*. Among the essayists were Matthew Arnold, W. S. Gilbert, and J. A. Symonds. In the face of fierce competition from periodicals similar to the *Cornhill*, particularly *Macmillan's** and *Temple Bar*,* the circulation dropped to about 20,000 by 1870, down from the record-setting 110,000 of the first issue.

A signficant change occurred in 1871 with the appointment of Leslie Stephen as editor. Some major fiction appeared in the magazine during this period: Thomas Hardy's *Far from the Madding Crowd* and *The Hand of Ethelberta* and Henry James's *Daisy Miller* and *Washington Square*. During this time the literary essay figured prominently in the *Cornhill* with the work of R. L. Stevenson, Edmund Gosse, Symonds, and, especially, Stephen himself. Many of the articles began to appear with authors' initials and even signatures. Despite the brilliance of the *Cornhill* under Stephen's management, the circulation dropped, having reached a low of 12,000 when he resigned in December 1882.

James Payn replaced Stephen and set about revitalizing the magazine by seeking a new readership. He began a new series with the July 1883 issue, reduced the price to six pence, and shifted the emphasis from high-quality literary essays to light fiction and articles aimed at a less literate audience. Because the *Cornhill* did not quite descend to the sensational level of the six-penny publications with which it was forced to compete, it failed to lure many of their readers. At the same time, it lost some of the faithful who had read it for classical essays, and the circulation fell disastrously low.

John St. Loe Strachey replaced Payn and attempted to return the magazine to its former position of dignity. With the July 1896 issue Strachey began a third series, made the *Cornhill* a shilling magazine again, and shifted the emphasis to belles lettres.

When Strachey resigned in 1898 to edit the *Spectator** (see *RA*), Reginald John Smith assumed the editorial duties. He filled the pages with second-rate essays and continued to serialize novels, a practice that had been abandoned by most other magazines by this time.

The *Cornhill* represents a major development in British periodical history. By offering to the readers in a single issue monthly installments of two novels by prominent novelists and well-written essays and short fiction by outstanding writers, the *Cornhill* effectively put an end to the separate-part issue of novels, a practice that had been in vogue since the great success of the *Pickwick Papers* in 1836. The innovations of George M. Smith reaped a readership of unprecedented size. [See also the article on the *Cornhill Magazine* in *MA*.]

Notes

1. Anthony Trollope, *An Autobiography*, ed. Bradford Allen Booth (Berkeley, 1947), p. 118.
2. For a fuller account of Thackeray's association with the *Cornhill*, see Gordon N. Ray, *Thackeray: The Age of Wisdom, 1847–1863* (New York, 1958), pp. 293–321.

Information Sources

BIBLIOGRAPHY

Cook, E. T. "Jubilee of the *Cornhill*." *Cornhill Magazine*, 3d ser., 28 (1910):8–27.
Houghton, Walter E., ed. *The Wellesley Index to Victorian Periodicals 1824–1900*. Volume 1. Toronto, 1966.
Huxley, Leonard. "Chronicles of the *Cornhill*." *Cornhill Magazine*, 3d ser., 52 (1922):364–84.
———. *The House of Smith Elder*. London, 1923.
Maitland, F. W. *The Life and Letters of Leslie Stephen*. London, 1906.
Maurer, Oscar. "Leslie Stephen and the *Cornhill Magazine*." *Studies in English* (University of Texas) 32 (1953):67–95.
Ritchie, Anne Thackeray. "First Number of the *Cornhill*." *Cornhill Magazine*, 3d ser., 1 (1896):1–16.
Scott, J. W. Robertson. *The Story of the "Pall Mall Gazette*." Oxford, 1950.
Smith, George M. *George Smith: A Memoir with Some Pages of Autobiography*. London, 1902.
———. "Our Birth and Parentage." *Cornhill Magazine*, n.s. 10 (1901):4–17.
Smith, Peter. "The *Cornhill Magazine*—Number 1." *Review of English Literature* 4 (1963):23–24.
Strachey, John St. Loe. *The Adventure in Living*. London, 1922.
Tiemersma, Richard R. "Fiction in the *Cornhill Magazine*—January 1860–March 1871." Ph.D. dissertation, Northwestern University, 1962.

INDEXES

Each volume indexed. 1860–1881 in *Poole's Index*. 1860–1900 in *Wellesley Index* 1.

REPRINT EDITIONS

Microform: Princeton Microfilm Corporation; UMI.

LOCATION SOURCES

American
Widely available.
British
Widely available

Publication History

MAGAZINE TITLE AND TITLE CHANGES

The Cornhill Magazine.

VOLUME AND ISSUE DATA
Volume 1, number 1–volume 47, number 6, January 1860–June 1883.
New series, volume 1, number 1–volume 26, number 6, July 1883–June 1896.
New series, volume 1, number 1, July 1896–.

FREQUENCY OF PUBLICATION
Monthly.

PUBLISHER
Volumes 1–18: Smith, Elder, and Co., 65 Cornhill St., London. Volume 19: 15 Waterloo Place, London.

EDITORS
William Makepeace Thackeray, January 1860–May 1862. Frederick Greenwood, George Henry Lewes, and George Smith, June 1862–1864 (?). Frederick Greenwood and George Smith, 1864 (?)–1868 (?). Edward Dutton Cook, George Henry Lewes, and George Smith, 1868 (?)–March 1871. Leslie Stephen, April 1871–December 1882. James Payn, January 1883–June 1896. John St. Loe Strachey, July 1896–December 1897. Reginald John Smith, January 1898–.

J. Don Vann

COSMOPOLIS

Cosmopolis: An International Review was created in 1896 to help protect the intellectual life of Europe from the destructive forces of nationalism. As its name suggests, *Cosmopolis* was intended as an appeal to interests "common to Europe at large" rather than to those defining any one linguistic or national culture (2:334). In a letter to the editor of *Cosmopolis*, French intellectual Jules Simon (who had been removed from his professorship at the Sorbonne for refusing to declare political allegiance to Louis Napoleon) declared his support for what he perceived to be this review's special mission in the last years of the nineteenth century:

Vous faites une revue cosmopolite pour contribuer à répandre les idées de paix et de concorde. . . . Jamais à aucune époque de l'histoire, la guerre n'a été à la fois aussi vraisemblable et aussi impossible qu'en ce moment: vraisemblable parce que les *casus belli* s'accumulent de tous les côtés, dans les Balkans, en Bulgarie, en Turquie, au Transvaal, en Chine.[You are making a cosmopolitan review in order to spread the ideas of peace and harmony. . . . Never in any period of history has war been at the same time so probable as well as impossible as at this moment: probable because the *casus belli* are increasing from all sides, in the Balkans, in Bulgaria, in Turkey, in the Transvaal, in China.] ["Lettre sur L'Arbitrage," 1:444]

Frederic Harrison, who in Arnold's *Culture and Anarchy* represents a narrow and negative understanding of culture, envisioned *Cosmopolis* as an attempt to give form to the ideal of cultural unity which technological and linguistic developments had virtually destroyed: what was once a culturally unified Europe was, by the end of the nineteenth century, a number of isolated nations, each motivated and controlled by "national pride, jealousy, and self-assertion," by "patriotic dreams of Empire, Victory, and Leadership of the World" ("The True Cosmopolis," 3:329). Typical of most reviews of its time, *Cosmopolis* welcomed contributions of fiction, drama, and poetry, as well as articles of literary and political criticism. Unusual among reviews of the time, *Cosmopolis* published in each issue contributions in English, French, and German. Had *Cosmopolis* continued as its early supporters hoped it would, contributions in yet more languages would eventually have been included within its covers, and its cultural representation would have extended to "eight or ten national centres in Europe, and two or three others in North and South America" (3:327). In the fall of 1896, at the very time when the Boer War broke out, Harrison looked forward to the time when "all the chief tongues of Europe and all the leading minds of both continents may one day find in [*Cosmopolis*] a common ground for interchange of thought" (3:327). Forces of history proved stronger than the desire for international cooperation that Simon, Harrison, and other contributors to the review hoped for. But by the time of its demise, in the winter of 1898, *Cosmopolis* had achieved a three-year history of publishing works of unusual artistic and intellectual merit.

The format of *Cosmopolis* changed little during its publication. Each issue consists of about three hundred octavo pages divided into three similarly designed and linguistically separate parts: the first in English, the second in French, and the third in German. Each of these three parts consists, first, of four or five signed pieces, at least one of which is an imaginative contribution (usually a short story, less often a drama, rarely a poem); one of literary criticism; and one on a political topic. Each of these three parts concludes with one or more review articles by a staff of writers who stayed with *Cosmopolis* throughout its publication life. These recurring articles are of three kinds: articles devoted to recent publications from the three cultures represented; articles on theatrical productions in those cultures; and articles on contemporary political events of great concern to each of those cultures. Of the review articles, only those devoted to political affairs appear in very nearly every issue; others—those devoted to literature and theater—appear quarterly. Beginning with volume 9, for January 1898, literary bulletins appear monthly: these consist of brief descriptions of current publications, including other literary periodicals. Andrew Lang, Emile Faguet (drama critic of *Journal des Débats*), and Anton Bettelheim were responsible for the literary review articles. A. B. Walkley, dramatist Jules Lemaître, and Otto Neumann-Hofer wrote regularly on theatrical productions, with occasional substitutions of William Archer, Francisque Sarcey, Felix Poppenberg, and Paul Schlenther. Journalist Henry Norman, political figure Francis de Pressensé, and "Ignotus" (pseudonym of Adam Muller-Guttenbrun, Austrian novelist and playwright) wrote on political events. The particular responsibility of these writers appears to have been to present an assessment of their countries' cultural life to readers of other countries. Emile Faguet explained:

> Je suivrai ici, mois par mois, aussi diligemment qu'il me sera possible, le mouvement de la littérature française. . . . Je n'oublierai pas que je parle par-dessus la frontière de mon pays et que, par ce seul fait, je suis obligé à une plus stricte et plus littérale définition des choses. Ce qu'un Français pense exactement des Français, voilà ce qu'un Anglais, un Américain, un Allemand, un Russe, un Italien ou un Espagnole demande à une revue comme celle-ci en l'ouvrant. . . . Sans sortir de mon departement et ne parlant qu'en mon nom, je peux assurer que je me considèrerai toujours ici comme m'adressant spécialement à mes voisins qu'à mes compatriotes. [I will follow here, month by month, as diligently as it will be possible for me, the movement of French literature. . . . I will not forget that I speak across the frontier of my country, and that by this single fact, I am bound to a stricter and more literal definition of things. What a Frenchman thinks exactly of the French is what an Englishman, an American, a German, a Russian, an Italian, or a Spaniard asks in a review like this one in opening it. . . . Without leaving the boundaries of my department and speaking only in my name, I can assure you I will always consider myself here as addressing myself especially to my neighbors rather than to my fellow-countrymen.] [1:184]

Though *Cosmopolis* might be considered as three mini-journals, each separate and complete in itself, it is clear that its editor, F. Ortmans, conceived of the periodical as one intended for readers who could appreciate the special intellectual richness that a command of three languages makes possible. Writers of one culture were aware of their responsibility to readers of another culture in various ways. Faguet and other regular contributors found their subject matter in their own cultures and their readers in other cultures. Other writers found both their subject matter and their readers in foreign places. *Cosmopolis* deals with events that transcend single cultures, and often provides the reader with an international symposium on a single topic. The death of Gladstone, for example, provokes responses among contributors to the three parts of *Cosmopolis*: Justin McCarthy in English, Francis de Pressensé in French, and Theodor Barth in German eulogize the statesman whose life influenced all of Europe (9:29–43, 114–35, 205–33). The sixty-year jubilee of the reign of Victoria serves as the subject for a similar international series of essays, by Richard Temple, Francis de Pressensé, and Theodor Barth (6:621–36, 788–810, 833–42). So too the centenary of the birth of Heine evoked essays by Israel Zangwill, Edward Dowden, Edouard Rod, and Karl Frenzel (8:617–44, 645–61, 739–47, 870–86). Dumas *fils* having died in 1895, *Cosmopolis* inaugurated its publication life with a three-month series of five articles devoted to the accomplishments and international influence of that writer: two by fellow countrymen, Francisque Sarcey (1:171–83) and a friend of Dumas, Gustave Larroumet (1:457–70); one by William Archer (1:363–72); one by Karl Frenzel (1: 553–60); and one written in French by Tolstoy (1:761–74).

There also appears in *Cosmopolis* a number of serialized articles the primary point of which derives from their international perspective. Published for the first time in *Cosmopolis*, for example, are J. S. Mill's letters to Gustave d'Eichthal (6:20–38, 348–66; 9:368–81, 780–808). Assessments of contemporary literature from a foreign perspective appear regularly, including two series: Edmund Gosse's "Current French Literature" (4:681–701; 6:637–54; 8:662–78; 10:660–74); and J. G. Robertson on current German literature (5:684–710; 7:657–73; 9:649–65; 12:31–48). A French view of English literature is provided in Augustin Filon's "Littérature d'Outre-Manche" (5:137–49), a German view of Hardy and Kipling in A. Brandl's "Vom englischen Büchertisch" (6:579–94), and a German view of French literature in J. J. David's "Die französische Litteratur im abgegangenen Jahre" (7:259–70). There are also frequent articles on literature from countries other than the three regularly represented: W. R. Morfill's "Russian Literature during the Last Year" (7:340–55); Ernest Tissot's "La Littérature Italienne d'Aujourd'hui" (12:452–74); Helen Zimmern's "Italian Literature" (12:352–66; coauthored with Enrico Corradini, 8:374–402); O. G. de Heidenstam's "Le Livre en Norvège" (7:404–24) and "Le Livre en Suède" (12:425–40); R. Nisbet Bain's "Contemporary Scandinavian Belles-Lettres" (8:66–94); R. Candiani's "Le Mouvement littéraire dans les Pays-Bas" (8:478–512); Lewis Sergeant's "Greek Contemporary Literature" (10:369–98). Among articles on literature of the past from a foreign or comparative perspective are George Moore's essay on French, Russian, and English novelists, with particular attention to Thackeray's influence on Tolstoy ("Since the Elizabethans," 4:42–58); J. J. Jusserand's series on "Shakespeare en France sous l'ancien Régime" (4:440–58, 752–74; 5:150–70, 448–66); and Clément Rochel's "La Renaissance dramatique en Espagne" (8:129–53).

Nowhere in *Cosmopolis* does there appear a statement of policy from its editor, nor is information about him easily found. F. Ortmans was probably French. Probably he is the same F. Ortmans who provided the index to G. V. Hertzberg's *Histoire de la Grèce sous la Domination des Romains*. The magazine itself suggests that Ortmans or someone acting in his place exerted clear and forceful control over the monthly, and that his connections with writers extended throughout much of Europe. Many contributors known for their political—generally liberal or radical—views as well as for significant scholarly or creative work were attracted to this monthly. If for no other reason, *Cosmopolis* is of great interest for the biographies of its contributors, many of whom were involved in important political events throughout Europe from the first half of the nineteenth century. Historian Theodor Mommsen was forced to resign his law professorship at Leipzig as a result of his political activities in 1848. He edited *Corpus Inscriptionum Latinarum* (1861–), and was to receive the Nobel Prize for literature in 1902. For *Cosmopolis* he wrote on a historical example of governmental control of civil disobedience in "Die Geschichte der Todesstrafe im Römischen Staat" (1:231–42). German socialist Eduard Bernstein, who lived some years in exile for political reasons, authored one of the letters of "Zukunfsstaatliches: Zwei offen Schreiben" (9:875–82). Hungarian novelist Maurus Jókai, whose political activities were severely curtailed as a result of his opposition to Austrian rule, provided *Cosmopolis* with an account of celebrations in Budapest in honor of the millennium of Hungary ("Ungarns Millennium und Landesausstellung," 3:851–56). The close friend of Marx and Engels, W. Liebknecht, spent years of exile in England for his participation in events of 1848; for *Cosmopolis* he wrote "Zukunfsstaatliches" (9:203–36). Bernard Shaw contributed an account of the 1896 International Socialist Congress in England, in which he criticizes socialists such as Liebknecht for their old-fashioned and unrealistic refusal to cooperate with other political parties and for reading history simplistically:

> Liebknecht's declaration that if the Alsace-Lorraine difficulty were left to the working classes it would be settled amicably in an hour, was received ... with acclamation. In nothing is the middle-class origin of the Socialist movement so apparent as in the persistent delusions of Socialists as to an ideal proletariat, forced by the brutalities of the capitalist into an unwilling acquiescence in war, penal codes, and other cruelties of civilization. [3:658–73]

As *Cosmopolis* was "ni Anglais, ni Allemand, ni Français" (Jules Simon, "Lettre sur L'Arbitrage," 1:446), neither was it Marxist, Fabian, socialist, or any other particular political advocate. As there was room in its pages for the leader of the French Socialist party, Jean Jaurès ("Le Socialisme français," 9:107–35) and for the English Liberal Charles Dilke, an outspoken critic of British colonial policy (1:21–40; 3:18–35), so was there room for a former editor of the *Pall Mall Gazette*, Frederick Greenwood, who disparages arbitration in favor of balance of power as a means of preventing war (2:346–60), and for the imperialist outcry of Henry Norman: "We are Imperialists first, and Liberals or Tories afterwards. I said this, for my own part, years ago, when the sentiment was not quite so popular. Now it has happily become a commonplace. The Jubilee is its culminating expression, and foreign observers should not fail to take note of this underlying significance of our national fête to-day" ("The Globe and the Island," 7:81).

The memory, the fact, and the fear of war mark *Cosmopolis* from its first through its last issues, and make it an extraordinarily rich repository of European thought on that subject during crucial transitional years in Europe's history. The reader is reminded again and again of events that made the century one of revolutions, both because of intensifying military threats throughout the world and because of the personal experiences with violence and the early dreams of peace among nations that contributors brought to the monthly. Historian Gabriel

Monod, in an account of his trip to the 1896 Bayreuth festival, recalls the dream
of his youth as he observes conflicting signs of what the future portends:

> Le rêve de ma jeunesse était, comme celui des meilleurs parmi mes com-
> pagnons d'étude, de travailler à l'union du génie allemand et du génie
> français pour des oeuvres communes de civilisation. ... Je reviens d'Al-
> lemagne très frappé par les signes de force, d'activité pacifique et de progrès
> que j'ai vu dans tous les lieux où j'ai passé. Il est necessaire que les
> Français sachent ce qu'est l'Allemagne actuelle, et ce qu'ils peuvent espérer
> ou craindre d'elle. [The dream of my youth was, like that of the best
> among my companions in study, of working to unite German talent and
> French talent for common causes of civilization. ... I return from Ger-
> many struck by the signs of force, of peaceful activity, and of progress
> which I saw wherever I went. It is necessary that the French know what
> the real Germany is, and what they can hope from her or fear from her.]
> [4:460, 476]

In a series of autobiographical essays that represent the convergence of culture
and personal history informing much of *Cosmopolis*, Max Müller presents detailed accounts of encounters with artists and thinkers of the cultures represented
in the magazine's three languages:

> All young poets in Germany were then liberal and more than liberal, all
> dreamt and sang of a united Germany. But being thirty years ahead of
> Bismarck, they were unmercifully sent to prison, and often their whole
> career was ruined. ... Living much in that society, I too, a harmless boy
> of eighteen, was sent to prison as a person highly dangerous to the peace
> of Europe. [4:638]

Between that kind of troubled past and World War I, *Cosmopolis* gave expression to a briefly realized hope that international understanding through cultural,
and particularly literary, exchange might prevail; in Edouard Rod's words: "Et
puis, l'avenir est si incertain, gros de tels orages, chargé de nuages si menaçants,
qu'il serait pueril de s'affliger en voyant la littérature se séparer en plus de la
vie générale" [And then, the future is so uncertain, pregnant with such storms,
charged with clouds so menacing, that it would be puerile to be distressed by
seeing literature separating itself more and more from life in general] (1:456).

In *Cosmopolis*'s thirty-five issues there appear about fifty contributions from
women. As a group these contributions are a fair representation of the diverse
interests of the periodical as well as of the cosmopolitan lives of many of its
contributors. There are, for example, a number of personal reminiscences by
women about men of international distinction, by Mary Robinson, Janet Ross,
Mrs. Freiligrath-Kroeker, Judith Gautier, and Malvida von Meysenbug.

Cosmopolis includes among its contributors some of Europe's most distinguished creative writers, as well as scholars and political writers. R. L. Stevenson's unfinished romance, *Weir of Hermiston*, with notes by his friend and editor Sidney Colvin, appears in serial through the first four issues of the monthly (1:1–20, 320–62, 640–63; 2:1–27), and the next to the last issue begins with a short story by W. Somerset Maugham, "Don Sebastian" (12:1–14). The high quality of writing to be found throughout *Cosmopolis* is especially noteworthy. English writers published in the magazine include Henry James (1:41–59, 373–92; 9:1–21, 317–32); Yeats (10:675–86); Gissing (3:309–26; 10:297–314); Kipling (6:1–19, 305–22); Conrad (6:609–20); and Meredith. French literary pieces came from similarly distinguished writers: Mallarmé (6:417–27); Paul Bourget (1:113–27; 2:401–24; 3:107–24, 705–27; 4:95–114, 719–46; 6:89–114, 707–27; 7:93–121); and Anatole France (1:128–41).

Twenty-four thousand copies of the first issue of *Cosmopolis* were sold, and eighteen thousand copies of the second issue were printed.[1] With no more than that meager information concerning the commercial history of *Cosmopolis*, one can only speculate on its failure to see a fourth year of publication. Throughout its life it maintained the high standards of intellectual and artistic excellence achieved in its first issues. It provided its readers with a remarkably rich and informed assessment of political and literary events of the time and with works by distinguished literary figures. Probably the direction that political history was taking did not favor the continuation of such a periodical. And perhaps, too, there was an insufficient number of readers of the kind *Cosmopolis* was created for: readers able to read in three languages, eager to follow the many connections among the three linguistically separated parts of the monthly, and interested in keeping abreast of literary and political events throughout Europe.

Note

1. J. R. Tye, comp. *Periodicals of the Nineties*. (Oxford, 1974), p. 4.

Information Sources

BIBLIOGRAPHY

Pondrom, Cyrena Norman. "English Literary Periodicals: 1885–1918." Ph.D. dissertation, Columbia University, 1965.

Tye, J. R., comp. *Periodicals of the Nineties*. Oxford, 1974.

REPRINT EDITIONS

Kraus Reprint, New York, 1974.

Microform: UMI.

INDEXES

Table of contents for volumes 1–11.

LOCATION SOURCES

American

Widely available.

British
> Widely available.

Publication History

MAGAZINE TITLE AND TITLE CHANGES
> *Cosmopolis: An International Monthly Review.*

VOLUME AND ISSUE DATA
> Volumes 1–12, numbers 1–35, January 1896–November 1898.

FREQUENCY OF PUBLICATION
> Monthly.

PUBLISHERS
> T. Fisher Unwin, London; and Armand Colin, Paris.

EDITOR
> F. Ortmans.

Carol de Saint Victor

COURT MAGAZINE AND MONTHLY CRITIC

The history of *Court Magazine*, which first appeared as a united series in January 1838, is complicated by a number of mergers and a change in publisher. When John Bell died in 1831, his 1806 *La Belle Assemblée** (see *RA*) became *Court Magazine and Belle Assemblée.*[1] This latter publication, edited by the Hon. Caroline Norton, changed its title in 1837 without notice to *Court Magazine and Monthly Critic.* In 1838 Edward Churton sold the periodical to Dobbs & Co. The new proprietor effected a general merger that resulted in the *Court Magazine and Monthly Critic and Lady's Magazine and Museum of Belles Lettres.* In December 1837 a brief note explained that, beginning in January, the publication would be expanded to include monthly fashion news, full-length portraits "splendidly coloured and jewelled, after original paintings of the most eminent old masters," and a new thirty-two page section of unspecified content. It seems clear that the sale from Churton to Dobbs and the revised format were caused by a drop in subscriptions; in July 1836, for example, the proprietor reminded his readers that a year before he had reduced the price of an issue in hopes of increased subscriptions, but that since new readers had not materialized, he planned to drop the fashion plates rather than raise the price.

The new magazine billed itself as a "family magazine," and, perhaps to assure a sophisticated cadre of readers, proclaimed itself to be under the patronage of the Duchess of Kent. It promised a selection of "original tales, reviews of literature, the fine arts, music, drama, fashions, etc., etc." It fulfilled all of these promises and more. Every issue contained original stories; in later years lengthy novels were published as well. The magazine also offered poems, extracts, memoirs, reprinted lectures, and discussions of literary matters. The "Monthly Critic" contained reviews of entertaining and informative books and publications. Long and short notices of plays and amusements ranging from pantomimes and cosmoramas to exhibitions of paintings were given as well. The end matter also contained a news miscellany, an alphabetical listing of births, deaths, and marriages, and "The Queen's Gazette," which provided court news. Perhaps most attractive to subscribers disappointed by the 1836 elimination of fashion news was an insert entitled "Le Follet, Courrier des Salons. Journal des Modes." Printed in French on pink paper, "Le Follet" carried up-to-date information about Parisian styles.

The balance between instruction and entertainment was more carefully preserved in the early years than in the later, when the body of the magazine contained a preponderance of fiction. In 1838, however, readers were offered pieces by Barbara Hofland, a friend of Mary Russel Mitford and a popular novelist in her own right. Her recommendations for "Hours of Convalescence" appeared in February 1838, and her "Wives, in their Varieties, Sentiments, Conduct, and Sufferings" in the issue for September-October 1838. Reminiscent of eighteenth-century character delineation, the latter essay lauds the cheerful and industrious wife against her "lamenting," over-economical, or "applauding" sisters. Carrying a different appeal, a long-running series of historical memoirs was accompanied by colored portraits; in the first half of 1838, for example, memoirs and portraits of Queen Mary II, William III, and Queen Anne appeared. Perhaps because of the expense of the illustration, the editor eventually fell into arrears; blank sheets were provided for portraits to be published and a pro forma apology ran volume by volume. Also illustrated was a series of essays by Sutherland Menzies, "Outlines of British Female Costume" (January 1838); drawings made from British Museum holdings were used "to render the page of history less arid" and "to diffuse among our readers generally a taste for that only which is historically true, as well as graphically excellent." Later essays included a series on the Admiralty (1846–1847) which featured detailed discussions of such military endeavors as Lord Exmouth's Algiers expedition and the siege of Gibraltar.

Much of the informative material appeared as reviews in the "Monthly Critic." More than simple notices, the reviews frequently incorporated lengthy extracts. Selections from the July 1838 "Monthly Critic" are typical of the editorial propensity for building an "educational library" on behalf of the readership. George Irvine's translation of Schiller's *Bride of Messina* appears first; the reviewer, who finds it "cast in the most dolorous style of the old awful Greek drama of the Oedipean class," disagrees with the general critical acclaim. On Henry Verlander's poem "The Vestal," the reviewer admits to a dislike for the coldness of classical subjects; on the play *Montezuma*, he comments that good grammar and morals are not equivalent to genius; and on Edward Jesse's *Gleanings of Natural History*, he objects to personifying animals. The review of *Madame Tussaud's Memoirs* seems calculated to satisfy the readership's taste for the bloodcurdling, containing as it does excerpts of how the venerable showwoman obtained casts of murderers' heads. Thomas Dick's *Celestial Scenery;*

or, the Wonders of the Planetary Systems Displayed alone is almost entirely satisfactory to the reviewer.

Discussions of literature took place outside of the "Monthly Critic" as well. In the issue for August 1838, for example, a critical discussion of Alexandre Dumas's *Caligula* begins. While deploring the "debased and humiliating position of national drama" and praising both Hugo and Dumas for their inventiveness, the reviewer nonetheless attacks the first for a lack of realism and the second for a dangerous morality. Despite the reviewer's fear of the "carpe diem" philosophy exhibited in *Caligula*, he gives long extracts from the play. In another instance, a public disagreement occurs between the editor and Count Carlo Pepoli, the Italian professor whose lectures (on the history of music, for example) were reprinted in *Court Magazine*. The exchange of letters was initiated by the editor's questioning the historical basis for Pepoli's interpretations in the lecture "Language and Literature of Italy," which *Court* reviewed in March 1839. Pepoli's charge that the editor was not a thorough master of Italian history appeared in April; in June the editor reminds the count that the British are a "fact loving people" and refuses to give up the privilege of anonymity.

The editor's taste for intellectual amusement is perhaps nowhere so aptly displayed as in the announcement for "the Knowledge Society" that appeared in August-September 1844. The stated purpose of the society, apparently occasioned by the editor's distress at an 1842 plague in Asia, was "to become familiar with the tract of country through which is made the land transit of India"; its motto was *Felix, quam faciunt aliena pericula cautum* [Fortunate is he whom foreign dangers make cautious]. Because of the duties involved in the new society, including organizing study groups and morning assemblies, the editor proposed to eliminate the year's October issue. Inquiries were to be sent post-free to G. Carden at 59 Lincoln's-Inn-Fields. At least one production of the Knowledge Society appeared in print; the June 1845 *Court Magazine* carried the House of Commons New Zealand debates, purportedly "printed for the Knowledge Society."

Despite this attempt to appeal to a bluestocking readership, perhaps the better part of *Court Magazine* was devoted to sentimental poetry and fiction of the sort unlikely to be acknowledged by the devotees of knowledge. *Court* published lamentations on the deaths of loved ones, such as "On the Death of the Young Casa Bianca," commemorating a commodore and his son lost in the sinking of the *Orient*; or of public figures, such as Mrs. Edmonds's "Lines on the Death of Dr. Southey" in April 1843: "Oh weep for him that sleepeth...." Long narrative Gothic poems—for example, Mrs. W. Bask's "The Count of Nicastro," a poem about a werewolf—were not uncommon. W. Ledger contributed a variety of poems, from "The Castle Tower" (April 1843) to "The Opening of the Royal Exchange" (December 1844). Translations from the German of Schiller and Friedrich von Matthison form a group in their own right, while patriotic poems form another. Readers were offered not only full-length descriptions of Victoria's coronation in the August 1838 "Queen's Gazette," but also Tennant Lachlan's 24 May 1838 birthday poem, "Victoria," and H.C.D.'s "The Crowned of the Isles" (July 1838), which began energetically, " 'Tis the Queen of the white cliffed shore, / The Queen of the free, the bold, the brave." Intentional humor is rare, perhaps confined to the satirical "Editor and the Shadow" (August 1838) by "Umbra," whose versified sketch of an overworked editor unfortunately becomes a moralistic injunction to finish the day's work in time.

As the years progress, the table of contents grows shorter while the works of fiction grow longer. In 1838 the editor struggled to complete an interrupted serial, Emma Whitehead's "Haunted House," and a historical series by Agnes Strickland, "Tales of the English Chronicles," whose first number appeared four years earlier. A shorter work by Whitehead, "The Bohemian; a Legend" (July 1838), is a typical tale of gypsy omens and blighted love, while Sutherland Menzies's "Hugues, the Wer-Wolf" (September 1838) deals with what was clearly a popular topic. Titles of sample tales are indicative of typical stories of love and intrigue in exotic or haunted places: two instances are "Emily Delany; or, the Prophetic Raven" (January 1843), by W. Ledger, and "The Bride-Widow; a Tale of the Old Mansions of Avondale" (February 1843), by W. Carey. In 1844 a 236-page novel appeared; complete with title page and introduction, it was entitled *The Excluded*, by "Theophilus Philocrapanthus Meredith Pry." After that, length seemed the rule rather than the exception. C. Sears Lancaster's 1846 "Who Are the Guilty?" whose last scene ends in "a pauper madhouse," ran for ten chapters; A. A.'s "Rosalie Vilancoeur; or, the Creature of Impulse," for sixteen; and B's 1845 "The Castle of Montebore; An Historical Romance of the 12th Century," for thirty-two. To be sure, some of the stories were moralistic: Emma Maria Sargent's 1846 "Slaves of Opinion" recounts a fashionable family's adjustment to financial reverses, and Barbara Hofland's 1838 "Charming Couple" is a warning to flirtatious husbands. On the whole, though, stories like Zavier Saintine's 1846 "The Slave of the Pasha," in which a Turkish slave becomes a dancer in the ballet corps of the Paris Opera, seem most common.

Perhaps one cause for the failure of the magazine in the 1840's was the irregular appearance of the issues. Another may have been the impossibility of wedding so many periodicals together, particularly insofar as a variety of interests were compartmentalized in, for example, the "Monthly Critic" and the fashion supplement. Indeed, the "many vexatious interruptions" that occasioned a lapse in the illustrated memoirs in 1844 may themselves have been ultimately responsible.

Note

1. Stanley Morison, *John Bell, 1745–1831* (Cambridge, England, 1930), p. 73.

Information Sources

INDEXES

Each volume indexed.

REPRINT EDITIONS

Microform: Early British Periodicals (UMI), reels 756–759.

LOCATION SOURCES
  American
    Partial runs: Widely available.
  British
    Partial runs: Widely available.

Publication History

MAGAZINE TITLE AND TITLE CHANGES
  Court Magazine and Monthly Critic and Lady's Magazine and Museum of Belles Lettres.
VOLUME AND ISSUE DATA
  United series, volumes 1–20 (also old series, 12–31), January 1838–1847.
FREQUENCY OF PUBLICATION
  Monthly.
PUBLISHER
  Dobbs & Co., 8 Carey St., Lincoln's Inn, London; 15 Gate St., Lincoln's-Inn-Fields, London.
EDITOR
  None cited.

                                                                                       Patricia Marks

CRITIC, THE

The *Critic* was one of a group of high-quality journals established or acquired by Sergeant Edward William Cox during the middle decades of the nineteenth century. Of a dozen or more of the Cox journalistic enterprises, the best known and the most successful were the *Law Times*, the *Field*, and the *Queen*. The *Critic* was his literary periodical. It originated as a department of the weekly *Law Times*, which Cox had founded in April 1843; under the title of "The Critic" appeared notices of new publications in legal and general literature, as well as music and works of art. After a short trial, the proprietor began to project an enlargement of that department into a monthly supplement containing the more general literary and artistic concerns so as to limit the parent journal wholly to legal subjects. In November 1843 the *Critic of Literature, Art, Science, and the Drama; A Guide for the Library and Book Club* was established as a distinct and separate periodical, to be issued monthly. With the second issue, in December 1843, John Crockford became its publisher, having supplanted Thomas Lauder as publisher and business manager of both journals. James Lowe was the editor of the *Critic* throughout the twenty years of its history,[1] although its content and character always reflected the interests and influence of its proprietor and it was conducted in a style similar to that of the *Law Times*.

The *Critic* inherited the readership of the parent paper, a "very wide circulation," it reported in the preface to the first number, "entirely among the educated and wealthy classes, from which are supplied the influential body of

Legislators, Magistrates, and Lawyers.'' Successive modifications in title, changes in frequency of issue, fluctuations in price, and continual experiment with subsidiary publications and projects marked its effors to expand its audience ''beyond the circulation for whose use it was immediately undertaken'' into the reading public formed by literary journals already in existence, particularly, in 1843, the *Literary Gazette** (see *RA*) and the *Athenaeum** (see *RA*). By the end of six years it considered itself fairly established in reputation, although, by its own account, eight years passed and more than 5,000 pounds had been invested to subsidize the journal before it became self-sustaining (n.s. 11:88). In 1851 it was reporting a ''steadily proceeding'' increase in circulation to 6,500 by November of that year. Three years later it put forth a claim to the largest circulation among the literary periodicals. This claim was challenged by its contemporaries. The *Athenaeum* was quick to point out that the *Critic* (''a paper of which few of our readers will have heard'') manipulated the figures of the Stamp Returns so as to compare the entire printing of the *Critic* with only the stamped figures of the *Athenaeum*, which also had a very considerable unstamped impression. The *Literary Gazette* reprinted the article from the *Athenaeum* and added a note calling attention to an attack in *Fraser's Magazine** (see *RA*) on Cox and his methods of conducting his journalistic enterprises, including the *Critic*. Despite the controversy, the *Critic* continued to insist upon its position as a major literary journal.[2]

Throughout the 1850s, occasional supplements were added to the issues of the *Critic*, apparently in an effort to make it more profitable: illustrated Christmas book supplements; an *Educational Supplement* (quarterly from July 1854 to July 1855); a full and detailed *Paris Exhibition Supplement* (15 August 1855); *Memoirs of the Literary, Artistic, and Scientific Societies*, accounts of the Royal Society and of the Royal Academy of Arts (1 May 1857–1 February 1858); and a *Booksellers' Record and Trade Register* issued as a weekly journal beginning 19 November 1859. *A Journal of the Exhibition* was separately issued in seven numbers from 9 November 1850 to 15 February 1851; and for six years, beginning in 1853, the editors of the *Critic* issued *Beautiful Poetry*, an anthology in monthly numbers, bound into a gift annual at the end of each year. Less successful was *Wit and Humour*, published on the same plan in 1853.

Nevertheless, there were indications that circulation was falling, rather than increasing, as the decade of the fifties wore on. There was reference to ''the necessities of our position,'' which forced a change from fortnightly to weekly publication in 1858; and in the following summer there were negotiations, subsequently abandoned, for merger with the *Literary Gazette*.[3] Beginning 15 July 1862 the *Critic* reverted to monthly publication and announced a total change in policy: the contents would be limited to literary, musical, and artistic intelligence. Then, abruptly, it was announced in the issue for December 1863 that the journal would suspend publication altogether.

A notice ''To Our Readers'' at the head of the *Critic* on 1 October 1849 announced its ''firm place in the periodical literature of Great Britain'' and followed this assessment with an outline of its plans for expansion. Up to this time, the journal had consisted of book reviews and somewhat journalistic reporting. It was now announced that leading articles on literary subjects and art would be part of each issue. A department of foreign literature would be added. The introduction of leaders marked a departure from the periodical's traditional authorial anonymity and the introduction of initials, pseudonyms, and, very occasionally, signatures. Thereafter, it becomes possible to identify certain of the writers associated with the periodical, for example, George Harris, William Maccall, George Gilfillan, and Francis Espinasse. In addition, William Michael Rossetti, Frederic George Stephens, and Alexander Gilchrist, each at a different time and for a brief period, wrote regularly for the *Critic*.

William Michael Rossetti wrote the art notices for the *Critic* from February to November 1850 and for some years thereafter contributed occasional book reviews. Rossetti's appointment proceeded from Cox's interest in the *Germ*,* review copies of which had been left for him. Cox himself reviewed the first two numbers of the *Germ* on 15 February 1850, and he was to follow with notices of numbers 3 and 4, under the revised title, *Art and Poetry* (1 June 1850). The February issue also contained Rossetti's first piece, a review of the exhibition of the British Institution. As the journal was still in a precarious situation, Rossetti was unpaid, but the position offered him an opportunity to promote Pre-Raphaelite interests. In November he left the *Critic* for more substantial arrangements as art editor of the *Spectator** (see *RA*). He continued, however, as occasional reviewer for the *Critic*. "I sometimes ponder with astonishment," Rossetti later wrote of his association with the *Critic*, that the paper "allowed me to instruct its public on matters of fine art before I was twenty-one years of age." Rossetti's art notices have been identified by R. W. Peattie. Some of his unsigned book reviews in the *Critic* are identified in Rossetti's letters, diaries, and journals; among them are reviews of William Allingham, Philip Bailey, and Meredith. Rossetti was succeeded as art editor of the *Critic* by Frederic George Stephens.[4] Stephens wrote weekly art notices during the early months of 1851 and did occasional reviewing, especially in the Pre-Raphaelite cause.

Alexander Gilchrist came to the *Critic* late in 1858 or at the beginning of 1859. He had recently been a contributor to the *Literary Gazette*. William Michael Rossetti had reviewed his biography of William Etty in the *Spectator*; and Gilchrist's preparations to write his biography of Blake led to his personal acquaintance with Dante Gabriel and William Michael Rossetti. According to William Michael Rossetti, the Pre-Raphaelites regarded Gilchrist as the "best-equipped and ablest of the various art-critics on the periodical press." He wrote the unsigned art notices in the *Critic* until his death at the end of November 1861.[5]

The leader writers for the *Critic* were less distinguished. A very early series of signed articles entitled "Historical Gleanings of the Georgian Era" was by George Harris, identified in the journal as a barrister and the biographer of Lord Chancellor Hardwicke. Most of the earliest leaders were written by William Maccall, under the pseudonym "Kenneth Morency." Maccall was also a regular reviewer for the *Critic* under the pseudonym of "Atticus."[6] Maccall's articles covered a wide range of subjects, many reflecting his theological background rather than his literary interests. Few of the essays are memorable; but three articles on "Obermann," in 1850, are of particular interest because of this early treatment of Senancour.

The Rev. George Gilfillan wrote regularly for the *Critic* for about seven years, beginning in 1851. "Apollodorus" was his usual signature, although many unsigned reviews have been identified.[7] He may be best remembered for the articles in the *Critic* that played a part in the Spasmodic controversy. He introduced to the reading public the name of Alexander Smith in an article, in December 1851, entitled "A New Poet in Glasgow"; and throughout 1852 he published from manuscript, serially, Smith's *A Life Drama*, before Bogue brought it out in book form in 1853. William Michael Rossetti attributed "the advance of the *Critic* in popularity" to its publication of *A Life Drama*.[8] Gilfillan also introduced, in the same style, "Another New Poet," J. Stanyan Bigg, and published serially, from manuscript, Bigg's "Night and the Soul." Shortly thereafter, in May 1854, William Edmondstoune Aytoun's "Firmilian" appeared in *Blackwood's Edinburgh Magazine** (see *RA*). Gilfillan's role in introducing these two Spasmodic poets had won him fame as the object of Aytoun's satire. Gilfillan's style is parodied in the language of the "reviewer" introducing the "coming poet," and the satire is pointed in the scene that follows the entrance of "Apollodorus, a Critic."

Francis Espinasse was introduced by Maccall to the *Critic* and quickly became, by his own account, "its chief, or at least its most copious contributor." From 1851 on, except for one period of absence, Espinasse wrote leaders and reviews under his own name or one of three pseudonyms, "Herodotus Smith," "Frank Grave," and "Lucian Paul." He was responsible for "The Critic Abroad," the department on foreign literature. A few unsigned articles can also be identified from his account of his association with the *Critic* in his *Literary Recollections and Sketches*, which also provides the fullest history of the *Critic* and its contributors.

Espinasse's first contribution to the *Critic*, on 1 June 1851, was the first of nine articles entitled "The Periodical and Newspaper Press: Sketches from the Literature of the Day." It was followed by a series of careful accounts, which included the *Quarterly** (see *RA*), *Westminster** (see *RA*), *North British**, *British Quarterly*, and *Prospective** reviews; *Blackwood's* and *Fraser's* magazines; and the *Times*, *Morning Chronicle*, and *Examiner** (see *RA*); the last concluded on 1 September 1852. A much shorter series of articles on "Notable Contemporaries" began with an essay of some importance on Thomas Carlyle (14 June 1851), followed by sketches of Emerson (1 August) and, in April of the following year, Disraeli. In an altogether different style, Espinasse conducted a regular feature, "Sayings and Doings of the Day," continued as "The Literary World: Its Sayings and Doings," modeled, he wrote in his *Recollections*, on "Lewes's agreeable literary causeries in the *Leader*.*" Espinasse also recorded in his *Recollections* his particular pride in one very early series which he called "Two Centuries Ago," an account based on research in the King's Pamphlets in the British Museum. The articles ran from December 1851 to February 1852. Had he been permitted to continue them, Espinasse speculated, they might have had lasting value. Instead, his early survey of the periodical press, his first contribution to the *Critic*, and his last, a series of "Histories of Publishing

Houses," were his most substantial contributions. His accounts of the firms of Murray, Longman, and Blackwood, from January to July 1860, were followed in May and July 1861 by a history of the house of Knight, which Frank Mumby and Ian Norrie attribute to Espinasse;[9] an anonymous article on Bentley, announced for later in 1861, never appeared before the journal suspended all articles and finally ceased publication altogether.

The *Publishers' Circular*, recording that the "publication of the *Critic* finally ceases with the present number," commented particularly on the considerable attention that had at times been drawn to the journal's treatment of various literary controversies. One of these had been the Payne Collier Shakespeare controversy, which the *Critic* had covered, in 1859 and 1860, with running commentary on the quarrel. Gilfillan's association with the Spasmodic controversy is another instance of such involvement. The repeated interconnection with Pre-Raphaelite history is a third. Espinasse's series on Victorian periodicals and his histories of nineteenth-century publishers are remembered, as are the *Critic*'s supplements of the 1850s, as important resources for information. As a literary journal, however, the *Critic* suffers by comparison with the *Athenaeum*, for example, or the *Reader**, among its contemporaries. Even literary news of the day was more effectively furnished by the more general periodicals. Nevertheless, the *Critic* remains a journal which by virtue of its documentary values merits more attention than it has usually been accorded in the history of Victorian periodicals.

Notes

1. *Dictionary of National Biography*, s.v. "Lowe, James"; *London Review* (1865):499.

2. *Critic*, 15 April, 1 May 1854; *Athenaeum*, 22 April 1854; *Literary Gazette*, 29 April 1854; *Fraser's Magazine* 46 (1852):571–85.

3. *Publishers' Circular*, 15 August 1859; *Critic*, 20, 27 August 1859; *Literary Gazette*, 1 September 1859.

4. *Dante Gabriel Rossetti: His Family Letters. With Memoir by William Michael Rossetti* (1895; rpt. New York, 1970), 1:132–33; R. W. Peattie, "William Michael Rossetti's Art Notices in the Periodicals 1850–1878: An Annotated Checklist," *Victorian Periodicals Newsletter* 8 (1975): 79–92; William Michael Rossetti, *Some Reminiscences* (New York, 1906), 1:101; *Athenaeum*, 16 March 1907.

5. Anne Gilchrist, "Memoir of Alexander Gilchrist," in Gilchrist, *Life of William Blake* (London, 1880), 2:373–74; W. M. Rossetti, Prefatory Notice in *Anne Gilchrist. Her Life and Writings*, ed. H. H. Gilchrist, 2d ed. (London, 1887), p. ix; *Critic*, 7 December 1861.

6. Francis Espinasse, *Literary Recollections and Sketches* (London, 1893), pp. 250–53, 366.

7. Robert Watson and Elizabeth S. Watson, *George Gilfillan: Letters and Journals, with Memoir* (London, 1892), pp. 464–66; T. Brisbane, *The Early Years of Alexander Smith* (London, 1869).

8. William Michael Rossetti, 1:94.

9. Frank A. Mumby and Ian Norrie, *Publishing and Bookselling*, 5th ed. (London, 1974), p. 618.

Information Sources

BIBLIOGRAPHY
Ellegård, Alvar. "The Readership of the Periodical Press in Mid-Victorian Britain." *Victorian Periodicals Newsletter*, no. 13 (1971):3–22.
Espinasse, Francis. *Literary Recollections and Sketches*. London, 1893.
Rosenberg, Henry, and Sheila Rosenberg. "Bibliography of Writings on Nineteenth-Century Periodicals." *Victorian Periodicals Newsletter*, no. 7 (1970):11–13.
INDEXES
Each volume indexed.
REPRINT EDITIONS
Microform: English Literary Periodicals (UMI), reels 856–863.
LOCATION SOURCES
American
Partial runs: Widely available.
British
Complete run: British Museum.
Partial runs: Birmingham Public Library; Bodleian Library; Cambridge Public Library; Manchester Public Library.

Publication History

MAGAZINE TITLE AND TITLE CHANGES
The Critic of Literature, Art, Science, and the Drama; A Guide for the Library and Book Club, November 1843–1 August 1844; *The Critic. Journal of British and Foreign Literature and the Arts: A Guide for the Library and Book-Club and Booksellers' Circular*, 15 August 1844–26 December 1846; *The Critic. Family Journal of British and Foreign Literature and the Arts: A Guide for the Library and Book-Club and Booksellers' Circular*, 2 January–26 June 1847; *The Critic. A Journal for Readers, Authors, and Publishers*, 3 July–25 December 1847; *The Critic. of Books, Society, Pictures, Music and Decorative Art; A Journal for Readers, Authors, Artists, Publishers, and Art-Manufacturers*, 1 January–15 December 1848; *The Critic of Books, Engravings, Music, and Decorative Art: A Journal for Readers, Publishers, Librarians, Artists, and Art-Manufacturers, and Booksellers' Circular*, 1 January 1849–15 October 1850; *The Critic: The London Literary Journal*, 1 November–15 December 1850; *The Critic: London Literary Journal*, 1 January 1851–29 May 1858; *The Critic; A Weekly Journal of Literature, Art, Science, and the Drama*, 5 June–23 October 1858; *The Critic; Weekly Journal of Literature, Art, Science, and the Drama*, 30 October 1858–31 December 1859; *The Critic*, 7 January 1860–1 October 1863; *The Critic: Guide to the Book-Club and Library*, 1 November 1863–1 December 1863.

VOLUME AND ISSUE DATA
Volume 1, numbers 1–14, November 1843–1 August 1844.
New series, volumes 1–25, 15 August 1844–1 December 1863.

FREQUENCY OF PUBLICATION
Monthly, November 1843–April 1844; semi-monthly, 15 April 1844–15 April 1845; weekly, Saturday, 3 May 1845–26 February 1848; semi-monthly, 1 March

1848–29 May 1858; weekly, 5 June 1858–28 June 1862; monthly, July 1862–December 1863.

PUBLISHERS

Volume 1, number 1, November 1843: Thomas Lauder, the *Critic* Office, London. Volume 1, number 2–new series, volume 25, December 1843–1 December 1863: John Crockford, the *Critic* Office, London.

EDITOR

James Lowe.

Charlotte C. Watkins

CRITIC, THE: (THE) LONDON LITERARY JOURNAL. See CRITIC, THE

CRITIC, THE; (A) WEEKLY JOURNAL OF LITERATURE, ART, SCIENCE, AND THE DRAMA. See CRITIC, THE

CRITIC OF BOOKS, THE. See CRITIC, THE

CRITIC OF LITERATURE, ART, SCIENCE, AND THE DRAMA, THE. See CRITIC, THE

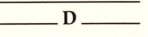

D

DANA

Dana: An Irish Magazine of Independent Thought was founded in 1904 as a forum for diverse observations and opinions on Irish life. Named for the pagan Celtic goddess of fertility and wisdom, whose name was borne by the Tuatha Dé Danann—People of the Goddess Dann—*Dana* suggests both the oneness of origin and the multiplicity of creation that the journal was to serve:

> We would have our magazine ... [be] not merely a doctrinaire but a literary, or rather a humanist, magazine; and we would receive and print contributions in prose and in verse which are the expression of the writer's individuality with greater satisfaction than those which are merely the belligerent expression of opinion.... We invite the thinkers, dreamers and observers dispersed throughout Ireland and elsewhere, who do not despair of humanity in Ireland, to communicate through our pages their thoughts, reveries and observations; and we venture to hope that a magazine, starting with such general designs, should profit by whatever is genuine in the new life and movement which of late years have manifested themselves in the country. [1:3–4]

In their introductory essay, the editors of *Dana*, John Eglinton (pseudonym of William Kirkpatrick Magee) and Frederick Ryan, place their journalistic endeavor in historical context. Since the days of Thomas Davis and the Young Irelanders, the Irish people, in the name of unity against their English oppressors, have avoided "fundamental questions of life and thought" (1:2). Rather than risk strife among themselves that political and religious disagreement might create, they have chosen to ignore issues on which they disagree while acquiescing to an unexamined opposition to England. Though not explicitly acknowledged, there is an Arnoldian spirit hovering about the first pages of *Dana*. Not for the propagation of dogmatic political views, but in the service of what Arnold called the "free play of thought" and the discernment of where reason lies, *Dana* was created. In a culture that had come to place much value on revival, *Dana* was to serve a revival of thought. Nothing less than the salvation of the country was at stake: "In a country warped and injured by lack of political freedom, it would be curious if intellectual freedom prospered. The Irish people, trampled by alien and unsympathetic rule, have looked with aching eyes to a heaven of bliss, and they have, more or less contentedly, lain down in their chains soothed by the hope of after-reward. If Ireland is to be saved we must change all that" (Ryan, "Political and Intellectual Freedom," 1:31).

Each of the twelve monthly issues of *Dana* consists of thirty-two pages and, on the average, eight or nine contributions: usually one or two poems, one or two articles devoted to recent publications on Irish issues or by Irish writers, an occasional imaginative piece, and four or five essays on political and religious issues. Most notable perhaps, given the statement of its editors concerning the kinds of contributions they invited, is the dearth of fiction or personal prose appearing in this magazine. Whether this fact reflects what has been cited as a characteristic scarcity of such kinds of writings from the Irish Renaissance or whether instead it reflects the choice of its editors is not clear.[1] Eglinton is generally recognized as one of three or four accomplished essayists of his time and culture, but little of his work transcends the troubled national life he participated in. Though as a poet and essayist he was closely allied with the Theosophical movement and A. E. (George W. Russell), Eglinton on at least one occasion failed to recognize the worth of another, if quite different, mode of Irish expression. Joyce offered him "the manuscript of a serial story" for publication in *Dana*, but Eglinton refused it with the comment that he did not want to publish anything that was incomprehensible.[2] Eglinton was to be one of Joyce's earliest and most perceptive admirers, but never was he to grant him unequivocal praise. Eglinton was, by his own admission, opposed to writing that created problems of interpretation rather than dealing with problems of life and thought.[3] Insistence on clarity of expression, so apparent throughout *Dana*, probably deprived us of the earliest version of what was to become *A Portrait of the Artist as a Young Man*.[4]

Only two pieces of fiction appear in *Dana*, both of minor importance. One is a modern English version of an ancient Irish hag myth (William Buckley, "King Diarmuid," 4:118–24), and the other, a lifeless character study (Jane Barlow, "Michael, A Mediatator," 12:357–63). Eglinton years later was to consider the "chief interest" of *Dana* to be George Moore's "Moods and Memories" (1:5–10; 2:55–61; 3:72–76; 4:106–10; 5:134–39; 6:170–75), a serialized and incomplete early version of *Memories of My Dead Life*, a fictionalized autobiography much in the manner of *Confessions of a Young Man*.[5] "Moods and Memories" is one of only two prose contributions to *Dana* that do not relate specifically to Irish issues or subjects, the other being a serialized lecture on the life and work of Jane Austen by T. W. Lyster, Chief of the Irish National Library, whose literary works consist mainly of translations from German, technical papers, and reviews ("Jane Austen," 8:245–51; 9:264–68; 10:303–4; 11:330–34). "Moods and Memories" is a paean to Paris, which Moore lyrically acknowledges as his literary and intellectual home (3:74). A close friend of Eglinton, Moore was to be one of *Dana*'s most frequent contributors. In addition to "Moods and Memories," he provided the monthly with a preface to a new edition of *Confessions of a Young Man* (7:200–204), and, concealed behind the name of Paul Ruttledge,[6] a mean-spirited attack—of the kind that blemished his later reputation—against Frank Fay, one of the founders of the Irish National Theatre ("Stage Management in the Irish National Theatre," 5:150–52). Though it is not acknowledged in the magazine, it was Moore who translated for *Dana* Edouard Dujardin's article on "The Abbé Louisy" (1:18–21), in which the writer, who was a major influence on Joyce, defends the cleric for his unorthodox efforts to reconcile science, history, and religion in *L'Evangile et l'Eglise* and *Autour d'un Petit Livre*.[7]

From the third issue on, there appears regularly in *Dana* a review article by F. M. Atkinson, titled first "Literary Notices" and later "A Literary Causerie," devoted for the most part to Irish writers and subjects. More substantial review articles appear less frequently, and include Thomas Koehler's censorious criticism of Synge's *The Well of the Saints* for encouraging belief in religious miracles (10:319–20; 11:351–52), as well as a defense in French of the same play for its use of symbol and its beauty of language (12:364–68). The first issue of *Dana* concludes with a typically brief review of *New Songs*, an important collection of poems by writers closely associated with the editor of the volume, A. E. The reviewer, Oliver Gogarty, was himself to be one of the magazine's frequent contributors of poems (5:144; 7:208–9; 10:308). He also gained a certain reputation as novelist, politician, physician, and wit, and appears in *Ulysses* as the medical student "Buck." Gogarty's assessment of the poems in *New Songs* might well serve for virtually all the poems that appear in *Dana*: technically proficient, musical, but lacking verve and originality. In fact, A. E. and poets represented in his *New Songs* provided *Dana* with the bulk of its poetry. Finely shaded landscapes of a spirit world typify A. E.'s contributions here ("Lightest of Dancers," 2:61; "Creation," 4:105; "In as Much," 9:279; and "Shadows," 11:329). The generally acknowledged debt of A. E. and his followers to Irish scholar and poet Edward Dowden is apparent in contributions from the latter (1:4; 3:71), particularly in their delicately rendered pantheistic quality. *New Songs'* Seamus O'Sullivan contributed six poems, most of which reveal clear affinities with A. E. (for example, "Dear they are praising your beauty," 5:140; and "Beside the Poplars," 10:302), as well as a sonnet on Parnell ("Glasnevin, October 9, 1904," 7:199), and a poem that anticipates some of his later and better known verse on the city as a vile and ungodly place ("In the City," 8:251). Padraic Colum, also a contributor to *New Songs*, provided *Dana* with three poems on rugged peasant life ("The Sower," 6:181; "An Old Woman of the Roads," and "The Pigeons," 10:313). Jane Barlow contributed a poem based on similar subject matter ("Wayfarers," 4:97–98), as well as a lyric based on an Italian sonnet by Carlo Maggi ("Porte after Stormie Seas," 9:268). Though Joyce's early fiction was not acceptable to *Dana*, one of his early poems was ("My love is in a light attire," 4:124).

Poems and "Moods and Memories" provide occasional lyric relief from the predominantly political tone of the magazine's brief essays, a good many of which were written by *Dana*'s editors. Eglinton and Ryan each contributed seven signed essays to the magazine's twelve issues, and other essays attributed to clearly fictitious names are strikingly similar in attitude and style to those signed by the editors: "A Reply to 'The Irish in America: An Open Letter to Sir Horace Plunkett,' " (6:161–69); Fergus, "Our Need of an Impersonal Judgment," (5:153–55); and Irial, "The Church and the Future," (8:233–38) and "The Catholic Silence," (9:335–38). Ryan is probably best remembered for his satirical drama on municipal life, *The Laying of the Foundations*, performed during the second season (1903) of the Irish National Dramatic Company. For *Dana* he wrote some of the magazine's most vociferous articles against institutions which in his view impeded progress toward Ireland's principal goal of self-government. He criticized the Catholic Church for its opposition to intellectual freedom ("Political and Intellectual Freedom," 1:27–31; "Criticism and Courage," 5:145–49; and "Church Disestablishment in France and Ireland," 10:289–94). He chastizes Ireland for its bigotry ("Political and Intellectual Freedom," 1:27–31), and England for its despotism: "The unvarnished truth is that no nation interferes from motives of philanthropy in the affairs of other nations, and the idea of world-rule is itself fundamentally vicious, since the rule of communities by themselves is fundamentally better in the long run than the most wise and benevolent outside despotism ("Empire and Liberty," 4:113). Ryan stands in outspoken opposition to the Gaelic Revival and any other endeavor that encourages people to turn away from the problems and conditions of the moment: "A nation is not morally raised by dwelling on its own past glories or its neighbors' present sins; it is raised by increasing its ability to deal with its present problems, political, economic, and social, in a spirit of equity and a spirit of knowledge" ("Is the Gaelic League a Progressive Force?" 7:220; see also "On Language and Political Ideas," 9:273–79).

Eglinton offers a more tempered view of Irish responsibility. To *Dana* he contributed his efforts as editor, essayist, and poet: a concern for national life could, by his example, accommodate a less directly political expression. His poetic contributions to *Dana* include a dozen epigrams (12:369–70), a brief verse (9:287), and a more ambitious lyric, "The Poet and the Citizen" (8:232), in which the Horatian image of the mariner's shield of triple brass is curiously attenuated:

> Of whom the Muse makes choice, I ween,
> About his bosom should have been

> A plate of brass and triple skin,
> More hard without for soft within.

The point of the poem seems to be that the political and poetic selves are
dissociated, the former being "a storm-proved mariner" and the latter "a feeble
thing." It is a point that *Dana*—and particularly Eglinton's contributions—
exemplify. The vigor lacking in *Dana*'s poetry is given expression in its political
prose. Like Ryan's essays, Eglinton's are animated by hostility toward religion
in general and Catholicism in particular, for having transformed mankind's religious impulse into a thoughtless acceptance of dogma ("The Breaking of the
Ice," 1:11–17). Eglinton's essays differ from Ryan's, however, in their emphasis
on individual rather than social endeavor, on poetic and intellectual rather than
political effort ("On Going to Church," 3:83–88). In some ways Eglinton's
essays may be read as enlarged and tangentially political statements deriving
from the Dublin mystics, as when he speaks of "the reciprocal connection
between the individual and the causal energy of the universe" ("A Way of
Understanding Nietzsche," 6:183). Willing to range far in time, from distant
past to present to distant future, Eglinton reveals himself to be a strict revisionist
and a daring—if false—prophet: "Celtic Ireland did not produce a religious
genius, the Irish language has no spiritual quality, and *Catholicism* and *Protestantism* will be obsolete terms in fifty years" ("The Island of Saints," 9:257–
63). He opposes celibacy among priests as a policy that deprives Ireland of much
of its evolutionary potential in "The Best Irish Poem 'The Midnight Court,' by
Brian Merriman," (10:296–302). As there is perhaps an echo of Arnold in the
pages of *Dana*, there is also an echo of Huxley—free thought is necessary, and
elsewhere than in tradition are we to find truth:

> In the decline of tradition and of authority we are indeed lost if a faculty
> of discrimination do not rise up in us of what is genuine and what is unreal
> in the world of men and of thought, who must take the place in us of the
> old respect for the Fathers, the Church, and the Bible. So far as we are
> sincere and genuine in ourselves we shall be able to recognise these qualities
> outside us, and to bring to bear on the men and things we have to do with
> a test more searching and more real than that of tradition. ["Sincerity,"
> 7:215]

As contributors Eglinton and Ryan identify themselves with specific political
principles, but as editors it is clear they welcomed articles presenting views
contrary to their own. Ryan's argument against the Gaelic League ("Is the Gaelic
League a Progressive Force?" 7:216–20) is preceded and followed by arguments
for the revival of ancient Irish (Alfred Webb, "The Gaelic League and Politics,"
5:141–44; and Stephen Gwynn, "In Praise of the Gaelic League," 8:239–44).
Though several articles assume opposition to English rule as a first principle (for
example, Gwynn, "In Praise of the Gaelic League"), arguments for Ireland's

participation in the British Empire find their place in *Dana* too (Ossorian, "Imperialism," 1:22–26, 2:50–54). Church disestablishment is advocated (Ryan, "Church Disestablishment in France and Ireland," 10:289–94) and forthwith opposed (W. Gibson, "Church Disestablishment in France: A Reply," 11:344–45). Though the editors' opposition to the Catholic Church finds frequent agreement among contributors (as in John M. Robertson, "Catholicism and Civilisation," 2:33–38), there also appear in the magazine articles defending the Church while advocating reform in it (such as F. Hugh O'Donnell, "The Facts of the Church-building Question in Ireland," 3:77–82; and, by "A Mission Priest in England," "Position of the Mission Priest in England," 6:176–80), and even unqualified defense of Catholic dogma (Maud Joynt, "Dogma," 10:309–13).

The importance of *Dana* derives mainly from its historical context. The year and city of its appearance—Dublin in 1904—alone make the magazine an important document to the reader of *Ulysses* as well as to anyone interested in the Irish Literary Renaissance. Dublin at that time was, as Eglinton observed, "a centre of vigorous potentialities."[8] The Irish Literary Theatre had recently been established. Dowden, representative of an older culture, was still alive and writing; Yeats, Synge, A. E., and Moore were well established; and a younger generation of writers, including Joyce and most of the writers represented in *New Songs*, was emerging. Political, social, and literary movements had progressed sufficiently to be called into question. "There was hardly anyone at that time," Eglinton later observed, "who did not believe that Ireland was on the point of some important transformation."[9] *Dana* was created as an instrument for determining what shape or direction that transformation would take, and while it cannot be argued that the magazine succeeded in its ambitious undertaking, it did provide a number of important Irish writers of the time with a modest and neatly designed and edited forum. Had the magazine survived longer, Shaw and Chesterton might have been counted among its contributors.[10] Yeats apparently refused to contribute to *Dana* because—though he remembered it as a "delightful" magazine—at the time of its appearance he considered it an organ of "Fleet Street atheism."[11] Though theoretically a forum for diverse thought, *Dana* is in the main a repository of anti-establishment polemic.

Perhaps, like the *Dublin University Review*, *Dana* died of "that pecuniary malnutrition which has so often been the lot of Irish reviews, however well nourished they may have been intellectually."[12] Or perhaps *Dana* failed because so few of its pieces individually suggested the kind of intellectual deference or political balance which is to be found by culling from its pages articles on a specific issue. As the publication in 1904 of *New Songs* proved to be a propitious event for evaluating the poetic contributions to *Dana*, the publication in the same year of Horace Plunkett's important account of the Cooperative Movement in Ireland—*Ireland in the New Century*—inspired essays that go far toward explaining a weakness of this publication. A review of *Ireland in the New Century* by a former worker in the Cooperative Movement censures Plunkett and others for having provided counsel to farmers and marketers that led to financial disasters

(Maurice Moore, "Ireland in the New Century," 2:39–44). In a later issue, A. E. takes up the philosophical issue raised by such an unqualified indictment of a writer and his commitment to social change ("Physical Force in Literature," 5:129–33). A. E.'s point is that the proper critical attitude is one that transcends personalities and demonstrates fairness and balance: "to fight well," he says, one must "be gentle" (5:129). A. E.'s other prose contribution to *Dana* is an artful demonstration of the attitude A. E. apparently found lacking in his friend Eglinton's magazine. The absence of spirituality in Ireland is to be explained by its failure to incorporate the female element of love in its religious life: unity, whether political, psychological, or religious, is the harmony of contraries; and proper political effort moves toward the unification of that which male and female represent ("Religion and Love," 2:45–49)—that which, in Eglinton's view, poet and citizen represent. Had *Dana* aspired to A. E.'s philosophical principles in its political articles as it did to his poetic principles in its poetry, it might not have survived any longer than it did, but it would have been a different magazine from what it was—and perhaps it would have come closer to achieving the ambitions of its editors.

Notes

1. Ernest A. Boyd, *Ireland's Literary Renaissance* (New York, 1916), pp. 374–75.
2. John Eglinton [pseud. of William Kirkpatrick Magee], "The Beginnings of Joyce," *Irish Literary Portraits* (London, 1935), p. 136.
3. John Eglinton, "A Glimpse of the Later Joyce," *Irish Literary Portraits*, pp. 157–58.
4. Richard Ellmann, *James Joyce* (New York, 1959), p. 149.
5. Eglinton, "Beginnings of Joyce," p. 136.
6. Robert Hogan and James Kilroy, *Modern Irish Drama: A Documentary History, 1902–04* (Dublin, 1976), p. 98.
7. *George Moore in Transition: Letters to T. Fisher Unwin and Lena Milman, 1894–1910*, ed. Helmut E. Gerber (Detroit, 1968), p. 286, n. 11.
8. Eglinton, "Beginnings of Joyce," p. 133.
9. Ibid.
10. Ibid., p. 135.
11. Ibid.
12. Boyd, p. 114.

Information Sources

BIBLIOGRAPHY

Boyd, Ernest A. *Ireland's Literary Renaissance*. New York, 1916.
Eglinton, John [pseud. of William Kirkpatrick Magee]. *Irish Literary Portraits*. London, 1935.
Ellmann, Richard. *James Joyce*. New York, 1959.
George Moore in Transition: Letters to T. Fisher Unwin and Lena Milman, 1894–1910. Edited by Helmut E. Gerber. Detroit, 1968.

Hogan, Robert, and James Kilroy. *Modern Irish Drama: A Documentary History, 1902–04*. Dublin, 1976.

Uncollected Prose by W. B. Yeats. Edited by John P. Frayne and Colton Johnson, Vol. 2. New York, 1976.

INDEXES
Article titles listed alphabetically as preface to reprint edition.

REPRINT EDITIONS
Lemma Publishing Corporation. New York, 1970.
Microform: New York Public Library.

LOCATION SOURCES
American
Widely available.

British
Complete runs: Bodleian Library; Cambridge University Library; Trinity College Library, Dublin.
Partial run: British Museum.

Publication History

MAGAZINE TITLE AND TITLE CHANGES
Dana: An Irish Magazine of Independent Thought.

VOLUME AND ISSUE DATA
Numbers 1–12, May 1904–April 1905.

FREQUENCY OF PUBLICATION
Monthly.

PUBLISHERS
Hodges, Figgis and Co., Ltd., Dublin; and David Nutt, London. Editorial address: 26, Dawson Chambers, Dawson St., Dublin.

EDITORS
John Eglinton (pseud. of William Kirkpatrick Magee) and Frederick Ryan.

Carol de Saint Victor

DICKENSIAN, THE

It would be hard to imagine a publisher today who could be convinced that a journal focused exclusively on the life and writings of one man, begun without capital on the strength of the interest expressed in 240 responses to a mailed survey, would have more than a very slim chance of survival. Yet such is the anomalous history of the *Dickensian*, begun in 1905 and in 1984 celebrating its eightieth year of uninterrupted publication, its focus still accurately represented by its title. Clues to the *Dickensian*'s surprising longevity lie in the charismatic personality of Charles Dickens himself, in his prolific and multifaceted artistic career, and in the complex interpenetration of popular taste, cultural change, and critical history. The *Dickensian*'s long standing as a periodical devoted both to the ideals of a fellowship of disciples and to the requirements of academic scholarship make it a fascinating study in literary history.

Little in the original plans of the magazine hints at the success it has since achieved. With the founding of the Dickens Fellowship in 1902, the need for some medium of communication to unite a growing membership began to be increasingly felt. At first, notices of Fellowship activities were carried in the columns of associated journals—in a revived *Household Words** until the management broke off the connection in 1903, after that in the *Golden Penny*, and finally again in *Household Words* under new ownership. The difficulties of securing a permanent mouthpiece made council members more receptive to an idea proposed earlier by F. G. Kitton, that the organization should sponsor its own independent publication. With B. W. Matz (on the staff of Dickens's original publishers, Chapman and Hall, and one of the prime movers of the Fellowship) to put his ideas into tangible form for him, Kitton outlined his proposal. The still extant dummies show a double-columned page, headed by the title *Our Mutual Friend*. "Notes By Cap'en Cuttle" were to occupy the four introductory pages, followed by Fellowship activities, each "reported" by Dickensian characters. Thus, Madame Mantalini and Mrs. Jellyby presided over the activities of "The Needlework and Charitable Guild," while Vincent Crummles reviewed "Dickens Plays."[1]

Kitton died before his ideas could come to fruition, and most Fellowship historians agree that it was well for the future of the journal that Matz ultimately shaped its course. Certainly, Kitton's "somewhat Gradgrindish mentality"[2] in matters of research, coupled with the limiting and parochial commitment to complete coverage of Fellowship doings, might have proved a fatal combination. When the first number, edited by Matz and published by Chapman and Hall, appeared in January 1905 after several further revisions of the original prospectus, it bore a significantly changed character. *Our Mutual Friend* had given way to the *Dickensian*, and the visual appeal of the magazine was enhanced by the introduction of a cover design featuring the original illustrative wrappers to Dickens's novels, used in rotation. Matz kept an abbreviated version of "Notes By Cap'en Cuttle"; "When Found . . ." now noted news of current interest, but readers were warned that for comprehensive and timely reporting of Fellowship activities, they must again turn to *Household Words*. The Dickensian personae were abandoned on the assumption that the humor would be difficult to sustain.[3] Matz's vision, as announced in the "Foreword" to the first number, was altogether broader and more imaginative than Kitton's:

It is intended that the magazine shall be . . . devoted to the vast subject of Dickens generally. In addition to original articles on the multifarious phases of Dickens's life and works, reproduction of pictures of places, portraits, and other illustrations, reprints will be given of contemporary reviews of his works, of articles bibliographical, biographical, topographical, by well-known writers of his time, . . . poetical tributes to the novelist—indeed anything and everything likely to interest the student and lover of England's greatest novelist. Thus it will be seen that in course of time subscribers to *The Dickensian* will gather together a library of Dickensiana on a scale practically impossible to acquire in the ordinary way by the isolated collector.[1:1]

How far the encyclopedic aspirations of Matz have been realized in three-quarters of a century of publication might have astonished even the first editor himself, but modern readers perusing these early volumes are more likely to be struck by the critical assumptions governing the selection and arrangement of material. If the minutiae of Fellowship expeditions, picnics, and lantern-lectures were to be subordinated to antiquarian studies of all aspects of Dickens's literary career, the *idea* of a fellowship was still paramount and supplied the spiritual thrust for such investigations. "Each unit in our thousands should be ... the centre of a circle, transmitting to all around the Dickens light, and promulgating the Dickens gospel," wrote J. Cuming Walter in the sixth volume of the *Dickensian*. And he reminded his colleagues that they were "Knights of the Round Table which Charles Dickens established" (6:287). Nor were these ideals mere sentiments or abstractions. The early volumes of the journal carry an astonishing number of articles and notices about charitable activities, dinners "to Waifs and Strays," pleas on behalf of the National Association for Promoting the Welfare of the Feeble-Minded, and fund-raising efforts to support "Tiny Tim cots" in local hospitals (2:45; 9:226).

This preoccupation with the impact of Dickens on the real world outside the library or study made these early disciples impassioned curators of a London from which Dickensian landmarks were fast disappearing; it also helps to explain their pronounced bias toward biographical and topographical criticism. Sylvere Monod counted 375 articles on topographical questions in the first sixteen volumes of the *Dickensian*, and Frank T. Dunn, whose task it was to index the journal in 1974, found his entries under this subheading swelling to quite surprising proportions (66:119; 71:134). Less interested in the imagination that created the landscapes and characters in the novels, the contributors to the *Dickensian* sought instead to identify the real-life correlatives for fiction. They tracked Little Nell's pilgrimages with a cartographer's zeal, and wrote in often heated terms defending their candidates for "The Prototype of Polly Toodle."

B. W. Matz retired as editor in 1925, and Walter Dexter took over the position until 1944. Under both, many valuable contributions to Dickens scholarship were made, most of them the result of the same amateur antiquarian zeal. In addition to portraits of Dickens never published before, illustrations from the novels, and bibliographical information on plagiarisms and continuations, the *Dickensian* printed recollections from contemporaries such as Hans Christian Andersen, Mary Cowden Clarke, and Edmund Yates. The Dickens canon was itself extended with the publication of hitherto unidentified essays, articles from the *Examiner*** (see *RA*), and other works. During Dexter's tenure the *Dickensian* served as a public display case for the numbers of Dickens's letters then coming to light at a surprising rate and unavailable to scholars through any other medium.

Not all of the discoveries in Dickens scholarship during this period were welcome ones—at least not to the faithful. Dickensians remained notably sensitive to suggestions that Dickens's life deviated in any way from what they perceived to be the ideals of his novels. When in 1928 C. E. Bechhofer Roberts published a fictionalized biography of Dickens portraying him as "selfish, grasping, vulgar, vain," the *Dickensian* countered with "Opinions That Count from Men Who Knew Dickens," accompanied by pictures bearing such captions as "The Good," "The Gentle," "Ever Friendly," and "Noble Dickens," and a series of stinging reviews of Roberts's book culled from the *Nation*, the *Athenaeum* (see RA)*, the *Spectator** (see *RA*), the *Times Literary Supplement*, and others (25:1–17). Such sledge-hammer blows, aimed at what was, after all, a rather silly book, suggest a blinding defensiveness that had more serious consequences elsewhere. For the scrupulous amassing of biographical data in the pages of the *Dickensian* had its tacit boundaries. In the early volumes of the journal, silence or a guarded reserve mark discussions of Dickens's youthful romance with Maria Beadnell or his ambiguously passionate attachment to his sister-in-law Mary Hogarth. Little wonder, then, that when Thomas Wright published his revelations about Dickens's liaison with Ellen Ternan in 1935, and when Gladys Storey substantiated the speculations in 1939, based on her interviews with Kate Perugini, the *Dickensian* reacted first with outrage and finally with an ill-disguised regret that such untidy and disturbing facts should surface at all (66:134–40).

By the time Leslie Staples took office as editor in 1944, the climate for Dickens studies had begun to change. The years 1925–1936 had marked the deaths of many prominent Dickensians, including most of Dickens's surviving associates. Staples was the last amateur Dickensian to edit the journal, but he was himself sensitive to the new perspectives offered by a generation of young academics. For Dickens was now academically respectable. Not the *same* Dickens, of course. K. J. Fielding, lamenting the "gulf . . . opening between those who turn to Dickens for enjoyment, and those who write about him with a critical axe to grind," noted that in a recent critical book there were index entries "for 'humours' but none for 'humor,' for 'class' and 'crime,' but not 'comedy,' nine lines of references to 'death,' none at all to 'life' " (56:160). Without changing the essential character of the journal, Staples straddled the chasm between the sometimes glib and superficial appreciators and the sometimes self-important and overly solemn critics, introducing such indispensable authorities as Humphry House, Philip Collins, K. J. Fielding, Kathleen Tillotson, John Butt, and Sylvere Monod. According to Fielding, Staples's "most important contribution has been that he has made this periodical one that nobody seriously interested in Dickens can do without" (64:68).

Under the two academic editors who followed Staples, Michael Slater and the present editor, Andrew Sanders, the value of the *Dickensian* to professional scholars has been enhanced. Apart from dozens of individual articles of note, the special centenary number deserves mention for its valuable perspectives on Dickens's literary reputation. Under Slater, the compilation of a cumulative index has provided the student with a helpful analytic key to the bewildering bits of data scattered through the *Dickensian*'s pages. Along with this emphasis on the needs of the professional scholar have come a renewed appreciation for the response of the general reader and a recognition of the *Dickensian*'s unique role as a historical record of a literary reputation whose development constitutes a study fascinating in its own right.

Not only the reputation of Dickens, but the reputation of the *Dickensian* has been a subject for scrutiny in these pages. The *Dickensian* is surely one of the most self-conscious of literary periodicals, and its many histories, retrospectives, and memoirs form a staple feature of its contents. Outside, it has often been subjected to condescension. A 1967 bibliography of Victorian studies ventured only a contemptuous nod toward "the enthusiastic concern of the Dickens Society [*sic*] for every scrap of information about the life of their idol, which they publish in *The Dickensian*."[4] Morton Zabel has written in similar terms of "the official piety . . . of the orthodox Dickens Society [*sic*] and its magazine *The Dickensian*.[5] From 1940 to 1960, according to Philip Collins, "when the sophisticated account and assessment of Dickens were markedly diverging from the popular and traditional, the Fellowship was generally good for a laugh, or a sneer, in books written by smarter guys than us" (66:146). Such judgments are not likely to stand. Indeed, the value of the *Dickensian*'s regular features—surveys of Dickens studies, reviews, reports on the acquisition and ownership of manuscripts, critiques of film and theatrical performances—has been convincingly outlined by Collins in the second edition of *Victorian Fiction: A Guide to Research*. His assessment echoes in concrete terms that of Ada Nisbet, who wrote the Dickens chapter in the first edition of the research guide: "Many professional scholars have tended to dismiss the *Dickensian* as the organ of amateur enthusiasts, but they do so now at their peril."[6]

Notes

1. Leo Mason, "*The Dickensian*: A Tale of Fifty Years," *Dickensian* 51 (1954):5–8.

2. J.W.T. Ley, "The History of *The Dickensian*," *Dickensian* 22 (1926):121.

3. Ley, p. 125; Mason, p.7.

4. Robert C. Slack, *Bibliographies of Studies in Victorian Literature for the Ten Years 1955–1964* (Urbana, Ill., 1967), p. xi.

5. Morton Zabel, *Craft and Character in Modern Fiction* (New York, 1957), p. 6.

6. Philip Collins, "Charles Dickens," in *Victorian Fiction: A Second Guide to Research*, ed. George H. Ford (New York, 1978), p. 41; Ada Nisbet, "Charles Dickens," in *Victorian Fiction: A Guide to Research*, ed. Lionel Stevenson (Cambridge, Mass., 1964), p. 71.

Information Sources

BIBLIOGRAPHY

"The Amateur Contribution." *Times Literary Supplement*, 13 February 1968, p. 157.

Collins, Philip. "Charles Dickens." In *Victorian Fiction: A Second Guide to Research*. Edited by George H. Ford. New York, 1978. Pp. 34–113.

————."1940–1960: Enter the Professionals." *Dickensian* 66 (1970):143–61.

Ford, George H. *Dickens and His Readers: Aspects of Novel-Criticism Since 1836*. Princeton, 1955.

Ley, J.W.T. "The History of *The Dickensian*." *Dickensian* 22 (1926):11–22; 121–29.

Mason, Leo. *"The Dickensian*: A Tale of Fifty Years." *Dickensian* 51 (1954):4–12.

Monod, Sylvere. "The Age of Chesterton." *Dickensian* 66 (1970):101–20.

Nisbet, Ada. "Charles Dickens." In *Victorian Fiction: A Guide to Research*. Edited by Lionel Stevenson. Cambridge, Mass., 1964. Pp. 44–153.

Slater, Michael. "1920–1940: 'Superior Folk' and Scandalmongers." *Dickensian* 66 (1970):121–42.

INDEXES

Doris Minards, comp., *The Dickensian: Index to Volumes I–XXX*, London, 1935. Doris Minards, comp., *The Dickensian: Index to Volumes XXXI–LVI*, London, 1961. Frank T. Dunn, comp., *A Cumulative Analytic Index to "The Dickensian"*: *1905–1974; Together with an Index to the Illustrations by Mary Ford and Michael Slater*, Hassocks, Sussex, 1976.

REPRINT EDITIONS

Kraus Reprint Corporation, New York, 1971.

Microform: Harvester Press Microfiche Edition, Hassocks, Sussex, 1975.

LOCATION SOURCES

American

Widely available.

British

Widely available.

Publication History

MAGAZINE TITLE AND TITLE CHANGES

The Dickensian: A Magazine for Dickens Lovers and Monthly Record of the Dickens Fellowship, volumes 1–14. *The Dickensian: A Quarterly Magazine For Dickens Lovers and the Official Record of the Dickens Fellowship*, volumes 15–22. *The Dickensian: A Quarterly Magazine for Dickens Lovers*, volumes 23–31. *The Dickensian: A Magazine for Dickens Lovers*, volumes 32–64. *The Dickensian*, volumes 65–.

VOLUME AND ISSUE DATA

Volumes 1–, January 1905–.

FREQUENCY OF PUBLICATION

Monthly, 1905–1918; quarterly, 1919–1956; three times a year, 1957–.

PUBLISHERS

1905–1921: Chapman and Hall, 11 Henrietta St., Covent Garden, London, W.C.

1922–1926: Cecil Palmer, 49 Chandos St., Covent Garden, London W.C. 2.

1927–: The Dickens Fellowship, The Dickens House, 48 Doughty St., London, W.C. 1. Editorial address: Birkbeck College, Malet St., London WC1E 7HX.

EDITORS

B. W. Matz, 1905–1925. Walter Dexter, 1925–1944. Leslie C. Staples, 1944–1968. Michael Slater, 1968–1977. Andrew Sanders, 1977–.

Nancy Aycock Metz

DOME, THE

The most famous English literary periodicals of the 1890s were the *Yellow Book** and the *Savoy**. A final attempt was made to create a worthwhile review by the publication of the *Dome*, which was issued in London by the Unicorn Press and which first appeared in 1897 and came to an end in 1900. Described as "A Quarterly containing examples of all the Arts" upon first appearance, after five quarterly issues it became a monthly, selling throughout at the price of one shilling. Compared with the *Yellow Book* at five shillings, the purchaser received very good value for a periodical which surveyed the various arts of the past as well as those of the present.

The *Dome* was financed and edited by the owner of the Unicorn Press, Ernest J. Oldmeadow, who was born in Chester in 1867 and died in London in 1949. In his twenties he became a Nonconformist minister and served in this capacity for some years in St. John's, Nova Scotia. While managing the Unicorn Press he was attracted to Catholicism and, guided and supported by the Meynells, he moved along the path of conversion. Oldmeadow became a welcome guest at Palace Court House, where Wilfrid and Alice Meynell regularly entertained leading literary figures of the period. The Unicorn Press under his direction carried on a tradition of publishing based on the aesthetic ideals and practices of William Morris and his circle. As the nineteenth century drew to a close, the Unicorn Press began to concentrate on the production of deluxe limited editions. None of these works is the most sought after by modern collectors. More noteworthy are titles published in ordinary and unlimited editions, such as Arthur Symons's *Aubrey Beardsley* (1898), Gordon Craig's *A Book of Woodcuts* (1898), Roger Fry's *Giovanni Bellini* (1899), and William Rothenstein's *Goya* (1900). The most impressive achievement of the press was its Artist's Library, the work of Laurence Binyon. Oldmeadow created several comic novels which are now forgotten, and was an occasional contributor to the *Westminster Gazette*, the *Nineteenth Century**, and the *Saturday Review**. In 1923 Cardinal Bourne invited him to become editor of the *Tablet*, a position he accepted and held for the next nineteen years. At the same time, drawing upon his expertise in the area of fine food and wine, he emerged as a wine merchant, in Dean Street, Soho, under the name of "Francis Downman."

As editor of the *Dome*, Oldmeadow was a frequent contributor, writing under the anagram "J. E. Woodmeald" several ephemeral one-act comedies with titles such as "Cousin Frederick" and "At the Sign of the Postboy's Horn" and a group of essays on art under the pseudonym "L. A. Corbeille."

Several writers, including Arthur Symons, Laurence Binyon, C. J. Holmes, J. F. Runciman, Gleeson White, Laurence Housman, Gordon Bottomley, and W. B. Yeats, were important contributors to the *Dome*. That most prolific writer and the recent editor of the *Savoy*, Arthur Symons, first contributed to the periodical in May 1897. Four poems and three essays were readily accepted. Laurence Binyon, though fully engaged in his work in the Department of Prints and Drawings of the British Museum, found the time to write appreciations of such artists as Martin Schongauer. Most of the verses he contributed to the *Dome* were gathered together in *Odes*, which also came from the Unicorn Press. His colleague in the Print Room of the British Museum, Campbell Dodgson, also contributed appreciations of Renaissance artists. C. J. Holmes, later the director of the National Gallery, journeyed further, at times, with essays on the great Japanese artists Hokusai and Utamaro. Gleeson White, a staunch supporter of Oldmeadow, also wrote of the great Renaissance artists, but, more important, he contributed an essay on Dante Gabriel Rossetti's "The Sea Spell." Laurence Housman, in the nineties, was best known for his illustrations, stories and poems, and art criticism. In early issues of the *Dome* appeared his drawing of "The Well in the Wall," his story, "Little Saint Michael," and a poem, "The Poison Tree." In 1899 he brought out *Rue*, which contained poems that had appeared in the *Outlook*, the *Spectator** (see *RA*) , and the *Dome*.

Roger Fry's one contribution was a serious essay on Giovanni Bellini, which he later rewrote in a more popular form as a chapter of his study of the artist's life, published by the Unicorn Press in 1899. All of the essays on art and artists in the *Dome* were accompanied by good quality reproductions.

Stephen Phillips contributed two poems; Francis Thompson published a like number; one of these, "An Arab Love Song," reappeared in the collection *Eyes of Youth* in 1910. Gordon Bottomley contributed "Three Sonnets for Pictures." Francis Vielé-Griffin, the French symbolist poet and translator of Swinburne's "Laus Veneris," forwarded two contributions. Voices of the Celtic world were represented by Fiona MacLeod (William Sharp) and W. B. Yeats.

Perhaps the most important contributor to the *Dome* was W. B. Yeats. Much of his thought at that time was devoted to developing his concepts for a poetic drama. He saw himself as a leading spirit in a movement which, using symbolism rather than realism, could restore and bring the poetic spirit back into the theater. This seminal idea is very much in evidence in his essay on the symbolist artist Althea Gyles, which he contributed to the *Dome* for its Christmas issue for 1898. In the April 1899 issue of the *Dome* appeared a note on the theater containing a definition of the theater Yeats was seeking:

Even if poetry were spoken as poetry, it would still seem out of place in many of its highest moments upon a stage, where the superficial appearances of nature are so closely copied; for poetry is founded upon conven-

tion, and becomes incredible the moment painting or gesture remind us
that people do not speak verse when they meet upon the highway. . . . The
theatre began in ritual, and it cannot come to greatness again without
recalling words to their ancient sovereignty.

It will take a generation, and perhaps generations, to restore the theatre
of Art; for one must get one's actors, and perhaps one's scenery, from the
theatre of commerce, until new actors and new painters have come to help
one; and until many failures and imperfect successes have made a new
tradition, and perfected in detail the ideal that is beginning to float before
our eyes. [P. 51]

After the success of *The Countess Cathleen* in the first season of the Irish
Literary Theatre, however, Yeats was emboldened to write in the *Dome* for
January 1900 that great vitality had already been restored to the Irish theater
scene:

Scandinavia is, as it seems, passing from her moments of miracle, and
some of us think that Ireland is passing to hers. She may not produce any
important literature, but because her moral nature has been aroused by
political sacrifices, and her imagination by a political pre-occupation with
her own destiny, she is ready to be moved by profound thoughts that are
a part of the unfolding of herself. [P. 235]

Most of the essays Yeats contributed to the *Dome* were reprinted in somewhat
revised form in *Ideas of Good and Evil* (1903). He also contributed some wonderful poems, such as "The Song of Monzan," which were reprinted in *The
Wind Among the Reeds* in 1899. The *Dome* also published two distinguished
translations from the work of Maurice Maeterlinck: "The Massacre of the In-
nocents" and "The Wanderers."

All references to the *Dome* emphasize how generously the editor supported
young composers. Two works by Edward Elgar appeared in the *Dome* just as
he came to prominence. A "Minuet" is here, as well as a song, "Love Alone
Will Stay," which later was transformed into "In Haven," the second of his
Sea Pictures. Frederick Delius contributed one of his early songs to the *Dome*
as "Fritz Delius."

Women writers were encouraged to submit their work. "Israfel," a Miss G.
Hudson, who was a prominent member of the Lyceum Club (a literary society
for ladies), contributed essays written in a rather extravagant style. Other members of the Lyceum Club's Poetry Circle were recruited by "Israfel." Norah
Hopper, an enthusiast of French literature, a member of the Irish Literary Society,
and much praised by Yeats, forwarded two contributions. Miss Ethel Wheeler,
a member of the staff of the *Academy** and a prolific journalist of the nineties,
also sent poems on the suggestion of "Israfel" to Oldmeadow. As Paul West
observes:

The three groups from which Oldmeadow drew his contributors were not exclusive of one another. Mrs. Meynell attended the dinners of the Lyceum Club. Yeats knew Mrs. Meynell; and Laurence Housman and Arthur Symons knew everybody. Oldmeadow went to neither the Lyceum Club nor the Irish Literary Society. But, so long as he was "persona grata" at Palace Court House, he had no need to find his contributors elsewhere.[1]

Note

1. Paul West, *"The Dome*: An Aesthetic Periodical of the 1890s," *Book Collector* 6 (1957):169.

Information Sources

BIBLIOGRAPHY

West, Paul. *"The Dome*: An Aesthetic Periodical of the 1890s." *Book Collector* 6 (1957):160–69.
Ziegler, A. P. *"The Dome* and Its Editor-Publisher: An Exploration." *American Book Collector* 15 (1965):19–21.

INDEXES

Each volume contains an index or table of contents.

REPRINT EDITIONS

Microform: Early British Periodicals (UMI), reel 184.

LOCATION SOURCES

American

Widely available.

British

Widely available.

Publication History

MAGAZINE TITLE AND TITLE CHANGES

The Dome: *A quarterly containing examples of all the arts.*

VOLUME AND ISSUE DATA

Numbers 1–5, March 1897–May 1898.

New series, volumes 1–7, numbers 1–19/20, October 1898–May/July 1900.

FREQUENCY OF PUBLICATION

Quarterly.

PUBLISHER

Ernest J. Oldmeadow, London.

EDITOR

Ernest J. Oldmeadow.

Cornelius P. Darcy

DOUGLAS JERROLD'S SHILLING MAGAZINE

The seven volumes of *Douglas Jerrold's Shilling Magazine* published between 1845 and 1848 maintained their distinctive character—a "consideration of the social wants and rightful claims of the People"[1]—even among the many ventures of Douglas William Jerrold's busiest journalistic decade.

In this decade *Punch** was launched by Jerrold's son-in-law Henry Mayhew and others. One of the short-lived predecessors of the famous comic weekly was an 1832 *Punch in London* (seventeen numbers between January and May) put out by a group including Douglas Jerrold and the illustrators George Cruikshank and Kenny Meadows. It is hardly surprising to find Jerrold a regular contributor to *Punch*, starting with its second number. Throughout the 1840s and 1850s, his grandson tells us, Jerrold "more definitely . . . than any of his confrères" stood for *Punch* to its readers.[2] "Punch's Letters to His Son" and "Punch's Complete Letter Writer" were Jerrold's. His serious articles, signed "Q," were as popular as his amusing pieces, and even his comic journalism served to raise the public's consciousness on significant political and social issues.[3] The thirty-seven installments of "Mrs. Caudle's Curtain Lectures" to her henpecked husband delighted readers in 1845, the year of the demise of the *Illuminated Magazine*, which Jerrold had edited since 1843.[4]

January 1845 saw the beginning of his new venture, *Douglas Jerrold's Shilling Magazine*. The title page of the low-priced monthly, "published at the Punch Office, for the Proprietors of Punch," bore a medallion of Queen Victoria with the Latin "by the grace of God" inscription around it, "Douglas Jerrold's" in fancy-quavery *Punch*-like script above it, and an elaborate "Shilling Magazine" below it. The table of contents on the reverse of the title page set the general pattern of the magazine, though no fixed order is observable among the typical items constituting any issue.

Number 1 opened with Jerrold's own "History of St. Giles and St. James," a story of poor and rich, illustrated by John Leech, one of the best artists on the staff of *Punch*. The serial concluded twenty-eight issues later and appeared, revised, in book form.[5] The author answered charges of setting class against class by declaring:

> It has been my endeavour to show, in the person of St. Giles, the victim of an ignorant disregard of the social claims of the poor upon the rich; of the governed million upon the governing few; to present . . . the picture of the infant pauper reared in brutish ignorance, a human waif of dirt and darkness. . . . I cannot think myself open to the charge of bedizening St. Giles at the cost of St. James; or of making Hog Lane the treasury of all the virtues, to the moral sacking of Mayfair.[6]

Another recurring feature was Jerrold's "Hedgehog Letters," as from a London cab driver to his far-flung family and friends, commenting sagely, wryly, preposterously upon what was going on at home. For example, the first letter makes amusingly dire predictions about the outcome of the Romanizing tendencies of certain Church of England clergy.

Among the few signed articles was Peter George Patmore's "Personal Recollections of the Late William Hazlitt," continued in the second issue. Patmore's poet son, the not yet distinguished Coventry, began at once to review for the *Shilling Magazine* and by June 1845 was represented by the first of his longer articles, "The Morbidness of the Age," signed "An Optimist." That no irony was intended seems evident from the concluding paragraphs, which call "morbidness" "an expression of the present age...as a period of transition....we would unwillingly exchange it for that healthfulness which expressed a lower state of reflection" (1:492). Assertions of "a sincere faith in the progress of humanity" are less likely to be even the youthful Patmore's, but are quite in keeping with the editor's views.

Poems in the magazine, not numerous and not very impressive, usually bore initials: E. O., E. R., J. K., L., and R.L.B. Coventry Patmore signed one of his "Rhymes for the Times" called "Young and Old England," and initialed another, "The Murderer's Sacrament," about the crowd at a public hanging.

Some idea of the range and tenor of the articles, whether signed, unsigned, or initialed,[7] emerges from sample titles: "The Finery of War," "Slavery the Only Remedy for the Miseries of the English Poor," "Music for the Million," "Art and Misery," "The Novelist and the Milliner," "Religion and Industry," "Short Story of the Allotment System," "Influence of Aristocracy on Literature," "Prospects of British Commerce in Japan," "Wives of Great Men," "The Worth of Statesmanship," "Man Was Not Made to Mourn," "Men of Letters and Their Abettors," "A Few Words on Early Shop-Shutting." Jerrold himself was vocal against luxury, corruption, war, flogging, and capital punishment, and advocated simple and healthful living, aesthetic education, and the amelioration of laborers' conditions, especially those of women and children.

The policy statement of the "Prospectus" urged the glory of aiding, "however humbly," the present epoch's "righteous and bloodless struggle" for redistribution of goods "provided for all men." It eschewed party politics as abusive and corrupt. By means of "all and every variety of literature," especially essays breathing "WITH A PURPOSE," even the "light reader" would be gently enlightened and need not "take alarm." A further aim of the publication was "to make every page exclusively British in its subject."

In fact, the *Shilling Magazine* consistently espoused social justice and social uplift, deploring what dehumanized the "lower orders" or denied them values beyond material improvement—"the books and lectures of Mechanics' Institutes" were "pervaded by a low prosaic tone of speciality: nothing higher than 'common sense' ... never ... higher or more ideal qualities" (5:366).

A circulation of 9,000 attested that it spoke to many.[8] Kathleen Tillotson gives an explanation of its short life: "It was probably too radical, and too 'low,' to offer a serious challenge to the half-crown monthlies in that period."[9] Jerrold's son suggested that the magazine was just not equal to its editor's ambition of making "its voice heard, not in boudoirs, but in the high places, where action for the good of the people might be the result."[10] Another practical reason might have been Jerrold's divided attention, as the success of his *Weekly Newspaper* persuaded him that the greater frequency and directness of this instrument made it more effective for his purposes. Indeed, he ended his days as editor of *Lloyd's Weekly Newspaper* (1852–1857).

There is a surprising breadth and variety of books reviewed in *Douglas Jerrold's Shilling Magazine*. Travel books, historical biographies, and translations from French and German relieved the "exclusively British" cast of the principal articles. The philosophy and aesthetics of Schiller, Schlegel, Richter, Emerson, and Hume would have appealed to an educated audience. Plays, poems, and novels (such as *Peers and Parvenus* by Mrs. Gore) stretched the didactic thread spun in the prospectus. The impression is of something for everybody in each number's ninety-odd octavo pages of text, about twenty of which were reviews of new books, exclusive of advertising. About fifteen more (unnumbered) pages contained notices of books and publishers' offers as well as promises about household products and patent medicines.

The magazine understandably repeated praises it earned in its column, "Opinions of the Press." The *Spectator** (see *RA*), for example, hails its "animating spirit" and the good quality ("for a shilling") of its articles as "earnest and real." It may sometimes verge "upon the theatrical clap-trap" but "only as a fault of manner. . . . the heart feels sound" (1, no. 2). Jerrold's reputation is cited as guarantee of worth.

A dozen years later James Hannay eulogizes this "wit with a mission" in the first number of the *Atlantic Monthly*—"not an artist" but a fighter with the weapons of the man of letters, "Jerrold and the century help to explain each other."[11]

Notes

1. From the "Prospectus," which was printed on the back cover of the first number of the *Shilling Magazine* and reprinted less prominently in several subsequent issues.

2. Walter Jerrold, *Douglas Jerrold and Punch* (London, 1910), p. vii.

3. See, for example, "How Mr. Chokepear Keeps a Merry Christmas" (1 [1841]:277), exposing pharisaism; "Groans of the People" (2 [1842]:88), prodding Sir Robert Peel to do more than "touch his hat"; "Blood" (2 [1842]:190), against glamorizing murder; and "The 'Sabre' and the 'Cross' " (3 [1842]:251), on the French in Algeria.

4. Published as a book in 1846 at the *Punch* office; included in volume 3 of Jerrold's *Works* (London, 1863).

5. Ibid, p. 1.

6. W. Blanchard Jerrold, *Life of Douglas Jerrold* (London, n.d.), p. 219.

7. E.g., Goodwyn Barmby, Paul Bell (several articles), Hepworth Dixon, R(ichard) H(engest) Horne, Richard Howitt, Horace Mayhew, Dinah Mulock, Angus B. Reach, John Wilson Ross, T. H. Sealy, Arthur Walbridge.

8. Jerrold, *Life*, p. 220.

9. Kathleen Tillotson, *Novels of the Eighteen-forties* (Oxford, 1954), p. 30 n.

10. Jerrold, *Life*, p. 220.

11. James Hannay, "Douglas Jerrold," *Atlantic Monthly*, November 1857, pp. 1–12.

Information Sources

BIBLIOGRAPHY

Hannay, James. "Douglas Jerrold." *Atlantic Monthly*, November 1857, pp. 1–12.

Jerrold, Douglas. *Works*, with an introductory memoir by his son, W. Blanchard Jerrold. 4 vols. London, 1863.

Jerrold, Walter. *Douglas Jerrold and "Punch."* London, 1910.

Jerrold, W. Blanchard. *Life and Remains of Douglas Jerrold*. London, 1859.

———. *Life of Douglas Jerrold*. London, n.d. There are at least two American editions: Boston, 1859; Philadelphia, n.d.

INDEXES

Each volume indexed.

REPRINT EDITIONS

None

LOCATION SOURCES

American

Widely available.

British

Complete runs: Aberdeen University Library; Birmingham Public Library; Bodleian Library; British Museum; Cambridge University Library; Newcastle-upon-Tyne Public Library; Norwich Public Library; Southampton Public Library.

Partial runs: Edinburgh Public Library; Leeds Public Library; London University Library; Manchester Public Library; Newport Public Library; Nottingham University Library; St. Andrews University Library.

Publication History

MAGAZINE TITLE AND TITLE CHANGES

Douglas Jerrold's Shilling Magazine.

VOLUME AND ISSUE DATA

Volumes 1–7, numbers 1–42, January 1845–June 1848.

FREQUENCY OF PUBLICATION

Monthly.

PUBLISHER

The *Punch* Office, 194 Strand, London; 92 Fleet Street, London.

EDITOR

Douglas Jerrold.

Mary Anthony Weinig

DUBLIN REVIEW, THE. See RA

DUBLIN UNIVERSITY MAGAZINE, THE. See RA

E

ECLECTIC REVIEW, THE. See RA

EDINBURGH REVIEW, THE. See RA

ENGLISH REVIEW, THE

The *English Review* began in 1908 under the founding editorship of Ford Madox Ford and lingered for some twenty-seven years as a political organ, first of the Liberal left and then of the illiberal right, before merging with the *National Review*.* The review was plagued by frequent changes of proprietors, editors, format, and price. Most accounts dismiss the post-Ford years and focus only on the first few volumes of the review. But however disjointed its career may appear, the *English Review* must be studied as an organic whole if one wishes the fullest understanding of British literature, culture, and politics from 1908 to 1937.

Ford Madox Ford (or Ford Madox Hueffer, until 1919) was unhappy with the established Edwardian literary periodicals. And when Thomas Hardy was unable to publish his poem, "A Sunday Morning Tragedy," Ford's desire to begin his own periodical crystalized. Paying Hardy twenty pounds for the poem, Ford included it in the inaugural issue of December 1908, along with James's "A Jolly Corner," the first of seven installments of Conrad's "Some Reminiscences," Galsworthy's "A Fisher of Men," the first part of Tolstoy's "The Raid," and a long installment of Wells's *Tono-Bungay*. For a year Ford and his subeditor, Douglas Goldring, working out of Ford's maisonette at 84 Holland Park Avenue (and occasionally out of a loge at a local music hall), published works of such writers as D. G. Rossetti, Anatole France, R. B. Cunninghame Graham, W. B. Yeats, Walter De la Mare, Violet Hunt, Hilaire Belloc, G. K.

Chesterton, Arnold Bennett, F. S. Flint, E. M. Forster, Max Beerbohm, George Meredith, Norman Douglas, Dostoevsky, D. H. Lawrence, and Ezra Pound. During Ford's editorship there were over a hundred contributors, more than half of whom appeared in the 1909 *Who's Who*. Ford had a genius for presenting between the same covers Victorian "Ancient Lights," Edwardians, and "les jeunes," the last group including his four major discoveries: Douglas (who succeeded Goldring as subeditor), Pound, Wyndham Lewis, and Lawrence.[1]

Unfortunately, Ford was a disaster at business, and after his original backer, Arthur Marwood, bowed out, Sir Alfred Mond, a wealthy politican, bought the review and replaced Ford with Austin Harrison. Ford was despondent in his final installment of his series, "The Critical Attitude": "But nothing will make the Englishman adopt a critical attitude.... In these islands critics have been extraordinarily rare.... So it has been with ... Hobbes, Matthew Arnold, and Mr. Ruskin, who, being dead, are nearly as much forgotten as ... the inventor of the safety bicycle" (4:532). Richard Aldington laid the blame for the failure of the review's circulation to rise above 1,000 copies a month on "the stupidity and genuine hatred of culture displayed by our countrymen."[2]

It is instructive reading how the *English Review*'s successive editors (listed below) attempted to take Ford's brilliant tenure into account without being apologetic for their own editorial goals and accomplishments. In June 1923 Austin Harrison recounted the "romantic" fortunes of the review ("The Old 'English,' " 36:512–15). He explained that under Ford the review's "only canons were quality," but that because the review was, after all, a school, after the master withdrew it languished. Named to succeed Ford by Sir Alfred Mond (later Lord Melchett), he saw his chief task as changing the review's attitude toward "the arts and matters generally" from "critical" to "adult." He recalls the public outrage and the boycott of the review which resulted from Frank Harris's article on Japanese morality, and from John Masefield's "The Everlasting Mercy," which he claimed had created more of a stir than any other poem since Byron's *Don Juan*. He also boasted of having been among the first to espouse the suffrage movement. And although he does not mention it, he could also have pointed to the review's having been "the *first to use in print*" the word "syphilis" (23:505) as further proof of his concern with an "adult" attitude. When the war came he stood for "a peace of reason," which did nothing to improve circulation, and after the "boom year" of 1920 the review fell from its "high estate." Complaining that "this is an age of mechanism," he acknowledges that the war has "opened all the windows, and the editorial glass-breaker no longer has a function." Political organs, however, always have a function, and with Harrison's successor, Ernest Remnant, the politics of the *English Review* took a sharp turn to the right and the quality of its literary contents nosedived.

The decline is readily apparent, for even though the *English Review* was purchased by Mond as a Liberal and reformist vehicle, Harrison (with the assistance until 1916 of his subeditor, Norman Douglas) maintained extraordinarily high literary standards.[3] In addition to publishing new works from many of the review's most famous early contributors, Harrison featured work from an international literary elite, including Richard Aldington, Sherwood Anderson, Chekhov, Gorky, Hesse, Aldous Huxley, Maeterlinck, Katherine Mansfield, Harold Monro, Nabokov, Yone Noguchi, Bertrand Russell, Shaw, May Sinclair, Arthur Symons, Turgenev, and Yeats.

Ernest Remnant, a businessman, was of an entirely different league than Harrison; for him the *English Review* would stand above all for "the national ideal" and "advocate a virile and independent Conservatism" (36:497, 501). In his obligatory sop to the review's previous literary importance, he promised that in addition to standing for England and her empire, the review would also "further the growth and the advance of those two priceless possessions of a people, their literature and their art." In practice, though, it seeems that Britannia first had to be made secure from socialists and Laborites, and Remnant's eight-year tenure is a desert between the literary oases provided by Harrison and Douglas Jerrold, Remnant's successor.

There is no mistaking the advent of Jerrold's editorship. He demonstrated the review's renewed commitment to literature by listing reviews and reviewers individually, and he scored something of a coup in obtaining three reviews by T. S. Eliot for his inaugural volume.[4] This same remarkable volume includes reviews of works by John Dewey, Theodore Dreiser, George Saintsbury, Frank Harris, Pearl Buck, William Faulkner, John Galsworthy, Ford, Edna Ferber, and Aldous Huxley. Among the reviewers are Herbert Agar, Osbert Burdett, Douglas Goldring, Hugh Kingsmill, and Horace Shipp. The subsequent eight volumes edited by Jerrold contain a wealth of reviews on works by or on Louis Golding, Lawrence, Eliot, James Joyce, Rebecca West, Gertrude Stein, Pound, Sholokhov, Robert Graves, John O'Hara, Faulkner, and Willa Cather, to mention only a dozen selected names.

The depressing state of contemporary criticism was discussed by Douglas Goldring in March 1932 in "Reviewers Reviewed" (54:290–95). He describes the times as a period when not only the authors are dissatisfied (as always) with the state of literary criticism, but when the reading public is even more dissatisfied than the authors. With 15,000 new books being issued each year, "silence is the lethal weapon," and those "novelist-reviewers who can dole out space to their competing colleagues are the financial bosses of their profession." Waxing nostalgic, he claims that before the war all literary criticism was governed by "the Standard of Value," a code of professional ethics he had learned from Ford. Because of the shortage of men during the war, he explains, "certain critics became pluralists." Even worse, though, were the practices of signing reviews and paying high rates to popular novelists to review their colleagues, the latter development being the fault of the "national newspapers." In the absence of responsible literary editing, he concludes somberly, "an author must push himself, must shove his way in—or stay outside." How authors are to do this he neglects to say.

After Jerrold's editorship the literary significance of the *English Review* effectively came to an end. Reviews and reviewers were no longer listed in the annual indexes, and the number of reviews fell from seventy-three in volume 61 to thirty-six in volume 62. Wilfrid Hindle's editorship lasted but six months before the review's final editor, Derek Walker-Smith, assumed his one-year custodianship. In October 1936, in an essay on the "Expansion of the *English Review*" (63:298–300), Walker-Smith proclaimed that the review was "the only paper in the English language which is expressing a Conservative philosophy that would be recognized as such by those who interpreted Conservative principles in the days when this country stood unquestionably supreme among the nations through its adherence to those principles." As was customary, he promised a "first-class monthly" which would include articles of literary interest besides fiction, book reviews, and poetry. Along with the review's expansion he announced a price increase of 150 percent, to two shillings and six pence, thus insuring the *English Review*'s demise. In July 1937 Walker-Smith informed his readers that the review would be amalgamated with the *National Review* the following month and gave his own summary of the review's history ("Current Comments," 64:755–63). In an extreme understatement, he explained that the *English Review* "was not always Conservative," and claimed that the war and "the logic of events" had converted Austin Harrison from Liberalism. It was not until Ernest Remnant became editor, however, that the review came into its own as "a definitely Right-Wing paper," and became the "organ of constructive intellectual Conservatism." Sadly, whatever gains the *English Review* brought to Conservatives were paid for dearly by the loss of its literary significance.

Notes

1. I am indebted for much of the information presented here to Ralph Herman Ruedy, "Ford Madox Ford and the *English Review*," Ph.D. dissertation, Duke University, 1976; and to Douglas Goldring, *South Lodge* (London, 1943), p. 18.

2. Frank MacShane, "The *English Review*," *South Atlantic Quarterly* 60 (1961):319.

3. In an amusing description of his life as editor ("Editorial Amenities," 15:615), Harrison maintains that "I've nothing to do, of course—all the *work* is done by Norman Douglas, who is sub-editor, and I have only to sit in a revolving chair for a few hours during a few afternoons in the week."

4. Eliot's three reviews in volume 53 are of Lawrence Hyde's *The Prospects of Humanism* (pp. 118–19), Belloc's *Essays of a Catholic Layman in England* (pp. 245–46), and E. E. Kellett's *Fashion in Literature: A Study of Changing Taste* (pp. 634–36).

Information Sources

BIBLIOGRAPHY

Bradbury, Malcolm. "The *English Review*." *London Magazine* 5 (August 1958):46–57.

Ford, Ford Madox. *Return to Yesterday*. New York, 1932.

Goldring, Douglas. *South Lodge: Reminiscences of Violet Hunt, Ford Madox Ford, and the "English Review" Circle*. London, 1943.

Hoffman, Frederick J., Charles Allen, And Carolyn F. Ulrich. *The Little Magazine: A History and a Bibliography*. Princeton, 1946.

Karl, Frederick R. "Joseph Conrad, Norman Douglas, and the *English Review*." *Journal of Modern Literature* 2 (1971–1972):342–56.

MacShane, Frank. "The *English Review*." *South Atlantic Quarterly* 60 (1961):311–20.

Mizener, Arthur. *The Saddest Story: A Biography of Ford Madox Ford*. New York, 1971.

Ruedy, Ralph Herman. "Ford Madox Ford and the *English Review*." Ph.D. dissertation, Duke University, 1976.

INDEXES

Each volume indexed, but incompletely.

REPRINT EDITIONS

Kraus Reprint Corporation, 1967.

Microform: Early British Periodicals (UMI), reels 286–300. Kraus Reprint.

LOCATION SOURCES

American

Widely available.

British

Complete runs: Birmingham Public Library; Bodleian Library; British Museum; Cambridge University Library; London University Library; National Central Library. Partial runs: Widely available.

Publication History

MAGAZINE TITLE AND TITLE CHANGES

The English Review. (Merged with *The National Review* in 1937.)

VOLUME AND ISSUE DATA

Volumes 1–64, December 1908–July 1937. (With the first number edited by Douglas Jerrold, June 1931, the review's cover format was altered and the designation "New Series, No. 1" was added. This "New Series" lasted only through "No. 7," December 1931, when the cover reverted to its previous format.)

FREQUENCY OF PUBLICATION

Monthly.

PUBLISHERS

December 1908–July 1909: Gerald Duckworth, Covent Garden, London. August 1909–November 1910: Chapman and Hall, Covent Garden, London. December 1910–December 1924: *English Review*, 11 Henrietta St., London. January 1925–January 1927: Eyre and Spottiswoode (Publications) Ltd., London. February–May, 1927: W. H. Berry, London. June 1927–December 1935: Eyre and Spottiswoode, Ltd., London. January 1936–July 1937: *The English Review*.

EDITORS

Ford Madox Ford, December 1908–December 1909. Austin Harrison, January 1910–May 1923. Ernest Remnant, June 1923–May 1931. Douglas Jerrold, June 1931–December 1935. Wilfrid Hindle, January–June 1936. Derek Walker-Smith, July 1936–July 1937.

Bruce A. White

EXAMINER, THE. See RA

EXAMINER AND LONDON REVIEW, THE. See EXAMINER,
THE (RA)

F

FOREIGN QUARTERLY REVIEW, THE. See RA

FORTNIGHTLY REVIEW, THE

The *Fortnightly Review* first appeared on 15 May 1865, as a result of the efforts of Anthony Trollope, Frederic Chapman, and others.[1] The founders modeled the new magazine after the French *Revue des Deux Mondes*, itself patterned on the *Edinburgh Review** (see *RA*) and the *Quarterly Review** (see *RA*), except that it published fiction and, more important, attempted to be nonpartisan. The prospectus for the *Fortnightly* declared that contributors would write for "cultivated readers of all classes" on the subjects of literature, art, science, philosophy, finance, and politics; and, though liberal in politics, the magazine would allow contributors complete freedom from editorial influence. Shortly after, the announcement of the forthcoming first issue added the significant and controversial stipulation, planned all along, chiefly at the insistence of Trollope, that reviews would be signed. It also promised a serialized story by Trollope, to run through the first sixteen issues; serial fiction had become quite profitable for magazines.

The first editor, George Henry Lewes, established the pattern that most subsequent editors were to follow. He enlisted well-known writers, and he was good at discovering those who were destined to become well known. Walter Bagehot led the first issue. Others who wrote for Lewes during the next two years were Thomas Henry Huxley, Herbert Spencer, George Meredith, John Stuart Mill, Frederic Harrison, and Anthony Trollope. Lewes himself wrote frequently. He argued for reform of the franchise and the school curriculum, where he wished more emphasis to be placed on physics, psychology, mathematics, and the natural sciences. Under Lewes the *Fortnightly* was not distinguished in literary criticism.

It favored Swinburne's *Atalanta in Calydon*. Trollope, reviewing Ruskin's *Sesame and Lilies* and *The Crown of Wild Olives*, objected that Ruskin had insufficient knowledge of economics and compared him unfavorably to Carlyle. During Lewes's editorship the *Fortnightly* did not notice Tennyson's *Enoch Arden*, Newman's *Apologia*, Carlyle's *Frederick*, Henry Thomas Buckles's *History of Civilization in England*, Arnold's *Essays in Criticism*, Swinburne's *Poems and Ballads*, or Browning's *Dramatis Personae*. Lewes recruited an excellent group of foreign correspondents, among them the foreign nationals Joseph Mazzini, Emilio Castelar, Karl Blind, Peter Kropotkin, Gustave Cluseret, and Emile de Laveleye. Karl Blind continued to write for the magazine during the rest of the century. In the last months of Lewes's editorship it became evident that the reading public preferred weeklies and monthlies, and beginning in November 1866 the *Fortnightly* became a monthly.[2]

When Lewes resigned at the end of 1866 because of ill health, John Morley succeeded him and created an excellent reputation for the *Fortnightly* during the next decade and a half. Like Lewes, he was strongly influenced by John Stuart Mill and Auguste Comte and believed deeply in progress, science, and rational thought. The *Fortnightly* criticized the Established Church, especially for its involvement in education and Irish affairs. Morley gave special emphasis to science (weather, anthropology, chemistry, physics, biology, medicine) and supported the evolutionists.[3] His publication of Huxley's "On the Physical Basis of Life" in the issue for February 1869 caused a notorious controversy.[4] The *Fortnightly* opposed war and militarism and favored land reform and trade unions, which it declared legal and saw as a means to better education and an escape from poverty and slavery.[5] It called on the universities to eliminate religious tests and to include science in the curriculum. Morley followed Lewes in encouraging women to contribute to the magazine and in publishing articles advocating women's rights.

While he strengthened the *Fortnightly* literary content, Morley insisted that it serve the magazine's progressive social philosophy. Trollope himself was accused of not observing human nature truthfully. Tennyson was attacked as being opposed to democracy, rational inquiry, reform, and freedom for women; Carlyle was disliked for his distrust of science and legislative reform; Arnold was praised for his poetry, but condemned for his social philosophy and lack of faith in legislative reform. The *Fortnightly* looked favorably on new writing and took as regular contributors Swinburne, Morris, and Rossetti. It was partial to the works of Browning, Walter Pater, and Victor Hugo, and it introduced Ibsen to English readers. Among the new contributors under Morley were Matthew Arnold, Leslie Stephen, Walter Pater, Joseph Chamberlain, Mark Pattison, Henry George, Andrew Carnegie, Andrew Lang, Edmund Gosse, and George Saintsbury. During the years 1865–1875 the *Fortnightly* published serially three novels by Trollope and two by Meredith, and poetry by Swinburne, Meredith, Rossetti, and Morris, among others. When Morley looked back on his editorship in 1882, he was proud that the *Fortnightly* had advocated "Free Labour, Free Land, Free

Schools, Free Church,'' and other broad reforms, and that the magazine had linked ideas and social and political action.[6]

During the four years of Thomas Hay Sweet Escott's editorship (1882–1886), the *Fortnightly* declined somewhat in quality and became more hospitable to conservative views, though it remained strongly liberal. Early in his tenure, Escott even went so far as to invite the conservative leadership to a dinner. But the *Fortnightly* retained its nature, running articles dealing with such matters as land reform, education for the poor, and church reform in Scotland. It published a series of seven articles on the Radical Programme during 1883–1885, which were extremely popular and which were reprinted separately in 1885 with an introduction by Joseph Chamberlain, who was a political influence on both Morley and Escott.

Frank Harris, editor from 1886 to 1894, took the *Fortnightly* in a more liberal, even radical direction, and strengthened its coverage of literary subjects, though the quality of the political and general intellectual commentary remained high. Among Harris's contributors were Arnold, Swinburne, Meredith, Wilde, Henry James, Hardy, Paul Verlaine, Kipling, H. G. Weils, Pater, Coventry Patmore, G. Bernard Shaw, William Archer, Andrew Lang, Leslie Stephen, Edmund Gosse, George Saintsbury, Austin Dobson, John Addington Symonds, Edward Dowden, Arthur Symons, and George Moore. Harris frequently contributed stories as well as essays, but did not get along well with the publishers, who complained about his story ''Modern Idyll'' in 1891 and then broke with him completely over an article by Charles Malato in September 1894 supporting anarchism.

Wiliam Leonard Courtney presided over the *Fortnightly* from 1894 to 1928. He restored the breadth lost under Harris, bringing back emphasis on political and intellectual subjects and creating a strong foreign correspondence. He retained many of Harris's writers and added James Joyce, George Gissing, Havelock Ellis, John Galsworthy, W. B. Yeats, and later, Ezra Pound, Hilaire Belloc, Arthur Quiller-Couch, and Edith Sitwell. [See also the article on *Fortnightly Review* in *MA*.]

Notes

1. Edwin M. Everett, *The Party of Humanity, ''The Fortnightly Review'' and Its Contributors, 1865–1874* (Chapel Hill, N.C., 1939), p. 17; ''*The Fortnightly Review*,1865–1900,'' *Wellesley Index to Victorian Periodicals, 1824–1900*, ed. Walter E. Houghton (Toronto, 1972), 2:173. I am indebted to Everett for much of the material presented in this essay.

2. D. W. Brogan, ''The Intellectual Review,'' *Encounter* 21, no. 5 (1963):11.

3. Everett, pp. 84, 114, 116, 134–35, 156.

4. John Morley, ''Valedictory,'' *Fortnightly Review* 38 (1882):518.

5. Everett, pp. 173, 204, 206-7, 225.

6. Morley, p. 519.

Information Sources

BIBLIOGRAPHY

Courtney, Janet. *The Making of an Editor, W. L. Courtney, 1850–1928*. London, 1930.

Escott, Thomas H. S. *Anthony Trollope; His Public Service, Private Friends, and Literary Originals*. 1913. Reprint. Port Washington, N.Y., 1967.

Everett, Edwin M. *The Party of Humanity, "The Fortnightly Review" and Its Contributors, 1865–1874*. Chapel Hill, N.C., 1939.

Hamer, D. A. *John Morley, Liberal Intellectual in Politics*. Oxford, 1968.

Harris, Frank. *My Life and Loves*. Edited by John F. Gallagher. New York, 1925.

Hirst, Francis W. *Early Life and Letters of John Morley*. 2 vols. 1927. Reprint. New York, n.d.

Houghton, Esther Rhoads. "John Verschoyle and the *Fortnightly Review*." *Victorian Periodicals Newsletter*, no. 3 (1968):17–21.

Lewes, George H. "Farewell Causerie." *Fortnightly Review* 6 (1866):890-91.

"M." "The *Fortnightly*—A Retrospect." *Fortnightly Review* 75 (1901): 104-17.

Morley, John. *Recollections*. 2 vols. New York, 1917.

———. "Valedictory." *Fortnightly Review* 38 (1882):511–21.

Sadleir, Michael. *Trollope: A Commentary*. Rev. ed., 1947. Reprint. Darby, 1980.

Trollope, Anthony. *An Autobiography*. 1947. Reprint. Los Angeles, 1979.

———. "George Henry Lewes." *Fortnightly Review* 31 (1879):15–24.

Waugh, Arthur. "The Biography of a Periodical." *Fortnightly Review*, n.s. 126 (1929):512–24.

———. *A Hundred Years of Publishing*. London, 1930.

Wellesley Index to Victorian Periodicals, 1824–1900. Edited by Walter E. Houghton. Vol. 2. Toronto, 1972.

INDEXES

Indexed by author in each bound volume. Volumes 1–37 in a *General Index to the "Contemporary Review," the "Fortnightly Review," and the "Nineteenth Century,"* comp. W. M. Griswold (Bangor, Me., 1802).1865–1881 in *Poole's Index*.1865–1900 in *Wellesley Index* 2.

REPRINT EDITIONS

Microform: Bell and Howell Co., Wooster, Ohio. Early British Periodicals (UMI), reels 785–799 and 857–868. Princeton Microfilm Corp., Princeton, N.J.

LOCATION SOURCES

American
   Widely available.
British
   Widely available.

Publication History

MAGAZINE TITLE AND TITLE CHANGES

The Fortnightly Review, 15 May 1865–July 1934. *The Fortnightly*, August 1934–December 1954. (Absorbed by *The Contemporary Review*,* January 1955.)

VOLUME AND ISSUE DATA

Continuous series (old series), volumes 1–182, 15 May 1865–December 1954. New Series, volumes 1 (vol. 7, o.s.)–175 (vols. 181/182, o.s.), 1 January 1867–December 1954.

FREQUENCY OF PUBLICATION
>   Biweekly (15 May 1865–15 October 1866); monthly (November 1866–December 1954).

PUBLISHERS
>   15 May 1865–December 1880: Chapman and Hall, 193 Piccadilly, London. January 1881–June 1931: Chapman and Hall, 11 Henrietta Street, Covent Garden, London. July 1931–December 1954: Horace Marshall, Temple House, Tallis Street, London.

EDITORS
>   George Henry Lewes, 15 May 1865–December 1866. John Morley, January 1867–October 1882. Thomas Hay Sweet Escott, November 1882–June 1886. Frank Harris, July 1886–October 1894. William Leonard Courtney, December 1894–October 1928. Unknown, November, 1928–June 1947. John Armitage, July 1947–December 1954.

Dickie A. Spurgeon

FRASER'S MAGAZINE FOR TOWN AND COUNTRY. See RA

FUN

The continuing success of *Punch** during the last half of the nineteenth century encouraged a mushroom growth of imitative comic periodicals. Of these, only *Fun* lasted long enough to become an institution in its own right. *Fun*'s first number appeared in September 1861, and its founding editor, Henry J. Byron, a prolific comic dramatist, intended to produce a weekly paper as much like *Punch* as he legally could. *Fun* therefore contained a full page topical cartoon (sometimes double, and usually political) in each issue; grotesque illustrations; smaller cuts (often on social subjects); sporting news; political, dramatic, literary, and art criticism; and puns, parodies, and light verse.

Just as Mr. Punch with his dog Toby presided over the elder periodical, so Mr. Fun, the jester with his cat, directed the younger, while the editorship was called "the Bauble." The *Punch* staff were scornful of their thriving rival, Thackeray referring to it as "Funch." Nevertheless, *Fun* was known as the poor man's *Punch*, its price being a penny to the other's three pence.

During its first dozen years, *Fun* had an upstart liveliness that *Punch* had lost. Under Byron, and especially under his successor, Tom Hood, *Fun*'s contributors were young, bohemian, and ebullient, and politically liberal where *Punch* was increasingly conservative. If *Punch* had its Thackeray, *Fun* had its W. S. Gilbert and Ambrose Bierce. *Punch* might have Tenniel, but *Fun* had Matt Morgan, and each magazine counted a Doyle among its artists. Unfortunately, *Fun*'s Tom Hood never equaled his father's "Song of the Shirt," published in an early number of *Punch*, but he wrote satirically compassionate verses such as "Nothing at all in the papers to-day! / Only a murder somewhere or other— / A girl who has put her child away, / Not being a wife as well as a mother.''[1]

Henry J. Byron's first editorial promise set *Fun*'s satiric tone: "rely upon it every one shall have his whack.'' When Hood became editor in 1865, he announced that "our first aim will be to secure 'the greatest laughter of the greatest number.' ... we shall constitute ourselves 'Whip' to all parties—when they deserve it.'' So Mr. Fun laughed at Derby Day and St. Valentine's Day, and whacked abuses in Workhouses ("Pauper or Prisoner,'' 3 January 1863) and repressive Sabbatarianism ("Trains of thought stopped by order of the Bishops,'' 7 February 1863). In 1870 Mr. Fun asserted that he "never jests about questions of faith—and he never strikes a woman!'' This did not preclude cartoons showing religious figures or jokes about foolish fashions and false hair.

Most comic periodicals of the day had a close connection with popular theater, but *Fun*'s was unusually close in its first decade. Its contributors then included not only Byron and Gilbert, but also T. W. (Tom) Robertson, who introduced domestic realism to the Victorian stage; Edward L. Blanchard, already the doyen of pantomime writers; Francis C. Burnand, burlesque writer and an early Sullivan librettist; and Clement Scott, with a penchant for sentimental verse and a future as the *Daily Telegraph* critic who hated Ibsen.

Little wonder, then, that *Fun*'s short reviews and longer theatrical articles were the best of their kind in the 1860s. Robertson and Byron occasionally practiced, and Gilbert perfected, the full-page parodistic review, treating play, production, and performance. In these highly amusing criticisms, Gilbert began to lay the foundation of his own dramatic methods.

Reviews were only part of Gilbert's contribution. He was a *Fun* artist, illustrating his own and others' works. Under such pseudonyms as "Snarler,'' "A. Dapter,'' and "A Trembling Widow,'' his prose ranged from filler to full-page series, including "The Comic Physiognomist.'' His verse included, but was not limited to, the "Bab Ballads,'' *Fun*'s lasting contribution to nonsense literature. These grotesque, topsy-turvy, but analytic depictions of human nature appeared from 1865 to 1871 and furnished Gilbert with material for later plays and libretti.

Arriving during a Gilbert lull, Ambrose Bierce ("Dod Grile'') was *Fun*'s second important satirist. His contributions included Western sketches, parodies, and "Laughorisms'' ("'Eccentric' is the solemn judgment of the stalled ox upon the sun-inspired lamb''), but his best work was his series "The Fables of Zambri, the Parsee'' (1872–1873). The style was Aesop "ironized'' with such morals as "People who begin doing something from a selfish motive frequently drop it when they learn that it is a real benevolence'' and "This fable teaches that its worthy author was drunk as a loon.''

Perhaps the most immediately popular *Fun* contributor was George Ross ("Arthur Sketchley''), whose Mrs. Brown papers began as stage monologues in 1863 and were a feature of *Fun* from 1865 to 1874. Middle-aged Mrs. Brown, loud, fat, complaining, and naive, indefatigably pushes herself into trouble, and comments on everything from dinner parties to Disraeli in her own eccentric dialect: "Mrs. Butler is a weazel-figgered woman as wears no cap, with grey hairs and not much on it" (23 December 1865). Mrs. Brown's adventures, collected into volumes, sold in the thousands.

Tom Hood died in November 1874, leaving "the Bauble" to a relatively new contributor, Henry Sampson. Although Sampson had taken over many of Hood's editorial functions during the last year, he was an unfortunate choice. Quarrelsome and vituperative, he was "constantly talking and writing about his 'enemies.' "[2] Gilbert, whose contributions had become infrequent, left *Fun* altogether, and many of the early *Fun* writers were dead or otherwise engaged.

Sampson left the magazine in February 1878, and the Dalziel family, already *Fun*'s proprietors and engravers, took over the editorship. Two generations of Dalziels wrote and drew for their periodical without arousing interest or controversy. *Fun* never regained its lost quality, although an occasional literary celebrity such as Charles Godfrey Leland, creator of "Hans Breitmann," might lighten an issue. There were still excellent artists, especially Jassef Sullivan, but even the dramatic reviews were sometimes merely pretexts for irrelevant puns. The tone had changed even in fillers such as "Lord Beaconsfield once gave *Sanitas Sanitatum* as the motto of his party. Surely, then, if a bath and wash-house kind of policy be the Conservatives' idea, the sooner they call themselves 'Lava-Tories' the better" (19 January 1881).

After the Dalziels sold *Fun* in 1893, it lingered through a long, obscure death until in July 1901 it was incorporated with *Sketchy Bits*. Mr. Punch had long since regained his superiority.

Notes

1. *Fun*, 13 March 1869. This poem is assigned to Hood on the basis of the proprietor's marked copies of *Fun*, 1865–1893, in the Henry E. Huntington Library. Edward S. Lauterbach, *"Fun" and Its Contributors: The Literary History of a Victorian Humor Magazine*, Ph.D. dissertation, University of Illinois, 1961, p. 62; see also chap. 1.

2. Carey McWilliams, *Ambrose Bierce: A Biography* (New York, 1929), p. 105.

Information Sources

BIBLIOGRAPHY

Adrian, Arthur A. *Mark Lemon: First Editor of "Punch."* London, 1966.

Barrett, Daniel, "T. W. Robertson [1829–1871]: The Dramatist as Critic." *Victorian Periodicals Review* 14, no. 4 (1981):144–49.

Burnand, Sir Francis C. *Records and Reminiscences: Personal and General.* 2 vols. London, 1904.

[Dalziel, George and Edward]. *The Brothers Dalziel.* London, 1901.

Gilbert, Sir William Schwenck. *The Bab Ballads.* Edited by James Ellis. Cambridge, Mass., 1970.

Jones, John Bush. "W. S. Gilbert's Contributions to *Fun*, 1865–1874." *Bulletin of the New York Public Library*, 73 (1969):253–66.

Lauterbach, Charles E. "Taking Gilbert's Measure," *Huntington Library Quarterly* 19 (1956):196–202.

Lauterbach, Edward S. *"Fun" and Its Contributors: The Literary History of a Victorian Humor Magazine*. Ph.D. dissertation, University of Illinois, 1961.

Lucy, Henry W. Letter quoted in "Table Talk." *Gentleman's Magazine*, n.s. 14 (1875):258–60.

———. "Tom Hood: A Biographical Sketch." *Gentleman's Magazine*, n.s. 14 (1875):[77]–88.

McWilliams, Carey. *Ambrose Bierce: A Biography*. New York, 1929.

Pemberton, T. Edgar. *The Life and Writings of T. W. Robertson*. London, 1893.

Roe, F. Gordon. *Victorian Corners: The Style and Taste of an Era*. New York, 1968.

Scott, Clement. *The Drama of Yesterday and To-Day*. 2 vols. London, 1899.

Spielmann, M. H. *The History of "Punch."* New York, 1895.

———. "The Rivals of *Punch*." *National Review* 25 (1895):654-66.

INDEXES

Each volume indexed.

REPRINT EDITIONS

Microform: English Literary Periodicals (UMI), reels 476–91.

LOCATION SOURCES

American

Partial runs: Widely available.

British

Partial runs: British Museum; Cambridge University Library; Harris Public Library (Preston); Manchester Public Library; Nottingham Public Library; Nottingham University Library; Southampton Public Library; St. Andrews University Library; Victoria and Albert Museum Library.

Publication History

MAGAZINE TITLE AND TITLE CHANGES

Fun

VOLUME AND ISSUE DATA

Volumes 1–7, numbers 1–191, 21 September 1861–13 May 1865.

New series, Volumes 1–73, 20 May 1865–10 August 1901. (Separately paged annual almanacs. Supplementary numbers through 1865.)

FREQUENCY OF PUBLICATION

Weekly (collected into bound volumes twice a year).

PUBLISHERS

September 1861–May 1865: Charles Maclean, 80 Fleet Street, London E.C. 20 May 1865–end 1869: Edward Wylam, 80 Fleet Street, London, E.C. 1870–9 August 1893: Dalziel brothers, 80 Fleet Street, London. No publisher identified until January 1901. January–July 1901: George Newnes (no editorial address).

EDITORS

Henry J. Byron, 1861–1865. Tom Hood, 1865–1874. Henry Sampson, 1874–1878. Charles Dalziel(?), 1878–1893. No other editors identified.

Jane W. Stedman

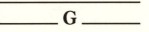

G

GENTLEMAN'S MAGAZINE, THE. See AAAJ

GERM, THE

In 1848 four young students in the schools of the Royal Academy decided to form a society. William Holman Hunt, John Everett Millais, and Dante Gabriel Rossetti were painters, Thomas Woolner a sculptor. They soon added to their number two other painters, James Collinson and Frederic George Stephens, as well as William Michael Rossetti, the brother of Dante Gabriel. Thus was formed the Pre-Raphaelite Brotherhood. The group was united by the desire to overthrow the reigning aesthetic principles and technical conventions of the Royal Academy. They believed that its principles stifled emotional sincerity and individual inspiration, and led artists away from the direct observation and representation of the truths of nature. Positive influences on the Brotherhood included the poetry of Keats and the early poetry of Tennyson, Ruskin's *Modern Painters*—the second volume of which had been published in 1846—and Ford Madox Brown, a somewhat older painter who while in Rome had come to know the leader of the Nazarenes, a group of German artists whose work combined technical simplicity and religious piety in ways congenial to the Pre-Raphaelites. An important rallying point was provided by the early Italian painters who, according to the Brotherhood, had perceived the natural world directly and represented it exactly. These painters did not place "between the eye and the visible fact the distorting artistic conventions created by Raphael, imposed by his followers, and fossilized into the theory and educational practice of the Royal Academy."[1]

It was not long before the seven members of the Pre-Raphaelite Brotherhood decided to start a journal to propagate their ideas. William Michael Rossetti was chosen editor. Several titles were considered, including *Monthly Thoughts in*

Literature and Art, Thoughts towards Nature: Conducted by Artists, the *Advent*, the *Spur*, the *Truth-Seeker*, and the *Scroll*. The title finally settled upon was the *Germ: Thoughts towards Nature in Poetry, Literature and Art*. The first issue came out in January 1850. It sold badly (around 200 of the 700 copies printed), but did better than the following February issue. In an attempt to attract more readers, the title of the March issue was changed to *Art and Poetry: Being Thoughts towards Nature Conducted Principally by Artists*, and most contributors were for the first time identified on the table of contents page. These changes were unsuccessful. The journal's last issue appeared in May 1850.

The statement on the back cover of the first issue announced: "This periodical will consist of original Poems, Stories to develope [*sic*] thought and principle, Essays concerning Art and other subjects and, analytic Reviews of current Literature—particularly of Poetry. Each number will also contain an Etching; the subject to be taken from the opening article of the month."[2] The Rossetti brothers were the most frequent contributors among the members of the Brotherhood. A number of Dante Gabriel's best-known poems, including "The Blessed Damozel" and "My Sister's Sleep," first appeared in the *Germ*. Other poets who contributed included Christina Georgina Rossetti, William Bell Scott, and Coventry Patmore. The verse contributions, W. M. Rossetti later explained, were to be written according to "the same principles of strict actuality and probability of detail which the Preraphaelites upheld in their pictures."[3] Further similarities between Pre-Raphaelite painting and the poems in the *Germ* are found in the religious ambiance and medieval flavor of a large number of them. The latter quality was accentuated by the medieval subjects of the etchings and by the gothic type used on the cover of each issue and for the titles of contributions.

The *raison d'être* of the *Germ* was not to be a poetry magazine but to make known the aesthetic ideals of the Brotherhood. In fact, the journal contains "the only attempts at a statement of aims ever put together by the Brotherhood, who had embarked on their revolutionary course two years earlier without issuing the customary manifesto."[4] To quote again from the back cover of the first issue: "The endeavour held in view throughout the writings on Art will be to encourage and enforce an entire adherence to the simplicity of nature." A corresponding emphasis on simplicity and sincerity of expression is found in the sonnet of W. M. Rossetti printed on the front cover of each issue. (Like his other metrical efforts, the sonnet is very poor; the editor's reviews of Clough's *Bothie of Toper-Na-Fuosich*, Arnold's *Strayed Reveller*, and Browning's *Christmas Eve and Easter Day* were far superior contributions.)

The principal articles on aesthetics published in the *Germ* were John Tupper's two-part "The Subject in Art," John Orchard's "A Dialogue on Art," and Stephens's "The Purpose and Tendency of Early Italian Art." Tupper argued that "works of Fine Art affect the beholder in the same ratio as the *natural prototypes* of those works would affect him; and not in proportion to the difficulties overcome in the artificial representation of those prototypes." He also urged artists not to turn away from contemporary subject matter (as did virtually all the contributors to the *Germ*) but to make their art "more directly conversant with the things, incidents, and influences which surround and constitute the living world" (3:118, 122). Orchard's speakers defended the arts as civilizing agents against "chemistry, steam-power, and the electric telegraph" and insisted that "Nature itself is comparatively pure; all that we desire is the removal of the factitious matter that the vice of fashion, evil hearts, and infamous desires, graft upon it" (4:149, 151). Stephens urged that the modern artist need not retire to monasteries to participate in "the same high feeling" as that of the early Italian artists. It could be reached by "the most just [artistic] method": the "firm attachment to truth in every point of representation." Furthermore, the sciences of geology and chemistry had "become almost exact within the present century" because of their experimental method. "If this adherence to fact, to experiment and not theory . . . has added so much to the knowledge of man in science; why may it not greatly assist the moral purposes of the Arts? . . . Truth in every particular ought to be the aim of the artist (2:59, 61).

Why did the *Germ* fail after only four issues? The immediate reason was financial. The members of the Pre-Raphaelite Brotherhood lacked business experience and large bank accounts. Nor did they have the entrepreneurial skill to realize that their journal would be perceived as a coterie publication. And except for D. G. Rossetti, none of them had real literary gifts. Another explanation was suggested by Edward William Cox in the *Critic**: "The truth is that [the *Germ*] is too good for the time. It is not *material* enough for the age."[5] But even if it had sold better, it is unlikely that the *Germ* would have gone on for much longer, for even two years after its founding the heterogeneity of interests among the Brotherhood was beginning to manifest itself. Collinson left in 1850, stating that membership was incompatible with his Roman Catholic beliefs. Not long after, Woolner went to Australia to look for gold; Hunt left for the Holy Land to paint religious pictures; and in 1853 Millais was ironically elected an associate of the Royal Academy. And D. G. Rossetti's consuming interest in something other than strict fidelity to external nature had been apparent since the first number of the *Germ*, in which had appeared his parabolic "Hand and Soul." Set in medieval Italy, the story is an allegory of the development of an artist, who had begun with "the imitation of any objects offered in nature," had gone through a phase in which he dedicated himself to moral and religious art, but was eventually granted a vision of a beautiful woman, "that was his soul," who tells him that his only duty as an artist is to be true to his own heart and soul (1:23, 31). That is, fidelity to inner experience supersedes fidelity to external nature or to moral concerns. In "Hand and Soul" one begins to hear the tones and the themes of Pater, the early Yeats, and the decadents.

During the last decades of the nineteenth century the fame and the influence of the Pre-Raphaelites grew, as did the reputation of their short-lived journal; reprints with substantial introductions were published around the turn of the century. From the vantage point of the later twentieth century, the *Germ* can be seen as a salient piece of literary history notable for its attempt to link literature and painting, as the ancestor of subsequent avant garde magazines, and as an epitome of one of those "returns to nature with which the course of poetry and painting is diversified."[6]

Notes

1. Herbert L. Sussman, *Fact into Figure: Typology in Carlyle, Ruskin, and the Pre-Raphaelite Brotherhood* (Columbus, Ohio, 1979), p. 40.
2. *The Germ*, no. 1 (January 1850):back cover. Photographically reproduced in Robert Stahr Hosmon, *"The Germ": A Pre-Raphaelite Little Magazine* (Coral Gables, Fla., 1970).
3. Quoted in the editor's introduction to James Sambrook, ed., *Pre-Raphaelitism: A Collection of Critical Essays* (Chicago, 1974), p. 2.
4. James Hardy, *The Pre-Raphaelites* (London, 1977), p. 6.
5. Quoted in Hosmon's introduction to *"The Germ": A Pre-Raphaelite Little Magazine*, p. 19.
6. Graham Hough, *The Last Romantics* (London, 1949), p. 46.

Information Sources

BIBLIOGRAPHY

Fredeman, William E., ed. *The P.R.B. Journal: William Michael Rossetti's Diary of the Pre-Raphaelite Brotherhood 1849–1853*. Oxford, 1975.
———. *Pre-Raphaelitism: A Bibliocritical Study*. Cambridge, Mass., 1965.
Hosmon, Robert Stahr, ed. *"The Germ": A Pre-Raphaelite Little Magazine*. Coral Gables, Fla., 1970.
Hough, Graham. "Books in General." *New Statesman*, 7 August 1948, p. 117.
———. *The Last Romantics*. London, 1949.
Stanford, Derek. *Pre-Raphaelite Writing: An Anthology*. London, 1973.

INDEXES

Index at end of run.

REPRINT EDITIONS

Facsimile reprint 1882, 1901. Numbers 3–4 reprinted as *Art and Poetry* (Portland, Me., 1898). AMS Press, New York. University of Miami Press, 1970.

Microform: Early British Periodicals (UMI), reel 21.

LOCATION SOURCES

American

Widely available.

British

Complete runs: British Museum; Cambridge University Library; Kensington Public Library; Newport Public Library; Nottingham Public Library; University College of Swansea Library.

Partial runs: National Library of Scotland.

Reprint editions: Birmingham Public Library; Birmingham University Library; Bristol University Library; British Museum; Edinburgh University Library; London University Library; Manchester Public Library; Queen's College (Belfast) Library.

Publication History

MAGAZINE TITLE AND TITLE CHANGES
> *The Germ: Thoughts towards nature in poetry, literature, and art*, January, February 1850. *Art and Poetry: Being Thoughts towards Nature Conducted Principally by Artists*, March, May 1850.

VOLUME AND ISSUE DATA
> Numbers 1–4, January–May 1850.

FREQUENCY OF PUBLICATION
> Four issues, January–May 1850.

PUBLISHERS
> Aylott & Jones, 8 Paternoster Row, London; Dickinson & Co. (volumes 3–4), 114 New Bond Street, London.

EDITOR
> William Michael Rossetti.

Kerry McSweeney

GOLDEN HYNDE, THE

When the *Golden Hynde* was first published in December 1913, the editors reminded the readers that its namesake was the ship of Sir Francis Drake. "Thus at first sight," the editors went on, "the title of the magazine may seem somewhat ambitious; but remember that 'The Golden Hynde' was the smallest ship of the fleet, and, moreover, to quote the words of the poet, that 'a man's reach should exceed his grasp.' " In a small way the magazine, it was hoped, would make a metaphorical voyage around the world and return home covered with glory and filled with treasure. The treasure—any profits made by the publishing venture—would "bring joy and health to many little lives that otherwise would be sad and dull. For all the wealth brought back by *The Golden 'Hynde'* will be devoted to sending poor London children away for holidays in the country" to get them out of the dirty and gloomy city atmosphere. While the editors hoped the readers would support the magazine for the joy it might bring poor children, they hoped, too, "to gain [their] interest for its own [the magazine's] sake" (1, no. 1:1–2). The editors were able to report in the second edition that seven pounds, three shillings, and seven pence were raised from sales of the first number and sent to the Children's Country Holiday Fair (1, no. 2:1).

The editors, identified only in the second number, were two young women—Beatrix Oliver and Marjorie Napier—who made the point that they were both under the age of twenty-five and hoped that the magazine would appeal to their contemporaries. Oliver was the daughter of Frederick Scott Oliver, a businessman who was also a man of letters. Interested especially in eighteenth-century history, Oliver published *The Statesman and the Bishop* in 1904 and *Alexander Hamilton* in 1906. He was involved in seeking a solution to the Irish problem through the federalization of the institutions of the United Kingdom. His one contribution to the *Golden Hynde* is a fictional conversation between upper-class Tories and Liberals in which the idea of federalization is discussed.

Political and social issues of this kind were often discussed in the publication. "The Policy of the National Service League," for example, is an article that outlines the league's belief in mandatory military service for all British males either in the regular forces or the Territorials. The league, founded in 1902, espoused peace through a strong national defense. Other articles praised the work of women's service organizations and called for more volunteers. Liberal policies and foreign missions were supported by various writers. Travel articles were featured as well. E. M. Forster's "Iron Horses in India," which describes the railroads on the subcontinent, is one such piece. Forster goes beyond the descriptive, however, as he comments on the railroad's effect on Hinduism. Once welcomed by the British as a means of breaking down caste barriers, the modern conveyances are seen by Forster as an asset to the native culture as they help increase attendance at religious gatherings. The railroad, with its first ("white-skinned and aloof"), second ("where the two races mingle"), and third ("many-coloured, brightly-clothed, and innumerable as the sand") classes, brings together all the elements of colonial society, according to the reporter.

The magazine published fiction and verse, much of it light-hearted or humorous. "Yuill Water," an adventure story by Henry Johnston, and "Homeward," a nostalgic poem by Hilaire Belloc, are examples. Political comment entered into the imaginative writing in the magazine at times. John Buchan, author of *The Thirty-Nine Steps* and other historical, poetic, and fictional works, contributed "Divus Johnson" to the *Hynde*. Told in Conrad's narrative style, the short story relates the adventures in far-off lands of Mr. Thomson, captain of a steamer, who eventually ends up in Scotland, a Liberal candidate for Parliament and a supporter of foreign missions.

The *Golden Hynde* was an entertaining, skillfully produced magazine containing work by competent authors. Its enthusiasm, optimism, and idealism were characteristic of the young generation of Britons just before the outbreak of World War I, and like many of the generation it sought to appeal to, the *Golden Hynde* became a casualty of that war.

Information Sources

INDEXES
    None.
REPRINT EDITIONS
    None.
LOCATION SOURCES
    American
        None.
    British
        Complete runs: British Museum; Cambridge University Library; Oxford University Library; Trinity College Library.

Publication History

MAGAZINE TITLE AND TITLE CHANGES
   The Golden Hynde.
VOLUME AND ISSUE DATA
   Volume 1, numbers 1–2, December 1913–June 1914.
FREQUENCY OF PUBLICATION
   Irregular.
PUBLISHERS
   Henry J. Glaisher, 55 and 57 Wigmore Street, London, W.
EDITORS
   Beatrix Oliver and Marjorie Napier.

James W. Parins

GOOD WORDS

Good Words (1860–1911) was a general magazine designed to be suitable not only for family reading but also, more specifically, for Sunday reading. At six pence per month, it cost only half as much as *Macmillan's** or the *Cornhill** and, during its best years in the 1870s, regularly sold between 80,000 and 130,000 copies per issue, which was more than any other monthly of that time. Although contributors to more intellectual magazines tended to sneer at *Good Words*, it printed illustrations by reputable artists (including Holman Hunt and J. E. Millais); articles by J. M. Ludlow, J. A. Froude, Bessie Parkes-Belloc, R. H. Hutton, and William Gladstone, as well as by clergymen; and fiction and verse from virtually all of the most popular middlebrow writers. *Good Words* records the literature of respectable bourgeois England.

The idea for *Good Words* was conceived by the young publisher Alexander Strahan at a time when Sunday was strictly observed, not only in Scotland, but also in many English households. Strahan asked Norman Macleod, one of Scotland's most eloquent preachers and later moderator of the Church of Scotland's general assembly, to edit the magazine. Their intention was to produce a periodical that would have as much variety as secular magazines and yet retain a distinctively Christian spirit, so that it could provide Sunday reading without insulting intelligent adults.

The magazine began in 1860 as an eight-page weekly (priced at three halfpence) with a decidedly religious emphasis, short essays, and a devotion for each day of the week. Full-page illustrations and serial fiction were added during the first year. At the beginning of its second year, in January 1861, *Good Words* became a monthly, usually running to seventy-two pages. In the editor's note explaining the change in format, MacLeod wrote that he wanted the magazine to "reflect the every-day life of a good man, with its times of religious thought and devotional feeling, naturally passing into others of healthy recreation, busy work, intellectual study, poetic joy, or even sunny laughter"(1:796).

When Norman Macleod died in 1872 his brother Donald Macleod, a slightly less eminent clergyman with very similar interests, took up the editorship and maintained continuity in policy and practice. In the early years each issue included some directly religious matter—a familiar sermon by a popular clergyman, a Bible commentary, an essay on Christian history or Biblical archaeology. As time passed the proportion of religious material gradually diminished and informative but undemanding articles on biography, natural history, travel, and science occupied more of the space reserved for nonfiction. Beginning in 1867 or 1868 there was an annual Christmas supplement, issued under the separate title *Good Cheer* and generally devoted to a single long story or novelette.

By the end of the century, Sunday was no longer strictly observed and "Sunday reading" had lost its unique place. *Good Words* tried a number of strategies—competitions, premiums, and so on—in an attempt to maintain circulation. By the 1890s a fair proportion of the readers were apparently English-speaking exiles in various outposts of the Empire; the stories often had colonial settings, and special Christmas numbers in 1902 and 1903 printed "Songs of Empire" and "Tales of Empire" submitted by the readers. Nearly half of the entries came from outside the British Isles.

In 1905 the magazine was sold to Harmsworth (the Amalgamated Press) and in May 1906 it was merged with Harmsworth's *Sunday Magazine* and issued weekly at a price of one penny. This version, which had much shorter articles, a simpler religious tone, collections of household hints, and advertisements for women's fashions and hair tonics, lasted until 8 April 1911.

Understanding the "distinctively Christian spirit" of *Good Words* during its most prosperous era helps to define mid-Victorian religious sentiment. Although Norman and Donald Macleod were Presbyterians, they did not use the magazine to promote any particular doctrine. Norman Macleod made his original reputation in the Church of Scotland by consistently occupying the middle ground in any heated controversy. When he accepted or commissioned material for *Good Words*, he avoided the narrow choice of subject and treatment that was typical of sectarian periodicals, but at the same time tried not to print anything that would "offend the prejudices, far more the sincere convictions and feelings of fair and reasonable Evangelical men."[1] The contributors represented various shades of belief; Macleod was guided, he said, by only one irrevocable principle: "never to accept the contributions of any writer, male or female, however talented, who is known to be anti-Christian in creed or life."[2]

Macleod's liberalism did not, of course, please evangelical extremists. The *Record* vehemently attacked *Good Words* for printing any fiction at all, and attempts were made to have it blacklisted by the tract societies because young people might be tempted to read the secular articles on Sunday. In a letter responding to one critic, Norman Macleod reiterated that *Good Words* was not designed, as most Christian periodicals were, for the young or uneducated, but rather for intelligent women and men. And he wryly suggested that "if any members of a Christian family are compelled to endure such severe and dry exercises on the Sunday as would make them long for even the scientific articles in 'Good Words,' '' they should protect themselves by locking up the magazine.[3]

But although the Macleods were not narrow in their views, both of them regarded editorship as part of their ministry and exercised care over every detail of the magazine's contents. As parish clergymen in Glasgow, both had initiated plans to improve the lot of the poor. (Norman established the first congregational penny savings-bank in Glasgow and opened refreshment rooms for working men; Donald organized women to do parish work in the Church of Scotland.) In *Good Words* they printed optimistic articles on social questions that promoted practical philanthropy; among the specific objectives were care for the children of female criminals; education for the blind; athletics for girls; prisoners' aid societies; protection of child performers; and the provision of medical women to work in India. Christian Socialists such as Charles Kingsley and J. M. Ludlow were regular contributors, and there was a deliberate effort to solicit articles from people who had first-hand experience: a judge, for example, wrote on the supervision of habitual criminals and a field officer on the problems of married soldiers.

When contacting authors, both editors were careful to state the aims of the magazine, and they sometimes indicated quite specifically what material would or would not be acceptable. In 1863 Norman Macleod asked Anthony Trollope for a novel; Trollope objected that his work was probably too worldly for *Good Words*, but Macleod persisted; and Trollope finally responded by submitting *Rachel Ray*. After careful reading and much thought—and after considering the recent attacks in the *Record*—Macleod rejected the novel. Trollope explained in his autobiography that "there is some dancing in one of the early chapters, described, no doubt, with that approval of the amusement which I have always entertained; and it was to this which my friend [Macleod] demurred.''[4]

Restrictions of that sort lessened as the century progressed; by 1875 Trollope said that he felt sure a book like *Rachel Ray* could be printed in *Good Words*. Donald Macleod, however, did continue to ask authors for permission to change unsuitable passages. In Thomas Hardy's *The Trumpet Major* (1880), for example, the day of the week on which the lovers have arranged to meet is altered from Sunday to Monday, and Trollope himself softened some language in *Kept in the Dark* when it was serialized in 1882.

This delineation of popular respectability gives the magazine a measure of significance in literary history. The fiction printed in *Good Words* was the fiction accepted for family reading by the broad mass of respectable, churchgoing people in the Victorian middle class. *Good Words* serialized Charles Kingsley's *Hereward* in 1865, Dinah Craik's *The Woman's Kingdom* in 1868, and J. M. Barrie's *The Little Minister* in 1891. It took Trollope's *Golden Lion of Granpère* after *Blackwood's Edinburgh Magazine** (see *RA*) declined it. It had novels by Margaret Oliphant and Thomas Hardy, by Amelia Edwards, Mrs. Henry Wood, Matilda Betham-Edwards, and Edna Lyell, by George MacDonald, James Payn, and John Buchan. The pages of *Good Words* index mid-cult taste at a level comparable to the *Saturday Evening Post* in the United States in the first half of the twentieth century.

Notes

1. Letter to Anthony Trollope, 11 June 1863, quoted in Michael Sadleir, *Trollope: A Commentary* (London, 1961), p. 248.

2. Donald Macleod, *Memoir of Norman Macleod, D.D.* (New York, 1876), p. 296.

3. Alexander Strahan, "Norman Macleod," *Contemporary Review* 20 (1872); reprinted in *Living Age* 114 (1872):438.

4. Anthony Trollope, *An Autobiography*, ed. Michael Sadleir and Frederick Page (Oxford, 1950), p. 188.

Information Sources

BIBLIOGRAPHY

Booth, Bradford Allen. *The Letters of Anthony Trollope.* London, 1951.
Macleod, Donald. *Memoir of Norman Macleod, D.D.* New York, 1876.
Sadleir, Michael. *Trollope: A Commentary.* London, 1961.
Smith, Sydney. *Donald Macleod of Glasgow: A Memoir and a Study.* London, 1926.
Strahan, Alexander. "Norman Macleod." *Contemporary Review* 20 (1872):291–306.
Trollope, Anthony. *An Autobiography.* Edited by Michael Sadleir and Frederick Page.
    Oxford, 1950.

INDEXES

Each volume indexed. 1860–1881 in *Poole's Index.*

REPRINT EDITIONS

Microform: Early British Periodicals (UMI), reels 300–315.

LOCATION SOURCES

American

Widely available.

British

Complete runs: British Museum; Edinburgh Public Library.

Partial runs: Birmingham Public Library; Birmingham University Library; Bradford Public Library; Cambridge University Library; Glasgow University Library; Leeds Public Library; London University Library; University of Hull Library; Victoria and Albert Museum Library.

Publication History

MAGAZINE TITLE AND TITLE CHANGES

Good Words, January 1860–April 1906. *Good Words and Sunday Magazine*, 5 May 1906–8 April 1911.

VOLUME AND ISSUE DATA

Volume 1, numbers 1–50, January–December 1860; volumes 2–47, January 1861–April 1906 (volume 47 includes November 1905–April 1906).

New series, volumes 1–10, 5 May 1906–8 April 1911.

FREQUENCY OF PUBLICATION

Weekly, January–December 1860; monthly, January 1861–April 1906; weekly, 5 May 1906–8 April 1911.

PUBLISHERS

Volumes 1–45, 1860–1904: Alexander Strahan and Company, 56 Ludgate Hill, London; William Isbister and Company, 56 Ludgate Hill; 15 and 16 Tavistock Street, London. Volume 46, January–October 1905: Sir Isaac Pitman and Sons, 1 Amen Corner, London. Volume 47–new series, volume 10, November 1905– 8 April 1911: Amalgamated Press, Carmelite House, London.

EDITORS

Norman Macleod, 1860–June 1872. Donald Macleod, July 1872–April 1906. Donald Macleod and Hartley Aspden, 1906–1907. No editor listed, 1907–1911.

Sally Mitchell

GRANTA, THE

The *Granta* emerged in 1889 as the newest in a long line of undergraduate journals at Cambridge. The first journal produced at the university, following Oxford's *Student** (see *AAAJ*) and its successor, the *Oxford and Cambridge Miscellany*, was the *Reformer* of 1776. However, it was not until the *Snob* that a publication was wholly controlled by students, *in statu pupillari*. From 1830 onwards undergraduate magazines flourished at Cambridge: the *Freshman*, the *Fellow*, the *Individual*, the *Tripos*, the *Sizar*, the *Realm*, and even an earlier *Granta* which was suppressed as too "scurrilous and obscene for publication."[1] By far the most important literary journal of the middle of the century was William Morris's *Oxford and Cambridge Magazine*,* which lasted only twelve months, but published the Pre-Raphaelites Edward Burne-Jones and Dante Gabriel Rossetti. In the 1880s arose, and almost as quickly subsided, a flurry of small undergraduate publications—the *Meteor*, the *True Blue*, the *Blue 'Un*— including the *Cambridge University Magazine* and the *Cambridge Fortnightly*, edited by Barry Pain, later one of the *Granta*'s leading writers. Most notable, however, was the emergence in 1879 of the *Cambridge Review*,* the one publication that outlasted all the others.[2]

The origins of the *Granta* are bound up with another journal of the period, a humorous weekly entitled the *Gadfly*. The first issue of *Granta*'s predecessor contained a rather disgraceful article on Oscar Browning, a fellow of King's College. Because of the essay, Browning managed to get the magazine suppressed by the university. The editor, Murray Guthrie, soon planned another journal, to be published in London, outside of university jurisdiction. Guthrie's new journal was without a name until in a chance interview with Browning he happened to learn that the don was planning to start an educational magazine to be called the *Granta*, an ancient name for the river Cam. Smarting under the knowledge that Browning was responsible for the destruction of his first magazine, Guthrie immediately registered *his* new one under the title of *Granta*, thereby denying Browning the use of the name.[3]

To describe the *Granta* as an undergraduate humor magazine is to do it a disservice. Unlike most ephemeral collegiate journals, it was topical and had a distinctive style, one that provided it with continuity from issue to issue. Unlike most other university publications, the *Granta* was not short-lived; with brief interruptions for two world wars, the magazine has survived up to modern times. The period from its founding in 1889 to the outbreak of the 1914–1918 war marks a special time not only for the journal but for the life at Cambridge which it reflected. Aside from the question of whether women should be allowed to take degrees, which was widely debated in the late 1890s, the most serious topic for the *Granta* contributors seems to have been to rag eccentric dons and those undergraduates who were too "keen" about their academic work. Although academic life in late Victorian and Edwardian Cambridge was experiencing rapid and substantial change, largely due to the rising importance of science in the curriculum, the *Granta*, at least, seemed to stand still and reflect an earlier period. Light verse, parodies of eminent Victorian writers, and attacks on the university powers bear the gentility and humor of another age. Unlike the *Granta* published between the wars or after World War II, before 1914 there was little about politics, religion, or the affairs of the world that graced its pages. Even the design of the cover remained relatively constant, changing little from 1895 until 1902.

The general format of the *Granta* was established with its first issue. The cover was designed from a bookplate of the poet Frederick Locker-Lampson and contained a jester, a symbol that the three editors thought appropriate for a humor magazine. Inside there was a three-color cartoon of the Master of Trinity, Dr. Butler, and the promise that each issue would provide a similar caricature, which turned into the popular series "Those in Authority" in which various Cambridge worthies were featured. Among the "Authorities" treated over the years were Edward VII, Rupert Brooke, Sir Arthur Quiller-Couch, R. C. Lehmann, J. M. Keynes, Arthur Balfour, F. M. Cornford, E. F. Benson, and Lord Kitchener. Two other columns appeared in the first issue which remained fixtures, the "Motley Notes" and the "Rowing Notes." In addition to such fixtures, a typical issue might contain light verse, often a literary parody or of local topical interest; portions of a serial of undergraduate life; information from the "Oxford Correspondent"; and the weekly doings of the various Cambridge colleges that had representatives to send in such material. The price was one shilling per copy and the magazine was to be published once a week during the term. During the first five terms, issues were printed in London so that the *Granta* should not be associated with the *Gadfly* and so that any attempts to suppress it would be minimized. From the beginning the journal was a success.[4]

One reason the *Granta* survived where similar literary efforts did not was the audacity of the editors during that first term. They not only contrived to get the journal discussed at the first Union debate, but they also ran a sabbath-breaking campaign against a university edict forbidding students to travel on Sundays, which shocked the academic community since it was unheard of for an undergraduate magazine to question the decisions of the university authorities. The editors increased the brashness of their fledgling journal by wading into college politics when the *Granta* took sides in the current election of the new dean at King's. The magazine received considerable publicity and the author of the articles was ducked in the King's Fountain. In nine weeks and in as many issues the *Granta* had become a journal of note, a thing to be reckoned with in university life. The May term went equally well. The price was dropped to six pence and the circulation doubled. At the end of June, R. C. Lehmann took over as editor for what was to be nearly the next six years.

Most new magazines begin publication with a heady sense of optimism, and the *Granta* was no exception. The opening number announced itself with a general greeting to the university community, took the first swipe at the *Cambridge Review*, and fired salvos at most of the major groups of the undergraduate society. By the third issue the editors were quoting George Trevelyan to the effect that if a university periodical got into a third number that was an instance of longevity. The *Granta* provided an alternative to the sober reflections of the *Review*—which rarely permitted itself a glimpse of humor—and furnished its readers with a genial view of undergraduate life, as well as an outlet for gentle complaint against the university authorities and community. That its reputation spread beyond the confines of Cambridge may be confirmed by the number of *Granta* contributors who later went on to serve on the staff of *Punch*.* At one time the connections were so strong that one wag described *Punch* as the London *Granta*. Among those who served on both journals were W. A. Darlington, Norman Davey, Anthony C. Deane, Charles Geake, Anstey Guthrie, H. S. Vere Hodge, R. P. Keigwin, F. O. Langley, R. C. Lehmann, Archibald Marshall, A. A. Milne, Barry Pain, Owen Seaman, A. A. Sykes, D. P. Turner, and P. Whitwell. It soon became obvious that a good training ground for budding humorists was on the staff of the *Granta*.

As with all undergraduate journals, the quality of the material fluctuated with the editors and the ever-changing student population. Certainly the early years from 1889 to 1895 produced the most distinguished group of contributors. The presence of A. A. Milne, who edited the *Granta* during the Lent and May terms of 1902, is proof that the journal still turned out established men of letters after 1895; but the fact remains that the initial "Lehmann years" were outstanding.[5] The writers working on the journal during this period and in the years immediately following produced a number of well-received books based on their *Granta* material. Barry Pain's *In a Canadian Canoe*, Owen Seaman's *Horace at Cambridge*, Archibald Marshall's *Peter Binney: Undergraduate*, E. F. Benson's *The Bake, B.A.*, and Lehmann's *In Cambridge Courts* all were based in part, if not wholly, on the contributions these writers had made to the *Granta*.[6] In addition, *Granta* writers were routinely anthologized in such collections as Theodore Cook's *An Anthology of Humorous Verse* and E. E. Kellett's *A Book of Cambridge Verse*.[7] The influence of the early issues of the magazine extended well beyond the narrow society of academic Cambridge.

If the editors after the turn of the century did not exhibit the audacity to pull another Math Tripos scoop of 1892—where by dint of an enormous intellectual effort the *Granta*, which appeared each Saturday morning, published the results of the set questions of the Problem Papers released the preceding Friday morning— the general quality of the journal remained high. Each succeeding anniversary was celebrated with a banquet of old contributors, often supplemented by such distinguished guests as G. K. Chesterton and Arthur Conan Doyle. Before officially ceasing to publish for the duration of World War I, the magazine was able to mark its twenty-fifth year. The journal was on a firm footing in the spring of 1914 and had even evolved a legal process by which the editors were to assume control and which replaced the rather quaint but basically haphazard method of passing on the editorship by merely signing the Agreement of Indemnity. At R. C. Lehmann's suggestion the process of electing succeeding editors and transferring the proprietorship was established by legal document. When the *Granta* resumed publication after the war it was to do so under much more professional circumstances.

The *Granta* of 1914 was a much different magazine from the fledgling journal of the 1890s. Gone were the days when the editorship appeared to be a sinecure of Trinity (between 1900 and 1907). By 1914 the editors and contributors were drawn from every college in the university and the editor was never at a loss for a successor or in want of material. Looking back on those days it is possible to lament the loss of the inspired amateurism that seemed to sustain the *Granta* through so many years of precarious existence. By 1918 the atmosphere of Cambridge, as well as of England itself, had changed profoundly. The *Granta*, which resumed publication as the universities resumed full operations, was markedly different from its prewar predecessor. Some of the light-heartedness, the gentleness, was gone. The youth of the *Granta* passed with the coming of the modern world. In many ways the contributors to the journal have been more distinguished, as a whole, since the war, and the *Granta* was perceived as a stepping-stone to a profession in writing. The diffidence that had characterized so much of the material in the *Granta*, as indeed it had characterized undergraduate life in general, was replaced by a new earnestness that culminated in the issues of the 1930s.

It is significant that among the first traditions to be revived at Cambridge after the dreary days of the war was the university humor magazine. The audacity of youth would once again be served. Perhaps it was because of their experiences in the war and the deaths of so many of their fellow *Granta* contributors that the "Old Contributors" looked back on their years at university with such nostalgia. To those who had survived the fighting and dying, the days of the *Granta* indeed must have seemed, as they did for A. A. Milne, a magical period of eternal youth.

Notes

1. F. A. Rice, comp., *"The Granta" and Its Contributors, 1889-1914* (London, 1924), p. 2. Rice's historical sketch of the *Granta* of this period provides a comprehensive

overview of the magazine from its beginnings to 1914. A. A. Milne, "Introduction" to *"The Granta" and Its Contributors*, p. xii. Charles Stuart Calverley came to Christ's from Balliol at Oxford. In the 1860s he published an influential series of parodies of eminent Victorian poets.

2. For a history of Cambridge magazines see Henry Curry Marillier, *University Magazines and Their Makers* (London, 1902).

3. See Oscar Browning, *"The Granta," Cambridge Review*, 24 January 1889, p. 158.

4. There is a certain irony that in the mid-1850s the *Granta* was suppressed for offending the authorities and was published from London under the name of the *Gadfly* until it was restored to official status in Cambridge. See Thom Gunn's article in *My Oxford: My Cambridge: Memories of University Life by Twenty-four Distinguished Graduates*, ed. Ann Thwaite and Ronald Hayman (New York, 1979), p. 356.

5. Lehmann actually went down in 1890 to join the staff of *Punch* and edited the journal with the aid of his "Cambridge staff," with whom he met at weekly Thursday evening dinners to plan the following issue.

6. Barry Pain, *In a Canadian Canoe: The Nine Muses Minus One and Other Stories* (London, 1891); Owen Seaman, *Horace at Cambridge* (London, 1895); Archibald Marshall, *Peter Binney: Undergraduate* (London, 1899); E. F. Benson, *The Bake, B.A.: Being the Uneventful History of a Young Gentleman at Cambridge University* (London, 1896); R. C. Lehmann, *In Cambridge Courts: Studies of University Life in Prose and Verse* (London, 1891).

7. Theodore A. Cook, ed., *An Anthology of Humorous Verse* (London, 1902); Ernest Edward Kellett, ed., *A Book of Cambridge Verse* (Cambridge, England, 1911).

Information Sources

BIBLIOGRAPHY

Browning, Oscar. *Memories of Sixty Years at Eton, Cambridge, and Elsewhere*. London, 1910.

Cook, Sir Theodore A., ed. *An Anthology of Humorous Verse*. London, 1902.

Kellett, Ernest Edward, ed. *A Book of Cambridge Verse*. Cambridge, England, 1911.

Lehmann, R. C. *In Cambridge Courts: Studies of University Life in Prose and Verse*. London, 1891.

Leslie, Shane. *The Film of Memory*. London, 1938.

———. *Mark Sykes: His Life and Letters*. London, 1923.

Marillier, Henry Currie. *University Magazines and Their Makers*. London, 1902.

Philip, Jim, John Simpson, and Nicholas Snowman, eds. *The Best of "Granta."* London, 1967.

Rice, F. A., comp. *"The Granta" and Its Contributors, 1889–1914*. London, 1924.

INDEXES

Each volume indexed.

REPRINT EDITIONS

None.

LOCATION SOURCES

American

Partial runs: Indiana University Library; New York Public Library; University of Minnesota Library; Yale University Library.

British
> Complete runs: Bodleian Library; Trinity College Library, Cambridge; University Library, Cambridge.
> Partial runs: Birmingham University Library; British Museum; St. John's College Library, Cambridge.

Publication History

MAGAZINE TITLE AND TITLE CHANGES
> *The Granta.*

VOLUME AND ISSUE DATA
> Volumes 1–66, numbers 1–1219, 18 January 1889–9 June 1962. (Hiatus during World Wars I and II.) New series, volumes 1–, numbers 1–, Michaelmas 1980–.

FREQUENCY OF PUBLICATION
> Weekly during Michaelmas, Lent, and May terms (October to June).

PUBLISHERS
> Lent 1889–May 1890: King, Sell and Railton, Ltd., 4 Bolt Court, Fleet Street, London. Michaelmas 1890–May 1914: W. P. Spaulding, Cambridge. June 1914–: unknown.

EDITORS
> Term, rotating editorship among students, who have included: Melville Balfour, 1899–1900. G. T. Boag, 1905. George Stewart Bowles, 1899–1900. K. M. Chance, 1900. L. S. Chanler, 1895. Norman Davey, 1909–1910. J. F. Dobson, 1899. M. D. Forbes, 1911–1912. K. J. Freeman, 1903. Dermot Freyer, 1912–1913. Denis Garstin, 1912. Charles Geake, 1889–1895. E. M. Gull, 1903–1904. Murray Guthrie, 1889. R.S.T. Haslehurst, 1906–1907. P.A.G. d'Hauteville, 1896–1897. H. S. Ver Hodge, 1902. Lionel Holland, 1889. F.M.H. Holman, 1911. Lord Howick, 1900. Clement Jones, 1901–1902. R. C. Lehmann, 1889–1895. Oliver Locker-Lampson, 1900. F. H. Lucas, 1899. H. G. Mackeurton, 1904–1905. R. P. Mahaffy, 1889–1895. J. H. Mandelberg, 1906–1907. C.F.G. Masterman, 1898–1899. A. A. Milne, 1902. E. S. Montagu, 1900–1901. G. W. Morrice, 1903, 1904. R. M. Pattison Muir, 1907–1908. E. A. Newton, 1889–1895. E. B. Noel, 1900. John Norman, 1914. W. M. Pryor, 1900. C. E. Raven, 1907–1908. C. S. Rewcastle, 1909. B. Fletcher Robinson, 1889–1895. C. H. Rodwell, 1896–1897. J.R.P. Sclater, 1899. Edward Shanks, 1912–1913. Raglan Somerset, 1908–1909. J. B. Sterndale-Bennett, 1910. J. C. Stobart, 1901. Eustace Talbot, 1895–1896. J. E. Harold Terry, 1905–1906. C. H. Tremlett, 1897–1898. A. C. Turner, 1902–1903. V. Whitaker, 1909. St. J. B. Wynne Willson, 1895. P. Whitwell Wilson, 1897. Harold Wright, 1909–1911.

Charles L. P. Silet

GREEN SHEAF, THE

In December 1902 W. B. Yeats wrote to Lady Gregory that a young American artist living in London was about to bring out a magazine for which he had conceived the idea. To be called the *Hour-Glass* (after his play by that name) and with a preface by him, the magazine was to be consecrated to the pictorial and written descriptions of life as its contributors would have it be. "Nothing is to be let in unless it tells of something that seems beautiful or charming or in some other way desirable," he wrote. Contributors "are not to touch the accursed Norwegian cloud in any way, even though they may be all good Ibsenites, and they are not to traffic in Gorky,"[1] No magazine called the *Hour-Glass* appeared, but the young American artist Yeats wrote about, Pamela Colman Smith, did come out with a slight and lovely periodical about which hovers the spirit of make-believe Yeats alluded to. Instead of a preface by Yeats, there is one by Smith—a versified editorial statement accompanied by a colored drawing, both of which appear on the cover of each issue of the *Green Sheaf*. The drawing is of gathered green strips of paper, and the verse transforms Yeats's distinction between happy and gloomy art into a more traditional distinction between instruction and entertainment. The *Green Sheaf* will be concerned with the latter:

> My *Sheaf* is small . . . but it is green.
> I will gather into my *Sheaf* all the young fresh things I can—
> *pictures, verses, ballads*, of *love* and *war*; tales of *pirates* and
> the *sea*.
> You will find ballads of the *old world* in my *Sheaf*. Are they not
> green for ever . . .
> Ripe ears are *good* for *bread*, but green ears are good for *pleasure*.

Pictures, poems and tales: such were to be the sheaves of Smith's magazine. There was to be no criticism or reviews of art or writing, and no attention to political or social events of the time. Smith's verse statement, quoted in its entirety above, is all that ever appears in the magazine that may be considered explanatory commentary on this or any other artistic endeavor. The *Green Sheaf* is a collection of imaginative pieces intended primarily to evoke or testify to experiences beyond reality, including examples of what Yeats hoped would be cheerful and desirable experiences, and examples of more fearful fantasies as well.

The contents of the *Green Sheaf* point to the artistically formative years of its energetic and variously talented editor as well as to important events in British cultural history at the turn of the century. Having been born in the United States in 1877 or 1878 and raised in Jamaica, Smith as a very young woman traveled with a Lyceum (London) Theater troupe during the last years that Ellen Terry and Henry Irving worked together as artistic directors of what was to be remembered as an extraordinary series of provincial tours.[2] If Ibsen and Gorky represented one aspect of artistic development of the time, the Pre-Raphaelites and their followers represented another. The latter group, according to one contributor to the *Green Sheaf*, John Masefield, "ruled that time."[3] It was probably with the Lyceum troupe that Smith came under the direct influence of

Burne-Jones, a friend of Terry and Irving and a consultant to the troupe on matters relating to costuming and set design.

Of more than sixty hand-colored drawings appearing in *Green Sheaf*, nearly half bear Smith's initials, and of these, most suggest the influence of Rossetti and his followers: attenuated and often elaborately costumed human forms, generous use of plant and flower motifs, brilliantly contrasted colors. From her association with the Lyceum troupe Smith probably learned a great deal concerning the possible integration of art forms, one of the informing ideals of the Pre-Raphaelites. The interplay of art forms becomes, in the *Green Sheaf*, an editorial imperative. On occasion, a drawing or a prose piece will appear in isolation, but clearly Smith's intent was as often as possible to provide the reader with an experience deriving from different modes of expression, to lead the reader to consider visual and verbal contributions as mutually enlarging. Smith's work with the Lyceum troupe prepared her to be most sympathetic to Yeats's hope of recovering ancient associations of the arts, to have "the painter painting what the poet has written, the musician setting the poet's words to simple airs."[4] Smith's many written contributions to the *Green Sheaf* do little to establish her as a poet, but they do indicate her dedication to the reciprocity of art forms and, more particularly, her interest in book illustration. Two or three years before *Green Sheaf*, Smith prepared what she considered to be her most successful artistic effort to date, illustrations for *Little Charles*, a children's book for which she failed to secure a publisher. In all probability three illustrated prose selections appearing in the *Green Sheaf* are taken from that work: one is dated 1901, when Smith was at work on *Little Charles*. Two of the prose selections (by Mrs. Barbauld) are but a few sentences long, and each of these is a woman's address to young children (no. 4:2, no. 9:6). The third prose passage by Mrs. Barbauld consists of a dialogue between a fisherman and young Charles ("Charles at the Seaside," no. 13:4–5). The colored drawings are typical of illustrations of children's books of the time: comfortable middle-class interiors, romanticized seascape, cherubic children. Smith's disappointment with commercial publishing marked the beginning of a very different period in her artistic life, which owed much to her experience earlier with the Lyceum troupe and perhaps more to her association with Yeats and others of his group in such organizations as the Rosicrucian Hermetic Order of the Golden Dawn, the Masquers' Society, the Irish Literary Society, and the Abbey Theatre. Like Yeats, Smith seems to have found the association with artistic groups appealing and profitable.

The *Green Sheaf* is, in fact, a repository of contributions from friends and acquaintances of Smith's who had formed artistic groups. Her early theatrical experience provided her with a number of important contributions for her magazine. Christopher St. John (pseudonym of Christabel Marshall), a close friend of Ellen Terry and her daughter, Ellen Craig, and editor of the Shaw-Terry correspondence as well as of Terry's memoirs, contributed to the *Green Sheaf* a number of pieces notable for their dark representation of the imaginative or dream life: a two-part narrative (with a colored illustration by Smith) of a medieval knight's arduous journey to his death as he tries to fulfill the command given him in a dream to seek the Princess of the North ("How Master Constans Went to the North," no. 1:6, and no. 2:12–13); a poetic narrative of a descent to hell—dedicated to Gorky ("A Ballad of a Night Refugee," no. 3:10); a brief excerpt from *The Good Hope*, a play by the Dutch playwright and novelist Herman Heijermans, in which Ellen Terry was eventually to play the unlikely role of an old peasant woman ("Cobus on Death," no. 6:12);[5] and an account of recurring dreams of violence ("The Gray Coat: A Dream," no. 8:8–9). Terry's son, Edward Gordon Craig, gave up a promising career as an actor to devote himself to other theatrical pursuits. Before leaving England for a distinguished career on the Continent as a stage designer and theatrical producer—he designed the set for Stanislavsky's *Hamlet* at the Art Theater in Moscow, for example— he collaborated with musician Martin Shaw, founder of the Purcell Operatic Society, on *The Masque of Love*, form Purcell's *Dioclesian*, and on *Dido and Aeneas*.[6] There appears in the *Green Sheaf* a description of another masque that Shaw and Craig apparently were advertising, based on a sixteenth-century ceremony of English harvest, with folk music accompaniment and featuring dance and song by Purcell ("A Masque: The Harvest Home," no. 3:2–3). There also appears a musical score arranged by Shaw (with illustration by Smith) for a song "given to John Masefield by Wally Blair, A.B." ("Spanish Ladies," no. 3:6–7).

In 1902 the Lyceum was closed as a legitimate theater, despite the best efforts of Henry Irving and others to keep it open. The next year, just two years before his death, Irving appeared as Dante in a scenario by that name written by Victorien Sardou.[7] Readers of the *Green Sheaf* doubtless understood allusions to those events in the otherwise puzzling narrative by Mary Brown, which is a Lyceum rodent's account of the appearance in the abandoned theater of characters played by Irving and their appeal to Dante that he continue his creative work ("The Lament of a Lyceum Rat," no. 5:8). Two colored illustrations by Smith accompany this piece, one of which is a large and powerfully conceived portrait of four characters in medieval costume.

Most of the identifiable contributors to the *Green Sheaf* are artists whom Smith met when she took up residence in London at the turn of the century. At Yeats's famous Monday evenings at 18, Woburn Bldgs., there gathered, among others, Lady Gregory, A. E., Synge, and Masefield, all of whom contributed to Smith's magazine. Smith, too, received artist friends at weekly "at-homes," and drew on those social occasions for advice on, and contributions to, her magazine. Artistic influences are acknowledged in a few contributions (for example, a reproduction of a drawing of Mrs. Sterling by Rossetti, offered as a supplement to no. 3; and brief passages from Blake and Keats, with uncolored illustrations by W. T. Horton, no. 2:2, and no. 6:11). William Horton's mystical drawings appeared in a number of small magazines of the time, and his work was important in Yeats's conception of "Symbolism in Painting."[8] One of Yeats's two contributions to the *Green Sheaf* is a pastel of "The Lake at Coole" (supplement to no. 4), probably one of two pastels Masefield was to remember seeing in Yeats's apartment when friends gathered to discuss art, to read their works, and to listen to tales "of strange things done by magicians in simpler lands than this"—including, probably, Jamaican folktales that Smith often recited at social gatherings.[9] "The Lake at Coole" is done in silvered grays and blues, and is a horizontal swath of sky, land, and water suggestive of early evening. Masefield contributed three relatively substantial pieces to the *Green Sheaf*, including one of its longest prose narratives—about twenty-five hundred words—about a sea captain who outwits the devil and thereby saves one of his sailors with whom the devil made a pact many years before ("A Deep Sea Yarn," with colored illustration by Smith, no. 6:4–9), and a poetic monologue of the lone and blind survivor of a treasure burial at Muertos ("Blind Man's Vigil," with colored illustration by Smith, no. 7:4–5). The latter contribution may have been inspired by "the nightly presence of a blind man" who offered small items for sale near Yeats's rooms, where Masefield often attended Monday evenings.[10]

Jack Yeats, with whom Smith earlier collaborated on *A Broad Sheet*, provided Smith with a colored drawing, an illustration for a St. Stephen's Day verse describing the custom of carrying a furze with wrens nested in it ("The wren! The wren!" no. 10:2). In addition to a lyric ("Reconcilement," no. 3:8) and a prose narrative ("A Dream of Angus Oge," with a colored illustration by Smith and a delicately arranged pair of sleeping nudes by Lewis Grant, no. 4:4–7), A. E. provided *Green Sheaf* with his drama, *Deirdre*, which had been produced the year before by the Irish National Dramatic Company along with Yeats's *Kathleen Ni Houlihan* (supplement to no. 7, with large colored illustrations, one by Smith and one by Cecil French); one of the directors of the Irish Dramatic Company, W. G. Fay, credited *Deirdre* with having begun the national drama movement in Ireland.[11] Also by A. E. is a colored pencil drawing ("A Million Years Hence," supplement to no. 2), perhaps the last in a series of symbolic drawings described by his close friend, John Eglinton (pseudonym of Irish essayist William Kirkpatrick Magee), as illustrations of mankind's history from its beginning to its dissolution.[12] "A Million Years Hence" presents a desolate landscape: a human figure sits on an enormous human skull contemplating the setting sun; and in the shadow of the plateau on which the skull rests are three other human figures, a woman holding an infant, and another child nearby. Lady Gregory's contributions to the *Green Sheaf* are a seven-sentence passage from a translation of Raferty, an Irish peasant poet of the early nineteenth century ("The Hill of Heart's Desire," with colored landscape by Smith, no. 1:3), and a much longer translation of an Irish story concerning the dream and song of a young suitor ("Cael and Credhe," with colored illustration by Smith, no. 5:3–5).

Perhaps the most interesting number of the *Green Sheaf* is the second. Of ten written pieces appearing in its sixteen folio pages, eight have to do with dream as the source of imaginative power and of mysteriously allusive experience. A colored drawing of a human face peering directly at the reader introduces the number and accompanies a prose passage from Blake in which the world of imagination is identified as the world of eternity (no. 2:2). An illustration by Smith accompanies a poem by "Lucilla," in which the moment of death is contemplated as a time of collecting one's memories of life as one prepares for "death's long dark, where we must go" ("At Departing," no. 2:3). London patron and artist Cecil French provides an illustration and poem in which dream is characterized as troublesome unrest ("A Prayer to the Lords of Dream," no. 2:4). Smith provides a precisely literal illustration of a brief, image-filled prose account of a death dream ("Once, in a dream, I saw a great church," no. 2:5). Then follow three unillustrated prose accounts of variously terrifying dreams, by Yeats, Synge, and Masefield. Yeats's dream is of the day of the world's end, in a city that reminds him of Paris, and of his flight to the countryside where he eventually awakes in terror ("Dream of the World's End," no. 2:6–7). Synge recounts the movement in drama from ecstasy to rage to agony as he tries unsuccessfully to refrain from dancing to insistent music ("A Dream of Inishman," no. 2:8–9). And Masefield tells of awakening in "the bright consciousness of vision" and of becoming part of the harmony of universal creation ("Jan a Dreams," no. 2:9–10). These powerfully wrought dream descriptions are followed by a simple uncolored seascape by Horton ("La Tranquillita," no. 2:11); the concluding part of Master Constans's voyage to death in the icy north ("How Master Constans Went to the North," no. 2:12–13); and a poem on the reluctance of a group of children to go to bed, framed by a rectangular colored drawing, both by Dorothy P. Ward ("Too Early to Bed—A Lament," no. 2:14). Of the thirteen numbers of the *Green Sheaf* that appeared, this number comes closest to suggesting the richness of texture and the intricacy of artistic interplay that Smith seems to have striven for throughout the magazine's brief life. Neither the contraries of happy and gloomy dream nor the contraries of instruction and entertainment that Yeats and Smith associated with the magazine suggests sufficiently the complex web of motifs that this number weaves. Here, artistic interplay is not limited to one written and one accompanying pictorial presentation: from the first page, with Horton's visual confrontation of the reader, to the last, with Ward's childhood lament on leaving consciousness, each contribution appears to assume a meaningful place in the larger context of the issue.

Six of the thirteen numbers of the *Green Sheaf* were issued with supplements, including the above-mentioned drawings by A. E. and Rossetti and pastel by Yeats, and A. E.'s *Deirdre*. Supplements carry two other accounts of personal and terrifying dreams. Irish poet and friend of Yeats, John Todhunter, recounts a "serial dream" that tormented him for years, concerning a fifteenth-century painting of the crucifixion and his attempt to escape both the painter and the event dramatized in the painting ("An Uncanny Dream," supplement to no. 9). In the last supplement, Todhunter offers the reader what he claims is an accurate dream account dictated to him by Frederick York-Powell, regius professor of modern history, whose death in 1904 occasioned this special supplement. The dream is one of violence and unexplained terrors surrounding an old man in a country house ("A Horror of the House of Dreams," supplement to no. 13:1–3). Accompanying this last prose account are a tipped-in drawing of York-Powell by Jack Yeats and a memorial essay by Todhunter ("Frederick York-Powell: A Reminiscence," supplement to no. 13). York-Powell had provided the *Green Sheaf* with a translation of a lyric by the twelfth-century troubadour Gerald of Bornelh ("The Dawn Song," no. 10:3), and Todhunter contributed two poems ("A May Madrigal," no. 5:7, and "The Nameless Ones," no. 12:7).

Besides Smith, Masefield, Horton, and Todhunter, frequent contributors to the *Green Sheaf* include Cecil French, who provided illustrations and verses, often together ("The Parting of the Ways," no. 1:5; "A Prayer to the Lord of Dreams," no. 2:4; "The Waters of the Moon," no. 6:14). Alix Egerton's numerous contributions include "The Lament of the Dead Knight" (no. 3:4); "The Calling Voice" (no. 7:3); "My Lady of Pain," (no. 9:4–5); "Memory" (no. 11:7); and "A Song of the Night" (no. 12:3). Dorothy P. Ward contributed poems with her own illustrations ("The Changed World," no. 11:2; "Around the World Is Spread the Sea," no. 13:2). Japanese-born Yone Noguchi provided the *Green Sheaf* with three poems: "The Violet" (no. 11:2), and "Evening" and "Mugen (Without Words)" (no. 12:4). American writer and literary executor of Mark Twain, Albert Bigelow Paine, whom Smith met in the late 1890s, when she returned to New York and studied art at the Pratt Institute in Brooklyn, provided a prose piece concerning two children who happily await a boat that will take them "to a fairy land that lies through the gates of evening, where all our dreams become realities, and all our realities dreams" ("The Boat of Dreams," no. 9:7).

There were to have been thirteen numbers of the *Green Sheaf* published each year (see back sheet of each issue). Thirteen numbers were published beginning at an unspecified time in 1903 and ending sometime in 1904. The magazine sold for thirteen pence per copy, a modest price for eight or, less often, sixteen pages of handsomely printed contributions and hand-colored drawings. But it was a price that may have forbidden further publication, especially given the apparent unpredictability of the quality of artistic execution with each issue. Beginning with the ninth number, each issue consists of only eight pages, and the number of contributions from distinguished artists diminishes. The supplements are of special interest and worth, but they appeared irregularly. Before its appearance, Yeats had foreseen that Smith's publication would probably not enjoy a long life.[13] It was, after all, a time of many small publications, and competition was doubtless keen. It began more grandly than it ended. The artistic worth of the *Green Sheaf* is uneven: there are far too many verses by its editors and too many drawings and poems by the likes of Cecil French and Alix Egerton. But as a brief periodical endeavor with artistic and historical associations of a most lively time in and around London, it deserves attention.

Notes

1. *Letters of W. B. Yeats*, ed. Allan Wade (London, 1954), p. 389.
2. Melinda Boyd Parsons, *To All Believers—The Art of Pamela Colman Smith* (Philadelphia, 1975), unnumbered pages. Virtually all the available biographical information

on this little-known artist is taken from this book, which is an illustrated catalogue for an exhibit of Smith's drawings and paintings at the Delaware Art Museum and the Princeton University Art Museum in 1975.

    3. John Masefield, *So Long to Learn* (New York, 1952), p. 84.

    4. W. B. Yeats, *Essays and Introductions* (New York, 1961), p. ix.

    5. Ellen Terry, *The Story of My Life* (London, 1908), p. 257.

    6. Edward Gordon Craig, *Index to the Story of My Days: Some Memoirs* (New York, 1957), pp. 222–32, 246–300.

    7. Austin Brereton, *The Life of Henry Irving* (New York, 1908), 1:306–11.

    8. Joseph Hone, *W. B. Yeats, 1865–1939* (New York, 1943), p. 161.

    9. Masefield, p. 108.

   10. Ibid., p. 104.

   11. W. G. Fay and Catherine Carswell, *The Fays of the Abbey Theater: An Autobiographical Record* (New York, 1935), pp. 115, 121.

   12. John Eglinton [William Kirkpatrick Magee], *A Memoir of A. E. (George William Russell)* (London, 1937), p. 61.

   13. Yeats, *Letters*, p. 389.

Information Sources

BIBLIOGRAPHY

Brereton, Austin. *The Life of Henry Irving.* 2 vols. New York, 1908.

Craig, Edward Gordon. *Ellen Terry and Her Secret Life.* London, n.d.

————. *Index to the Story of My Days: Some Memoirs.* New York, 1957.

Eglinton, John [William Kirkpatrick Magee]. *A Memoir of A. E.* London, 1937.

Fay, W. G., and Catherine Carswell. *The Fays of the Abbey Theater: An Autobiographical Record.* New York, 1935.

Hone, Joseph. *W. B. Yeats, 1865–1939.* New York, 1943.

Letters of W. B. Yeats. Edited by Allan Wade. London, 1954.

Letters to W. B. Yeats. Edited by Richard J. Finneran, George M. Harper, and William M. Murphy. 2 vols. London, 1977.

Masefield, John. *So Long to Learn.* New York, 1952.

Parsons, Melinda Boyd. *To All Believers—The Art of Pamela Colman Smith.* Philadelphia, 1975.

Terry, Ellen. *The Story of My Life.* London, 1908.

Yeats, W. B. *Essays and Introductions.* New York, 1961.

INDEXES
None.

REPRINT EDITIONS
None.

LOCATION SOURCES

American

    Complete runs: Dartmouth College Library; Harvard University Library; Henry E. Huntington Library; Princeton University Library; University of Buffalo Library; University of Minnesota Library; Yale University Library.

    Partial runs: Newberry Library; New York Public Library.

British

    None.

Publication History

MAGAZINE TITLE AND TITLE CHANGES
   The Green Sheaf.
VOLUME AND ISSUE DATA
   Numbers 1–13, with supplements to numbers 2, 3, 4, 7, 9, and 13; 1903–1904
   (months unspecified).
FREQUENCY OF PUBLICATION
   Thirteen numbers a year.
PUBLISHER
   Pamela Colman Smith, 14, Milborne Grove, The Boltons, London, S.W.
EDITOR
   Pamela Colman Smith.

Carol de Saint Victor

──── H ────

HOBBY HORSE, THE

Herbert Percy Horne, editor of the *Hobby Horse*, was an architect, designer, poet, and art collector; but most important of all, he was a founding member of the Century Guild, a group of artists who banded together to promote their work and to encourage the appreciation of "crafts" as an art form. Formed in 1882, the Century Guild of Artists was strongly influenced by the work of William Morris and included among its members Horne; Arthur Mackmurdo, a young architect who was also to be instrumental in founding the Home Arts and Industrial Association; Selwyn Image, artist; Benjamin Creswick, sculptor; Clement Heaton, designer and craftsman in stained glass and metals; and George Esling and Kellock Brown, both metalworkers. Two nonmembers closely associated with the guild were William De Morgan, creator of pottery and tiles, and George Heywood Sumner, designer, painter, and etcher. When the guild was formed, the stated aim was "to render all branches of art the sphere no longer of the tradesman but of the artist. It would restore building, decoration, glass-painting, pottery, woodcarving, and metal to their right place beside painting and sculpture."[1]

One means that the Century Guild utilized that set them apart from other such arts organizations in England was the publication of a little magazine of their own: the *Century Guild Hobby Horse*. The first issue appeared in April 1884, and it continued as an annual publication thereafter from 1886, the year of volume 1, until 1892, with the publication of volume 7. The *Century Guild Hobby Horse* was published in quarto size at the Chiswick Press by J. Kegan Paul; Mackmurdo edited the April 1884 issue, shared the editorial responsibilities with Horne for the 1886 issue, and abdicated in favor of Horne as sole editor for the issues printed from 1887 through 1892. When the *Century Guild Hobby Horse* ceased publication, a new series simply entitled the *Hobby Horse* appeared in 1893.

This new publication was also edited by Herbert Horne, and was published by the Bodley Head Press.

Only the year of publication appears on the covers of the new series: 1893 on numbers 1 and 2, 1894 on number 3. Although the names of Elkin Mathews and John Lane as publishers appear on the title pages of 1 and 2, only Mathews's name is on 3. Although there is also some confusion as to the number of issues of the *Hobby Horse*, most listings account for three: bibliographical listings such as the *Union List of Serials* and the *British Union Catalogue of Periodicals* cite 1894 as the final year of publication; the reprint by Frank Cass contains only three numbers for the new series; and in a catalogue prepared for an auction of Thomas Bird Mosher's library, "the complete set" is advertised with "Nos. I–III of the New Series."[2]

Unlike the issues of the *Century Guild Hobby Horse*, the *Hobby Horse* was also published in America by Copeland and Day of Boston, the same firm that published the *Yellow Book** in America. According to a letter from Mackmurdo to Lillian Block, "Copeland and Day published a few American copies entirely on their own account." The American edition was not set up from new type, however, but was composed of sheets of the English issue.[3]

Under the leadership of its editor, the *Hobby Horse* was an attractively designed little magazine that published some of the outstanding poets of its day. Contributors included Ernest Dowson, who published "The Statute of Limitations," "A Requiem," "Terre Promise," and "Benedicto Domini" in the magazine. Paul Verlaine published his "Visiteurs," and Laurence Binyon contributed "Quid, Quae Te Pura Solum Sub Nocte Canenten Audieram." In addition to poetry, critical essays were published in the magazine, including Horne's "An Essay on the Life of Inigo Jones, Architect," and the journal also published illustrations, including designs by Simeon Solomon and C. H. Shannon.

While the magazine was not intended to solicit business for any particular artist, each issue did contain a list of endorsed artists and artisans as part of an effort to promote the relevance of the Arts and Crafts movement in England. Indeed, the idea of artist-as-knight-going-into-battle dominates the cover of each issue of the *Hobby Horse* in a design by Selwyn Image: the central part of the design depicts two mounted knights in armor, carrying standards. The emblem of a hobby horse was never graphically depicted in the magazine, but Horne was quoted in the *Studio* explaining the significance of the title:

> The principle which gives the paper its name is that of free expression; each writer is supposed to utter only his sincerest opinions, and such opinions affect only the writer, for the editors hold with Uncle Toby that the true translation of "De gustibus non est disputandum" is "there is no disputing about hobby-horses", and so they endeavour to make it a quiet garden of literature, kept free from arguments, for the setting forth of high principles.[4]

All numbers of the *Hobby Horse* reflect Horne's interest in art for art's sake, not in the terms of Walter Pater, but in those employed by Morris, Ruskin, and Matthew Arnold. When writing of his philosophy on the Arts and Crafts movement, Horne affirmed:

> Certainly the greatest Art is that which interests itself most deeply in the conduct of life, which, while it is striving to satisfy our need of beauty, its chief matter of concern, is also mindful of our other needs. ... For this end, therefore, Art must exist for its own sake, as an expression and ornament of life. [4:1–2]

If there is one single message in the *Hobby Horse*, as in its predecessor, the *Century Guild Hobby Horse*, that message is in praise of the unity of art. In a paper delivered by Horne to the Whitechapel Craft School, the editor of the magazine explained his and the journal's point of view:

> There are not *many* Arts. As there is but one proper study of mankind, which is man; so is there but one art; the art of a fine and various expression of the human spirit; *multipartia sed indivisibilis*; of many forms, no doubt, but never possible to divide. [6:84–85]

According to an announcement on the inside covers of the *Hobby Horse*, the annual subscription to the magazine was one pound. It was an expensive publication, but artistically and mechanically produced with care and precision. Everything about the magazine was consistent, and unity in art was stressed.

Although the diverse contributors to the magazine were obviously free to pursue their personal convictions, no essay, poem, or illustration contradicted Horne's editorial policy. Unity in art meant unity in the magazine, and the magazine was the device, indeed the "weapon," to promote that policy:

> Artists must make more direct appeal to the people; to a people not slow to be touched by the idealization of those sentiments which spiritualize its workaday life—sentiments which it holds yet unconsciously, till the artist comes to give the consciousness, by striking their key note upon the strings of art. [7:17]

Why the *Hobby Horse* failed is not known. Perhaps after the guild lost interest in it and the new series appeared, Horne could not or would not shoulder the responsibilities all by himself for more than the final three issues of the magazine. Perhaps it was a philosophical decision, where Horne acutely understood the changing trends in Victorian England. With the arrival of the *fin de siècle*, artists and writers were no longer interested in the past; symbolism and Paterism were becoming a part of the 1890s, and little magazines like the *Hobby Horse* had lost their audience.

Notes

1. *Exhibition of Victorian and Edwardian Decorative Arts* (London, 1952), p. 58.

2. Lorraine R.L. Hunt maintains that there were four numbers of the *Hobby Horse*. *"The Century Guild Hobby Horse*: A Study of a Magazine," Ph.D. dissertation, University of North Carolina, 1965, p. 50. Cf. the Parke-Bernet catalogue (10 May 1948) of the "Library of the Late Thomas Bird Mosher," 1, item 71.

3. Lillian R. Block, "Pursuit of Beauty," Master's thesis, Columbia University, 1941, p. 141. Ms. Block exchanged letters with Arthur Mackmurdo in preparation for her thesis, and much of the correspondence is printed here. According to Katherine Lyon Mix, Copeland and Day were "young and enterprising"; Copeland was "a Harvard man with modern ideas, and Fred Holland Day had plenty of money and was willing to use it." *A Study in Yellow* (Lawrence, Kans., 1960), p. 72.

4. "The Work of Mr. Selwyn Image," *Studio* 14 (1898):8.

Information Sources

BIBLIOGRAPHY

Casford, E. Lenore. *The Magazines of the 1890's*. Eugene, Ore., 1929.

Harbron, Dudley. "Minor Masters of the Nineteenth Century: Herbert P. Horne." *Architectural Review* 81 (1937):31–34.

Muddiman, Bernard. *The Men of the Nineties*. London, 1926.

Vallance, Aymer. "Mr. Arthur H. Mackmurdo and the Century Guild." *Studio* 16 (1899):183–92.

INDEXES

In Lillian R. Block, "Pursuit of Beauty," Master's thesis, Columbia University, 1941; in Cyrena Norman Pondrom, "English Literary Periodicals: 1885–1918," Ph.D. dissertation, Columbia University, 1965.

REPRINT EDITIONS

Microform: Early British Periodicals (UMI), reel 235; Kraus Reprint Corporation, New York.

LOCATION SOURCES

American

Widely available.

British

Complete runs: Bodleian Library; British Museum.

Partial runs: Widely available.

Publication History

MAGAZINE TITLE AND TITLE CHANGES

The Century Guild Hobby Horse, 1884; 1886–1892. *The Hobby Horse*, 1893–1894.

VOLUME AND ISSUE DATA

Number 1, 1884; volumes 1–7, 1886–1892. Numbers 1 and 2, 1893; number 3, 1894.

FREQUENCY OF PUBLICATION

Annual (volumes 1–7, 1884–1892); quarterly (numbers 1–3, 1893–1894).

PUBLISHERS

1884–1892: J. Kegan Paul, Chiswick Press, London. 1893–1894: Elkin Mathews and John Lane, The Bodley Head Press, Vigo Street, London. (American edition: Copeland and Day, Boston.)

EDITORS

Arthur Mackmurdo, number 1, April 1884. Arthur Mackmurdo and Herbert P. Horne, 1886. Herbert P. Horne, 1887–1891. Arthur Mackmurdo, 1892. Herbert P. Horne, 1893–94.

Robert Stahr Hosmon

HOOD'S MAGAZINE

Hood's Magazine (1844–1849) was a half-crown monthly containing fiction, poetry, sketches, and reviews. The first issue, under the title *Hood's Magazine and Comic Miscellany*, appeared in January 1844, when Thomas Hood was riding the crest of popularity that grew from the publication of "The Song of the Shirt." His prospectus said that the magazine was intended to supply relief to a public pressed by "hard times" and "heavy taxes"; he promised that it would contain neither religion nor politics, and that it would be comic "without raising a Maiden Blush . . . or trespassing, by wanton personalities, on the parks and lawns of Private Life."[1] The magazine had a distinctive, lively energy as long as Hood was publishing his own work and eliciting contributions from his friends. However, the last piece he was able to write appeared in February 1845, and after his death the magazine became simply another monthly with nothing particular to recommend it.

Thomas Hood had left the editorship of Henry Colburn's *New Monthly Magazine** (see *RA*) in the summer of 1843 because Colburn did not allow him full control over the magazine's contents. After looking unsuccessfully for another editorial post, he found a financial backer for a magazine that would be Hood's own and that would give him the absolute freedom of action that he wanted.

The first number had a modest sale of 1,500 copies. Hood was disappointed; he believed that the booksellers were refusing to put the magazine in their windows and that publishers were conspiring against him because of the messy disagreement with Colburn and because he had decided to issue the magazine from its own office in order to remain independent from the publishing establishment.

There was worse to come. Thomas Flight, the "wealthy" backer, turned out to be a fraud. He was either unwilling or unable to pay the printer for the first issue, and two other printers were tried before the February number finally made a belated appearance. Flight also failed to pay Hood and apparently made off with much of the income received from the first issue. Finally, after a great deal of stress and confusion, the printer Andrew Spottiswoode agreed to back the magazine for twelve months and to pay Hood twenty-five pounds a month as editor as well as twenty pounds per sheet for his own contributions to the magazine.

The strain and uncertainty told on Hood's already poor health. By the end of May he had collapsed and was spitting blood. Frederick Oldfield Ward managed the magazine without salary from June through September, and various friends and admirers of Hood contributed pieces as a way of helping him out. Hood recovered sufficiently to take some part in the editorial work and write a few more contributions, but he was never again well. The last chapters of his unfinished novel, *Our Family*, appeared in February 1845; he died on 3 May.

For a time after Hood's death the magazine was largely written by Charles Rowcroft and featured his serials *The Bushranger of Van Dieman's Land* and *Chronicles of the Fleet*. In January 1846 the subtitle "and Comic Miscellany" was dropped. The magazine's energy and vitality declined; it had little verse and no distinguished contributors, and depended heavily on the kind of book review that fills space by printing long extracts. The editorial voice retained the personal tone that Hood had established, but did not have a strong personality to make it distinctive. Toward the end of 1848 the magazine began to print extensive notices of exhibitions, opera, and theater. The issue for January 1849 was described as the first of a new series and given a new title—*Hood's Magazine and Literary, Scientific, and Dramatic Journal*—but it was, in fact, the last issue that appeared.

The first three volumes of *Hood's Magazine* (January 1844–July 1845) are noteworthy for the distinctive Thomas Hood blend of comic inventiveness and social passion. For the first few months Hood wrote nearly half of the material and displayed his talents in all their variety. The first issue began with "The Haunted House," a poem in the Edgar Allan Poe mode, and one which Poe himself admired. Hood also produced brief parodies of popular literature (for example, "Mrs. Burrage. A Temperance Romance"), a mock letter in brogue on the Irish rebellion, epigrams, pen-and-ink sketches, jocular notices of Dickens's Christmas books, and tongue-in-cheek reviews of such items as the London Post Office Directory. In his other vein, he wrote "The Workhouse Clock," "The Lay of the Labourer," and, for the issue of May 1844, his second most famous poem, "The Bridge of Sighs."

Hood's editorial choices provided the same mixture in the rest of the contents. There were comic narratives about an Oxford undergraduate written by "Suum Cuique, Esq." (J.T.J. Hewlett), sentimental poems by the blind Irishwoman Frances Browne, and local-color sketches in dialect by Mrs. S. C. Hall. The interest and variety of these early issues also grows from the efforts of Hood's friends to do what they could to help him. Mrs. S. C. Hall offered to contribute only if she could name her own terms, which were "the pleasure she will feel in assisting however humbly, in the success of his periodical: as a tribute of veneration to the author of the Song of the Shirt."[2] Charles Dickens supplied a virulent attack on Thomas Hood written by an old gentleman; R. Monckton Milnes, Robert Browning, and Walter Savage Landor sent poems; Bulwer-Lytton offered a dramatic sketch; G. H. Lewes wrote "A Word to Young Authors"; and the possessor of some of Keats's manuscripts provided the poem "Old Meg," which had not previously been published.

Hood's poems of social protest were impassioned but politically neutral. He objected strongly when, during his illness, F. O. Ward pledged himself to a series that reflected the ideas of Young England; he repeatedly urged Ward to avoid religious or political topics. Hood had also originally intended to avoid serial fiction, and although he did eventually begin writing and running a novel of his own, he much preferred pieces that were independent but linked, such as the Oxford sketches by "Suum Cuique." This characteristic form was continued in later volumes. In 1848, for example, there was a series of "Hospital Reminiscences, by a Late Student." There was also a novel entitled *The Times; or Modern Philosophy* by the (unidentified) editor, which mildly and episodically satirizes the political behavior of aristocrats. There were also, in 1848, overt but moderate expressions of middle-class support for Chartist aims. Thus, to an extent the subsequent editors reflected the Thomas Hood tradition, but, lacking his talent and energy, they could not reproduce his mood of genial good humor combined with deeply felt social sympathy.

Notes

1. Walter Jerrold, *Thomas Hood: His Life and Times* (New York, 1901), p. 372.
2. Ibid., pp. 374–75.

Information Sources

BIBLIOGRAPHY
Jerrold, Walter. *Thomas Hood: His Life and Times*. New York, 1901.
Morgan, Peter F., ed. *The Letters of Thomas Hood*. Toronto, 1973.
Reid, John C. *Thomas Hood*. London, 1963.
INDEXES
Each volume indexed.
REPRINT EDITIONS
Microform: English Literary Periodicals (UMI), reels 904–907.
LOCATION SOURCES
American
Partial runs: Widely available.
British
Complete runs: Bodleian Library; British Museum.
Partial runs: Cambridge University Library; Edinburgh University Library; Trinity College Library.

Publication History

MAGAZINE TITLE AND TITLE CHANGES
Hood's Magazine and Comic Miscellany, 1844–1845. *Hoods's Magazine*, 1846–1848. *Hood's Magazine and Literary, Scientific, and Dramatic Journal*, January 1849.

VOLUME AND ISSUE DATA
> Volumes 1–10, January 1844–December 1848.
>
> New series, number 61 (volume 11, number 1), January 1849.

FREQUENCY OF PUBLICATION
> Monthly.

PUBLISHERS
> Volumes 1–4: H. Renshaw, 356 Strand, London. Volumes 5–9: H. Hurst, 27 King William Street, London. Volumes 10–11: E. Churton, 26 Holles Street, London.

EDITORS
> Thomas Hood, January 1844–May 1845. (During this period, after May 1844, Frederick Oldfield Ward was nominal editor.) Charles Rowcroft, May 1845–(?).

Sally Mitchell

HOUSEHOLD WORDS

When the first issue of *Household Words* appeared on 30 March 1850, Charles Dickens had already served an editorial apprenticeship on three magazines.[1] The new miscellany was the first totally planned and executed by Dickens, who maintained firm editorial control for nine years, until a dispute with the publishers Bradbury and Evans prompted him to found *All the Year Round** in 1859. Dickens's initial plan for *Household Words* was discussed in some detail with his friend and biographer, John Forster, to whom Dickens sent an informal outline on 7 October 1849. The magazine was to be "in part original and in part selected, and always having, if possible, a little good poetry." The selected material would include "extraordinary," "romantic," or "remarkable" subjects; the original material was to bear a strong imprint of Dickens's own personality and was, in effect, to be a guide to public opinion, all "as amusing as possible, but all distinctly and boldly going to what in one's own view ought to be the spirit of the people and the time." The incipient social reformism of the magazine was almost obscured for Forster by the whimsical way in which Dickens proposed that its binding spirit or personality be conceived of as a "Shadow, which may go into any place, . . . and be in all homes, and all nooks and corners, and be supposed to be cognisant of everything, and go everywhere, without the least difficulty." More than a fancy, this embodiment of "common-sense and humanity" had a serious mission: "to issue his warnings from time to time, that he is going to fall on such and such a subject; or to expose such and such a piece of humbug."[2]

Forster's misgivings about a conflict between the miscellaneous content and the imaginative freight it was expected to bear were tempered when Dickens chose *Household Words: A Weekly Journal* as the title and substituted a Conductor for a Shadow.[3] An experienced journalist, William Henry Wills (Dickens's secretary on the *Daily News*), became the subeditor for a salary of eight pounds a week and 12.5 percent of the profits, the same percentage offered to Forster for occasional contributions.[4] Bradbury and Evans owned 25 percent of the periodical; Dickens, who drew a yearly salary of 500 pounds, was half-owner, but virtually controlled 75 percent. The other members of the staff included Richard Henry Horne, John Dickens, and George Hogarth (Dickens's father-in-law). Henry Morley, poet and essayist, joined the staff in 1851, the novelist Wilkie Collins in 1856. In the latter year Forster resigned his interest.[5]

Dickens's "Preliminary Word" to the reader announced a two-fold purpose: on the one hand, the articles in *Household Words* were "to help in the discussion of the most important social questions of the time"; on the other, "no mere utilitarian spirit, no iron binding of the mind to grim realities" would deter the magazine from "cherish[ing] that light of Fancy which is inherent in the human breast." To achieve his goals, Dickens enrolled almost four hundred contributors[6] and counted on an "uncompromising humanitarian radicalism" rather than on attractiveness of format.[7] For a twopenny piece, readers purchased a plain, twenty-four page issue printed in double columns, with no illustrations. Inside, however, they found on the average six full-length pieces: installments of travelogues or novels, scientific explanations for laymen, short tales, poetry, and essays. On the readers' behalf, the Conductor waged a number of campaigns. He advocated free education (kindergartens, Ragged Schools, and mechanics' institutes) to cure poverty and immorality; public sanitation to cope with epidemics arising from tainted drinking water, poor sewage disposal, and unhealthy funerary practices; and unionization, law enforcement, and employer responsibility to reduce mutilation and death in unsafe factories.

Dickens himself wrote much of the original matter, including two long works—*Hard Times* (4 April 1854–12 August 1854) and *A Child's History of England* (25 January 1851–10 December 1853). He publicized Angela Burdett-Coutts's efforts on behalf of destitute women (23 April 1853); he expostulated with Lord Palmerston in "The Thousand and One Humbugs" (21 April–5 May 1855); he wrote the obituary for Justice Talfourd. He is directly credited with over 170 pieces, just under half published during the first two years. Some were jointly authored, sometimes with Wills, who may indeed have been instrumental in planning at least the first year's layout and content, as pre-publication plans in his handwriting suggest.[8] Wills's more than a hundred collaborations included articles on the Bank of England, Chancery, education, and emigration. Forster contributed only seven pieces before he severed his connection in 1853; during his tenure, however, he was responsible for the *Household Narrative of Current Events*, a news supplement compiled by George Hogarth. Forster also introduced new contributors; Percy Fitzgerald, the first president of the Dickens Fellowship, was one of these.

Elizabeth Cleghorn Gaskell was an important contributor; the first issue featured an installment of her *Lizzie Leigh*. Along with other tales, the series that became *Cranford* appeared in 1851–1853 and *My Lady Ludlow* in 1858. *North and South*, whose unsuitability for serialization probably caused sales figures to drop, was published in 1854–1855.[9] Harriet Martineau, while disliking the narrative style Dickens demanded, contributed a successful series on manufacturing processes (reprinted as *Health, Husbandry, and Handicraft*) in 1851–1852. Arguing with Dickens over his political acumen, she dissociated herself from *Household Words* in 1855.[10] Along with Gaskell and Martineau, one of Dickens's best-known contributors was Wilkie Collins, whose *Dead Secret* appeared in 1857. He and Dickens collaborated on a number of the Christmas issues, as well as on "A Lazy Tour of Two Idle Apprentices" (October 1857). Another popular contributor was Eliza Linton; while Dickens sometimes edited out her Balzacian touches, he regularly published her short stories, articles on French manners and customs, and a series on witchcraft. Charles Knight also contributed at Dickens's request; Dickens especially liked his 1850 "Illustrations of Cheapness" (from matches to steel pens) and his 1851 "Shadows" biographical series.

Among the writers who came to *Household Words* with ready-made reputations was Henry Morley, who had contributed public health articles to Forster's *Examiner** (see *RA*). He adopted the persona of a talkative, slipshod old woman for his first article and eventually contributed articles on the Poor Laws, tobacco, and the Factory Act. Many other writers, however, were like John Hollingshead, who considered himself a "Dickens young man"; valued for his penchant for accuracy, he contributed on a variety of topics, including cruelty to animals, photography, the railroads, and the navy.[11] George Augustus Sala came under Dickens's special protection; thirty-two of his miscellaneous items were reprinted as *Gaslight and Daylight*. Sala also served as a foreign correspondent in Russia, but antagonized Dickens by arguing about his expenses and failing to deliver his articles on time. Wills's suggestion brought another foreign correspondent to *Household Words*: Grenville Murray's successful "Roving Englishman" series, which explored, among other countries, Germany, Greece, and Turkey, began his journalistic career.

Aside from staff members, the rate of payment for the new and the experienced writer was nominally the same: one guinea for a single page of prose, with poetry and material for the Christmas issues receiving a higher rate. Wills, however, frequently allowed fractional pages to go unreimbursed and translated guineas into pounds unless Dickens intervened, as he often did.[12] Dickens's generosity extended further than financial equality, however; he was well known for his continuing encouragement of new, promising writers. He wrote long rejection letters to some, like Holme Lee, to whom he suggested plot and stylistic changes.[13] To others, like Sheridan Le Fanu, Coventry Patmore, and Adelaide Anne Proctor, he offered minor revisions before publication.

As a general rule, works by both the famous and the forgotten appeared anonymously, although Dickens revealed authorship when asked. While some, like Douglas Jerrold, objected to the then common practice,[14] for Dickens it had an important advantage: his contributors seemed to speak with one voice, even on controversial issues. The consistently sympathetic and reformistic point of view they maintained was, of course, achieved by much editorial revision on

Dickens's part; in 1854 alone he supposedly read 900 submissions, completely rewriting some for publication.[15] He edited poetry as well as prose, routinely deploring the distance between the poets' vision and language in the submissions, many plagued by stylistic peculiarities. To Laman Blanchard, who submitted "Orient Pearls at Random Strung," he wrote, "Dear Blanchard, too much string,—yours, C. D."[16] His efforts to cherish the "light of Fancy" were matched by his desire for accuracy. He refused, for example, to retract a 14 September 1850 interview with Inspector Field, relying on witnesses to verify his transcription; and when "Gold and Silver Diets" (5 March 1853) proved inaccurate, he ordered Wills to check the author's subsequent submission fact by fact.[17] Likewise, he asked Henry Austin, secretary of the Sanitary Commission, to read drafts of a series on sanitation and requested the use of Michael Faraday's notes for an explanation entitled "The Chemistry of a Candle" (3 August 1850).[18]

Circulation figures demonstrate Dickens's success; the first number and some of the Christmas numbers were said to reach 100,000; average circulation was apparently around 40,000.[19] Despite the magazine's popularity and the enthusiastic support of such critics as Edmund Yates, Percy Fitzgerald, Walter Savage Landor, and Leigh Hunt, others, including Henry Morley and Henry Crabb Robinson, objected to the literary standards and management of the periodical and complained that Dickens's attempt to present facts by the light of fancy resulted, at times, in an exaggeration of style and misproportion of attack, especially when novice contributors aped his comic style without his genius. Even more to be expected, special interest groups—slumlords and mill-owners, for example, smarting from such articles as "Death's Doors" (10 June 1854) and "Death's Cyphering-Book" (12 May 1855)—strongly objected to Dickens's views on social issues. Such criticism had, however, little to do with the demise of *Household Words*; rather, Dickens's marital difficulties and consequent quarrel with Bradbury and Evans seem to be at fault.[20] On 12 June 1858 the first page of the magazine was devoted to the famous statement of Dickens's "domestic trouble . . . of long standing" that shocked friends and enemies alike. In the statement Dickens attempted to quash rumors that the failure of his marriage was due to his affair with the actress Ellen Ternan. Because the statement was not also published in *Punch*,* Dickens quarreled seriously with his friend Mark Lemon, the editor, and Bradbury and Evans, who also published the comic miscellany. In November 1858 Dickens began action to dissociate himself from Bradbury and Evans and to renew his contract with Chapman and Hall. Forster advised the publishers that their refusal to sell their shares would prompt Dickens to undermine *Household Words* by starting a rival publication. Even before a legal decision forced the sale of the *Household Words* property at auction on 16 May 1859,[21] Dickens had announced the beginning of *All the Year Round*.

Household Words, which had been initiated with so much hope and enthusiasm, ended on a note of bitterness that reflected Dickens's personal troubles. Throughout its tenure, however, it exerted an incalculable influence. Although many of the reform issues were certainly not initiated by Dickens, his readable style assured that progressive ideas about public health, employment, and education would be understood and perhaps adopted by those who had the power to make changes. In addition, his openness to contributions encouraged the development of many young, talented writers. In the words of Lord Northcliffe, he was "the best magazine editor of his own or any other age."[22]

Notes

1. Dickens left *Bentley's Miscellany** in 1839 over a disagreement about editorial responsibility; *Master Humphrey's Clock*, underwritten by Chapman and Hall in the same year, devolved into a vehicle for *The Old Curiosity Shop* and *Barnaby Rudge*; and his association with the *Daily News*, which he founded in 1846, ended after three weeks, again because of a question about editorial responsibility. See Harry Stone, *Charles Dickens' Uncollected Writings from "Household Words," 1850–1859* (Bloomington, Ind., 1968), 1: 6–11.

2. John Forster, *The Life of Charles Dickens*, ed. A. J. Hoppé (London, 1969), 2:63–66.

3. Forster, 2:66.

4. For an index to the contents of *Household Words* based on Wills's office-book, see Anne Lohrli, *"Household Words": A Weekly Journal, 1850–1859, Conducted by Charles Dickens* (Toronto, 1973). Her introduction is especially helpful.

5. Forster, 2:702; Lohrli, p. 25. See Gerald Giles Grubb, "The Editorial Policies of Charles Dickens," *Publications of the Modern Language Association of America* 58 (1943):1119, n.46 for a discussion of the redistribution of shares.

6. Lohrli gives biographies and contributions of each.

7. Edgar Johnson, *Charles Dickens: His Tragedy and Triumph* (New York, 1952), 2:703.

8. Philip Collins, "W. H. Wills' Plans for *Household Words*," *Victorian Periodicals Newsletter*, no. 8 (1970):33–46.

9. Lohrli, p. 278.

10. Lohrli, p. 358; Johnson, 2:854–55.

11. Lohrli, p. 306; Johnson, 2:712–13.

12. Lohrli, p. 21.

13. Forster, 2:384; Grubb, pp. 1120–21.

14. Johnson, 2:704.

15. Ibid., 2:712.

16. Arthur A. Adrian, "Charles Dickens as Verse Editor," *Modern Philology* 58 (1960):100.

17. Grubb, pp. 1111–12.

18. Johnson, 2:708.

19. Johnson, 2:946; Lohrli, p. 23; Stone, p. 21.

20. Many accounts are available. See Forster, 2:465–67, n.22; Johnson, 2:943–45.

21. A notice appears in the London *Times* for 29 April 1859, p. 11.

22. Gerald Giles Grubb, "Dickens' Influence as an Editor," *Studies in Philology* 42 (1945):819.

Information Sources

BIBLIOGRAPHY

Adrian, Arthur A. "Charles Dickens as Verse Editor." *Modern Philology* 58 (1960):99–107.

Buckler, William E. "Dickens' Success with *Household Words.*" *Dickensian* 46 (1950):197–203.

Fitzgerald, Percy Hetherington. *Memories of Charles Dickens, with an Account of "Household Words" and "All the Year Round" and of the Contributors Thereto.* 1913. Reprint. New York, 1973.

Forster, John. *The Life of Charles Dickens.* Edited by A. J. Hoppé. 2 vols. London, 1969.

Grubb, Gerald Giles. "The Editorial Policies of Charles Dickens." *Publications of the Modern Language Association of America* 58 (1943):1110–24.

Johnson, Edgar. *Charles Dickens: His Tragedy and Triumph.* 2 vols. New York, 1952.

Lehmann, Rudolph C. *Charles Dickens as Editor; Being Letters Written by Him to William Henry Wills His Sub-Editor.* New York, 1912.

Lohrli, Anne. Introduction to *"Household Words": A Weekly Journal, 1850–1859, Conducted by Charles Dickens.* Toronto, 1973.

Stone, Harry. Introduction to *Charles Dickens' Uncollected Writings from "Household Words," 1850–1859.* Bloomington, Ind., 1968.

INDEXES

Poole's Index. *Index to Legal Periodical Literature.* In Anne Lohrli, ed., *Household Words*, Toronto, 1973.

REPRINT EDITIONS

Ed. Anne Lohrli, Toronto, 1973. *Charles Dickens' Uncollected Writings from "Household Words,"* ed. Harry Stone, Bloomington, Ind., 1968.

Microform: Early British Periodicals (UMI), reels 47–50. AMS Press, New York.

LOCATION SOURCES

American

Widely available.

British

Widely available.

Publication History

MAGAZINE TITLE AND TITLE CHANGES

Household Words: A Weekly Journal.

VOLUME AND ISSUE DATA

Volumes 1–19, 30 March 1850–28 May 1859.

FREQUENCY OF PUBLICATION

Weekly.

PUBLISHER

Bradbury and Evans, Whitefriars, London.

EDITOR

Charles Dickens.

Patricia Marks

I

IDLER, THE

When he was asked to edit the *Idler*, a new sixpenny monthly, Jerome Klapka Jerome had behind him years as an unsuccessful actor with provincial theater companies, the production of miscellaneous journalism, and several moderately successful plays. He had received his first major acclaim with the publication in 1889 of a book of essays, *Idle Thoughts of an Idle Fellow*, and consolidated his reputation in the same year with *Three Men in a Boat*. The latter blended Jerome's typical facetiousness with the humor, sentiment, and descriptive passages attendant on the trials of three citified young men as they cope with nature during a trip up the Thames from Kingston to Oxford. Jerome later wrote in *My Life and Times* that Robert Barr, the *Idler*'s proprietor, had asked him to assume the editorship rather than Kipling, "thinking that I should be the easier to manage."[1] As with many of Jerome's statements, this one should be accepted with caution. The title *Idler** (see *AAAJ*) first belonged to a series of essays which had been contributed by Dr. Johnson to the *Universal Chronicle and Weekly Gazette* in the mid-eighteenth century. The spirit and content of Jerome's magazine is suggested by the subtitle of a short-lived periodical of 1856: the *Idler: Magazine of Fiction, Belles Lettres, News and Comedy*.[2]

Jerome had been an early beneficiary of the National Education Bill of 1870, which made the provision of education for all the responsibility of the government. Although he had to leave school shortly after his own fourteenth birthday because of his father's death, Jerome owed his education up to that point to the new free Board Schools.[3] By the 1890s these schools had developed a new class of readers—a class rather cruelly pilloried by George Gissing in his novel *New Grub Street* (1891). Literate rather than literary, these educationally enfranchised millions turned to journalism for amusement and information. The lengthy and serious articles in the reviews and quarterlies did not interest the majority of them, nor were they an audience for the many esoteric little magazines that flourished in the 1890s. The *Yellow Book** of Henry Harland is the best known of these but there were many transient titles as well, such as the *Hobby Horse** and *Rose Leaf.* Jerome's mixture of irreverence, facetiousness, and knowledge did appeal to these new readers. He knew how to hold these qualities suspended in the medium of invincible sentimentality. Part of his originality as a writer and editor lay in his ability to give a certain charm to the "shabby genteel" poverty many of his readers knew, or had known, first hand. He also exploited the idea of "idleness" as a positive quality and used the cognomen of the "Idler" in three volumes of sketches he published between 1886 and 1905. After his career as an editor ended, Jerome later enjoyed a flourishing career as a dramatist and novelist. *The Passing of the Third Floor Back* (1908), a play based on his own short story of the same name, had great success. Indeed, this drama of supernatural intervention into the lives of residents of a boarding house was performed in St. Paul's Cathedral in 1928.

In the first number, which set the pattern the *Idler* followed throughout its nineteen years, no piece is more than a few pages long, with the exception of serials by Mark Twain and Bret Harte. Indeed, Arnold Bennett wrote later that it was "an era of paragraphs."[4] Numerous illustrations within the text, in addition to full-page pictures, give the pages a lively appearance. Typical of the sophistication of tone is a story, "A Suicide," published in the first number for February 1892. Here, as in many fictional works appearing in periodicals for the middle class, marital infidelity is narrowly averted. With "The Adventures of Sherlaw Kombs," Jerome began a series, "Detective Stories Gone Wrong." Robert Barr, who was at that time the coeditor, used the pseudonym "Luke Short" in order to reduce Holmes's methods to absurdity.[5]

The *Idler*'s most enduring contribution to literary journalism is probably not found in any specific piece, but in the number of new names to whom Jerome opened his pages. Conan Doyle himself contributed an article in 1892 to a series entitled "My First Book," in which successful authors recounted their difficulties in breaking into print. Eden Philpotts, Israel Zangwill, Barry Pain, Marie Corelli, Anthony Hope, Grant Allen, John Davidson, Robert Louis Stevenson, and W. W. Jacobs wrote for the *Idler.* Many of them appeared as members of the "Idler's Club," a feature Jerome incorporated into the first issue and which might be considered the keynote of the periodical. In the first issue the Club consisted of writers informally indulging in "unorganized table-talk."[6] By the second volume the discussions were taking place around an actual library table and the Idlers addressed themselves to specific topics in each issue. Over the years these topics ranged from smoking to the durability of corrupt governments, and included stories about skating, the benefits of procrastination, and accidents. Doyle was a member of the early Idler's group and also contributed medical stories—later collected as *Round the Red Lamp.* His "study of thoughts, hopes, feelings and above all religious doubts of a young doctor"[7] was serialized during 1894–1895 as the *Stark Munro Letters.*

Jerome was fond of series of all kinds and devised one which provided "inside information" about literature and the theater. In addition, the *Idler* in its first years featured accounts of rehearsals contributed by G. B. Bayin and another series, "Why Did I Write ———?" Marie Corelli's essay, "Why Did I Write *Barabbas*?" (7:120) was probably the most sensational of these essays and she became a steady contributor to the *Idler* of the late 1890s.

In 1893 Jerome collected and published the pieces he had written for "Novel Notes" during the *Idler*'s first year. The framework, the tone, and the topics of the "Notes" are quintessentially Jerome, and their flavor permeated the *Idler* for many years to come. The narrator collaborates with three bachelor friends who write a novel, encouraged by his wife's remark, "Look how silly all the novels are nowadays. I'm sure you could write one."[8] This quartet's ongoing discussions result in the telling of anecdotes about dreams, ghosts, cats, and so on, and stories that range from the comic to the grim. There is a large proportion of tales about "ghosts, doubles and dual personalities," which were very popular in the 1890s.[9] Typically, grim stories that raise points of moral ambiguity are always rendered harmless by the narrative frame. The *Idler* let its readers flirt with sophistication and moral and social problems, but always brought them back to the comforting certainties of the library table and the teapot.

In November 1893 Jerome started a weekly paper, *To-day*,* which sold for two pence and used many contributors associated with the *Idler*. In 1897 the paper was involved in a libel suit over an advice column for investors that Jerome did not write but for which, as editor, he was responsible. Jerome lost the case and, while the damages were negligible, he was forced to sell his interest in both magazines in order to pay court costs. Jerome wrote in his autobiography that "Barr's friends took over the *Idler*,"[10] but this was only for a short period. Arthur Lawrence, the journalist who became an authority on Sir Arthur Sullivan, and the artist Sidney H. Sime continued it between May 1899 and January 1901. After another hiatus, Barr resumed the editorship in October 1902. During this period, Sime was embarking on a successful career as an artist of fantasy and the fantastic. He is perhaps best known for his illustrations for the works of Lord Dunsany. He embellished the *Idler* during his editorship with tail pieces of mannered and slightly sinister insects and birds. The illustrations in the *Idler* do not rise above the general level found in many periodicals of the time, but Jerome used more female illustrators than did other editors.

Robert Barr, primarily an author of light tales and novels, has the distinction of having collaborated with Stephen Crane. Their *O'Ruddy* appeared in 1903. In the words of his good friend Sir Arthur Conan Doyle, Barr was a "volcanic Anglo or rather Scot-American, with a violent temper, a wealth of strong adjectives, and one of the kindest natures underneath it all. He was one of the best raconteurs I have ever known, and as a writer I have always felt that he did not quite come into his own." While his "Sherlaw Kombs" parody was so heavy-handed as to be tiresome, Barr showed a much lighter touch in the stories he collected under the somewhat ironic title *The Triumphs of Éugene Valmont*

(1906). After the custom of Sherlock Holmes, his "semi-comic" investigator, the French Valmont, is consulted "unofficially" by Scotland Yard. Sometimes his solutions are correct, sometimes ambiguous, but they generally end in Valmont's discomfiture. Agatha Christie's Belgian detective, Hercule Poirot, bears more than a passing resemblance to Valmont.[11] Barr serialized many of his own works in the *Idler*. "The Man Who Convinced Himself," which appears in the March 1911 issue, was the last of his many "light tales and extravagant romances" to be published initially in his own magazine.

The *Idler* never took on the *fin de siècle* look sported by periodicals which were influenced by the self-conscious decadence of Beardsley. However, Jerome and Barr accepted the aesthetic movement into their pages in the person of Richard Le Gallienne. His "Revolving Bookcase" was a feature of the last years of the century. During this same period Barr obtained Chesterton as a contributor. A typical example of his paradox and playful fantasy is "The Singular Speculations of the House Agent," which appeared in yet another *Idler* series, "The Club of Queer Trades," in 1905.

By the time the *Idler* ended its run in 1911 it had shifted to fewer but longer articles and added a new feature, "The Vanity Pages," on fashion. At the same time that Barr was welcoming writers such as Doyle and Chesterton to the pages of the *Idler* he also accepted such amateurish stories as "Rose Garden" by Herbert Holt. Considering the parodistic tendencies of the earlier *Idler*, the reader might expect statements such as "My love found me a girl and transformed me into a woman" to reflect satiric intent; however, the story is nothing if not sincere. The last issue typifies the unevenness: along with Barr's "The Man Who Convinced Himself" appeared an exposé of the oil industry, "Millions in Petroleum," and "The Fauna of London," a would-be facetious account of the rats, cockroaches, and similar vermin which bedeviled Londoners.

The *Idler* and the Edwardian Age virtually ceased together. The *Idler*'s demise was probably precipitated by Barr's final illness. Many journals were foundering at that time—intellectually if not financially. Many of the older, serious periodicals, such as the *Saturday Review*,* had lost their impetus and excitement, and the underlying ferment in politics, literature, and art would soon change the face of literature.[12] That the *Idler* lasted for nineteen years with virtually the same content and format is a tribute to Jerome's sensitivity. He fashioned the periodical to serve the tastes and aspirations of an era in which general education and leisure became widely available to more Britons than ever before.

Notes

1. Jerome K. Jerome, *My Life and Times* (New York, 1926), p. 166.

2. For this entry, see *National Union Catalog of Pre-1956 Imprints*, 263:467.

3. Ruth Marie Faurot, *Jerome K. Jerome*, Twayne's English Authors Series (New York, 1974), p. 21.

4. Quoted in John Gross, *The Rise and Fall of the Man of Letters: English Literary Life Since 1800* (Harmondsworth, 1969; rpt. 1973), p. 233.

5. This identification is made in Stanley J. Kunitz and Howard Haycraft, *Twentieth Century Authors: A Biographical Dictionary of Modern Literature* (New York, 1942), p. 77.

6. Faurot, p. 60.

7. John Dickson Carr, *The Life of Sir Arthur Conan Doyle* (New York, 1949), p. 80. Carr identifies Stark Munro with Doyle himself.

8. Jerome K. Jerome, *Novel Notes* (New York, 1893), p. 3.

9. Faurot, p. 71.

10. Jerome, *My Life and Times*, p. 194.

11. Kunitz and Haycraft, p. 77.

12. Gross, p. 249.

Information Sources

BIBLIOGRAPHY

Doyle, Arthur Conan. *Memories and Adventures*. Boston, 1923.

Faurot, Ruth Marie. *Jerome K. Jerome*. Twayne's English Authors Series. New York, 1974.

Gross, John. *The Rise and Fall of the Man of Letters: English Literary Life Since 1800.* Harmondsworth, 1969. Reprint. 1973.

Jerome, Jerome Klapka. *My Life and Times*. New York, 1926.

"Robert Barr." *Times* (London), 23 October 1912, p. 11.

INDEXES

In *Poole's Index*.

REPRINT EDITIONS

Microform: Early British Periodicals (UMI), reels 391–398.

LOCATION SOURCES

American

Complete runs: Columbia University Library; Free Library of Philadelphia; Historical Society of Pennsylvania; Michigan State Library; Milwaukee Public Library; New York Public Library. U.S. Library of Congress; University of Illinois Library; Walters Art Gallery.

Partial runs: Widely available.

British

Complete run: Cambridge University Library.

Partial runs: Widely available.

Publication History

MAGAZINE TITLE AND TITLE CHANGES

The Idler Magazine: An Illustrated Monthly Magazine, February 1892–July 1898. *The Idler: An Illustrated Magazine*, August 1898–January 1899. *The Idler*, February 1899–January 1901. *The Idler: An Illustrated Monthly Magazine*, February 1901–March 1911.

VOLUME AND ISSUE DATA

February 1892–March 1911. Two volumes per year for a total of 38 volumes. Number of issues to a volume varies.

FREQUENCY OF PUBLICATION

Monthly. Sometimes irregular in last years.

PUBLISHERS

February 1892–January 1898: Chatto & Windus, 214 Piccadilly, London. February–September 1898: J. M. Dent & Co. October 1898–(?): W. R. Russell & Co. Later, dates not certain: Horace Marshall & Son, 125 Fleet Street, London E.C.; Chatto & Windus, 214 Piccadilly, London.

EDITORS

Jerome Klapka Jerome and Robert Barr, February 1892–July 1895. Jerome Klapka Jerome, August 1895–November 1897. Arthur Lawrence, May 1899–August 1900(?). Sidney H. Sime, September 1900(?)–January 1901. Robert Barr, October 1902–March 1911.

Barbara J. Dunlap

J

JOHN BULL. See RA

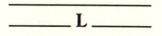

L

LADY'S WORLD, THE. See WOMAN'S WORLD, THE

LEADER, THE

In Autumn 1849 Thornton Hunt apparently originated the idea for a weekly journal that would serve as a record of radical causes and a forum of advanced opinion. W. J. Linton, G. H. Lewes, and G. J. Holyoake soon joined him in promoting the proposed journal. Financial support came from various sympathetic middle-class radicals, chiefly Northern businessmen, and most prominently from the Rev. E. R. Larken, a well-connected Christian Socialist parson who became the major shareholder and managing director of the Leader Newspaper Corporation.

The *Leader* first appeared on 30 March 1850 and quickly developed a following among radical artisans. Its first two years afford an especially vivid picture of the ferment of radicalism, both English and Continental (the latter as particularly reflected in the political exile community of London), in the aftermath of 1848 and the decline of militant Chartism. Linton, Hunt, and Holyoake were all active in interlocking radical organizations of the time, such as the People's International League and the Society of Friends of Italy. All three men were members of the executive board of the National Charter Association in 1851–1852. Given such shared sympathies, a more or less collective editorial position was achieved under the general editorship of Hunt on political issues (although Linton was dropped early on for his extreme republicanism. One feature of the journal was the ''Open Forum'' where readers were invited to contribute their views to continuing debates on controversial social and political issues such as feminism. The *Leader* soon enjoyed the distinction of being branded ''socialist'' in the *Edinburgh Review** (see *RA*) of January 1851, perhaps because one could read the radical manufacturer W. E. Forster (a son-in-law of Thomas Arnold and a future cabinet minister) expounding at length the "rights of labour" and the duty of the state to provide work to every member of the community (9 November–7 December 1850).

The *Leader* very ably filled a gap between the arts-oriented *Athenaeum** (see *RA*) and the more political—and more conservative—*Spectator** (see *RA*), of which Hunt had previously been an editor. Its content was fairly evenly divided between political and cultural matters. The latter was the particular sphere of G. H. Lewes, literary editor and drama and opera critic, who wrote under the pseudonym "Vivian." Hunt was the art critic. An indifferent actor, minor playwright, and mediocre novelist, Lewes displayed great critical talent in each of these areas. His drama criticsm is the most impressive and informative of the period. His literary judgments have held up remarkably well. He spoke out very early for *Wuthering Heights*, and he was the first and best of the few who recognized *Moby Dick*'s greatness. He did not hesitate immediately upon its publication to place *In Memoriam* above the elegies of Milton and Shelley in a review that is recognized as the most important of the early criticisms of that poem. He recognized in the young Browning a "gigantic talent" and he gave the young George Eliot an opportunity to sharpen her critical skills as a regular *Leader* reviewer from 1854 to 1857.

The *Leader* can in fact be called the self-conscious voice and champion of realism, a term Lewes was the first to use regularly in English. Interestingly, Hunt (the most probable attribution), in a discussion of the Pre-Raphaelites, criticized them for going beyond realism to "naturalism"—the "truth of nature without the truth of art" (14 May 1853, p. 477). In his drama criticism, the "representation of life" was Lewes's criterion both for acting and authorship, and he constantly upheld French plays and players as examples for the English theater to follow—an attitude in keeping with the journal's generally cosmopolitan and anti-insular tone. However, in his novel criticism Lewes did not look abroad, for Fielding and Jane Austen were regularly invoked as touchstones of realism.

These high standards and sureness of judgment did not apply to the original literary work that the *Leader* published, especially in its earlier years, which included poetry and some short stories and novels. J. A. Froude anonymously published the charming fables "The Cat's Pilgrimage" (June–July 1851). Lewes himself contributed some poems and an uncompleted novel, *The Apprenticeship of Life*, which is of some interest as a thematic counterpart to its contemporary, Flaubert's *Education Sentimentale*. It demonstrates very clearly Lewes's inability to animate his own theories in fiction. Occupying the border between fact and fiction were the journalist Harriet Martineau's documentary series, "Sketches from Life" (November 1850–March 1851), which were fictionalized reports of social case histories. Even in its factual stories, especially reports of crimes and trials, the *Leader* dwelt frequently on the problematic relationship of truth and fiction, noting of one lawsuit, for instance, that it showed truth "departing more from verisimilitude than fiction safely can" ("How to Get Rid of a Wife," 9 February 1856), or observing that the notorious "Rugeley poisoner," Thomas Palmer, played out his role in court as a "consummate artist."

It was in the *Leader* that Lewes, in the name of realism and science, challenged Dickens's use of spontaneous combustion in *Bleak House* (5:12), thereby eliciting Dickens's important prefatorial response, a major document in the history of realism in England. Lewes was responsible for the very full attention paid to science in the *Leader*'s early years. Spiritualism and other such "unscientific" follies were subjected to a steady barrage of criticism and ridicule. The *Leader* also served as the major vehicle for introducing the work of Auguste Comte to England. Lewes published an extensive analysis (under his own name, though it was largely the work of George Walker, a young Scots lawyer) of Comte's *Philosophie Positive* (3 April–14 August 1852). It was also in the *Leader* that Lewes's close friend Herbert Spencer published (anonymously) some of his earliest sociological studies, including the important "Development Hypothesis" (March 1852) in which he defended the theory of organic evolution.

In 1851 ownership of the *Leader* shifted from the founding partners to E.F.S. Pigott, a bohemian younger son of gentry family, who subsidized the journal, according to Holyoake, to the amount of forty-one pounds a week. In January 1852 he replaced Hunt as editor, though the staff remained essentially the same. However, the political complexion of the journal began to shift perceptibly toward a sort of militant middle-class consciousness. This was most vividly embodied in the writing of E. M. Whitty, a newcomer to the staff in 1852. He wrote a brilliantly sardonic parliamentary commentary, "Stranger in Parliament," from 14 August 1852 to 27 August 1853, which irreverently provided an insider's view of Parliament, even to the point of indicating which members were drunk. (These pieces were later reprinted as a book.) Whitty followed up with "The Governing Classes" (3 September 1853–28 January 1854), which contained scathing portraits of the country's leading aristocratic politicians. It spared only Lord Palmerston and Prince Albert from general accusations of gross political incompetence. These works were very much in tune with the contemporary disenchantment with aristocratic mismanagement so vividly demonstrated by the Crimean War. In June 1853 Whitty became editor of the journal, which at this time enjoyed perhaps its most brilliant period. It had lost some of its original radical artisan readership along with some of its political idealism, but had increased its middle-class readership and gained a reputation for "smartness."

Whitty departed from the journal early in 1854 under a cloud. He later attacked his former colleagues and their journal, "The Teazer," in his amusing but self-indulgent novel, *Friends of Bohemia* (1857). Shortly afterward Lewes and Hunt left also, Hunt to edit the new *Daily Telegraph*. Lewes later returned to work as drama and literary critic (but not editor) from May 1855 to March 1857. Holyoake remained a frequent contributor throughout.

From the mid-1850s the *Leader* declines appreciably in interest. Very probably the newly founded *Saturday Review** (1856) eroded its position. An attempt was made to define a new readership by attempting to unite bohemian and business interests through the advocacy of mutual insurance companies, bankruptcy law reform, and limited liability legislation. Criminal reports, with special attention to wife-beating and fraud, were increasingly relied on to combine human interest with reformist moralizing. The literary and cultural coverage became more gossipy and less distinguished.

Pigott took advantage of the new Companies Act to create a limited liability company early in 1857, but was unable to sell many shares. In June 1858, having exhausted his private means, he lost control of the *Leader*. Henceforth its ownership and editorship are not certain, but it seems very probable that the journalist-publisher F. G. Tomlins became both until early 1860, when a relative (possibly his son), C. N. Tomlins, took over. He made a last attempt to restore the paper under a new title to its smart mid-1850s style. The result did not catch on and the last issue of the *Saturday Analyst and Leader* appeared on 24 November 1860.

Information Sources

BIBLIOGRAPHY

Brick, Allan R. "*The Leader*: Organ of Radicalism." Ph.D. dissertation, Yale University, 1957.
Eliot, George. *Letters*. Edited by Gordon Haight. New Haven, 1954–1978.
Espinasse, Francis. *Literary Recollections*. London, 1893.
Holyoake, G. J. *Sixty Years of an Agitator's Life*. London, 1906.
Kitchel, Anna T. *George Lewes and George Eliot: A Review of the Records*. New York, 1933.
McCabe, Joseph. *The Life and Letters of G. J. Holyoake*. London, 1908.
Smith, F. B. *Radical Artisan: William James Linton, 1812–1897*. Manchester, 1973.
Whitty, Edward M. *Friends of Bohemia*. London, 1857.
Yates, Edmund. *Recollections and Experiences*. London, 1884.

INDEXES
Annual indexes for 1850, 1851, 1853, and 1854.

REPRINT EDITIONS
Microform: English Literary Periodicals (UMI), reels 530–534. Harvester Press Microfilm (Hassocks, Sussex, 1979), reels 5–15 of Rare Radical and Labour Periodicals of Great Britain, pt. 2.

LOCATION SOURCES
American
Complete run: Boston Athenaeum.
Partial runs: Boston Public Library; California State Library; Harvard University Library; Library Company of Philadelphia; New York Public Library; State Historical Society of Wisconsin; U.S. Library of Congress; Yale University Library.
British
Complete runs: British Museum; Manchester Public Library.
Partial runs: Birmingham Public Library; Cambridge University Library; Glasgow University Library.

Publication History

MAGAZINE TITLE AND TITLE CHANGES

The Leader, 30 March 1850–31 December 1859. (Subtitle 17 July–21 July 1858: *A Political and Literary Review*; subtitle 24 July 1858–31 December 1859: *A Political and Literary Review, Mercantile Journal, Record of Joint Stock Companies, Banks, Railways, Mines, Shipping, etc.*)

The Leader and Saturday Analyst: A Review and Record of Political, Artistic and Social Events, 7 January–30 June 1860.

The Saturday Analyst and Leader (subtitle unchanged), 7 July–24 November 1860.

VOLUME AND ISSUE DATA

Volume 1, number 1, 30 March 1850–volume 2, number 557, 24 November 1860.

FREQUENCY OF PUBLICATION

Monthly, October 1869–December 1870; fortnightly, 15 January 1871–15 December 1873; weekly, 3 January 1874–24 November 1860.

PUBLISHERS

30 March 1850–1 November 1851: Joseph Clayton Jr., 265 Strand, London. 15 November 1851–14 October 1854: Thornton Leigh Hunt, 10 (later 7) Wellington St., Strand, London. 21 October 1854–17 July 1856: Alfred Edmund Galloway, 7 Wellington Street, Strand, London/154 (later 352) Strand, London. 24 July 1858–18 December 1858: Frederick Guest Tomlins, 352 Strand, London/18 Catherine Street, Strand, London. 7 January 1860–24 November 1860: Charles Nuttall Tomlins, 18 Catherine Street, Strand, London.

EDITORS

Thornton Leigh Hunt, 30 March 1850–ca. January 1852. Edward Frederick Smyth Pigott, ca. January 1852–ca. July 1853, ca. March 1854–June 1858. Edward Michael Whitty, ca. July 1853–March 1854, ca. 1860. Frederick Guest Tomlins (probable), ca. June 1858–ca. January 1860.

Christopher Kent

LEADER AND SATURDAY ANALYST, THE. See LEADER, THE

LEIGH HUNT'S JOURNAL. See LEIGH HUNT'S (LONDON) JOURNAL (RA)

LIBRARY, THE

The purpose of the *Library*, as declared in a prospectus circulated during November 1888, was to treat bibliographical subjects. As the official publication of the Library Association of the United Kingdom, the journal would deal with all questions related to the profession of librarian, and it would advocate the Free Library Movement. Moreover, it would offer articles on all aspects of bibliography: reviews of books on libraries and bibliography, news of interest to librarians, and a section for correspondence on bibliographical topics. The prospectus included the names of forty-two potential contributors, among whom were some who would have a long and important association with the *Library*: Alfred W. Pollard, W. J. Hardy, W.E.A. Axon, Austin Dobson, Richard Garnett, Falconer Madan, William Blades, Charles Sayle, E. C. Thomas, H. R. Tedder, and Richard C. Christie.[1] John Young Walker MacAlister was appointed editor, a position he held through the year 1919. Near the end of the first year of publication, Richard Christie, president of the Library Association, provided more specific information on the purpose of the *Library* in his annual report, where he named as some of the more important objectives of the association and the *Library* the development of (1) a general catalogue of English literature; (2) systems for the classification and arrangement of books; and (3) guidelines for descriptive and analytical bibliography. The *Library* would promote bibliographical research, publish library statistics, encourage the founding of new libraries, and seek to raise librarians' professional status.[2]

The first series (1889–1898) of the *Library* combined some of the functions of *Transactions, Monthly Notes*, and the *Library Chronicle*, each of which had preceded it as the official publication of the Library Association. Following the two to five short articles that began each number was a second section entitled "Library Chronicle," composed of news items, reviews, lists of books, notices of meetings, information about legislation, reports from local libraries, and correspondence. Occasionally there were obituaries, "Legal Notes and Queries," "Library Economics," and short lists of anonyms and pseudonyms. The monthly numbers of the first series varied from thirty to forty pages in length.

J.Y.W. MacAlister was faithful to the statement of purpose in the Library Association prospectus, although he apparently had increasing doubts during the first series. He published articles, reviews, notes, and items of news, and listed books on indicators, library administration, statutes, reference libraries, periodical literature, catalogues, women librarians, discounts, training, classification, and the Library Movement.[3] An unusually large number of articles and items dealt with the demand for fiction in libraries and the objections to it.[4] MacAlister gave attention to book production, subject and author bibliographies, and descriptions of books, libraries, and collections.[5] Frank Campbell's "The Bibliography of the Future" (1st ser., 7:33–48) is a good summation of what the term *bibliography* meant and how far the *Library*'s interests in bibliographic skills extended. The book reviews of the first series, while not as large a part of each issue as they were to become in later years, were nevertheless significant.[6] Among the more important contributors of articles to the first series were A. H. Bullen, Alfred W. Pollard, E. Gordon Duff, W.H.K. Wright, William Blades, F. G. Fleay, W.E.A. Axon, Charles Welch, Richard Garnett, W. J. Hardy, E. Maunde Thompson, Richard Christie, Ernest Chester Thomas, Henry R. Tedder, and Miss S. T. Prideaux.

MacAlister had many problems during his term as editor. Numbers were frequently late.[7] He was continually short of good copy, especially after Pollard began *Bibliographica* (1895–1897). MacAlister also did not find it easy to combine the interests of librarians and bibliographers, or to serve the needs of the Library Association. He disapproved of publishing, regardless of quality, those papers accepted by the Library Association Council. He wanted to treat library subjects more systematically, and found that he often had to scrape up copy to meet the monthly deadline. Evidently as a result of these problems, MacAlister announced that the *Library Association Record*, up to this point carried in the *Library*, would be published separately as the new official organ of the Library Association, and that the *Library* would cease with the tenth volume of the first series in 1898.[8]

A second series (1899–1909, "New Series") appeared nevertheless. After encouragement from friends, MacAlister decided to continue as editor but only with changes stipulated in conditions. The *Library* would be issued quarterly and would contain quality articles, or would not appear until it did. Although no longer sponsored by the Library Association, it would provide systematic treatment of "practical librarianship," for example, library history, legislation, architecture, government, cataloguing, classification, formation, and management. It would be illustrated. It would give equal treatment to bibliography and would place more emphasis than formerly on reviews, which were to be the responsibility of Alfred W. Pollard.[9]

The first volume of the second series appeared in December 1899, opening with a photogravure and brief biographical sketch of Richard Garnett, followed by almost a dozen articles on bibliographical and library subjects. Following was a section entitled "Notes on Books and Work: Bibliography, Literary History, and Collecting," containing subtitles for various subject areas—for example, "American Notes" and "Science Notes"—depending on the content of the particular issue, edited by Pollard.[10] The photogravures were dropped after volume 2, and MacAlister, still not able to find enough suitable copy, went to larger type in order to fill up the 112 pages with fewer articles.[11] He was for the most part unable to implement his plan to provide a more systematic treatment of library topics, though the first volume does give attention to American libraries, while some of the later volumes contain concentrations on specific subjects, and bibliographical subjects receive increasing emphasis in the second series.

In 1903 MacAlister once again announced the cessation of the *Library*, but once again publication was resumed, this time immediately, with Alfred W. Pollard as coeditor. Pollard wrote of the difficulty of pleasing both librarians and bibliographers in the same journal, but planned to continue those dual emphases.[12] Under MacAlister and Pollard, the quality of the *Library* improved steadily, especially in bibliography. During this period (second series to 1909, third series, 1910–1919), Walter W. Gregg, Ronald B. McKerrow, Henry Plomer, E. Gordon Duff, Gilbert Redgrave, Melvil Dewey, Victor Scholderer, Muriel St. Clare Byrne, John Dover Wilson, and other scholars of comparable stature wrote substantial articles for the *Library*. Pollard himself contributed frequently. The length of individual articles increased. The reviews fluctuated in number and emphasis.[13] In volume 4 of the second series (1904), Elizabeth Lee began a series of reviews of foreign literature that continued until the end of the third series (1919).[14] Although MacAlister and Pollard had planned to continue to cover "practical library problems," the articles and items on these matters gradually declined and ultimately all but disappeared. During this time the journal began to focus on the bibliography of English literature before 1640, an emphasis that was to grow stronger in the 1920s and 1930s, chiefly through the work of Gregg, Pollard, and McKerrow.[15]

When the *Library* merged with the *Transactions* of the Bibliographical Society in 1920, the transition was an easy one. As early as 1891, MacAlister and W. A. Copinger discussed the formation of a bibliographical society, the first announcements of which appeared in the *Library* during 1892, and the first meeting of which was held in the *Library* offices at 20 Hanover Square. Pollard and many others connected with the *Library* over the years were also members of the Bibliographical Society. William Osler, president of the society, strongly favored the merger. It would eliminate delays in publication by the society resulting from the fact that the *Transactions* came out only every other year. The *Library* (the title appears under "The Transactions of the Bibliographical Society") adopted the typographical format of the *Transactions*, permitting more words per page, and kept a reduced adaptation of Michelangelo's drawing of the entrance to the Laurentian Library in Florence on the front cover, adding the works "Founded by J.Y.W. MacAlister in 1888."[16] Issues now typically contained a series of bibliographical articles, followed by obituaries, reviews, reports and notices of the society, and correspondence. Beginning with volume 23 of the fourth series (September/December 1942), a section of "Bibliographical Notes" was introduced just after the longer articles, and increased rapidly in size in subsequent volumes.

During the two decades after the assumption of the *Library* by the Bibliographical Society and the appointment of Alfred W. Pollard as editor, the journal developed a strong reputation for bibliographical studies of English literature before 1640. Pollard, Gregg, McKerrow, and others were joined by Fredson T. Bowers, R. C. Bald, Maynard Mack, Michael Sadleir, James G. McManaway, Geoffrey Keynes, J. D. Jump, William A. Jackson, H. T. Price, and Don Cameron Allen. Later came John Dover Wilson, Charleton Hinman, Giles Dawson, Stanley Morison, J. B. Leishman, Joseph Quincy Adams, Graham Pollard, Leo Kirschbaum, J. M. Nosworthy, William B. Todd, William White, G. K. Hunter, Arthur Freeman, E.A.J. Honigman, W.H. Bond, Vinton A. Dearing, Robert K. Turner, Franklin B. Williams, G. Thomas Tanselle, and others. They wrote on printing and printers, paper, booksellers, handwriting, plays, Bibles, romances, almanacs, liturgies, medicine, woodcuts, and many other topics.[17] Perhaps the single greatest offshoot of this activity was Alfred W. Pollard and Gilbert R. Redgrave's *Short-Title Catalogue of Books Printed in England, Scotland, and Ireland, and of English Books Printed Abroad* (London, 1926). The more than seventy articles on Shakespeare's texts that appeared between 1892 and 1943 are, for example, an unmatched contribution to Shakespeare bibliography.[18] After World War II the *Library* began to cover an increasingly wide range of modern literature, though it continued to maintain its strength in earlier literature, especially that of the eighteenth century.

Aside from the attention to modern works, the *Library* has made few changes since World War II, however. The reference to MacAlister on the cover was dropped in June 1946, and the drawing of the Laurentian Library in December 1965. The practice of naming the place of residence of authors of articles began in 1966; "Projects in Progress" was added in 1972, and the journal began to use a lighter weight paper, to number notes continuously, and to increase the number of lines on each page.

Notes

1. Alfred W. Pollard, *"The Library*: A History of Forty Volumes," *Library*, 4th ser., 10 (1930):398–417.

2. "Annual Report," *Library*, 1st ser., 1 (November 1889):335.

3. On the Library Movement, see *Library*, 1st ser., 7 (1895):97–109, 110–19, 223, 282–83, 296. *Encylopaedia Britannica*, 9th ed., provides a background of the movement.

4. *Library*, 1st ser., 2 (1890):178, 373; 5 (1893):49; 6 (1894):236–37, 252, 410, 411; 7 (1895):52, 97, 110, 120, 128, 276–81.

5. A good example of the work on author bibliographies is W.E.A. Axon, "The Spenser Society and Its Work," *Library*, 1st ser., 7 (1895):201–10.

6. See *Library*, 1st ser., 9 (1897):157–63, for a survey of the books reviewed from 1889 to 1897 and a supplementary list of books overlooked.

7. See the announcement in *Library*, 1st ser., 4 (1892):355. The index to volume 4, 1st ser., is published in the January issue of volume 5.

8. J.Y.W. MacAlister, *"The Library* Redivivus," *Library*, 1st ser., 10 (1898):398–400.

9. Pollard, pp. 398–400.

10. In volume 2 only there is a section of book reviews immediately before Pollard's "Notes."

11. Pollard, pp. 408–9.

12. *Library*, 2d ser., 3 (1902):440–41; 4 (1903):94–96.

13. After volume 1, 3d ser. (1910), the section "Notes and Reviews" becomes "Reviews."

14. French and German books were reviewed alternately up to January 1915, when German books were dropped.

15. Walter W. Gregg's important articles on the Shakespeare quartos appear in 2d ser., 9, nos. 34 and 36 (1908); Phoebe Sheavyn's *The Literary Profession in the Elizabethan Age* (1909) was a revision of her articles in 2d ser., 7 (1906), 8 (1907).

16. Pollard, p. 415; see also *Library*, 1st ser., 4 (1892):1–7, 230–32, 294–97; 4th ser., 6 (1926):375–80.

17. F. S. Ferguson, "English Books Before 1640," in *The Bibliographical Society, 1892–1942* (London, 1945), pp. 42–75, discusses these contributions in detail.

18. F. P. Wilson, "Shakespeare and the 'New Bibliography,' " in *The Bibliographical Society, 1892–1942*, pp. 76–135.

Information Sources

BIBLIOGRAPHY
The Bibliographical Society, 1892–1942. Studies in Retrospect. London, 1945.
MacAlister, John Young Walker. *"The Library* Redivivus." *Library*, 1st ser., 10
    (1898):398–400.
Pollard, Alfred W. "Sir John MacAlister: Some Reminiscences." *Library*, 4th ser., 6
    (1926):375–80.
INDEXES
    Each volume indexed. Index of authors for 3d series (1910–1919) in volume 10,
    3d ser. (1919). *General Index* (Oxford, 1932) covers 4th ser., volumes 1–10
    (1920–1930). George Watson Cole, *An Index to Bibliographical Papers Published
    by the Bibliographical Society and the Library Association, London, 1877–1932*
    (Chicago, 1933).
REPRINT EDITIONS
    Kraus Reprint Ltd., Nendeln, FL-9491, Liechtenstein.
LOCATION SOURCES
American
    Widely available.
British
    Widely available.

Publication History

MAGAZINE TITLE AND TITLE CHANGES
    The Library: A Magazine of Bibliography and Literature, January, 1889–Decem-
    ber 1893. *The Library: A Magazine of Bibliography and Library Literature*,
    January, 1894–November 1899. *The Library: A Quarterly Review of Bibliography
    and Library Lore*, December 1899–March 1920. *The Library: A Quarterly Review
    of Bibliography*, June 1920–December 1963. *The Library: A Quarterly Journal
    of Bibliography*, March 1964–.
VOLUME AND ISSUE DATA
    First series, volumes 1–10, January 1889–December 1898; second series, volumes
    1–10, December 1899–October 1909; third series, volumes 1–10, January 1910–
    October 1919; fourth series, volumes 1–26, June 1920–March 1946; fifth series,
    volumes 1–33, June 1946–December 1978; sixth series, volumes 1–, March 1979–
FREQUENCY OF PUBLICATION
    Monthly, January 1889–December 1898; quarterly, December 1899–.
PUBLISHERS
    January 1889–December 1891: Elliot Stock, 62 Paternoster Row, London. January
    1892–December 1893: Library Association, 20 Hanover Square, W., London.
    January 1894–December 1895: Simpkin, Marshall and Company, 4 Stationers
    Hall Court, London, E.C. January 1896–December 1898: Library Bureau, 10
    Bloomsbury Street, London, W.C. December 1899–October 1902: Kegan Paul,
    Trench, Trubner and Company, Limited, Paternoster House, Charing Cross Road,
    London, W.C. January 1903–October 1907: Unknown. January 1908–October

1919: Alexander Moring, Limited, 32 George Street, Hanover Square, London, W. June 1920–December 1978: Humphrey Milford, Oxford University Press.

EDITORS

John Young Walker MacAlister, January 1889–October 1902. John Young Walker MacAlister and Alfred W. Pollard, January 1903–October 1919. Alfred W. Pollard, June 1920–March 1935. Ronald B. McKerrow, June 1935–March 1936. Ronald B. McKerrow and F. C. Francis, June 1936–March 1937. F. C. Francis, June 1937–December 1953. J.C.T. Oates, March 1954–Decemberr 1960. Desmond G. Neill, March 1961–December 1964. R. A. Sayce, March 1965–December 1970. Peter H. Davison, January 1971–.

Dickie A. Spurgeon

LITERARY GAZETTE, THE. See RA

LITERARY GUIDE

Charles Albert Watts founded the *Literary Guide* in 1885, calling it for its first nine years *Watts Literary Guide.* In 1898 Watts and fellow freethinkers organized the Rationalist Press Association to further promote the ideals for which the *Literary Guide* stood. From 1898 to the present, the story of the *Literary Guide* parallels the development and successes of the Rationalist Press Association. Adam Gowans Whyte, with Watts one of the original founders of the Rationalist Press Association, for which the *Literary Guide* became first an unofficial and then an official organ, summarized Watts's early editorial policy in this way: "His main ambition in those early days was to bring the treasures of Rationalism within the reach of everybody" (64:118). In a defense of the *Literary Guide*'s nonpolitical emphasis, F.C.C. Watts, the son of C. A. Watts, and the second editor, stated: "Like the [Rationalist] movement of which it may be regarded as the chief mouthpiece, the *Literary Guide* must concern itself first and foremost with those fundamental questions raised by religion and philosophy" (65:232). Hector Hawton, third editor of the *Literary Guide*, summarized the periodical's goal in this way: "When the *Literary Guide* was founded it served the valuable purpose of calling attention to unorthodox books which, in those days, were usually kept out of shop windows. It was considered shocking to profess doubts about Christianity. If you believed in the new-fangled theory of evolution you were looked at askance. It was daring to call yourself an agnostic and it might be socially disastrous to describe yourself as an atheist" (71:6). Though transformed in time from being a journal that "cater[ed] mainly for members of a movement" (69:22) into one "with a public appeal and general sale" (69:22), the magazine, as *Literary Guide* and then as the *Humanist* and the *New Humanist*, continued to encourage the goals of the Rationalist Press Association:

> To promote the study of rational thinking
>
> To encourage the spread of rational thinking in human conduct
>
> To fight irrationality and superstition wherever they affect human conduct
>
> To defend freedom of thought and inquiry, particularly where a rational approach to human affairs may conflict with traditional creeds and beliefs
>
> To advance a secular system of education, the main object of which shall be to cultivate in the young moral and intellectual fitness for social life
>
> [83 (April 1968): front cover]

With its origins in the freethinking atmosphere of late Victorian culture, struggling for a place and a voice in a still predominantly theistic society, the *Literary Guide* presents the impression, even in its later years, of an embattled but on the whole happy crowd of rationalists and atheists. In its twenty-six to thirty pages, the *Guide* presented editorials ("The Open Window," by "Protonious"— most frequently A. G. Whyte), signed articles, "Notes and News" (of the Rationalist Press Association), book reviews, short notices, and correspondence. The *Literary Guide* evaluated issues, books, and figures from the rather selective perspective of how these furthered or impeded the progress of rationalism. Always something of a family affair, the magazine found many of its regular contributors among the authors of books published by Watts and Company; and while book reviews in the journal considered many major works in science, philosophy, religion, and literature of the times, a fair number of books reviewed were those published by Watts, a company known particularly for its reprints of important scientific or controversial works by such authors as R. G. Ingersoll, Sir Arthur Keith, Albert Einstein, and Charles Darwin. Reviewer D. Stark Murray, for instance, claimed that H. G. Wells's *Short History of the World* sold 250,000 copies in Watts's Thinkers' Library edition (65:41).

Topics of the *Literary Guide*'s signed articles tended to be philosophical, scientific, or anti-Christian—at least anti-Revelation—in the tradition of T. H. Huxley, rather than political or purely literary. Lord Raglan might contribute a brief anthropological note; Maurice Burton might discuss "The Return of the Predators" (65:85), or Llewelyn Powys might complain about the dimunition of the heroic figure of Christ as presented in American sermons (64:93–95). Reviews, seldom running longer than a thousand words, treated many of the same topics. E. Royston Pike, a regular contributor for years, reviewed Watts's 1949 reprint of Lord Raglan's 1936 classic, *The Hero* (64:152–53); Hector Hawton, later editor of the *Literary Guide*, reviewed Lancelot Law Whyte's *The Unitary Principle in Physics and Biology* (64:174); and Archibald Robertson reviewed Bronislaw Malinowski's *Magic, Science, and Religion* (64:130). C. D. Darlington reviewed Julian Huxley's *Soviet Genetics* (65:38).

When the *Literary Guide* did treat literature or literary figures, the articles tended to be highly partisan, if not tendentious. They emphasized the rationalistic or humanistic rebellion of authors such as Robert Louis Stevenson (65:253) or Goethe, Wordsworth, and Coleridge (68:187). As the *Humanist*, the periodical printed articles on the stoicism of Hemingway and a rationalist investigation by Robert Graves and Joshua Podro of "How the Gospels Were Written" (October 1954). A series by Kathleen Nott (September 1954–March 1955) considered the orthodoxy or lack of orthodoxy among some modern and not so modern writers.

Before 1954, when the magazine sought to de-emphasize its role as organ of the Rationalist Press Association, the topical notes in individual issues said much about the character of the magazine, its contributors, and the intellectual and social milieu of which they were a part. In the late 1940s, for instance, the magazine was full of self-congratulatory material as the association approached its jubilee year. Issues devoted to the yearly conferences in London and then in Oxford listed the participants (often with photographs) and recorded the speeches laudatory of the editors, the association, and the special speakers. The issue for 20 May 1949 includes a summary of Bertrand Russell's speech, the keynote address of the jubilee year conference.

At the yearly conferences A. E. Heath, Lord Raglan, and J. C. Robertson Scott, biographer of the *Pall Mall Gazette*, were among the guests. At the conference on irrationalism, held in 1950, the guest list included A. J. Ayer, one of the speakers, and the Albert Schweitzers. In other issues the "Notes and News" columns included announcements of or retrospectives on the Rationalist Press Association's many social functions. One such announcement, for instance, solicits interest in a visit to the haunts of famous nineteenth-century scientists and rationalists such as Darwin and Bentham. In numerous issues the careful reader can also find plotted the relation of the *Literary Guide* and the Rationalist Press Association to other periodicals of the time. As a single example, in 1950 (65:103) Royston Pike gives a memorial tribute to Harold Laski, who was president of the Rationalist Press Association from 1929 to 1933, but who was also, during the same years, a contributor to the more important and well-known *New Statesman*.*

Over the years, the most notable contributors to the *Literary Guide* and the names most often referred to with manly and rational reverence by the magazine's less well known contributors were Bertrand Russell (a member of the Rationalist Press Association since the 1920s), Sir Arthur Keith, Julian Huxley, J.B.S. Haldane, Lord Raglan, Maurice Burton, A. E. Heath, W. Glanville Cook, and the scientist Raymond Firth. Writers like Haldane and Huxley also contributed to the Rationalist Press's more prestigious *Rationalist Annual*, and, as noted, well-known thinkers like A. J. Ayer had their speeches at the yearly conferences synopsized in the pages of the *Literary Guide*.

In the 1950s some notable contributions were those by Jacob Bronowski (June–September 1954) and William Empson ("The Elizabethan Stage," March 1955). Bronowski's "Human Values" appeared in November 1955 (70:11). Into the

1960s the magazine was still treating issues dear to the hearts of old-time atheists and principled rationalists. The June 1968 issue included an editorial heralding the death-of-God theologian, J.A.T. Robinson; the July 1968 issue interspersed the new and the old, including articles on "Killing Animals," "Euthanasia," "Juvenile Delinqency," and "Jewish Anti-Semitism." For a small, highly specialized journal which has nevertheless survived for nearly one hundred years, the *Literary Guide/Humanist/New Humanist* is fairly easy to characterize, and its transformations in response to the changing importance of rational and antireligious issues make an interesting study of the ways in which ideas and partisanships maintain continuity through history.

Information Sources

BIBLIOGRAPHY
Whyte, Adam Gowans. *The Story of the R.P.A.* London, 1949.
INDEXES
    None.
REPRINT EDITIONS
    None.
LOCATION SOURCES
    American
        Partial runs: Widely available.
    British
        Partial runs: British Library of Political Science; British Museum; Liverpool Public Library; University College of South Wales Library; University College of Swansea Library.

Publication History

MAGAZINE TITLE AND TITLE CHANGES
        Watts Literary Guide, 1885–1894. *Literary Guide and Rationalist Review*, 1894–1954. *Literary Guide*, 1954–1956. *Humanist*, 1956–1971. *New Humanist*, 1972–.
VOLUME AND ISSUE DATA
        Numbers 1–105, 1885–15 August 1894.
        New Series, numbers 106–126, October 1894–June 1896.
        New Series, numbers 1–546, 1 July 1896–December 1941; volumes 57–, January 1942–.
FREQUENCY OF PUBLICATION
        Monthly.
PUBLISHERS
        1885–1954: C. A. Watts and Co., Ltd., 5 and 6 Johnson's Court, Fleet Street, London E.C. 4. 1954–1959: Rationalist Press Association, 40 Drury Lane, London W.C. 2/H. I. Thompson Co. Ltd., 12 St. James Place, London S.W. 1. 1959–1964: Rationalist Press Association, 28 St. James Place, London W. 1/H. I. Thompson Co., Ltd. 1965–1966: Rationalist Press Association, 2 Ellis St., Sloane St., London S.W. 1. 1967–: Rationalist Press Association, 88 Islington St., London, N. 1 8EW.

Ed Block, Jr.

LITERATURE

Four days before the appearance of its first issue in October 1897, *Literature* was heralded in the London *Times*, its proprietor, as a periodical of a kind that did not then exist in England: a critical literary weekly. Its frequent appearance and its exclusive attention to literature would, it was hoped, make it "the organ of the literary classes": "Books, alike and equally in their relation to the world of authors, of publishers, and of readers, will be its exclusive concern; and no effort will be spared to win recognition for it as an impartial and authoritative organ of literary criticism and a comprehensive and trustworthy medium of literary intelligence."[1] As its name was meant to indicate, its function was not to be solely critical. It was to take up, in various forms, "any literary subject, either of permanent or of current interest to the writing, publishing, or reading world."[2] It also was to serve as a record of current publications by means of a classified index providing information on the author and publisher, and on the size, number of pages, and price of each title it received. Book criticism was, however, to be its chief concern. Two articles in the first issue of *Literature* take up the subject of critical reviewing. Augustine Birrell, in "A Colloquy of Criticism," discusses its difficulties, and *Literature* editor H. D. Traill, in "Author and Critic," argues for its necessity:

> *Literature* . . . owes its existence in some measure to the conviction that, in an effort to satisfy every one of the innumerable applicants, deserving and undeserving, for its notice, contemporary criticism is running a real danger of neglecting its discriminative functions, and of forgetting that the special recognition which it owes to writers of genuine literary merit is necessarily depreciated in value by association with a too liberal complaisance of attention to all writers whatsoever. [No. 1:2]

As it turned out, the role of mediator between reader and writer, whether as literary critic or as teacher, became the subject of a number of articles in *Literature*. Articles on criticism and the critic include two more by Traill ("International Criticism" and "What Is a Critic?") as well as W. D. Howells's "Nature of American Literary Criticism," Stephen Gwynn's "Qualifications of a Critic," Harry Quilter's "Review of Reviewing," and "A" 's "On Certain Defects in Modern Criticism." In the last of these articles are echoes of historical allusion and of the critical attitude found in the first issue of *Literature*: "The most startling feature of modern reviewing is not its harshness, its scorn, its implacability, but rather its universal indulgence, and its discriminate and excessive language of eulogy" (no. 7:209). The abiding critical principle of *Literature* is that criticism should avoid the extremes of intellectual narrowness and appreciative effulgence—that the merit of books be assessed according to "principles which can be defined and analysed" (no. 120:98).

Related to *Literature*'s concern with the duties of the critic is its more general concern with the duties of the educator. Among articles related to this subject are H. A. Dalton's "Inspection of Secondary Schools," F. Frankfort Moore's "An Extinct Type" (on boys' books as teachers of hypocrisy), and two articles by Traill, "The Teaching of English Literature" and "A Holiday Task for Parents" ("If at least half of the school books now current were piled upon a great bonfire, education would certainly not suffer. It might even survive if a few teachers perished in the flames" [no. 9:258]). Books on education and more especially books for young readers were regularly reviewed in *Literature*, and in time an "Educational Supplement" became an established addition to the weekly.

Normally twenty-five or more titles were anonymously reviewed in *Literature* by writers chosen for their authority in the subject of the review. The importance of the book and the eminence of its writer determined the review's length. Thus, as many as one to three thousand words were devoted to about half the reviews, and as few as half a dozen lines to others. In a six-month period, notices of nearly a thousand books by more than nine hundred writers appeared in *Literature*, with the greatest attention given to fiction (about one-fourth of the total number), biographies, art and archaeology, and books for young readers. The usual format of *Literature* provided that the large central section devoted to reviews be preceded by a leading article (unsigned, but by Traill), another signed article by or about a writer of note, and often a poem or a short story. Following the review section were obituaries of literary figures (including ones on Nietzsche, Mallarmé, Eliza Lynn Linton, and R. D. Blackmore, and Henry James's memorial articles on Daudet and Frederic Harrison's on Ruskin); brief notes on literary events; a bibliographical article, correspondence, and a concluding list of new books and reprints.

Traill's leading articles reveal the editor's wide-ranging knowledge of literary matters and the breadth of literary subjects that *Literature* was to claim as its own. He wrote on particular writers (for example, Burns and Tolstoy), genres (autobiography, history, the novel, poetic drama, and travel books), literature and culture (women's journals and "Culture and the Classics"), and contemporary literary issues ("The Domination of the Novel," "The Bookselling Question," and "An English Academy") as well as on criticism. A lawyer by training, Traill served briefly as inspector of returns in the Education Office. Most of his career he spent as a journalist, having served as regular contributor and staff member for several journals, including the *Observer* and *Saturday Review*.* In the years immediately preceding the founding of *Literature* he served as editor of a sociological and historical series, Social England. He wrote plays, poems, and literary biographies, as well as innumerable articles, most of them literary.

During the first years of *Literature* signed articles appeared regularly under the title "Among My Books" and, later, "Personal Views." These articles comprise a remarkably varied series of personal records by known writers of their reading and literary views. These include Leslie Stephen's "Perishable Books" ("Will our grandchildren have any cause for sorrow if ninety-nine hundredths of all the publications of today should disappear like a bad dream?" [no. 6:177]); Andrew Lang's "History as It Is Written"; Edmund Gosse's appreciation of Addison's *Travels*; Eliza Lynn Linton's "Montaigne"; Vernon Lee's "Keys to the Universe" (the "only universe we can ever really know is the universe which we know not through processes of induction or deduction, but through thoroughgoing enjoyment or weary longing or bitter grief" [no. 13:49]); George Gissing's "Dickens in Memory"; Hilaire Belloc's "The Historian"; Jerome K. Jerome's "The German Schoolboy"; and Max Beerbohm's "A Pathetic Imposture." Other articles in this series include astronomer Agnes Clerk's "Scientific Women" (in which she hails women's contributions to knowledge as now habitual rather than exceptional occurrences); Lionel Tollemache's reminiscences of Gladstone and Lewis Carroll; Hannah Lynch's "The Drama as a Moral Force"; H. F. Carlill's "A Plea for the Consideration of Walt Whitman"; and Mrs. E. T. Cook's "Women's Journalism."

Though the publication of poems and short stories makes up a small part of *Literature*, the contributors include Kipling and Meredith as well as Emily Lawless, Fiona MacLeod, Evelyn Nesbit, Ernest Rhys, Alice Herbert, and Grace Ellery Channing.

Having named a Leipzig agency (Brockhaus) for its distribution in Germany, Austria, and Switzerland, and Harper and Brothers of New York for an American edition, *Literature* committed itself early on to reporting on important publications from across the Channel and the Atlantic.[3] Reviews of foreign publications appeared regularly in *Literature*, and there began with its second number a regular series of "Foreign Letters," some signed and some not, on literary events in the United States, France, and—less frequently—other countries. Two important individual series that developed from this column were "American Letters" by Howells and James. In anticipation of these series Traill wrote in "Literature in America" on events and conditions leading to differences between American and English books. James discussed "The Novel of Dialect," "The Question of the Opportunities," and Hamlin Garland, as well as the letters of General Grant to a friend, of Walt Whitman to Peter Doyle, and of Harding Davis. Howells's subjects include "The Politics of American Authors," "The Southern States in Recent American Literature," and "Puritanism in Fiction."

Following Traill's sudden death in early 1900, *Literature* underwent some substantial changes, including the abandonment of the leading article, the introduction of a larger number of signed non-review articles, and, beginning in May 1901 and continuing through the last issue, the publication of a series of "Literary

Portraits." Embellished with photographs, these studies by critics of "authority" were of thirty-six "chief writers of the day, English and Foreign" (no. 185:353). These portraits came to represent the major non-review article of *Literature*. Included in this series were portraits of Arthur Symons, Emerson, Ibsen, and Stevenson (all by Egan Mew); of Carlyle, Whitman, H. W. Lucy, Stanley J. Weyman, and H. G. Wells (by E. H. Lacon Watson); of Edmund Gosse, Hardy, and Stephen Phillips (by Stephen Gwynn); of Ruskin and Morris (by Wallace L. Crowdy); of Gissing, by Morley Roberts; of Swinburne, by W. E. Garrett Fisher; of Mrs. Humphry Ward, by Laurie Magnus; and of Andrew Lang, by G. K. Chesterton. For a while these illustrated literary portraits threatened to transform *Literature* into a quite different weekly from what it had been under Traill's editorship and the year following his death: personal reminiscences as well as biographical and critical articles in this series sometimes verged on the appreciative and eulogistic. Another series of articles, on "Principal Movements of Victorian Poetry," by Arthur Waugh, also contributed to the new character of *Literature* as a less varied and less critical review of contemporary publications than it had been originally. Another regular feature of the later *Literature* was a drama article by A. B. Walkley, who, in the spirit of the original *Literature*, wrote often about contemporary books on drama, but also wrote about dramatic productions. In its later years, *Literature* began to move away from the principles of literary focus and critical analysis with which it had begun.

With its 221st issue of 11 January 1902, *Literature* ceased as an independent publication and was, the next week, absorbed by the *Academy** under the name *Academy and Literature: A Weekly Review of Literature and Life*. The *Academy* had begun publication in 1869 as a monthly literary review whose contributors included Matthew Arnold, W. M. Rossetti, William Morris, and J. A. Symonds. By 1890 it had become a "weekly review of literature, science and art" which counted among its contributors Andrew Lang, George Saintsbury, A. C. Swinburne, Arthur Symons, Lionel Johnson, Richard Le Gallienne, and Michael Field (joint pen name of Katherine Harris Bradley and Edith Emma Cooper). Though *Academy and Literature* maintained for a while the distinction the two separate reviews had enjoyed previous to their merger, by 1916, when it ceased publication, it had degenerated into a gossip-filled penny paper bearing little evidence of its admirable parentage.[4] The important lineage, however, is from *Literature* to the *Times Literary Supplement*, whose predecessor *Literature* was. The original intent of *Literature* to serve as the chief critical literary weekly of the literary classes was assumed by *TLS*, the first issue of which appeared on 17 January 1902, six days after the last issue of *Literature* appeared.

Notes

1. London *Times*, 19 October 1897, p. 5.

2. Ibid.

3. The American edition of *Literature* is identical to the English one except for the year 1899, when the American edition assumed a different format altogether from the English one.

4. Cyrena Norman Pondrom, *English Literary Periodicals: 1885–1918*, Ph.D. dissertation, Columbia University, 1965, pp. 39–40.

Information Sources

BIBLIOGRAPHY
Graham, Walter. *English Literary Periodicals*. New York, 1930.
London *Times*, 19 October 1897, pp. 5, 7.
Pondrom, Cyrena Norman. *English Literary Periodicals: 1885–1918*. Ph.D. dissertation, Columbia University, 1965.
INDEXES
Each volume indexed.
REPRINT EDITIONS
Arno Press, New York, 1974.
LOCATION SOURCES
American
Widely available.
British
Complete runs: Birmingham Public Library; Bodleian Library; British Museum; Manchester Public Library; Queen's University of Belfast Library; Sheffield Public Library; University College (London) Library; Victoria and Albert Museum Library. Partial runs: Aberdeen University Library; Cambridge University Library; Dundee Public Library; Roborough Library (University College of Exeter); University of Hull Library.

Publication History

MAGAZINE TITLE AND TITLE CHANGES
Literature. (Merged with *Academy* after 11 January 1902.)
VOLUME AND ISSUE DATA
Volumes 1–10, numbers 1–221, 23 October 1897–11 January 1902.
FREQUENCY OF PUBLICATION
Weekly.
PUBLISHER
London *Times*, Printing House Square, London E.C.
EDITORS
H. D. Traill, 1897–1900. Subsequent editor(s) of *Literature* unknown.

Carol de Saint Victor

LONDON AND EDINBURGH WEEKLY REVIEW. See WEEKLY REVIEW

LONDON QUARTERLY AND HOLBORN REVIEW, THE

As early as 1839 a young Methodist theological student at Leeds, James Harrison Rigg, urged the editor of the Tory Methodist publication, the *Watchman*, to further the establishment of a review within which Methodism could defend its system and doctrine after the fashion of other religious groups.[1] In the thirty years prior to the founding of the *London Quarterly Review* in 1853, Methodism had been torn by "a quarrel between the growing radicalism of the rank and file and the Toryism of the Chiefs."[2] The review was nonpolitical in the sense that it supported neither party, but it did advocate ever more strongly a "social Gospel" at variance with Wesley's own views. In the nineteenth century Methodism did not, on the whole, consider itself to be a "dissenting" religion, but rather a supplementary order which supplied the deficiencies of the Church of England. A reviewer in the October 1872 issue of the *London Quarterly* argued, in his discussion of a book about dissent and its relation to the Church of England, that Methodism was not mere dissent, but had its roots in the "Mother Church."[3] John Wesley himself had remained an Anglican priest until he was expelled in 1784 for ordaining his own priests. While Methodism had split into several sects, it was still possible to speak of a "Methodist Church," and only a church— rather than a collection of unrelated chapels—could support an erudite periodical such as the *London Quarterly Review*.

The gradual repeal of the stamp and paper taxes between 1836 and 1861 had substantially lowered the cost of periodicals and favored the growth of the religious press. The decades preceding the founding of the *London Quarterly* saw the establishment of periodicals by several denominations, including a new one by the Church of England, the *Guardian*, and the Roman Catholic *Tablet*. It was out of this background that the *London Quarterly Review* was launched in September 1853 under the sponsorship of the Methodist Connexion. It lacked any editorial statement of purpose. Wesley had established his own *Arminian Magazine* in 1778, and by 1900 over ninety Methodist periodicals had appeared, serving both geographical and sectional interests.[4] Names such as the *Wesleyan Methodist Penny Magazine* (1853), *Cornish Methodist Church* (1892–1895), and *Methodist Temperance Magazine* (1868–1906) suggest their variety. In the 1850s reviews were still what the name implies—journals devoted to lengthy discussions of new books. The *London Quarterly Review* from its inception put its readers in touch with most of the social and intellectual currents of the day. It also was designed to provide through its theological reviews, intellectual rigor, which many both inside and outside the Church felt Methodism to be lacking.

The first number of September 1853 demonstrated how this plan was to be carried out (see 1, no. 1: articles 1, 2, 4, and 6). A long review of a travel book on Turkey and the lower Danube "by a British Resident Twenty Years in the East" occasioned a discussion of Mohammedan theology and of the social order consequent on a philosophy which believes that "despotism is the law of the universe." An omnibus review of six books about Wesley and Methodism allowed the reviewer to clarify many points of Methodist doctrine. He noted that while Robert Southey's unimpeachable credentials as a member of the British religious and political establishment had given final respectability to Wesley when Southey chose him as the subject of his 1820 biography, Southey's characterization of Wesley as a "Protestant Loyola" was a gross misrepresentation.

From such concerns the reader was swept into a review of ten recent books on natural history in which topics such as the reproduction of fungi were discussed in extensive detail. The *London Quarterly*'s reviewing of scientific works tended to be objective. It was more concerned to present the matter of the book than to discuss the theological implications arising therefrom. Reviews of the Registrar General's reports on cholera fatalities, births, deaths, and infant mortality did occasion conclusions, however. The reviewer advocated teaching "public and individual hygiene" in the schools and said unequivocally that the Gospel of Christ must also bring "physical regeneration." During 1859, the last year of Thomas M'Nicholl's editorship, the *London Quarterly* reviewed favorably both the *Idylls of the King* and John Stuart Mill's *On Liberty*. They faulted Mill's ideas only for their defect in "practical application" owing to the fact that not everyone is equipped by intellect or circumstance to test all ideas for himself (ser. 1, 13:270ff).

At the end of 1859 M'Nicholl resigned the editorship. At his death in 1863 his successor, William Burt Pope, praised his "nervous, discriminating, accurate and always graceful writings" and hailed them as the cornerstone on which the *London Quarterly*'s reputation had been formed (ser. 1, 20:419). Pope adhered to the high standards of his predecessor and carried on the periodical until 1886, when his health broke. For the last three of those years he shared the editorship with James Harrison Rigg, who was then sole editor until 1898. Both Pope and Rigg were Methodist clergymen. Pope was also a teacher and translator who took special interest in making the work of the evangelical German theologians known in England at the very time when the writings of skeptics such as Friedrich Strauss "were awakening the fears of the unlearned."[5] As a student of the Gospel, Pope's particular interest was the Risen Christ. One of his earliest contributions to the *London Quarterly* in July 1858 was an unsigned article, "The Risen Saviour—Works on the Forty Days," in which his review of new books was mingled with the results of his own study and observation.[6]

During his years of editorship, James Harrison Rigg was also principal of the Westminster Training College. This position helped him gain the financial support of laymen, as well as theologians, who were eager to see Methodism gain intellectual standing and to increase the cultivation of its ministers. The circulation of the *London Quarterly Review* was probably never over 1,200 copies and Methodism reaped prestige rather than pounds from it. Throughout the nineteenth century the editors sponsored long omnibus reviews on topics of current interest. British journalism was the topic, for example, in October 1859, with special concern shown for books and articles that confronted the question of making books affordable to the masses. In any one issue a scholarly review of a new edition of a Greek text might precede a notice of a popular Methodist devotional work, thus appealing to the reader's scholarly and devotional concerns.

William Burt Pope commissioned the Methodist artist and writer James Smetham to write a review of Alexander Gilchrist's *Life of William Blake*. It was
widely read and commented on far outside the usual circle of *London Quarterly*
readers. Dante Gabriel Rossetti, who had helped Gilchrist's widow in the completion of the volume, regarded Smetham's piece as the "most penetrating"
review of the artist's life and character that had appeared to date.[7]

By the latter part of the century the *London Quarterly* had ceased to be a pure
review and published original articles as well. These remained anonymous until
1898 when William Lonsdale Wilkinson became editor, but the reviews themselves continued to be unsigned for some years. With the accession to the
editorship of John Telford, Rigg's son-in-law, in 1905 each issue contained an
article by a non-Methodist theologian. Telford wrote many reviews himself and
specialized in biographies ("Editorial Comments," ser. 6, 168 [October
1943]:357). His successor noted that he had also a talent for "literary gossip"
and that his review of *At John Murray's: Records of a Literary Circle* in 1932
was declared to be the finest notice the book had received ("John Telford: An
Appreciation," ser. 6, 159 [October 1934]:434). After glancing over the history
of the *London Quarterly* in 1943, Wilbert F. Howard lamented the decline in
the reading of serious biblical and theological books among the contemporary
clergy and, indeed, the decline of "solid reading" generally. He noted that the
periodicals of all denominations were increasingly given to a "jumble" of comments on miscellaneous works, "humourous paragraphs and domestic prattle."
The editors of these papers knew their audience: "If the axe is laid at the root
of the tree of knowledge it is because the taste for that kind of fruit has been
lost" (ser. 6, 168 [October 1943]:359). "Solid reading" remained an accurate
description of the *London Quarterly and Holborn Review*, and it offered it on
a wide range of topics: philosophy, history, literature, and science, in addition
to the biblical studies and theology.

In 1932, at the time of the union of Methodist sects in Britain, the *London
Quarterly Review* amalgamated with the *Holborn Review*, an organ of the group
known as Primitive Methodists. The *Holborn*'s history included a series of
mergers extending back to 1858 when Colin C. M'Kechnie inaugurated the
Christian Ambassador. A Methodist organ, the *Ambassador* was straightforward
in its aim: "to defend the cause of Evangelical godliness against hostile assault
... to constrain to practical conformity to the image of Christ."[8] Under the
editorship of Arthur S. Peake from 1919 to 1929 the *Holborn* benefited from
his wide friendship with contemporary theologians and had a reputation far
outweighing its circulation. In 1932 the first issue of the joint *London Quarterly
and Holborn Review* looked beyond Methodism. In his article on William Inge,
the "gloomy Dean" of St. Paul's Cathedral, Henry W. Forbes commented that
"he makes clear how far today we have deviated from the Christianity of Christ."
Inge's views that religion was impotent to redeem the world and that "social
legislation lies simply outside the range of our Lord's teachings" were attacked
as false to the nature and needs of man (ser. 6, 157:1–12). Inge's views were,

in fact, compatible on these points with Wesley's own, but not with the tradition of social consciousness that had developed in British Methodism since the industrial revolution had begun to transform British life. Thus the *London Quarterly* interested itself in President Roosevelt's economic recovery plan as an example of the pursuit of social justice (J. S. Richardson, "President Roosevelt's Recovery Experiment," ser. 6, 159 [1934]:1ff).

In its last years the *London Quarterly and Holborn Review* became more narrowly a quarterly of theology, although other areas were not ignored. In an age that offered a bewildering array of secular periodicals, the decision to emphasize theology was a logical one, although a departure from the ideal of earlier editors. Telford in particular had wished to appeal to all aspects of the reader's nature (ser. 6, 159 [October 1934]:434). In its last three years the review confronted the challenge presented by the theology of Karl Barth and the elevation of humanism to a religion. In the January 1937 issue it scored a coup for a periodical of its kind when Barth himself chose its pages for his attack on the Oxford Group movement led by Frank Buchman. The *London Quarterly* took up the cause of liturgical reform in its last years, a topic previously neglected among Methodists. When it was absorbed into the new *Church Quarterly Review* in 1968, William Strawson asserted that his retrospective article on its last forty years was "not an obituary notice. The *L.Q.H.R.* is beginning a new stage in its journey; it is evolving out of its past into a new future."[9]

Notes

1. John Telford, *The Life of James Harrison Rigg, D.D.: 1821–1909* (London, 1909), p. 19.

2. E. E. Kellet, "The Press," in *Early Victorian England, 1830–1865*, ed. G. M. Young (London, 1934), 2:85–86.

3. See the review of George Henry Curteis's *Dissent in Its Relation to the Church of England* in *London Quarterly Review*, ser. 1, 39 (October 1872):213.

4. See Samuel J. Rogal, "A Survey of Methodist Periodicals Published in England, 1778–1900," *Victorian Periodicals Review* 14 (Summer 1981):66–69. Rogal's list omits the *London Quarterly*.

5. Richard Woddy Moss, *The Rev. William Burt Pope, D.D.: Theologian and Saint*, Library of Methodist Biography (London, n.d.), pp. 110–11.

6. Ibid., p. 110.

7. See [James Smetham], *"Life of William Blake: Pictor Ignotus,"* *London Quarterly Review*, ser. 1, 25 (1869):265–311. The first edition of Gilchrist's book had appeared in 1863 (London). In the edition of 1880 Smetham's essay was reprinted without many of the quotations appropriate to the review.

8. Quoted in William Strawson, *"The London Quarterly and Holborn Review*, 1853–1968," *Church Quarterly Review* 1 (1968):43.

9. Ibid., p. 41.

Information Sources

BIBLIOGRAPHY
Aquila-Barber, B. "John Telford: An Appreciation." *London Quarterly and Holborn Review*, ser. 6, 159 (October 1934):443–40.

Howard, Wilbert F. "Editorial Comments." *London Quarterly and Holborn Review*, ser. 6, 159 (October 1934):356–59.

Moss, Richard Woddy. *The Rev. William Burt Pope, D.D.: Theologian and Saint*. Library of Methodist Biography. London, n.d.

Peake, Arthur S. *Recollections and Appreciations*. Edited by Wilbert F. Howard. London, 1938.

Rogal, Samuel J. "A Survey of Methodist Periodicals Published in England, 1778–1900." *Victorian Periodicals Review* 14 (Summer 1981):66–69.

Strawson, William. *"The London Quarterly and Holborn Review, 1853–1968."* *Church Quarterly Review* 1 (1968):41–52.

INDEXES

Some volumes indexed. 1853–1881 in *Poole's Index*. 1853–1900 in *Wellesley Index* 4 (projected).

REPRINT EDITIONS

Microform: American Theological Library Association, Princeton, N.J.; Early British Periodicals (UMI), reels 259–275.

LOCATION SOURCES

American

Widely available.

British

Complete runs: Aberdeen University Library; Birmingham Public Library; British Museum; Cambridge University Library; Manchester Union Library; National Library of Scotland; Newcastle-upon-Tyne Public Library.

Partial runs: Widely available.

Publication History

MAGAZINE TITLE AND TITLE CHANGES

The *London Quarterly Review*, 1853–1857, 1863–1931. *The London Review*, 1858–1862. *The London Quarterly and Holborn Review*, 1932–1968. (The *Holborn Review*, 1910–1931, was a continuation of the *Primitive Methodist Quarterly Review and Christian Ambassador*, 1879–1910, which had absorbed the older *Christian Ambassador*, 1858–1878.)

VOLUME AND ISSUE DATA

Series 1, volumes 1–60, September 1853–July 1883; series 2, volumes 1–30, old series volumes 61–90, October 1883–July 1898; series 3, volumes 1–12, old series volumes 91–102, January 1899–October 1904; series 4, volumes 1–12, old series volumes, 103–114, January 1905–October 1910; series 5, volumes 1–42, old series volumes 115–156, 1911–1931; series 6, volumes 1–35, old series volumes 157–191, 1932–1968.

FREQUENCY OF PUBLICATION

Quarterly.

PUBLISHERS

Volumes 1–90: Methodist Connexion, London. Volumes 91–156: Methodist Book Room, London. Volumes 157–191: Epworth Press, London.

EDITORS

Thomas M'Nicholl, 1853–1859. William Pope, 1860–1883. William Burt Pope and James Harrison Rigg, 1883–1886. James Harrison Rigg, 1886–1898. William Lonsdale Wilkinson, 1898–1904. W. T. Davison, 1904–1905. John Telford, 1905–1934. Unknown, 1934–1968.

Barbara J. Dunlap

LONDON REVIEW, THE. See MIRROR OF LITERATURE. . . , THE (RA)

LONGMAN'S MAGAZINE

In September 1882 a quarterly listing of publications from Longmans, Green and Company announced a new magazine to appear that November. The monthly, to be known as *Longman's Magazine*, promised "a full share of that intellectual entertainment which may be obtained in the study of pure literature."[1] The intent of the publishers was "to contribute something to the amusement of an age which has been held by some to be too much in earnest" and to meet the needs of the large new class of readers "reinforced in England since the passing of the Elementary Education Act in 1870." The new magazine superseded *Fraser's Magazine** (see *RA*), which had been owned by Longmans since 1863. For twenty-three years *Longman's* enjoyed only moderate success, and ultimately failed because of an ambivalence in what it attempted to accomplish.

Between November 1882 and October 1905, 276 monthly issues of *Longman's Magazine* appeared. The price was six pence throughout the run of all 46 volumes. Fiction was abundant, with one or two short stories and an installment of at least one novel in each issue. A few poems, two or three nonfiction articles, and a number of regular features rounded out a typical month's offering. One hundred thousand copies of the first issue were run (in two printings), though a steady decline in sales tapered press runs to 4,000 during the last year of publication.[2]

Nonfiction in *Longman's* reflected the publisher's intent. The magazine was not to be "devoted to the interests of any party or of any particular school of thought, whether political, religious, or social." The policy was to avoid politics, "which mainly occupy the attention of the daily and weekly press," and religious subjects, "which are fully dealt with by the organs of the various religious sections and by the graver monthly reviews."

The plan to offer larger amounts "of literature of a high standard at so low a price" and to a new audience was risky. Longmans acknowledged that it was a "bold step" but remained confident that there was an audience "anxious to procure literature of this kind, provided it is offered at a reasonable price."

Perhaps Longmans' experience during the last few years of *Fraser's Magazine* convinced them that lowering the price would be a significant advantage. Additionally, Longmans had enjoyed success in the recent sale of moderately priced fiction, such as the sixpenny edition of Lady Brassey's *Voyage in the Sunbeam* a year earlier. The coincidence of all these factors provided encouragement "that there may be room for *Longman's Magazine*."

At first there was considerable "room" for the popular fiction, the gossip, and the serialized novels among an enthusiastic readership of moderate size. The premier issue included the first installment of *Thicker Than Water*, one of the many novels by James Payn to appear in the coming years. Two short stories were included, as well as W. D. Howells's article "Lexington." "Atoms, Molecules, and Ether Waves," by John Tyndall, and an article on American speech and customs, "Our Origins as a Species," were perhaps more heavy-going than the new, more popular image would warrant. Lighter reading included R. L. Stevenson's "A Gossip on Romance." *Longman's* never carried illustrations, a decision that seems to have shortened the life span of the magazine. With the resources of a large publishing firm behind it, publicity was good, and the first issue reached a wide audience. There was a consensus that Longman's new venture was "welcomed as an attempt to provide popular literature, that its success was likely to depend on the appeal of its fiction, and that the serious articles were too difficult for the kind of public which the editor had in mind."[3]

Many notables published in *Longman's*, among them Edmund Gosse, Thomas Hardy, Bret Harte, William Dean Howells, W. H. Hudson, Henry James, Rudyard Kipling, Robert Louis Stevenson, Walter Besant, Eden Philpotts, Margaret Oliphant, Walter De la Mare, John Masefield, Rider Haggard, M. E. Francis, James Froude, Grant Allen, Austin Dobson, Jean Ingelow, and Richard Jefferies. But the editors never succeeded in getting what the 1882 announcement hoped would be "a plentiful supply of shorter stories by the best novelists." There were exceptions. Readers were treated to "The Pupil," by Henry James, two stories by Bret Harte, three novels by Robert Louis Stevenson, and a story by Thomas Hardy. However, predominantly there was an abundance of popular fiction that is studied today (if at all) only as popular culture rather than as part of the canons of British fiction.

The nonfiction displays a wide range of topics. The editors promised articles on physical science and natural history, and "occasional papers" on field sports and games. Representative titles included R. A. Proctor, "The Earth in Meteroic Shadow"; A. W. Pollard, "The First English Book Sale"; and Ford M. Hueffer (later Ford), "D. G. Rossetti and His Family Letters." Articles on language, such as Edward A. Freeman's "On Some Modern Abuses of Language," were frequent. Cyprian Blagden finds the nonfiction significant: "If I had to compile from the 46 volumes of *Longman's Magazine* an anthology to be published in 1963, I would fill it largely from the serious articles." He adds a note of caution, however, when he admits "regretfully" that the articles "must have frightened away many thousands of readers at their first appearance."[4]

Several features illustrate the tone and the extra-literary commitment of the magazine. The first issue carried "A Gossip on Romance" and subsequent "Gossips" were to appear on a variety of literary genres and topics. *Longman's* was also committed to unemployed dock workers; it arranged for a stall with hot food, collected donations, and published news and lists of donors from time to time. The most notable and controversial regular feature was Andrew Lang's "At the Sign of the Ship," a monthly essay of opinion that began in January 1886 and appeared regularly until the last issue.

Lang's opinions about people and ideas were eclectic, sometimes stimulating, and frequently infuriating. Eleanor De Selms Langstaff calls Lang's column "a chatty accumulation of paragraphs on assorted subjects, poems by Lang and books Lang liked."[5] Each month he offered commentary on recent publications and research. He summarized his travels and offered serious and whimsical human interest stories. It is easy to see even now why Lang's musings were popular, but scholarship is mixed both on public response and on the effects "Ship" had on readers. Blagden believes that the column did not attract the new kind of readers "at which the editor aimed," while Langstaff feels that Lang's "dribbles of anthropology and droplets of psychology" provided "useful information for readers who liked their education short and striking."[6]

Lang's influence on *Longman's* was enormous. It is generally believed that he had more say in editorial decisions than Charles Longman, who was editor throughout the entire run of the magazine. Longman was never acknowledged as editor in the pages of the magazine, and he contributed only one signed review.[7] Posterity has found Lang's influence to be significant but his judgment idiosyncratic and anti-intellectual: "by precept, by practice, and by quasi-editorial selection, Lang made *Longman's* a vehicle for the expression of his own tastes, opinions, and prejudices." Oscar Mauer notes that Lang barred from *Longman's* "fiction with a purpose" and selected "historical romance," "adventure," and "stories that end happily and can be read without the aid of a dictionary."[8] Lang's early columns are likened to *La Vie Littéraire* and *Impressions de Théâtre*, but "much of what he wrote was obviously dictated by whim and prejudice." He was capable of "an understanding and an imaginative sympathy as delicate as they are illuminating," but "perverted by a determination to discourage realism at any cost," and even "jaded and indifferent" from "the constant strain of overproduction."[9]

The omnipresence of Lang may have contributed to the failure of the magazine to bring to its intended audience "literature of a high standard." Referring sarcastically to the opposition between popular writing and "cultured" literature, Lang called the latter "a manner of writing so refined and tormented that very few people want to read it." The intent of *Longman's* to reach new readers with the best literature was repeatedly undermined by Lang's "nonliterary anti-intellectual" standards. He "did harm by helping to widen the split between the general reader and the serious artists in fiction."[10]

With continued support coming from the large publishing firm, why did *Longman's Magazine* suspend publication with its October 1905 issue? Longmans' reasons can be found in their statement in that last issue. "The times have changed in many respects" since the first issue twenty three years earlier, the editor maintains, and "none perhaps more than in regard to periodical literature." Though *Longman's* may have been one of the first monthlies to initiate the "competition for the patronage of the six penny public," there soon followed a different kind of competition: "The great advance made in cheap processes for the reproduction of drawings and photographs has called into existence a number of magazines and papers depending largely upon their illustrations." In short, a mass medium of visual dimensions was arriving. In the era of illustrations, *Longman's* was "an anachronism from the beginning."[11] Longmans' announcement further lamented that "the mere endeavor to keep up a high literary standard is nowadays not sufficient." The editors chose not to follow "the prevailing fashion," feeling that longstanding readers would not have liked the change.

Several factors no doubt contributed to the discontinuation after 276 issues. Several newer magazines capitalized on the popularity of photographs—notably the *English Illustrated Magazine* in September 1883. The nonfiction articles in *Longman's* were often too difficult for, or tangential to the interests of, the larger popular audience early on. Serialization may actually have hurt sales. Many readers may have preferred to wait for complete editions of novels published after (or often during) serialization rather than have their reading continuity "chopped into ten or a dozen sections . . . at monthly intervals."[12] Finally, the decline in copies printed seems to indicate that *Longman's Magazine* never really attracted the steady growth of new readers that the editors hoped it would. The idea may have been right, but other illustrated magazines with more popular features were destined to have at least a measure of the success for which the Longmans had hoped.

Notes

1. *Notes on Books*, May 1855, a brochure distributed quarterly by Longmans, as quoted in Cyprian Blagden, "*Longman's Magazine*," *Review of English Literature* 4 (1963):9–10. I am much indebted throughout this discussion to Blagden's informative and thorough study of all facets of *Longman's Magazine*.

2. Unless otherwise noted, Blagden has compiled the statistics cited herein.

3. Blagden, p. 13.

4. Ibid., p. 18.

5. Eleanor De Selms Langstaff, *Andrew Lang* (Boston, 1978), p. 117.

6. Ibid.; Blagden, p. 18.

7. See Blagden, p. 19; Oscar Maurer, "Andrew Lang and *Longman's Magazine* 1882–1905," *Texas Studies in English* 34 (1955):152; Forrest Reid, "Andrew Lang and *Longman's*," *London Mercury* 37 (1938):502.

8. Mauer, pp. 158–59, 175.

9. Reid, pp. 503–5.

10. Maurer, pp. 170–72.

11. Ibid., p. 155.

12. Blagden, p. 17. See also Fader and Bornstein, *British Periodicals of the Eighteenth and Nineteenth Centuries* (Ann Arbor, Mich., 1972), pp. 86–87.

Information Sources

BIBLIOGRAPHY

Blagden, Cyprian. "*Longman's Magazine.*" *Review of English Literature* 4 (1963):9–22.

Cox, Harold. "The House of Longman." *Edinburgh Review* 240 (1924):209–42.

Fader, Daniel, and George Bornstein. *British Periodicals of the Eighteenth and Nineteenth Centuries.* Ann Arbor, Mich., 1972.

Graham, Walter. *English Literary Periodicals.* New York, 1930.

Green, Roger Lancelyn. *Andrew Lang: A Criticial Biography.* Leicester, 1946.

Langstaff, Eleanor De Selms. *Andrew Lang.* Boston, 1978.

Maurer, Oscar. "Andrew Lang and *Longman's Magazine* 1882–1905." *Texas Studies in English* 34 (1955):152–78.

Parker, W. M. "Lang and *Longman's,*" *Scots Magazine* 40 (1944):451–63.

Reid, Forrest. "Andrew Lang and *Longman's.*" *London Mercury* 37 (1938):502–8.

INDEXES

Volume 6 on, each volume indexed; volumes 1–46 at end of volume 46; 1882–1900 in *Wellesley Index* 4 (projected).

REPRINT EDITIONS

Microform: Early British Periodicals (UMI), reels 21–28.

LOCATION SOURCES

American

Widely available.

British

Widely available.

Publication History

MAGAZINE TITLE AND TITLE CHANGES

Longman's Magazine.

VOLUME AND ISSUE DATA

Volumes 1–46, November 1882–October 1905. (Christmas issue following the December 1884 edition.)

FREQUENCY OF PUBLICATION

Monthly.

PUBLISHER

Longmans, Green and Co., London.

EDITOR

Charles J. Longman.

Ronald Primeau

M

MACMILLAN'S MAGAZINE

The idea that Macmillans, founded by the brothers Daniel and Alexander Macmillan in 1843, should branch out from book publication and produce a magazine seems to have been mooted first in 1855. In May of that year Alexander wrote to Daniel about a suggestion made by Isaac Todhunter, the Cambridge mathematician, that they start "a weekly, or at any rate a fortnightly publication. ... My idea is to make a thing like the *Revue des Deux Mondes* and call it 'The World of Letters.' ... I believe a thing of that kind might be got up to an enormous scale if made tolerably cheap, ls. or ls. 6d."[1] Daniel was less than warm toward the project, and clearly saw the setting up of a London branch of the Cambridge-based business as a more pressing priority. The idea was therefore shelved for a while.

The next documented suggestion comes in a letter in November 1856 from J. M. Ludlow to Alexander Macmillan. Ludlow, a close friend of Thomas Hughes, whose *Tom Brown's Schooldays* was about to give Macmillans one of their greatest successes, writes:

Look at this *Tom Brown*, first rate as it is,—I suspect you will still have some difficulty in getting for it all the success it deserves off hand, coming from an entirely new author. Now if that same Tom Brown had been published in a magazine, for which it is admirably adapted, not only would it have increased the sale of the magazine largely as it went on, but by the time it had got to the end it would *no longer be* a book by a new hand,—it would on being republished as a whole, just step into success, instead of having to fight its way into it.[2]

Nonetheless, it was not until after Daniel's death in 1857, and the setting up of a London branch soon afterward, that plans hardened into firmer shape. Every Thursday evening Alexander Macmillan kept open house in the office in Henrietta Street, and these "tobacco parliaments" of what came to be known as the Round Table attracted an impressive cross-section of the important literary and academic figures that the Macmillans had gathered around them in their Cambridge years. The setting up of a monthly magazine soon became one of the recurrent topics of conversation, and by the early summer of 1859 serious preparations were being made. David Masson had established a solid reputation as a contributor to reviews, succeeded Arthur Clough as professor of English literature at University College, London, and published the first volume of his six-volume *Life of Milton*. He accepted the position of editor. Alexander Macmillan, who was very active in soliciting contributions, favored calling the new magazine the *Round Table* (the first of Tennyson's *Idylls* had recently been published), while David Masson suggested *Macmillan's Monthly*.[3] In any event, the title *Macmillan's Magazine* was adopted. The new publication made its first appearance on 1 November 1859 and an inaugural dinner was held at Henrietta Street in its honor. It was the first of the shilling monthlies, preceding the *Cornhill** (under Thackeray's editorship) by two months. Until 1864 Thomas Hughes had a financial interest in it.

During the forty-eight years of its publication, *Macmillan's* had only four editors: David Masson, George Grove, John Morley, and Mowbray Morris. The fact that the editors, with the exception of John Morley, who was in transit to higher political office, had such lengthy terms in control resulted in a consistency of content which was one of the strengths, and perhaps at the last one of the weaknesses, of the magazine. Each issue usually contained a political article, a serial, a literary or philosophical article, a historical or travel article, and a poem or short story—a range that indicates the limits of the *Athenaeum** description of *Macmillan's* as "a review of political affairs from the philsophical rather than from the partisan point of view."[4] Partisan it was not, but it became cautious about offending delicate sensibilities. One of the minor flurries came toward the end of Masson's editorship when editorial caution dictated the excision of three lines from Tennyson's *Lucretius* (May 1868).[5] Charges of Grundyism were from time to time leveled at the magazine, perhaps with more justice during Mowbray Morris's time in office at the end of the century, when times were beginning to change and *Macmillan's* seemed reluctant to change with them. But this problem was less apparent in the early stages, and *Macmillan's* rapidly became noted for the variety and exceptional quality of its articles.

Masson and Macmillan clearly took to heart Ludlow's earlier comments on the suitability of Tom Brown for serialization; the first serial to appear in *Macmillan's* was the less popular sequel, *Tom Brown at Oxford*. The first number also included an article by Ludlow on Tennyson's *Idylls*, and the first of what was to have been a regular feature, "Colloquies of the Round Table." The coterie banter of Macmillan's Thursday night guests failed to spark in print, and the feature was quietly dropped after the second number. The third number was to be a particularly important one since the *Cornhill*'s first issue was scheduled for January 1860, but Alexander Macmillan had been sufficiently politic to acquire Tennyson's *Sea Dreams* and hold it back for this issue. The *Cornhill* competition was a very real one, but there was a tendency for the two magazines to appeal to slightly distinct markets. As the *Wellesley Index* suggests, the fiction in *Macmillan's* was initially not as distinguished as that in the *Cornhill*, although its serious articles were untouchable.[6] For the first half of 1861 *Tom Brown at Oxford* was still running concurrently with Henry Kingsley's *Ravenshoe*. *Ravenshoe* was followed by Charles Kingsley's *The Water-Babies*. Novels by Margaret Oliphant, Charlotte Yonge, R. D. Blackmore, and Henry Kingsley were among the best of those published under Masson's editorship. At the same time the *Cornhill* was publishing Trollope and Thackeray, *Macmillan's* was enjoying regular contributions from Matthew Arnold (including, in April 1866, *Thyrsis*), F. D. Maurice, G. O. Trevelyan, and Masson himself. It was not until the 1880s that *Macmillan's* would begin publishing literary work of the importance of James's *The Portrait of a Lady* (1880–1881) or Hardy's *The Woodlanders* (1886–1887). Nor were the early years without their controversy. An article by Charles Kingsley, published in *Macmillan's* in January 1864, provoked not only an exchange of letters with an irritated John Henry Newman, who felt that his integrity had been impugned by Kingsley, but also, ultimately, Newman's *Apologia Pro Vita Sua*.

Masson's appointment to the chair of English literature at Edinburgh University necessitated his resignation of the *Macmillan's* editorship, and in 1868 he was succeeded by George Grove, who had already acted as his assistant for some months. Grove held the position for fifteen years, resigning in 1883 to become the first director of the Royal College of Music. While Grove is more famous for the latter appointment, and for his *Dictionary of Music and Musicians*, his editorship of *Macmillan's* saw some of its most productive days. Arnold continued his association; poetry by George Eliot and George Meredith appeared, as did prose by Walter Pater. As Grove's biographer indicates, the last volume to appear during his editorship contained work by Arnold, Christina Rossetti, Mrs. Humphry Ward, J. H. Shorthouse, and J. R. Seeley,[7] and it was Grove's editorship that introduced Henry James to *Macmillan's*.

John Morley had been associated with *Macmillan's* as a reader since the 1860s, and he was editor of the English Men of Letters series. His brief editorship produced, predictably, a larger number of political and historical articles, and was a relatively slack period for literature. One of Morley's most important innovations was the introduction of a feature entitled ''Review of the Month''— written at first by W. T. Stead, but from October 1883 by Morley himself— which dealt with ''current politics from the standpoint of Philosophic Radicalism.''[8] This increasingly political orientation of the magazine, reflecting Morley's earlier work as editor of the *Fortnightly Review** and the *Pall Mall Gazette*, changed when the rigors of his own political campaigning necessitated his resignation from the *Macmillan's* editorship.

Over the years Alexander Macmillan had been having increasingly less direct involvement with the magazine; indeed, by the mid-1880s the next generation of Macmillans had substantially taken over direction of the publishing company as a whole, so that Mowbray Morris was left very much to his own devices as editor. While *Macmillan's* continued to attract important names, Mowbray Morris, a conservative mind dealing with an age of transition, was perhaps not the best figure to have as editor at a time when the monthlies were soon to be encountering major market changes. Charles Morgan's history, *The House of Macmillan*, sums up what was perhaps the key limitation: "There are in existence opinions by Mowbray Morris written with a violence that men do not use except subconsciously in defence of a closed mind, and Frederick Macmillan might have been warned by them."[9] Those opinions were expressed on works by, among others, Hardy, Yeats, and Meredith. *Tess of the d'Urbervilles* was one of the potential serials that fell victim to Morris's fastidiousness. But blind spots notwithstanding, Morris did change the primary direction of *Macmillan's* toward literature, and did publish work by James, Hardy, and Kipling.

In 1905, in an attempt to respond to competition from the new cheap press, *Macmillan's* reduced its price to six pence, at the same time reducing its contents by the same ratio by the simple expedient of using larger type and printing each page in one column rather than two. The change was a response to wider trends that could only have been turned to advantage, if at all, by a much younger man than Mowbray Morris. Within two years, *Macmillan's* quietly ceased publication.

Notes

1. Charles L. Graves, *Life and Letters of Alexander Macmillan* (London, 1910), pp. 69–70.

2. Ibid., pp. 91–92.

3. Ibid., pp. 132–33.

4. A. J. Gurr, "*Macmillan's Magazine,*" *Review of English Literature* 6, no. 1 (1965):50.

5. Gurr, p. 45.

6. *The Wellesley Index to Victorian Periodicals 1824–1900*, ed. Walter E. Houghton (Toronto, 1966), 1:554–55.

7. Charles L. Graves, *The Life and Letters of Sir George Grove, C.B.* (London, 1903), p. 285.

8. F. W. Hirst, *Early Life and Letters of John Morley* (London, 1927), 2:180.

9. Charles Morgan, *The House of Macmillan (1843–1943)* (London, 1944), p. 144.

Information Sources

BIBLIOGRAPHY

Francis, John Collins. "*Macmillan's Magazine.*" *Notes and Queries*, 11th ser., 1 (1910):141–42.

Graves, Charles L. *Life and Letters of Alexander Macmillan*. London, 1910.

———. *The Life and Letters of Sir George Grove, C.B.* London, 1903.

Gurr, A. J. *"Macmillan's Magazine." Review of English Literature* 6, no. 1 (1965):39–55.

Hirst, F. W. *Early Life and Letters of John Morley*. 2 vols. London, 1927.

Houghton, Walter E., ed. *The Wellesley Index to Victorian Periodicals 1824–1900*. Vol. 1. Toronto, 1966.

Morgan, Charles. *The House of Macmillan (1843–1943)*. London, 1944.

Young, Percy M. *George Grove 1820-1900: A Biography*. London, 1980.

INDEXES

Indexed by title in bound volumes. 1860–1881 in *Poole's Index*; 1859–1900 in *Wellesley Index* 1.

REPRINT EDITIONS

Microform: English Literary Periodicals (UMI), reels 816–826. EP Microform Ltd., Wakefield, England.

LOCATION SOURCES

American

Widely available.

British

Widely available.

Publication History

MAGAZINE TITLE AND TITLE CHANGES

Macmillan's Magazine.

VOLUME AND ISSUE DATA

Volumes 1–92, numbers 1–522, November 1859–October 1905; new series, volumes 1–2, numbers 1–24, November 1905–October 1907.

FREQUENCY OF PUBLICATION

Monthly.

PUBLISHER

Macmillans, London.

EDITORS

David Masson, November 1859–April 1868. George Grove, May 1868–April 1883. John Morley, May 1883–September 1885. Mowbray Morris, October 1885–October 1907.

Keith Wilson

METROPOLITAN MAGAZINE, THE. See RA

MIRROR MONTHLY MAGAZINE, THE. See MIRROR OF LITERATURE ..., THE (RA)

MIRROR OF LITERATURE, AMUSEMENT, AND INSTRUCTION, THE. See RA

MONTH, THE

In July 1864 the *Month*, a new "Illustrated Magazine of Literature, Science and Art," moved into place between the quarterly *Dublin Review** (see *RA*) (1836–1969) and the weekly *Tablet* (1840–)—all published in London—as a Catholic counterpart of Thackeray's *Cornhill Magazine** (1860–1975) and, like it, a monthly directed to an educated readership.

Its launching editor was Frances Margaret Taylor, a literary woman who from 1862 to 1871 was proprietor and editor of the *Lamp: An Illustrated Catholic Journal of General Literature* of popular appeal. She also wrote, edited, or translated some twenty-two books, mostly religious. Her first, *Eastern Hospitals and English Nurses* (1856), argued the need for drastic reform in military hospitals: she had nursed under Florence Nightingale during the Crimean War. The High Church daughter of a Lincolnshire clergyman, Fanny Taylor became a Catholic in 1855 in Crimea. She worked as a laywoman among the poor in London in close collaboration with Lady Georgiana Fullerton and under the spiritual guidance of the Jesuits at Farm Street. The latter encouraged her to start the *Month* and relieved her of it after one year. Miss Taylor considered Peter Gallwey, S. J., its "real founder": "After the first number was out, I heard too many rivals were in the field, so I wanted to stop; but Father Gallwey urged me on, and before No. 3 . . . he told me he hoped the Society would take it over, and asked me to carry it on *pro tem.*. . . . The Jesuits, when they finally took it over paid all expenses from the beginning" (174:14).

The *Month*'s first year more than fulfilled its promoters' expectations. Besides poems and fiction—short stories and serialized novels including Lady Georgiana Fullerton's *Constance Sherwood: An Autobiography of the Sixteenth Century*—there were articles on art, literature, and historical subjects. Henry J. Coleridge's "Few Words for Mary Stuart" opened the first issue and his name or initials appeared often; he became the first Jesuit editor the following year. Travel sketches of Italy were signed Julia Kavanagh, sketches of Ireland and France, Bessie Rayner Parkes (the future Mrs. Belloc), who also contributed poems. C. W. Russell, who had been a mainstay of the *Dublin Review*, provided an account of a Scottish Benedictine who was a secret agent in the Napoleonic Wars. Three stories were almost certainly by Fanny Taylor herself: "A Glimmering Dawn," on the evils of the workhouse system, especially for girls; "Hope for the Prisoners," praising an Irish model; and "Middle-Class Lunatic Asylums." John Henry Newman's "Saints of the Desert," collections of their sayings, was a regular feature until it was parodied, albeit "respectfully," by *Punch.**

Wood engravings by Walter Crane sometimes accompanied a story or poem. By the third volume (Father Coleridge's first) the engravings had disappeared, to be replaced only very occasionally thereafter by maps or diagrams or by photographs of portraits (in an 1882 supplement on saints) or of art works and architecture. The cover illustration of St. George and the dragon, designed by

James Doyle, remained until it was displaced in 1882 by the table of contents; it was restored in 1897 and succeeded five years later by a new half-page "St. George" by Paul Woodroffe, allowing space for a list of articles below it.

With its title modified to *The Month: A Magazine and Review*, the July–December 1865 volume admirably exercised the dual function suggested. As a magazine it continued to offer original material: a two-part article on "Art and Beauty" by "J.H.P."; and "Fine Arts at the Dublin International Exhibition of 1865" by John Hungerford Pollen, Sr., a well-known artist and Oxford convert, father of the celebrated Jesuit historian. His son's works appeared in the *Month* from 1887 to 1924. Other works included "Sir Joshua Reynolds and Dr. Johnson. By the Author of 'Wild Times' "; "Early Married Life of Marie Antoinette," unsigned; "Railway Reform," unsigned; a translation into Latin of a Wordsworth quatrain, signed "Q. C."; the last five installments of *Constance Sherwood*; and poems by Aubrey de Vere and others.

As a review the *Month* dealt with Arnold's *Essays in Criticism*; "Thoughts on St. Gertrude" by Aubrey de Vere, on the newly translated *Life and Revelations* of the abbess; Henry Taylor's *Poetical Works*; Trollope's last novel, *Can You Forgive Her?*; "A Few Words About Smoke" (arising from *Our Domestic Fireplaces* and *A Treatise on Smoky Chimneys*, "useful" books by Frederick Edwards); "Oakeley's *Lyra Liturgica*"; and many other topics of general or special interest. Several of the pieces were signed with Greek letters in lieu of the names of various Jesuits who helped from time to time.

John Henry Newman's concern for the *Month* is evident less from his contributions to the magazine than from his letters (1864–1881) to his friend Henry James Coleridge before and during the latter's editorship. Coleridge, the great-nephew of the poet, was himself an Oxford man and a former Anglican curate who became a Roman Catholic in 1852. He went to Rome to study theology and was ordained there in 1856. Returning to England with a doctorate in 1857, he entered the Jesuit novitiate. After making his vows he taught scripture for five years at St. Beuno's Theological College in Wales. Coleridge was more interested in writing than in teaching. Known to be "always urging the establishment of a literary organ of Catholic opinion" (78:173), he was the obvious choice when the *Month* needed a Jesuit editor in the summer of 1865. As a member of the Farm Street community he was instrumental in starting a Jesuit "house of writers," a pool of talent responsible for some significant *Month* articles and reviews.

Fortunately, Coleridge's reverence for Newman did not extend to the latter's advice about a hypothetical periodical, which he was "little disposed to encourage" and "less and less sanguine about" (101:3). To Father Gallwey, Newman wrote in February 1865 as the project materialized: "As to direct inculcation of Catholic truth . . . in such a periodical, I should dread its effects. . . . What is to be aimed at, is to lay a Catholic *foundation* of thought— and *no* foundation is above ground (101:5). To Coleridge in June 1865: "I am sorry you are going to introduce theology into *The Month*. . . . it will deprive the magazine of the chance of influence in the Protestant world'' (101:10). But Newman did in fact approve of Coleridge as controversialist, and thanked him for discerning notices and occasional defense. There is actually more about Newman than by him in the *Month*; his *Grammar of Assent* drew fire—''I think I see that the main argument of my book does not fall within the philosophical and theological traditions of the Society,'' Newman wrote to Coleridge in 1870 (101:238).

The initial promise to ''deal with all questions interesting to Catholics,— politics alone excepted'' (102:2), gave subsequent editors plenty of scope. Richard Frederick Clarke was Coleridge's successor. Though a more ebullient personality, he had a similar background. An Oxford fellow, he renounced Anglican orders and was received into the Catholic Church by Henry J. Coleridge in 1869. A Jesuit, Clarke began and edited the Stonyhurst Philosophical Series; his own *Logic* (1889) ''is perhaps the most interesting book ever written on that dry subject'' (96:337). He also opened and headed (for the last five years of his life) the Jesuit house at Oxford, Clarke's Hall, now generally referred to as Campion Hall.

Under such learned editors, the *Month* presented equally distinguished writers. John Morris, who was drawn by the Tractarian Movement and Gothic revival into the Catholic Church, published historical work, especially on the English martyrs, and set the direction for some very productive scholarship by his colleagues as well. John Gerard, Sydney Fenn Smith, and Herbert Thurston were long-term contributors who extended the range of the *Month* even into science and the occult. The arts were not neglected, despite the famous refusal of Gerard Manley Hopkins's ''Wreck of the Deutschland'' in 1875. Stories and poems appeared occasionally. Books reviewed included belles lettres. Articles like A. M. Clark's ''The Imagination: Its Nature, Uses, and Abuses'' or ''A Modern Poetess'' by the Westphalian Annette van Droste-Hülhoff share space with ''Characteristics of Bears'' and ''The River Niger and Its Future.'' Education, Church affairs, history, philosophy, and theology took up the most space. Travel and science essays were represented in nearly every number. For the first fifteen years of the twentieth century, the *Month* excluded poetry, but editor Joseph Keating, himself a poet, reinstated the genre.

The long editorship of his predecessor John Gerard (from 1894 to 1897 and from 1901 to 1912, with Sydney Smith filling the interim while the Scottish Gerard was provincial of the English Jesuits) covered the controversial modernist years when the ''Abelardian spell'' of George Tyrrell waxed and waned. Tyrrell, a youthful convert to Roman Catholicism, ordained as a Jesuit in 1891, was a sought-after spiritual director and an appealing writer. He contributed nearly forty articles to the *Month* and was on its staff from 1896 to 1900. His ''Relation of Theology to Devotion'' was a straw in the wind. He identifies the '' 'deposit' of faith'' as ''not merely a symbol or creed, but ... a concrete religion left by Christ to His Church ... perhaps in some sense more directly a *lex orandi* than a *lex credendi*,'' and goes on to declare that ''theology as far as it formulates and justifies the devotion of the best Catholics, and as far as it is true to the life of faith and charity as actually lived . . . is a law and corrective for all. But where it begins to contradict the facts of that spiritual life, it loses its reality and its authority; and needs itself to be corrected by the *lex orandi*" (94:473). Although at least one article did not pass censorship at this time (1899), and although Tyrrell was sent from Farm Street to a parish outside London, work of his still appeared in the *Month* through 1903. In May 1906, shortly after Tyrrell's dismissal from the Jesuits, the *Month* reviewed very appreciatively his book *Lex Credendi*, a sequel to *Lex Orandi*: "Father Tyrrell looks forwards rather than backwards. He writes for the coming generation, whose minds can hardly fail to be storm-tossed by the daring theological discussions that now surround us. . . . But of his zeal for what is highest and what is truest we have no doubt" (107:553). Tyrrell incurred ecclesiastical censure in 1907 for publicly attacking the condemnation of modernism. (His friend Henri Brémond, also a former Jesuit and eventually a French Academician acclaimed for his *Histoire littéraire du sentiment religieux en France* (1916–1933), was temporarily suspended by the Bishop of Southwark in 1909 for unofficially officiating at Tyrrell's funeral.) A lifetime later, and in the light of the Second Vatican Council, the *Month* characteristically reexamined the whole controversy in articles such as "Did Modernism Die?" referring to Pius X's 1907 encyclical *Pascendi* and decree *Lamentabile*. It quoted Tyrrell's simple definition of his own brand of modernism as "a philosophy of Catholic experience or practice, distinguishing what is life-giving and permanent in belief and usages—what saints have lived on" (n.s. 39:272). Previously unpublished letters of Tyrrell appeared in the *Month* and shed sympathetic light on his Jesuit days, while retrospective letters of Friederich von Hügel illuminated the friendship and divergences of the two thinkers (n.s. 40:178–85; 2d ser. 1:95–101, 138–49; 2d ser. 3:111–15, 119; 2d ser. 4:178–80). Other articles, on "Tyrrell's Dublin Days" and "Tyrrell's 'Medievalism' " (n.s. 42:8–22), fill in with interest and compassion a little more of a complex picture whose handling by the *Month* is an example of the magazine's strong sense of historic continuity, which is also a sense of how the present modifies the past.

From time to time the *Month* explicitly recapitulates its own history in its pages, restating goals and adjusting its direction. The December 1902 issue celebrates the completion of its 100th volume. The first four months of 1903 have a series of Newman letters dealing with its beginnings. The preface to an index to *Month* (1864–1908) reviews changes "in price and size, in shape and in the character of its contents" for the first forty-five years. The January 1914 issue announces its jubilee year six months before its fiftieth anniversary. The July 1939 issue marks a "fourth quarter of a century" with John Murray replacing editor Joseph Keating. The issue for December 1941 explains wartime exigencies and the shift to bimonthly publication (as once before, 1871–1873), in an effort "to serve this country in its time of need and to serve too the ever abiding cause of the Church" (p. 330); the November-December 1946 issue heralds the resumption of monthly issues. (A double July-August number became standard for a while—through 1948, and again from 1964 to 1969.) January 1949 starts a new series under Philip Caraman as editor, "providing for those interests which go to make a complete culture . . . imaginative writing, criticism, and theology which the layman can understand" (p. [4]).

In December 1950 "The Thousandth Issue" attributes the *Month*'s survival partly "to its connection with a permanent institution" and reiterates its commitment to "an authentic humanism," broadening again the focus which the sheer weight of historical scholarship in its pages had made too specialized and which contemporary international problems had tended to overwhelm (p. 364). The January 1964 centenary-year editorial by Ronald Moffat, who had taken over in May 1963, spoke of "a larger view of our responsibilities towards the society in which we live" and less sheer controversy, quoting yet again Newman's ideal of taking part in "all the questions of the day."

In July 1969 the *Month* incorporated the *Dublin Review* and a year later *Herder Correspondence*. In July 1970 Peter Hebblethwaite assured his readers that "the emphasis on reporting and information does not mean that we intend to abandon cultural tasks. . . . The most interesting and important developments often happen on the frontiers of disciplines, where two or more competencies meet in the same person or in a team. Sociology can supply irreplaceable data. The novel can put flesh on the too tidy concepts of theologians" (p. 3). The role of the *Month* to inform and challenge the educated continues to be vital.

Information Sources

BIBLIOGRAPHY
Altholz, Josef L. "*The Month*, 1864–1900." *Victorian Periodicals Review* 14 (1981):70–72.
Corbishley, Thomas. "Marriage of True Minds." *Month*, n.s. 42 (1969):4–7.
[Gerard, John]. "A 'Century' and a Retrospect." *Month* 100 (1902):561–67.
[Murray, John]. "*The Month*, July, 1864–July, 1939." *Month* 174 (1939):13–24.
Special "Commemoration Number." *Month*, n.s. 32 (1964):Editorial, 14–17; James Brodrick, "Frescoes from the Past," 18–27; John Murray, "Wartime Production," 27–33; Ronald Moffat, "Post–war Renewal," 34–38.
INDEXES
Volumes 1–112, separately published in 1909; volumes 113–38, separately published in 1922. Volumes 1–130 indexed (by contents) at end of volume. 1864–1881 in *Poole's Index*.
REPRINT EDITIONS
Microform: Early British Periodicals (UMI), reels 320–344.
LOCATION SOURCES
American
Widely available.
British
Complete runs: Birmingham Public Library; British Museum; Cambridge University Library.
Partial runs: Widely available.

Publication History

MAGAZINE TITLE AND TITLE CHANGES

The Month: An Illustrated Magazine of Literature, Science and Art, July 1864–
June 1865. *The Month: A Magazine and Review*, July 1865–1873. *The Month
and Catholic Review*, 1874–1881. *The Month: A Catholic Magazine and Review*,
1882–June 1897. *The Month: A Catholic Magazine*, July 1897–1912. *The Month*,
1913–March 1971. *The Month: An International Review of the Christian World*,
April 1971. *The Month: A Review of Christian Thought and World Affairs*, May
1971–.

VOLUME AND ISSUE DATA

Volumes 1–11, July 1864–December 1869; new series, volumes 1–8, January
1870–December 1873 (also called by original numbers 12–19); (not called "new
series") volumes 1–24, January 1874–December 1881 (also called by original
numbers 20–43); volumes 44–186, January 1882–December 1948; new series,
volumes 1–42, January 1949–December 1969 (also called original numbers 187–
228); 2d new series, volumes 1–, January 1970– (also called original numbers
229–).

FREQUENCY OF PUBLICATION

Monthly.

PUBLISHERS

Volumes 1–6, July 1864–June 1867: Simpkin, Marshall, and Co., Stationers' Hall
Court, London/Burns, Lambert, and Oates, 17-18 Portman Street, London (Burns,
Lambert, and Oates at 63 Paternoster Row for volumes 4 and 5; Lambert's name
does not appear on volume 6). Volumes 7–8, July 1867–June 1868: *The Month*
office, 50 South Street, Grosvenor Square, London/Simpkin, Marshall & Co.
(same address as above). Volumes 9–43 (n.s. 24), July 1868–December 1881:
Simpkin, Marshall, and Co., Stationers' Hall Court, London/Burns and Oates,
63 Paternoster Row. (Simpkin, Marshall dropped after 1882; foreign agents named
intermittently from 1882 to 1960; Burns and Oates replaced by Longmans, Green
& Co. by 1912; editorial office frequently given along with Longmans, Green &
Co. from 1912 until April 1960.) April 1960–January 1982: *The Month* office,
31 Farm Street/114 Mount Street, London. January 1982–: *The Month*, 114 Mount
Street, London W1Y 6AH.

EDITORS

Frances Margaret Taylor, 1864–1865. Henry James Coleridge, 1865–1881. Richard Frederick Clarke, 1882–1894. John Gerard, 1894–1897, 1901–1912. Sydney
Fenn Smith, 1897–1901. Joseph Keating, 1912–March 1939. John Murray, April
1939–December 1948. Philip Caraman, 1949–April 1963. Ronald Moffat, May
1963–March 1967. Peter Hebblethwaite, April 1967–January 1974. Michael Walsh,
February 1974–1975. Hugh Kay, 1976–.

Mary Anthony Weinig

MONTHLY CHAPBOOK, THE. See CHAPBOOK, THE

MONTHLY CHRONICLE, THE

The *Monthly Chronicle; A National Journal of Politics, Literature, Science and Art* was one of many efforts to capitalize on the development of a new and broader reading public in early Victorian England. It was conceived by Dionysius Lardner, an Irishman possessed of a broad range of knowledge and a wide interest in the latest developments in science and technology. He published many popular works on various sciences and inventions and edited several encyclopedias, including his popular *Cabinet Cyclopaedia*, published in 133 volumes between 1829 and 1849. In 1827 he was appointed professor of natural philosophy in astronomy at the new Long University.[1]

In 1832 Lardner, as he later recalled, had conceived of a periodical that would survey current developments in politics, literature, science, and the "useful arts." Over the next few years, he discussed the project with Henry Lytton Bulwer, Edward Lytton Bulwer (later Bulwer-Lytton), Albany Fonblanque, and others. In 1837 Bulwer-Lytton wrote, "Lardner is much at me about the Quarterly. I cannot make up my mind. At all events, I shall steer clear of the responsibilities of editorship." A few months later, however, Bulwer-Lytton agreed to join Lardner as joint editor and proprietor of the paper, encouraged, no doubt, by the promise of Whig financial support.[2]

The first issue, appearing in March 1838, contained sixteen articles grouped under various headings similar to the "cabinets" in Lardner's encyclopedia. Bulwer-Lytton contributed an article on current politics, another on the reign of Queen Victoria, and a third on fiction.[3] He also published the first part of "Zicci— a tale," which was continued in several additional monthly installments until he stopped it, unfinished. A few years later, revised and completed, it was published as Bulwer-Lytton's first mystic novel, *Zanoni*.[4] Lardner contributed articles on team navigation and on a heating apparatus; and other articles dealt with music and theaters, crime, weather, and the press.

The contents of later issues remained eclectic, but changed as Bulwer-Lytton and then Lardner withdrew from the enterprise, Bulwer-Lytton in October 1838 and Lardner in April 1839. Bulwer-Lytton's initial reluctance in joining the project and his dissatisfaction with his novel are adequate explanations for his departure. Lardner's withdrawal, in view of his origination of the project and his strong advocacy of it, is more difficult to explain. Complications in his private life may have contributed to his decision. He was romantically involved with the wife of a cavalry officer, and in March 1840 eloped with her to France. They married, after each was divorced, some years later. Lardner's last articles for the *Monthly Chronicle*, published in January, March, and April 1840, were written just before his departure.[5]

Lardner was succeeded by another Irish journalist, Robert Bell, who edited the journal, except for one issue, for the remainder of its life. Bell had contributed to Lardner's *Cyclopaedia* and had edited the *Atlas*, a successful radical weekly, for many years.[6] His work at the *Atlas* and at the *True Sun* had made Bell a well-known figure among radical journalists. The circle of friends who gathered for dinner on Sundays at his home a few miles out of London included, among others, Richard Horne, Leigh Hunt, Southwood Smith, and William and Mary Hazlitt, most of whom wrote for the *Monthly Chronicle*. Horne, in particular, was a major contributor to the journal and an early admirer of Elizabeth Barrett's poems, some of which he tried to place in the *Chronicle*.[7]

Other contributors included Jefferson Hogg, who wrote a series of essays entitled "Some Recollections of Childhood," as well as a fragment of a novel and an article entitled "The Socratic Irony" for the journal.[8] Giuseppe Mazzini, struggling to establish himself in London, also wrote numerous articles. In reviewing French literature, he praised Lamennais and George Sand, and in another review he criticized his friend Carlyle's *French Revolution*. Between May and September 1839 Mazzini also published four articles entitled "Letters on the State and Prospects for Italy," in which he set the agenda for Italian nationalists for the next generation, urging confrontation with Austria.[9]

When G. H. Lewes and Laman Blanchard are added to the list of contributors, it is clear that the *Chronicle* published some of the major writers and journalists of the age. Despite so much talent, the magazine lasted just over two years, its last issue appearing in June 1841. Why did it fail? It was "self-slain," wrote Elizabeth Barrett Browning, "because it wouldn't condescend to be lively. There was power enough in it for three or four magazine popularities—but the taste of *caviare* predominated, and people turned away their heads. They said of it, as my own ears witnessed, 'dull and heavy.' Then it was such a fatal mistake to keep back the names! "[10]

These factors no doubt contributed to the journal's demise, as did its creators' inability to establish an independent identity for it. With its usual exclusion of fiction and its short articles on a variety of subjects, it seemed much like a weekly paper, but it did not appear often enough to be competitive with them. The variety of subjects treated in its articles raises further questions about what specific group of readers it was intended for or who would have been attracted to such a journal. The editors' further refusal to allow "personal vituperation," though admirable, surely contributed to the *Monthly Chronicle*'s reputation for being "dull and heavy."[11] It remains an intriguing though unsuccessful experiment in nineteenth-century journalism.

Notes

1. *Dictionary of National Biography*, s.v. "Lardner, Dionysius."
2. E. L. Bulwer to Albany Fonblanque, 30 September 1837, in *The Life and Labours of Albany Fonblanque*, ed. Edward Barrington De Fonblanque (London, 1874), p. 53; Walter Houghton, ed., *The Wellesley Index to Victorian Periodicals, 1824–1900* (Toronto, 1972), 3:109–12.
3. See *Wellesley Index*, 3:116–34, where the authors of most articles are identified.
4. Lord Lytton, *The Life of Edward Bulwer, First Lord Lytton*, (London, 1913), 2:32.

5. *Dictionary of National Biography*, s.v. "Lardner." Although the preponderance of evidence indicates that Lardner left the editorship in March 1839, some doubt remains because of a slight confusion in the *Wellesly Index* account. Citing evidence from the Commission Ledger, the *Wellesley* indicates that Robert Bell took over in April 1839 (pp. 110, 114). But elsewhere (p. 113), it lists Bell as editor from April 1840, and mistakenly lists Lardner's last three articles as appearing in January, March, and April 1841 (p. 114) instead of 1840, as they are identified in the detailed list of the journal's contents (pp. 128–30).

6. *Dictionary of National Biography*, s.v. "Bell, Robert."

7. Ann Blainey, *The Farthing Poet: A Biography of Richard Hengist Horne, 1802–84* (London, 1968), pp. 97, 118.

8. Winifred Scott, *Jefferson Hogg* (London, 1951), pp. 182, 185–86.

9. Harry W. Rudman, *Italian Nationalism and English Letters* (London, 1940), p. 47.

10. Letter to Richard Hengist Horne, 14 August 1841, in *Letters of Elizabeth Barrett Browning Addressed to Richard Hengist Horne* (New York, 1877), p. 28.

11. The *Wellesley Index*, 3:112, notes that with its short articles and its exclusion of fiction, the *Monthly Chronicle* was "more like the *Athenaeum*[* (see *RA*)] than *Blackwood's*"* (see *RA*).

Information Sources

BIBLIOGRAPHY

Blainey, Ann. *The Farthing Poet: A Biography of Richard Hengist Horne, 1802–84.* London, 1968.

Lytton, Lord. *The Life of Edward Bulwer, First Lord Lytton.* 2 vols. London, 1913.

Rudman, Harry W. *Italian Nationalism and English Letters.* London, 1940.

Scott, Winifred. *Jefferson Hogg.* London, 1951.

INDEXES

Wellesley Index 3.

REPRINT EDITIONS

Microform: English Literary Periodicals (UMI), reels 595–596.

LOCATION SOURCES

American

Complete runs: Boston Athenaeum; Detroit Public Library; Library Company of Philadelphia; New York Public Library; Princeton University Library; U.S. Library of Congress.

Partial runs: Newberry Library; State University of Iowa Library; Tulane University, Howard-Tilton Memorial Library; University of Illinois Library; University of Virginia Library; Yale University Library.

British

Complete runs: Bodleian Library; British Museum; Cambridge University Library; Edinburgh University Library; Manchester Public Library; St. Andrews University Library.

Partial runs: Dr. William's Library; Glasgow University Library.

Publication History

MAGAZINE TITLE AND TITLE CHANGES
> *The Monthly Chronicle; A National Journal of Politics, Literature, Science, and Art.*

VOLUME AND ISSUE DATA
> Volumes 1–7, March 1838–June 1841.

FREQUENCY OF PUBLICATION
> Monthly.

PUBLISHER
> Longman, Orme, Brown, Green, and Longmans, London.

EDITORS
> Edward Bulwer-Lytton and Dionysius Lardner, March–October 1838. Dionysius Lardner, November 1838–March 1839. Robert Bell, April–August 1839. Richard Hengist Horne, September 1839. Robert Bell, October 1839–June 1841.

> *Darwin F. Bostick*

MONTHLY MAGAZINE, THE. See RA

MONTHLY REVIEW, THE

In 1900, when John Murray summoned Henry Newbolt to his office to discuss a new journalistic venture, he was doubtless aware that the partnership he contemplated was a risky one. Concerning literary and intellectual standards these two men—one a distinguished publisher, the other a barrister turned full-time man of letters—were in agreement. The monthly magazine was to be "open to everything which is good of its kind, except what is contrary to good taste, sound morals, and the fullest respect for religious feeling."[1] Murray may have had in mind a nonpartisan version of the *Quarterly Review** (see *RA*), begun three generations earlier by the publishing house of the Murray family. Murray was an avowed Conservative, and Newbolt was a Liberal sympathizer with friends in high political places. The new monthly would, Murray hoped, benefit from the far-reaching political connections of both publisher and editor, and escape the political bias of either: "The initiative as to subjects and writers should rest with the Editor, but here ... we should be prepared to render assistance, and—though I do not anticipate any such crisis—I presume that neither party would press a point in the teeth of a strong protest from the other in a case where personal convictions or principles were at stake." Newbolt appears to have been of two editorial minds from early on. To Liberal statesman Edward Grey he confessed his political ambition as an editor: he hoped "to do something for the Liberal cause, if not for the Liberal party"; and at the same time he envisioned himself as a twentieth-century Addison, whose *Spectator** (see *AAAJ*) would address readers "on a wide range of topics; leaning to the Arts rather than to Parties or Orthodoxies: surveying Public Affairs and Politics when necessary, but from the library-window rather than from the drill-ground point of view."[2] For four years Murray and Newbolt worked amicably if at times uneasily together to produce what Walter Graham considered to be one of the most attractive and distinguished periodicals of its time.[3] The *Monthly Review* eventually fell on financial hard times. In 1904 Newbolt resigned as editor, having served in that capacity from the beginning of publication in 1900. Charles Hanbury-Williams took over the editorship until 1907, when publication ceased.

Despite Newbolt's and Murray's agreement to make the *Monthly Review* nonpartisan, readers from the beginning perceived it to be a Liberal organ.[4] Newbolt created a format that allowed him the opportunity to begin each issue with two or three editorial statements, usually on political issues. And if his intention was to speak as a disinterested observer, readers seem to have judged him to be, if not a drill-ground participant in political battles, at least a sideline partisan. The war in South Africa, army and navy reform, and Liberal party divisions were issues Newbolt took up as editorial writer and editorial manager— issues that scarcely encouraged disinterested commentary. Important political events in other countries led Newbolt to ask a number of distinguished foreigners to contribute articles to the *Monthly Review*: for example, five political leaders from Eastern Europe contributed commentaries on "Austro-Hungarian Leaders of the Habsburg Monarchy": Austrian Christian Socialist leader Albert Gesmann, Young Czech party leader Adolf Stransky, Hungarian Ex-Premier N. Banffy, Hungarian Independence party leader Franz Kossuth, and Polish Conservative party leader Stanislas Ritter von Starzynski (10 [February 1903]: 42–61; 10 [March 1903]: 17–25). A Russian journalist and anti-Semite, M. O. Menchikoff, and M. Tugan-Baronowsky, a liberal Russian writer, provide opposing statements concerning "The Jewish Peril in Russia" (14 [January 1904]:70–77; 14 [February 1904]:91–95.)

Of all the political issues Newbolt took up as editor, the one that finally led to his resignation was that of free trade. During the latter half of 1903, following Chamberlain's call for protective tariff legislation, no fewer than eight major articles by free trade advocates appeared in the *Monthly Review*. Former director of the Bank of England and author of *Theory of the Foreign Exchanges* (1861), George Goschen revised for the *Monthly* a speech he delivered in Parliament in opposition to Chamberlain's proposal ("Mr. Chamberlain's Proposals," 12 [July 1903]:38–55). Thereafter appeared free trade articles from, among others, M.P. Henry Hobhouse ("The Position of Unionist Free Traders," 12 [August 1903]:55–63); and Liberal Imperialist Council president Edward Grey ("Mr. Chamberlain's Fiscal Policy," 13 [October 1903]:11-25); as well as from Conservative Free Traders such as M.P. Michael Hicks-Beach ("A View of the Fiscal Controversy," 12 [September 1903]:28–39); and Winston Churchill ("Sheffield and Its Shadow," 13 [November 1903]:17–31). Newbolt's contribution to the foray was an imitation of Swift, "Gulliver's Last Voyage" (12 [July 1903]:1–17), which, though intended as impartial satire, did little to temper the decidedly partisan view reiterated from issue to issue of the *Monthly Review* concerning trade and tariffs. These articles in particular caused Murray some embarrassment among his friends and longtime clientele, but he was businessman enough to recognize the commercial opportunity the articles provided. The decision was made to run another printing of those issues containing articles on trade. The reprinting of issues proved to be an expensive gamble that the *Monthly Review* lost: by the time reruns were available, public interest in them had apparently waned—or perhaps publisher and editor overestimated initial public interest in an issue that preoccupied a number of Britain's statesman.[5] By 1904 Newbolt was forced to acknowledge that the *Monthly* had failed to create a sufficiently large and faithful clientele to warrant his continuation as editor. It seems unlikely that the *Monthly Review* was a greater commercial success under its second editor than it had been under its first. A severe curtailment of photographic illustrations after 1904 suggests an enforced financial retrenchment. Other changes suggest a loss of the intellectual vigor that had characterized the magazine during its first four years.

In addition to Newbolt's editorials, the format of the *Monthly Review* provided for a regular article, "On the Line," a series of brief descriptions of books recommended to readers of broad interests and unspecialized training:

> We shall give a list; the books will be recent; they will be such as in our opinion no one can ignore without loss; among them will be found foreign books, especially books in French; all classes of literature will be eligible. On the other hand, the list will not claim to be an exhaustive one; it will not necessarily be confined to books appearing within the month; it will not consider the interests of the expert in any branch, but the pleasure of the general or omnivorous reader. It will contain comments, but brief and not detailed; the mere report of a patrol, so that the reader may not feel he is being led to attack entirely unknown positions; it is far from our intention merely to add one more to the chorus of critics. The books we do not like we shall leave others to advertise. [2 (February 1901):22]

Though unsigned, these appreciative reviews were written by various hands, including Newbolt and a number of his regular contributors, among them A. T. Quiller-Couch, Mary Coleridge, Edith Sichel, and Roger Fry ("On the Line," 6 [February 1902]:7–8). "On the Line" normally presents as many as a dozen titles, about a third of which are of poetry and fiction, and two-thirds of memoirs, biography, the arts, philosophy and religion, natural history, economics, antiquities, and military matters. About a third of the total number of books hung "On the Line" are of non-British origin (examples are Anatole France's *M. Bergeret à Paris*, 3 [April 1901]:12–13; Tarkington's *M. Beaucaire*, 3 [June 1901]:17–18; and Chekhov's *The Black Monk*, 15 [April 1904]:16–19). Following these fixed opening editorial and review articles are normally ten to twelve signed contributions and, occasionally, pseudonymous attributions (for instance, "Eques" and "Cavalry" debate cavalry modernization in "The Cavalry and Its Principal Arm," 13 [December 1903]:50–73, and 14 [February 1904]:78–90). The ratio of literary and journalistic pieces in each issue is roughly the same as that which prevails in "On the Line": about two of the latter for each of the former. A distinctive feature of this magazine is its occasional publication of long poems: Laurence Binyon's "The Death of Adam" (6 [February 1902]:171–90); Robert Bridges's "Epistle to a Socialist in London" (12 [July 1903]:150–67) and "Recollections of Solitude" (10 [February 1903]:123–27); Yeats's "Baile and Aillinn" (8 [July 1902]:156–64); a newly published poem by Blake, "The Passions" (12 [August 1903]:123–29); and two selections from Meredith's *A Reading of Life* (2 [March 1901]:155–64).

Under Hanbury-Williams's editorship, the partisan tone of the *Monthly* was considerably muted. Editorials were dropped, and articles dealing with political issues or personalities were apt to be more deferential than had been the case earlier: for example, Tory Herbert Maxwell's memorial of Liberal M.P. "Sir William Harcourt" (17 [November 1904]:15–27). "On the Line" continued, but in substantially reduced form; and it was moved from its early position in an issue to the back pages. For good or ill, with Newbolt's resignation the *Monthly Review* lost its identifiable character as a magazine reflecting the views and tastes of a strong-minded editor and a coterie of close literary and political friends. There is something charmingly naive, if blatantly self-serving, in the frequent recommendation to be found in "On the Line" of books that have appeared in the *Monthly Review* before their independent publication: T. A. Cook's *Spirals in Nature and Art*, on the source of the staircase design of the Chateau de Blois, appeared in the *Monthly Review* in serial form under the title "The Shell of Leonardo" (7 [April 1902]:133–58; 7 [May 1902]:102–25), and a portion of Leslie Stephen's *Studies of a Biographer* appeared as "In Praise of Walking" in *Monthly Review* (4 [August 1901]:98–116): both books are warmly recommended in "On the Line" (11 [April 1903]:9–15).

A number of Newbolt's most frequent contributors of signed articles are prominent literary figures of the time. Roger E. Fry provided a series of elaborately illustrated articles that count among his most important early essays. These include "Art before Giotto" (1 [October 1900]:126–51); "Giotto" (1 [December 1900]:139–57, and 2 [February 1901]:96–121); "Florentine Painting of the Fourteenth Century" (3 [June 1901]:112–34); "A Note on an Early Venetian Picture [Bellini's 'The Annunciation']" (4 [July 1901]:86-97); "The Symbolism of Signorelli's Pan" (5 [December 1901]:110-14); and "Art and Religion" (7 [May 1902]:126–39). Drama critic William Archer wrote on the need for public discussion of a national pantheon ("An Academy of the Dead," 1 [December 1900]:118–27); on military and educational reforms ("A Plain Man's Politics," 5 [November 1901]:66–85); and on "The Case for National Theaters" (8 [July 1902]:140–55). Havelock Ellis contributed three essays to the early *Monthly Review*: a preliminary study of the significance of geography and race in determining national ability ("The Distribution of British Ability," 3 [April 1901]:91–104); a study of portraits in the National Portrait Gallery to determine the connection between physical coloring and mental aptitude ("The Comparative Abilities of the Fair and Dark," 4 [August 1901]:84–97); and a study of the historical origins of the idealistic and realistic modes of British painting ("The Evolution of Painting in England," 6 [March 1901]:123–41). Yeats contributed two poems: "Adam's Curse" (9 [December 1902]:112–13) as well as the much longer "Baile and Aillinn" (8 [July 1902]:156–64), based on a story from Lady Gregory's *Cuchullain of Muirthemne*, which the poet describes as "the most important book that has come out of Ireland in my time" (8 [July 1902]:156). Yeats also contributed two autobiographical essays: "Magic" (4 [September 1901]:144–62), on personal experiences demonstrating the interconnectedness of minds through symbols; and "Speaking to the Psaltery" (7 [May 1902]:94–99), on the poet's resolution to write his shorter poems with a form of musical notation in order to achieve certain rhythmic effects. Bridges provided his friend Newbolt with several poems (including "To Robert Burns," 6 [March 1902]:157–63, and two sonnets, "To the President of Magdalen College, Oxford" and "To Joseph Joachim," 15 [June 1904]:159–60), as well as an article advocating the inclusion of specific lessons in elementary schools for the purpose of forming a national taste for good music ("English Music: A Practical Scheme," 16 [July 1904]:105–10). Former classmate and longtime friend A. T. Quiller-Couch contributed review articles on Thomas Edward Brown ("T.E.B.," 1 [October 1900]:152–64) and Coventry Patmore (2 [January 1901]:149–66). Friend Edith Sichel provided articles on various topics, among them memorial articles on "Charlotte Yonge as a Chronicler" (3 [May 1901]:88–97) and on biographer Canon Ainger ("A Personal Impression," 14 [March 1904]:64–74); "The Religion of Rabelais" (1 [December 1900]:128–38), on his beliefs and influences, particularly as they found their way to England; and a wide-ranging essay on the history of women painters and its present culmination in the work of Miss Fortescue-Brickdale, whose works were being exhibited in a Bond Street gallery ("A Woman Painter and Symbolism," 4 [September 1901]:101–14). Arthur Symons contributed articles on various artists and works of art ("Robert Bridges," 4 [July 1901]:114–27; "John Keats," 5 [October 1901]:139–55; "A Study at Toledo" [on the seventeenth-century painter Theotocopuli], 2 [March 1901]:144–54; "A New Art of the Stage" [on Purcell Society musical productions], 7 [June 1902]:157–62; and "The Music of Richard Strauss," 9 [December 1902]:80–91).

Some of De la Mare's first published poems and fiction appeared in the *Monthly*, including the short story "The Riddle" (10 [February 1903]:156–60) and several poems: "Ten Characters from Shakespeare" (7 [May 1902]:153–62), "Memories of Childhood" (14 [January 1904]:155–64); "Goliath" (15 [April 1904]:160), and "The Happy Encounter" (16 [July 1904]:125). De la Mare and Newbolt became close friends as a result of their first meeting through the *Monthly Review*, and Newbolt was largely responsible for De la Mare's subsequent full-time devotion to writing. Other distinguished writers whose works appear in the *Monthly Review* include Gorky ("Makar Chudra," 5 [November 1901]:173–87; and "The Kahn and His Son," 6 [February 1902]:163–70); Edward Garnett ("The Contemporary Critic," 5 [December 1901]:92–109, in which the distinction is drawn between the scholarly and the journalistic critic); Kipling ("Below the Mill Dam," 8 [September 1902]:23–41: a short story); Lady Gregory ("West Irish Folk Ballads," 9 [October 1902]:123–35); Fiona Macleod ("The Magic Kingdoms," 10 [January 1903]:99–112, on sources of knowledge and intuitive power); Percy Lubbock and Arthur Benson ("Julian Sturgis," 16 [July 1904]:111–23: two short aricles); and H. G. Wells ("George Gissing: An Impression," 16 [August 1904]:159–72).

Under Newbolt's editorship there appeared in the *Monthly Review* four serialized novels. Every issue Newbolt edited, in fact, concludes with an installment of about thirty pages of a long piece of fiction, not one of which suggests, except in its manner of publication, the richness of texure or density of action of its Victorian forebears: Anthony Hope's historical fiction, *Tristram of Blent* (1–5 [October 1900–October 1901]); Alfred Ollivant's *Danny*, a sequel to his most famous novel, *Bob, Son of Battle*, for which the novelist was given the dubious epitaph of a one-dog writer (6–10 [April 1902–January 1903]); William Hurrel Mallock's anonymously published serial, *The Veil of the Temple*, a lengthy dialogue on free will and Christianity (11–13 [April–December 1903]); and Quiller-Couch's historical novel on the Seven Years' War, *Fort Amity* (12–15 [August 1903–May 1904]).

Under Hanbury-Williams's editorship, a few of Newbolt's contributors continued to provide material for the *Monthly Review*. De la Mare, for example, provided the new editor with a short story, "An Ideal Craftsman" (19 [June 1905]:92–106). Symons continued to provide the review with essays on various artists: "Beethoven" (19 [April 1905]:31–47), "Gustave Moreau" (20 [July 1905]:125–32), "Dante and Botticelli" (26 [February 1907]:49–60); and "A Forgotten Poet [John Clare]" (27 [May 1907]:45–62). After a brief hiatus following Newbolt's resignation from the *Monthly Review*, Hanbury-Williams recommenced publication of serialized long fiction: H. C. Bailey's historical novel, *Beaujeu* (18–21 [January–November 1905]); Horace Annesley Vachell's *Face of Clay* (21–23 [December 1905–May 1906]), a novel based on a legend concerning the model of a well-known artist's mask; and Mrs. Henry de la Pasture's novel, *The Lonely Lady of Grosvenor Square* (23–26 [June 1906–February 1907]). Also published in installments were G. S. Street's *Ghosts of Piccadilly* (25–27 [November 1906–June 1907]), a series of essays on important figures of British history who lived in London.

Among Hanbury-Williams's most frequent contributors were two journalists, Basil Tozer (who occasionally wrote elsewhere under the beguiling pseudonym of *Villain Regardant*) and Michael MacDonagh, each of whom provided the *Monthly Review* with at least nine articles. Tozer wrote primarily on literary topics: "The Increasing Popularity of the Erotic Novel" (20 [September 1905]:53–59); "A Plea for Shorter Novels" (27 [May 1907]:34–44). MacDonagh wrote on political topics: "The Fascination of Parliament" (22 [February 1906]:1–18); "House of Commons at Work" (25 [October 1906]:55–76). Tozer's slightly sensational essays and MacDonagh's chatty ones suggest that Murray's and Newbolt's hope of creating a magazine of the highest intellectual standards did not last through the life of the *Monthly Review*. Still, articles occasionally appeared during Hanbury-Wiliams's editorship that, either by authorship or by topic, cause even a late twentieth-century reader to pause: W. H. Hudson's imagistic study of "The Serpent in Literature" (20 [August 1905]:118–30); Gorky's short story, "Man" (18 [March 1905]:1–7); William Archer's personal account, "Ibsen as I Knew Him" (23 [June 1906]:1–19); Lucy Gardner Paget's spirited defense of women's suffrage, "The Coming Power" (24 [July 1906]:35–42); and E. Maud Simon's equally spirited condemnation of suffrage as a detriment to the nation's welfare, "Women's Suffrage" (27 [May 1907]:22–33).

Why the *Monthly Review* failed to gain sufficient readership under Newbolt is a question to which there is no satisfactory answer. Under his editorship, virtually every issue of the *Monthly Review* offered its readers at least one literary contribution of great merit and several pieces of high intellectual quality. Under Hanbury-Williams, the *Monthly Review* could make fewer claims to literary or intellectual excellence.

Notes

1. Henry Newbolt, *My World as in My Time* (London, 1932), p. 232.
2. Newbolt, pp. 239, 271, 240.
3. Walter Graham, *English Literary Periodicals* (New York, 1930), p. 266.
4. Newbolt, pp. 241–43.
5. Ibid., pp. 245–75.

Information Sources

BIBLIOGRAPHY
Graham, Walter. *English Literary Periodicals*. New York, 1930.
Mallock, W. H. *Memoirs of Life and Literature*. New York, 1920.
Newbolt, Henry. *My World as in My Time*. London, 1932.
Vachell, Horace Annesley. *Fellow-Travellers*. New York, n.d.
INDEXES
Index of authors and index of subjects, alphabetically arranged, precede each volume of three issues.
REPRINT EDITIONS
Microform: Early British Periodicals (UMI), reels 496–500.
LOCATION SOURCES
American
Widely available.
British
Widely available.

Publication History

MAGAZINE TITLE AND TITLE CHANGES
The Monthly Review.
VOLUME AND ISSUE DATA
Volumes 1–27, October 1900–June 1907.
FREQUENCY OF PUBLICATION
Monthly.
PUBLISHERS
Volumes 1–6: John Murray, Albermarle St., W., London. Volumes 7–27: John Murray, London/George N. Morang (or Morang and Co.), Toronto.
EDITORS
Henry Newbolt, volumes 1–16, October 1900–September 1904: Charles Hanbury-Williams, volumes 17–27, October 1904–June 1907.

Carol de Saint Victor

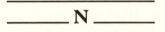

N

NATIONAL OBSERVER. See SCOTS OBSERVER, THE

NATIONAL REVIEW (1855)

Some time in 1854, the Unitarian proprietors of the *Prospective Review*,* seeing steadily decreasing numbers of subscribers and a consequent steady decrease in the impact of their journal on public thought, decided on drastic measures: they would either merge the *Prospective* with another, healthier journal, or terminate it and start over. James Martineau, the influential Unitarian minister who was one of the review's principals, first attempted to buy the *Westminster Review** (see *RA*) in order to merge it with the *Prospective*. Failing that, he joined with J. J. Tayler, Henry Crabb Robinson, S. D. Darbishire, Lady Byron, and several others in putting together a sufficient fund for founding an entirely new quarterly out of the anticipated ashes of the *Prospective*.

In 1855 W. R. Greg agreed to edit the as yet unnamed successor to the *Prospective*. However, at the last moment Greg backed out, and Martineau approached Richard Holt Hutton, then the *de facto* editor of the *Prospective*, and his friend Walter Bagehot, with the offer of a joint editorship. Hutton, a former student of Martineau's, had worked with J. L. Sanford from 1851 to 1853 editing the *Inquirer*, then the leading Unitarian weekly. Bagehot, who had published several articles in the *Prospective*, had helped Hutton get the editorship there for its last few numbers.

Hutton and Bagehot accepted the offer, although Bagehot considered Hutton to be the working editor. In March 1855 he wrote to Hutton:

I am much obliged to you for engaging to take the Editorship of the *National* at my request, though I own I think you will like it better than you think you shall. Of course you may count on my doing anything for you in the way of cooperation—literary or practical locomotion which is not in my absolute power, always excepted. Even if it were offered me I could not have the responsibility of the *Review* absolutely on me. . . . The only part I think I could be of any use would be perhaps in planning the secular articles for each number at first and I shall be most willing to do all I can in this.[1]

As Alastair Buchan describes the working relationship: "Hutton offered to share the chair with Bagehot, who declined the formal appointment but nevertheless interfered with vigor in most of Hutton's editorial decisions."[2]

Hutton continued as editor until 1862, when a combination of his increasing duties as coeditor of the *Spectator** (see *RA*) and his growing Anglicanism caused him to resign his chair. Of the two reasons, the religious was probably the more telling. Martineau was a serious Unitarian, and Hutton was becoming a serious Anglican. Although neither he nor Bagehot was directly responsible to Martineau, both felt that, as Unitarian money had founded the *National* and continued to support it, and as a preponderance of subscribers were Unitarian, the quarterly should normally take a Unitarian slant, for which Hutton felt a growing abhorrence.

Hutton was replaced by Charles Henry Pearson, who edited the *National* ably from July 1862 until July 1863. Pearson brought several new contributors, including Goldwin Smith, W. W. Story, Edward Dicey, and others, many of whom were dissatisfied with the *Saturday Review*'s* editorial policies and had quit there in protest. In fact, M. E. Grant Duff, one of the original *Saturday Review* group, recommended Pearson for the *National* editorship. Pearson lasted for four issues, then resigned in a dispute with Bagehot over the balance of articles in each issue. Bagehot insisted on two religious articles (as had been the custom until then), while Pearson said that "theology was the dead weight against which the 'Review' had to struggle, and . . . one article at a time was all it could bear."[3]

Bagehot struggled to keep the *National* going, but, faced with declining subscriptions—a large part of the circulation was American, and the American Civil War effectively closed off that market—and other interests, he closed it in 1864. Unitarian backing had all but disappeared by this time with the founding of a purely Unitarian journal, the *Theological Review*. The last regular number of the *National* appeared in April 1864. Bagehot tried one more number in November 1864 that included signed articles (relatively innovative at the time), but by then reader support had evaporated. The Unitarian subscribers lost interest as the Unitarian content diminished, and the general readers found a number of lively weeklies, fortnightlies, monthlies, and quarterlies covering the same intellectual territory as the *National*, and covering it well.

The *National* began life with a great deal of promise. In an announcement published in June 1855 in the *Athenaeum,** *Spectator* (for both, see *RA*), *Inquirer*, and several other weeklies, the new review was described as "a new Quarterly

Journal of General Literature, Politics, and Social and Religious Philosophy.'' It was not characterized as a Unitarian organ, nor were its politics announced. According to Martineau, its purpose was to cover an area "of unrepresented feeling and opinion between the heavy Whiggism and decorous church-latitude of the *Edinburgh* [*(see *RA*)] on one hand and the atheistic tendency and refugee politics of the *Westminster* on the other."[4] The first issue ran about 250 pages and contained political articles by Greg, Martineau, and Sanford; literary reviews by Bagehot, W. C. Roscoe, and Tom Taylor; theological articles by J. J. Tayler (a review of Charles Ewald's *Life of Christ*), Hutton, and T. S. Osler; and a science article, "The Planets," by Hutton. That wide range of interests characterized the *National* throughout its existence—there were always at least two political and two theological essays, and a mix of social, literary, and general interest commentary.

Bagehot and Hutton solicited articles on specific subjects from particular writers, thus assuring that the articles would be of uniform high quality. Quality was also ensured by the core of brilliant contributors recruited by Bagehot. Eight men—Bagehot, Hutton, Roscoe, Greg, Martineau, Sanford, Tayler, and E. A. Freeman—wrote 20 percent of the articles appearing in the *National*. Other contributors wrote regularly for the *Saturday Review, Spectator, Westminster*, and other influential contemporary periodicals (as, incidentally, did the *National* eight).

At its height, the *National* attained a respectable circulation and a reasonable amount of influence, thanks to Bagehot's incisive essays and his ability to persuade the best writers of the day to write for him. The January 1856 issue sold 540 copies. By 1860 the *National* was regularly selling 1,000 copies an issue, slightly fewer than the 1,250 that Martineau felt were needed to make it financially independent. Independence was finally achieved in the summer of 1861, with a circulation of 1,500. Unfortunately, that was to be a high-water mark. Events in Charleston Harbor immediately crippled circulation and Martineau and his friends once again had to underwrite the *National*'s publication.

Mrs. Russell Barrington describes the review's readership as "a refined and cultured minority."[5] Clearly, however, the majority of readers were American and English Unitarians. After losing the American market, the editors decided to balance the Unitarian position with an appeal to the English Broad Church market. The experiment failed; as described by then editor Pearson, "the genuine Unitarian clientele found the articles by 'liberal parsons' . . . as distasteful as the Nicene Creed itself. On the other hand, the Anglican reviews, which had treated the 'National' in its old days, when it was an avowed opponent, with great courtesy, declared open war against it."[6] Although the review remained Liberal in its politics to the end, this shifting of theological positions probably caused its ultimate demise.[7]

J. J. Tayler privately spoke for a large number of Unitarians when he wrote to Martineau that "the 'National' has now passed out of our hands, and represents really a section of the Broad Church party."[8] The *Christian Reformer*, a Unitarian periodical, noted that "unless we are very greatly mistaken, there will speedily be a great change in the readers of this periodical [the *National*]. . . . It is now to be the mouthpiece of those who would fain persuade themselves and the world that their iron handcuffs are only silver bracelets."[9] The Unitarians perceived the *National* as becoming an Anglican organ, and the Anglicans simply never picked it up.

In its heyday, the *National* provided an important forum for the best minds of the day. Virtually all of Bagehot's most important essays appeared in it. Martin Tupper was debunked in an important literary essay entitled "Charlatan Poetry" in 1858; "Owen Meredith" was exposed in 1863. Augustus de Morgan, Herbert Spencer, W. S. Jevons, F. W. Newman, Mark Pattison, Thomas Hughes, and Fitzjames Stephen are just some of the leading intellectuals of the era who published in the *National*. Finally, Matthew Arnold's "The Function of Criticism at the Present Time" appeared in the very last issue; it was perhaps the most important literary paper produced in the journal.

The most famous of the *National*'s encomiums came from Arnold, who wrote to his brother in 1856 that "there is nothing here in literature worth speaking of—except that the *National Review* is doing well."[10] Other contemporaries also praised it at various times, including the *Spectator*, the *Guardian*, and the *Morning Post*. The *New Monthly Magazine** (see *RA*) perhaps summarized most thoughtful reaction to the *National* in an article on Bagehot published in 1858:

> The *National Review* does not appear as the organ of any definite class, though its readers will be at no loss to determine the drift of its sympathies, literary, theological, moral, and political. Without passing any opinion upon the scope of these opinions, we are free to pay our tribute to the literary character of its general contents, in virtue of which it ranks second to none of its contemporaries, in the intrinisic value of essays distinguished by thinking broad and deep, impartiality and independence of spirit, searching critical discernment, a refined and eloquent style, and an earnest advocacy of what it holds to be just and true, with as stringent an opposition to whatever it accounts corrupt and fallacious.[11]

The *National*'s death was perhaps unfortunate after so short a life, but while it existed it "made a distinguished contribution to the trenchant analysis of the thought, literature, and society of an age famous for its self-criticism."[12] Its end left a definite void in the intellectual life of England and America.

Notes

1. Mrs. Russell Barrington (Emilie Isabel Wilson), *Life of Walter Bagehot* (London, 1914), p. 219.

2. Alastair Buchan, *The Spare Chancellor: The Life of Walter Bagehot* (East Lansing, Mich., 1960), p. 75.

3. Charles Henry Pearson, *Charles Henry Pearson, Fellow of Oriel and Education Minister for Victoria: Memorials by Himself, His Wife, and His Friends*, ed. William Stebbing (London, 1900), p. 96.

4. James Martineau, *The Life and Letters of James Martineau*, ed. James Drummond and C. B. Upton (London, 1902), 1:269. One might conclude from this statement either that Martineau had attempted to purchase the *Westminster* to quiet its atheism, or that he still resented the *Westminster*'s rejection of his offer.

5. Barrington, p. 219.

6. Pearson, p. 96.

7. See Barrington, p. 219, and Buchan, p. 75.

8. *John James Tayler: Letters Embracing His Life*, ed. J. H. Thom (London, 1872), 2:233.

9. "*National Review*, 1855–1864," in *The Wellesley Index to Victorian Periodicals 1824–1900*, ed. Walter E. Houghton (Toronto, 1979), 3:143.

10. *Unpublished Letters of Matthew Arnold*, ed. Arnold Whitridge (New Haven, 1923), p. 33.

11. *New Monthly Magazine* 112 (1858):340–41.

12. *Wellesley Index*, 3:144.

Information Sources

BIBLIOGRAPHY

Barrington, Mrs. Russell. *Life of Walter Bagehot*. London, 1914.

Buchan, Alastair. *The Spare Chancellor: The Life of Walter Bagehot*. East Lansing, Mich., 1960.

Martineau, James. *The Life and Letters of James Martineau*. 2 vols. Edited by James Drummond and C. B. Upton. London, 1902.

McLachlan, Herbert J. *The Unitarian Movement in the Religious Life of England 1700–1900*. London, 1934.

"*National Review*, 1855–1864." In *The Wellesley Index to Victorian Periodicals 1824–1900*. Vol. 3. Edited by Walter E. Houghton. Toronto, 1979.

Pearson, Charles Henry. *Charles Henry Pearson, Fellow of Oriel and Education Minister for Victoria: Memorials by Himself, His Wife, and His Friends*. Edited by William Stebbing. London, 1900.

St. John-Stevas, Norman. *Walter Bagehot*. London, 1959.

Sisson, C. H. *The Case of Walter Bagehot*. London, 1972.

INDEXES
Wellesley Index 3.

REPRINT EDITIONS
Microform: Early British Periodicals (UMI), reels 240–243.

LOCATION SOURCES
American
Widely available.
British
Widely available.

Publication History

MAGAZINE TITLE AND TITLE CHANGES

> *National Review*, informally related, but not formal successor, to *Prospective Review* (1845–1855); informally succeeded by *Theological Review* (1864–79).

VOLUME AND ISSUE DATA

> Volumes 1–18, July 1855–March, 1864; volume 19, November 1864.

FREQUENCY OF PUBLICATION

> Quarterly.

PUBLISHERS

> Volumes 1–2, July 1855–April 1856: R. Theobald. Volumes 3–19, July 1856–Nov. 1864: Chapman and Hall.

EDITORS

> Walter Bagehot, 1855–1864; R. H. Hutton, 1855–1862; Charles H. Pearson, 1862–1863.

Richard D. Fulton

NATIONAL REVIEW, THE (1883)

In the spring of 1881, Benjamin Disraeli remarked to a visitor in his home that he found it curious and even perplexing that well-considered periodicals of the day were philosophically inconsistent: in a periodical lying on a nearby table, for example, there was one article denying the existence of God and another proclaiming the pope as God's vice-regent (1 [March 1883]:24).[1] Before the conversation ended between the statesman whose death Victoria and the nation were soon to mourn and the journalist-poet she was later to name as Tennyson's successor as Poet Laureate, the idea of the *National Review* took preliminary shape. It was to be a monthly review devoted to political and literary matters, and it was to be unashamedly committed to Tory principles. Disraeli was firmly opposed to party affiliation for the monthly, however, or to its presuming to proffer political policies: "Above all, no Programme," he cautioned (1 [March 1883]:25). Alfred Austin was to remember Disraeli's admonition, but he was not to follow it: " 'Above all, no Programme' applies, not to Conservatism or to the Conservative Party, but only to the first number of this Review" (1 [March 1883]:36).

During its long life the *National Review* was to be a forum primarily for Conservatives who wished "to speak the thought that is in them on all subjects that interest the community" (1 [March 1883]:35). The purpose was, according to editor Austin, to promote Conservatism "by the demonstration that Conservatives have capacity, and not only political capacity, but capacity of the large and generous sort," and in so doing, "to go a long way towards converting people to Conservatism" (1 [March 1883]:35–36). Though answerable to no party control, the review was to persist from 1883 until 1960 as an outspoken advocate of rightist views on virtually all the important political issues of that era. Different editors and changing times would effect different intellectual and political emphases in the *Review*; on occasion there were to appear in its pages contributions calling into question the proper Conservative stance concerning an issue; and—though rarely—contributors with decidedly radical views were to find space in the *National Review* (for example, the issue of women's suffrage). In general, however, the *National Review*—which survived, as Disraeli did, for seventy-seven years—stands among periodicals of its era as he did among Victorian statesmen: a long-lived, eloquent, and self-confident Tory spokesman.

If Disraeli is to be acknowledged as the magazine's spritual father, then the Carlton Club should perhaps be credited as its financial guardian, at least during its first year or so: before the first issue of the *National Review* appeared, the Carlton Club pledged payment of 1,000 annual subscriptions (131 [October 1948]:267–71). Of about ten articles in each issue of about 160 pages, as many as eight may be called Conservative in Austin's broad understanding of that term—either for being written by a prominent Conservative or for presenting a Tory view on an issue of the day: for example, A. J. Balfour's "Bishop Berkeley's Life and Letters" (1 [March 1883]:85–100, [April, 1883]:299–313), and Robert Cecil's "Labourers' and Artisans' Dwellings" (2 [November 1883]:301–16). Austin served as editor during the first decade, with the help, until 1887, of W. J. Courthope, who served as literary editor and who, with Austin, was the principal contributor of literary articles.

Conservatism pervades the literary essays as well as the political ones. In literature as in politics, Austin's preferences were allied to tradition and law (cf. 2 [September 1883]:81–96; 3 [March 1884]:61–77; 4 [November 1884]:330–41). Courthope's contributions emphasize the analytical usefulness of political designations in understanding literature, and they, more than Austin's essays, are responsible for whatever claim is to be made for the achievement of the *National Review* as a critically probing monthly as well as a politically biased one. Just as in political thought extremists of left and right engage mistaken attitudes, whether of passive obedience to tradition or thoughtless denial of it, so "the representatives of the various arts seem to fall naturally into two divisions, corresponding to the Liberals and Conservatives in politics": every "real work of art," Courthope avers, "requires an union of liberty and order" ("Conservatism in Art," 1 [March 1883]:72). Most notable among Courthope's contributions is a serialization of what was later published as a book, *The Liberal Movement in English Literature*, a study of Romanticism based on politically derived critical concepts.

Of course, there do appear, during Austin's tenure as editor, literary articles that neither adhere to Austin's political bias nor concern themselves with Courthope's effort to apply political structures to literature. The names of the writers of many of these articles suggest that the *National Review* is to be compared with the most distinguished literary periodicals of the last years of the nineteenth century: among them are Violet Paget, William Archer, George Saintsbury, Arthur Symons, A. Conan Doyle, Andrew Lang, and Edmund Gosse. Among literary articles relating politics and art are Mortimer Dyneley's *"Locksley Hall and Liberalism,"* (8 [January 1886]:641–47) and statesman George N. Curzon's "Poetry, Politics, and Conservatism" (6 [December 1885]:502–18). A frequent contributor (and Courthope's replacement as literary editor in 1887) is William Watson. Several of Watson's literary essays to appear in the *National Review* were later reprinted in his *Excursions in Criticism*.

Among the *Review*'s political articles of the late 1880s are twenty-five or more on women's suffrage. They comprise a far more broadly based political discussion than the *Review* ordinarily provides. Nina H. Kennard discusses the sociological reasons for women having achieved less than men in all disciplines other than imaginative writing (3 [July 1884]:694–706). A ranking Conservative opposes women's suffrage as a threat to national character (4 [January 1885]:631–41), and is answered by an advocate of suffrage, Philip Vernon Smith (4 [March 1885]:60–70). "A Woman" asserts that motherhood is woman's highest calling (4 [January 1885]:669–82), and is answered by "A Man" (4 [February 1885]:289–92). Arch-antifeminist Eliza Lynn Linton—introduced to readers as an "avowedly advanced Liberal"—contributed at least four articles on the issue of feminism, including an attack on women who aspire to invade men's political territory (8 [September 1886]:1–15). A leader of the suffrage movement compares the past and present influence of women in national affairs (8 [November 1886]:392–99); and feminist Millicent Garrett Fawcett replies (11 [March 1887]:44–61) to what is perhaps the most outrageously bigoted article of the lot, by a former regius professor of modern history, Goldwin Smith (10 [February 1888]:735–52): "For my own part I confess that rather than see English women become like some of the public women of America, I would see them turn black" (10 [February 1888]:746).

In 1893 Frederick Maxse (whom Meredith immortalized as the protagonist of *Beauchamp's Career*) bought the *National Review* for his son, Leopold J. Maxse, whose ill health prevented him from pursuing a career as a politician. Instead, he was to serve, during nearly forty years as editor of the *Review*, as one of Britain's foremost Conservative journalistic spokesmen. As editor he attracted to the periodical some of his country's most prominent Conservative advocates, and through his monthly lead article, "Episodes of the Month," he provided readers with a sustained commentary on many of the most important domestic and international events during the two decades before World War I and for more than a decade after. The *National Review* thrived under Maxse's editorship as it did not do under any other of its editors. During the Edwardian years, the *Review* "lay in the drawing-rooms of a governing class whose wealth and influence were still virtually intact" (154 [June 1960]:203), in no one of which, it may be presumed, was a reader moved to repeat Disraeli's remark to Austin concerning the lack of a philosophically consistent periodical. During this time, circulation rose to more than 10,000—more than twice what it had been under Austin. When, in 1929, Leo Maxse fell ill, his successor found herself responsible for a magazine that had finally fallen on financial hard times, but before then—

and most particularly before World War I—the *National Review* achieved its greatest commercial—and perhaps even its greatest intellectual—success. Probably the single most important reason for that success was "Episodes of the Month," which expanded during Maxse's tenure from about fifteen pages to forty-five, approximately a quarter of an issue's total volume. Maxse spoke for tariff reform, a militarily strong Britain, and friendship with France; and against a return to the gold standard, the League of Nations, and Germany, whom he perceived from early on as a threat to the rest of Europe. Articles he wrote and published concerning the German menace were later published as a book, *"Germany on the Brain,"* or, *The Obsession of "A Crank": Gleanings from the "National Review," 1899–1914*, a tribute to his political prescience and tenacity.

Though Maxse's genius and interests were political rather than literary, the monthly continued to offer its readers articles on literary interest for a number of years after Maxse became editor. During World War I and for some years afterwards, fewer literary contributions appeared in the *National Review*. Before then, the magazine upheld the tradition of the British monthly in generous fashion, offering its readers literary as well as political criticism, personal essays, fiction, poetry, and even an occasional drama. Among pieces of short fiction are works by the Irish Renaissance writer, Jane Barlow (23 [July 1894]:708–18, and 24 [October 1894]:278–88), and by George Gissing (23 [April 1894]:273–84, and 24 [February 1895]:847–62). Poems include Meredith's "Foresight and Patience" (23 [April 1894]:164–74) and several pieces of occasional verse. Most issues contain at least one literary article, and while literary articles of this period are on the whole less interesting than those published under Austin's editorship, they reflect many of the literary concerns of the time: Arthur Tilley's "Gogol, the Father of Russian Realism" (23 [July 1894]:640–61); Evelyn Underhill's defense of May Sinclair, "The Cant of Unconventionality," (50 [January 1908]:751–60); Edward Dowden's response to the Shakespeare-Bacon controversy, "Shakespeare as a Man of Science: A Study in Higher Criticism," (39 [July 1902]:799–813); W. L. Courtney's "Vicissitudes of the Hero in Drama" (39 [April 1902]:305–13); and, among a number of outcries against contemporary fiction, Basil Tozer's "The Coming Censorship of Fiction" (51 [April 1908]:236–42) and Maxwell Gray's "Plea for the Silence of the Novelist" (39 [May 1902]:429–37).

Among frequent contributors of literary criticism during Maxse's years are Austin Dobson, H. C. Biron, novelist Jane H. Findlater, and Leslie Stephen. Dobson's fairly frequent contributions between 1901 and 1920 are often review articles, particularly on eighteenth-century literature, for which he was particularly known; they include an article on one of Fielding's journalistic ventures, "The Covent Garden Journal" (37 [May 1901]:383–96) and "[George] Lyttelton as Man of Letters" (55 [June 1910]:593–610). Biron's contributions include two articles on Dickens (59 [May 1912]:514–23; 73 [August 1919]:806–13) and others on "Dr. Johnson and [the forger] Dr. Dodd" (58 [November 1911]:455–63), "Clarissa Harlowe" (74 [September 1919]:71–81), "Anthony Trollope"

(75 [March 1920]:76–88), and "Evelyn of Wooton" (76 [September 1920]:83–95). Findlater's contributions are often concerned with the contemporary corruption of literary forms. Her essay on Gissing—"The Spokesman of Despair" (44 [November 1904]:511–22)—however, is largely favorable, as is her article, "On Religious Novels" (39 [March 1902]:88–98). Stephen contributed many essays, including critical and autobiographical ones: two essays on Shakespeare (37 [April 1901]:220–39; 38 [November 1901]:402–6); "Anthony Trollope" (38 [September 1901]:68–84); "Robert Louis Stevenson" (38 [January 1902]:725–43); "William Godwin's Novels" (38 [February 1902]:908–23); "Young's *Night Thoughts*" (39 [August 1902]:908–26); and a series of autobiographical essays on his university years and his experiences as a journalist and editor: "Some Early Impressions," (42 [September 1903]:130–46; [October 1903]:208–24; [November 1903]:420–36; [December 1903]:563–81). Stephen's essays may lay claim to being the most significant group of literary essays published in the *National Review* during Maxse's editorship.

From 1929, when Maxse fell seriously ill, until 1932, when he died, his sister Violet Milner assumed the tasks of editor, with her brother Ivor serving as business manager. In 1932 Milner assumed the title of editor, and until 1948 she served in that capacity. Thus, for fifty-five years the *National Review* was very much the enterprise of one family. Milner shared her brother's political views, but she achieved a reputation for allowing personal animosities to interfere with her political judgments. While an honest and justifiable fear of Germany's military intentions led Milner to attack the Baldwin and Chamberlain governments for their appeasement of Germany, her bitter memory of Churchill's unflattering remarks about her husband Alfred Milner prevented her from acknowledging Churchill's accomplishments as prime minister: "Lady Milner resembled her brother in outlook: in temperament she was, perhaps, more venomous and vindictive when her righteous indignation was engaged" (154 [June 1960]:206). At its most effective, Milner's prose recalled the unsentimentalized, clearly phrased, allusive writing so characteristic of her brother: "We are not fighting to make the world safe for democracy. We are fighting to keep ourselves safe for democracy. We are fighting to save England and France; to keep alive the forces of civilisation; to keep Europe from subjection to a horde that has brought five aggressive wars on peaceful neighbours within a life time, each war more treacherously prepared and more evilly conducted than the last" ("Episodes of the Month," 113 [October 1939]:406).

Under Milner's editorship, literary pieces comprise no more than about 5 percent of the articles in the *National Review*. Nearly all of the literary criticism of this period appears under "Books Old and New," a regular monthly series of short articles, with quite brief notices of recent publications listed under "National Review Library." Frequent contributors of literary criticism under "Books Old and New" are Orlo Williams and Bonamy Dobrée, both of whom wrote from an impressive knowledge of literary history. As seems fitting, Kipling was both contributor to and subject of articles in the *Review*. He contributed several poems, including "Canada" and "What Happened" (130 [January 1948]:35, 47), as well as an essay on the importance of the monarchy to the English spirit ("Let Us Face Facts," 107 [September 1936]:305–8). Articles on Kipling include Ian D. Colvin's comparison of him to Shakespeare ("Rudyard Kipling," 106 [February 1936]:188–92) and a two-part article on Kipling's early reading ("This Bore Fruit Afterwards" and "The Old Shekarry," 110 [February 1938]:215–21, [March 1938]:362–65).

Perhaps a telling sign of the magazine's age during Milner's editorship—in addition to the reduction of the number of its pages by about half—is the frequent reprinting of literary pieces from its earlier and more vigorous past: Stephen's "On Biography" in August 1933, which first appeared in 1893; A. E. Gathorne-Hardy's "Fallow Deer at Home" in September 1934, first published in 1884; and several of Austin's early contributions, including his essay on "Matthew Arnold," first published in 1888; and "Tennyson's Sensitiveness," first published in 1893. A more congenial note of nostalgia is struck with a number of personal essays in which the present era is judged deficient by comparison with the past: E. Lyttelton's "A Schoolboy Seventy Years Ago" (104 [April 1935]: 507–12); Mary Maxse's "The Books We Lose" (104 [April 1935]:540–44); Charles Pendrill's "A City Lane That Was" (124 [March 1945]:233–41); and Basil Tozer's "Will Fox-Hunting Survive the War?" (125 [September 1945]:239–45).

Poems appear occasionally during this period, but often by mediocre poets such as Gladys Doreena Wilkinson and E. Mary Prister-Cruttwell. Rarely does short fiction appear during this period, but one notable example is an early story by Marguerite Yourcenar, "Witchcraft" (112 [April 1939]:503–16).

In August 1937, the *National Review* absorbed the *English Review*,* created in 1908, edited by Ford Madox Ford and others, and regarded in its earliest days as a brilliant literary journal. Thereafter it bore the title, the *National Review, incorporating The English Review*. In 1950, the monthly absorbed the *English Review Magazine*, and thereupon assumed the less cumbersome title, the *National and English Review*. In 1948 Milner relinquished proprietorship of the magazine to Edward Grigg. In 1955, following Grigg's death, his son, John Edward Grigg, became editor. Father and son could trace their journalistic and political associations with the monthly back to the days of Leo Maxse. Edward Grigg had served as foreign and imperial editor of the *Times* and, in 1923, had been elected to Parliament as a Liberal. Following a term as governor of Kenya, he was elected to Parliament again, this time as a Conservative. He and his son adapted their Tory stance to what they considered to be a realistic acknowledgment of Britain's limited control over the Empire and social movements. Of the son it was said that he suffered "more than his predecessors from the tension between a radical temperament and the conventional spirit of Toryism" (154 [June 1960]:206). He favored the relinquishment of imperial power when it could be retained only through violence. He argued for India's independence and against the Suez ultimatum, issues that dated back, ironically, to Disraeli: under his administration, Victoria had been named Empress of India, and Britain had taken possession of the Suez Canal. By 1960 the monthly that had been a gleam in the dying Disraeli's eye had, in its own words, "completed its life-cycle": "It dies swiftly and without self-pity. The means to keep it alive, for several years at least, have been offered—and declined.... it would be wrong to sustain through the charity of well-wishers a form of journalism which is no longer viable" ("Episodes of the Month," 154 [June 1960]:201).

Under Edward Grigg the magazine continued for a while its perfunctory attention to literary articles and poetry, the former limited almost exclusively to brief reviews of current publications under "Books Old and New." Beginning in 1950, however, when the *English Review Magazine* brought to the *National Review* the reputation of an important literary publication as well as the services of one of its literary editors, Christopher Sykes, more of the monthly's pages were devoted to literary matters. "Books Old and New" continued, with frequent contributions from Orlo Williams, Ruby Millar, Eric Gillett (who served for a time as literary editor of the *National and English Review*), and Sykes. Occasional contributions to the review column came from better-known writers, including E. M. Forster ("Fen, Forest, and Field," 136 [August 1951]:109–10). Walter De la Mare contributed to the monthly three poems ("Time, Love and Life," 142 [June 1954]:355–56; and "Tares" and "Derelict," 143 [July 1954]:40–42), as well as two essays, the second of which appeared in the year of his death ("Essay on Prose," 144 [January 1955]:11–17; [February 1955]:95–100; [March 1955]:155–60; and "Metrical Techniques," 146 [February 1956]:89–97; [March 1956]:156–67). In the last years of the monthly, whole issues were often devoted to a single subject, and of these, two are of particular interest. One issue devoted to British universities includes articles by Asa Briggs ("Redbrick and Old Lace"), Kingsley Amis ("Sherry, Mild, and Coffee"), and Iris Murdoch ("The Equal Woman," 150 [May 1958]). Another special issue consists of an anthology of contemporary poetry, and includes works by Patricia Beer, Edmund Blunden, C. Day Lewis, Geoffrey Hill, Herbert Read, Stephen Spender, John Wait, and David Wright ("Life and Language: An Anthology of New Work by Contemporary Poets," 150 [April 1958]). In the preface to this anthology is acknowledged the "responsibility of any periodical that appeals to the literate public to make some of its space available for new poetry" (150 [April 1958]:2). This monthly, the preface continues, has published poetry from time to time, but from now on it will be one of its regular features. And so it was, with one or two poems appearing in most issues, including works by Edward Lowbury ("Fog," 151 [August 1958]:58), Peter Levi ("Longwall Street," 151 [September 1958]:118), Gloria Evans Davis ("Coast: Prelude," 152 [January 1959]:23), and others. But the effort was too late and too small. The *National Review* was to cease publication without having achieved the literary appeal it had enjoyed in its Victorian years.

Note

1. Most of the information in this article derives from the pages of the periodical itself. Of varying usefulness are several articles scattered throughout the magazine on its history and its proprietors and editors. See especially Alfred Austin, " 'Above All, No Programme,' " 1 (March 1883):24–39; John Satterfield Sandars, "Our Brilliant Friend [Leopold J. Maxse]," 98 (February 1932):156; Wilson Herbert Wrigley, "L. J. Maxse as Editor," 100 (February 1933):175–82; "The *National Review* Luncheon," 106 (April 1936):468–77; "The *National Review* Luncheon," 108 (April 1937):480–87; Violet Milner, "Fifty-Five Years: An Historical Note," 131 (October 1948):267–71; and "The *National Review*," 154 (June 1960):203–9.

Information Sources

BIBLIOGRAPHY
Austin, Alfred. *Autobiography*. 2 vols. London, 1911.
Christian, Robert Murray. *Leo Maxse and the "National Review": A Study in the Periodical Press and British Foreign Policy, 1893–1914*. Ph.D. dissertation, University of Virginia, 1940.
Crowell, Norton B. *Alfred Austin: Victorian*. Albuquerque, 1953.
Hardinge, Arthur H. *Life of Henry Howard Molyneux Herbert, Fourth Earl of Carnarvon*. 3 vols. London, 1925.
Hutchinson, John A. *Leo Maxse and the "National Review."* Ph.D. dissertation, University of North Carolina, 1973.
Kebbel, T. E. *Lord Beaconsfield and Other Tory Memories*. New York, 1907.
Maxse, Leopold J., ed. *"Germany on the Brain," or, The Obsession of "A Crank": Gleanings from the "National Review," 1899–1914*. London, 1915.
Milner, Violet. *My Picture Gallery, 1886–1901*. London, 1951.
REPRINT EDITIONS
Microform: UMI.
INDEXES
1883–1900 in *Wellesley Index* 2.
LOCATION SOURCES
American
Widely available.
British
Complete runs: British Museum; Dr. William's Library; Manchester College Library.
Partial runs: Widely available.

Publication History

MAGAZINE TITLE AND TITLE CHANGES
The National Review, March 1883–July 1937. *The National Review, incorporating The English Review*, August 1937–May 1950. *The National and English Review*, June 1950–June 1960.
VOLUME AND ISSUE DATA
Volumes 1–154, numbers 1–928, March 1883–June 1960.

FREQUENCY OF PUBLICATION
  Monthly.
PUBLISHERS
  March 1883–February 1891: W. H. Allen, 13 Waterloo Place, London, S.W.
  March 1891–December 1891: Edward Arnold, 37 Bedford St., Strand, London,
  W.C. March 1892–February 1894: W. H. Allen, 13 Waterloo Place, London,
  S.W. March 1894–February 1904: Edward Arnold, 37 Bedford St., Strand, Lon-
  don, W.C. March 1904–February 1914: Proprietor [Leopold J. Maxse], 23 Ryder
  St., St. James's, London, S.W. March 1914–February 1916: Proprietor [Leopold
  J. Maxse], 14 Tavistock St., Covent Garden, London, W.C. March 1916–February
  1922: Proprietor [Leopold J. Maxse], 43 Duke St., St. James's, London, S.W.
  March 1923–August 1929: Proprietor [Leopold J. Maxse], 8 John St., Adelphi,
  London, W.C. 2. September 1929–June 1932: Proprietor [Leopold J. Maxse], 14
  Burleigh St., Strand, London, W.C. 2. July 1932–June 1935: Proprietors [Violet
  Milner et al.], 18 York Bldgs., Adelphi, London, W.C. July 1935–June 1941:
  Proprietors [Violet Milner et al.], 35 Wellington St., Strand, London, W.C. 2.
  July 1941–October 1948: Proprietors [Violet Milner et al.], Rolls House, 2 Breams
  Bldgs., London, E.C. 4. November 1948–November 1954: Proprietors [Edward
  Grigg et al.], Rolls House, 2 Breams Bldgs., London, E.C. 4. December 1954–
  June 1960: Proprietors [John Edward Grigg et al.], 2 Breams Bldgs., London,
  E.C. 4.
EDITORS
  Alfred Austin with literary editor William John Courthope, March 1883–August
  1887. Alfred Austin, September 1887–July 1893. Leopold J. Maxse, August
  1893–January 1932. Violet Milner, February 1932–October 1948. Edward Grigg,
  November 1948–November 1954. John Edward Grigg, December 1954–June 1960.

Carol de Saint Victor

NEW AGE, THE

In 1894 a new weekly, edited by Frederick A. Atkins, joined the ranks of
several journals that espoused new liberal policies. Called the *New Age*, the
journal described itself in its subtitle as a "Weekly Record of Culture, Social
Service, and Literary Life." In 1895 its socialist bent under A. E. Fletcher's
editorship became more manifest; as a "Journal for Thinkers and Workers," it
represented the views of Ramsay MacDonald. A rapid succession of editors was
never able to make the magazine prosper, and in 1907 mounting debts to the
printer mandated its sale.

The new owners—A. R. Orage, and, briefly, Holbrook Jackson, backed by
banker Lewis Wallace and dramatist George Bernard Shaw—began to transform
the magazine into one of the most important reviews of its time. The first issue,
for 2 May 1907, may have seemed merely an extension of the older *Age*. Its
contributors included Sidney Webb and the Fabian Society secretary, Edward
Pease; the masthead proclaimed it "An Independent Socialist Review of Politics,
Literature, and Art"; its format resembled other political weeklies; its topics

included conventionally radical ones of feminism and laws against homosexuality. But Orage had a larger purpose, to separate the *New Age* from other narrow liberal journals, and transform it into a "socialist *Spectator*"* (see *AAAJ*), as standard for its time as Steele and Addison's paper had been for the eighteenth century.[1] Jackson, who wanted to promulgate a narrower Fabianism, left the *New Age* in 1908 and in a few years began to edit another popular journal, *T. P.'s Weekly*, later called *To-Day*.*

Under Orage's sole editorship, which lasted until September 1922, the magazine exhibited two distinct periods. Wallace Martin, who has provided the most complete study of Orage's editorship, recognizes that "Orage's most valuable work as an editor was done before 1918." From 1907 until 1918, Orage believed that everything "cultural" contributed to the solution of social problems. After 1918, in a "radically oversimplified conception" of social reform, the editor turned more and more to economics or to mystical solutions.[2]

To demonstrate that the "new" *New Age* was more than the organ of a narrow socialist position, Orage began to publish in 1908 a series of divergent opinions on socialist policies. G. K. Chesterton contributed to the issue for 4 January an essay, "Why I Am Not a Socialist." His paper adumbrated the views of Hilaire Belloc, who pointed out a dangerous authoritarianism in some of the policies of Fabian socialists. In the next issue, for 11 January, H. G. Wells contributed an essay, "About Chesterton and Belloc." And in the issue for 15 February 1908, George Bernard Shaw attacked both Chesterton and Belloc in an essay that instantly became a classic for its fabulous parody, the "Chesterbelloc," a four-legged beast-prophet that appeared to save civilization from the dangers of liberal collectivism. The debate among such notable figures lasted, sporadically, well into 1909. Orage was able to orchestrate the controversy, elevate it to Swiftian mock-heroics, and keep it philosophical and literary, above mere editorial issues. While early twentieth-century social movements, particularly that of Guild socialism, remained a vital concern of the *New Age*, they never dominated the magazine and never served to proselytize.

Early in 1908 Orage began to enlarge the scope of the *New Age* as a literary magazine as well, with more essays on art and literature, and with philosophical considerations of aesthetics. He made a coterie of his contributors, holding weekly meetings with them at various cafés. Two of the circle—A. E. Randall (pseud. John Francis Hope) and J. M. Kennedy—contributed, with Orage, almost half of each issue. Others, minor figures who surrounded Orage—some of whom one contributor described as "social reformers, economic wizards, votaries of philosophy, bores, and cranks"—included Ashley Dukes, J. C. Squire (of the *London Mercury*), Will Dyson, Clifford Sharp, Cecil Chesterton, E. Balfort Box, and Marmaduke Pickthall.[3] More important socializers included H. G. Wells, Arnold Bennett, Beatrice Hastings, Ezra Pound, T. E. Hulme, Katherine Mansfield, and W. B. Yeats. Many of them have left written acknowledgments of their debt to Orage's literary parties. Edwin Muir, for example, describes Orage's extraordinary editorial talents. His mind was "peculiarly lucid and sinuous.... From a few stammering words he could divine a thought you were struggling to express, and, as if his mind were an objective clarifying element, in a few minutes he could return it to you cleansed of its impurities and expressed in better words than you could have found yourself."[4]

Orage's genius for synthesizing the thought of the best intellectuals soon made the *New Age* the center for critical discussion in London literary circles. Arnold Bennett became fiction critic; William Archer, L. Haden Guest, and Ashley Dukes analyzed drama; F. S. Flint discussed poetry. Bennett's column "Books and Persons," appearing pseudonymously as by "Jacob Tonson," introduced to the English literati the works of the new French writers Anatole France, Rémy de Gourmont, and Paul Valéry, and the Russians Chekhov and Dostoevsky. Almost singlehandedly Bennett was responsible for Constance Garnett's translations of the Russian masters into English.[5] Archer called, less successfully, for a revival of realism in the English theater. His successor, Ashley Dukes, could find only three English playwrights worthy of praise—Shaw, Barker, and Galsworthy—and wrote instead, at Orage's encouragement, a series of reviews of Continental dramatists. Later the essays were collected and published separately as *Modern Dramatists*, one of the first surveys in English of modern Continental dramatists.

F. S. Flint's importance to the *New Age* rests primarily in his attraction to the magazine of T. E. Hulme (and through Hulme, later, of Ezra Pound). In the issue for 11 February 1909 Flint attacked a volume published by the Poet's Club (4:327); in the next issue Hulme answered Flint's charges (4:350). By July 1909 Hulme was the *New Age* reviewer of the philosophical works of William James and Henri Bergson (5:198–99). Bergson's concept of the image led to Hulme's development, from 1909 to 1911, of the English counterpart to the French movements of *imagisme* and *symbolisme*.[6] Flint would later document the movement in his *History of Imagism*, and Hulme's many essays in the *New Age* were collected in *Speculations*.

The remarkable impact of the *New Age* on drama, fiction, and poetry in the years 1908–1910 was, however, only a prelude to the golden years of 1911–1914. In the issue for 30 November 1911 Hulme's friend, Ezra Pound, made his first contribution: his translation of "The Seafarer." In subsequent issues, it was announced, he would publish other translations under the rubric "The New Methods" (10:107); and there followed the famous translations of Cavalcanti and so many additional essays on the techniques of poetry that one critic labels the *New Age* "a semi-official organ of the Imagists."[7] Under the pseudonyms "B. H. Dias" and "William Atheling" Pound also served the *New Age* as art and music critic. Simultaneously, as the magazine welcomed imagism in poetry, it celebrated the post-Impressionist movement in art. From the first exhibitions in France and England in 1910, the *New Age* recognized the radical philosophical changes that post-Impressionism embodied (8:89–90). In 1910 it published a sketch by Picasso. The reviews and the reproduction touched off a letter-writing campaign. Both advocates and detractors were given editorial space;

meanwhile, Orage went on to publish not only artwork by Auguste Herbin and Edward Zier, but also some of the first critical essays about their works—by John Middleton Murry and, more important, Walter Sickert (see, for example, 8:225, 15:35). Fast on the heels of the post-Impressionist controversy came Marinetti's futurism. The *New Age* first parodied Marinetti (10:524, 12:63–64) and then offered him a forum for his views (15:16). The magazine began a series of "Contemporary Drawings," edited by Hulme, and at the same time allowed its own critic, Sickert, to denounce many of them (14:65, 632).

In the midst of such radical change, the *New Age* aimed not only to reflect the heterogeneity of the new century, but to detect in that variety some indication for the future (14:722). Orage was concerned, like T. S. Eliot, not with promoting the new, but with absorbing it into tradition. He admired the eighteenth-century rational essays, and incorporated their tone in his own writings in *New Age*. Typical are his "Tales for Men Only," witty, refined observations on the sexes, and the column by P. E. Richards ("Holbein Bagman"), a twentieth-century Roger de Coverley. In the flux of new, misunderstood literature, and on the eve of war, Orage admitted that he could detect "no common problem . . . posed for practical solution" and "no currents of literary opinion" (15:62). World War I, and the attendant depression, soon provided that "common problem" and, increasingly, Orage retreated from his belief that culture might transform society. During the war years various new factions of socialism, led by G.D.H. Cole and others, tried to politicize the *New Age*, but Orage resisted. In 1917, however, appalled by the economic collapse, Orage began to study the "social credit" scheme of C. H. Douglas. The solution for a depressed economy was to print more money, distribute it directly to the people, and, at the same time, control prices. In January 1919 Douglas's first essays appeared in the *New Age*. That same year Orage and Douglas proposed a social credit scheme to save the mining industry, a plan which the National Guilds League rejected.[8]

In the issue for 6 November 1919 Orage mapped out the direction of a "present momentum" of a *New Age*:

> to carry us forward in two directions simultaneously and equally: in the direction of a more radical and simple analysis and synthesis of modern industrial society, and in the direction of a more profound analysis and synthesis of human psychology. [26:12]

As essays on economics replaced those on politics, so much of the space that had been given to literature and philosophy was given over to psychoanalysis. During the time that Orage embraced economic ideas, he also fell under the tutelage of G. I. Gurdjieff, who had returned from Russia after the war, full of the occultism of Ouspensky. He also met Dmitri Mitrinovíc, who held a peculiar, anthropomorphic conception of the universe. In a *New Age* column, "World Affairs," Orage began to report Mitrinovíc's theories; after several months Mitrinovíc himself wrote the feature.[9]

Increasingly, Orage's private interests usurped the public concerns of *New Age*. Literary strengths remained in the works of such reviewers as Edwin Muir (assistant editor from 1920) and Herbert Read, novelists St. John Gogarty and Michael Arlen, and poets, most notably Pound. The *New Age* was still a "clearing-house for information regarding new writers"; Orage referred to the work of Joyce and Eliot in 1921 and told his readers of the American little magazines publishing their work.[10] But the *New Age* had declined in size, in part because of a postwar paper shortage, to as few as twelve pages. It had to compete with such younger, more vigorous literary magazines as *Arts and Letters*,* *Coterie*,* and *Wheels** (for all, see *MA*), as well as the Fabian *New Statesman*.* And it had lost the sense of cultural relevance it had possessed before the war. In October 1922 Orage left London and entered the Gurdjieff Institute, near Fontainbleau. From 1923 to 1931 he worked as an instructor for Gurdjieff in New York, and then returned to London, where from 1932 until his death in 1934 he edited the *New English Weekly** (see *MA*).[11]

Although the *New Age* survived until 1938, its literary importance ended soon after Orage's departure. Edwin Muir continued to contribute his essays, most of them on literary subjects, until 1924; his weekly column of social comment ended, however, with Orage's editorship. Pound had published his "intellectual will and testament" to England, *Axiomatica*, in the issue for 13 January 1921; and except for a review, "The New Therapy," in the issue for 16 March 1922, no other work by Pound appeared in the *New Age* until 1935. (Soon after Orage began his *New English Weekly*, however, Pound contributed two essays.) For the decade 1910–1920, no other magazine equaled the *New Age* for its blend of literature and social criticism, or for its sense of timeliness and a concomitant awareness of tradition. And, except for Ford Madox Ford's *English Review*,* no other magazine displayed the editorial acumen of Orage's magazine.

Notes

1. Philip Mairet, *A. R. Orage: A Memoir* (London, 1936), p. 48.

2. Wallace Martin, *The "New Age" Under Orage* (New York, 1967), p. 292. I am indebted to Martin's work for much of the discussion below.

3. Paul Selver, in *Orage and the "New Age" Circle* (London, 1959), estimates the three wrote half of the contents. Martin, p. 125, says that Orage, Kennedy, Randall, and Beatrice Hastings "wrote approximately one-third" of the contents. In a fictionalized treatment of the *New Age* circle by Carl Bechhofer-Roberts, *Let's Begin Again* (London, 1940), Orage is the model for Whitworth, Kennedy for Harrison, and Randall for Davies. For an idiosyncratic account of Hastings's role, see her *Old "New Age"* (London, 1936).

4. Edwin Muir, *An Autobiography* (London, 1954), p. 172.

5. Martin, pp. 92–94.

6. See ibid., pp. 166–181, for a larger discussion of Hulme, Flint, and Orage.

7. Ibid., p. 252.

8. See Mairet, pp. 66–77, for a larger discussion of Orage and Douglas.

9. See Martin, pp. 284–85, 285, n. 2.

10. Ibid., pp. 14–15.

11. For Orage's work in New York, see Charles King, *The Oragean Vision* (New York, 1951).

Information Sources

BIBLIOGRAPHY

Bechhofer-Roberts, Carl. *Let's Begin Again*. London, 1940.
Hastings, Beatrice. *The Old "New Age": Orage and Others*. London, 1936.
Hobson, S. G. *Pilgrim to the Left*. London, 1938.
Hynes, Samuel. *Edwardian Occasions*. London, 1972.
King, Charles. *The Oragean Vision*. New York, 1951.
Mairet, Philip. *A. R. Orage: A Memoir*. London, 1936.
Martin, Wallace. *The "New Age" Under Orage*. New York, 1967.
————., ed. *Orage as Critic*. Boston, 1974.
Muir, Edwin. *An Autobiography*. London, 1954.
Orage, A. R. *The Active Mind*. New York, 1954.
————, in *New Age* 38 (1926):235–36, 246–47, 258, 271–72, 283–84, 295–96.
Selver, Paul. *Orage and the "New Age" Circle*. London, 1959.
    Swinnerton, Frank. *Figures in the Foreground: Literary Reminiscences*. Garden City, N.Y., 1964.

INDEXES
None.

REPRINT EDITIONS
Microform: British Library (Newspaper Library), Colindale Ave., London NW9 5HE.

LOCATION SOURCES
American
Partial runs: Widely available.
British
Complete run: British Museum.
Partial runs: Birmingham Public Library; Cambridge University Library; Edinburgh Public Library; Leeds Public Library; Manchester Public Library; National Library of Scotland, Edinburgh.

Publication History

MAGAZINE TITLE AND TITLE CHANGES
The New Age. Subtitle varies: *A Weekly Record of Culture, Social Service, and Literary Life*; *A Journal for Thinkers and Workers*; *A Review of Literature, Religion and Politics*; *An Independent Socialist Review of Politics, Literature, and Art*; *A Democratic Review of Politics, Religion, and Literature*; *A Weekly Review of Politics, Literature, and Art*.

VOLUME AND ISSUE DATA
Volumes 1–19, numbers 1–659, 4 October 1894–25 April 1907; new series, volumes 1–62, 2 May 1907–7 April 1938.

FREQUENCY OF PUBLICATION
Weekly.

PUBLISHERS
> Volumes 1–19: Unknown (printer is C. B. Bonner). New series, volumes 1–62: Frank Palmer, 139 Fleet Street, London. E.C.

EDITORS
> Frederick A. Atkins, 4 October 1894–23 May 1895. A. E. Fletcher, 30 May 1895–? July 1898. Arthur Compton-Rickett, 28 July 1898–(?). Joseph Clayton, (?)–25 April 1907. Holbrook Jackson and A. R. Orage, 2 May 1907–December 1907. A. R. Orage, January 1908–September 1922. Arthur Moore, October 1922–1923. Arthur Brenton, 1923–1938.

Alvin Sullivan

NEW FREEWOMAN, THE. See EGOIST, THE (MA)

NEW MONTHLY MAGAZINE, THE. See RA

NEW QUARTERLY REVIEW

Early in 1852 there appeared in London a new journal that was aimed, the *Examiner** noted, at the same class of readers as those of the *Quarterly Review,** the *Edinburgh Review,** and the *Westminster Review** (for all, see *RA*). Called the *New Quarterly Review*, it was "a half-crown digest of current English literature, with a short notice of French books and a shorter one of German publications. This new quarterly review contains a large amount of matter in double columns of tolerably close print, and its criticisms seem to be written with ability."[1] The new journal was, in Walter Graham's words, "an ambitious effort to revive the eighteenth-century methods exemplified in the *Critical Review* [* (see *AAAJ*)] and *Monthly Review*"* (see *AAAJ*), one which "attempted to notice everything of importance in the world of books."[2] As Graham noted, the reviews averaged a page in length, though many were no more than a paragraph. Reviews were grouped under headings that tended to disappear in later years: history and biography; voyages and travels; novels, tales, and romances; poetry; and miscellaneous. Other headings were used as demanded for books on art or education or even on modern conveniences such as railroads and gas lights. In the early issues there were long lists of books received which the editors had not had time to consider, but these lists soon disappeared.

As time passed, the editors became less encyclopedic in their approach, publishing fewer but longer articles. In 1857 there was a notable increase in the political content in the *New Quarterly Review*. This took the form of lengthy reviews of works on recently deceased statesmen, such as Sir Robert Peel; but it also involved reviews of parliamentary papers and the like. Some reviews focused on topics of current international interest, such as those in Italy and

Austria in 1859, or articles on the situation in Turkey in the 1850s. On occasion, there was a simple political article, such as that on "The Political Dictatorship of Lord Palmerston" (6:124).

Although the *New Quarterly Review* lasted about ten years, little is known about its editors and staff. There is some reason to believe that it was founded and edited for a number of years by Frederick William Haydon, the second son of Benjamin R. Haydon, the painter. Frederick Haydon spent his youth in the navy, but in 1849 he transferred to the civil service, where he became an inspector of factories. In 1857 he succeeded D. C. Coulton as editor of Disraeli's *Press*, a position that lasted only until the following year, when the paper was sold. Haydon was later dismissed from the civil service for publishing a letter critical of the Home Office. He died in the Bethlehem Hospital in 1886.[3]

In its decline, the *New Quarterly Review* was edited by John Kesson, a translator and scholar noted for his mastery of nearly a dozen languages. A native of Aberdeen, Kesson had been private secretary to Joseph Hume and a cataloguer at the British Museum. He had the dubious distinction of editing the last numbers of the *Critic** in 1863, of the *Literary Gazette** (see *RA*) in 1863, and of the *New Quarterly Review* in 1862.[4]

Notes

1. *Examiner*, 10 January 1852, p. 20.
2. Walter Graham, *English Literary Periodicals* (New York, 1930), pp. 256–57.
3. Clark Olney, *Benjamin Robert Haydon, Historical Painter* (Athens, Ga., 1952), p. 181; Alan J. Lee, *The Origins of the Popular Press in England, 1855–1914* (London, 1976), p. 149; *Dictionary of National Biography*, s.v. "Haydon, Benjamin."
4. Frederick Boase, *Modern English Biography* (London, 1965), 2:212–13.

Information Sources

BIBLIOGRAPHY
Boase, Frederick. *Modern English Biography*. Vol. 2. London, 1965.
Dictionary of National Biography. S.v. "Haydon, Benjamin."
Graham, Walter. *English Literary Periodicals*. New York, 1930.
Lee, Alan J. *The Origins of the Popular Press in England, 1855–1914*. London, 1976.
INDEXES
    Each volume is indexed; 1853–1861 in *Poole's Index*.
REPRINT EDITIONS
    Microform: English Literary Periodicals (UMI), reels 921–922.
LOCATION SOURCES
    American
        Partial runs: Boston Public Library; Carnegie Library of Pittsburgh; Chicago Public Library; Library Company of Philadelphia; Milwaukee Public Library; New York Public Library; Public Library of Cincinnati and Hamilton County; Union Theological Seminary Library; U. S. Library of Congress.

British
>   Complete runs: Bodleian Library; British Museum; Trinity College Library.
>   Partial runs: Cambridge University Library; Guildhall Library; St. Andrews University Library.

Publication History

MAGAZINE TITLE AND TITLE CHANGES
>   *New Quarterly Review and Digest of Current Literature, British, American, French and German.*

VOLUME AND ISSUE DATA
>   Volumes 1–2, numbers 1–41, 1852–1862.

FREQUENCY OF PUBLICATION
>   Quarterly.

PUBLISHERS
>   1852–1854: Hookham and Sons, 15 Old Bond Street, London. 1855: Thomas Bosworth, 215 Regent Street, London. 1856–1858: Bosworth and Harrison, 215 Regent Street, London. 1859–1862: Robert Hardwick, 192 Piccadilly, London.

EDITORS
>   Frederick William Haydon, 1852–(?). John Kesson, (?)–1862.

Darwin F. Bostick

NEW REVIEW, THE

When William Ernest Henley assumed editorship of the *New Review* in January 1895, it was the hope of his friends and fellow directors that the editorial virtues he had so consistently displayed in the *Scots Observer*,* and then in the *National Observer*, would make the *New Review* as distinguished as the earlier journals. Its very name was appropriate to the period to which it belonged; as Holbrook Jackson suggests in his study of the 1890s, it was the era of the "new"—the "new drama," the "new woman," the "new spirit," the "new Unionism," the "new Party."[1]

The *New Review* had been established in 1889 and was edited by Archibald Grove, a Liberal and a member of Parliament for West Ham, with Arthur Waugh as assistant editor. The prospectus stated: "The object of the *New Review* is to place within the reach of all a critical periodical of the first order," and to publish articles on "Politics, Science, and Art."[2] The fact that Grove intended to sell an issue for six pence, in contrast, for example, to the *Nineteenth Century*'s* price of two shillings, six pence, indicates another intention on his part, "to outstrip even the half-crown reviews, not so much in quality as in profits, through a large volume of sales."[3]

One of Henley's biographers has described the *New Review* under Grove as "a monthly of established reputation and quite remarkable dullness," and Grove himself as "respectable and uninspired" as an editor.[4] But if there were a number of titled or merely popular—and today unknown—contributors, there were also stories and essays by Henry James, Tolstoy, Edmund Gosse, and Hardy. Symposiums were a regular feature: "The Tree of Knowledge" (on female education), "Candour in English Fiction" and "The Science of Fiction" (Hardy contributed to both), "The Science of Preaching," and "Women and Work." While Mrs. Lynn Linton continued her campaign to preserve the purity of the English girl, "new woman" fiction and ideology was represented by Olive Schreiner. James's fiction and his review of the first English production of *Hedda Gabler* appeared. Shaw wrote on the socialist ideal and on the theater, and there were essays by Zola and Yeats. A scene from the recently translated *Master Builder* was published, and Hauptmann's play, *Hennele*, ran in three numbers. The "new drama," in fact, was well represented, with contributions from William Archer, Henry Arthur Jones, and A. B. Walkley. Ellen Terry's memoirs appeared, and Beardsley defended it in his 1894 essay, "The Art of the Hoarding": "Beauty has laid siege to London," he insisted (11:53).

But by 1894 the *New Review* had failed either to make money or to gain a reputation equal to the *Nineteenth Century*'s. In volume 10 Grove announced a new series, and offered a free issue to any reader who acquired six new subscribers for the magazine. A "novel departure" was also promised—the inclusion of a short story in every issue, chosen "on its merit alone regardless of the author's name." Nevertheless, Grove's parliamentary duties were absorbing more of his time, and he was willing to sell when a group of Henley's friends collected enough money to buy the magazine for him. In the group was William Heinemann, who had had a hand in publishing the *New Review* during the previous year, and who had already made a reputation as an enlightened publisher.

If the more immediate response to the 1890s is to think of Wilde and Beardsely, John Lane and the *Yellow Book*,* there was another equally articulate and "organized" group of writers—and a publisher—some of whom, as Jerome Buckley points out, "would outwear the greatest of the 'decadents.' "[5] Heinemann had in his list, by 1894, Henley himself, Robert Louis Stevenson, Israel Zangwill, Ibsen, and Kipling. A "Realist" and Tory, Henley had collected around himself a group of young and energetic writers and journalists, dubbed by Max Beerbohm the "Henley Regatta." Dining at Solferino's Restaurant, they challenged their rivals, the Rhymers, meeting at the Chesire Cheese. Both met, according to Kipling, to "regulate all literature till all hours of the morning."[6] The group included Charles Whibley, George Wyndham, Kipling, G. S. Street, George Steevens, Wilfred Pollock, Gilbert Parker, Vernon Blackburn, Leslie Cornford, W. B. Yeats, and H. B. Marriott-Watson. Yeats acknowledged that "Henley got the best out of us all,"[7] and it was this quality, as well as his editorial genius, that promised success for the *New Review*.

For the first issue under the new editor, William Archer wrote an obituary for Henley's old friend and collaborator, Robert Louis Stevenson. Henley, encouraged by Shaw's praise of the Henley-Stevenson *Macaire*, in contrast to the "old third-class version" that Irving was playing at the Lyceum, published the "melodramatic farce" in the June number. But if Henley retained many of his old

contributors and ties with his past, he also continued to discover and encourage
new writers such as H. G. Wells, whose novel *The Time Machine* was the first
serial Henley ran in his new magazine. Besides fantasy, and perhaps more in
sympathy with Henley's own lyrics of city life, Arthur Morrison's *A Child of
the Jago*, a work of harsh urban realism, ran for thirteen numbers, and Stephen
Crane was also added to the list of contributors. Even Kipling's father was
represented by an essay, "The Novel of the Mutiny." Henley's "organic
loathing"[8] of Gladstone did not keep him from publishing the statesman's last
essay on literature, "Man-Making and Verse-Making."

The circulation of the *New Review* "dropped like a stone" when a story
appeared that gave a rather more explicit description of a housemaid's seduction
than some readers could approve. But Henley had never supported the notion
that the "theory and practice of British art" should be influenced by the "British
schoolgirl."[9] He had been the editor, after all, who had printed the christening
scene from *Tess* in the *National Observer*, when the *Graphic*, which was running
the serial, refused to publish it. "About love as they handled it," Ford Madox
Ford has written of Henley and his supporters, "there was nothing mystic."
And in the same essay Ford added that it was this group of writers who had
"introduced into the English writing mind the idea that a man of action was
something fine and a man of letters a sort of castrato."[10] Yet one notes, reading
through the table of contents for Henley's years, not only the poetry of Kipling,
but that of Yeats, as well as essays by or about Arthur Symons, Valéry, and
Verlaine.

If, in Jerome Buckley's words, "the quality of its contributors . . . was hardly
less remarkable than the *National Observer*,"[11] an earlier biographer claimed
that Henley's "heart was never in 'cultured' Billy Heinemann's venture as it
had been in the *Scots Observer*," though Henley maintained "a very high
standard."[12] But Henley had no place in the *New Review* for his anonymous
notes and comments; and the men who had purchased the magazine for him had
done it at least as much to give him time to do his own writing as to salvage
the magazine."[13]

Henley wrote to Whibley that Heinemann was "too bloody cultured," adding,
"he wants to edit the magazine—not to sell it."[14] And to Whibley he wrote
again in January 1897, the last year of the *New Review*, that his directors had
"landed" him with "100 pages of Henrietta James," adding, "So I fear the *N.
R.* will scarce survive the year."[15] It was to *What Maisie Knew* that he referred.
But in the very same issues that carried the James novel, a new writer, encouraged
by Henley's interest, appeared: Joseph Conrad, represented by *The Nigger of
the Narcissus*. As Henley had introduced Wells when he first took over the *New
Review*, now in its final days he "offered a hand" to Conrad.

The final issue also contained the last of a series of crayon portraits by William
Nicholson. The sitters had included Sarah Bernhardt and Whistler, Kipling, Lord
Roberts, Cecil Rhodes, and Prince Bismarck. It was fitting, perhaps, that Ni-
cholson and Conrad should end Henley's career as an editor. It was Nicholson's

portrait of Henley that had so delighted the editor, depicting him as "a brigand, a land pirate";[16] and it was Conrad who had written to Edward Garnett on the acceptance of his novel: "Now I have conquered Henley, I aint fraid of the divvle himself."[17]

Notes

1. Holbrook Jackson, *The Eighteen Nineties* (New York, 1966), p. 22.
2. *The Wellesley Index to Victorian Periodicals 1824–1900*, ed. Walter E. Houghton (Toronto, 1979), 3:301, contains the fullest account of the editorial organization and financial management of the *New Review* now available.
3. Ibid.
4. John Connell, *W. E. Henley* (London, 1949), p. 290.
5. Jerome H. Buckley, *William Ernest Henley: A Study in the "Counter-Decadence" of the 'Nineties* (Princeton, 1945), p. 152.
6. Rudyard Kipling, *Something of Myself* (New York, 1937), p. 90.
7. William Butler Yeats, *Autobiography* (New York, 1958), p. 85.
8. Kipling, p. 90.
9. Buckley, p. 157.
10. Ford Madox Ford, *Memories and Impressions* (New York, 1911), p. 192.
11. Buckley, p. 196.
12. Connell, p. 310.
13. *Wellesley Index*, 3:305.
14. Connell, p. 300.
15. Ibid., p. 316.
16. Buckley, p. 149.
17. Joseph Conrad, *Letters from Joseph Conrad, 1895–1924*, ed. Edward Garnett (Indianapolis, 1928), p. 81.

Information Sources

BIBLIOGRAPHY

Buckley, Jerome H. *William Ernest Henley: A Study in the "Counter-Decadence" of the 'Nineties*. Princeton, 1945.
Connell, John. *W. E. Henley*. London, 1949.
Conrad, Joseph. *Letters from Joseph Conrad, 1895–1924*. Edited by Edward Garnett. Indianapolis, 1928.
Ford, Ford Madox. *Memories and Impressions*. New York, 1911.
Houghton, Walter E., ed. *The Wellesley Index to Victorian Periodicals 1824–1900*, Vol. 3. Toronto, 1979.
Jackson, Holbrook. *The Eighteen Nineties*. New York, 1966.
Kipling, Rudyard. *Something of Myself*. New York, 1937.
Mackail, J. W., and Guy Wyndham. *Life and Letters of George Wyndham*. 2 vols. London, 1925.
Stephen, Herbert. "William Ernest Henley as a Contemporary and an Editor." *London Mercury* 13 (February 1926).
Waugh, Arthur. *One Man's Road*. London, 1931.
Whyte, Frederic. *William Heinemann*. London, 1928.

INDEXES
>   Each volume indexed. *Wellesley Index* 3.

REPRINT EDITIONS
>   Microform: UMI.

LOCATION SOURCES
> *American*
>>   Widely available.
> *British*
>>   Widely available.

Publication History

MAGAZINE TITLE AND TITLE CHANGES
>   *The New Review.* (In 1898 George Wyndham turned the *New Review* into the *Outlook and New Review*, which became simply the *Outlook*, and continued as a weekly until 1928.)

VOLUME AND ISSUE DATA
>   Volumes 1–9, June 1889–December 1893; volumes 10–11, new series, January 1894–December 1894; volumes 12–17, January 1895–December 1897.

FREQUENCY OF PUBLICATION
>   Monthly.

PUBLISHERS
>   Volumes 1–11: Longmans. Volumes 12–17: Heinemann.

EDITORS
>   Archibald Grove; Arthur Waugh, assistant editor, June 1889–December 1894. William Ernest Henley; J. W. Gilmer, assistant editor, January 1895–December 1897.

Mary Heath

NEW STATESMAN

Beginning publication on Saturday, 12 April 1913, the *New Statesman* promised in its editorial that it would not "ignore the traditions long associated with English weekly reviews" (1:5). It did, however, clearly assert its originality:

> Our critical standpoint will be fresh. We shall deal with all current political, social, religious, and intellectual questions; but in doing so we shall be bound by no ties of party, class, or creed. Naturally, like everyone else, we have certain prepossessions of our own, a definite point from which we view each new issue as it arises. Indeed, we have more than that; we have a definite ideal at which we are consciously aiming. We believe that the steps which this country and all the foremost communities of the world have lately been taking in the direction of a greater corporate responsibility, a greater corporate activity, and a greater corporate control of the resources and the social conditions of the nation are steps in the right directions,

and we look forward to a time when this growing corporate life will be developed to a point far beyond anything that has yet been carried out or even planned in any part of the world. In common with every thinking man and woman to-day we recognize that vast social changes are imminent, and for our part we welcome them. That we welcome them is our bias. But it is not in any sense whatever a party bias. The world movement towards collectivism is altogether beyond and above party. [1:5]

To underline its socialist bias, the *New Statesman* also began with an acknowledgement that "Mr. G. B. Shaw and Mr. Sidney Webb will as a rule write editorially in our columns" and followed this announcement by serializing the Webbs' "What Is Socialism?" in the first twenty numbers, from 12 April to 6 September 1913. The energetically socialist, determinedly scientific, and virulently rationalistic purpose expressed in the periodical's opening editorial statement characterizes the *New Statesman*'s style and interests through much of its first decades. This common purpose marks a relatively fixed point from which to judge the tone of many contributions by writers otherwise often widely diverse.

From the beginning, the first editor enjoyed a fairly free rein despite the periodical's loyalties to the socialist cause. In fact, Clifford Dyce Sharp was an active Fabian with Shaw and Webb, and the *New Statesman* was essentially a successor to an earlier socialist newspaper, the *Crusade*.[1] Yet, because of the freedom he enjoyed, Dyce was able to make the *New Statesman* a place where Victorian, Edwardian, and early modern, as well as more narrowly socialist perspectives, could coexist within a scientific and socially conscious milieu. Contributors such as Edmund Gosse, Maurice Baring, and Havelock Ellis represented a predominantly Victorian perspective. Shaw and the Webbs effectively spanned the two ages. Among notable Edwardians were Hilaire Belloc, Arnold Bennett, W. H. Hudson, Rupert Brooke, Walter De la Mare, and Siegfried Sassoon. Early modern contributors included Richard Aldington, I. A. Richards, D. H. Lawrence, and T. S. Eliot. Bloomsbury and its associates were conspicuously present in the contributions of Desmond MacCarthy, Clive Bell, Roger Fry, E. M. Forster, Lytton Strachey, John Maynard Keynes, and Leonard and Virginia Woolf. Above or outside ordinary categories were such contributors as W. B. Yeats, Bertrand Russell, and Rebecca West.

By the time the *New Statesman* became the *New Statesman and Nation* in 1931, the contributors had come to include some of the most notable names of the socialist thirties: Harold Laski, Eric Blair, Stephen Spender, and Cyril Connolly, and some notable names from outside that category, among them Peter Quennell and V. S. Pritchett. In every decade since the 1930s, the *New Statesman* has attracted a host of writers, many of whose names have become synonymous with major socialist or left-liberal movements of the present or recent past; they include Louis MacNeice, Malcolm Muggeridge, Raymond Williams, and art critic John Berger. While any list that is less than comprehensive may falsify the impression of a periodical's contributors, it is also worth noting such other well-known names of the last two decades as Edwin Muir, Noel Annan, and H. R. Trevor-Roper.

In keeping with its original socialist bias, the *New Statesman*'s editorial and "Comments" sections bristled from the start with reports and commentaries on the major issues of the decade: political and economic unrest in Africa, Ireland, America, and Mexico, as well as the fortunes and misfortunes of Sylvia Pankhurst and the suffragettes. In fact, in its news and political features especially, the *New Statesman* fulfilled one of the goals set forth by the Webbs, providing a forum for the work of the Fabian Research Department.[2] Somewhat surprisingly, its editorial response to the onset of World War I (3:545) was less pugnaciously "I told you so" and more reverently shocked than might have been expected from a publication that welcomed "vast social change."

From the beginning down to the present day, the *New Statesman*'s regular weekly features have included correspondence, summary reviews of books, and individual reviews, variously divided at different times into reviews of new novels, special signed reviews, shorter notices, and "Miscellanies"—into which a variety of other matters could be introduced as well. In the early years, the *New Statesman* included a column entitled "The City," afterwards to be called "London Diary." This local perspective has remained to the present day in similar features and columns. At the start, the *New Statesman* also issued monthly supplements, summarizing Acts of Parliament (Blue Book Supplements), developing perspectives on major social issues ("Women in Industry," 21 February 1914), and highlighting literature. The *New Statesman* also remained alert to many of the newest statements of modernism. It published, for instance, a futurist manifesto in the issue for 21 February 1914, including a disclaimer, and it regularly reported on developments in international socialism. Many of the contributors to early issues assumed a distinctly social perspective when writing for the *New Statesman*. Academic critic and fiction writer Vernon Lee, for instance, showed her interest in social and political issues, reviewing Rudolph Goldscheid's *Menschenökonomie* for the 23 August 1913 issue.

Other features of the *New Statesman* developed around areas of special significance or around particular contributors. Science was first put in perspective by Bertrand Russell's "Science as an Element in Culture" (24 and 31 May 1913). In a column over the by-line "Lens," the *New Statesman* followed up this position statement by reviewing issues in contemporary science: "Energy of Atoms" (16 January 1914), "Radium and Cancer" (24 January 1914), and "The Problems of Organic Evolution" (1 and 8 August 1914). When, in 1916, scientists like A. J. Thomson, Alexander Findlay, and Julian Huxley began to appear as regular or occasional contributors, the coverage of science became more sophisticated. Hugh Elliot, for instance, reviewed the "Reality of Atoms" (9:250) and discussed "Lord Haldane on Relativity" (17:573), giving the *New Statesman* added credibility in its treatment of modern science. As a result, the "Lens" column became more concerned with science and technology and their social implications. See, for instance, "Suppression of Quackery" (9:226).

For a paper founded under the banner of socialism, the *New Statesman*'s cultural and literary features were far less socialist than one finds in other politically oriented periodicals. "Old" socialist "Hubert Bland" reviewed popular, predominantly middle-class novels from a social perspective until his death in 1914. The Webbs and Russell continued to contribute to the *New Statesman* into the 1920s. However, the forces of modernism and the influence of Bloomsbury came to dominate the treatment of literature and the fine arts. As the most consistent contributor for the first twenty years, Desmond MacCarthy became virtually identified with the *New Statesman*'s reviews of drama. Besides writing features, feuilletons, and a wide-ranging review and critical column over the pseudonym "Affable Hawk," MacCarthy reported regularly on productions of the most important classics from Shakespeare to Shaw, and on productions of the most important modern dramas from Joyce's *Exiles* (26:581) and Jean Cocteau's *Orpheus* (31:45–46) to Eugene O'Neill's *Strange Interlude* (36:552–54) and *Desire Under the Elms* (n.s. 1:62–63). In reviewing *Orpheus*, MacCarthy expressed a typical *New Statesman* reaction to apparently febrile or incoherent aestheticism. After having summarized the details and ideas of Cocteau's play, he concluded:

I understand only too well how profound and sympathetic all this would appear to a generation unwilling or unable (I don't know which it is) to think consecutively. He [Cocteau] seemed to me no lion, I confess; rather a pretty azure dragon-fly, poising for a quivering instant in front of this art or that, and darting at it like a needle. [31:46]

In issue after issue, through at least 1928, MacCarthy filled the major role of drama critic, or a dual role of drama critic and "Affable Hawk," affecting the character of the *New Statesman*'s review so dramatically that its significance has yet to be determined accurately.

Fine arts were less consistently reviewed at first. Randall Davies, Clive Bell, and Roger Fry contributed occasional signed pieces on art or aesthetics. From about mid-1916, W. J. Turner regularly reviewed music and musical productions. The *New Statesman* also occasionally took note of advances in cinema and dance. By the time "Arts and Entertainment" had become a regular feature in the 1940s, the *New Statesman* was attracting more searching and professionally acute reviews of the fine arts. Art critic and novelist John Berger, who began contributing in the late 1950s, inaugurated a significant series of *engagé* art reviews which may be said to characterize at least one facet of the paper's modern approach to the fine arts.

In literature and in the reviewing of literature, the *New Statesman* was most consistently eclectic. Its allowance of poetry grew from about ten poems per (six months') volume in volume 18 and about twenty-four poems per volume in volume 34, to about thirty-five per volume in 1957 and about fifty in 1979. From the start the magazine gave space to Victorians and Edwardians as well as to modernist poets. In time the *New Statesman* was to attract major poets of many persuasions. The early volumes included poems by Edward Thomas, T. Sturge Moore, Robert Bridges, John Masefield, Walter De la Mare, W. H. Davies, and Siegfried Sassoon. Robert Graves, Vachel Lindsay, and W. B. Yeats also published poems (the latter represented by "Paudeen," "The Magi" [vol. 3], and "Ego Dominus Tuus" [vol. 9]). Down to the present, the *New Statesman* has attracted the best and the most characteristic poets of modern Britain, including Stephen Spender, Louis MacNeice, D. J. Enright, Donald Davie, and Ted Hughes.

Among authors of signed literary articles, the central figures were at first Edwardians and Bloomsburians. Arnold Bennett contributed, and the *New Statesman* gave Hilaire Belloc space and opportunity to force a late flowering of the English familiar essay. Next to MacCarthy, Belloc was probably the best-known frequent contributor, failing to appear in only one volume in the decade between 1918 and 1928. Among Bloomsburians, Virginia Woolf was the most famous contributor, but her fiction reviews were few and only occasionally brilliant. In its "Miscellany" feature, as well as in longer signed articles of 3,000 to 4,000 words, the *New Statesman* also gave space to the work of Wyndham Lewis (22:474–76; 22:601–2), I. A. Richards ("On Teaching English," 29:478), T. S. Eliot ("Vers Libre," 8:518–19; "The Borderline of Prose," 9:157–58), and a host of even younger writers. The modernity and informed, no-nonsense tone of "The Borderline of Prose" is perhaps best explained by its context in the social-critical and unabashedly rational *New Statesman* of 1917. Although Eliot's objectivity in the survey of innovations in artistic prose from Mallarmé, Rimbaud, and Wilde to Claudel may be questioned when he finds in Richard Aldington's work the epitome of the trend, still this 2,000-word article is paradigmatic of Eliot's interests, approach, and style in the formative years of his public criticism. Not a little of what he learned about tone and style ought to be related to his coming to terms with the distinct tone and slant of the *New Statesman*.

Among newer writers, the case of Peter Quennell is instructive. From writing occasional short notices and signed reviews in 1927, Quennell graduated to longer and more frequent contributions, with six in volume 31 (1928) alone. With Pritchett, Anthony West, and Ralph Partridge, Quennell was doing "Books in General" for the *New Statesman* by 1949. And Quennell's history of association with the *New Statesman* is only one story of how the occasional contributor came to develop a style, a perspective, and an audience from having consistently written for the pages of the same paper.

Despite changes in format, perspective, and emphasis, the *New Statesman* has maintained a consistency of outlook and an enviable record of quality for over seventy years. While Clifford Dyce Sharp might not recognize the modern look and format of the *New Statesman*, if he turned its pages and read its contents, he would find in it a social and political stance, and a commitment to excellence which would be familiar from the early days of this remarkably successful and popular weekly.

Notes

1. Margaret Cole, *Beatrice Webb* (London, 1945), p. 124.
2. Kitty Muggeridge and Ruth Adam, *Beatrice Webb* (New York, 1968), p. 202.

Information Sources

INDEXES
> Each volume indexed.

REPRINT EDITIONS
> Microform: Princeton Microfilm Corporation; UMI.

LOCATION SOURCES

American
> Widely available.

British
> Complete runs: Birmingham Public Library; Bodleian Library; Bradford Public Library; Bristol Public Library; British Library of Political Science; British Museum; Cambridge University Library; Manchester Public Library; Newcastle-upon-Tyne Public Library.
> Partial runs: Widely available.

Publication History

MAGAZINE TITLE AND TITLE CHANGES
> *New Statesman*, 1913–1931. *New Statesman and Nation*, 1931–1957. *New Statesman*, 1957–.

VOLUME AND ISSUE DATA
> Volumes 1–36, 12 April 1913–21 February 1931; new series, volume 1–, 28 February 1931–.

FREQUENCY OF PUBLICATION
> Weekly (Saturday).

PUBLISHERS
> 1913–1931: The Statesman Publishing Co., Ltd., 10 Great Queen Street, Kingsway, London. 1931–1949: Statesman and Nation Publishing Co., Ltd. 1949–1982: Statesman Publishing Co., Ltd., 10 Great Turnstile, London W.C. 1. 1983–: Statesman Publishing Co., Ltd., 14–16 Farringdon Ln., London E.C. 1.

EDITORS
> Clifford Dyce Sharp, 1913–February 1930. Kingsley Martin, 1930–1963. John Freeman, 1963–1968. Paul Johnson, 1969–1970. Richard Crossman, 1971–1972. Anthony Howard, 1973–1978. Bruce Page, 1978–1982. Hugh Stephenson, 1983–.

Ed Block, Jr.

NINETEENTH CENTURY, THE

Writing of the *Nineteenth Century: A Monthly Review*, whose founding editor and owner, Sir James Thomas Knowles, had just died, Frederic Harrison took no eulogistic license in assessing this influential monthly: "It grew to be a literary power in the New World as well as in the old; and it exercised a very striking influence not only on periodical literature but on liberal thought."[1] The prominence and reputation of Knowles's *Nineteenth Century* has not diminished with time. The magazine, as distinguished from its successors, the *Nineteenth Century and After* (1901–1950)* (see *MA*) and the *Twentieth Century* (1951–1972), has been cumulatively indexed and catalogued. It has also been anthologized and commemorated. Furthermore, in the recent biography of Knowles by Priscilla Metcalf, a seventy-eight-page chapter is devoted to the *Nineteenth Century* in a book that is a model of readable scholarship.[2]

James Knowles was both a journalist and an architect, which was not unusual in an age that produced painter-poets such as D. G. Rossetti and Edward Lear, a poet-designer-politician like William Morris, and the engineer-musicologist George Grove. For over six years before starting the *Nineteenth Century*, Knowles edited the *Contemporary Review*.* This monthly was a general review whose policies putatively reflected those of the Established Church. No bargain at a half-crown an issue, the *Contemporary* was foundering until Knowles assumed its editorship. Before his forced resignation in late 1876, he quadrupled its circulation to 8,000, an unimpressive figure by today's standards, but sufficient then to make it profitable. The *Contemporary*'s publisher, Alexander Strahan, and one of its principal owners, Samuel Morley, thought Knowles expendable. Their breach of contract and ideological prejudice enriched Knowles by 1,500 pounds and inspired him to begin the *Nineteenth Century*.

In 1877 Knowles was more than a successful architect and an editor with an idea for a new journal. For nearly eight years he had been the honorary secretary of the Metaphysical Society, a peculiarly high Victorian entity that discussed the weightiest of theological and ethical problems. Its membership—limited to forty—included some of England's best thinkers and writers—statesmen, churchmen, editors, lawyers, academicians, scientists, and philosophers. Original members included W. E. Gladstone, Henry E. (Cardinal) Manning, Alfred Tennyson, Richard H. Hutton, Thomas Henry Huxley, James Anthony Froude, Walter Bagehot, and, of course, Knowles, among a distinguished complement. "Newman, Arnold, Lewes, Mill, and Spencer all refused to join."[3] Later, the Eighth Duke of Argyll (George Douglas), Frederic Harrison, John Ruskin, Leslie Stephen, Arthur James Balfour, and George Grove were among those elected to replenish the ranks of the society, which was dissolved in December 1880.[4]

Much of the *Contemporary*'s success was attributable to the contributions of individual members of the Metaphysical Society. Sharing Knowles's sense of injury at Strahan's and Morley's hands, they rallied around him, ensuring the *Nineteenth* an auspicious debut. In fact, long after the society's demise, its erstwhile members were the strength of Knowles's monthly. Harrison's statement is no exaggeration: "For a short time indeed this review was almost the literary organ of the Metaphysical Society; and of the sixty-two members of the Society there were few who, at one time or another, have not appeared as contributors to the pages of this Review."[5]

The *Nineteenth Century* was a successful sole proprietorship of owner-editor.[6] Accordingly, the consistency of its format is unsurprising. Typically it contained 172 octavo pages with neither photographs nor advertising. Each issue included about ten articles on diverse topics and occasionally a poem or a concession to belles lettres. Neither novels nor other serial fiction was ever printed, although on a single occasion a one-act play was offered, and dialogues appeared infrequently. Although no photos were used, charts, maps, plans, music, and diagrams, usually as folded and bound inserts, were not uncommon. Clearly, it was not the format but the intellective content that intrigued readers.

Nevertheless, the magazine did change over its run of 286 monthly numbers. Diversity was always the hallmark, yet the balance shifted. Early in its history it was theological; later, political. In its fifth year the *Nineteenth* matured as an editorial force with its campaign against the proposed Channel tunnel. Throughout Knowles's editorship it periodically launched other campaigns. Over the years the tone of the journal became less reflective and more pragmatic as it descended from Olympus to the arena. The *Nineteenth* remained an open forum, but in the last years of Victoria's reign the views of the establishment dominated the debate.

The early issues were redolent of the Metaphysical Society. Gladstone, Manning, and Tennyson, as well as such lesser Metaphysicals as Sir John Lubbock, the Bishop of Glouchester and Bristol (C. J. Ellicott), George Croom Robertson, and Sir M. E. Grant Duff were among the contributors to the maiden number (March 1877). But it was the tone of the society more than its roster that permeated the *Nineteenth*. For instance, Manning's "True Story of the Vatican Council" went on for five numbers in the Metaphysical tradition of inexhaustible argument. Similarly, when Gladstone wrote a review of the recently reissued *Essay on the Influence of Authority in Matters of Opinion* by George Cornewall Lewis, James Stephen wrote a twenty-seven page response for the next issue. Controversy in the *Nineteenth* was generally dispassionate and fair-minded, although some departures from the standards in the 1890s became celebrated. Sometimes even the format of the Metaphysical Society's proceedings was approached. For example, four of its members engaged in one of the *Nineteenth*'s many symposiums, the earliest (April and May 1877) on "The Influence upon Morality of a Decline in Religious Belief" and a second, in succeeding issues, on "The Soul and Future Life." The first symposium was a series of responses to a society paper by J. F. Stephen. The second emanated from a reading by Harrison. Most of the respondents were Metaphysicals, and their comments differed from those presented at the meetings principally in their formality.

It is hard to exaggerate the influence of the Metaphysical Society on the *Nineteenth Century*, yet the magazine was much more than the views of the society in print. Matthew Arnold, in the first issue, eulogized Lord Falkland, Charles I's secretary of state, who fell at Newbury; Arnold remembered him as a "martyr of sweetness and light." The early issues included not only theological controversy, but also essays on science, geography, politics, literature, law, medicine, and theater. Any topic that would appeal to a serious and educated English reader seemed suitable to Knowles.

Noteworthy contributors before 1880 included historian James Anthony Froude; R. H. Hutton, who edited the *Spectator** (see *RA*); Browning devotee Mrs. Sutherland Orr; Rabbi Herman Adler ("Can Jews Be Patriots?"); atheist George Jacob Holyoake; the prominent Catholic editor and layman, Dr. W. G. Ward; Francis Galton, the eugenicist; and Frederick Leighton, the artist and, later, president of the Royal Academy. Tennyson continued to send poetry, and Arnold both essays and poetry. Anthony Trollope noted the accomplishments of Dickens and Thackeray, as well as the new prestige of the novel.

After 1880 new names were added to the list of contributors, including Wilfrid Scawen Blunt, not yet an Irish partisan, but an acknowledged Orientalist and breeder, who wrote in 1880 on "The Thoroughbred Horse—English and Arabian." The same year Tennyson's son Hallam reflected on "Earl Russell During the Eastern Question, 1853–1855." The next year socialist Harry Hyndman saluted "The Dawn of the Revolutionary Epoch," and Paul Janet contributed "La Philosophie de Diderot" (in French). Meanwhile, Huxley was supervising his column on "Recent Science," which appeared irregularly, although at least twice a year. Cardinal Manning opposed the parliamentary seating of Charles Bradlaugh. Scientist John Tyndall wrote on the history and significance of "The Sabbath," and Gladstone in separate articles discussed both the importance of free trade and railways to commerce, and relations between Russia and England.

The year 1882 was a turning point for the *Nineteenth Century*, as it began a campaign against the proposals for a Channel tunnel. The specific fear of an invasion from France had never been dissipated, and Francophobia was more than a military disease. In the February 1882 issue Admiral Lord Dunsany deplored the impact of a tunnel on English defenses, and a March symposium presented both sides of the issue. However, the April issue contained "The Proposed Channel Tunnel, A Protest," with over fifty signatures, initially including Tennyson, Browning, Harrison, Holyoake, Huxley, Manning, the Marquis of Bath, the Marquis of Sligo, and the Bishop of Gloucester and Bristol. Among the hundreds of notables who later signed were Cardinal Newman, William Morris, Alfred Austin (Tennyson's eventual successor as Laureate), Blunt, and Leighton. In addition, innumerable clergymen, military men, and trade union leaders signed. The last were apprehensive of an influx of cheap labor. Knowles buttressed his opposition with a personally written six-page editorial. Like all material in the *Nineteenth Century*, it was signed. The controversy was continued in the May issue. It included more signatures; an article by the Frenchman Joseph Reinach, which impugned English insularity and motives in general; and three other articles, including one by a military engineer, whose antipathy took the patriotic high road, not the commercial low one.

The dramatic success achieved through the journal inspired its editor to take up other causes, which included an 1888–1889 campaign against the undue reliance on examinations in the civil and military services; opposition to women's suffrage later in 1889; and a 1900 proposal to form "an association having for its object to fix public attention upon some of the most important lessons taught by the South African War." This conflict, like its Crimean predecessor, reminded England how ineptly its expeditionary forces were organized, administered, and led. The same format was repeated. First came the statement or manifesto and the small petition signed by influential people. Next, a secondary group subscribed and supporting articles were written. Finally, in the spirit of fairness, not totally effective rejoinders were published and, sometimes, still further signatures. If the *Nineteenth Century* never again attained the mass influence it had with the tunnel issue, its failure was one of topic, rather than a decline in literary standards, intellectual respectability, or tactics.

Quality, not excitement, sustained the journal through the 1880s. As the excitement over the tunnel subsided, Matthew Arnold published "Literature and Science" in the August issue, and during the next year anarchist Prince Kropotkin twice discussed Russian prisons. Artists G. F. Watts wrote "On Taste in Dress," and Tennyson submitted "Frater Ave Atque Vale" (not a translation of Catullus LI, but a nine-line lyric on Catullus' life). That year Knowles printed his publisher, C. Kegan Paul, on "Clergymen as Headmasters," and historian Sir Henry Taylor reviewed the abortive 1835 attempt to establish "An Academy of Literature for Great Britain." The many-talented Gladstone translated Cowper's hymn, "Hark, my soul!" into Italian—"Senti, senti, anima mia!"—but one suspects that Knowles accepted it only because he could not risk offending Gladstone.

Throughout the 1880s fundamental questions of religion pervaded the journal. Spencer refined his concept of the unknowable. Huxley articulated agnosticism. Mrs. Humphry Ward (*Robert Elsmere*) explored "The New Reformation," and Gladstone combated all of these heresies, especially Huxley's. The Duke of Argyll, the Bishop of Peterborough (William Connor Magee), Henry Wace, and Harrison also involved themselves in the magazine.

It is ironic that two of Victorian England's more notorious literary figures, A. C. Swinburne and Oscar Wilde, should have helped sustain the staid *Nineteenth*'s critical reputation in the 1880s, even though the period followed Swinburne's rehabilitation and preceded Wilde's disgrace. Swinburne contributed over forty pieces during his lifetime. These included not only poetry, but also valuable Tudor and Stuart literary history and comment, especially on drama. Wilde, too, treated the Elizabethan stage in "Shakespeare and Stage Costume" (May 1885), although his later famous dialogue "The Critic as Artist" did not appear in the *Nineteenth* until 1890.

Despite its ostensible demise, for a decade the Metaphysical Society seemed to mesmerize the *Nineteenth Century*; but the death in the 1890s of three Metaphysical stalwarts—Tennyson, Huxley, and Gladstone—inevitably diminished the society's influence. By 1890 Knowles was conscious of his own value, not merely as a useful organizer and arranger, or as a provider of an "open court," but more significantly as an editor and *de facto* publisher who knew important Englishmen in every walk of life and who controlled an influential organ of opinion. As such, his interests were more topical, and a subtle movement from the general to the particular is observable in his editorial selections during the nineties, although the old spirit is evident in Huxley's "On the Natural Inequality of Man" and Spencer's "Absolute Political Ethics" in the first issues of 1890 and in Argyll's diatribe, "Professor Huxley on the Warpath," as the lead article for 1891. Labor leader Tom Mann appeared twice in 1890; Prince Kropotkin became a regular contributor as Huxley's successor in "Recent Science"; Harrison (December 1890) urged that England should "Give Back the Elgin Marbles" in lieu of proselytizing for positivism; and Francis Seymour Haden, Whistler's brother-in-law and arch-enemy, submitted his "Presidential Address of the Royal Society of Painter-Etchers for 1890."

Topics for 1892 included "Cardinal Manning in the Church of England," by R. G. Wilberforce; a symposium on the mid-year election; Anglo-Egyptian relations as interpreted by Blunt; and, most notably, the death of Tennyson, which prompted seven verse tributes for the November issue, including effusions by Huxley and Knowles.

A more professional if less heartfelt elegy was furnished by Swinburne for the January 1893 number. That issue also included "A Personal Reminiscence" by Knowles, complete with an early draft of "The Dolorous Stroke" and marginalia for *In Memoriam* (which the Tennyson family thought presumptuous). Further reminiscences of Tennyson by other contributors appeared in February, March, and May.

The next two years, 1894–1895, were memorable for a symposium on the House of Lords, which included proposals to abolish its veto and even to abolish it; Gladstone's translation of "The Love Odes of Horace, Five Specimens"; and presentations of the platforms of "The Independent Labour Party" (January 1895) and the Conservative party, in part, represented by "The Conservative Program of Social Reform" (July 1895). Yet the old spirit, however diminished, survived. Huxley wrote in March 1895 of "Mr. Balfour's Attack on Agnosticism," his final contribution.

Foreign affairs were prominent in 1896. "The True Motive and Reason of Dr. Jameson's Raid" foreshadowed the *Nineteenth Century*'s keen concern with South African affairs, whereas a September article on "The Jew-Baiting on the Continent," a symposium on "The Massacres in Turkey" the next month, and two further articles on "Turkish Misgovernment" reaffirmed the breadth of its readers' interest in foreign affairs. Closer to home Wilfrid Ward, the son of Huxley's Catholic Metaphysical antagonist W. G. Ward, wrote "Thomas Henry Huxley: A Reminiscence" for the August issue, and Gladstone's essay in the

Turkish symposium was that old campaigner's valedictory to the journal, although Gladstone did not die until 1898.

The *Nineteenth*'s diamond jubilee year was not notable. The February issue featured two articles on "Law and the Laundry," a wage-hour and women's labor issue that involved Beatrice Webb. Argyll persisted with "Mr. Herbert Spencer and Lord Salisbury on Evolution" (March and April), and Havelock Ellis made an unremarkable appearance with "Genius and Stature."

The next year provided a renewal of Knowles as controversialist. In January he published a four-part symposium with the inflammatory title "The War Office and Its Sham Army." It outlined a plan to reorganize the War Office, criticized the recruiting system and the general state of military preparedness, and made specific suggestions. Two further articles that month discussed the proper roles of the army and the navy and "A Recruiting Sergeant's Suggestions." Other topics for early 1898 included the Millais retrospective and "Deaths under Chloroform."

But Gladstone's death became the event of the year. In June Knowles himself wrote of "Mr. Gladstone as a Contributor to the 'Nineteenth Century,' " cataloguing his sixty-seven contributions and praising his personal modesty, punctuality, charm, consideration, and open-mindedness, while acknowledging his official "imperious certitude." The next month Wilfrid Meynell and Guiness Rogers respectively recalled Gladstone's relationships with Catholicism and Nonconformism, and in August Emyss Reid discussed "Mr. Gladstone and His Party." The subject seemed inexhaustible. Meynell quoted Lord Rosebery's apothegm "that a limited liability company will be needed to write a biography of Mr. Gladstone."

Although anticipating the end of the century and despite its title, the *Nineteenth* was commendably unretrospective. In January 1899 it castigated the French government for its persecution of Dreyfus, and in April and May explored a feminist topic, "Woman as an Athlete." Still venturesome, in September it published "The American Negro and His Place," a defense by an American woman of separation with equality in the South, and a December rebuttal, "A Negro on the Position of the Negro in America."

The ambivalence of the *Nineteenth Century* persisted until the magazine ended. In July 1900 there was another salvo: "The Lesson of the War: A Proposed Association." A manifesto with sixty signatures was published, focusing on defense policy and the affirmation of "ordinary business principles" in "conducting the business of the country." The next issue contained an additional 400 signatures, and for the balance of the year articles critical of the administration of the war appeared. But the old note was also heard when in the December issue Leslie Stephen, in "Thomas Henry Huxley," reviewed Leonard Huxley's biography of his father. Characteristically, the *Nineteenth Century* looked both forward and backward. It is not strange that when the *Nineteenth Century and After* appeared in January 1901, it employed Janus as its trademark.

Notes

1. *Nineteenth Century and After* 63 (1908):695–96.

2. The Victorian years have been indexed in *The Wellesley Index to Victorian Periodicals 1824–1900*, ed. Walter E. Houghton (Toronto, 1972), 2:621–722, except for poetry, which is indexed by Priscilla Metcalf in *James Knowles: Victorian Editor and Architect* (New York, 1980), pp. 368–69. Knowles's earlier index (1903?) is now superseded.

The anthology is *Nineteenth-Century Opinion: An Anthology of Extracts from the First Fifty Volumes of the "Nineteenth Century," 1877–1901*, ed. Michael Goodwin (Harmondsworth, 1951). A long list of commemorative articles is given in the introductory essay to the *Wellesley Index* entry, pp. 625–26; Metcalf's history appears in *James Knowles*, pp. 274–351.

3. Metcalf, p. 215.

4. The definitive history is an older work, Alan Willard Brown, *The Metaphysical Society: Victorian Minds in Crisis, 1869–1880* (1947; rpt. New York, 1973.) See chap. 3, "The Founding of the Society," pp. 20–33.

5. *Nineteenth Century and After* 43 (1908):695.

6. When Knowles founded the magazine, his father placed 2,000 pounds on reserve, a sum that remained untouched. When the editor died in 1908, he left over 30,000 pounds. Metcalf, pp. 275, 363.

Information Sources

BIBLIOGRAPHY

Brown, Alan Willard. *The Metaphysical Society: Victorian Minds in Crisis, 1869–1880*. 1947. Reprint. New York, 1973.

Goodwin, Michael, ed. *Nineteenth-Century Opinion: An Anthology of Extracts from the First Fifty Volumes of the "Nineteenth Century," 1877–1901*. Harmondsworth, 1951.

Metcalf, Priscilla. *James Knowles: Victorian Editor and Architect*. New York, 1980.

INDEXES

List of contents in each bound volume. Volumes 1–11 in *A General Index to the "Contemporary Review," the "Fortnightly Review," and the "Nineteenth Century,"* comp. W. M. Griswold (Bangor, Me., 1882). Volumes 1–50 in *"The Nineteenth Century": Catalogue of Contributors and Contributions* (London, 1903). 1877–1881 in *Poole's Index*. Prose in *Wellesley Index* 2. Poetry in Priscilla Metcalf, *James Knowles: Victorian Editor and Architect*, New York, 1980.

REPRINT EDITIONS

Microform: Early British Periodicals (UMI), reels 505–523.

LOCATION SOURCES

American

Widely available.

British

Widely available.

Publication History

MAGAZINE TITLE AND TITLE CHANGES
The Nineteenth Century: A Monthly Review.
VOLUME AND ISSUE DATA
Volumes 1–43, numbers 1–286, March 1877–December 1900.
FREQUENCY OF PUBLICATION
Monthly.
PUBLISHERS
Volumes 1–2, March–December 1877: Henry S. King & Co., London. Volumes 3–9, January 1878–June 1881: C. Kegan Paul & Co., 1 Paternoster Square, London. Volumes 10–28, July 1881–December 1890: Kegan Paul, Trench, & Co., 1 Paternoster Square, London. Volume 29, January–June 1891: Kegan Paul, Trench, Trübner, & Co., Ltd., 1 Paternoster Square, London. Volumes 30–48, July 1891–December 1900: Sampson Low, Marston & Company (Limited), St. Dunstan's House, Fetter Lane, Fleet Street, London E.C.
EDITOR
James Knowles

Daniel Rutenberg

NORTH BRITISH REVIEW, THE

The history of the *North British Review* begins on 18 May 1843, when Dr. Thomas Chalmers led 474 ministers out of the Church of Scotland to form the "Free Kirk." The founders of this evangelical wing established their own university, the New College of Edinburgh, and, in 1844, their own literary journal, the *North British Review*.

Their prospectus began:

For a considerable time past, there have been, on the part of a large proportion of the public, a growing feeling of the want of a Periodical accomodated to the character of the times. The professedly religious Magazines have been chiefly devoted to theological subjects, and generally address themselves to the peculiar views of one sect; and the literary, scientific, and political Journals—though some of them conducted with admirable talent—have excluded religion altogether from their pages, or allowed it only a subordinate place; and no attempt has been hitherto made to meet the increased intelligence in connection with the strong religious feelings of the age.

To remedy these defects the present Work has been undertaken. It is not intended to be a Theological Journal. No subject that can occupy the interest of a well-cultivated mind will be excluded. But topics of every kind will be treated of by individuals accustomed to view them in their highest relations; and Papers of a more strictly religious character will be frequently introduced.

W. G. Blaikie, the editor from 1860 to 1863, was more concise and specific: "Neither the *Edinburgh*[* (see *RA*)] nor the *Quarterly Review*[* (see *RA*)] was quite satisfactory to a considerable number of gentlemen, . . . for the *Edinburgh* was too secular, and the *Quarterly* too conservative. They longed for an organ of a high class that would be both liberal in politics and Christian in tone."[1] But from the beginning, the *North British Review* did but slenderly know itself. Thus, the Reverend William Hanna, the editor from 1846 to 1850, ingenuously wrote that the review did not want "articles on religious subjects half so much as articles on common subjects, written with a decidedly Christian tone," and spoke of "its pure and independent, its Christian yet unsectarian aim." Likewise, Blaikie said, "The projectors of the *Review* were mostly Free Churchmen, but it never was designed to be a Free Church organ." Henry Cockburn was more forthright when he commented, "It is a Free Church review." They may claim the reverse, "but indirectly the general impression of the work will be against the Church, and in favour of all dissent that is honest and pious."[2]

The fundamental belief of the *North British* was that "truth does not change with time. . . . What was once true is true for ever" (28:272). Thus, the outstanding trait of a "great man" like Zwingli, "indicating in fact his position as a Reformer, is his profound reverence for the Word of God. He regarded it as the lone standard of truth and duty" (29:305). Similarly, the rightness of Wesleyan Methodists is contrasted with the blindness of infidels, papists, and all "enemies of evangelical religion" (32:86). As for Catholics, "in serving the Church, they ought to have been serving Christ. . . . He who would devote himself to the historical Church of Christ, must give up the attempt to serve Christ himself" (28:273). In an article on "Recent Rationalism in the Church of England," the evangelical review claims that "nothing but the cordial and unreserved recognition of the supernatural element . . . in Scripture, can lead to a sound exegesis, or furnish a secure foundation for a saving faith in its truths, bringing the soul into vital union with God through the medium of His own word" (33:135). At the other end of the religious spectrum, "Socinianism, Unitarianism, 'Liberal Christianity,' or whatever other name may be devised to hide its nakedness, passes away . . . by a process of self-destruction. . . . '*But the word of the Lord endureth for ever*' " (30:268–69). Predictably, in an article on Mormonism, the review warns that "the noble principle of Protestantism, that of private judgment, may in fact be carried to excess. . . . Religious liberty may be abused, as well as political liberty" (39:113).

The *North British* always claimed to be a liberal review and was, in fact, consistently Whiggish in politics. But its religious conservatism caused it to reject many of the most advanced scientific and social theories of the times. For example, in "Literature and the Labor Question," a review of Henry Mayhew's *London Labour and the London Poor* and Charles Kingsley's *Alton Locke*, the review dismisses the emphasis on social change: "We hear little of the new heart and the right spirit." All of our efforts for the good of mankind "must be mean, physical, and partial." Instead, suffering workers are admonished, "Seek ye first the Kingdom of God, and His righteousness; and all other things shall be added unto you" (14:226–27). Marx could have been referring to the *North British* when he spoke of religion as the opiate of the people. Likewise, the review attacks Mill's *On Liberty* for "the gross ignorance and audacity of his attack on the morals of Christ's teaching, and on the system of Calvinism." His advocacy of "Drunkeness, Sabbath-breaking, and Mormonism" is only to be expected from a man who avows "that the Bible is not a complete rule of moral conduct" (30:219–20). Similarly, *On the Origin of Species* is condemned because "Mr. Darwin's work is in direct antagonism to all the findings of a natural theology, formed on legitimate induction in the study of the works of God; and it does open violence to everything which the Creator Himself has told us in the Scriptures of truth, of the method and results of His working." The publication of Darwin's work "is a mistake" (32:263).

In literature, as the prospectus stated, "the moral and religious tendency of works under review, will always be the first subject of consideration." Thus, Coventry Patmore begins his review of American novels: "The responsibility of the poet and the novelist, for the wholesomeness of their instructions, is also scarcely inferior to that of the preacher," and, on this basis, rates the novels of Harriet Beecher Stowe and Elizabeth Wetherell above those of Nathaniel Hawthorne (20:44). The *North British* was wary of Dickens, especially his "speculative doctrine." As David Masson states:

> In his antipathy to Puritanism, Mr. Dickens seems to have adopted a principle closely resembling that which pervades the ethical part of Unitarianism, the essence of which is, that it places a facile disposition at the centre of the universe. . . . any man or artist who shall enter upon his sphere of activity, without in some way or other realizing and holding fast those truths which Puritanism sets such store by, and which it has embodied . . . in the words sin, wrath, and justice, must necessarily take but half the facts of the world along with him, and go through his task too lightly and nimbly." [15:43]

Similarly, Charles Kingsley defends the Puritans' hatred of the morally degraded Stuart stage, including Shakespeare's "low art, the foul and horrible elements which he had in common with his brother play-writers" (25:13). The *North British* maintained this bias in its numerous considerations of modern poetry. Shelley, for example, was a master of language but "was throughout wrong in all his speculations on religion and morals" (8:133–37). Keats is underrated because he had "powers of merely sensual perception and expression." Patmore claims that Keats's "mind, like Goethe's, was 'lighted from below.' Not a ray of the wisdom that is from above had, as yet, illumed it" (10:38–39). In contrast,

Gerald Massey speaks of "Browning as a great religious poet. We have had too many poets who were endowed with the sense of beauty, without the fitting reverence for the Creator of all beauty; and there is too great a divorce between our poetry and religion for us not to rejoice over a poet who possesses the clearest of all seeing faculties—religious faith" (34:194).

But of all the subjects covered by the review, literature enjoyed the greatest freedom. The *North British* was always on the side of the angels, but individual critics disagreed over who the angels were. Thus, in the 1850s a controversy raged over the "Spasmodic Poets" and the proper subject of modern poetry. In an article of August 1853, David Masson praised the poetry of Alexander Smith, a leading Spasmodic, and claimed that "the subject chosen by a poetical writer . . . is a kind of allegory of the whole state of his mental being at the moment" (19:321). It was this statement that so riled Arnold in the famous "Preface" to his poems of 1853: "An allegory of the state of one's own mind, the highest problem of an art which imitates actions! No assuredly, it is not, it never can be so: no great poetical work has ever been produced with such an aim."[3] But J. C. Shairp, writing in the *North British* in August 1854, denied Arnold's premise that true poetry contemplates noble actions of heroic times and insisted that the poet should mend the present by strengthening whatever is good in the men of his own time.[4] In contrast, Coventry Patmore, a major reviewer for the *North British*, finally attacked the Spasmodics in the *Edinburgh Review* in 1856, using Arnold's poems as "very refreshing and instructive contrasts" to the Spasmodics' "unreadable" works.[5] Patmore also made several derogatory references to the Spasmodics in the *North British* during the late 1850s. But it was Gerald Massey who wrote the major attack against the Spasmodics in the *North British* in 1858 and, like Arnold, called for "a return to the lasting and true subject-matter of poetry, and a firmer reliance on primal truths" (28:135). What accounts for this radical shift in the *North British* during the 1850s from an advocacy of Spasmodic poetry to a return to classical principles? Was it simply that Masson and Shairp were different critics from Patmore and Massey? Or is it attributable to the change in editorship from A. C. Fraser to John Duns in 1857? Or is the *North British* simply reflecting the change in the critical climate after the publication in 1854 of Aytoun's famous parody of the Spasmodics, *Firmilian*? Or was it perhaps a combination of these factors? Once beyond the religious and moral priorities of the review, it becomes extremely difficult, if not impossible, to speak of "a *North British* position" in literature.

The *North British Review* offered good, comprehensive literary criticism from the start. Henry Cockburn noted the excellence of the first number and estimated "nearly 4,000 copies have been sold," being only about 1,000 fewer than its great exemplar, the *Edinburgh*.[6] In fact, its Scottish circulation was larger, perhaps because the *North British* had a provincial air during the 1840s. David Welsh, the first editor, had occupied the chair of the General Assembly at the Disruption. William Hanna, the editor from 1847 to 1850, was a disciple of Thomas Chalmers and undertook the office because of "the large promises of counsel and aid held out by Dr. Chalmers.''[7] Likewise, most of the writers during the 1840s were Scottish advocates and Scottish theologians. By 1849, the number of printed copies had dropped to 1,650.[8] Still, the quality of its literary criticism was consistently high, and sometimes outstanding. De Quincey, for example, published some of his finest essays in the *North British* in 1848, including ''The Poetry of Pope,'' which contains his most mature consideration of the distinction between the literature of power and the literature of knowledge.

A. C. Fraser, the editor from 1850 to 1857, turned the *North British* into a more sophisticated and broadly based review. He solicited and obtained articles from men of letters all over Great Britain, including (in literature) Nassau Senior, Charles Kingsley, J. M. Ludlow, E. S. Dallas, J. C. Shairp, and David Masson. Masson, the chief literary critic during Fraser's tenure, and Coventry Patmore, who had held that position under Hanna and who continued to contribute in the 1850s, provided the *North British* with literary criticism just below the best in mid-century Britain. Although it was now a respectable challenger of the *Edinburgh* and the *Quarterly*, it could not pay its contributors as generously, and consequently had to settle for some leftovers from the two great reviews.[9] The reign of Fraser came to an end in February 1857 because Isaac Taylor's liberal interpretation of Chalmers's religious works roused the anger of William Cunningham, principal of the Free Church College, who believed in the verbal infallibility of Scripture. In Fraser's view, ''censure fell chiefly on Taylor's hopeful anticipation of a 'biblical theology' ready to recognize in an open spirit the mysterious facts in divine revelation, liberated from 'superannuated logical or deductive theology.' ''[10] Cunningham forced Fraser's resignation, indicating that the review remained under the aegis of the Church.

The *North British* struggled under the editorship of John Duns, an obscure country clergyman, from 1857 to 1860, when printings declined to an all-time low of 1,250. But it returned to prominence during the 1860s. W. G. Blaikie and David Douglas provided ''enlightened leadership''; circulation rose to 3,000 again by the middle of the decade.[11] On 31 December 1864 the London *Times* commended the review in a four-column study:

> They avail themselves more freely than formerly of the products of English contributors.... we hail the recent numbers of the *North British* as a sign of their advance, and a proof that a true Scot is as ready as ever to cross the Tweed and to vie successfully with his English competitors. It is seldom, if ever, that one sees so good a series of reviews—so good substantially in nearly all of their articles, from the first page to the last.

The *North British Review* became most free, liberal, and cosmopolitan at the end of its career when, in late 1869, a group of liberal Catholics took control. T. F. Wetherell, the editor, was supported by Lord Acton's advice and contributions and by the same band of writers who had been associated with him on the *Home and Foreign Review* and the *Chronicle*. The original prospectus of

1844 had stressed the religious attitude and the immutable nature of truth; the new prospectus emphasized the scientific attitude and the historical evolution of truth. It claimed that the aim of a literary organ "must be the victory of scientific truth.... And it must be animated by that spirit of genial tolerance and various adaptiveness which is taught by the analysis of human nature, and the manifold permutations of history." The new *North British* employed foreign critics and reviewed foreign literature. It admitted "that wide diversity of view which is inseparable from the process of honest investigation" (30:602–5). Although Cardinal Newman chided Wetherell for the new secularism of the review, he admitted that it was "exceedingly able and careful" and "wonderful in point of matter and conscientious hard work."[12] But sales dropped, perhaps because the traditional readers of the *North British* would not support such radical changes. When Wetherell became seriously ill in early 1871, the *North British Review*, which had never been healthier as a literary organ, died.

Notes

1. W. G. Blaikie, *An Autobiography*, 2d ed. (London, 1901), p. 136.

2. William Hanna, *Memoirs of the Life and Writings of Thomas Chalmers* (New York, 1853), 4:422; Blaikie, p. 137; Henry Cockburn, *Journal* (Edinburgh, 1874), 2:70.

3. Matthew Arnold, "Preface to First Edition of Poems," in *Irish Essays and Others* (London, 1882), p. 293.

4. See Walter E. Houghton, "The Authorship of Two Reviews of Arnold's Poetry in the *North British Review*," *Victorian Periodicals Newsletter* 8 (1975):17–20.

5. *Edinburgh Review* 104 (1856):173–86.

6. Cockburn, 2:71.

7. Hanna, 4:422.

8. Walter E. Houghton, ed., *The Wellesley Index to Victorian Periodicals 1824–1900* (Toronto, 1966), 1:663n.

9. On the editorship of Fraser, see Joanne Shattock, "Spreading It Thinly: Some Victorian Reviewers at Work," *Victorian Periodicals Newsletter* 9 (1976):84–87, and "Editorial Policy and the Quarterlies: The Case of *North British Review*," *Victorian Periodicals Newsletter* 10 (1977):130–39.

10. A. C. Fraser, *Biographia Philosophica: A Retrospect*, 2d ed. (Edinburgh, 1905), p. 161.

11. Houghton, 1:663.

12. Quoted in Abbot Gasquet, ed., *Lord Acton and His Circle* (London, 1906), p. lxxxii.

Information Sources

BIBLIOGRAPHY

Shattock, Joanne. "Editorial Policy and the Quarterlies: The Case of *North British Review*." *Victorian Periodicals Newsletter* 10 (1977):130–39.

——. "Spreading It Thinly: Some Victorian Reviewers at Work." *Victorian Periodical Newsletter* 9 (1976):84–87.

The Wellesley Index to Victorian Periodicals 1824–1900. Vol. 1. Edited by Walter E. Houghton. Toronto, 1966.

INDEXES
  Poole's Index. Wellesley Index 1.
REPRINT EDITIONS
  Microform: English Literary Periodicals (UMI), reels 728–735.
LOCATION SOURCES
  American
    Widely available.
  British
    Widely available.

Publication History

MAGAZINE TITLE AND TITLE CHANGES
  The North British Review.
VOLUME AND ISSUE DATA
  Volumes 1–53, May 1844–January 1871. (No issue, May 1857.)
FREQUENCY OF PUBLICATION
  Quarterly.
PUBLISHERS
  Volumes 1–32: W. P. Kennedy, Edinburgh. Volumes 33–38: T. and T. Clark, Edinburgh. Volumes 39–49: Edmonston and Douglas, Edinburgh. Volumes 50–53: Williams and Norgate, London.
EDITORS
  David Welsh, May 1844–May 1845. Edward F. Maitland, August 1845–November 1846. William Hanna, February 1847–February 1850. A. C. Fraser, May 1850–February 1857. John Duns, August 1857–May 1860. Mr. Forster, August 1860. W. G. Blaikie, November 1860–August 1863. David Douglas, November 1863–July 1869. T. F. Wetherell, October 1869–January 1871.

Mark A. Weinstein

NOTES AND QUERIES

After an unsuccessful attempt in 1841 titled the *Medium*, the first issue of *Notes and Queries*, subtitled *A Medium of Inter-Communication for Literary Men, Artists, Antiquaries, Genealogists, etc.*, appeared at the beginning of the publishing season, on 3 November 1849. Three years earlier W. J. Thoms (under the pseudonym "Ambrose Merton") had begun in the *Athenaeum** (see *RA*) a column of folklore items submitted by readers of the magazine. Anticipating a large number of contributions, the *Athenaeum* recommended brevity. The items submitted soon became so numerous that, even though kept short, they required more space than was available. Thoms then established *Notes and Queries* as a vehicle for these and other short notes, using the *Somerset House Gazette* (1823) as a model.[1]

The purpose of *Notes and Queries* in matters of folklore was to collect items feared about to be lost and to make them available to students of the subject, joining the efforts of amateur collectors with the disciplined researches of the anthropologists. Emphasis in *Notes and Queries*, given the limitation of space, was on collection. An indication of the success of the effort was the publication in 1859 of *Choice Notes from "Notes and Queries": Folklore*, containing over 500 items, indexed by subject and county.

But the content of *Notes and Queries* was not restricted just to folklore. Thoms's intent was, as he said in the first number, to provide "a cheap and frequent means" for the exchange of "the Notes of the writer and the reader, whatever be the subject-matter of his studies, of the antiquary, and the artist, the man of science, the historian, the herald, and the genealogist, in short, Notes relating to all subjects but such as are, in popular discourse, termed either political or polemical." The first index (to volumes 1–12) reveals a wide range of topics indeed, including almost 200 items on photography, but others on matters as various as the body weight of officers in the American revolutionary army, the presence of Scotchmen in Poland, and the derivation of *Czar* and *Tsar*. However, the main subjects of these volumes and most of those following, through the first part of the next century, were language, literature, history (especially local history), and genealogy (biography). The classifications that commonly recur in the indexes are anonymous works, epigrams, epitaphs, folklore, proverbs, quotations, Shakespeare, and songs and ballads. Less frequent classified headings show an emphasis on literature: Macaulay, Popiana, Swift (1st series), parallel passages (7th, 8th, and 9th series), Dickensia, editorial, Scott's works, Thackeray's works (10th series), rimes (11th, 12th, and 13th series), and theatre (13th series). Offering as it did a means for a relatively quick exchange of information, *Notes and Queries* helped many among the rapidly growing reading public who did not have access to large libraries or distant sources of information.

Much of the material that appeared in *Notes and Queries* has been judged to have permanent value. Many of the early articles on history are collected in *Choice Notes from "Notes and Queries": On History* (1858). In 1896 W. W. Skeat collected in *A Student's Pastime* his several hundred contributions on etymology during the years 1866–1896. Through its activity in the areas of language, literature, and biography, the periodical played an important role in the founding of the English Dialect Society and in the preparation of the *English Dialect Dictionary*, the *Dictionary of National Biography*, and the *Oxford English Dictionary* and its supplements. W. C. Boulter's corrections to the *DNB* were published quarterly in *Notes and Queries* between 1882 and 1900.

Though *Notes and Queries* is generally regarded as having changed relatively little over the years, there have been changes. The contents are first listed in issue number 3, 17 November 1849. Beginning in January 1851, the editors went to a supplementary number in those months in which there were only four Saturdays. The names of contributors are listed for the first time in the index to the ninth series (1904). The names of the editors are not printed until number 6 of new series volume 6 (June 1959). Book reviews first appeared under the heading "Notes on Books," then under "Library," and finally, after 1965, under "Reviews." The number of books reviewed increases gradually from just a few, on various topics, to more than fifty, exclusively on literature, in the latest numbers. The size of issues increased from sixteen pages (1849), to twenty-four (1942), to forty-eight (1953), to the present ninety-six pages. Individual numbers appeared weekly through April 1917, monthly (because of the war) through December 1919, weekly again through June 1942, every two weeks (because of the war) through December 1952, monthly through December 1976, and since January 1977 every other month. After 1900 the number of American contributors increases significantly,[2] and the number of items on literature (belles lettres), relatively large from the beginning, becomes even larger, especially after 1930. As the preface to the fifteenth series index notes, volumes after 1948 give more space to notes and reviews, and less space to queries and replies. With the policy of emphasizing a particular literary period in each issue, begun in September 1959 in an effort to help in the preparation of the new supplement to the *Oxford English Dictionary*, *Notes and Queries* became almost entirely literary in content.

Notes

1. Thoms describes the founding of *Notes and Queries* in a rambling account published there between 1 July 1876 and 21 April 1877. See also *Athenaeum*, no. 982 (22 August 1846), pp. 862–63, and no. 983 (29 August 1846), pp. 886–87; *Notes and Queries* 2, no. 42 (1850):193; *Notes and Queries* 2, no. 46 (1850):242–43. The *Somerset House Gazette* (1823) should not be confused with the *Somerset County Gazette* (1836).

2. There have been several American publications modeled on *Notes and Queries*. Perhaps the first was *American Notes and Queries* (1857), edited by William Brotherhead. The most recent is *American Notes and Queries* (1962), edited by Lee Ash.

Information Sources

BIBLIOGRAPHY

Algar, F., and Wilfred H. Holden. "W. J. Thoms: Our First Editor." *Notes and Queries* 198 (1953):125, 223.

Bell, Edward. *George Bell, Publisher: A Brief Memoir*. London, 1924.

Dorson, Richard M. "The First Group of British Folklorists." *Journal of American Folklore* 68 (1955):1–8, 333–40.

Francis, John C. *Notes by the Way: The Memoirs of Knight and the Rev. Joseph Woodfall Ebsworth*. London, 1909.

Hale, B.F.R. "Joseph Knight." *Notes and Queries* 194 (1949):464.

Hayllar, Florence. "N & Q." *Times Literary Supplement*, 17 August 1922, p. 533.

Notes and Queries 190 (1946):275–76; 191 (1946):1, 101–2; 192 (1947):429–30; 195 (1950):353.

Thoms, William J. "The Story of *Notes and Queries*." *Notes and Queries*, 5th ser., 6 (1876):1, 41, 101, 221. *Notes and Queries*, 5th ser., 7 (1877):1, 222, 303.

INDEXES

Each volume indexed. Series 1–15 (12 volumes each), separately published, 1856–1955. 1849–1923, rpt. separately (Burt Franklin & Co.).

REPRINT EDITIONS
    Microform: Brook Haven Press, La Crosse, Wis. Princeton Microfilm Corp.,
    Princeton, N.J. UMI.
LOCATION SOURCES
    American
    Widely available.
    British
    Widely available.

Publication History

MAGAZINE TITLE AND TITLE CHANGES
    *Notes and Queries: a medium of inter-communication for literary men, artists,
    antiquaries, genealogists, etc.*, 1st series, volume 1–3d series, volume 2, Novem-
    ber 1849–December 1862. *Notes and Queries: a medium of intercommunication
    for literary men, general readers, etc.*, 3d series, volume 3–13th series, volume
    1, January 1863–December 1923. *Notes and Queries for readers and writers,
    collectors and librarians*, 13th series, volume 2–new series, volume 28, number
    6, January 1924–December 1981. (The title-page epigraph [" 'When found, make
    a note of.'—Captain Cuttle."] was dropped after December 1923.)
VOLUME AND ISSUE DATA
    Continuous series, volumes 1–226, November 1849–December 1981: series 1–
    13, volume 1, November 1849–December 1923; continuous volumes 146–198,
    January 1924–December 1953; new series, volumes 1–28, number 6, January
    1954–December 1981 (new series volume 1 begins with volume 199 in the con-
    tinuous series).
FREQUENCY OF PUBLICATION
    Weekly through April 1917; monthly, May 1917–December 1919; weekly, January
    1920–June 1942; semi-monthly, July 1942–December 1952; monthly, January
    1953–December 1976; bimonthly, January 1977–.
PUBLISHERS
    Volume 1, 1st series–volume 4, 3d series, November 1849–December 1863: George
    Bell, London. Volume 5, 3d series–volume 4, 12th series, January 1864–Decem-
    ber 1918: John Francis, London. Volume 5, 12th series–volume 11, 12th series,
    January 1919–December 1922: Times Publishing Company, London. Volume 12,
    12th series–volume 157 continuous volumes, January 1923–December 1929: Bucks
    Free Press, Wycombe. Volume 158–volume 175, number 14, January 1929–
    October 1938: Rolls House Publishing Company, London. Volume 175, number
    15–volume 176, number 12, 8 October 1938–25 March 1939: Guardian and Church
    Quarterly Review, London. Volume 176, number 13–volume 28, number 6, n.s.,
    1 April 1939–December 1981: Oxford University Press, London.
EDITORS
    William John Thoms, 1849–1872, assisted by James Yeowell, 1852–1872. John
    Doran, 1872–1878, assisted by H. F. Turle, 1873–1878. H. F. Turle, 1878–1883.
    Joseph Knight, 1883–1907, assisted by Vernon Rendall, 1899–1907. Vernon

Rendall, 1907–1912. Florence Hayllar 1912–1942. F. J. Page, 1943–1959. John C. Maxwell and R. W. Burchfield, 1959–1962. John C. Maxwell and Eric G. Stanley, 1963–1977. Eric G. Stanley, J. D. Fleeman, and D. Hewitt, 1977–1981.

Dickie A. Spurgeon

NOVEL REVIEW, THE. See TINSLEY'S MAGAZINE

O

ONCE A WEEK

Publishers Bradbury and Evans put out their first issue of *Once A Week* on 2 July 1859 under the editorship of Samuel Lucas. Just prior to this, they had been partners with Charles Dickens in the publication of *Household Words*.* After a quarrel between them and Dickens, the latter took legal action to discontinue *Household Words*, continuing the journal under a new name, *All the Year Round*.* Counter-attacking with *Once A Week*, Bradbury and Evans were accused by Dickens of producing a poor imitation of *Household Words* and *All the Year Round*. Thus, *Once A Week* was born in controversy.

In seeking a successor to *Household Words* and a competitor to *All the Year Round*, Bradbury and Evans, proprietors of *Punch*,* marshalled a distinguished band of artist-illustrators, including John Leech, John Tenniel, Charles Keene, Hablot K. Browne, and John Millais. In their prospectus for the new "Illustrated Miscellany of Literature, Art, Science, and Popular Information," they announced that they would feature "a considerable proportion of Fiction, including serial tales by Novelists of celebrity" and "discussions of Social characteristics," along with history, travel narratives, and biographies. Some foreign literature, art notices, and articles on natural history would be included, but "information on the popular aspects of Science and of new Inventions will be especially sought for, and it is confidently hoped, contributed by our most eminent discoverers and scientific authorities."[1]

Thus, to distinguish *Once A Week* from Dickens's publications, Bradbury and Evans would stress illustrations and charge a slightly higher price, give opportunities to unknown contributors, allow writers the option of signing their contributions, and avoid programs of social reform or party allegiances. The content would be general articles of good quality, to appeal to generally middle-class, liberal-minded readers of fair educational standard.

Introducing the first issue (2 July 1859) was an eleven-stanza poem by Shirley Brooks, illustrated by John Leech, the chief illustrator from 1859 to 1861.

> With no pregnant words, that tremble,
>   With awful Purpose, take we leave to come:
> Yet, when one enters where one's friends assemble,
>   'Tis not good manners to be wholly dumb.
> So, the bow made, and hands in kindness shaken,
>   Accept some lightest lines of rhyme, to speak
> Our notion of the work we've undertaken,
>   Our new hebdomadal—our *Once A Week*.

The poem goes on to pledge discretion, avoiding extremes of "madness," and to assure doctors, lawyers, and kings, as well as ordinary families of both "the rich" and "other thousands," that the magazine will provide pleasant entertainment and escape from dull routine,

> For quiet wanderings where the woodbine flowers,
>   And for the Altar, with its teachings meek;—
> Such is the lesson of this page of ours,
>   Such are the morals of our *Once A Week*.

Brooks's poem reflected the editorial principles of Samuel Lucas. Lucas came to *Once A Week* as a proven literary critic of the *Times*. He sought an Aristotelean decorum and unity in the stories, a balance between actual and imagined truth in the fiction. Thus, he preferred Thackeray's more realistic structuring to Dickens's convenient use of accident and improbability. He disapproved of sensationalism with "melodramatic surprises" and was therefore impressed by George Meredith's more philosophical and reflective approach. Lucas, a man with good taste in book illustration, sought artists whose drawings would be in harmony with the work they illustrated. Under his editorship, this was remarkably well achieved. One of the admirable features was the magazine's fine story illustrations, especially during the earlier years.

Shirley Brooks, who also worked on *Punch* and who became *Punch*'s second editor in the early 1870s, was a staff member of *Once A Week* and a regular contributor of poems, articles, and fiction, including his serialized *The Silver Cord*. Other "Punchites" publishing poems for *Once A Week* included Mark Lemon and Tom Taylor, *Punch*'s first and third editors. Other regular writers included George Henry Lewes, A. A. Knox (who contributed a "Last Week" review of national and international events), W. Bridges Adams, Edward Jesse, R. A. Benson, A. Stewart Harrison, Dr. Andrew Wynter, Albany Fonblanque, Jr., Dutton Cook, George Meredith, and Harriet Martineau.

During its first month of publication, the magazine contained papers on the scientific philosophy of Lewes and Huxley; a poem by Tennyson ("The Grandmother's Apology") and others by Theodore Martin, Caroline and Christina

Rossetti, and George Meredith; and the serialization of Charles Reade's *A Good Fight*, later to become *The Cloister and the Hearth* (1861).

Although Lucas wanted to publish "tales complete in one number," he gave in to pressure and the popular trend to serialize by using Reade's *A Good Fight*, followed by Meredith's *Evan Harrington*[2] and Brooks's *The Silver Cord*, all in early issues. In later volumes the magazine aimed toward shorter pieces, but eventually catered to popular taste with more sensational serialization, such as A. W. Dubourg's *Lillian's Perplexities* and Mrs. Henry Wood's *Verner's Pride*.

The most regular contributor under Lucas was Harriet Martineau, who, in addition to signed contributions, wrote a monthly feature, "The Months"; continued the news survey "Last Week" after Knox; provided national and international commentary in "From the Mountain"; and did a delightful series of "historiettes," provided with interpretive drawings by Millais.

Millais also did the illustrations for Tennyson's "The Grandmother's Apology" and Meredith's "Crown of Love." However, the most frequent illustrators of the first few volumes were Leech, Browne, Tenniel, and Keene, the latter of whom excelled in character drawings for fictional serials. Other *Once A Week* artistic contributions came from an impressive group including Hablot Browne ("Phiz"), J. Wolf, H. G. Hine, Frederick Walker, George du Maurier, M. J. Lawless, Charles Green, Percival Skelton, Frederick Sandys, Holman Hunt, James M. Whistler, E. J. Poynter, T. Sulman, G. J. Pinwell, M. E. Edwards, F. Eltze, R. T. Pritchett, and F. J. Slinger. Thus, along with its role as a vehicle for popular literature, *Once A Week* deserves a special place in the history of English book illustration. The fine engravings by Messrs. Swain add to this reputation.

Following Lucas's editorship, the magazine was guided by Lucas's chief assistant, Edward Walford, from 1865 to 1867, and by E. S. Dallas from 1868 until mid-1869.[3] Further research is needed on the leadership of the second decade, but examination of the magazine itself suggests that from August 1869 through its final issue in May 1880, *Once A Week* was guided by Mark Lemon and George Manville Fenn.

During the second decade, far fewer illustrations appeared. Smaller drawings were abandoned for one large two-page drawing, often not as good as the smaller ones had been. Some issues of the 1870s contained no illustrations at all. Periodic "postscripts" announced that "increasing popularity" demanded alterations of format, including the expansion from twenty-four to thirty-two pages in 1870, a larger size and cartoon cover in 1877, and the use of the magazine to publish complete novels during the final two years. But these postscripts on success, at least in the financial sense, were questionable. Financially *Once A Week* was failing, carrying seemingly desperate articles on life insurance and features on "products of the earth."

However, on 6 January 1872 a special series of marvelous drawings began. While these did not save the magazine from its demise a few years later, they deserve special recognition. Throughout 1872 Frederick Waddy contributed a series of full-page caricatures of various men of the day, each accompanied by biographical notes. Waddy's drawings, collected and published in 1873 under the title *Cartoon Portraits and Biographical Sketches of Men of the Day*, are among the finest examples of Victorian caricature. His commentaries, especially those on such literary figures as Tennyson, Browning, and Arnold, remain remarkably perceptive. But competition in magazine caricature art was stiff, especially from *Vanity Fair*,* which was publishing weekly chromolithograph cartoons by Pellegrini and others.

As William Buckler points out, *Once A Week* was, in spite of its literary merits, a commercial failure.[4] The total circulation for the first six months, July to December 1859, was about 570,000. During the next six months, this declined by more than 150,000; and it continued to decline by an average of about 35,000 a year until the mid-1860s. Thereafter, the decline was less dramatic, but steady. Several factors may account for this. Charles Dickens was competing with serializations of *A Tale of Two Cities* and *Great Expectations* in *All the Year Round*. Bradbury and Evans interfered with editorial matters; both Lucas and Walford were hampered by this.[5] *Once A Week* was not a crusader for social causes. The magazine made much use, perhaps too much, of unknown talent. And it was, as Meredith complained, too diverse, lacking a pointed purpose and characteristic tone.

Nonetheless, *Once A Week* was a respectable literary miscellany. Its writers were among the finest of those contributing to any popular Victorian periodical. And its contribution to the history of book-illustration art was outstanding.

Notes

1. For information on the early years of *Once A Week*, see William E. Buckler, "*Once A Week* Under Samuel Lucas, 1859–65," *Publications of the Modern Language Association of America* 67 (1952):924–41.

2. For accounts of the appearances of these two novels in *Once A Week*, see Royal A. Gettman's "Serialization and *Evan Harrington*," *Publications of the Modern Language Association of America* 64 (1949):963–75, and "Serialization of Reade's *A Good Fight*," *Nineteenth Century Fiction* 6 (1952):21–32.

3. See William E. Buckler, "E. S. Dallas's Appointment as Editor of *Once A Week*," *Notes and Queries* 195 (1950):279–80.

4. Buckler, "*Once A Week*," pp. 938–99.

5. Ibid. See also Buckler, "Edward Walford: A Distressed Editor," *Notes and Queries* 198 (1953):536–38.

Information Sources

BIBLIOGRAPHY

Buckler, William E. "E. S. Dallas's Appointment as Editor of *Once a Week*." *Notes and Queries* 195 (1950):279–80.

———. "Edward Walford: A Distressed Editor." *Notes and Queries* 198 (1953):536–38.

———. *"Once A Week* Under Samuel Lucas, 1859–65." *Publications of the Modern Language Association of America* 67 (1952):924–41.

Gettman, Royal A. "Serialization and *Evan Harrington." Publications of the Modern Language Association of America* 64 (1949):693–75.

———. "Serialization of Reade's *A Good Fight." Nineteenth Century Fiction* 6 (1952):21–32.

Whiteley, Derek P. "Du Maurier's Illustrations for *Once A Week." Alphabet and Image* 5 (September 1947):17–29.

INDEXES

Each volume indexed. 1859–1874 in *Poole's Index.*

REPRINT EDITIONS

Microform: Datamics, Inc., New York. Early British Periodicals (UMI), reels 725–732.

LOCATION SOURCES

American

Complete runs: Goucher College Library; Lloyd Library and Museum; Newberry Library.

Partial runs: Widely available.

British

Partial runs: Widely available.

Publication History

MAGAZINE TITLE AND TITLE CHANGES

Once A Week.

VOLUME AND ISSUE DATA

Volumes 1–13, 2 July 1859–30 December 1865; new series, volumes 1–4, 6 January 1866–28 December 1867; third series, volumes 1–13, 4 January 1868–29 August 1874; fourth series, volumes 1–11, 5 September 1874–27 December 1879; fifth series, volume 1, numbers 1–19, 1880.

FREQUENCY OF PUBLICATION

Weekly.

PUBLISHERS

1859–(?): Bradbury and Evans, London. (?)–1873: James Rice, London. 1873–1880: George Manville Fenn, London.

EDITORS

Samuel Lucas, 1859–1865. Edward Walford, 1865–1867. E. S. Dallas, January 1868–July 1869. Mark Lemon, 1869–1873(?). George Manville Fenn, 1873–1880.

Jerold J. Savory

OPEN WINDOW

A new illustrated monthly with plain blue cover and silver title, the *Open Window*, appeared in London in October 1910, a "little magazine" (before this designation was common) in its physical format, sedecimo, 6″ × 4 1/2″ as trimmed for binding. Without fanfare or manifestoes it identified its bent as "imaginative rather than controversial," opting for art whose "free vision" title and frontispiece suggest. Maxwell Armfield's black-and-white drawing is of an open casement window with sill wide enough for a book, clasped shut, on the left, and on the right a bird feeding from a dish, three other birds near, and more in the distance. The view includes a castle on a rock in the foreground, fields and clumps and lines of trees in the middle distance, a town on a winding river just beyond, mountains and clouds in the background, and a large patch of empty sky. The side frames and slightly arched top frame of the window appear to be of stone. Four hinges show on the right side, and there are two rings to fasten the casements to each other. The carefully delimited perspective, the orderly range of detail, and the uncrowded specificity characterize the scope and format throughout the two small volumes, whose tacit "cease publication" notice is the concluding illustration that immediately precedes the index of volume 2—in Keith Henderson's "Closing the Window" a woman is drawing the curtains on a nine-pane sash window with only the rising moon visible through the middle pane.

Each bound volume lists its contents in page order for its six consecutive numbers. Art titles are italicized; written pieces appear in capitals, with authors and illustrators in lower case. The noncommittal title page gives no editorial information but names the publisher as Locke Ellis of 18 Whitcomb Street, Leicester Square. Although Frederick Hoffman finds the "editor not established,"[1] there is no reasonable doubt that publisher and editor are the same person, Vivian Locke Ellis.

Ellis was a craftsman and a man of taste. While most of his career lay ahead of him at the time of *Open Window*, the young editor was able to attract considerable talent to his pages. Reviewing the principal contributors we get a sense of a network of artists and writers, earnest and competent, who would publish substantial volumes over three or four decades and actively promote the arts. Some of them undoubtedly found a first public in the hospitable and critically well-accepted monthly issues of *Open Window*. The influential weekly *Athenaeum** (see *RA*) followed with interest the fortunes of "this tiny magazine, which tries to keep, and succeeds in keeping, up well the tradition of belles lettres."[2]

The list of *Open Window* poets includes Ellis, Walter De la Mare, W. H. Davies, James Stephens, and John Drinkwater. Less familiar names include Robin Flower, whose *Eire and Other Poems* Locke Ellis published in 1910. His major interest was Celtic and medieval texts; during his thirty-eight years in the British Museum Department of Manuscripts, he undertook the catalogue of Irish manuscripts which was completed only after his death. Geoffrey Arundel Whitworth, who contributed both prose and verse, also helped Ellis with the publishing of *Open Window*, and his wife, Phyllis Grace Bell, performed secretarial chores. Whitworth's own books range through fiction, children's poetry, translations from the French, plays, and theater subjects. Yone Noguchi, art historian, poet, and fiction writer, is represented in verse and prose, with particularly charming pieces reflecting Japanese seasonal costumes. Edward Thomas, interestingly enough, contributed only prose.

There were plays by Lord Dunsany, Gilbert Cannan, and the versatile Hugh de Selincourt. Harold Hannyngton Child, actor, critic, and editor, published two stories in *Open Window*. E. M. Forster and Frank Swinnerton each contributed one story.

Further variety was provided by still others among the sixty-odd writers: Alfred Zimmern, Oxford professor of industrial relations; V. M. Garshin, translated from the Russian by C. Ratner; Douglas Goldring; F. Tennyson Jesse; William Shirlaw. Katherine Mansfield, already recognized by *New Age** as a promising new writer, moved out of that magazine to *Open Window* in the issue for December 1910 with "A Fairy Story," which one of her biographers spoke of as "an ironical little fable written in a manner . . . by no means acceptable to the New Age," which she signed "Katherina Mansfield" as though for a new start.[3]

Equally important were the many artists whose works graced *Open Window*. Jack Butler Yeats and Auguste Rodin permitted the magazine to use photo-reproductions of their work. Maxwell Armfield contributed three drawings and the frontispiece of volume 1. Keith Henderson, who illustrated Ellis's 1910 poems, published his drawings, poetry, and prose in *Open Window*. Charles March Gere, landscape painter and an illustrator for Kelmscott Press, long associated with William Morris, contributed, as did Sir Charles John Holmes, a landscape painter and art critic and director of the National Portrait Gallery and the National Gallery. Muirhead Bone, who became official artist for the War Office, produced the frontispiece for volume 2.

The service rendered to arts and letters by *Open Window* went well beyond the single year of its existence. Its integrity, balance, and good workmanship, appreciated as solid, but not hailed as particularly avant garde, achieved a measure of permanence in the two small but sturdy volumes of 390 and 370 pages which, selling for a modest four shillings and six pence each, were available as instant gift anthologies or permanent library acquisitions in the fall of 1911. Their makers had reason for satisfaction as they turned their creative hands to further work, leaving the magazine field open for a host of successors in the second decade of the twentieth century.

Notes

1. Frederick J. Hoffman, *The Little Magazine* (Princeton, 1947), p. 239. Vivian Locke Ellis seems to have many publications but no biography. The usual sources of dates and data are silent about him; a vain search for an obituary suggests that perhaps he is still alive at close to 100.

2. *Athenaeum*, no. 4351 (18 March 1911):316.

3. Antony Alpers, *Katherine Mansfield* (London, 1954), p. 134.

Information Sources

BIBLIOGRAPHY
Dictionary of National Biography. S.v. "Ellis, Locke."
Hoffman, Frederick J., et al. *The Little Magazine: A History and a Bibliography.* Princeton, 1947.
INDEXES
Each volume indexed.
REPRINT EDITIONS
None.
LOCATION SOURCES
American
Complete runs: Columbia University Library; Harvard University Library; Ohio State University Library; University of California Library, Berkeley; University of Michigan Library; University of Minnesota Library; Yale University Library. Partial runs: Henry E. Huntington Library; U.S. Library of Congress.
British
Complete runs: Birmingham University Library; Bodleian Library; British Museum; Cambridge University Library.
Partial run: National Library of Scotland, Edinburgh.

Publication History

MAGAZINE TITLE AND TITLE CHANGES
Open Window.
VOLUME AND ISSUE DATA
Volume 1, numbers 1–6, October 1910–March 1911; volume 2, numbers 1–6, April–September 1911.
FREQUENCY OF PUBLICATION
Monthly.
PUBLISHER
Locke Ellis, 18 Whitcomb St., Leicester Square, London, W.C.
EDITOR
Vivian Locke Ellis.

Mary Anthony Weinig

OXFORD AND CAMBRIDGE MAGAZINE, THE

William Morris, who was to cofound the *Oxford and Cambridge Magazine* in 1856, was a student at Exeter College at Oxford University in 1852. There, while studying Holy Orders, he began a lifelong friendship with a fellow student, Edward Burne-Jones of Birmingham. In 1853 Morris and Burne-Jones shared lodgings in the town, and their intellectual attraction for one another flourished. Of the beginnings of that friendship, Burne-Jones wrote: "One by one, for one cause or another, I dropped apart from my contemporaries there [Exeter], and by a fortnight's end it seemed settled that Morris and I only would be companions. . . . at Exeter we were very isolated, and before many weeks were past there were but three or four men in the whole College whom we visited or spoke to."[1]

Distraught at their choice of colleges and careers, the two young men turned to Cambridge University for intellectual and artistic companionship, and found friends at Pembroke College who shared their common interests in art and literature. Together the seven young men—Burne-Jones, Morris, Richard W. Dixon, Cormell Price, Charles J. Faulkner, Harry Macdonald, and William Fulford—formed a loose alliance that was to ultimately turn into a "new" Brotherhood, fashioned after the defunct Pre-Raphaelite Brotherhood which had preceded them.

The idea of forming an official "organization" of the seven compatriots first occured to Burne-Jones, and in May 1853 he wrote to Cormell Price about the idea:

> Remember, I have set my heart on our founding a Brotherhood. Learn Sir Galahad by heart. He is to be the patron of our Order. I have enlisted *one* [Dixon] in the project up here, heart and soul. You shall have a copy of the canons some day.
>
> > [Signed] General of the Order
> > of Sir Galahad[2]

A little later Burne-Jones wrote of his idea, and to some extent Morris's, of founding a "monastic settlement," and of enlisting "yet others in this Crusade and Holy Warfare against the age."[3] Like the Pre-Raphaelites, Burne-Jones wished to war against contemporary materialism, and judging from his letter to Price, his *modus operandi* included transcending the present and returning to medieval art for the true and pure.

It was not long before three sympathizers joined the original seven "Brothers": Godfrey Lushington of Balliol, and Vernon Lushington and Wilfred Heeley of Trinity College, Cambridge. On 16 October 1854 Burne-Jones wrote again to Price: "I was sick of home and idleness and longed with an ardent longing to be back with Morris and his glorious little company of martyrs—the monastery stands a fairer chance than ever of being founded; I know that it will be some day."[4]

While the Brotherhood was to become an effective force, it was not to follow the scheme Burne-Jones had originally suggested. Rather, early in 1855 Burne-Jones and Morris attended an exhibition at the Clarendon Press, which included two paintings on display from William Holman Hunt and Dante Gabriel Rossetti's watercolor of Dante drawing the head of Beatrice.[5] From that time on, their interest in the Pre-Raphaelite school of art was on the ascendancy.

At about the same time, the Brotherhood also came into possession of a copy of the *Germ*,* the short-lived little magazine of the Pre-Raphaelite Brotherhood, and their reading of "The Blessed Damozel" and "Hand and Soul" fanned their interest in the Pre-Raphaelites, and in Rossetti in particular. In the summer of 1855, when Morris, Burne-Jones, and Fulford were in France, they visited the Beaux Arts Department of the Paris Exposition, and on 25 July Fulford wrote from Chartres: "Conceive our delight to find no less than seven Pre-Raphaelite among the English pictures; three by Hunt, including the Light of the World, three by Millais, one by Collins."[6]

By the time the trio returned to England in August 1855, Morris and Burne-Jones had abandoned their plans to study Holy Orders and had instead embraced the world of art; Morris was to devote his talents to architecture, Burne-Jones to painting. The two were joined daily by the Oxford group, and when the men were alone, much of their time was passed in discussing plans for the Brotherhood.[7]

Although Richard Dixon was the first to advance the idea of a magazine to be published by the group, his action was only the final stage in a logical process that had been followed by the Brotherhood as a whole. They welcomed Dixon's proposal; were promised help from Heeley at Cambridge; chose a banal but descriptive title: the *Oxford and Cambridge Magazine: Conducted by Members of the Two Universities*; and immediately began plans for publication.

Meetings were held at the home of Cormell Price in Birmingham, where it was "unanimously agreed that there shall be no shewing off, no quips, no sneers, no lampooning in our Magazine." Dr. Birbeck Hill, a professor at Oxford and a friend of the group, recorded his impressions of one of those meetings of the Brotherhood in which the very eager young men were discussing their proposed magazine: "It was a new world into which I was brought. . . . The subjects I had always heard discussed were never discussed here, while matters on which I had never heard anyone speak formed here the staple of the talk."

The group agreed that the magazine was not to be used as a political forum, but rather was to contain "mainly Tales, Poetry, friendly critiques and social articles," divided in much the same way as the *Germ*. In September 1855 Burne-Jones wrote to his cousin, Maria Choyce, giving her complete details of the magazine and projecting its future:

> Shall I tell you about our Magazine, as you are so good as to take an interest in it? In the enclosed envelope I have sent you a prospectus. It appeared in nearly all the magazines of the month, and will be in the Quarterly reviews of January and in the Times. We have thoroughly set ourselves to the work now, banded ourselves into an exclusive Brotherhood of seven. Mr. Morris is proprietor. The expenses will fall heavily upon him, I fear, for it cannot be published under 500 per annum, exclusive of engravings which we shall sometimes give; he hopes not to lose more than 300, but even that is a great deal. Not one magazine in a hundred pays, but we are full of hope. We have such a deal to tell people, such a deal of scolding to administer, so many fights to wage and opposition to encounter that our spirits are quite rising with the emergency. We shall restrict ourselves to our present contributors, and not receive any indiscriminate

contributions, for we wish to keep before us one aim and end throughout the Magazine.[8]

Years later, Richard Dixon wrote to T. Hall Caine, outlining those "aims and ends" of the magazine:

Of this undertaking, the central notion was, I think, to advocate moral earnestness and purpose in literature, art, and society. It was founded much on Ruskin's teaching: it sprang out of immaturity and ignorance: but perhaps it was not without value as a protest against some things. The Pre-Raphaelite movement was then in vigour: and this Magazine came to be considered as the organ of those who accepted the ideas which were brought into art at that time; and, as in a matter, the successor of *The Germ*, a small periodical which had been published previously by the first beginners of the movement.[9]

The aims and ideals of the Pre-Raphaelites had been adopted by this new Brotherhood; the medievalism of Morris's prose and poetry, Burne-Jones's defense of Ruskin against the prominent critics of the day, Heeley's abhorrence of the materialism of his day, Fulford's adoption of Pre-Raphaelite heroes (especially Shakespeare) as subject matter, and Lushington's praise of Madox Brown and Dante Gabriel Rossetti all support the idea that Pre-Raphaelitism was the force behind the Morris/Burne-Jones Brotherhood. The *Oxford and Cambridge Magazine* was intended to be—and indeed was—a continuance of the philosophy of Rossetti and Hunt. Though the original Pre-Raphaelite Brotherhood had dissolved, the ideas that had been postulated had found a new place with this group of young men from the two universities.

Burne-Jones continued his description and explanation of the magazine for Maria Choyce:

We have bound ourselves to continue it for one year, and then if it does not turn out such a very great failure we have no limits to its continuance. It will go on till we are dead, I hope, and perhaps afterwards. I will send you the first number. . . . You will find a good deal of it very dry sometimes, but you will not mind that. For my part I have not much esteem for things done without labour.

And as for the Brotherhood, Burne-Jones wrote:

We may do a world of good, for we start from new principles and those of the strongest kind, and are as full of enthusiasm as the first crusaders, and we may perish in a year as others have done before. Well, if we are wanted I suppose we shall remain, and if not, what have we to want? Nothing, I know, for I can safely affirm for all that no mean and contemptible desire for a little contemporary fame, no mere purpose of writing for writing's sake has prompted one amongst us, but a sole and only wish to teach others principles and truths which they may not know and which have made us happy.[10]

The first issue of the magazine was published on 1 January 1856 under its full title by Messrs. Bell and Daldy of 186 Fleet Street. With a total of sixty-four pages of poetry, short stories, essays, and book reviews, all printed in double columns, the magazine sold at one shilling, a figure that was considered "too high for the amount of matter by some purchasers, and was thought to have injured circulation.[11] As in all issues of the magazine, contributors were not identified, but included Burne-Jones and Morris, as well as Georgiana Macdonald, future wife of Burne-Jones. Unlike the *Germ*, the *Oxford and Cambridge Magazine* contained no illustrations or etchings, but photographs of medallions of Carlyle and Tennyson executed by Thomas Woolner were mounted for binding with the first issue and were sold separately.

Before the second issue of the magazine appeared, Morris named William Fulford as editor, as explained in a letter from Burne-Jones to Price:

Topsy [a nickname for Morris] has surrendered active powers as editor to Fulford, who is now to be autocratical master of the magazine, with full powers to accept or reject or modify anything or everything submitted to his imperial jurisdiction—it will be a good thing for all of us, and a great relief to Topsy.

Having been assigned the task of editor at an annual salary of a hundred pounds, Fulford, in his new capacity, sent a copy of the January issue of the magazine to Tennyson, soliciting the Poet Laureate's opinion of its quality. He was understandably pleased with Tennyson's reply: "I find in such of the articles as I have read, a truthfulness and earnestness very refreshing to me: very refreshing likewise is the use of the plain 'I' in lieu of the old hackneyed unconscientious editorial 'we'. May you go on and prosper."

John Ruskin was another who received a complimentary copy of the first issue, and a note that he sent to Burne-Jones is paraphrased in Fulford's unpublished diary: "Ruskin has sent a most jolly note to Jones, promising to write for us when he has time, which won't be at present. But he is very despondent: he thinks people don't want honest criticism; and he has never known an honest journal get on yet."[12] Burne-Jones was ecstatic over Ruskin's response and wrote to Price in January, 1856: "I'm not Ted any longer, I'm not E.C.B. Jones now—I've dropped my personality—I'm a correspondent with RUSKIN, and my future title is "the man who wrote to Ruskin and got an answer.""[13]

Burne-Jones's enthusiasm was, of course, shared by the other members of the Brotherhood, if in varying degrees, and an optimistic view of the magazine's future was adopted. Seven hundred and fifty copies of the journal were printed initially; Morris requested 250 more copies of the first issue later in January.[14]

If the magazine was favorably received by some important literary figures of the day, the reviews in the periodical press were less than enthusiastic. The *Press* of London reviewed each of the twelve monthly issues, and at least one article appeared in the *Guardian, John Bull** (see *RA*), the *Athenaeum** (see *RA*), the *Saturday Review,** and the *Spectator** (see *RA*).

The first issue was met with mixed reactions, including an unfavorable review in the *Spectator* (which called the contents "amateur-like") and a prediction of an early demise in the *Athenaeum*: "New Year's Day is the flowering time of Periodical literature. . . . year after year we see the blossoms put forth . . . and cannot but regard them with a melancholy akin to that which we feel at the sight of a youth smitten with consumption." Others were kinder: the *Guardian* called the magazine "a remarkable publication" showing "reflection and care." *John Bull* noted that it possessed "warmth and youthful sentiment" which imparted life and interest to its contents.[15]

After its January issue, the major journals took no further notice of the *Oxford and Cambridge Magazine*, but an interesting development can be seen in the changing attitude of the *Press* (London), the only publication to review each issue of the periodical. The *Press* admired the first issue, and its critical acclaim increased with its review of the second issue: "The second number bears even more than the first unmistakable marks of high literary genius. . . . the magazine will soon rise to the front rank, if not to the very highest place among its contemporaries." Yet as each subsequent issue emerged, and as it became more apparent that the magazine was to be no more than an outlet for a group of undergraduates, the favorable criticism of the *Press* began to wane. The April issue, which contained a major piece on Carlyle by Lushington and a piece on Ruskin by Burne-Jones, was dismissed as "sickly discontent and affected enthusiasm, bred of idleness and inexperience." And the August issue, which included D. G. Rossetti's "The Burden of Nineveh" and a serious essay by Fulford entitled "Woman, Her Duties, Education, and Position," was criticized for being "coloured by the affectation which pervades this . . . unequal periodical."[16]

As praise and interest faded, so did the enthusiasm of the Brotherhood for the magazine. As early as August 1856 Burne-Jones wrote in his journal: "The Mag is going to smash—let it go. The world is not converted and never will be. It has had stupid things in it lately. I shall write not for it again, no more will Topsy—We cannot do more than one thing at a time, and our hours are too valuable to spend so."[17] Burne-Jones and Morris had come under the spell of Dante Gabriel Rossetti by the time that entry was recorded in the journal, and, ironically, the association of Rossetti and the Morris Brotherhood was at once the high point and the disruptive force for the periodical. In addition to "The Burden of Nineveh" in the August issue, Rossetti also contributed a revised version of his "Blessed Damozel" to November's issue (the original version of the poem had previously appeared in the *Germ*) and "The Staff and the Scrip" to the final issue of the magazine in December.

Yet, as a result of Rossetti's interest in the magazine, the attentions of Burne-Jones and Morris were diverted from the *Oxford and Cambridge* and toward the project of assisting Rossetti in the painting of decorative murals on the walls of the Oxford Union. Art had always been a principal interest of Burne-Jones, and, encouraged by Rossetti, Morris too was entertaining ideas of entering the field. In a letter to Andreas Scheu on 5 September 1883, Morris gave the Austrian socialist a brief sketch of his life, in which he described his brief flirtation with painting: "Having been introduced by Burne-Jones, the painter, who was my great college friend, to Dante Gabriel Rossetti, the leader of the Pre-Raphaelite school, I made up my mind to turn painter, and studied the art but in a very desultory way for some time."[18]

It was not lack of attention from Morris and Burne-Jones, however, that was the sole cause for the failure of the *Oxford and Cambridge Magazine*. The interests of other members of the Brotherhood also began to drift, beginning with Heeley, who married and left for India in September 1856. The magazine actually died of neglect by virtually everyone involved, with the possible exception of Fulford, who continued to edit it until its demise. Ultimately, that neglect, plus a gradual dissolution of the Brotherhood—and the fact that the magazine was operating at a deficit underwritten by Morris—forced the magazine to fold.

In December 1856 the twelfth and final issue of the *Oxford and Cambridge Magazine* was printed. In a letter to William Allingham on 18 December 1856, Rossetti announced the fate of the magazine that he had unwittingly helped to destroy: "You will see no more of the poor *Oxford and Cambridge*. It was 'too like the Spirit of *Germ*. Down, down;' and has vanished into the witches' cauldron."[19]

Two months after the cessation of the periodical, the *Saturday Review* published the definitive critique on the *Oxford and Cambridge Magazine*, evaluating its merits and shortcomings in proper balance and with an unbiased perspective:

> During the course of the last year a publication issued in monthly numbers from the two Universities bearing the title of the *Oxford and Cambridge Magazine*. . . . The issue having ceased, the separate numbers have been collected into a volume, which has recently been published. It is a volume worth looking into—not so much on account of its literary merits, as because, having been written almost entirely, we believe by undergraduate members of the Universities, it affords a curious specimen of the kind of thoughts and language current among the young men who are now preparing at those seats of learning, to fill offices in Church and State. . . . All the contributors wrote sermons, and securing the pulpit one after another, tell us what we should think and say. . . . They are gentle with us, but

firm—they are compassionate while they rebuke. It is one of their fancies to call the reader "brother."

... they are trying, in their own way, to get at what is good; and they are preserved by a familiarity with the great authors from the petty frivolity of smart writing.... In two or three years we may prophesy that these essayists will be excellent, sensible, humdrum creatures, and about as likely to think it a sacred duty to offer little sermons to an ungrateful public as to walk in cap and gown along Pall Mall.[20]

The critic for the *Saturday Review* was applying a hasty prophesy to the fifteen contributors to the *Oxford and Cambridge Magazine*, and certainly to Morris and Burne-Jones. At least that critic would live to see his predictions proven false.

Notes

1. Georgiana Macdonald Burne-Jones, *Memorials of Edward Burne-Jones* (New York, 1904), 1:72; hereafter cited as *Memorials*.

2. Ibid., 1:77.

3. Quoted in Lloyd Wendell Eshleman, *A Victorian Rebel: The Life of William Morris* (New York, 1940), p. 37.

4. J. W. Mackail, *The Life of William Morris* (London, 1899), 1:64; hereafter cited as *Life*.

5. Ibid., 1:71.

6. Ibid., 1:72.

7. *Memorials*, 1:115.

8. Ibid., 1:116–22; for quotations, see 1:116, 118, 121–22.

9. T. Hall Caine, *Recollections of Dante Gabriel Rossetti* (Boston, 1898), p. 36. For other opinions that the *Oxford and Cambridge Magazine* was an extension of the *Germ*, see F. S. Boase, *Rossetti and His Poetry* (London, 1918), p. 55; Graham Hough, *The Last Romantics* (London, 1949), p. 83; G. Maurey, *D. G. Rossetti et les Pre-Raphaelites Anglais* (Paris, n.d.), p. 19; William Michael Rossetti, "Introduction" to *The Germ: Being a Facsimile Reprint of the Literary Organ of the Pre-Raphaelite Brotherhood, Publ. in 1850* (London, 1882), p. 101; and Evelyn Waugh, *Rossetti: His Life and Works* (New York, 1928), p. 81.

10. *Memorials*, 1:122–24.

11. *Life*, 1:88.

12. Ibid., 1:88–89, 90 for correspondence of Burne-Jones, Tennyson, Ruskin.

13. *Memorials*, 1:127.

14. *Life*, 1:89.

15. *Spectator* (Supplement), 19 January 1856, p. 85; *Athenaeum*, 12 January 1859, p. 43; *Guardian*, 30 January 1856, p. 87; *John Bull*, 16 February 1856, p. 108.

16. *Press*, no. 145 (9 February 1856):140; no. 155 (19 April 1856):378; no. 172 (16 August 1856):787.

17. *Memorials*, 1:108.

18. *The Letters of William Morris*, ed. Philip Henderson (London, 1950), p. 185.

19. *Letters of Dante Gabriel Rossetti*, ed. Oswald Doughty and John R. Wahl, 2 vols. (Oxford, 1965–1967), 1:311.

20. T. C. Sander, "Undergraduate Literature," *Saturday Review*, 28 February 1857, pp. 196–97.

Information Sources

BIBLIOGRAPHY

Burne-Jones, Georgiana Macdonald. *Memorials of Edward Burne-Jones*. 2 vols. New York, 1904.

"Cambridge Periodicals." *Notes and Queries*, 6th ser., 11 (1885):133–34.

Gordon, Walter Kelly. "Pre-Raphaelitism and the *Oxford and Cambridge Magazine*." *Rutgers University Library Journal* 29 (1966):42–51.

Hosmon, Robert Stahr. "*The Germ* (1850) and *The Oxford and Cambridge Magazine* (1856)." *Victorian Periodicals Newsletter*, no. 4 (1969):36–47.

Mackail, J. W. *The Life of William Morris*. 2 vols. London, 1899.

INDEXES

Wellesley Index 2. In W. K. Gordon, "A Critical Selected Edition of William Morris's *Oxford and Cambridge Magazine*," Ph.D. dissertation, University of Pennsylvania, 1960.

REPRINT EDITIONS

Gordon, W. K., "A Critical Selected Edition of William Morris's *Oxford and Cambridge Magazine*," Ph.D. dissertation, University of Pennsylvania, 1960. AMS Press, New York.

Microform: English Literary Periodicals (UMI), reel 680.

LOCATION SOURCES

American

Widely available.

British

Complete runs: Birmingham Public Library; Bodleian Library; British Museum; Cambridge University Library; Edinburgh Public Library; Edinburgh University Library; Glasgow University Library.

Publication History

MAGAZINE TITLE AND TITLE CHANGES

The Oxford and Cambridge Magazine. Conducted by Members of the Two Universities.

VOLUME AND ISSUE DATA

Numbers 1–12, January–December 1856.

PUBLISHER

Messrs. Bell and Daldy, 186 Fleet Street, London.

EDITORS

William Morris, January 1856. William Fulford, February–December 1856.

Robert Stahr Hosmon

___ P ___

PAGEANT, THE

Each of the founders of the *Pageant* magazine came to the new journal with a wealth of credentials in the publishing business and a solid background in "little magazines" of the late nineteenth century. Charles Ricketts had established a reputation as an illustrator from his designs for a number of Oscar Wilde's books, including *The Picture of Dorian Gray* and *A House of Pomegranates*. In addition, Ricketts was in partnership with Charles Hazlewood Shannon in the ownership of the Vale Press, a significant little press of the time, and in the editorship of the *Dial* magazine. Charles Hazlewood Shannon, like Ricketts, was an illustrator and artistic designer with a solid reputation in the British arts community. Both men were members of the prestigious Royal Academy. Like Ricketts, Shannon was also involved in several of Oscar Wilde's projects, and he designed the binding for most of Wilde's plays, including *The Importance of Being Earnest*. In 1895 the two artists enlisted the aid of a third party, J. W. Gleeson White, in publishing a new journal to be called the *Pageant*. White was an established literary editor and had experience with magazines as well; he was the first editor of the *Studio* magazine in 1893.

It was agreed among the three that Shannon would be the artistic editor for the *Pageant*, White the literary editor, and Ricketts cover designer for what was to be a hardbound magazine in the style of a gift book. The publisher was to be Henry and Co. of London, a firm that included J. T. Grein as a partner and that had a reputation for publishing quality art books.

In matters of content, the editors agreed to include poetry, short stories, essays, plays, and reproductions of art, selected from among their friends and from some of the new, emerging artists and writers of the day. To this end, they solicited assistance from their coterie of contacts for material and for advice on contents within the magazine. One of those contacts, William Rothenstein, writes of those efforts in his memoirs: "Soon after my return from Spain I found that Ricketts and Shannon were planning a new annual, *The Pageant*. . . . Several of us younger men, [Charles] Conder, Max Beerbohm and myself, were to contribute. Shannon asked me to write to Whistler to induce him to give us a lithograph, and to Verlaine for a poem; Verlaine, he suggested, might write on Whistler's *Symphony in White*."[1]

Rothenstein also wrote to the poet Robert Bridges regarding the magazine and received a cautionary letter in return:

> I had forgotten all about the Pageant. What you told me at Oxford interested me very much, and made me wish to help in any way that I could—and I am of course extremely gratified by your wish to associate my small talents.
>
> There are real difficulties in the way of making such a magazine artistically successful. . . . I should like to have some sort of prospectus or scheme from the Editor, by way of assurance, e.g. that he is not coming out at the Kelmscott Press in "Troy type." That would be a Pageant indeed. Then if . . . he could tell me whether a poem of 50 or 60 lines would be too long. I have one of that length which I should like to send.[2]

When the first annual issue of the *Pageant* appeared in 1896, Bridges's poem, "The South Wind," was there, as were a number of selections by established as well as emerging artists. In style, the contents of that issue reflected the various interests of the *fin de siècle* in England and included works that could be termed symbolist, decadent, or aesthetic, as well as Pre-Raphaelite.

Writers contributing to the first issue included Algernon Swinburne ("A Roundel of Rabelais"), W. B. Yeats ("Costello the Proud, Oona Macdermott, and the Bitter Tongue"), John Gray ("Niggard Truth"), Lionel Johnson ("Four Quatrains"), and Max Beerbohm ("Be It Cosiness"). Paul Verlaine contributed, not a poem to accompany Whistler's *Symphony in White*, but "Monna Rosa," to complement Dante Gabriel Rossetti's painting by the same name, a reproduction of which appeared in the magazine. Reflecting the intellectual background of its audience, the *Pageant* printed Verlaine's poem in the original French, without translation, and also printed Maurice Maeterlinck's "Et S'il Revenait" in the original. Maeterlinck's play, *The Death of Tintagiles*, was printed in English, however, with a translation by Alfred Sutro.

In addition to works by Rossetti and Whistler, the first issue of the *Pageant* also included reproductions of art by Ricketts (an accompanying essay by Gleeson White on "The Work of Charles Ricketts" also appears), Rothenstein, Shannon, John Everett Millais, Charles Conder, G. F. Watts, and Sir Edward Burne-Jones. Selwyn Image, who had been involved in a number of little magazines in the past, including the *Hobby Horse*,* designed the title page, and Lucien Pissarro prepared the end-papers to complete the artistic presentation of the *Pageant*.

By the time the second and final issue of the *Pageant* appeared in 1897, Image's title page had been omitted, but Pissarro's and Ricketts's work remained; in addition, Gleeson White designed a paper wrapper to cover the hardbound volume. Like the first issue of the *Pageant*, the 1897 edition contained a mixture of 1890s literature and art. Notable contributions in literature included Edmund Gosse's "Jules Barbey d'Aurevilly," Austin Dobson's "A Postscript to Retaliation," John Gray's "On the South Coast of Cornwall" and "Light," Max Beerbohm's "Yai and the Moon," Maurice Maeterlinck's *The Seven Princesses* (translated by Alfred Sutro), Ernest Dowson's "On a Breton Cemetery," and Lionel Johnson's "The Lilies of France." Also included were art works by Gustave Moreau, Dante Gabriel Rossetti, Edward Burne-Jones (including two illustrations for the "Perseus" series), G. F. Watts, and Walter Crane, as well as by Shannon, Ricketts, and Pissarro.

The reasons for the demise of the *Pageant* are unknown, but speculation could lead to the conclusion that the publishers and editors perhaps never intended for the magazine to enjoy a long run. The hardbound, slick paper edition, including some art reproductions in color, was limited to 150 copies and sold for one pound, one shilling. Despite its short run, however, the *Pageant* remains one of the most attractive, one of the most professional, and one of the best little magazines published during the periodicals-rich 1890s.

Notes

1. William Rothenstein, *Men and Memories: Recollections of William Rothenstein, 1872–1900* (London, 1931), p. 226.
2. Ibid., p. 227.

Information Sources

BIBLIOGRAPHY

Le Gallienne, Richard. *The Romantic Nineties*. London, 1926.

Rothenstein, William. *Men and Memories: Recollections of William Rothenstein, 1872–1900*. London, 1931.

Winwar, Frances. *Oscar Wilde and the Yellow Nineties*. New York, 1940.

INDEXES

In Cyrena Norman Pondrom, "English Literary Periodicals: 1885–1918," Ph.D. dissertation, Columbia University, 1965.

REPRINT EDITIONS

Microform: Somerset House, Teaneck, N.J.

LOCATION SOURCES

American

Widely available.

British

Widely available.

Publication History

MAGAZINE TITLE AND TITLE CHANGES
   The Pageant.
VOLUME AND ISSUE DATA
   Number 1, 1896; number 2, 1897.
FREQUENCY OF PUBLICATION
   Annual.
PUBLISHER
   Henry and Co., 93 Saint Martin's Lane, London.
EDITORS
   J. W. Gleeson White, literary editor. Charles Hazlewood Shannon, arts editor.

Robert Stahr Hosmon

PALL MALL MAGAZINE

Name the *Pall Mall Magazine* to modern readers, and if the title seems familiar, they are probably confusing it with the *Paul Mall Gazette*, that crusading (and sensationalist) London evening paper whose famous late Victorian editors included John Morley and W. T. Stead. The monthly *Pall Mall Magazine*, first published in 1893, numbered Hall Caine, Arthur Conan Doyle, Kier Hardie, Bret Harte, Rudyard Kipling, Lewis Morris, Roden Noel, A. C. Swinburne, Theodore Watts-Dunton, and Israel Zangwill among the literary contributors to its first volume, as well as thirteen members of Parliament. Some of its early artists were Aubrey Beardsley, Sir Frederick Leighton, and Laurence Housman. Later writers included George Meredith, Thomas Hardy, W. E. Henley, W. H. Mallock, Joseph Conrad, Robert Louis Stevenson, Arthur Symons, John Davidson, C. W. Dilke, W. M. Rossetti, Katharine Tynan, Olive Custance, Ford Madox Hueffer (later Ford Madox Ford), William Sharp, Hilaire Belloc, Austin Dobson, G. K. Chesterton, Jack London, and John Masefield.

Yet, recently, when eleven scholars of Victorian periodicals listed over 400 important nineteenth-century serials, none thought enough of *Pall Mall* to mention it.[1] The magazine's oblivion among these period specialists may be partially attributed to its being more Edwardian than Victorian, but this critical disregard is also a judgment of *Pall Mall*'s uneven quality. From auspicious beginnings there was a rapid decline that was reversed only as the century waned. And in its final years, before *Pall Mall* was absorbed by *Nash's*, work by H. G. Wells, P. G. Wodehouse, G. B. Shaw, Chesterton, Belloc, and Kipling appeared, and if circulation did not reach the early mark, at least the literary standard of the first years was approached.

Pall Mall wrote its autobiography in May 1914: "Coming of Age: Twenty-One Years of the *Pall Mall Magazine*" (53:569–80). Ironically, in view of its absorption that September by *Nash's*, it was almost an obituary. Albert Kinross, in his encomium, recalls how William Waldorf Astor founded *Pall Mall*:

Here we had an American gentleman of culture and vast fortune, who, like Lorenzo the Magnificent or the Duke of Weimar, was eager to encourage the noblest that was being sung in verse or written in plain prose. In default of a court, he had to content himself with a plain magazine; it seems to be the modern equivalent. Associated with Mr. Astor were Lord Frederic[k] Hamilton and Sir Douglas Straight; these were our first Editors. [53:570]

Kinross's view is retrospective. By 1914 the concept of the 1890s as Bodley Head versus the Henleyites was well established. Holbrook Jackson's *The 1890's* had been published three years earlier, so it was easy enough to reconstruct the establishment of *Pall Mall* as a deliberate attempt to stay above the fray between the decadents and the imperialists.

Another perspective on the 1890s could show a period of contention between the disengaged (aesthetes) and the involved (Henley's school at the *National Observer* [*Scots Observer**]), and in this respect anyone who stood aloof from the controversy was in the aesthetic camp. Of course, by 1914 critics were already hyphenating ''aesthetic-decadent.'' Hamilton and Straight's position was stated in an October 1893 editorial preface to the first volume: ''The Magazine was started in the belief that there was a large and influential section of the reading public who would cordially welcome and heartily support a periodical that aimed at securing and maintaining a high and refined literary and artistic standard.''

Initially, the publishers were largely faithful to this statement, printing quality work from across the spectrum. Thomas Hardy's short story, ''An Imaginative Woman,'' and George Meredith's *Lord Ormont and His Aminta* appeared in the next two volumes. The decadents were poetically represented by Arthur Symons's ''Flowers'' and Paul Verlaine's remembrance (in French) of Oxford. On the other side was Kipling with ''Back in the Army Again'' and ''Follow Me 'Ome.'' Also in these late 1893 and early 1894 volumes was work by W. H. Mallock, Bram Stoker, and Robert Hichens, as well as by such mediocrities as Grant Allen, Alfred Austin, Richard Le Gallienne, Edmund Gosse, and Ouida (Louise Ramé). The standards of the earliest volumes could therefore be described as relatively, but not uniformly, high.

Two trends were observable as early as 1895. First, *Pall Mall* was increasingly relying on serials by such popular writers as H. Rider Haggard, Ouida, and Allen. Few major figures, literary or political, contributed in 1894–1895, as the editorial thrust of the periodical seemed to shift. Evidently the editors or publishers were increasingly unwilling or unable to remunerate major writers. Instead, Hamilton and Straight relied on serial fiction to develop and maintain readership, although they did run R. L. Stevenson's posthumous ''St. Ives: The Adventures of a French Prisoner in England'' (completed by Arthur Quiller-Couch) in 1896, the year Hamilton became sole editor. Second, *Pall Mall* became unabashedly philistine, catering to readers interested in cricket, yachting, field sports, and art collectibles, among other middle-class interests. An article on silver nefs was "sanctioned and personally revised by H.R.H. the Duke of Saxe-Coburg-Gotha." The "Sport of the Month" articles separately addressed "Partridge Shooting" and "Pheasant Shooting." Monthly photographs and descriptions of great houses—Longleat and Belvoir Castle, for example—became a regular feature.

There were few redeeming aspects to a periodical that published the "Zenda" fiction of Anthony Hope, "A Duel with Snakes," by Captain D. Beames and Edgar Jepson, and especially "The Prayer of the Cattle Smitten with Rinderpest" (with three illustrations). Yet one was the 1898 presentation of some previously unpublished poems by D. G. Rossetti, with critical comments by his brother, William Michael. Fortunately, this decline was reversed, and if *Pall Mall* never realized its early promise, in 1899 it resumed the regular publication of significant work. Henley briefly became the regular bookman, replacing Quiller-Couch, who had supplanted Israel Zangwill.

From 1901 until 1905 *Pall Mall* was edited by George R. Halkett, who deserves credit for publishing work by Max Beerbohm, George Meredith ("The Voyage of the Ophir"), Leslie Stephen, William Archer, Hueffer, Henley, Masefield, and Zangwill. *Typhoon*, by Joseph Conrad, was serialized in volume 26 (1902), and under Halkett's editorship Jack London became a regular contributor.

The last acknowledged editor of *Pall Mall* was Charles Morley, in 1905. Beginning in 1906, no editor was listed through the eight years the magazine remained an autonomous enterprise. The editorial anonymity remains unexplained, but it did not reflect the quality of the periodical, at least for a few years. Davidson, Dobson, and Masefield sent poetry; London, Conrad, Wells, and Mrs. Ward published fiction; and notables as divergent as Sylvia Pankhurst and Count Zeppelin contributed nonfiction.

However, readership declined, and less revenue dictated a greater reliance on journeymen. Furthermore, if circulation were to be restored, a new format seemed desirable. Accordingly, beginning in July 1909, each monthly issue ended with the *Pall Mall Story Book*—belles lettres, short fiction, and poetry intended for a less discriminating audience. The balance of the magazine was largely unchanged, as fiction, poetry, and articles of the usual kind were published. Through 1912 the *Story Book*, rather than prominent contributors, was relied on to attract younger readers and families. Perhaps the most notable authors in this insipid period of *Pall Mall* were Laurence Housman, Kate Perugini, the Rev. Sabine Baring-Gould, and Lt. Gen. Sir Robert Baden-Powell.

The effulgence of 1913 was brief, but in its last full year of autonomy *Pall Mall* was again a distinguished periodical. G. K. Chesterton published "The Wisdom of Father Brown" and four more stories about this most lovable detective. Kipling, Wodehouse, Belloc, Alfred Noyes, and Mrs. Tynan appeared, as did a new poet, Rupert Brooke, whose career proved as brief as *Pall Mall*'s. A symposium on "Why Woman Should Have the Vote" included such contributors as Shaw, Granville Barker, Zangwill, Arthur Pinero, and Mrs. Ward, the last named opposing the idea. If this penultimate level was not sustained in 1914, at least no one had to apologize for a magazine that published Desmond MacCarthy, Compton Mackenzie, Belloc, Wodehouse, and Chesterton in its final issues.

When *Pall Mall* merged with *Nash's* in September 1914, the publishers could scarcely be blamed for pretending that the demise was a happy event. Ironically, it was an appropriate ending. The besetting fault of *Pall Mall* was its uncertain identity. Beginning as a serious literary and artistic periodical, an illustrated journal of belles lettres and significant nonfiction, it gradually lost its purpose. Originally eclectic and claiming indifference to aesthetic quarrels and cultural pettiness, it became the organ of the philistines, as it glorified stately houses, silver nefs, and shooting. Recovering from this lapse of taste, it again published significant work by important authors: Meredith, Conrad, Hueffer, and London, to name only a few. However, when circulation ebbed, the publisher once more sought a mass audience, this time through the *Story Book*, only belatedly to restore quality to its writing in the final volumes. In its twenty-one years, *Pall Mall* altered its personality too often, so there may be retributive justice in its last identity as an appendage—the lesser half of a hyphenated title. *Pall Mall* was not silenced by the guns of August, but by its own diffidence or reluctance to declare itself.

Note

1. Michael Wolff, "The 'Key' Serials Project: A Finite Experiment in Victorian Periodicals Bibliography," *Victorian Periodicals Review* 13 (1980):95–102.

Information Sources

INDEXES
    Each volume indexed.
REPRINT EDITIONS
    Microform: Early British Periodicals (UMI), reels 732–745.
LOCATION SOURCES
American
    Partial runs: Widely available.
British
    Complete runs: British Museum; Cambridge University Library.
    Partial runs: Widely available.

Publication History

MAGAZINE TITLE AND TITLE CHANGES
    Pall Mall Magazine. (Merged with *Nash's* in October 1914 to form *Nash's and Pall Mall*.)
VOLUME AND ISSUE DATA
    Volumes 1–53, numbers 1–253, May 1893–August 1914.
FREQUENCY OF PUBLICATION
    Monthly.

PUBLISHERS
>May 1893–December 1912: George Routledge & Sons, Limited, 18 Charing Cross Road, London W.C./Newton Street, Holborn, London W.C. January 1913–August 1914: Iliffe & Sons, Ltd., 20 Tudor Street, London, E.C.

EDITORS
>Lord Frederick Spencer Hamilton and Sir Douglas Straight, May 1893–November 1896. Lord Frederick Spencer Hamilton, December 1896–December 1900. George Roland Halkett, January 1901–August 1905. Charles Robert Morley, September 1905–December 1912. No editor is listed from January 1913 to August 1914.

Daniel Rutenberg

PEARSON'S MAGAZINE

Sir Arthur Pearson sought out the "public created by compulsory education, unused to reading, and demanding stories and information which could be appreciated and understood without any great initial culture or without any great necessity for thought."[1] To please that public, Pearson created several magazines, beginning with *Pearson's Weekly* (1890), which bore the motto "To Instruct, to Elevate, to Amuse." This magazine became the prototype for those that followed: *Home Notes* (1894), *Pearson's Magazine* (1896), an American *Pearson's Magazine* (1899), and *Novel Magazine* (1905). All of his publications, which included newspapers, were intended for popular rather than high-brow reading. He aimed to make people feel good about his publications and himself through name recognition and gimmickry. Pearson's Pipes, Pearson's Cigars, Pearson's Soap, Pearson's Puzzle, and Pearson's Patent Penholder were made available to the public, and the Missing Word Competition gave the circulation a tremendous lift. Mr. Chamberlain described him as "the greatest hustler I have ever known."[2]

The son of a poor clergyman, Pearson was educated by his father after only two years at Winchester. He won a clerkship offered as a prize in a competition in George Newnes's *Tit-Bits*, a new species of popular journal. A year later he became manager. With Peter Keary and Ernest Kessell, also from *Tit-Bits*, he established Pearson's Limited, initially financed by Stephen Mills's 3,000 pounds. Mills grew apprehensive when he saw his money swiftly disappearing and dissolved the partnership. However, Sir William Ingram, the proprietor of the *Illustrated London News*, lent Pearson another 3,000 pounds, and six years later Pearson's was converted into a limited liability company with a capital of over 400,000 pounds.[3]

Pearson was involved in all areas of the new magazine from the first issue, writing several articles, editing, publishing, running a competition for clergymen and ministers with annuities for prizes, including a free Railway Insurance Policy of 1,000 pounds, and visiting every newsagent of importance in the United Kingdom. In number 3, "Home Notes" began on the women's page and became popular enough to evolve into a weekly. Pearson had great energy, ambition, and the common touch; he knew how to appeal to ordinary people's desire to identify with the famous, and to their need for security, recognition, and self-esteem. In addition to contests to be won, there was also an annual appeal to the reader's generosity via the Fresh Air Fund, which provided a week in the country for poor city children. His magazines were also very direct in their appeal: "How to Become Rich," for example, was written by leading self-made millionaires of America.

Pearson was an entrepreneur who showed concern for the readers. During an influenza epidemic, Pearson and fifty others sprayed eucalyptus oil on copies of *Pearson's Weekly* because a doctor maintained that the best preventative for influenza was eucalyptus. Yet Pearson also had shortcomings:

> Apart from its admirable philanthropic aspect, Pearson's career is perhaps more alarming than edifying. Intellectually he was unfitted to guide, much less to form, public opinion. He knew nothing of philosophy, little of history, and less of literature and art. His opinions were the caprice of his uncriticized intuitions, and he was resentful of opposition, impatient of argument. Happily for his readers, whom he sought to stampede rather than to inform, his tastes were harmless and his nature wholesome. ... He paid in his own person most of the penalties which nature exacts of the "hustler."[4]

An audience of "men, women and elder children of every class, creed and profession" were assured that in Pearson's magazines "no word or suggestion will ever appear that is capable of giving offense to the most fastidious."[5] To enhance its appeal to a popular audience, *Pearson's* included photographs that often depicted a process so clearly that the idea could be understood from simply looking at the pictures and reading only the captions. Such titles as "Multiplication Made Easy," "Nature's Practical Jokes," "Study of Splashes," and "Photographing Flying Bullets" were often more novel than educational, although the emphasis on scientific discovery showed a concern for the education of readers. Other picture series frequently presented famous people, depicting their families, their houses, or their art. To create wonder about the ordinary and tell a good story was an editorial goal. For example, "The Story of the Umbrella" in volume 6 showed the use of state umbrellas in China and Abyssinia and the worship of umbrellas in India.

The fiction was sometimes complete in one issue and sometimes serialized. Its emphasis on romance and adventure was indicated by such titles as "A Trooper in Love" by Roger Pocock, "The Last of the Borgias" by Fred M. White, and the very popular *Adventures of Captain Kettle* by Cutcliffe Hyne. Contributing writers included Rudyard Kipling, Max Pemberton, and Rafael Sabatini. None of the writers first introduced in *Pearson's Magazine*—Hyne, Baroness Orazy, Ethel M. Dell, and Ralph Hodgson—achieved a lasting reputation. The only fiction to retain its popularity was Kipling's *Stalky and Company*, and that honor had to be shared with the *Windsor Magazine*,* which actually serialized more of the book.

The drawings that accompanied these stories usually depicted fashionably or exotically costumed pretty young women in the company of handsome young men or menacing villains. The cover featured a colored picture of a pretty girl and carried titles of special items within the issue.

Normally issues averaged 120 pages. In a typical issue from 1898 there appeared one short story and articles on art, travel, religion, exercise or sport, and science. In general, the magazine celebrated discovery, including new inventions and the strange wonders of other countries. Like other family-oriented magazines, it was patriotic and immensely proud of royalty and the military. Fascination with the famous led to such articles as "The German Emperor and His Hobbies," and concern for the ordinary was shown via pictures in "Self-Protection on a Cycle."

Whole issues were sometimes printed in red, blue, or brown ink, including the pictures, although occasionally only the pictures were colored. In 1901 an illustrated article on "How a Woman Journalist Faced Death" (she was rescued by men) suggests an early use of a tantalizing title device. Each December issue began the new volume number and was expanded to include more stories. The cover and a few items at the front were on a Christmas theme, and some Christmas issues also had items for younger children. In general, the magazine both created and satisfied curiosity in order that the reader would feel simultaneously informed and entertained.

Notes

1. Sidney Dark, *The Life of Sir Arthur Pearson* (London, 1918), p. 73.
2. *Dictionary of National Biography*, s.v. "Pearson, Cyril Arthur."
3. Dark, p. 61.
4. *Dictionary of National Biography*, s.v. "Pearson, Cyril Arthur."
5. Dark, p. 50.

Information Sources

BIBLIOGRAPHY
Dark, Sidney. *The Life of Sir Arthur Pearson*. London, 1918.
Dictionary of National Biography. S.v. "Pearson, Cyril Arthur."
Tye, J. R. *Periodicals of the Nineties*. Oxford, 1974.
INDEXES
   None.
REPRINT EDITIONS
   None.
LOCATION SOURCES
   American
      Partial runs: Chicago Public Library; University of Illinois Library; U. S. Library of Congress.

British

Complete run: British Museum.

Partial runs: Birmingham University Library; Cambridge University Library; Dundee Public Library; Manchester Public Library.

Publication History

MAGAZINE TITLE AND TITLE CHANGES
   Pearson's Magazine.
VOLUME AND ISSUE DATA
   Volumes 1–88, January 1896–November 1939.
FREQUENCY OF PUBLICATION
   Monthly.
PUBLISHER
   C. Arthur Pearson, Henrietta Street, London.
EDITOR
   C. Arthur Pearson.

Barbara Quinn Schmidt

POETRY AND DRAMA. See CHAPBOOK, THE

POETRY REVIEW, THE

Originally published in May 1909 as the *Poetical Gazette*, the *Poetry Review* is the official journal of the Poetry Society (London). The title was changed to *The Poetry Review* in January 1912 and to the shorter *Poetry Review* in 1970. From its inception the journal has published critical essays on poetry and poetics, reviews of books of poetry, poetical drama, and selections of poetry by both known and unknown authors. Early issues of the *Poetry Review* from 1912 to 1916 incorporated sporadic numbers of the *Poetical Gazette* that contained news of interest to members of the society, ranging from announcements of poetry competitions and subjects for lectures to reports on readings and recitals to short critical book notices of recent publications of poems.

The journal's early emphasis was primarily elocutionary and belletristic, tempered frequently by a tumidly precious tone. One book notice in the *Gazette* section of the first issue, for instance, offered the hope that the "daintily produced volume" in question might "open the magic casement to eyes that have not looked hitherto upon the faery land of poesy" (1:51).

Officially, the *Poetry Review*, like the Poetry Society, was designed to assist in the "general recognition and appreciation of Poetry" by encouraging public and private readings (1:52). The members of the society wanted to bring together lovers of poetry, to encourage public recitals, to publish poems, to offer premiums for poetry, and to popularize interest in poetry. Their objective was nothing less than a complete poetic renaissance, and to that end they diligently formed local centers and reading circles all over Great Britain and the world. From the outset, much of the emphasis was placed on poetry recitals that were largely excuses for extravagant social events for superannuated votaries of the muse. At its inception the journal proposed to provide more than news of readings and society announcements. It published a wide variety of poetry with an international focus; issues were projected for American, German, French, and Italian verse. One issue was devoted to women poets and another to the Celtic Renaissance, in full swing at the time. Other issues dealt with such diverse topics as Christian mystic poets, the "school of Whitman," the Elizabethans, and poetry recitation.

In 1912 the Poetry Society numbered among its extraordinarily lengthy list of distinguished vice-presidents Herbert Trench, Henry Newbolt, Wilfrid Blunt, G. K. Chesterton, Ellen Terry, Maurice Hewlett, E. de Selincourt, Edmund Gosse, W. W. Skeat, F. S. Boas, Sir H. Beerbohm Tree, W. M. Rossetti, Alfred Noyes, Gilbert Murray, John Galsworthy, Arnold Bennett, T. Sturge Moore, and Israel Zangwill. A similarly lengthy list of patrons and honorary members included, among others, Sir Arthur Pinero, Oscar Browning, Theodore Watts-Dunton, Marie Corelli, W. H. Lever, Sir Lawrence Alma-Tadema, A. C. Benson, and W. H. Hudson.

In spite of the many famous literary figures who were listed as vice-presidents and honorary members, the most powerful single force behind the magazine was the relatively unknown William Galloway Kyle, the founder and director of the society from its beginnings until his death in 1967 at the age of ninety-two, and editor of the *Poetry Review* for thirty-one years, from 1916 to 1947. During his editorship the journal prospered and circulation increased. The *Review* enlisted the assistance of prominent, wealthy literary enthusiasts from both England and America and generally fulfilled its charge as a public relations instrument tailored to the rather antiquated tastes and traditional wishes of the society.

For the purpose of literary history, however, the initial year of the journal's publication and the years that followed Kyle's tenure as editor, were by far the most interesting in terms of contributors and quality. Initially the *Poetry Review* promised to provide in England the brand of literary excitement that Harriet Monroe's *Poetry*, also founded in 1912, was soon to provide for America. But the promise went unfulfilled. The first editor was Harold Monro. Prior to his involvement with the *Poetry Review*, while living abroad, Monro had developed a desire to publish a journal devoted mainly to poetry criticism. It would attempt to explain poetry in relation to life in the twentieth century. When he returned to England in 1911, he was approached by the Poetry Society and asked to edit the *Poetical Gazette*. He refused, offering instead to start an independent monthly review that he argued would greatly benefit the members of the society. The idea for the formation of the *Poetry Review* was thus conceived, and Kyle and the society agreed to the venture. Monro would be the editor, but he would be overseen by a committee from the society. Monro was not sympathetic with the major interests and objectives of the society. He was a Georgian, but also a friend and supporter of the experimentalists, rebelling against what he believed were outmoded literary interests and objectives. He perceived that his task as editor was to provide a public forum for the serious critical discussion of poetry, and to restore the public interest in the art of poetry as something more than flat echoings of nineteenth-century traditions, many of which the Poetry Society at the time obligingly and uncritically supported.[1] As Marvin Magalaner has pointed out, "One need look no further than the second page of Monro's first number ... for evidence that modern English poetry was in the doldrums." An advertisement placed by John Lane, the prominent publisher, listed as the "Best Poetry" of the time works by Alfred Austin, who was still writing 1890s *fin de siècle* poetry; William Watson, the atrabilious traditionalist who by 1910 was already an anachronism; and Olive Custance, Ethel Clifford, and Francis Coutts, all of whom have long since been forgotten.

From the outset, Monro and the Poetry Society were destined to part company. To begin with, he was never pleased with the necessity of incorporating the *Poetical Gazette*, the society's newsletter, into the journal. He objected to its tone and, as he would later admit, "to the irrelevant snobbery of the Society's list of patrons."[2] He had no legal agreement and, hence, no protection from the society, consenting on his own to defray expenses for one year. Early meetings with the committee formed to oversee his work resulted in bitter stalemates. Eventually the meetings ceased altogether. From November 1911 to January 1912 Monro and Arundell del Re, his assistant editor, worked tirelessly toward a scheduled January 1912 publication deadline. When the the first number of the *Poetry Review* appeared—on schedule—it was bound in brown paper and cost six pence. By the end of the year, Monro was objecting openly to the inclusion of the *Gazette*, disturbed particularly by a *Gazette* notice in the February issue that offered for a fee "authoritative critical opinion" of manuscripts sent to the society. He was also arguing for the need to publish the journal quarterly instead of monthly because it would give him more time for preparation. The society insisted, however, that the *Gazette* continue to be included, along with the offensive offer to criticize manuscripts for a fee, and that the *Poetry Review* remain a monthly. In the December number the following notice appeared: "Mr. Harold Monro, having decided to enlarge the scope of his periodical by issuing it quarterly under the title POETRY AND DRAMA [,] THE JOURNAL OF THE POETRY SOCIETY Beginning with the next number, JANUARY, will be issued under the Editorship of MR STEPHEN PHILLIPS and a brilliant list of contributors has been secured. . . . " In addition to his editorial duties, Phillips, who had "thrilled the world," according to the notice, with "Marpessa," "Herod," "Ulysses," and "Nero," would "contribute a monthly leading article on the eternal significance of Poetry" (1:563). Monro's short career as editor of the *Poetry Review* was ended.

Monro was now free to publish a journal according to his own design. *Poetry and Drama*, a quarterly, made its appearance in the spring of 1913. Monro acknowledged the problems he had encountered with the editorship of the *Poetry*

Review, admitting that by September of the preceding year it had become quite clear to him that "the future of the *Review* depended entirely on the degree to which it could be kept clear of the influence of the Poetry Society."[3] Though it was short-lived (the last issue appeared in December 1914), Monro's new journal moved forward to include in its pages works by the emerging Imagists and other experimental writers. In the years following Monro's editorship, the *Poetry Review* moved backwards, miring itself in an outworn tradition of decorative and high-blown verse written in poor imitation of Victorian and Romantic predecessors.

For the one year that Monro had control, the journal demonstrated the potential for a quality of excellence that was both timely and exacting. Monro had been supported in his efforts that year by Ezra Pound, who was in England espousing Imagism. Though Pound and Monro did not agree philosophically on the social function of poetry, Pound, along with F. S. Flint and T. E. Hulme, threw the full weight of his support behind Monro and his new magazine.[4] Early numbers of the *Poetry Review* for 1912 contained critical essays on poets and poetics written by Monro, Lascelles Abercrombie, Henry Newbolt, Trevor Blakemore, and John Drinkwater. The October number included an article by Harriet Monroe on "Modern American Poetry" that Monro had solicited as part of his enthusiastic support for the publication of *Poetry* magazine. The February issue published a selection of poems and a "Prologomena" written by Pound. Poems by Maurice Hewlett, John Drinkwater, Katharine Tynan, James Stephens, and T. Sturge Moore also appeared in the journal. A sampling of William Carlos Williams's work appeared in the October issue with a foreword on Williams's poetry submitted by Pound. Other writers whose work appeared in the *Poetry Review* in 1912 were Rupert Brooke, G. K. Chesterton, W. H. Davies, James Elroy Flecker, W. W. Gibson, J. C. Squire, Walter De la Mare, and Laurence Binyon. Richard Aldington, Monro's personal friend, submitted reviews; del Re, the journal's assistant editor, acted as chief translator. The 1912 volume included quality items written by recognizable, exciting, and innovative writers who were establishing new directions along which the main traditions of twentieth-century poetic theory would progress.

The first number to appear in 1913 under the editorship of Stephen Phillips made it clear that the new editorial policy for the *Poetry Review* would proceed along directions quite distinct from those that had been advocated by Monro. Not only is there a noticeable decrease in the number of recognizable names publishing in the *Poetry Review* after 1912, but the quality of the contributions deteriorates. Phillips was somewhat of an anachronism, a throwback to the nineteenth century, unable to see beyond his Victorian literary inheritance. He consciously aped the style and sentiments of earlier nineteenth-century writers, appealing solicitously to tradition with a naive, quasi-religious zeal for the preservation of highly decorative, rhetorical verse, against what he and the Poetry Society feared were the intentions of the new literary iconoclasts bent on the destruction of traditional Western literary ideals. He saw himself as a sentinel guarding revered literary traditions from those who would destroy them if they were left unprotected. His primary literary interest was verse drama—lengthy, austere pieces full of the pomp of empire, with wooden characters, predictable themes, and conventional moral sentiments. His tastes are reflected in the pages of the journal, overloaded more often than not with tediously long poetic dramas. The January issue for 1915, for instance, included B. L. Bowhay's *The State Supreme: A Poetic Play in Three Acts*, all sixty-three pages of it, followed by a turgid six-page patriotic poem by Douglas Spens Steuart written "To the Prussianizers of Germany." The poem, capitalizing on the strong anti-German sentiment produced by the war, was a poor imitation of Browning. The December 1915 issue included a review of periodicals that dismissed much of the new Imagist poetry that had appeared in the *British Review* as so much perversity (6:585). Earlier, in 1914, the journal had subscribed to the view that Florence Earle Coates was "the leading living poet of the United States" and had openly advanced the position that the pages of the *Poetry Review* would preserve the grandeur of a tradition of verse associated with the greatest poets in the English language from "futurists" bent on the destruction of traditional European art. It was also in 1914 that the journal, in order to increase circulation, started to publish, along with the notes and announcements of the Poetry Society appearing in the *Gazette*, the proceedings of the British Empire Shakespeare Society. But it must be remembered that in the eyes of Kyle and the Poetry Society, the purpose of the journal was not to provide, as Monro had hoped, a forum for critical debate, poetic reform, and written attempts to relate poetry to life in the modern world. The conservative Poetry Society from the outset saw the *Poetry Review* as a means of providing printed journalistic support for its efforts to promote the appreciation of poetry primarily through public readings. To that end, Phillips, in spite of the wearisomeness of the journal under his editorship, was true.

When Phillips died in December 1915, the editorship went to Galloway Kyle, the director of the Poetry Society and the most powerful single influence behind the journal's editorial posture. Kyle promptly went on record welcoming the appearance in America of *Contemporary Verse* as "an admirable antidote to the extreme 'modernism' of the more pretentious *Poetry* of Chicago" (7:166). In 1917 he finally eliminated the *Gazette* section to which Monro had objected so strenuously in 1912, replacing it with the less pretentious "Reports and Announcements" of the society. He also opened the pages of the *Poetry Review* during the war years to a rather fascinating selection of war poetry of mixed quality written by soldiers at the front, poetry that in 1916 was no longer characterized by the type of patriotic bravado found in war poems published in the *Review* and elsewhere during the early war years but that dealt instead with the misery, oppressiveness, and frustration experienced by soldiers involved in the now seemingly endless conflict.

The years 1916–1947, during which Kyle edited the journal, were years of expansion. By 1920 he had become increasingly interested in the potential for a poetic outlet for the society's interests in America. In 1923 he appointed Alice Hunt Bartlett, a wealthy New York socialite, as American associate editor, assuring his readers that she had no ties to "any of the many freakish schools" of American verse (14:157). Not only did she submit lengthy regular feature articles on American poetry and poets; she also provided the money for a series of poetry contests on an exceptionally wide variety of subjects, including everything from domestic pets to sonnets about life in the city.

The years immediately following her appointment were marked by a distinct change in the tone of the journal. Though still staunchly conservative in his editorial policies, Kyle, perhaps somewhat influenced by American marketing tactics, initiated a series of efforts designed to "popularize" poetry. The *Poetry Review* sponsored the Bartlett prizes as publicity schemes, and in 1925 ran a crossword puzzle on the works of Browning and a contest on the best poem on Poe. A contest was devised in 1926 to explain the meaning of De la Mare's "The Listeners," as well as a Tennyson crossword puzzle; and in 1928 a contest was held for the best poem about flying achievements. Kyle's tenure as editor ended in 1947. During the thirty-one years of his editorship he brought a distinct American presence to the journal, and he made a sincere effort to extend the journal's marketability. But few recognizable poets appeared in the journal during those years, the exceptions being an undistinguishable single poem published by A. Conan Doyle in 1917, a poem by Herbert Read in 1922, one by Kipling in 1930, and one by Edmund Blunden in 1943. Vita Sackville-West won the Bartlett sea-sonnet award in 1923 and contributed a number of other selections over the years, as did Edwin Markham, the winner of the best poem on Poe in 1925. Other notable inclusions during Kyle's editorship were a series of articles on a variety of wide-ranging literary subjects written by Federico Olivero, the distinguished Italian scholar-critic, and a verse drama contributed by T. Sturge Moore in 1942. In 1946 Muriel Spark published her first poem in the journal, followed by others in 1947, the year she won the premium poem prize for a selection of sonnets on "Autumn." When Kyle retired as editor that year, Muriel Spark was chosen to replace him.

Murial Spark's involvement with the journal was short-lived.In 1949 she was replaced by John Gawsworth. Ironically, one of his first acts was to acknowledge his debt to Harold Monro, his "old mentor." During the years Gawsworth was editor (1949–1952), the quality of the journal improved noticeably, with poems by De la Mare, Hilaire Belloc, Hugh MacDiarmid, Richard Aldington, Herbert Read, Frank O'Connor, and Robert Graves, and critical articles by Iain Fletcher, G. S. Fraser, and Lawrence Durrell. In 1952 the *Poetry Review* went from a bimonthly to a quarterly, exactly what Monro had hoped would happen thirty years earlier. That same year, fourteen of Lionel Johnson's previously unprinted poems, written between the ages of seventeen and nineteeen, appeared in the journal.

From 1952 to the early 1960s, the *Poetry Review* returned to its lackluster format. By 1962, however, noticeable changes began to occur. The journal included fewer essays and reviews, and a more selective body of poetry. In 1969, under the editorship of Derek Parker, the journal published work by W. H. Auden and John Heath-Stubbs, and in 1970, poems by Robert Graves, Lucien Stryk, Hugh MacDiarmid, Thom Gunn, Stevie Smith, and A. L. Rowse, and essays by Philip Hobsbaum and Colin Wilson. The journal had become wide ranging, experimental, colorful, and innovative. By 1972, when Eric Mottram assumed the editorship, the *Poetry Review* looked like a new publication. Mottram published the work of Allen Ginsberg, Denise Levertov, John Wieners, Lawrence Ferlinghetti, Muriel Rukeyser, Gary Snyder, and Gilbert Sorrentino. John Ashbery contributed an essay to the 1971 edition. The editorial emphasis had shifted from a journal designed to please the casual reader of poetry to one that was in the center of the poetry revival of the 1960s and 1970s. Later volumes would publish poetry written by Michael McClure (1973) and Ed Sanders (1975).

By 1978 Mottram was out as editor and the journal underwent another conservative turn, marked by the inclusion, once again, of fewer experimental writers and fewer well-known names. The journal also returned to its more traditional format, including reviews of recent publications, poetry contests, interviews with writers, and autobiographical essays.

Notes

1. See Joy Grant, *Harold Monro and the Poetry Bookshop* (Berkeley, 1967), pp. 26–52; see also Marvin Magalaner, "Harold Monro and *The Poetry Review*," *Poetry Review* 40 (1949):340–47; and Magalaner, "Bookshop in the Slums," *New Mexico Quarterly Review* 18 (1948):421–28.

2. *Poetry and Drama* 1 (March 1913):10.

3. Ibid.

4. See Arundell del Re, "Georgian Reminiscences," *Studies in English Literature* (Tokyo, 1932, 1934); Grant, p. 44.

Information Sources

BIBLIOGRAPHY

del Re, Arundell. "Georgian Reminiscences." *Studies in English Literature*. Tokyo, 1932, 1934.

Grant, Joy. *Harold Monro and the Poetry Bookshop*. Berkeley, 1967.

Magalaner, Marvin. "Bookshop in the Slums." *New Mexico Quarterly Review* 18 (1948):421–28.

———. "Harold Monro and *The Poetry Review*." *Poetry Review* 40 (1949):340–47.

INDEXES

The following volumes are indexed: 1913, 1914, 1915, 1919, 1920, 1924, 1926, 1927, 1929, 1930, 1931, 1932, 1933, 1935, 1936, 1937, 1938, 1939, 1940, 1941, 1953, 1954, 1971, 1972. 1928–1946 in *Subject Index to Periodicals*.

REPRINT EDITIONS

Volumes 1–61, 1912–1970/71, Kraus Reprint, Nendeln, Liechtenstein. Scholars' Facsimiles and Reprints, Delmar, New York.

LOCATION SOURCES
American
    Widely available.
British
    Widely available.

Publication History

MAGAZINE TITLE AND TITLE CHANGES
    The Poetical Gazette, 1909–1912. *The Poetry Review*. 1912–1969. *Poetry Review*,
    1969–.
VOLUME AND ISSUE DATA
    Numbers 1–15, May 1909–1911; volume 1–, January 1912–.
FREQUENCY OF PUBLICATION
    Volumes 1–5, 1912–1914, monthly; volumes 6–42, 1915–1951, bimonthly; vol-
    umes 43–, 1952–, quarterly.
PUBLISHERS
    The Poetry Society, 21 Earls Court Square, London, S.W.5/9BY.
EDITORS
    Harold Monro, 1912–1913. Stephen Phillips, 1913–1915. Galloway Kyle, 1916–
    1947. Muriel Spark, 1947–1948. John Gawsworth, 1949–1952. Thomas Moult,
    editorial board chairman, 1952–1962. John Smith, 1962–1965. Derek Parker,
    1966–1970. Guest editors: Adrian Henri, Martin Booth, Anthony Rudolf, Eric
    Mottram, 1971. Eric Mottram, 1972–1977. Guest editors: Edwin Brock, Harry
    Chambers, Douglas Dunn, Roger Garfitt, 1978. Roger Garfitt, 1979–1981. An-
    drew Motion, 1982–.

Franklin E. Court

PROSPECTIVE REVIEW, THE

The *Prospective Review: A Quarterly Journal of Theology and Literature* was
a Unitarian journal that did not really wish to be known as Unitarian. It was
descended from the *Christian Teacher*, which started as a Unitarian monthly in
1835 and became a quarterly in 1838, edited by the Reverend J. H. Thom. By
1845, however, a number of the younger clergymen felt that Unitarianism had
become too sectarian and stagnant, and they reacted by fixing their attention on
broader ranges of rational inquiry, not only into religion but into philosophy,
literature, and ethics as well. Reflecting this newer trend, the *Christian Teacher*
changed its name to the *Prospective Review* in 1845, and added three new
editors—the Reverends J. J. Tayler, Charles Wicksteed, and James Martineau—
to support Thom's general editorship. In their prefatory note to the first new
volume (1845) the editors commented that the name was changed because the
old title was "deficient in modesty," created a wrong impression of dogmatism,
and continued to suggest "the old ideas." In effect, the name was being changed
to accommodate the change in spirit, as well as format, of the journal, for the

editors announced their wish that their new quarterly should be "catholic, spiritual, progressive." It would, they said "restrain by no rigid orthodoxy the free expression of different forms and tendencies of mind. The comprehensive and philosophic method in which an inquiry is conducted, the spirit it breathes, and the new thoughts it opens may often be deemed of more vital importance than exact agreement with its conclusions."

In keeping with these large, fair-minded aims, the editors almost immediately weeded out all the "local news" of Unitarians that had been a feature of the old *Christian Teacher*, as they were to exclude all sectarian or provincial considerations. The format of the first issue, for example, had the journal consist almost entirely of lengthy review-articles—six in all—prompted by topics such as "Historical Christianity," "Religion in the Age of Great Cities," "The Evidences of the Genuineness of the Gospels," "An Inquiry Concerning the Origin of Christianity," A. P. Stanley's "Life and Correspondence of Thomas Arnold, D.D.," and the explosive "Vestiges of the Natural History of Creation," by Robert Chambers (at the time anonymous). A final section is called "Notices of New Publications," and contains brief descriptions of contemporary books about religion, ethics, and related subjects. The rest of the issues continued in this approximate format for the entire ten-year run of the journal, although there was a gradual introduction of broader and more literary topics over the years, as the *Prospective* fought for its life.

Indeed, the combination of steadily enlarging range and steadily decreasing support from its readers forms a persistent thread of ironic suspense throughout the *Prospective*, for the nature of its aims put much against it. Its insistence on performing "on the borders of parties" gave it little allegiance from readers of any sect; and its serious and thorough treatment of subjects and issues made it unattractive to the general reader. James Martineau, who was the most important guiding spirit of the journal, summarized the problem well in later years:

> The great object of [the *Prospective Review*'s] conductors was to prevent the course of liberal theology from slipping into the rut of any Unitarian or other sect, and to treat its whole contents and all cognate topics with philosophical and historical impartiality, apart from all ecclesiastical or party interests.
> ... this breadth of purpose, while securing it some circulation and marked respect among studious persons in various connections, caused it to be coldly looked upon by the very people it was supposed to represent.[1]

Eventually, the *Prospective* reached out so far beyond its nominal religious base that it transformed its whole nature, and with it once again its name, in 1855.

For the modern reader, the literary value of the journal's articles is in itself not very great, although many of the essays are well written. Their greatest value is to the student of English literature who wants to be thoroughly acquainted with the intellectual and spiritual milieu from which emerged the great works and writers of mid-Victorian England. Readers especially of Matthew Arnold, Robert and Elizabeth Barrett Browning, George Eliot, John Ruskin, Thomas Carlyle, Arthur Hugh Clough, and even James Martineau's more famous sister Harriet, will find much aid to their understanding in the pages of the *Prospective*, for in them nearly every major issue and problem of the mind of the age is explored with thoroughness and dependable, impartial justice. And most of the major literary works that appeared during the ten-year life of the journal are reviewed with similar impartiality.

The article on Chambers's "Natural History of Creation," for instance, in the first issue of volume 1 for February 1845, calmly summarizes that book's central idea that "the old-fashioned idea of Creation must ... be remodeled"; that reasons based on the "surface of Natural History" forbid us "to believe that organic life was originally ... produced by a *special* act of Creation"; and that man's growth has been a "diverging development out of a common root." No further comment is added, and the startled mid-Victorian reader is left to ponder his past and present for himself, at the dawn of a decade leading to Darwin.

Volume 2 of the *Prospective* contains a valuable review of Thomas Carlyle's *Oliver Cromwell's Letters and Speeches* (no. 5, February 1846). Calling the book "very original," and recoiling a bit from some of its "questionable and extravagant notions" and its "strange, outlandish diction," the reviewer still credits it with "the deepest interest" and "an earnest wisdom," and praises Carlyle for his courage in trying to vindicate Cromwell throughout. In what must surely be one of the great understatements in English letters, the reviewer then adds his opinion that "on the whole, Mr. Carlyle is hardly just to writers whose cast of mind and general object are different from his own." Volume 2 also contains, in issue number 8 for November 1846, a fair and receptive review of yet another mid-Victorian religious bombshell, David Friedrich Strauss's *Life of Jesus*. After providing a faithful survey of the book, the reviewer wonders why England has produced no valuable, simple reply to Strauss, and goes on to warn England against both smugness and blindness. The translation from the German, which we now know to have been done by George Eliot, is praised as "faithful, elegant, and scholar-like."

Nineteenth-century social and economic thought fill volumes 3 and 4. Issue 11 in volume 3, for August 1847, contains a long review of a collection of essays by the European thinker J.C.L. Simonde de Sismondi, entitled *Political Economy and the Philosophy of Government*; and issue 16 of volume 4 (November 1848) contains a forty-three-page review of John Stuart Mill's *Political Economy*. Of the two, the reviewers prefer Mill, whom they rank with Adam Smith and David Ricardo, though their praise is not unqualified. What is admired most in Mill's book is that it "evades no difficulty, and of the problems which occur solves rightly a proportion ... beyond all precedent large" (p. 501). Sismondi, an unorthodox economist who influenced Carlyle and Ruskin, is frankly called "absurd" by the reviewer, but his central economic ideas are given a long, fair survey, and he is praised for the timely reproof he casts upon England "on account of the degradation of the British poor, in town and country" (p. 326).

The *Prospective*'s flexibility in dealing with what it disagrees with is demonstrated in volume 5, issue 18 (August 1849): it carries reviews of both Macaulay's *History of England* and James Anthony Froude's two novels of religious doubt, *Shadows of the Clouds* and *The Nemesis of Faith*. Macaulay is commended for his "lively style, and gay narrative," as well as other virtues; but the reviewer is much shocked by "so forensic a manner and intonation" throughout the book, and opines that "it is not the fitting tone of an historian to write systematically as at an opponent." The grand defect of the history, he finds, is its "want of moral weight," though another limitation bothers him almost as much. "To Mr. Macaulay," he says, "the constitution is the world . . . a limitation . . . unpardonable in an historian" (p. 139). Froude's novels, however, though they are said to contain "some questionable theories" and many sentiments that the reviewer "resents," are still on the whole praised for their "new and clear manifestation of genius." Their pages are cited as being "full of beauty and of interest" (p. 181), while Froude himself is admired as a man of "deep and true sympathy with all that is good, gentle, pure, and noble." The review must have refreshed Froude, whose novels had recently been burned by an irate Oxford clergyman.

Reviews of poetry in the *Prospective* are comparatively rare, and not so astute as the reviews of prose. They are generally preoccupied with the spiritual and emotional content of the poems, and they measure all works against the criterion of high seriousness or inspirational effect on the reader. Thus the review of Tennyson's *In Memoriam* in volume 6 (1850) stresses the poet's recovery from his grief, and draws exclusive attention to the faith and sweetness of the work, rather than to its struggles and doubts. The review of Wordsworth's *Prelude* in volume 7 (1851) goes so far as to say that "a poet could surely tell the story of his mental growth more clearly and effectively in prose" (p. 95). After commending Wordsworth for his significance in literary history, it ranks him as less than "transcendently great" because "in him the Poet and the Philosopher are never wholly blended; they always stand somewhat apart" (p. 100). And the review of Matthew Arnold's three volumes of poetry in volume 10 (1854), while praising Arnold's "keen and refined sense of beauty," finds his poems too personal, too superficial in their emotions, and too incomplete in their "meditations on life." "His mourning notes over the perplexities and distorting influences [of modern life]," the reviewer says, "are apt to degenerate into mere bewailments. It is the part of a true and manly poet to raise us above these troubles" (p. 106).

Much more congenial to the *Prospective*'s spirit is Ruskin's *Stones of Venice*, which is enthusiastically reviewed in the first issue of volume 10 for February 1854 as the work of "a very Titian of language" who surpasses every prose writer since Milton "in the serious splendour of his style." Ruskin is especially cited for the "great service" he is performing in initiating an investigation into the "right exercise of some of the noblest mental functions, in methods and from points of view congenial to the English mind" (p. 19). As such, the reviewer ranks Ruskin in the high continuous tradition of Wordsworth and Tennyson.

Perhaps the best, and final, sense of the *Prospective*'s temperament can be attained by noting two reviews that appeared fairly late in the journal's life. Just after Harriet Martineau, with coauthor Henry George Atkinson, published her *Letters on the Laws of Man's Nature and Development* in 1851, her brother James pondered long and decided to review the book negatively in the *Prospective Review*. When he did so, his allegiance to fair-mindedness caused his sister to avoid speaking to him for the rest of her life. And when *Uncle Tom's Cabin* was reviewed in the last issue of volume 8 (November 1852), the reviewer not only praised the book, but wrote a lengthy essay on American slavery, ending by declaring unhesitatingly that "it is the greatest wrong now perpetrated upon God's earth; the foulest possible blot upon Anglo-Saxon civilization" (p. 513).

Ultimately the widening of interests into the more secular realms of literature and politics had its effect, and the *Prospective*'s readers became too restless while its editors became more ambitious. In the last issue of the tenth volume (November 1854), the editors announce with new inspiration that they feel they have even more work to do in "diffusing the more catholic spirit." "There are symptoms of a coming conflict of opinion," they proclaim prophetically, "which will draw off the chief combatants to the extremes of rigid orthodoxy and mere atheism. We mean to hold the field against both." Accordingly, they declare that they will try "enlarging the scope of [their] review, and giving it all the variety and interest of a first-class Quarterly." The *Prospective Review* then ran for only one more issue—that of February 1855 (volume 11)—before it became that "first-class Quarterly" and changed its name to *National Review*,* which first appeared in July 1855.

Note

1. *Biographical Memoranda*, quoted in James Drummond and Charles B. Upton, *The Life and Letters of James Martineau* (London, 1902), 1:264.

Information Sources

BIBLIOGRAPHY
Carpenter, J. E. *James Martineau: Theologian and Teacher*. London, 1905.

Drummond, James, and Charles B. Upton. *The Life and Letters of James Martineau*. 2 vols. London, 1902.

McLachlan, Herbert. *The Unitarian Movement in the Religious Life of England*. London, 1934.

Stephen, Leslie. *The English Utilitarians*. 3 vols. London, 1900.

INDEXES
List of contents at beginning of bound volumes. *Poole's Index. Wellesley Index* 3.

REPRINT EDITIONS
Microform: English Literary Periodicals (UMI), reels 761–762.
LOCATION SOURCES
American
Complete runs: Boston Public Library; Enoch Pratt Library; Harvard University Library; Michigan State Library; Newberry Library; U. S. Library of Congress; University of Minnesota; Yale University.
Partial runs: Widely available.
British
Partial runs: Widely available.

Publication History

MAGAZINE TITLE AND TITLE CHANGES
The Prospective Review: A Quarterly Journal of Theology and Literature. Changed to *National Review*, July 1855.
VOLUME AND ISSUE DATA
Volumes 1–11, numbers 1–41, February 1845–February 1855.
FREQUENCY OF PUBLICATION
Quarterly (February, May, August, and November).
PUBLISHERS
February 1845–November 1854: John Chapman, 121 Newgate Street/142 Strand, London. February 1855: R. Theobald, 26 Paternoster Row, London.
EDITORS
John Hamilton Thom (general editor). James Martineau, John James Tayler, Charles Wicksteed, 1845–1855. William L. Roscoe, 1855.

George Allan Cate

PUNCH

From its first number on 17 July 1841, the weekly *Punch* has remained in continuous publication as the venerable superstar of English comic periodicals. The subject of three fine book-length historical studies, several volumes on its art, artists, and editors, and numerous articles on its contents and publication history, *Punch* has been the most fully studied of British humor magazines.[1] So numerous are the names of *Punch*'s distinguished writers and artists during its 160-year survival that a brief survey can do little more than trace some of the magazine's significant features and contributors that appeared under its eleven editors, ranging from Mark Lemon to Alan Coren.

Although details of *Punch*'s origin are somewhat uncertain, several names associated with its initial ownership include the engraver Ebenezer Landells, the printer Joseph Last, and three coeditors: Henry Mayhew, Mark Lemon, and Stirling Coyne. In 1842 Bradbury and Evans (Bradbury, Agnew and Co. from 1872 on) acquired control, and Mark Lemon became the editor. *Punch*'s subtitle, *The London Charivari*, suggests kinship with the famous Parisian journal. The first cover, by Archibald Henning, shows a group of grotesques watching a Punch and Judy show. Mr. Punch, the magazine's animated logo, continued to appear in various personalities through the years. Various artists have depicted in him their concepts of the spirit of the magazine—from buffoon and showman to high-minded clown and piquant dwarf.

Introducing the first issue, Mr. Punch announces that he "has no party prejudices—he is conservative in his opposition to Fantoccini and political puppets, but a progressive whig in his love of *small change*." In addition to being "a form of refuge for destitute wit" and "the asylum for thousands of orphan jokes" and "perishing puns," the magazine included commentary and cartoons on politics, fashion, fine arts, music, drama, sporting news, and current events. "The Moral of Punch," wrote Lemon in his lead editorial for 17 July 1841, was to be the voice of the oppressed, especially victims of debtors' prisons, capital punishment, the Poor Law, Sabbatarianism, and other earnest abuses. As a "polite whig," the magazine would ridicule royals, and appeal largely to an upper-middle-class readership.

The format, which remained fairly constant for over three decades, included "a big cut by Tenniel, surrounded by comic articles of less than a page in length, a Paliamentary column, drama criticism, and the spaces filled with pars and socials that dealt with the funny side of hunting, housekeeping, social climbing, or the idiocies of servants, cabmen, and lower-class drunks."[2] The initial circulation of about six thousand increased to about forty thousand by 1860.

In addition to Lemon, Beckett, and Mayhew, other early writers included William Thackeray, Douglas Jerrold, and Shirley Brooks, the latter of whom assumed increased responsibility under Lemon and became the magazine's second editor. Thackeray, who was an able illustrator as well as writer, was a man of tremendous output, producing four of his novels while writing regularly for *Punch* and establishing the *Cornhill Magazine*.* His light-hearted poem, "The Mahogany Tree," celebrated *Punch*'s weekly convention of editorial dinners held around the famed wooden table with its carved initials of staff members and contributors:

> Here let us sport,
> Boys, as we sit,
> Laughter and wit
> Flashing so free
> Life is but short—
> When we are gone,
> Let them sing on,
> Round the old tree.[3]

"Round the old tree" also sat artists John Leech, Richard Doyle, John Tenniel, and Charles Keene, Leech, who loved comic scenes of low life, contributed about three thousand cartoons (a term first applied under his signature to humorous magazine drawings). Tenniel provided such now famous symbolic personifications as Father Time, Britannia, and the British Lion.

By 1850 *Punch* was securely established with brilliant talents, satirizing everything in sight. Often anti-Catholic and anti-Jewish, it was consistently anti-privilege and -pomposity, whatever the source. However, the satiric outrage and radicalism of the first three decades gradually tamed during the remaining three decades of the nineteenth century as the magazine shifted toward respectability and moderation under editors Tom Taylor and Francis Burnand. Taylor brought a scholarly and academic touch to the Mahogany Table, and Burnand brought a humor more kindly toward royalty, Jews, and Catholics. They led the magazine away from its earlier political punch and toward a more establishment policy of "animated moderation." But they also brought such writers as E. J. Milliken, Henry Lucy, A. A. Milne, and W. S. Gilbert, and some of *Punch*'s finest artists: George du Maurier, Edward Linley Sambourne, Bernard Partridge, Harry Furniss, and Phil May.

Through the latter part of the nineteenth century, *Punch* shifted its emphasis from writing to cartoons, the quality of which helped to retain the magazine's popularity in spite of competition from such rivals as the *Tomahawk*, the liberal *Fun*,* and the conservative *Judy*. During this time of somewhat complacent prosperity, *Punch*'s major attraction was George du Maurier. Tenniel was established as the magazine's political cartoonist, and Keene followed in Leech's tradition of low-life comedy. Du Maurier, on the other hand, was the society cartoonist, focusing on the world of the social climber, the vulgar *nouveau riche*, the pretentious aristocrat, and the romantic woman. Some of du Maurier's finest work was his often cruel lampooning of the *poseurs* in the aesthetic movement during the 1870s and 1880s. In 1866 he burlesqued the art and poetry of the Pre-Raphaelites in a delightful three-part series, "A Legend of Camelot." Later he created such comically incompetent snobs as the Bunthorne-like poet Jellaby Postlethwaite, the dreadful painter Maudle, and the arty hostess Mrs. Cimabue Brown.

Closely following du Maurier in popularity, especially capturing the lively spirit of the 1890s, was Phil May who, with economy of lines and memorable expressions on his cartoon characters' faces, produced the forerunners of the modern cartoon. By the 1890s, over a hundred different artists had signed their *Punch* cartoons. Two of them, G. L. Stampa and Bernard Partridge, continued to contribute until the middle of the twentieth century.

During the first half of the twentieth century, *Punch* was under the editorship of Owen Seaman (1906–1932) and E. V. Knox (1932–1949). In these years, the world changed drastically, but *Punch* did not—save for expanded advertising and an ever-increasing dependence upon cartoons. The magazine became more of a commentator than a critic and was faced with competition from a growing number of magazines carrying cartoons, amusing drawings, and literary criticism. The chief threat was the *New Yorker*, started in 1925.

The first "new look" for the magazine's format came with Kenneth Bird's editorship from 1949 to 1952, and under Malcolm Muggeridge (1953–1957) a trend of lagging sales was gradually reversed. Since then, under the leadership of Bernard Hollowood, William Davis, and Alan Coren, *Punch* has managed to weather continued storms, as it has throughout its remarkable long life. In 1957, R.G.G. Price wrote:

> *Punch* is a National Institution in a way that no purely commercial magazine can be. Look at *Punch* as the early Editors saw it and you see a miracle of survival. Look at it as it seemed in its middle period and you see something as majestically unchanging as cliffs, and as liable to erosion. To-day, whether *Punch* lives or dies it will obviously do it with a bang, which means it will live, and if it lives it will grow. *Punch*'s future is more interesting than its past.[4]

Punch, has, of course, continued to live on into the 1980s, and the yearly bibliographies based on it suggest a yet unexhausted reservoir of studies availing students of the history of English literature, art, and popular culture.

Notes

1. M. H. Spielmann's *The History of "Punch"* (1895; rpt. New York, 1969) provided a detailed account of the magazine's first fifty years. In 1955 R. E. Williams edited an extensive collection of *Punch*'s cartoons in *A Century of "Punch"* (London). This was followed by R.G.G. Price's *A History of "Punch"* (London, 1957), a commentary on the magazine and its editors from Mark Lemon to Malcolm Muggeridge. Most recently, Alan Prager, in *The Mahogany Tree: An Informal History of "Punch"* (New York, 1979), gives yet another perspective on the magazine from its beginnings until the 1970s.
2. Prager, p. 135.
3. Quoted by Spielmann, p. 53.
4. Price, p. 338.

Information Sources

BIBLIOGRAPHY

Adrian, Arthur A. *Mark Lemon, First Editor of "Punch."* London, 1966. [Good resource for *Punch*'s early years.]
Madden, Lionel, and Diana Dixon. *The Periodical Press in Britain: A Bibliography of Modern Studies.* New York, 1976.
Ormond, Leonee. *George du Maurier.* London, 1969.
Prager, Arthur. *The Mahogany Tree: An Informal History of "Punch."* New York, 1979.
Price, R.G.G. *A History of "Punch."* London, 1957. [One of the standard histories.]
INDEXES

Each volume indexed. Indexes reprinted separately (Punch Publications).

REPRINT EDITIONS

Microform: Bell and Howell Co., Wooster, Ohio. UMI.

LOCATION SOURCES
American
>Widely available.

British
>Widely available.

Publication History

MAGAZINE TITLE AND TITLE CHANGES
>*Punch, or the London Charivari.*

VOLUME AND ISSUE DATA
>Volume 1, 17 July 1841–.

FREQUENCY OF PUBLICATION
>Weekly.

PUBLISHERS
>July 1841–December 1842; Ebenezer Landells and Joseph Last, 13 Wellington Street, Strand, London. December 1842–1872: Bradbury & Evans, 11 Bouverie Street, London/*Punch* office, 85 Fleet Street, London. 1872–: Bradbury & Agnew, London/*Punch* offices, 23 Tudor Street, London.

EDITORS
>Mark Lemon, 1841–1870. Shirley Brooks, 1870–1874. Tom Taylor, 1874–1880. Francis Burnand, 1880–1906. Owen Seaman, 1906–1932. E.V. Knox, 1932–1949. Kenneth Bird, 1949–1952. Malcolm Muggeridge, 1953–1957. Bernard Hollowood, 1957–1968. William Davis, 1968–1977. Alan Coren, 1977–.

Jerold J. Savory

Q

QUARTERLY REVIEW, THE. See RA, MA

QUIVER, THE

During John Cassell's 1854 journey through the United States, he observed the American taste for religious magazines, a taste encouraging to the publisher of the *Biblical Educator, Family Bible, Family Prayer Book*, and many other such titles. The *Quiver*, with its subtitle, *Designed for the Defence of Biblical Truth, and the Advancement of Religion in the Homes of the People*, first appeared on 7 September 1861. The magazine's subsequent career can readily be inferred from the changes in its subtitle: in 1864 it became "An Illustrated Magazine of Social, Intellectual, and Religious Progress"; in 1866, "An Illustrated Magazine for Sunday and General Reading." In the opening number, editor Cassell proclaims that "the religion will be that of the New Testament—spiritual, evangelical, catholic—free alike from bigotry on the one side and latitudinarian on the other." Nonsectarian in its aims, then, the *Quiver* studiously avoided political and doctrinal questions in order to promote proper appreciation of the Bible: "To those who know how to read the Bible, it is in itself the most interesting of all books; many may be led to discover this by being guided as to its use, or being shown how it is corroborated by modern science, ancient inscriptions, recent travel, geology, botany, comparative chronology, and other sources of Scriptural illustration. We are the advocates of progress." Despite this bravado, articles of scientific interest appeared infrequently, and the tone of the *Quiver* remained moderate, calmly denying any mechanistic creation or evolution, still urging in the 1880s that young Darwinists should not be driven from the churches.

The cover design of the *Quiver* includes a quiver of arrows labeled "Progress of Truth," "Fireside Lectures," "Appeals to the Heart," and "Treasures for the Young,'' a fair representation of the contents, designed in part to appeal to children and in part to address both the intellects and the feelings of adults. Temperance articles, reports of missionary projects, historical articles on churches and religious figures, book reviews (always at least tepidly favorable), and requests for donations to charitable causes such as the Cotton Famine Relief Fund provided the bulk of its weekly numbers. To appeal to the heart, the *Quiver* published a good deal of serial fiction. Its best-known writer was also one of its earliest—Mrs. Henry Wood agreed to write *The Channings* for the *Quiver* just before her *East Lynne* came out in the three-volume edition.[1] She subsequently published several more series in the *Quiver*, including ''Mrs. Halliburton's Troubles'' (19 April–6 December 1862), ''William Allair: Or Running Away to Sea'' (13 December 1862–31 January 1863), and ''Squire Trevlyn's Heir'' (7 February–19 September 1863). Fiction in the second and third series issued from less distinguished pens. Mrs. C. L. Balfour contributed, for instance, ''The Family Honour'' (3 September 1865) and ''Kate Ormond's Dower'' (28 April 1866). The *Quiver* did not aim at being a literary journal, of course, and poetry very rarely appeared. The 26 November 1864 reprinting of Wordsworth's ''We Are Seven'' (with illustrations by one J. Cooper) is a rare exception in the first series. The short-lived second series contained almost no poetry. The third series carried some original poetry, often of the sort typified by A. W. Hume's alexandrine couplets, ''On the Death of Little Nell'' (1 December 1866).

Cassell at first edited the journal himself, and he oversaw the second editor, C.H.H. Wright. By the summer of 1864 Cassell's partners, Petter and Galpin, decided to revamp the *Quiver* in hopes of boosting its sales. John Willis Clark, then editor, added illustrations to lighten the appearance and changed the subtitle to accentuate progress and de-emphasize religious combativeness. Because of Cassell's displeasure with the first number of Clark's new series, Clark was replaced. Thomas Teignmouth Shore was the firm's chief editor from 1865 to 1888, but a subeditor, H. G. Bonavia Hunt, really controlled the *Quiver* until 1905. It continued as a weekly until 1926, after which Cassell's ceased to publish it. Another publisher issued annuals into the 1950s.[2]

The new series of 1864 was more visually attractive but not substantively different from its predecessor. Though Cassell died in 1865, his designs for the *Quiver* persisted through the turn of the century. The new series frequently featured an illustrator of Continental but not British reputation, Gustave Doré, several of whose works Cassell, Petter, and Galpin published between 1864 and 1866. In 1866 the *Quiver* ran a cover portrait of Doré and a laudatory article concentrating on his biblical illustrations, then being published by the firm. This inclusion of a Catholic artist marked something of a moderation of the rather aggressively Protestant tone and content of the magazine. The third series mellows further, so that by March 1869 the *Quiver* could run ''Twickenham Church and the Grave of Pope'' and criticize, not Pope's Catholicism, but his arrogance.

In 1866 the *Quiver* included for the first time a list of contributors to its volume of 1865 numbers, and from this time forward the list preceded the first article of every regular number. Unfortunately, the contributors are not connected to their works in a table of contents. Articles are thus often not identified at all, although they sometimes carry initials or mention another of the author's works, as in the immortal " 'Pinktottens, and How She Put Her Money in Heaven,' by the Author of 'Doddlekins.' " (Authors' names are generally of no particular value since the lists of contributors read like a vast *Who's Nobody 1865–1900*.) In the third series, the available special Christmas numbers, always named for some object or quality associated with archery, do include tables of contents with authors listed.[3] "The Mark" (1868) and "The Silver Bow" (1870) include respectively, "The Child Jesus," by His Grace the Lord Archbishop of York and "Christ Standing at the Door," by His Grace the Archbishop of Canterbury, facts that might suggest that the *Quiver* here departs from its usual format to appeal to well-bred religious readers with social and literary pretensions or ambitions. These Christmas numbers, with their heavier emphasis on literature and illustrations, were harbingers of the later magazine.

The character of the *Quiver* changes substantially in the 1880s and 1890s, becoming more sedate, less demanding of its readers, and in the main, more genteel. The contrast between the early and late periods of the magazine is most apparent in the attitudes toward poverty. An 1866 series, frequently the leading story, "The Deeper Depth; or Scenes of Real Life Among the Very Poor," condemns the smugness which denies the existence of poverty or blames the poor. It recommends individual charity unaccompanied by lectures on thrift and duty. "The Deeper Depth" probably reflects the growing cultural awareness of the effect on everyday life of continual physical drudgery without the hope of social advancement. Henry Mayhew's *London Labour and the London Poor* (1851–1864), Charles Dickens's *Bleak House* (1853), and John Ruskin's lecture "The Work of Iron, in Nature, Art, and Policy" (1858) had earlier expressed this same social consciousness in the parliamentary, literary, and aesthetic worlds; they had helped to create a climate in which the *Quiver* could accent understanding rather than righteousness. Aware of its mission to avoid controversy and therefore wary of originality, the *Quiver* repeats the accepted dicta with added religious overtones. Thus, when the temper of the times became more conservative, the 1896 *Quiver* ran a "Poverty in Gloves" series on the genteel poor ruined "through no fault of their own" in bank failures.

As gentility became more important, the magazine expanded its offerings. In 1877 music becomes an important enough continuing section of the *Quiver* to merit a list of composers among each volume's contributors. In the third series articles without explicit religious intent begin to appear frequently. Although these appear very occasionally in the second series, they are there limited to amusement for children—an article illustrating the anaconda, for example. The issues from the 1880s contain more of these articles, which are now directed toward women. At first the focus remains serious and reform-minded. In 1881 Phillis Browne (author of "What Girls Can Do") pleads for day nurseries to insure physical survival for the infants of the poor, among whom, she claims, the mortality rate for children under four years of age reached 40 percent. This article, "Day Nurseries for Poor Children," aims at soliciting the support of middle-class mothers. An 1882 article, "Working Girls of London," lists charities supplying cheap lodgings, a rare appeal to working-class rather than middle-class readers.

Gradually, however, the emphasis of this "woman's section" shifted from current social problems to either historical or upper-class subjects with a religious gloss. The 1883 series "Good Wives of Great Men" thus includes Mary and Elizabeth Bunyan, the wife of Ulrich Zwingli, and Lady Rachel Russell. In a series which might have been written by the Veneerings of *Our Mutual Friend*, a woman visitor to the courts of Europe describes sabbath celebrations of various European monarchs, thus combining the appeals of travelogue, social snobbery, and genteel religion. The exemplars of virtue change too, with emphasis now on the successful religious man—eminent religious men among poets, composers, and so on.

The older, less genteel approach to society never vanishes entirely. The Rev. S. A. Swaine discusses occupational diseases and the lack of industrial safety standards, for example, in "The Seamy Side of Civilization" (1884). And in 1889 the Rev. W.T.A. Baker, a missionary, in "A Walk Down a Chinese Street," mentions not only the natives' definition of whites as devils but the horrors of opium and England's partial reponsibility for opium addiction and traffic. The *Quiver* does not maintain this level of cultural understanding, however, for the 1880s also brings "Picaninny," a children's story about a black East Indian woman who sells her child because, as a non-Christian, she cannot love it. As the social criticism loses momentum in the 1880s and 1890s, the solicitations for charity become articles by eminent philanthropists in a "Work in Which I Am Interested" format, and missionary reports de-emphasize religious fervor in favor of descriptions of native customs.

John Cassell's prospectus for the new series of the *Quiver* drew fire from the *London Review* (see *Mirror of Literature, Amusement, and Instruction** [*RA*]) as a publication promoting equally Christianity and Cassell.[4] Just as that mixture of religious and commercial interest typifies the middle class of 1861, so the *Quiver* of the 1880s and 1890s reveals the domestication of the middle-class evangelical impulse.

Notes

1. Simon Nowell-Smith, *The House of Cassell 1848–1958* (London, 1958), p. 60.

2. Letter received by the author from Norman Lamber, archivist for Cassell Ltd., July 1981.

3. These Christmas issues are not reprinted in the microfilm reproduction.

4. Nowell-Smith, p. 62.

Information Sources

BIBLIOGRAPHY
Eliott-Binns, L. E. *Religion in the Victorian Era*. London, 1936.
Nowell-Smith, Simon. *The House of Cassell 1848–1958*. London, 1958.

INDEXES
     None.
REPRINT EDITIONS
     Microform: Datamics Inc., New York. Early British Periodicals (UMI), reels 817–
     825 and 869–877.
LOCATION SOURCES
  American
     Partial runs: Widely available.
  British
     Complete runs: Bodleian Library; British Museum.
     Partial runs: Birmingham University Library; Cambridge University Library; Edin-
     burgh Public Library.

Publication History

MAGAZINE TITLE AND TITLE CHANGES
     The *Quiver, Designed for the Defence of Biblical Truth and the Advancement of
     Religion in the Homes of the People,* 1861–September 1864. *The Quiver: An
     Illustrated Magazine of Social, Intellectual, and Religious Progress,* October
     1864–October 1865. *The Quiver: An Illustrated Magazine for Sunday and General
     Reading, 1866–1926.*
VOLUME AND ISSUE DATA
     Numbers 1–6, September 1861–September 1864; new series, volumes 1–2, Oc-
     tober 1864–October 1865; third series, volumes 1–131, 1866–1926.
FREQUENCY OF PUBLICATION
     Weekly.
PUBLISHER
     Cassell, Petter, and Galpin, 596 Broadway, New York/Ludgate Hill, E.C., London.
EDITORS
     John Cassell, 1861–(?). C.H.H. Wright, (?)–summer 1864. John Willis Clark,
     summer 1864–July 1865. H. G. Bonavia Hunt, 24 July 1865–1905. David Wil-
     liamson, 1905–(?). H. D. Williams, (?).

                                                            Missy Dehn Kubitschek

R

RAMBLER, THE

Founded in 1848 by John Moore Capes, the *Rambler* was "essentially the organ of the lay converts, men of Oxford," and would mirror throughout its nearly fifteen turbulent years of existence the bracing tension of faith and intellect, of fealty to Roman Catholicism and an insistence upon the independence and scope of a cosmopolitan catholicity.[1] This adamant stance regarding liberty for educated Catholics to be questing and questioning laity led to conflicts with English "old Catholics" and the Church hierarchy, particularly after a proprietor, Richard Simpson, became a regular contributor in 1854.[2] The readers of the journal were deftly apprised of the leading events and issues of the mid-Victorian years from 1848 to 1862. Topics elucidated for them included architecture (with important items on Augustus Pugin and the Gothic), art (notices and essays on Gustave Doré, John Ruskin, J.M.W. Turner, and Diego de Silva y Velázquez), geology, education, music (a notice on Hector Berlioz, in addition to many items on sacred music), philosophy, philology, science, travel (many items on accounts of gold prospecting, and several on the works of Richard F. Burton), and political events (with as many as twenty-five pages an issue being devoted to domestic and foreign contemporary events).

The publication's original title was *The Rambler, A Journal of Home and Foreign Literature, Politics, Science, and Art*, and the first number for Saturday, 1 January 1848, sold for four and a half pence, with stamp.[3] The price went to five pence with the tenth number (4 March 1848), when an *Ecclesiastical Register* and *Journal of the Week* were introduced. With the first number of the second volume (6 May 1848) the title was expanded to include "Music," "Art" was upgraded to "The Fine Arts," and the price was raised to six pence. The first monthly number appeared in September 1848, for eighteen pence.

While the word *theology* is in neither of the titles, it was, of course, the editors' religious views and the journal's unavoidable encroachment on issues of religious import that dogged its publication, and it is the journal's theological and political aspects that have received most study.[4]

A two-part review of John Stuart Mill's *On Liberty* by Thomas Arnold reflects some of the characteristics of this liberal Catholic journal. Arnold suggested that there was perhaps "no single moral question upon which a greater medley of opinions is afloat among Catholics than that of individual liberty" and boldly asserted that the citizens of Western Europe "are all bound to assume,—and must be permitted to assume,—the burdens and dangers of freedom" (November 1859, pp. 62, 75).[5] Arnold's essay is indicative of the editors' high regard for their readers' intelligence and their conscientious mission to keep their readers informed not only of matters pertaining to their faith and Church, but of the heady intellectual trends of the 1850s and early 1860s. Arnold explained that his article was written partly to combat the "imputations of mental torpor which are so freely made against" Catholics (p. 62), imputations which Richard Simpson (and Sir John Acton, another proprietor and editor of the *Rambler*) felt had some validity. Another characteristic of this review is that it was "communicated"; that is to say, it appeared in that section of the journal which supposedly bore least editorial responsibility, a possibly unique journalistic experiment initiated by John Henry Newman upon assuming his short-lived editorship of the *Rambler* in the spring of 1859.[6] This subterfuge to stem official censure failed utterly. Writing to Rome on 8 July 1861, Bishop Ullathorne boasted of having removed three editors (Capes, Simpson, and Newman), and Cardinal Wiseman, in a letter to Rome later that year, on 25 November, complained of the journal's four major "mistakes": its "tendency toward rationalism," its "boldness or, rather its erroneousness in matters of dogma," its series of articles on ecclesiastical education, and its "madness" in discussing contemporary politics, especially as displayed in its articles concerning "the Kingdom of Italy, and the temporal power of the Pope."[7]

Although the journal professed to cover both home and foreign literature, the proportion of foreign reviews (outside of the many notices of French religious and historical works) is actually quite small. Perhaps of most interest are the scattering of items on Heinrich Heine, Goethe, and François Chateaubriand, and a number of reviews of the works of François Guizot. The foreign literature that received greater coverage than that of the Continent was that of the United States.

American themes and writers receive appreciable study in the pages of the *Rambler*. In addition to the expected notices of books about missionary work among the Indians, and many glowing references to Orestes Brownson and his *Quarterly Review* (which ran roughly coterminously with the *Rambler*), there are discussions of such topics as the American Revolution, the Negro, slavery, and spiritualism. The last topic attracted considerable and intriguing attention. The writer of "The Spirit-Rappers," after approving of Oliver Wendell Holmes's dictum that "spiritualism is the modern plague of theology" (September 1860,

p. 357), notes that this fascination with spiritualism, also prevalent in England, is the result of the "materialism of men of science," and warns against "this exaggerated respect for the anormal [sic] and unregulated parts of our nature" (p. 362). An earlier article, "Table-Turning and Table-Talking" (November 1853, pp. 384–406), mocked Protestants' fascination with spiritualism and their groping with the possibility "that spiritual agencies may be going on all round us, even in the midst of this material world" (p. 384); the writer (possibly J. S. Northcote) concluded scornfully that the Catholic Church had never lost sight of such agencies.

Among the American men of letters receiving notice are the historians William H. Prescott and George Ticknor Curtis, and the editors George Ripley and Charles A. Dana. The range of the *Rambler*'s interests is illustrated by its enthusiastic praise for *The Hundred Boston Orators*, on the one hand, and, on the other, a winsome review of P. T. Barnum's *Life*: though it is a "cynical exposition of all his tricks of trade, justified by quotations from the Bible," Barnum at least "is good-natured enough not to show up any one but himself" (February 1855, p. 166).[8]

American authors were generally poorly received. Cooper and Longfellow were excoriated for their deplorable habit of painting "imaginary beings" when they write of Indians. The reviewer of *The Bee-Hunter; or, Oak Openings* berates Cooper for his "prosiness and preachiness," and states his preference for the earlier sea stories, in which Cooper "paints men" (November 1848, p. 202). Longfellow, as "a romance-writer," receives no mercy in the reviews of *Song of Hiawatha* and *Miles Standish*. The faithfulness of the former to the genuine traditions of the Indians is doubted (January 1856, p. 75), and the Puritans of the latter are, observes Richard Simpson, "no more the real Puritans of the seventeenth century than they are Chinese mandarins or Hindoo fakirs" (November 1858, p. 314). Simpson goes on to lash out at Longfellow's sentimental romanticism and his "weakness. . .for the Peter-Bell school of insipid innocence and sincere milk-and-water" (p. 321). Emerson comes off no better; in a review of *English Traits* Simpson asserts that the author, insofar as he is a transcendental seer and a disciple of Carlyle, is "dreary and dull"—his writing can be terse and vigorous, but only when he remains "on this side of the moon in his mother-sense" (October 1856, p. 319). And Harriet Beecher Stowe (whose *Uncle Tom's Cabin* was reviewed, probably by Northcote, in November 1852, pp. 413–24) was taken to task for her melodrama and sentiment in a mixed review of *Tales and Sketches of New-England Life* (July 1855, p. 79).

The majority of the literary notices in the *Rambler* are, of course, devoted to "home" literature, most of them appearing in the "Literary Notices" that concluded most numbers. These notices ran from two to nine pages, and were prepared by a variety of hands. Besides Dickens and Thackeray, those novelists receiving prominent attention are Cecilia Caddell (whose *Seymour's Curse* appeared in four installments, one of the journal's many serializations), Lady Georgiana Fullerton, and Charles Kingsley.

As for poetry, the triad of great Victorian poets, Arnold, Browning, and Tennyson, receives sparse notice. Arnold's verses, complained the reviewer of *Poems*, were "rugged, and read like translations" (January 1855, p. 81). Browning's *Men and Women* was warmly assessed in a seventeen-page essay: "For ourselves, we thank Mr. Browning, sceptical and reckless as he is, for a rare treat in these thoughtful and able volumes. . . . there is an undercurrent of thought that is by no means inconsistent with our religion" (January 1856, p. 71). Tennyson's *Princess* was negatively reviewed as a "curious little freak of fancy . . . confounding what is true in fact with what is truly poetical, and degrading the *natural* into the merely *animal*" (11 March 1848, pp. 210–11); *Maud, and Other Poems*, however, was well received (September 1855, p. 240). In a long article, "Modern Poets" (March 1858, pp. 188–207), Charles Meynell, a philosopher, points to Tennyson's *In Memoriam* as an exemplar of the "black demon" of "unhealthy poetry," and, in view of his hatred for "the spasmodic school," hopes that Longfellow's rising influence will succeed in banishing this demon (p. 196). Frankly admitting that he seeks a Catholic literature, Meynell praises the poetry of Father Faber and Father Caswall and prays for their success, for the "unhealthy atmosphere of Protestantism" makes the modern poets by turns "morbid, frantic, sullen, and ecstatic" (p. 207).

Other than the poets (and Dickens and Thackeray), the male writers who receive significant attention are Thomas Carlyle, Leigh Hunt, Charles Kingsley, Anthony Trollope, and Wilkie Collins, and only Collins receives any approval.[9] The article "Carlylism," a review of the first two *Latter-Day Pamphlets*, declares that Carlyle is blind to "all that comes from heaven," and, though clever and witty, is "not so clever as to know himself, or to be aware that he is but one imposter discoursing to his fellow-imposters" (April 1850, p. 355). It comes as little surprise when his *History of Frederick the Great* receives unfavorable notice from Sir John Acton (December 1858, pp. 429–31).

Leigh Hunt's *The Old Court Suburb* contained "a good deal of twaddle," and "his spite against Catholicity" was, the critic hoped, "too prominent . . . to serve his turn" (August 1855, p. 155). Charles Kingsley, whose association with Carlyle was already a strike against him, was similarly scored for his hatred of Catholicism and, predictably, his *Yeast, A Problem, Westward Ho!*, and *Glaucus, or the Wonders of the Shore* were all denounced (June 1851, pp. 525-33; June 1855, p. 508; August 1855, pp. 156-57). Trollope was berated for *La Beata* (September 1861, p. 402), and described by J. M. Capes as a "goose" who has "entirely mistaken his vocation" as a writer of historical biographies (January 1857, p. 62); Capes subsequently praised *Doctor Thorne* (August 1858, pp. 142–43). Collins alone was highly praised. His *Hide and Seek*, a story about a deaf girl, was extolled as an "interesting novel, written with true artistic care" (August 1854, p. 184), and *After Dark* merited this encomium: "We can seldom speak in a so high terms of a book of tales as of these two volumes" (April 1856, p. 317).

Dickens and Thackeray receive approximately equal notice in the *Rambler*, but there is no mistaking the journal's preference for Thackeray. Both receive generally favorable notices in the late 1840s, but subsequently comparisons of the two are biased against Dickens.[10] The turning point in their valuation is most clearly expressed in J. A. Stothert's "Living Novelists," an eleven-page review of the works of Dickens, Thackeray, Bulwer-Lytton, Lady G. Fullerton, and Currer Bell (Charlotte Brontë) that appeared in the first number of the first "new series" (January 1854, pp. 41–51).

Stothert begins by making two points clear: these five novelists are in the "second rank," behind Walter Scott and Jane Austen, and their relative popularity is "no test whatever of their respective merits" (p. 41). He classifies Dickens as a farcical writer, and Thackeray as a satirist; leaving no doubt as to which type of writer he rates higher, Stothert continues by belittling Dickens as the product of his age: "He is at once the creation and the prophet of an age which loves benevolence without religion, the domestic virtues more than the heroic, the farcical more than the comic, and the extravagant more than the tragic.... [He is a] product of a restlessly observant but shallow era" (p. 42). Being not a man of "*thought*" he usually "overdoes it," and is capable of only "melodrama instead of tragedy, and penny-a-lining (clever though it be) instead of powerful writing" (pp. 43–44). Moreover, Dickens is guilty of the following litany of ills: "nastiness"; a belief in "amiable jollity" as the "*beau-ideal* of human perfection"; ignorance of the "elements of a religious faith"; an inability to draw religious hypocrites; and last, but not least, a superficial knowledge of human nature (pp. 44–45). It is by now very clear that the reviewer is unhappy with *Bleak House*.

In juxtaposition to this trouncing of Dickens appears a laudatory appraisal of Thackeray, whose "power lies in the dissection of human motives and the developing of human infirmities" (p. 45). What makes Stothert's praise of Thackeray all the more clearly a result of disdain for Dickens rather than of an unbridled enthusiasm for Thackeray is the admission that Thackeray was apparently misogynic, the fact that he had savagely attacked Cardinal Wiseman in *Punch*,* and his failure with *Esmond*: its "Addisonian style...is, after all, only a very clever schoolboy's exercise in the manner of the *Spectator*"* (see *AAAJ*) (p. 46).

Frederick Capes (brother to J. M. Capes) continues in this strain a few years later in a review of J. Cordy Jeaffreson's *Novels and Novelists*. Capes claims that Thackeray "describes men as they actually are," while Dickens "draws them as they appear" (September 1858, p. 206). In opposing "the 'Boz' ophicleide," he echoes Stothert's prejudice against popularity when he explains that the secret of Dickens's popularity is the same as that of the *Times*: "He does not lead or form public opinion, but he follows it with unerring certainty" (p. 204). Thackeray's bent for realism had been praised earlier by a reviewer (possibly John C. Whyte) of *The Newcomes* (October 1855, pp. 277–84). While noting the wide range of differences of opinion over Thackeray, the reviewer includes himself among those "who regard his picture of human life . . . as substantially accurate in an extraordinary degree. English society is, we are convinced, no better and no worse than Mr. Thackeray describes it" (p. 278). As with Stothert, this praise is forthcoming in spite of Thackeray's serious shortcomings; for example, the reviewer deplores his "little knowledge of religious principle in its heroic or its manly types" (p. 278), a complaint echoing that made by Stothert against Dickens. What was pleasing, however, was the change in Thackeray's treatment of things Catholic; indeed, it now seemed that the satirist "detected the boundless humbug which belongs to some of the peculiarities of Protestantism" (p. 280).

Women and their works receive extensive coverage and analysis in the pages of the *Rambler*. Those rating appreciable explication are Charlotte Brontë, E. B. Browning, Caddell, Dinah Maria Mulock Craik, George Eliot, E. C. Gaskell, and Harriet Martineau. Martineau was rather extravagantly vilified in the second part of a review of *Eastern Life, Past and Present* as "the enemy of Christianity and of all existing religions" (3 June, 1848, p. 106), although a later reviewer (Daniel Parsons) praised her *Playfellow, The Settlers at Home*, and *Feats on the Fiord* (March 1854, p. 300). Craik fared poorly: in dismissing *A Woman's Thoughts about Women*, Richard Simpson wrote, "When a woman publishes three hundred and fifty pages of advice to her 'sect,' she can hardly avoid being dry, didactic, and boring" (March 1858, p. 215). Simpson liked better Caddell's *Home and the Homeless* (December 1858, pp. 431–32), Browning's *Aurora Leigh* (February 1857, pp. 152–54), and Fullerton's *Grantley Manor, A Tale*, the last which, he felt, showed Catholics in "their every-day life, without controversy or any of that obtrusiveness which characterises the 'religious novel' " (October 1854, p. 363). Gaskell's *Lizzie Leigh, and Other Tales* was well received (December 1855, p. 470), but Frederick and J. M. Capes expressed impatience with her *Life of Charlotte Brontë*: "Mrs. Gaskell and Miss Brontë profess to instruct the world, and must abide the consequences. . . . If women write as men, they must be judged as men" (July 1857, p. 79).

Brontë's works received mixed reviews. In 1848 *Jane Eyre*, because of the "radical *coarseness* of feeling which pervades the story," was described (in an item on *The Christian Remembrancer*) as "one of the most offensive books we ever read" (8 April 1848, p. 313). A few years later, however, J. A. Stothert classified Brontë as a representative of the psychological school, and described her as a "remarkable and powerful writer" who can penetrate "into the *depths* of a mind such as she desires to depict" (January 1854, p. 50). He praised also her "dramatic power in the development of character," but her spite against the Belgians in *Villette* made him wonder "what Brussels has done to Currer Bell" (p. 51). And in a revealing comment regarding the anti-Catholicism of his time, he noted that, "unfair as are her representations of Catholicism and Catholics, they are not so bad as are generally to be found in the current popular literature of the day" (p. 51). Finally, complaining of her narrowness of mind and paucity of conceptions, he warned that her popularity would decline almost as rapidly as it had arisen unless "a decided change is shown in her next work" (p 51).

Turning at last to George Eliot, J. M. Capes observed of her in 1858 that he did not know who the writer of *Scenes from Clerical Life* was, but opined that he was "unmistakably an Anglican clergyman of the broad-church school in theology" (August 1858, p. 143). Two years later, in a "communicated" article on her novels, H. N. Oxenham claims to have known the author's sex since the appearance of *Adam Bede*, and credits her (along with Miss Yonge and Currer Bell) with the capacity for "spiritual photography," a "graphic power of de-lineating fine shades of character" (November 1860, p. 81). Asserting that the promise shown in *Scenes from Clerical Life* has been amply fulfilled, he notes that he, contrary to prevailing opinion, does not rank *The Mill on the Floss* inferior to *Adam Bede*. Closing his essay, he professes that the religious tend-encies of Eliot's writings "bear a striking indirect evidence . . . to the truth of Catholicism as alone answering the deeper needs of the heart of man" (p. 98).

Any assessment of the literary concerns of the *Rambler* must take into account the journal's isolation and precariousness. As dispiriting as the rise of unbelief might have been to many mid-Victorian Protestants, their discomfort must have been exceeded by the anguish of those new and idealistic Catholics connected with the *Rambler*, who had to contend not only with the prevailing rationalist and "infidel" Protestant press, and prejudicial literary treatments by non-Catholic writers, but also with the incessant hounding by those of their own Church (the *Rambler* being driven at last to a Protestant publisher for its final four numbers).[11] Beleaguered as they were, the journal's contributors may be excused if they were sometimes tempted, too readily, to see crypto-Catholics, possible converts, or the "truth of Catholicism" in the Victorian writers and works they reviewed. The importance of the *Rambler*'s literary reviews and essays may lie in their concern with the health and sanative worth of literature, with the obligations of writers to their readers. Not that fiction and poetry had to be sermonic; in fact, reviewers tended to be emphatic about the need to keep "preachiness" out of literature. They did not want works of art to be burdened with theology: from writers of fiction they expected unadorned and unexaggerated realism, with no forced melodrama or artificial sentiment; and from poets they demanded restraint and responsibleness, in many ways anticipating John Morley's condemnation of Swinburne (in the *Saturday Review** for 4 August 1866) and Robert Buchanan's famous review of Rossetti (in the *Contemporary Review** for October 1871).

Sadly, despite the *Rambler*'s crusade against rationalist journalism and irre-sponsible fiction and poetry, and despite its support of Catholic publishers and publications (though not given unreservedly, as its all but suicidal strictures of the *Dublin Review* * [see *RA*] prove), the ill-fated journal was not viable. Its successor, the *Home and Foreign Review*, lasted but two years. The following wistful comment by Thomas Hardy, who despaired, as these liberal Catholics must have, of ever seeing an English alliance between religion and rationality, may serve as an epitaph for them and their journal:

The historic and once august hierarchy of Rome some generation ago lost its chance of being the religion of the future by ... throwing over the little band of New Catholics who were making a struggle for continuity by applying the principle of evolution to their own faith, joining hands with modern science, and outflanking the hesitating English instinct towards liturgical restatement.[12]

Notes

1. Josef L. Altholz, *The Liberal Catholic Movement in England: The "Rambler" and Its Contributors, 1848–1864* (London, 1962), p. 9.

2. Ibid., p. 26.

3. The essay on the *Rambler* in the *Wellesley Index* implies that the original title included "Music" and (in place of "Art") "The Fine Arts." These additions to the title are indeed on the title page of the bound volume 1, but were not effective until number 19 (6 May 1848), which was the first number of volume 2.

4. See Altholz, *Liberal Catholic Movement*; and Walter E. Houghton, ed., *The Wellesley Index to Victorian Periodicals, 1824–1900*, vol. 2 (Toronto, 1972). I am indebted to the *Wellesley Index* for my assignment of contributors' names to selected items highlighted in this profile.

5. Because the *Rambler* went through three series, with the second and third both called "New Series," I have simplified parenthetical documentation in the text by limiting such documentation to the date of the issue, followed by the page number(s). With this data, one can quickly find the appropriate denominations of series and volume by consulting the *Wellesley Index* (2:742–84). Subsequent textual documentation for the same citation will give only page number(s).

6. Josef L. Altholz, "On the Use of 'Communicated' in the *Rambler*," *Victorian Periodicals Newsletter*, no. 8 (1968):28.

7. Vincent Ferrer Blehl, "Newman, the Bishops and *The Rambler*," *Downside Review* 90 (1972):24–25, 30–35.

8. The short reviews are often cleverly done, sometimes caustically so, as in this unmerciful dismissal of S. W. Fullom's *The History of Woman*: "Mr. Fullom is one of those preposterous funguses that every now and then will ooze forth from the hoary trunk of our literature, and engage more attention than they deserve" (April 1855, p. 329).

9. Disraeli is occasionally mentioned in the pages of the *Rambler*, but primarily in his political capacities. There is an interesting article entitled "The Hebraisms and Catholicisms of Disraeli's Novels" (May 1854, pp. 439–53), in which W. F. Finlason, a legal writer, harshly reviews (in their new editions) *The Young Duke, Coningsby, Sibyl, Tancred*, and other works, but the article's literary value is limited.

10. Among these early notices are the following: *Dombey and Son* (22 January 1848, pp. 64–65); *David Copperfield* (September 1849, pp. 333–35); *Our Street* (15 January 1848, p. 44); *Book of Snobs* (12 February 1848, p. 116); and *Pendennis* (May 1849, pp. 48–51). Later notices include a negative review of *Hard Times* (October 1854, pp. 361–62), and praise for both *The Rose and the Ring* (January 1855, pp. 79–80) and *Miscellanies, Prose and Verse*, volume 1 (December 1855, p. 470).

11. The following inventory of the Protestant press appears in the review of Kingsley's *Yeast* (June 1851, p. 526): "Of the chief quarterly reviews, the *Edinburgh* [*(see RA)]

is rationalist; the *Westminster and Foreign Quarterly* [see *Westminster Review** (*RA*)] all but infidel, if not quite so. Of the weekly journals, the *Spectator* [*(see *RA*)], the *Athenaeum* [*(see *RA*)], and the *Examiner* [*(see *RA*)] are infidel all but in name; the *Weekly Dispatch* and the *Leader* [*] are professedly infidel. Among the daily papers, the *Daily News* is rationalist, the *Chronicle* puseyiticorationalist, while the *Times* believes in nothing whatsoever.''

12. This passage is from Hardy's "Apology" in the preface to his *Late Lyrics and Earlier* (London, 1922).

Information Sources

BIBLIOGRAPHY

Altholz, Josef L. *The Liberal Catholic Movement in England: The "Rambler" and Its Contributors, 1848–1864*. London, 1962.
———. "On the Use of 'Communicated' in the *Rambler*." *Victorian Periodicals Newsletter*, no. 8 (1968):28.
Altholz, Josef Lewis, and Damian McElrath, eds. *The Correspondence of Lord Acton and Richard Simpson*. Cambridge, England, 1971–1975.
Blehl, Vincent Ferrer. "Newman, the Bishops and *The Rambler*." *Downside Review* 90 (1972):24–35.
Houghton, Walter, ed. *The Wellesley Index to Victorian Periodicals, 1824–1900*. Vol. 2. Toronto, 1972.
McElrath, Damian. "Richard Simpson and John Henry Newman: *The Rambler*, Laymen, and Theology." *Catholic Historical Review* 52 (1967):509–33.
Newman, John Henry. *The Letters and Diaries of John Henry Newman*. Edited by Charles Stephen Dissain. London, 1961–1976.

INDEXES

Each volume is indexed (not all items in the short literary notices are included in the indexes). *Wellesley Index* 2.

REPRINT EDITIONS

Microform: English Literary, Periodicals (UMI), reels 519–524.

LOCATION SOURCES

American

Partial runs: Widely available.

British

Complete runs: British Museum; Cambridge University Library.
Partial runs: Birmingham Public Library; Bodleian Library; Dr. William's Library; Edinburgh Public Library; Glasgow University Library; Manchester Public Library; St. Andrews University Library; Trinity College Library, Dublin; University College Library, London.

Publication History

MAGAZINE TITLE AND TITLE CHANGES

The Rambler, A Journal of Home and Foreign Literature, Politics, Science, and Art, 1 January 1848–29 April 1848. *The Rambler, A Journal of Home and Foreign Literature, Politics, Science, Music, and The Fine Arts*, 6 May 1848–26 August 1848. *The Rambler, A Journal and Review of Home and Foreign Literature, Politics, Science, Music, and The Fine Arts*, September 1848–December 1849.

The Rambler, A Catholic Journal and Review, January 1850–June 1854. *The Rambler*, July 1854–May 1862.

VOLUME AND ISSUE DATA

Volumes 1–12, 1 January 1848–December 1853; new series (2d ser.), volumes 1–11, number 2, January 1854–February 1859; new series (3d ser.), volumes 1–6, May 1859–May 1862.

FREQUENCY OF PUBLICATION

Weekly, 1 January 1848–26 August 1848; monthly, September 1848–February 1859; bimonthly, May 1859–May 1862. (Succeeded by the *Home and Foreign Review*, July 1862–April 1864.)

PUBLISHERS

1 January 1848–December 1849: James Burns, 17 Portman St., Portman Sq.; January 1850–September 1861: Burns and Lambert, 17 Portman St., Portman Sq.; November 1861–May 1862: Williams and Norgate, 14 Henrietta St., Covent Garden.

EDITORS

John Moore Capes, 1 January, 1848–1852. James Spencer Northcote, 1852–September 1854. John Moore Capes, October 1854–October 1857. (Simpson acting editor, October 1856–January 1857 and November 1857–January 1858.) Richard Simpson, February 1858–February 1859. (Capes acting editor, July 1858.). John Henry Newman, May–July 1859. Sir John Acton, September 1859–May 1862.

Bruce A. White

READER, THE

The *Reader: A Review of Current Literature* appeared for the first time on Saturday, 3 January 1863. It has been described as "unquestionably, one of the finest literary journals of the nineteenth century." "Designed to notice all books," the *Reader* shared similarities with the *Monthly Review** (see *AAAJ*) and *Critical Review** (see *AAAJ*) of the previous century. "The fullness of this critical plan is important," writes Walter Graham, "in the light of later-day attempts and achievements." Its audience was upper-middle-class, highly educated, politically liberal, and philosophically radical. The *Reader* was considered "a worthy competitor to the *Athenaeum*"* (see *RA*), which it resembled in design and purpose.[1] It proposed to fill a journalistic need existing in the 1860s, following Darwin's *On the Origin of Species*. According to the *Annual Register*, "The *Athenaeum* and the *Reader* are the two journals now representing literature, art, and popular science; the old *Literary Gazette* [* (see *RA*)], which in 1862 assumed the name of the *Parthenon*, having come to an end in 1863, after an existence of forty-six years. The *Critic*,[*] another literary paper of later origin, also expired in this year."[2]

The *Reader* was perhaps the only literary journal in England during the years 1863–1867 to carry free and open discussion of both scientific and religious subjects—along with a comprehensive digest of scientific and learned news—into the homes of educated, liberal-minded laymen. It began, following the clarion call of Darwin's *Origin of Species*, in a decade of expansion, of transition from sail to steam, of scientific experimentation, of "revolutionary agencies in thought," including philosophy, biblical criticism, and educational reform. It was an age of oppositions: science versus religion; utilitarian versus idealistic concepts of culture; and the "free play of the intellect versus the abject deference . . . for authority." It was, in short, an age of reform.[3]

The *Reader* reflects several different traditions, including the belles lettres or literary tradition of the *Spectator** (see *AAAJ, RA*) and *Athenaeum*; the polemical emphasis of the Christian Socialist's journals and tracts; and the scientific discussions from learned journals and their proceedings. Its history suggests three distinct phases, observed from the first issue to the 211th number, which appeared on 12 January 1867. The first period (3 January 1863–10 December 1864) was dominated in the first year by the Christian Socialists and Broad Churchmen gathered around F. D. Maurice, J. M. Ludlow, and Thomas Hughes. During the second year, dominance shifted to the vigorous leadership of Thomas Henry Huxley, Frederick Norman Lockyer, Francis Galton, and other scientists, whom J. D. Hooker called the "Young Guard of Science."[4] The second period (17 December 1864–29 July 1865) comprised the direct control and ownership of the "Young Guard."[5] The third period (5 August 1865–12 January 1867) comprised the ownership and editorial control of Thomas Bendyshe, a fellow of King's College, Cambridge, and a barrister of the Inner Temple.

The first number of the *Reader* appeared on 3 January 1863, "commanding the services of distinguished writers in every branch of literature and science, in an attempt to review all contemporary progress in the march of human endeavor. This ambitious essay in cultural synthesis was at first piloted by J. M. Ludlow with the old brigade of Christian Socialists stocking the columns: Llewelyn Davies, Lowes Dickinson, [F. J.] Furnivall, [Charles] Kingsley, Maurice, [E. V.] Neale, [John] Westlake, and of course, Hughes."[6] These Christian Socialists, along with others, were the direct source of support for the *Reader* during the first two years of its existence. More than a decade of cooperation, polemical writing, and education of working people lay beneath the basic proposal setting forth the principles of the new review. Yet, in spite of Ludlow's lofty purpose, he "could not get it organized in the business-like manner he wished and finding 'manager, publisher and printer impossible' very soon resigned, 'after having gathered' he claimed, 'a list of contributors such as was never known for a newspaper.' "[7]

A list of the most prolific of these contributors suggests the range of the reviewers during 1863–1865, the most significant years. Contributors included C. C. Blake, anthropologist and secretary of the Anthropology Society of London; Sidney Blanchard, son of Laman Blanchard and private secretary at one time to Disraeli; H. R. Foxbourne, noted journalist, who reviewed historical and governmental works; Frances Power Cobbe, feminist and philosophical writer (travel and social science); J. L. Davies, Broad Churchman and supporter of Cooperation (theological subjects; theological editor during early 1865); Edward Dicey, war correspondent in Europe and America (fiction and Civil War books); Frederick J. Furnivall, philologist and Christian Socialist (novels and early English literature); Edward L. Garbett, Oxford divine and editor of the *Record*, 1854–1867 (architectural and scientific subjects); Frederick W. Gibbs, tutor to the Prince of Wales, 1851–1860; Thomas Hughes, proprietor and editor (U.S. Civil War and general subjects); Charles Kingsley and his brothers George and Henry; Andrew V. Kirwan (fiction, travel, food, wines, and naval history); David C. Lathbury (fiction); Joseph N. Lockyer, science editor and contributor on scientific subjects; John F.M. Ludlow, proprietor and editor (fiction and social science); Edward V. Neale, Christian Socialist (religious subjects); George Rawlinson, Canon of Canterbury (theological subjects); J. F. Robertson (fiction); William M. Rossetti, art critic; and Tom Taylor (poetry and fiction).[8]

From the beginning, the *Reader* was committed to the scientific viewpoint. It was merely a question of time until Ludlow's "band of brothers" gracefully capitulated to the "Young Guard" of science. The guard was headed by "Darwin's Bulldog," Thomas H. Huxley, whose association with the *Reader* gave it the proper amount of secular moral tone necessary for popularizing the scientific epoch: a liberal theology willing to put dogma to the scientific test and a scientific frame of reference capable of preserving the provable truth of Christian tradition. The mere presence of Huxley should have guaranteed the growth and success of the new science. Most of his efforts were directed to one end—producing a journal that would collect and disseminate the projects, discoveries, and advances of science. To that end he joined Lockyer on the *Reader* sometime in 1863, leaving the *Natural History Review*, which weakened and expired two year later.

A combination of factors contributed to making the second phase in the *Reader*'s history, November 1864–July 1865, the shortest and perhaps the most significant in its four-year existence. Sometime during the summer of 1864, Lockyer and Huxley probably saw the *Reader* approaching its end as the organ of Broad Church liberal social reform. The Christian Socialists were concerning themselves more and more with the education of working men and women, cooperation, and trade unionism. It is a reasonable conjecture that the British Association meeting at Newcastle-on-Tyne in August 1863 gave encouragement to Lockyer and Huxley a year later to form a proprietorship composed of the best young scientists in England—the "Young Guard." The meeting of the British Association at Bath in 1864 could only have reinforced their earlier convictions.

At the first meeting of the "X" Club, 3 November 1864, Huxley and eight other prominent scientists—George Busk, Edward Frankland, Thomas A. Hirst, John L. Lubbock, William Spottiswoode, John Tyndall, Herbert Spencer, and Joseph D. Hooker—discussed the reorganization of the *Reader*. During the same week, a decision was made by at least five of the "X" group (Huxley, Lubbock, Spencer, Tyndall, and Spottiswoode) to purchase the *Reader* and turn it into a limited liability company. Huxley is credited with bringing the original "X" group together. His contributions to science through the club and the *Reader* are equally important, reflecting his mutual concern for the advancement of scientific information and the control of its dissemination. These men were undoubtedly the intellectual bank behind what became the new *Reader*.

Little information is available on the transfer of the *Reader* proprietorship to Thomas Bendyshe. It is known that he purchased it sometime in July 1865, but details are sparse. During his tenure, from August 1865 to the final number for 12 January 1867, the *Reader* issues reflect a growing, changing attitude toward science and, especially, religion.

Little is known about Bendyshe himself except that he was a close friend of Swinburne, a founder of the Anthropological Society of London, and the author of a number of anthropological treatises; he was also a member of the infamous Cannibal Club, along with Swinburne, J. F. Collingwood, James Hurst, Nicholas Trubner, Charles Carter Blake, Richard Burton, Charles Duncan Cameron, and Winwood Reade.[9] Swinburne calls him "a raging and devoted atheist,"[10] while W. M. Rossetti refers to him as "a singular unconventional-minded man."[11] But there was certainly something about this eccentric, "aggressively atheistic . . . notoriously strong-minded and (apparently) unpopular senior fellow of King's"[12] that led to the dissolution of the final proprietorship on 12 January 1867. If a cause can be discovered for the end of the *Reader*, it may provide a connection between Bendyshe's behavior at the Westminster election in July 1865 when, in what can only be construed as an act of defiance, he voted for J. S. Mill, who was elected to Parliament as a Liberal; his incomplete "Memoirs of a Suicide," in which he exercised a mind apparently fascinated by the possibilities of heterodoxy; and F. J. Furnivall's bizarre review of Latham's edition of Dr. Johnson's *Dictionary*, in which the reviewer, presumably Furnivall, misread Johnson's famous preface, castigating its author unmercifully under the apparent notion that it had been written by the editor, R. G. Latham. The *Reader* never appeared again after that issue, number 211, for 12 January 1867.

At first glance it would appear that the *Reader* was a valiant, albeit ill-fated journalistic venture, a scientific "experiment" that failed. Too often, however, journalistic success is measured in volumes and lines of type. In a quantitative sense, perhaps, the *Reader* was a failure. But in a qualitative sense, the *Reader* deserves a higher place in the history of Victorian literary journalism than it has been given. Its pages preserve the recognizable efforts of liberal theologians, Darwinian disciples, and dreamers of treason awakened to a "Hymn of Man."

In spite of its farcical end, the *Reader* contains sufficient evidence that, like its more successful rival, the *Athenaeum*, it, too, "mirrored" the culture of the 1860s. Its brief four years' run suggests a microcosm of Victorian scientific journalism; its more than 5,600 pages of reviews preserve an eclectic adventure; its three proprietorships reflect the inevitable movement of the Victorian periodical away from the theological, toward scientific subject matter. More importantly, the *Reader* made a serious attempt to create a scientific center of disinterested discussion; indeed, it might be termed a truly scientific *Athenaeum*. Careful attention to its reviews indicates its liberalizing spirit. Common to all three periods is a marked tendency to reflect the reality of the Darwinian revolution. Whether in matters of theological discussion, scientific speculation, or the milder forms of heterodoxical proselytizing, the *Reader* was in the vanguard of post-Darwinian thought and action. Coming as it did just a few years after the *Origin of Species*, the *Reader* was undoubtedly the clearest expression of the youthful fervor of Huxley, Darwin, Spencer, and the Young Guard of science. By combining the elements of liberal theology, conservative scientific inquiry, and mild heterodoxy, the *Reader* gave its audience a preview of the elements of diversity destined to hold the attention of Victoria's subjects for the remainder of the century.

Notes

1. Walter Graham, *English Literary Periodicals* (New York, 1930), p. 331.
2. *Annual Register for 1863* (London, 1864), p. 360.
3. G. M. Young, *Victorian England: Portrait of an Age*, 2d ed. (New York, 1960), pp. 81–82.
4. Leonard Huxley, *Life and Letters of J. D. Hooker*, 2 vols. (London, 1918), 1:541.
5. An approximation; the source mentions August 1865 as the date of purchase by Thomas Bendyshe. T.H.S. Escott, *Platform, Press, Politics and Play* (Bristol, 1895), pp. 238–41.
6. E. C. Mack and Walter H. G. Armytage, *Thomas Hughes* (London, 1952), p. 125.
7. N. C. Masterman, *John Malcolm Ludlow* (Cambridge, England, 1963), p. 159.
8. During the final period, Bendyshe, as owner and editor, seems to have operated almost single-handedly.
9. Cecil Y. Lang, ed., *Swinburne Letters*, 6 vols. (New Haven, 1959–1962), 1:288.
10. Lang, 2:4–5.
11. W. M. Rossetti, ed., *Rossetti Papers: 1862–1870* (London, 1903), pp. 379–80.
12. Lang, 1:227.

Information Sources

BIBLIOGRAPHY

Bibby, H. Cyril. *Thomas Henry Huxley, Scientist, Humanist, and Educator*. New York, 1960.

Byrne, John F. "The Reader: A Review of Literature, Science and the Arts, 1863–1867." Ph.D. dissertation, Northwestern University, 1964.

Galton, Francis. *Memories of My Life*. 3d ed. London, 1909.

Irvine, William. *Apes, Angels, and Victorians: A Joint Biography of Darwin and Huxley*. London, 1955.

Lang, Cecil Y., ed. *Swinburne Letters*. 6 vols. New Haven, 1959–1962.

Lockyer, T. M., and W. L. Lockyer. *Life and Work of Sir Norman Lockyer*. London, 1928.

Mack, E. C., and Walter H. G. Armytage. *Thomas Hughes*. London, 1952.

Masterman, N. C. *John Malcolm Ludlow*. Cambridge, England, 1963.

Maurice, Frederic M.M., ed. *Life of Frederic D. Maurice Chiefly Told in his Own Letters*. 2 vols. London, 1884.

Pearson, Karl. *Life and Letters and Labours of Francis Galton*. 3 vols. in 4. Cambridge, England, 1914–1930.

Pollock, Sir Frederick. *Personal Remembrances*. 2 vols. London, 1887.

INDEXES

Volumes 1–6 indexed. (John F. Byrne has prepared an index not yet published.)

REPRINT EDITIONS

1961, University of Chicago.

Microform: English Literary Periodicals (UMI), reels 608–609 and 617–618.

LOCATION SOURCES

American

Complete runs: Boston Athenaeum; U. S. Library of Congress.

Partial runs: Widely available.

British

Partial runs: Widely available.

Publication History

MAGAZINE TITLE AND TITLE CHANGES

The Reader: A Review of Current Literature.

VOLUME AND ISSUE DATA

Volumes 1–8, numbers 1–211, 3 January 1863–12 January 1867.

FREQUENCY OF PUBLICATION

Weekly.

PUBLISHERS

3 January 1863–16 June 1866: James Bohn, 112 Fleet Street, London, E.C./24 Tavistock Street, Covent Garden, London, W.C. (5 December 1863–16 June 1866). 23 June 1866–12 January 1867: A. Lawler ("for the proprietor"—Thomas Bendyshe), 24 Tavistock Street, Covent Garden, London, W.C.

EDITORS

J. M. Ludlow, 3 January–end of March, 1863. David Masson, April–summer 1863. W. F. Rae, summer 1863–fall 1864. No editor-in-chief, but a nominal editor, unknown, 17 December 1864–29 July 1865. Thomas Bendyshe, 5 August 1865–12 January 1867.

John F. Byrne

RETROSPECTIVE REVIEW, THE. See RA

REVIEW OF REVIEWS, THE

The Victorian journalist-politician T. P. O'Connor was one of many who rated the *Review of Reviews*, which began in 1890, as "one of the most interesting and ... most instructive periodicals ever published,"[1] Others noted that while readers of the journal never quite knew what new men, movements, or causes its editor, W. T. Stead, would espouse, he always presented his appeals with "a freshness, vitality and resourcefulness" that were difficult to deny. The *Review* had special appeal to the lower middle class because it provided a comprehensive digest of the most important periodicals.[2]

Following two decades in daily journalism as the renowned editor of the Darlington *Northern Echo* (1871–1880) and the London *Pall Mall Gazette* (1880–1889), Stead decided to publish and edit a monthly periodical that would exert the power of the press in politics.[3] In mid-December 1889 Stead explained that the projected *Review* would seek to impart to the reading public his "gospel and ideals" while presenting "a readable and compendious summary of all [that is] best . . . in the magazines and reviews. . .[and] the best writers of our time."[4] The project was indeed the result of a scheme for a monthly supplement to the *Pall Mall Gazette* that Stead had evolved in 1888 to arrest the declining circulation of the paper. When its proprietor, Henry Yates Thompson, rejected the scheme, Stead sought financial assistance to launch independently a six-penny journal, hoping that Thompson would permit him to edit the periodical while continuing as the editor of the *Pall Mall Gazette*.[5] As Thompson refused his proposal, Stead left, declaring that the monthly periodical had replaced the daily paper as the best means to exert influence on national and international affairs. To assure publishers of other periodicals that his new journal would neither cannibalize nor prejudice their circulation, Stead asserted that his venture would serve as "a guide to those already in existence" by publicizing "their wares" and by providing work for writers unable to secure publication in the older monthlies and quarterlies.[6]

Failing to interest the Cassell publishing house in the project, Stead secured the support of George Newnes, the publisher of the very successful weekly, *Tit-Bits*. Newnes agreed to finance Stead's scheme, and on 6 January 1890 the first issue of the *Review of Reviews* was produced. In this new venture, Newnes was publisher, Stead his partner and editor, and C. A. Pearson business manager. Sixty thousand copies of the first issue were sold and it was soon apparent that the *Review* was indeed a "triumph of journalistic skill and industry." The publisher of the *Star*, T. P. O'Connor, who knew Stead well, hailed the *Review* as a valuable "six-penny poor and busy man's guide to monthly literature."[7]

The first issue of eighty-four pages set the pattern for subsequent issues. It began with a news commentary ("The Progress of the World") that reflected Stead's view of events. In addition to the commentary, there were articles on Stead's special projects, including a keen "Character Sketch" of a prominent personality (often written by Stead); some thirty pages of summaries of "Leading Articles" in major British and foreign periodicals; a section ("The Reviews Reviewed") presenting brief summaries of the contents of British, American, and Continental magazines; the condensation of a new book (during the first year this included Mark Twain's *Connecticut Yankee in King Arthur's Court*, Tolstoy's *Kreutzer Sonata*, and *The Journal of Marie Bashkirtseff*); an annotated list of new books; and a checklist of significant periodical articles. Such rich fare greatly increased the circulation of the *Review*, notwithstanding the cavalier sneer that it appealed only to the "below-stairs intelligence."[8]

The most significant feature in the first issue of the *Review* was Stead's editorial pronouncement "To All English-Speaking Folk," which averred that a major objective of the journal was "the universal diffusion of the ascertained results of human experience in a form accessible to all men" (pp. 15–20). While the *Review*, explained Stead, would seek to facilitate "the expression of individual conviction upon men and things" and to reflect "the best thought of our time," it would be neither a party organ nor "a colorless reflection of public opinion." Its greatest mission was to promote the "English-speaking race" as "one of God's chosen agents for the improvement of mankind" by working to achieve the union of all English-speaking peoples, the expansion of the British Empire, and Irish home rule. But, since the *Review* was also dedicated to other great "needs"—the "revival of civic faith, a quickening of spiritual life," and morality in political life—Stead invited readers to join him in an Association of Helpers to aid in the achievement of these objectives.[9]

During the early months of the *Review*, Stead assiduously cultivated the goodwill of other periodicals, expanded periodical exchanges, and (much to the distaste of Newnes) published reviews and summaries of such controversial books as Twain's *Connecticut Yankee*. Stead thus belied the predictions of some critics that the *Review* was doomed because the journals on which it fed would refuse to cooperate.

Meanwhile, Newnes, the hard-headed businessman, was rapidly becoming disenchanted with his ebullient partner.[10] He would not tolerate Stead's haste to establish overseas affiliates of the *Review*, or his use of the *Review* to propagate his own ideas, or his penchant for controversy. Above all, Newnes feared that Stead's persistence in making the *Review* "an independent organ of opinion" would lessen its financial value. The breach occurred in February as a result of Stead's acid "Character Sketch" of the *Times* for the March issue, which Newnes feared might provoke a libel suit. Although Stead made some minor concessions to Newnes, he protested his "interference" with the editorial direction of the *Review*. Stead respected Newnes's business acumen, but had no faith in his intellect or devotion to "high ideals." This attitude was apparent in their quarrel over Stead's arrangement to publish a condensation of Count Leo Tolstoy's provocative novel, *The Kreutzer Sonata*. Following the tsarist government's refusal to permit the publication of the book, Stead sought to achieve a journalistic coup by arranging for its translation and unexpurgated publication in the *Review*. When Newnes sharply objected to the publication of a work that might offend Victorian sensibilities, Stead moved to terminate their partnership.

After a month of hard bargaining, Newnes agreed on 3 April to accept 10,000 pounds for his share, and the partnership was dissolved. But a major problem for Stead was obtaining the money to defray the purchase. In spite of Stead's persistent denials, he secured most of the funds through a loan from his friends, the leaders of the Salvation Army, "General" William Booth and his heir apparent, Bramwell Booth, on the condition that "it [was] to remain absolutely private" lest it be harmful to both parties in the transaction.

Since separation from Newnes deprived Stead of the able Pearson and the *Tit-Bits* staff and quarters, he moved the *Review* office to Mowbray House and hurriedly recruited a staff that included the young Grant Richards to handle subscriptions, Edmund H. Peers as business manager, Marie Belloc Lowndes as office manager, and a corps of young women as clerical assistants. Always generous and considerate, Stead was very popular with his staff. Devoted to the concept of absolute equality for women, Stead hired them at the same salary he paid to men. Unfortunately he was much too generous and wasteful with his time. He was as available to beggars and cranks as he was to cabinet officers and contributors. To establish order and procedure, Grant Richards assumed the responsibility of getting the *Review* to press well before printing deadlines.

A circulation crisis in December 1890, caused by Stead's and Peers's miscalculations, convinced Stead of the urgent need for efficient management of the *Review*. Thus, early in 1891, the incompetent Peers was replaced by Edwin H. Stout. It was a most fortunate change and the beginning of Stout's long and devoted service (1891–1913). Although Stead had complete confidence in Stout, their relationship was always formal, largely because Stout was careful and frugal and attempted to restrain or interdict Stead's prodigality. Stout labored valiantly to keep the *Review* and Stead solvent, a task made doubly difficult by Stead's enthusiasms, campaigns, conflicts, illnesses, and family. Fortunately, Stout could make use of handsome annual dividends from Stead's holdings in the very successful *American Review of Reviews*, established in partnership with Dr. Albert Shaw in late 1890.

The *Review*'s circulation and its revenues decreased because of Stead's unrelenting "social purity" campaigns, such as those to oust Charles Stewart Parnell from politics and to prevent Sir Charles Dilke's resumption of his political career; his Association of Helpers scheme to improve the spiritual and moral condition of British life; his long absence from Britain while waging a crusade against political corruption and sin in Chicago (1893–1894); and his increasing preoccupation with spiritualism. Not even Stout could limit or control Stead's hero-worship of Cecil Rhodes, his vendettas against Dilke and Joseph Chamberlain, and his spiritualist interests. But some redeeming factors were the work of Stead's able younger brother, the Christian Socialist Rev. F. Herbert Stead, as acting editor of the *Review* during Stead's absences and illnesses, and Stead's huge capacity for work. Stout later recalled that, in addition to writing the monthly "Progress of the World," scores of "Character Sketches," "Book of the Month" reviews, and numerous articles for the daily and periodical press, Stead personally wrote or dictated over 80,000 letters during the years 1890–1912. Moreover, during the first two years of the *Review*, affiliates were established in Australia (*Review of Reviews for Australia*), in France (*Revue des Revues*), and especially in the United States (*American Review of Reviews*).[11]

The American affiliate, under the shrewd management of Albert Shaw, became a valuable property yielding handsome semiannual dividends that Stout always feared might be lost as a result of Stead's bickering with Shaw over editorial policy and Stead's mortgaging of his investment of 5,000 pounds in the *American Review*.[12]

Stead, however, was not impossible. Those who knew him well tolerated his prejudices and eccentricities because "they knew that there was nothing mean or bitter or ill-tempered in his make-up" and they were convinced that he was honest, sincere, and loyal. His consistently strong support of women's rights and suffrage was valued by the suffragettes, who always knew that the *Review* would uphold their cause. But while many admired Stead's honesty and fidelity, some (like Josephine Butler and Andrew Carnegie) exploited his biases and friendship. Yet neither his affection for his friends nor the interventions of his confidant, Reginald Brett, could dissuade Stead from assailing what he was convinced was wrong.[13]

Stead's strong sense of loyalty impelled him to help friends by publicity in the *Review*. Thus he accorded a laudatory review to *England in Egypt*, by his former colleague on the *Pall Mall Gazette*, Sir Alfred Milner; publicized the efforts of his longtime friend, Mme. Olga Novikov, to promote Anglo-Russian friendship; supported the political career of his former *Gazette* chief, John Morley; assisted Cardinal Manning in publicizing Pope Leo XIII's *Rerum Novarum*; ardently supported the temperance crusades of Frances Willard and Lady Henry Somerset; "ghosted" and publicized General William Booth's *In Darkest England and the Way Out*, and defended the Salvation Army; and, inspired by the courtier Brett, undertook a spirited defense of the Prince of Wales during the Tranby Croft baccarat affair.[14]

As in the Dilke and Parnell affairs, the Prince's indiscretions and the baccarat scandal had aroused Stead's interest. Thus, in May 1891 he was easily persuaded by Mrs. Josephine Butler and friends in the "Social Purity" movement to undertake a "Character Sketch" of the Prince of Wales for the *Review*. To accomplish his purpose, Brett arranged a meeting for Stead with the Prince's private secretary, Sir Francis Knollys, on June 22. Stead assured Knollys that he desired only "to set forth the facts" of the Prince's life in order to dispel the conviction of most Nonconformists that the Prince was an immoral wastrel. Pledging to write an impartial "Character Sketch," Stead quickly completed a draft and submitted copies of it to Knollys, Brett, Gladstone, and the prominent Nonconformist leaders Hugh Price Hughes and Dr. John Clifford. All rejected the draft and advised drastic revision; Knollys declared that it was unfair to the Prince. Following another meeting with Knollys and drastic revisions, the sketch was approved by Knollys and published in July 1891. Unfortunately, while the Prince, the government, and Cardinal Manning felt that Stead had skillfully dealt with major criticisms of the Prince, many Nonconformists, "Social Purity" partisans, and some sectors of the press rejected Stead's efforts as "a shameless whitewash" of royalty.[15]

The Prince of Wales was only one of Stead's concerns. Until his death in 1912, Stead remained an ardent advocate of women's suffrage and belabored the major political parties for their reluctance to acknowledge "the complete enfranchisement of Women as the most important issue" in British politics.[16] Other causes and issues that Stead championed in the *Review* included the ideas and work of Cecil Rhodes; penny postage for the British Empire; Anglo-Russian amity; Poor Law reform; Irish home rule; Anglo-American alliance and reunion; efficiency and modernization of British industry; international arbitration and limitation of armaments; the Boer Republics during the South African War; the October Manifesto of Tsar Nicholas II during the Russian Revolution of 1905; beleaguered Turkey in the Italo-Turkish War of 1910–1911; psychic phenomena and experimentation; and political and social reform in Britain. Stead remained steadfast in his advocacy of these causes despite the fact that some of them severely decreased the *Review*'s circulation and advertising revenues. His self-righteous prose and alleged inconsistencies provoked the ire of such prominent contemporaries as Frederic Harrison, Charles Algernon Swinburne, James Knowles (editor of the *Fortnightly Review**), W. E. Henley, Sir William Harcourt, T. H. Huxley, Joseph Chamberlain, H. F. Battersby, Gladstone and his son Herbert, George Bernard Shaw, and William Archer.[17]

Nevertheless, until his death on the *Titanic*, Stead made the *Review* interesting, readable, entertaining, and instructive. His perceptive "Character Sketches," informative book reviews, and lead articles distinguish the *Review* as a major source on the culture, politics, thought, and journalism of the late Victorian and Edwardian decades. Unfortunately, under Stead's successors the decline in the quality and variety of the *Review* was precipitous. Following his death, his sons Alfred and John unsuccessfully edited the journal until their departure in 1914 for war service. They were succeeded by Charles Peers who, after three months, gave way to Stead's eldest daughter, Estelle; she occupied the editorial chair for three and a half years until, on behalf of her mother, she sold the *Review* for 25,000 pounds to Daniel O'Connor. Even with the help of the able Philip Gibbs, O'Connor was unable to arrest the decline of the *Review* and, after failing to sell a half-share to Dr. Albert Shaw, sold the property to the renowned *Times* political editor, Henry Wickham Steed, in 1923. Steed served the *Review* as editor-publisher until 1930, when he was succeeded by Lovat Dickson, who in turn was succeeded by W. W. Hindle during 1933. In March 1936 the *Review* was absorbed by the *World* and briefly (March–August 1936) became the *World Review of Reviews*. The journal was again renamed the *World Review* in September 1936, and it came under the direction of the *World*'s editor, Vernon Bartlett. He continued as editor until the periodical was purchased in 1940 by Sir Edward Hulton, and it remained under his aegis until it ceased publication in May 1953.[18]

Notes

1. T. P. O'Connor, "Reminiscences of Stead—II," *T. P.'s Weekly* 21 (1913):657–58.

2. See S. K. Ratcliffe, "W. T. Stead," *Modern Review* 12 (1912):55; Harold Herd, *The Making of Modern Journalism* (London, 1936), p. 33. This essay is in part based on my article, "W. T. Stead as Publisher and Editor of the *Review of Reviews*," *Victorian Periodicals Review* 12 (1979):70–83.

3. On the life and career of William T. Stead (1849–1912), see Frederic Whyte, *The Life of W. T. Stead*, 2 vols. (New York, 1925); Estelle W. Stead, *My Father: Personal and Spiritual Reminiscences* (London, 1913); J. W. Robertson Scott, *The Life and Death of a Newspaper: An Account of the . . . Editors of the "Pall Mall Gazette"* (London, 1952), pp. 72ff.; and the following works by Joseph O. Baylen: "W. T. Stead's *History of the Mystery* and the Jameson Raid," *Journal of British Studies* 4 (1964):104–32; "W. T. Stead and the 'New Journalism,' " *Emory University Quarterly* 21 (1970):1–13; *The Tsar's "Lecturer-General": W. T. Stead and the Russian Revolution of 1905*, Georgia State University, School of Arts and Sciences Research Paper no. 23 (Atlanta, 1969); "The 'New Journalism' in Late Victorian Britain," *Australian Journal of Politics and History* 18 (1972):367–85; "Stead's 'Penny Masterpiece Library,' " *Journal of Popular Culture* 9 (1975–1976):710–25.

4. Mr. Stead's Enterprise," *Manchester Guardian*, 19 December 1889.

5. See Hulda Friederich, *The Life of Sir George Newnes, Bart.* (London, 1911), pp. 112–13; and Stead to Editor of *Blackwood's Magazine*, 9 December 1889, Blackwood's Publishers Archives, National Library of Scotland (NLS) MS. 4542.

6. See Stead's remarks to Frank G. Carpenter, "A Chat with Stead," *Evening Star* (Washington, D.C.), 2 December 1892; Reginald Pound, *"The Strand Magazine," 1891–1950* (London, 1966), p. 28.

7. *Star* (London), 8 January 1890; also Stead, "To All English-Speaking Folks," *Review of Reviews* 1 (1890):15–20.

8. Stead to Newnes, 7 January 1890, W. T. Stead Papers (Courtesy W. K. Stead); Frank Luther Mott, *A History of American Newspapers* (Cambridge, Mass., 1930), 4:403.

9. See Stead to Editor of *Blackwood's Magazine*, 7 January 1890, Blackwood's Publishers Archives, NLS MS. 4561; [Stead], "Mark Twain's New Book. A Satirical Attack on English Institutions," *Review of Reviews* 1 (1890):144–56; also William Archer, "A New Profession: Soul-Doctoring," *Daily Graphic* (London), 22 January 1890.

10. For the biographical and historical details in the following paragraphs I am indebted to unpublished correspondence in several collections. In the Stead papers at Falmouth, Cornwall, see the exchange of letters between Newnes and Stead, 6 January–3 April 1890; Bramwell Booth to Stead, 25 March, 4 April 1890. In the Stead papers at the Humanities Research Center at the University Texas, Austin, see letters of Stead to Grant Richards, 6 October, 23 December 1891.

In the collection of E.E.J. Dillon's papers see Stead's letters to Dillon: 3 March, 12 March, 31 March, 14 April, 25 August, 26 October, 20 December 1890.

In the Albert Shaw papers at the New York Public Library see letters of Stead to Shaw, 4 February 1891, 7 February 1894; Bramwell Booth to Stead, 25 March, 4 April 1890.

In the Robertson Scott papers (in my possession) I have used letters of Edwin H. Stout to Scott, 18 November 1944, 13 November 1947; Scott to Frederic Whyte, 8 September 1921.

In the F. Herbert Stead papers, courtesy of Miss Theodora Stead, I have relied on letters of W. T. Stead to F. Herbert Stead, 17 February, 14 April, 16 April, 2 May 1890.

See also Scott's letter to John Clifford, 28 August 1892, in James Marchant, *Dr. John Clifford, C.H., Life, Letters, and Reminiscences* (London, 1942), pp. 86–87; Friedrich, pp. 116–17; Grant Richards, *Memories of a Misspent Youth* (London, 1932), pp. 124–28, 132–34, 147, 186, 263; W. Roberts, "Leading London Papers and Their Editors: The *Review of Reviews* and Mr. Stead," *Great Thoughts* 18 (1893):444. In the *Review of Reviews* see 1 (1890):330–47; 42 (1910):13; 44 (1911):613; 45 (1912):483.

Stout published a two-part reminiscence in *News-paper World* for 28 November and 5 December 1936. Henry Stead's reminiscence of his father appears in the *Review of Reviews for Australia* 42 (1913):357–58. And see Baylen, "A Victorian's 'Crusade' in Chicago, 1893–94," *Journal of American History* 51 (1964):418–34.

11. See Mott, 4:658–59 n.; Lloyd J. Graybar, "Albert Shaw and the Founding of the *Review of Reviews*. 1891–97," *Journalism Quarterly* 49 (1972):692–97.

12. In the Albert Shaw papers, Stead to Shaw, January–December 1892. In the Stead papers, Shaw to Stead, 25 October 1892. See also Graybar, *Albert Shaw and the Review of Reviews* (Lexington, Ky., 1974), chap. 4.

13. In the Stead papers: Josephine Butler to Stead, 15 June, 16, 29 September, 16 December 1892; Andrew Carnegie to Stead, 11, 16 August 1892; Sir Garnet Wolseley to Stead, 10 June, 16 August 1892; Reginald Baliol Brett to Stead, ? November 1891. Stead's letter to Carnegie on 9 August 1892 is in the Carnegie collection at the New York Public Library.

In the Olga Novikov collection at the Central State Archives of the U.S.S.R. (Moscow) see W. C. Edgar to Olga Novikov, 23 December 1892.

See also Philip Gibbs, "Crusader of the Pen," *News Chronicle* (London), 5 July 1949; David Mitchell, *Queen Christabel: A Biography of Christabel Pankhurst* (London, 1977), p. 30; Elizabeth Robins, *Both Sides of the Curtain* (London, 1940), p. 305.

14. In the Stead papers: John Morley to Stead, 18 August 1892; Cardinal Manning to Stead, 15, 25 May, 3 June, 18 July 1892. In the Viscount Milner papers at the Bodleian Library, Oxford, see F. Edmund Garrett to Alfred Milner, 17 December 1892. In the Gladstone papers at the British Library (Add. Mss. 44268, vol. 183), see Olga Novikov to W. E. Gladstone, 12 March 1892. In the Frances Willard papers at the W.C.T.U. House in Evanston, Ill., see Stead to Frances Willard, 15 September 1892. See also Stead's essays in the *Review of Reviews* 3 (1891):14–17, 443–55.

15. In the Stead papers: Knollys to Stead, 28, 29 June, 1, 3, 23 July 1891; Stead to Knollys, 16 July 1891; Stead to Gladstone, 27, 29 June, 2 July, 17 August 1891; Gladstone to Stead, 28, 30 June 1891; Manning to Stead, 19 July 1891; interview with Knollys, 22 June 1891.

In the W.S.P.U. Archives at Fawcett Library at the City of London Polytechnic, see Josephine Butler to Mrs. M. Clarl, 15 July 1891. In the Viscount Bryce papers at the Bodleian Library, see Stead to Bryce, 14 July 1891.

See also Stead's essay on the Prince of Wales in the *Review of Reviews* 4 (1891):22–34: Kinley Roby, *The King, the Press, and the People: A Study of Edward VII* (London, 1974), pp. 227, 238, 258; Henry S. Lunn, *Chapters from My Life* (London, 1918), p. 136.

16. In the Stead papers: Stead to Gladstone, 16, 23 April 1892; Mrs. Butler to Stead, [May 1892]. In the Millicent Garrett Fawcett papers: Stead to M. G. Fawcett, 7 May 1890. In the W.S.P.U. Archives (Misc. Autographs vol. 13): Stead to Mrs. E. Wolstenholme Elmy, 10 November 1891.

17. In the E.E.J. Dillon papers: H. F. Battersby to Dillon, 13 January 1891. At Lambeth Place Library (34:2866), see the entry in W. E. Gladstone's diary for 2 April 1890.

18. In the Albert Shaw papers: E. W. Stead to Shaw, 23 June 1919; Daniel O'Connor to Shaw, 15 November 1922; memorandum of Shaw to Charles Lanier, 17 November 1922. For a succinct history of the *Review* after Stead's death, see Robertson Scott, *Life and Death of a Newspaper* (London, 1952), p. 224n.

Information Sources

BIBLIOGRAPHY
Baylen, Joseph O. *"Borderland*: A Quarterly Review and Index of Psychic Phenomena, 1893–1897." *Victorian Periodicals Newsletter*, no. 4 (1969):30–35.
————."Stead's 'Penny Masterpiece Library.' " *Journal of Popular Culture* 9 (1975–1976:710–25.
————."W. T. Stead and the 'New Journalism.' " *Emory University Quarterly* 21 (1970):1–13.
————."W. T. Stead as Publisher and Editor of the *Review of Reviews.*" *Victorian Periodicals Review* 12 (1979):70–83.
————."W. T. Stead's *History of the Mystery* and the Jameson Raid." *Journal of British Studies* 4 (1964):104–32.
Scott, J. W. Robertson. *The Life and Death of a Newspaper: An Account of the ... Editors of the "Pall Mall Gazette."* London, 1952.
Stead, Estelle W. *My Father: Personal and Spiritual Reminiscences.* London, 1913.
Whyte, Frederic. *The Life of W. T. Stead.* 2 vols. New York, 1925.

INDEXES
Each volume indexed.

REPRINT EDITIONS
Microform: Bell & Howell Co., Wooster, Ohio. Datamics Inc., New York. Early British Periodicals (UMI), reels 675–682 and 900–902.

LOCATION SOURCES
American
Complete runs: Buffalo and Erie County Public Library; Colgate University Library; Free Library of Philadelphia; Harvard University Library; Lafayette College Library; Los Angeles Public Library; New York State Library.
Partial runs: Widely available.

British
Complete runs: Birmingham Public Library; Bodleian Library; British Library of Political Science; British Museum; Manchester Public Library.

Publication History

MAGAZINE TITLE AND TITLE CHANGES
The Review of Reviews, 1890–1936. *World Review of Reviews*, 1936. *World Review*, 1936–1953.

VOLUME AND ISSUE DATA
Volumes 1–88, numbers 1–553, January 1890–February 1936; volume 1, numbers 1–6, March–August 1936; volume 2, numbers 1–50, September 1936–April/May 1953.

FREQUENCY OF PUBLICATION
Monthly.

PUBLISHERS

W. T. Stead, Mrs. W. T. Stead, Daniel O'Connor, Henry Wickham Steed, and Sir Edward Hulton, Mowbray House, London, W.C. (1890–1908); Bank Buildings, Kingsway, London, W.C. 1 (1909–1936); 43 Shoe Lane, London, E.C. 4 (1936–1953).

EDITORS

W. T. Stead, 1890–1912. Alfred Stead and John Stead, 1912–1914. Charles Peers, 1914. Estelle W. Stead, 1915–1919. Philip Gibbs, 1919–1923. H. Wickham Steed, 1923–1930. Lovat Dickson, 1930–1933. W. W. Hindle, 1933–1936. Vernon Bartlett, 1936–1940. Sir Edward Hulton, 1940–1953.

Joseph O. Baylen

RHYTHM

In June 1911 Oxford undergraduate John Middleton Murry brought out the first number of *Rhythm*, a handsomely printed quarterly of art, music, and literature from the St. Catherine Press in London. Its small but cosmopolitan readership was earnest enough to prompt a second printing of the first issue and, in a year, to support monthly publication. Although financial difficulties cut short its life, including its brief reincarnation as the *Blue Review** in 1913, the new journal was not merely "a youthful literary magazine," as Murry himself later referred to it, but in significant measure "the first literary periodical to come directly out of that new mood of artistic euphoria and commitment to artistic change that immediately preceded the First World War."[1]

Murry was not alone in this undertaking. He and an interested fellow student, Michael T.H. Sadler (later Sadleir) visited in 1910 the Paris studio of the Scottish painter John Duncan Fergusson, to ask permission to use one of his pictures on the cover of the new magazine. Fergusson promised a new design and offered to be art editor, finding in Murry a willing proponent of the doctrine "that rhythm was the essential quality of a work of art."[2] With a title thus pointing to "a common aesthetic focus," Murry's editorial efforts would seek "to produce contact right across the arts."[3]

Fergusson's enthusiasm for the new group of French artists whom Roger Fry was soon to christen post-Impressionists gave further direction. In retrospect, the First Post-Impressionist Exhibition in the Grafton Galleries in the autumn of 1910 certainly seems to have been a catalyst for renewal of the arts and reformulation of aesthetic theory in English critical circles. "The English public became for the first time fully aware of the existence of a new movement in art, a movement which was the more disconcerting in that it was no mere variation upon an accepted theme but implied a reconsideration of the very purpose and aim as well as of the methods of pictorial and plastic art."[4] It was in this direction particularly that the first issue of *Rhythm* pointed its "Aims and Ideals":

Its title is the ideal of a new art.... Aestheticism has had its day and done its work.... it has been inevitably submerged by the surge of life that lay beyond its sphere.... Our intention is to provide art, be it drawing, literature or criticism, which shall be vigorous, determined, which shall have its roots below the surface, and be the rhythmical echo of the life with which it is in touch. [P. 36]

Murry opted for finding art in "the strong things of life," including "its pity and its brutality," coming to grips with which was "the triumph of sanity and reason"—"art is not made of feeble blood."

Although professing to "leave protest for progress" (p. 36), the first number opened with a denunciation of "Golden Age yearnings" and "the never-never land of the theologian" (p. 1) in a "New Thelema" by Frederick Goodyear, an interested associate and occasional contributor to *Rhythm*. "Thelema, the soul's ideal home ... lies in the ordinary human future that is perpetually transmuting itself into the past.... Men shall build it ... artists have to create the free minds that may dwell therein" (no. 1:1–2).

Two other essays, slight but tendentious, followed. Murry himself on "Art and Philosophy" at last hailed the "tardy recognition in England of Bergson's philosophy as "the open avowal of the supremacy of intuition, of the spiritual vision of the artist in form, in words and meaning" (no. 1:9–12). Michael T.H. Sadler wrote on "Fauvism and a Fauve," preferring to avoid the "futile and misleading" term "post-Impressionism" and stressing "art and not literature ... erratically individual and not mechanical," with the example to hand of cubist and Fauvist artist Anne Estelle Rice, whose work was currently on exhibition in the Baillie Gallery—a sample was her "Schéhérazade" in the midst of Sadler's article (no. 1:14, 16–18).

Most of the first number contents qualify as literature rather than criticism. A reverie on "Aix en Provence" and a dreamy description of "Les Huit Danseuses," in French, appeared from Francis Carco, later to be listed as one of *Rhythm*'s French correspondents. Arthur Crossthwaite wrote on "Ennui" that "strangles and kills." In Hall Ruffy's dialogue, "The Death of the Devil," the latter discovered that he was "really trying to create something beautiful" and died because philosophy took over. Sadler and Crossthwaite also contributed poems to number 1, respectively "Sic Transit ..." in six stanzas and an irregular "Songe d'Été" about crimson anemones fading. An untitled poem by Hardress O'Grady proclaimed "Life is but a little loving." Rhys Carpenter—whose considerable poetic output preceded his many works of classical scholarship—had a two-page free-verse work, "Autumn in Three Lands."

Probably the strongest feature of the new journal was the art work, which included some Picasso studies.[5] Albert Marquet and Othon Friesz, both well-established artists associated with Matisse and the Fauves, and Auguste Herbin, who joined Picasso's "Groupe du Bateau-Lavoir" in 1909 and exhibited cubist work by 1911, were represented in *Rhythm*. Black-and-white reproductions may not have done justice to the paintings of these color-loving French artists, but their drawings were effectively presented, as were those of Anne Estelle Rice, S. J. Peploe, Jessie Dismorr, Georges Banks, and J. D. Fergusson himself.

Number 2 for autumn 1911 featured poems by Francis Coutts, John Harvey, Julian Park, and Carpenter. The prose still ran to the arts, Murry reviewing *The Aesthetics of Benedetto Croce* (pp. 11–13) and Sadler *The Letters of Vincent Van Gogh* (pp. 16–18), while Rollo Myers discussed "The Art of Claude Debussy" (pp.29–34). Vincent O'Sullivan's "Anna Vaddock's Fame" (pp. 1–7) and Arthur Crossthwaite's "Three Eclogues" (pp. 22–25) were an approach to fiction.

With the fourth issue Katherine Mansfield began to contribute to *Rhythm*. She had been "discovered" by A. R. Orage, editor of the *New Age*,* and the bulk of her prose output for two years—sixteen stories and sketches—was published there from 1910 to 1911. Understandably, the *New Age* accused her of desertion when she became associated with *Rhythm*. Her introduction to Murry came about when the novelist W. L. George sent Murry one of her stories. Murry rejected the "fairy story," which he "did not understand," and asked Mansfield to send him something else.[6] She did so, and "The Woman at the Store" pleased him mightily, as did her first volume *In a German Pension*, which he soon read. They met, and a partnership of sorts quickly developed between them. *Rhythm* for spring 1912, number 4, contained the accepted New Zealand murder story and two poems by Katherine Mansfield, supposedly translations from the Russian of "Boris Petrovsky."

June 1912 found *Rhythm*'s acute financial problems ephemerally solved when Mansfield's publisher, Stephen Swift, assumed "responsibility" and paid Murry and Katherine a joint salary as editors of what was henceforth to be a monthly journal. As number 5 began the second volume, the masthead (*Rhythm*'s first) listed John Middleton Murry as editor, assisted by Katherine Mansfield and Michael T.H. Sadler (whose name had disappeared by the next month), with John Duncan Fergusson as art editor. New blue covers replaced the original elephant gray. There were poems by Katherine Mansfield, Wilfrid Wilson Gibson, and W.H. Davies; stories by Frank Harris and Gerda Morgan; a "Letter from France" (in French as a regular feature) by Tristan Derème on Ronsard and Pascal; an article by Dan Phaër on "Types of Artists"; and Murry himself on "The Meaning of Rhythm," which, eternally quested for, is "ultimate and unassailable . . . unity of art and artist in freedom, reality, individuality," possible since "true intuition . . . is an inevitable and infallible directness of vision" (pp. 19–20). In his book reviews Murry pronounced James Stephens "the greatest poet of our day" and Mansfield declared "Mr. Galsworthy . . . wise in that he avoids all mention of the word 'poetry' in connection with his verses." The July contents were previewed, and the issue featured caricatures of contributors by Georges Banks.

For the next three issues the magazine did indeed provide, as Murry wanted, "contact across the arts." In the July number Francis Carco wrote the "Lettre de Paris'' and Murry praised Frank Harris extravagantly. The editors jointly considered "Seriousness in Art" and separately reviewed some half dozen books. A play by W. W. Gibson provided variety of genre. The Russian ballet appeared among the illustrations. The issue for August 1912 offered a Mansfield story, the "Observations and Opinions" of Gilbert Cannan, and a brace of "foreign correspondents" extending beyond France to Poland and Russia, with Julian Park for America. The September number had Gaudier-Brzeska drawings, articles on Russian writers and artists, and several reviews signed "F. G."— Frederick Goodyear, who was faithful to the last.

Catastrophically, in September Stephen Swift was declared bankrupt, and Murry found himself not only without salary but with large printing debts left in his name. Instead of dying on the spot, the magazine rallied with generous financial assistance from Edward Marsh (whose first *Georgian Anthology* appeared in 1912). Martin Secker offered to be the publisher, and many literary figures came forward with monetary contributions. Murry and Mansfield moved the editorial office to a tiny flat at 57 Chancery Lane, and *Rhythm* carried on into 1913; its monthly issues reached fourteen (in the original number sequence) in March. Additionally, two supplements appeared in December 1913 and March 1914, while one announced for January 1913, "dealing with various forms of House Decoration," apparently never materialized.

In the spring of 1914 financial difficulties again overtook Murry's magazine. Seeking to establish a new focus—and with the aid of D. H. Lawrence—Murry and Mansfield transformed *Rhythm* into the *Blue Review*, but it lasted for only three issues. In its short life, *Rhythm* nevertheless accumulated an impressive roster of contributors. Mansfield was the most prolific, with ten poems, seven stories, and numerous signed and anonymous reviews. Other writers included H. G. Wells, Ford Madox Ford, Frank Swinnerton, Walter De la Mare, J. D. Beresford, Lascelles Abercrombie, Rupert Brooke, Yone Noguchi, Maurice Hewlett, Bernard Kellerman, Max Plowman, Thomas Moult, and Lord Dunsany.

Although in later life even Murry did not insist powerfully on the intrinsic significance of *Rhythm*—for him its retrospective interest seemed to lie largely in its association with his first wife, Mansfield, whose work he strongly believed in—the little magazine played no undistinguished role among its serious and quality-conscious peers.

Notes

1. John Middleton Murry, *The Short Stories of Katherine Mansfield* (New York, 1937), p. vi; Malcolm Bradbury, "*Rhythm* and *The Blue Review*" [part of a series of articles on early little magazines], *Times Literary Supplement*, 25 April 1968, p. 423.

2. Frank A. Lea, *Life of John Middleton Murry* (London, 1959), pp. 23–24; for the quotation, see Bradbury, p. 423. See also Anthony Alpers, *Katherine Mansfield* (London, 1954), p. 151.

3. Bradbury, p. 423.

4. Roger Fry, Preface to Catalogue of the Second Post-Impressionist Exhibition, Grafton Galleries, 1912, rpt. in *Vision and Design* (1920; rpt. Cleveland, 1956).

5. According to Anthony Alpers, in *Katherine Mansfield* (London, 1954), p. 148, *Rhythm* was the first English magazine to publish his work.

6. *The Letters of Katherine Mansfield to John Middleton Murry*, ed. John Middleton Murry (London, 1951), p. 1. See also Murry, *Between Two Worlds: An Autobiography* (London, 1935).

Information Sources

BIBLIOGRAPHY

Alpers, Anthony. *Katherine Mansfield*. London, 1954.

Bradbury, Malcolm. "*Rhythm* and *The Blue Review*." *Times Literary Supplement*, 25 April 1968.

Fry, Roger. *Vision and Design*. 1920. Reprint. Cleveland, 1956.

Hoffman, Frederick J., Charles Allen, and Carolyn F. Ulrich. *The Little Magazine: A History and a Bibliography*. Princeton, 1947.

Lea, Frank A. *Life of John Middleton Murry*. London, 1959.

Mansfield, Katherine. *Letters of Katherine Mansfield to John Middleton Murry*. Edited by John Middleton Murry. London, 1951.

Murry, John Middleton. *Between Two Worlds*. London, 1935.

Swinnerton, Frank. *Background with Chorus: A Footnote to Changes in English Literary Fashion Between 1901 and 1917*. London, 1956.

INDEXES
None.

REPRINT EDITIONS
None.

LOCATION SOURCES

American

Complete runs: Enoch Pratt Library; Henry E. Huntington Library; New York Public Library; Princeton University Library; Stanford College Library; University of North Carolina Library.

Partial runs: Columbia University Library; Newberry Library; Ohio State University Library; Philadelphia Museum of Art; Yale University Library.

British

Complete runs: British Museum; Leeds Public Library; Victoria and Albert Museum Library.

Partial runs: Bodleian Library; Cambridge University Library; Glasgow University Library.

Publication History

MAGAZINE TITLE AND TITLE CHANGES
Rhythm.

VOLUME AND ISSUE DATA

Volume 1, numbers 1–4, summer 1911–spring 1912; volume 2, numbers 5–14, June 1912–March 1913. Supplements December 1912, March 1913.

FREQUENCY OF PUBLICATION

Quarterly, summer 1911–spring 1912; monthly, June 1912–March 1913.

PUBLISHERS

Summer 1911–spring 1912: The St. Catherine Press, Norfolk Street, London.
June–August 1912: Stephen Swift and Co., Ltd., 16 King St., Covent Garden,
London. September 1912–March 1913: Martin Secker, 5 John Street, Adelphi,
London W.C.

EDITOR

John Middleton Murry.

Mary Anthony Weinig

S

ST. MARTIN'S REVIEW

St. Martin's Review, which first appeared in January 1890 and transformed a lowly parish magazine into a respected literary journal, has lasted for nearly a hundred years. Generally, people who read parish magazines do not have a literary background. "It would disgrace a parish magazine" sums up a hostile verdict often passed on an essay by a reader with rather sophisticated literary taste, but as the critic, writing for the *Spectator** (see *RA*), went on to remark in his adjudication of "The Parish Magazine":

> The Editor [of *St. Martin's Review*] has brought his parish magazine up to the level of a serious review. His short articles are full of information and thought, but they are not above the understanding of any ordinary man who will try his hardest to think. They do not make appeal to the stupid or the careless, neither do they presuppose learning. They are written for every man who calls himself a Christian, and seek to throw light upon every question and controversy which stirs the religious world.[1]

Reverend John Kitto, M.A., vicar of St. Martin-in-the-Field (that little church known the world over and located at the heart of London in Trafalgar Square), founded the *Review*. The first number was entitled the *St. Martin-in-the-Field Monthly Messenger* and was chiefly concerned with parish activities—notably that the Repair Fund had fallen short of 300 pounds. The vicar-editor wryly asks if anyone could suggest ways of getting money from those who have not contributed. Even in its earliest issues, *St. Martin's* went beyond the usual scope of a parish magazine by considering nonchurch matters; the April 1890 issue discusses the progress in the construction of the National Portrait Gallery, and the visit of the Prince and Princess of Wales.

By the second year of publication, fuller coverage was given to broader issues, and the four-page magazine had more than doubled in size. In its descriptions of social and cultural activities *St. Martin's* transcends its parochial boundaries, featuring a ten-page description of Gladstone's opening of the new Free Public Library (March 1891) and notice of Balfour's opening of the new Town Hall (January 1892). But in that same January 1892 edition there is evidence that the plucky parish magazine had a growing sense of self-consciousness. Kitto noted that in his little publication he was "astonished to find how various and how complete is the record of parochial history." He also rather proudly reiterated the aim of his *St. Martin-in-the-Field Monthly Messenger*: "Our endeavour has been to make it a means of announcing and recording whatever occurs in the parish which is likely to be of real interest to the parishoners" (p. 3).

The real founder of the *St. Martin's Review* was the Reverend H.R.L. Sheppard, who came to St. Martin's in 1914. From the outset he realized that the magazine catered chiefly to those who went to church regularly. He wanted not only to reach the "saved," but to preach a new, rich doctrine of the Incarnation to all the earth. From the very beginning he attempted to deal with every human matter under the sun. He reveled in art, music, drama, and literature. If people were bored with going to church, then he would not be adverse to writing that an afternoon at the National Gallery or at Covent Garden might be more of an act of worship than going to hear a sermon. In his book *H.R.L. Sheppard: Life and Letters*, R. Ellis Roberts, writing of the period when Sheppard first came to St. Martin's, claims:

> Old St. Martin's represented a tradition of which Dick was almost completely ignorant, the old-fashioned Evangelical family parish church . . . ; and when he first saw the church, St. Martin's, although it was not dead, it was allied with a tradition that was hopelessly defunct. It was middle-period Victorian, and that period in 1914 was to share in the doom of all things Victorian, the pity or contempt, or complete indifference of the young. Dick was in impulsive, gay opposition to that tradition; and he was blissfully innocent of any knowledge of the ordinary parochial life and services in the Church of England.[2]

From the moment he arrived, Sheppard began changing things: a daily Eucharist, a sung Eucharist on Sunday, cross and candles on the altar. But it was to the parish magazine, the *St. Martin-in-the-Field Monthly Messenger*, that Sheppard directed most of his genius. He was a brilliant editor and an astute manager. In order not to waste spare copies of the *Messenger* he had his workers deposit them in the letter boxes of Harley Street, with a note from the vicar asking that they be put in the doctors' waiting rooms.

In the January 1920 edition of the magazine, which was now called simply the *St. Martin's Review*, Sheppard wrote:

With this number we launch into the deep—that is to say, we aspire to become seriously considered as a piece of Christian literature, issued monthly. It will cost 6 [shillings] for each copy now, instead of 2 [shillings] though parishioners and members of the Guild of Fellowship will obtain their Review at the old rate. One of the urgent needs of to-day is for Christian literature; that all problems may be brought to the touch-stone of Christ. We hope to attempt this. [N.p.]

During Sheppard's editorship, which continued even after ill health forced him to resign as vicar, some of the age's best writers contributed to the *Review*: Thomas Hardy, John Masefield, Bernard Shaw, Robert Cecil, Laurence Housman, Beatrice Webb, J. A. Spender, G. M. Trevelyan, Arnold Bennett, and Harley Granville-Barker. Every subject, from sport to science, from the theater to the church, was investigated. Sheppard moved the *Review* out of the office of the vicarage into a home of its own. Its first office was in the gallery of the church, and from here his assistant editor and manager, Bertine Buxton, carried out the instructions of Sheppard. Writing of him, Buxton noted that "his vision amounted almost to prophecy and he had an amazing way of knowing what the public was thinking before its thoughts had crystalized into actual expression of opinion, while he was a genius at saying the right thing at the right psychological moment."[3]

Moving the office of the *St. Martin's Review* from the vicarage underscored Sheppard's belief that a Christian review should embrace the whole world. He aimed to bring the Christian message into the wider parish of the casualty ward of the Charing Cross Hospital, into the courts of Bedfordbury, even into the public houses. In one of the first letters he ever wrote to his parishioners, in the issue for January 1915, he made his views known:

> I very much want *St. Martin's in-the-Field Monthly Messenger* to be one of the links by means of which the whole parish will be united into a whole....I feel very strongly that a Church like ours which belongs to London as well as to the parish of St. Martin-in-the-Field should have a large staff of responsible clergy, some of whom are giving themselves to the parish and some of whom are being given by the parish to the big problems that are not limited by parochial boundaries.

The parish and its magazine would be remarkable not only in Charing Cross or in London, but even throughout the world. By means of his own letters and the many literary friends whom he persuaded to write for the *Review*, in a seemingly effortless way, he recalled to all his parishioners that St. Martin's Church was not an independent, self-sufficient entity; it was part of the world. Consequently, there was always the usual parochial news, but the major part of the *Review* was given up to articles to make St. Martin's parishioners acquainted with the world in which they lived and moved and had their being. Remarkably, under

Sheppard, the *Review* achieved its highest circulation. On an average it was 10,000 copies a month, while special double numbers sometimes reached 30,000 copies.[4]

Sheppard guided the *Review* until 1927, when W. Patrick McCormack became editor and vicar of St. Martin's. McCormack was a close friend of Sheppard and had worked with him over the years on the magazine; the ideal to unite the City of God with the city of men was passed from Sheppard to McCormack; thence, in 1941, to Eric S. Loveday, in 1948 to L. M. Charles-Edwards and, in 1956, to its present vicar, Austen Williams, whose wife, Daphne, now edits the *Review*.

St. Martin's Review still prides itself on its international outlook. Although the circulation is smaller than in the past (1,500–2,000 copies), the *Review* goes much farther afield. Since 1975 the vicar's monthly World Service Broadcast sermon, requested by readers throughout the world, has been published. Dick Sheppard would have rejoiced that the *Review*'s influence is still transcending St. Martin's parish boundaries.

Notes

1. "The Parish Magazine," reprint of a *Spectator* article published in the *St. Martin's Review*, February 1921, pp. 59–62.

2. R. Ellis Roberts, *H.R.L. Sheppard: Life and Letters* (London,1942), p. 90.

3. Ibid., p. 110.

4. Ibid., p. 107.

Information Sources

BIBLIOGRAPHY
Roberts, R. Ellis. *H.R.L. Sheppard: Life and Letters*. London, 1942.
Williams, Daphne (acting editor of the *St. Martin's Review*). Interview with author. London. 15 July 1983.

INDEXES
Each volume indexed. *Index of Contributors to the "St. Martin's Review," 1920– 1925*.

REPRINT EDITIONS
None.

LOCATION SOURCES
American
Partial runs: New York Public Library; U.S. Library of Congress.
British
Complete run: *St. Martin's Review* editorial office, 5 St. Martin's Place, London W.C. 2.
Partial runs: British Museum; Selly Oak Colleges Library.

Publication History

MAGAZINE TITLE AND TITLE CHANGES
St. Martin-in-the-Field Monthly Messenger, January 1890–June 1919. *St. Martin-in-the-Field Monthly Review*, July–December 1919. *St. Martin's Review*, January 1920–.

VOLUME AND ISSUE DATA

Volume 1, numbers 1–36, January 1890–December 1892; volume 2, numbers 37–72, January 1893–December 1895; volume 3, numbers 73–105, January 1896–December 1898; volume 4, numbers 106–141, January 1899–December 1901; volume 5, numbers 142–176, January 1902–December 1904; volume 6, numbers 177–209, January 1905–December 1907; volume 7, numbers 210–241, January 1908–December 1910; volume 8, numbers 242–275, January 1911–December 1913; volume 9, numbers 276–286, January–December 1914 (11 months: August/September combined). Beginning in 1915 volumes are numbered annually and consist of twelve issues. January 1915 is numbered 287.

FREQUENCY OF PUBLICATION

Monthly.

PUBLISHER

1890–: Church of St. Martin-in-the-Field.

EDITORS

John F. Kitto, 1890–1903. Leonard F. Shelford, 1903–1914. Hugh R.L. Sheppard, 1914–1927. W. Patrick McCormack, 1927–1941. Eric S. Loveday, 1941–1948. L. M. Charles-Edwards, 1948–1956. Austen and Daphne Williams, 1956–.

Martha Westwater

SAINT PAUL'S MAGAZINE

Saint Paul's Magazine was founded by the Victorian printer James Virtue and first published in October 1867. The much celebrated novelist Anthony Trollope was its first editor and most famous contributor. Other regular contributors of note included Leslie Stephen, Margaret Oliphant, Robert Buchanan, and G. H. Lewes. In his *Autobiography* Trollope supplies some excellent commentary on the origins of the magazine: "I very strongly advised James Virtue to abandon the project, pointing out to him that a large expenditure would be necessary to carry on the magazine in accordance with my views....He listened to my arguments with great patience, and then told me that if I would not do the work he would find some other editor."[1] Trollope's initial skepticism about the economic feasibility of starting another journal is reflected in his "Introduction" to the first issue:

He begs to assure such of the public as will kindly interest themselves in the matter, that Saint Pauls is not established on any rooted and matured conviction that such a periodical is the great and pressing want of the age. The ... Magazine is not started because another special publication is needed to satisfy the requirements of the reading public, but because the requirements of the reading world demand that there shall be many publications to satisfy its needs. [1:1]

The reading public, it was hoped, would prove sufficiently large to support *Saint Paul's*, but the hope or expectations of the editor were not enough to sustain the journal, and after three changes of both editors and owners, the magazine closed down in March 1874.

Trollope may have been skeptical about the prospects of the magazine, but he was a shrewd choice for editor. He had just finished a term on the editorial board of the successful *Fortnightly Review** and was at the crest of his reputation as a novelist.

The range of interests covered in *Saint Paul's*, while very broad, was not as inclusive as that of the *Fortnightly* or the *Contemporary Review.** Trollope compensated for the general absence of materials on the Victorian church by emphasizing new works of fiction. And although he may have been turned away from the growth of liberalism in the Church of England, he noted in the "Introduction" that the "preaching of the day is done by the novelists" (1:5). If that is so, *Saint Paul's* is a deeply religious magazine, for it overflows with fiction. The leading issue has the first installment of Trollope's latest novel, *Phineas Finn*; after his retirement as editor he contributed *Ralph the Heir*. Other novelists published included George MacDonald (C. S. Lewis's mentor), Margaret Oliphant, and Nathaniel Hawthorne, whose *Septimius* was published after Trollope had relinquished the editorship. Trollope's *Phineas* was described by the editor-author as a "slight story . . . a love ditty" (1:5).

In addition to the emphasis on publishing new fiction, there is a fair amount of novel criticism throughout various issues. Essay-reviews on Jane Austen (March 1871), George Eliot (August 1868), and Richardson's *Clarissa* were published. Trollope wrote an especially fine essay, "Charles Dickens," published on the occasion of his death in July 1870, in which he praises Dickens for his ability to create "great prototypes" for the English: "A 'boots' at a hotel," said Trollope, "is more of a boots the closer he resembles Sam Weller." What puzzled Trollope about Dickens was his lack of belief in politics or political systems, though he was "a radical at heart" (6:372–74). There is a commercial motif in the essay on Dickens as well as in Trollope's essay on Richardson's *Clarissa* in November 1868. Trollope cites Richardson's denial of the title "greatest of all novelists," which his most recent editor had made for him, for Richardson had never achieved any widespread popularity (3:172). By comparison, one of the distinctive elements in Dickens's claims to greatness was to be found in his close understanding of the tastes of his reading public (6:374).

There is not much poetry in *Saint Paul's*. According to one scholar, Trollope was not a good critic of poetry. "He fell between two stools," said Michael Sadleir, for he tried to "adjust by verbal alteration work written from pure literary impulse."[2] The remarks seem fair. Trollope did ask his only poet, Henry Dobson, to change some materials in his "Pyramus and Thisbe": "No one should have to pause a moment to look for interpretation. If it is not fit to be read aloud so as to catch the intellects of not very intellectual persons, it does not answer its professed object." Having listed a series of words and phrases that he found obscure, Trollope concluded: "Allow me to ask you to remember that did I not like the piece much, I should not descend to such a picking of holes—which is unpleasant work. Pray let me have it again."[3] Dobson made the corrections, and the poem, according to George Eliot, was a masterpiece.

As far as can be discovered, Dobson was the only poet published in *Saint Paul's*, but there is an abundance of poetic criticism. Browning's *The Ring and the Book* and his poetry in general received a lengthy review, as did Tennyson's poetry, praised for its "charm" in contrast to the many hard "lyric nut[s]" in the work of Browning. The reviewer held that both men were great poets, and if Browning was less attentive to the requirements of beauty in his poems, he was never unfaithful to that of truth. In "Browning Poems" of March 1872, the reviewer wrote that "deep moral convictions" were the ultimate source of his "severer satire," and he was in effect "the Carlyle of verse," though Trollope himself had become disillusioned with Carlyle by that time (10:259).

In the "Introduction" Trollope remarked that there would not be a great amount of literary criticism in his magazine (1:6); however, *Saint Paul's* has many reviews of English writers, poets, novelists, and critics. George Buchanan, among others, wrote several essays on the theory of criticism, and there is an even longer series of essays on "Literary Legislators" of the nineteenth century, most of whom a modern reader would not recognize.

Trollope had promised that *Saint Paul's*, "if it be anything, will be political," and every issue has at least one essay on a political question. Many of these essays were written by Trollope himself, and a number were on "the Irish Question," one of his most pressing interests. Trollope supported Gladstone's Irish Land Bill (March 1870) and a system of liberal justice for the Irish farmers as the only antidote for the "rabidly-rebellious newspapers in Dublin." He stated in "What Does Ireland Want?" (March 1870) that the basic endeavor of English statesmen should be "to regulate the law between landlord and tenant as to make it evidently the landlord's interest to give his tenant a lease if demanded" (5:645–52). Combined with this restrained advocacy of justice for the Irish is a series of attacks on Benjamin Disraeli, as a politician and as a novelist. Disraeli must have been something of a cynic to have written such trash for a reading public which bought his novels only because they came from "good or lofty hands."[4]

There are numerous essays on travel and sports, and it is hard to think of a subject or interest that is not covered in *Saint Paul's*. The most interesting exception is the limited interest in the political and religious affairs of the Church of England. This is especially surprising if one remembers that Trollope came to his term as editor fresh from the *Barchester* series. There are only two mentions of this subject—an obituary on F. D. Maurice (who is praised) and a lengthy review in March 1870 of the life of Henry Phillpotts, Bishop of Exeter, also recently deceased. There are factual errors in the essay on Phillpotts—he was not a High Churchman of the Caroline type—and there are some devastating comments on the first leaders of the Oxford Movement, including John Henry Newman, John Keble, and others. They are described as "perverse schoolboys.'' But the reviewer considered Phillpotts himself a great man, for though he had spent much of his life in theological disputes which the reviewer did not approve of, he illustrated one of the most endearing features of the national church, its comprehensiveness. There is also an attack on the latest phase of ''Puseyism'' (Anglo-Catholicism)—the founding of monasteries and convents. Unmarried priests, the reviewer said, were ''a vile moral nuisance,'' and the Church had many features of a large social club in which the ''good tempered, pure-minded . . . hostesses'' (wives of the clergy) ministered to the needs of the parish. Yet, ultimately Phillpots was touted as a ''stout-hearted Englishman'' who understood the church and its real mission in the world (5:645–52).

Scholars have suggested that *Saint Paul's* went into a decline after Trollope resigned as editor in May 1870. However, the contributors in the post-1870 period are generally the same as those who worked under Trollope. A few of the original contributors had died, but the decline owing to their absence is not obvious. Michael Sadleir has suggested that Trollope himself went into a decline because of his dealings with Strahan and King, his successors as editors of *Saint Paul's*. Trollope did nothing immoral, but ''implications'' stemming from his association with these persons and the firms they represented were bad for his reputation. Sadleir remarked that ''as a serious novelist he was slightly blown upon.''[5] Yet none of Trollope's later associates seemed to have noticed this demise in his reputation. According to Margaret Oliphant and her circle, he was still the great master of Victorian fiction, and *Blackwood's** (see *RA*) was very happy to later have him on its staff.[6] Furthermore, Trollope seemed to gain personally from his editorial experience, as he produced a small and now forgotten volume based on his work with *Saint Paul's*, entitled *An Editor's Tales*. It was, as a contemporary observed, ''as convincing a proof of the genius of the author as anything he wrote.''[7]

Yet *Saint Paul's* was a failure in the mind of Trollope, James Virtue, and its later owners: ''It never paid its way.'' And there is no easy answer to the question: ''Why did so good a magazine fail to succeed?''[8] One might suggest that Trollope's name and that of his family lost its charm after a time, for the editor himself was the most conspicuous contributor, closely followed by Francis and Henry Trollope. As Henry Dobson observed, Trollope was ''too ready to buy manuscripts from himself and the Tom Trollopes.''[9] Another suggestion might be that while the first editor was characterized by ''fantastic energy,'' he was not especially subtle in catching ''so many of the nuances of one of the most revolutionary periods in history.''[10] As good as it was, *Saint Paul's* perhaps failed precisely because it was so cautionary.

Notes

1. Anthony Trollope, *Autobiography*, ed. Bradford Booth (Berkeley, 1947), p. 238.
2. Michael Sadleir, *Anthony Trollope: A Commentary* (New York, 1947), p. 297.
3. *The Letters of Anthony Trollope*, ed. Bradford A. Booth (Westport, Conn., 1979), p. 248.

4. Quoted in Walter Houghton, ed., "Saint Paul's Magazine," *Wellesley Index to Victorian Periodicals* (Toronto, 1979), 3:375.

5. Sadleir, p. 300.

6. G. Porter, *William Blackwood and His Sons* (Edinburgh, 1898), pp. 335ff.

7. Quoted in Sadleir, p. 302, n.1.

8. Houghton, 3:360.

9. Quoted in Lucy Stebbins, *The Trollopes: The Chronicle of a Writing Family* (New York, 1945), p. 249.

10. Robert Polhemus, *The Changing World of Anthony Trollope* (Berkeley, 1968), p. 248.

Information Sources

BIBLIOGRAPHY

ApRoberts, Ruth. *The Moral Trollope*. Athens, Ohio, 1971.

Booth, Bradford A. *The Letters of Anthony Trollope*. Westport, Conn., 1979.

Houghton, Walter E. *Wellesley Index to Victorian Periodicals, 1824–1890*. Volume 3. Toronto, 1979.

Porter, G. *William Blackwood and Sons*. Edinburgh, 1898.

Sadleir, Michael. *Trollope: A Commentary*. New York, 1947.

Stebbins, Lucy P. *The Trollopes: The Chronicle of a Writing Family*. New York, 1945.

Trollope, Anthony. *Autobiography*. Edited by Bradford A. Booth. Berkeley, 1947.

INDEXES

List of contents in each bound volume. *Poole's Index. Wellesley Index* 3.

REPRINT EDITIONS

Microform: English Literary Periodicals (UMI), reels 960–961, 969.

LOCATION SOURCES

American

Widely available.

British

Complete runs: Birmingham Public Library; Bodleian Library; British Museum; Edinburgh Public Library; West Ham Public Library.

Partial runs: Bristol Public Library; Cambridge University Library; Glasgow University Library; Hull University Library; Leeds University Library; Sheffield University Library.

Publication History

MAGAZINE TITLE AND TITLE CHANGES

Saint Paul's, October 1867–March 1870. *Saint Paul's Magazine*, April 1870–March 1874.

VOLUME AND ISSUE DATA

Volumes 1–14, October 1867–March 1874.

FREQUENCY OF PUBLICATION

Monthly.

PUBLISHERS

1867–1869: Virtue & Co., London. 1869–1871: Strahan and Co., London. 1872–1874: Henry S. King & Co., London.

EDITORS
Anthony Trollope, October 1867–July 1870. Alexander Strahan, August 1870–
October 1872. Henry S. King, November 1872- March 1874.

John R. Griffin

SAMHAIN

Samhain was the journal of the Irish National Theatre Society from 1901 to
1906, with a final issue in 1908. Edited by William Butler Yeats, it followed
on the heels of *Beltaine* (1899–1900), which had served the same function and
which Yeats had also edited.[1] Because it was the chief promotional and theoretical
publication of the early national theater movement in Ireland, it remains a significant document for scholars and students of Irish drama and literary history.

Even if *Samhain* were not rich in theoretical and historical information, however, it would undoubtedly endure because of the dramatical pieces it published
and because of the names associated with it. Plays by Yeats (*Cathleen ni Hoo-
lihan*), J. M. Synge (*Riders to the Sea; In the Shadow of the Glen*), Douglas
Hyde (*The Poorhouse; The Lost Saint*), and Lady Gregory (translations, one
tragedy, and several comedies) appeared in the pages of *Samhain* during its
seven-year run.

Yeats's prose, though, constituted the heart of the journal. For the first number,
he contributed a series of paragraphs entitled "Windlestraws" that reported the
state of the Irish national theater movement as it was developing out of the Irish
Literary Theatre, which Yeats, Edward Martyn, and Lady Gregory had founded
just before the turn of the century. "Windlestraws" was also to some extent a
call to arms for the Irish dramatic movement: "Whether the Irish Literary Theatre
has a successor made on its own model or not, we can claim that a dramatic
movement which will not die has been started" (1:3). Martyn's "A Plea for a
National Theatre in Ireland," in the same issue (pp. 14–15), was also a kind of
manifesto; one scholar of Irish drama, in fact, has called the "Plea" "the most
important feature in *Samhain* 1901."[2] George Moore's somewhat fretful essay,
"The Irish Literary Theatre" (pp. 11–13), acts as ballast in the issue, for he
openly refers to the economic and artistic shortcomings of the theatrical movement. He, too, however, is ultimately proud of the work that has been done to
date: "Since we began our work plays have been written, some in Irish and
some in English, and we shall be forgiven if we take a little credit for having
helped to awaken intellectual life in Ireland. Many will think I am guilty of
exaggeration when I say that the Irish Literary Theatre has done more to awaken
intellectual life in Ireland than Trinity College" (p. 13).

The prose contributions of Martyn and Moore were special to the first issue,
and it was Yeats who provided virtually all of the commentary, criticism, and
theory in the subsequent issues. The "Windlestraws" title was dropped, but its
format was not; Yeats continued to arrange several paragraphs loosely, variously

titling them "Notes," "Notes and Opinions," "The Dramatic Movement," and "First Principles." His topics ranged from Irish nationalism to censorship in England to dramatic performances themselves.

At least two significant issues recur throughout these pieces, both having as much to do with Yeats's own poetics as with the national theater movement. First, Yeats seems to have recognized the need for Irish writers to become political, to think both in terms of an Irish *nation* and an Irish *moment* in history. He seems to have realized, too, however, that becoming political could drain a writer's creative power: "How can we create like the ancients, while innumerable considerations of external probability or social utility or of what is becoming in so meritorious a person as ourselves, destroy the seeming irresponsible creative power that is life itself?" (3:25–33). This tension between political awareness and creative "irresponsibility" is accompanied by another conflict—one between the pragmatic demands of starting a theater and the mystical interests that informed Yeats's own ideas of drama. As Richard Ellmann has observed:

> Yeats's endeavours to found an order and to found an Irish theatre came about the same time, and the synchronization is significant. Occultism, or, to use a more generalized expression, spiritual ideas, underlie all his early plays and his theories of what the national theatre should be. . . . His original intention was to present a series of miracle plays, by which he meant plays not necessarily Christian but manifesting in one way or another the existence of an invisible world.[3]

In any event, the prose pieces with which Yeats began each issue of *Samhain* are remarkable for a variety of reasons; they record the difficulties and triumphs of the theater movement, and they express Yeats's ideas of "moment," nation, and spiritual drama.

Aside from Yeats's commentary, the plays themselves were the other regular feature of *Samhain*. Typically, at least two plays appeared in each issue, one in Irish and one in English. Most of these are very much of the *literary* theater, often better read than performed, although there are some notable exceptions, such as Synge's *Riders to the Sea* (3:25–33). Lady Gregory is perhaps the most surprisingly talented of the contributing playwrights, displaying a gift for comedy in *The Rising of the Moon, Spreading the News*, and *Hyacinth Halvey* (4:45–52, 5:15–28; 6:15–35).

The format of *Samhain* was consistent. Yeats would lead off with his commentary, occasionally following this with another essay of his own or one by another contributor. Two or three short plays would then follow, and the issue would be complete. The issues ranged in length from thirty to fifty-five pages. The magazine could risk being so unassuming and straightforward, perhaps, because it drew its readership chiefly from those already committed to, or at least interested in, the national theater movement. Curiously enough, however, *Samhain* owes much of its importance to this very simplicity. Far from having to compromise, its contributors—particularly Yeats—could muse and experiment. Yeats's "Notes" could accommodate anything that was on his mind, and the drama section could allow an inexperienced playwright like Lady Gregory to try her hand. Even the design of the magazine was unassuming, reflecting Edward Gordon Craig's typography, "large black type on coarse brown paper."[4]

The last number of *Samhain* appeared in 1908, although the regularity of appearance had already been broken in 1907, when the *Arrow** took over the role of the national theater magazine.[5] Yeats wrote some paragraphs, which he labeled "private and confidential," for a 1909 *Samhain* that never materialized. In them he speaks of how the dramatic movement is becoming financially independent—independent, specifically, of Annie E.F. Horniman's subsidy. He also speaks of his weariness, which was perhaps the more fundamental reason for the ending of *Samhain*: "For many years now Lady Gregory and I, helped by the late Mr. Synge, as far as his health allowed, have done a great deal of the work and borne all the responsibility. We have done this unpaid, and this and the expenses it entailed were only made possible in my own case by the success of a lecturing tour in America. Our proper work, for we are writers, has been neglected more and more."[6] No one then could have begrudged Yeats his wish to return to his "proper work," nor can we begrudge him that wish, knowing that many of his greatest poems were to appear after the editorship of *Samhain*. Nonetheless, *Samhain* was a lively, important magazine that drew excitement from the national theater movement it sought to shape and inspire.

Notes

1. " 'Beltaine' is the name of an ancient Irish Spring festival while 'Samhain' refers to the Autumn and both correspond to theatrical seasons given by the Irish Literary Theatre." G. C. Bloomfield, "Editor's Note," *Samhain* (London, 1970), p. i.

2. Liam Miller, *The Noble Drama of W. B. Yeats* (Dublin, 1977), p. 55.

3. Richard Ellmann, *Yeats: The Man and the Masks* (1948; repr. New York, 1978), p. 131.

4. Miller, p. 55.

5. The last issue (pp. 34–35) lists the "Dates and Places of the First Performances of Plays Produced by the National Theatre Society and Its Predecessors." Fifty-seven plays are listed; many of them appeared in *Samhain*.

6. "Paragraphs from the Forthcoming Number of 'Samhain.' " *Samhain* (London, 1970).

Information Sources

BIBLIOGRAPHY

Bloomfield, B. C. "Editor's Note." *Samhain*. London, 1970.

Ellmann, Richard. *Yeats: The Man and the Masks*. 1948. Reprint. New York, 1978.

Hogan, Robert, and James Kilroy. *The Irish Literary Theatre 1899–1901*. Dublin, 1975.

Hogan, Robert, Richard Burnham, and Daniel P. Poteet. *The Rise of the Realists 1910–1915*. Dublin, 1979.

Miller, Liam. *The Noble Drama of W. B. Yeats*. Dublin, 1977.

REPRINT EDITIONS
London, 1970.
INDEXES
None.

Publication History

MAGAZINE TITLE AND TITLE CHANGES
Samhain.
VOLUME AND ISSUE DATA
Number 1, October 1901; number 2, October 1902; number 3, September 1903;
number 4, December 1904; number 5, November 1905; number 6, December
1906; number 7, November 1908.
FREQUENCY OF PUBLICATION
Irregular annual.
PUBLISHERS
Numbers 1–4: Sealy, Bryers, and Walker, Middle Abbey Street, Dublin/T. Fisher
Unwin, London. Number 5: Maunsel and Co., Ltd., 60 Dawson St., Dublin/A.
H. Bullen, London. Number 6: Maunsel and Co., Ltd., 60 Dawson St., Dublin.
Number 7: Maunsel and Co., Ltd./T. Fisher Unwin, London.
EDITOR
W. B. Yeats.

Hans Ostrom

SATURDAY ANALYST AND LEADER, THE. See LEADER, THE

SATURDAY REVIEW, THE

The *Saturday Review* was founded in 1855 by A.J.B. Beresford Hope, whose
aim was to establish a weekly newspaper of literature, opinion, science, and the
arts, "not bound to any party," he said, "but written by a combination of Peelite
Conservatives and Moderate Liberals, and to be the mouthpiece of the middle
moderate opinions of thoughtful and educated society."[1] He was joined in the
enterprise by John Douglas Cook and Philip Harwood, both earlier associated,
as was Beresford Hope, with the *Morning Chronicle* of London. Cook would
become the editor of the new paper, Harwood the coeditor. They were invading
a field, that of the weekly reviews, that was dominated by the *Athenaeum*,* the
Literary Gazette,* and Leigh Hunt's *Examiner*,* along with the *Spectator** (for
all, see *RA*).

Appearing under its full title, the *Saturday Review of Politics, Literature,
Science, and Art*, the paper's first issue came out on 3 November 1855. It scorned
the correspondence and gossip features of the *Spectator* and filled its columns
exclusively with full-scale articles, two to four columns long, dealing with
subjects from British foreign policy to critiques of individual poems by Tennyson.

By March 1858 its circulation had reached 5,000, more than the rival *Spectator*'s, slightly less than the prestigious *Athenaeum*'s. Among its early contributors were G. H. Lewes, Walter Bagehot, James Fitzjames Stephen, Max Muller, Mark Pattison, R. W. Church, and Leslie Stephen. Later additions included the critic John Morley and novelist Eliza Lynn Linton. Even for such distinguished writers, the almost inflexible policy was that the *Saturday*'s reviewing was done anonymously, for leaders and reviews alike, at least partly to contribute to a tone of unity with which the paper professed to speak. That tone not only rang with authority but was sometimes slashingly critical, earning the review its various nicknames: the "Saturday Snarler," "Saturday Scorpion," and "Saturday Reviler."

Addressing the educated and privileged classes, the *Saturday Review* generally took a moderate line, opposed democratic innovations but favored "prudent" social reforms, sympathized with the prerogatives of the Church, and advocated free trade and voluntary education. Before the passage of the Reform Bill of 1867, the paper cautioned that "freedom depends on the political supremacy of the upper and middle classes" (2:449). The *Saturday* ridiculed socialism and bitterly opposed the labor union movement. On the "woman question" it could see nothing but evil resulting from proposals to grant women equal rights with men. One review states, "It seems very doubtful to us whether anything which draws women away from their firesides may not, in the end, be more productive of harm than good" (1:116). In its view, women, being intellectually inferior to men, existed to furnish the elegant graces of Victorian domesticity and to be admired for their "fine gloss of innocence and delicacy" (20:602).

In literature the *Saturday Review* maintained, in general, a moderately critical outlook on the great figures of the age. It approved the writings of Thomas Carlyle as "works of art" but found that he falsified history by "excess of imagination" (5:638–40). Both *Past and Present* and *Latter-Day Pamphlets* were criticized as being unjust to modern English society, which the *Saturday*, notwithstanding its reputation as the "Reviler," believed was not nearly so desperately sick as Carlyle diagnosed. Ruskin was more severely dealt with. His *Modern Painters* escaped censure, but *Unto This Last* was attacked in such scathing terms by the *Saturday* and other journals that Ruskin's "socialist" criticism of English society was prematurely withdrawn from the pages of the *Cornhill*.* As for Matthew Arnold, the *Saturday*'s commentary on "The Function of Criticism at the Present Time" takes objection to his faulting the English for provincial narrowness of thought. *Essays in Criticism* as a whole, however, was kindly received.

Among novelists, Charles Dickens was taken to task for meddling ignorantly in social reform. The reviewer, Fitzjames Stephen, denied that Dickens's fiction had any hand in remedying social ills such as the harsh Poor Laws or the existence of debtors' prisons. Reforms would have come in any case, he argues; Dickens merely exercises a "very wide and very pernicious political and social influence" to sentimentalize the poor while castigating the educated governing class as the fount of "folly and stupidity" (3:8–9). The reviewer of *Great Expectations*, however, found it "original, powerful, and very entertaining" (12:69–70). Of Thackeray the paper was more respectful. He was not seen as a propagandizer against established institutions and he did not set up as a prophet. George Eliot, in a review by John Morley, is awarded a place in "the very first rank among English novelists" (21:722–24).

The *Saturday Review* accepted the general view of Alfred Tennyson as the chief poet of the age. A review of *Idylls of the King* in 1859 consists mostly of admiring comment and quotation of the poem; his powers of "musical composition" are lavishly praised (3:75–76). Browning did not fare so well; his *Men and Women* was reviewed shortly after the *Saturday* was launched in 1855. Attacking Browning for obscurity, the reviewer cries: "It is really high time that this sort of thing should, if possible, be stopped. Here is another book of madness and mysticism—another melancholy specimen of power wantonly wasted, and talent deliberately perverted" (1:69–70). In later years, however, the *Saturday*'s tone grew softer, and it helped usher in a belated public acceptance of Browning's work. In contrast with the review of *Men and Women*, a notice of *Dramatis Personae* nearly a decade later praises the "felicity of expression" with which the poet expresses complex ideas (17:735).

A. C. Swinburne, after winning praise from the *Saturday* for his *Atalanta in Calydon*, was excoriated in a review by John Morley that would become one of the most famous attacks on a nineteenth-century poet. The review, expressly ordered by the editor, Cook, charged that in *Poems and Ballads* (1866) Swinburne could be seen "grovelling down among the nameless, shameless abominations which inspire him with such frenzied delight." While granting Swinburne's musical and imaginative powers, Morley condemns the poet as "either the vindictive and scornful apostle of a crushing iron-shod despair, or . . . the libidinous laureate of a pack of satyrs."[2] So severe was Morley's criticism, so weighty the reputation of the *Saturday Review* in the mid-1860s, that the blast against Swinburne has been given more credit than it deserves for casting a shadow over the rest of Swinburne's long life.

Upon the death of Cook in 1868, subeditor Philip Harwood took control of the *Saturday*. Although Harwood added such men as Walter Besant and Andrew Lang to the list of contributors, the paper seems to have grown more concerned with remaining the most influential of English reviews, less concerned with keeping up the adventurous quality of its first thirteen years. From 1883 to 1894, under editor Walter Herries Pollock, the once independent *Saturday Review* became a predictable supporter of the Conservative party, though its still able staff included the likes of George Saintsbury as literary subeditor. Reviews became shorter and often included notices of several books in one brief article.

The paper enjoyed a brief renaissance from 1894 to 1898, with Frank Harris taking the helm as both owner and editor. Under Harris's predecessor, the *Saturday Review* had seen its influence wane as it lost both advertising and circulation. Harris, flushed with previous success as the editor of the *Fortnightly*

Review,* assembled a new staff whose brightest luminary was George Bernard Shaw, whose articles, signed "G.B.S.," appeared from 1895 to 1898. Max Beerbohm took Shaw's place as dramatic critic when he resigned, and H. G. Wells also was recruited by Harris to write for the paper. Having built it to a position of renewed prominence, Harris was able to sell the *Saturday Review* at a handsome profit in 1898.

Despite the Harris interlude, the *Saturday Review* would never regain its old stature as spokesman for England's upper classes. Again it began to lose money as circulation fell and as daily newspapers made inroads on the advertising potential of the weekly reviews. Gifts of money from individuals and groups were necessary to keep the paper in operation. In the twentieth century the *Saturday Review* changed hands a number of times, but with no reversal of the publication's failing fortunes. The nadir was reached when the eccentric heiress Lady Houston took over the paper in 1933, introduced red ink and a sensational tone to the once venerable review, and used her new acquisition to praise the machinations of Mussolini and Hitler. From its old status as the voice of England's establishment, the paper at its demise in 1938 had lost the attention, as well as the respect, of its old audience.

Notes

1. M. M. Bevington, *"The Saturday Review" 1855–68: Representative Educated Opinion in Victorian England* (New York, 1941), p. 16. Bevington's book, to which the present account is indebted, is the standard work on the *Saturday*. See also William Henry Law and Irene Law, *The Book of the Beresford Hopes* (London, 1925).

2. Morley's essay appears in 22 (1866):145–47. For a Swinburnean perspective, see Georges Lafourcade, *Swinburne* (New York, 1932), pp. 132–44, and Clyde K. Hyder, *Swinburne's Literary Career and Fame* (Durham, N.C., 1933), pp. 34–84.

Information Sources

BIBLIOGRAPHY

B., A. A. [A. A. Baumann]. *"The Saturday Review* as I Knew It." *Saturday Review* 156 (1933):686–87.

Bennion, S. C. *"Saturday Review*: From Literature to Life." Ph.D. dissertation, Syracuse University, 1968.

Bevington, M. M. *"The Saturday Review" 1855–68: Representative Educated Opinion in Victorian England.* New York, 1941.

Grant, James. *"The Saturday Review,"* Its Origin and Progress: Its Contributors and Character, with Illustrations of the Mode in Which It Is Conducted. London, 1873.

Jump, J. D. "Weekly Reviewing in the Eighteen-Fifties." *Review of English Studies* 24 (1948):42–57.

Law, William Henry, and Irene Law. *The Book of the Beresford Hopes.* London, 1925.

"Our Early Days." *Saturday Review* 150 (1930):583.

"The *Saturday* and Swinburne." *Saturday Review* 134 (1922):749–50.

"Seventy-Five Not Out." *Saturday Review* 150 (1930):581.

INDEXES
Some bound volumes contain indexes.
REPRINT EDITIONS
Microform: British Library (Newspaper Library), London.
LOCATION SOURCES
American
Widely available.
British
Complete runs: Bristol Public Library; British Museum; Cambridge University Library.
Partial runs: Widely available.

Publication History

MAGAZINE TITLE AND TITLE CHANGES
The Saturday Review of Politics, Literature, Science, and Art.
VOLUME AND ISSUE DATA
Volumes 1–66, numbers 1–4319, 3 November 1855–16 July 1938. (16 January 1937–16 July 1938 published without volume numbering.)
FREQUENCY OF PUBLICATION
Weekly.
PUBLISHERS(All in London)
1855–1887: A.J.B. Beresford Hope. 1887–1891: Philip Beresford Hope. 1891–1894: Lewis Humfrey Edmunds. 1894–1898: Frank Harris. 1898–1904: Earl of Hardwicke. 1904–1917: Sir Gervase Beckett. 1917–1921: A. A. Baumann. 1921: Grant Morden. 1921–1924: Sir Edward Mackay Edgar. 1924–1931: George Pinckard. 1931–1932: A. Wyatt Tilby. 1932–1938: Chawton Publishing Co.
EDITORS
John Douglas Cook, 1855–1868. Philip Harwood, 1868–1883. Walter Herries Pollock, 1883–1894. Frank Harris, 1894–1898. Harold Hodge, 1898–1913. G.A.B. Dewar, 1913–1917. A. A. Baumann, 1917–1921. Sydney Brooks, 1921. Filson Young, 1921–1924. Gerald Barry, 1924–1930. A. Wyatt Tilby, 1930–1932. Guy Pollock et al., 1932–1933. J. Wentworth Day, 1933–1934. Lady Houston, 1934–1936. George Freeman, 1936–1938.

Kerry Powell

SAVOY, THE

The idea of establishing a literary and artistic periodical to rival the *Yellow Book** was conceived in 1895 by Leonard Smithers, an unsuccessful solicitor turned bookseller and publisher, who advertised himself in the *Savoy* as a "Dealer in Rare and Valuable Literary and Artistic Property." In the late summer of 1895, Smithers, currently publishing Arthur Symons's controversial third collection of poems, *London Nights*, sought Symons out in Dieppe and asked him, in Symons's words, "to form and edit a new magazine." Symons gives the following account of the next steps in the creation of the *Savoy*: "As this magazine was to contain not only literature but illustration, I immediately went to Mr. Beardsley, whom I looked upon as the most individual and expressive draughtsman of our time, and secured his cordial co-operation. I then got together some of the writers, especially the younger writers, whose works seemed to me most personal and accomplished; deliberately choosing them from as many 'schools' as possible'' (''A Literary Causerie: By Way of Epilogue,'' no. 8:91). Beardsley, delighted to be working on the new magazine after having been recently dismissed by Henry Harland from the *Yellow Book*, named the magazine the *Savoy*. The first issue was ready by December 1895, but it was held up because friends of the project advised Smithers to remove the insult to Henry Harland that Beardsley had incorporated into the cover drawing: in the foreground a chubby little male figure, with full front exposed, was standing spread-legged over a copy of the *Yellow Book*.[1] By the time the offending details were removed and the issue made ready for sale, it was January—the Christmas trade had been missed. Still, the editors and publisher of the *Savoy* were fairly well pleased with the reception of the first issue by the public, to whom they were appealing by offering the magazine at an inexpensive price. Although they were puzzled by the outrage in many of the reviews of the first number (no. 8:91), they proudly quoted statements from some of the reviews in press notices at the end of the second number, such as this one from *Sketch*: ''We should describe it briefly as a 'Yellow Book' redeemed of its puerilities—and a 'Pageant' in which the illustrations are mainly original.'' The sales of the first two issues were good enough to embolden Smithers and his editors to transform their quarterly into a monthly, but over the next five months sales declined, and Symons sadly announced in the November issue that the December issue would be the last (no. 7:i). The last issue contained eighty pages of literary material, all written by Symons—an original poem, his translation of a poem by Mallarmé, a story, a descriptive essay, a critical essay, and the epilogue. The cover, the title page, and all twelve illustrations were done by Beardsley. Explaining in the epilogue why publication of the magazine could not be sustained, Symons states:

> Our first mistake was in giving so much for so little money; our second, in abandoning a quarterly for a monthly issue. The action of Messrs. Smith and Son in refusing to place ''The Savoy'' on their bookstalls [in railway stations], on account of the reproduction of a drawing by Blake [''Anteus Setting Virgil and Dante upon the Verge of Cocytus,'' no. 3:55],[2] was another misfortune. And then, worst of all, we assumed that there were very many people in the world who really cared for art, and really for art's sake. The more I consider it, the more I realize that this is not the case. Comparatively very few people care for art at all, and most of these care for it because they mistake it for something else.[No. 8:92]

Symons's intention from the beginning had been to provide good art, for art's sake. In his editorial note at the beginning of the first issue, he dissociates the

Savoy from philosophical and critical schools by stating: "We have no formulas, and we desire no false unity of form or matter. We have not invented a new point of view. We are not Realists, or Romantists, or Decadents. For us, all art is good which is good art." But of course the eclecticism implied in this statement is itself a philosophical stance, and the selection by aesthetic characteristics a critical stance. The combination of the two relates the *Savoy* to the eclectic, aesthetic tradition of Goethe, Mme. De Staël, Ernest Renan, and Walter Pater.

The literary content of the *Savoy* is truer to Symons's eclectic pronouncement than the art content, and the prose is more diverse and significant than the poetry. Among the stories that can be classified as Romantic are W. B. Yeats's slight but haunting tale, "The Binding of the Hair" (no. 1:135–38), portraying the young Queen Dectira, who even during a bloody war thinks only of the bard Aodh and his romantic songs; and the ballad-like "Morag of the Glen" (no. 7:13–34) by Fiona Macleod [William Sharp], concerned with a proud, stern father, his long-suffering wife, and their two beautiful daughters, one of whom dies a desperate death after being seduced by the landowner's son and the other of whom, in vengeance, drives the seducer, whom she too has loved, to suicide. Yeats's "The Tables of the Law" (no. 7:79–87) twists the Romantic theme of questing for ideal truth by having the seeker, a nineteenth-century disciple of Joachim of Flora, find what he is looking for. Ironically, however, he is now miserably isolated, because in his new state of mind he has lost the power of committing a sin and is therefore no longer "among those for whom Christ died" (no. 7:86).

Most of the stories can be classified as realistic, although there is a good deal of variety in them. Symons's "Pages from the Life of Lucy Newcome" (no. 2:147–60) and Hubert Crackanthrope's "Anthony Garstin's Courtship" (no. 3:15–39) deal with the "fallen" woman, but the former concentrates on the sufferings and the essential goodness of the woman, and the latter, in a seriocomic vein, on a middle-aged man whose good luck it is to be accepted in marriage by a pretty, spirited young woman with whom he is infatuated, because he will cover her "sin." Frederick Wedmore's epistolary stories, "To Nancy" (no. 1:31–41) and "The Deterioration of Nancy" (no. 2:99–108), deal with a similar theme—a girl's loss of "innocence." In these stories Wedmore reflects, through the letters of a fashionable portrait painter, the age's admiration of decorative girlhood and its fear of full-grown women. Seefang, in Ernest Dowson's "The Eyes of Pride" (no. 1:51–63), like Wedmore's painter, is a man in whom "the fine and the gross were so strangely mingled" (p. 53). Seefang wants two kinds of women: one type (of the lower class) to appeal to his grossness, and another (of his own, genteel class) to appeal to his fineness; but it is his fate to become attracted to a woman rather like himself. He is indignant: "Grudgingly, he had admitted that she was beautiful, but it was a beauty that repelled him in a girl of his own class, although he would have liked it well enough in women of less title to respect" (p. 53). Wedmore and Dowson present the traditional ideal of purity in women with utter seriousness, not satirically. Amid the stories about fallen women and the women who slip from the girlish ideal, there is Ernest Rhys's "A Romance of Three Fools" (no. 5:57–69), a comic satire on a male writer's admiration of the actress who plays the heroine in his sentimental drama, "Sweet Cinderella," and Rudolf Dircks's "Ellen" (no. 1:103–8), an astute portrayal of a waitress who is complex enough to be shy, lacking in self-confidence, lonely, and in need of a confidant and a child, but proud of her independence and not disposed toward marriage. All of these realistic short stories are well crafted. The best story, however, is Joseph Conrad's "The Idiots" (no. 6:11–30), a stark domestic tragedy heightened by religious terror and the absence of scientific enlightenment.

If there is a decadent story in the magazine, it is Yeats's "Rosa Alchemica" (no. 2:56–70). The isolation of the persona from all of the normal procedures of life, the feverishness of his search for meaning, the delirium of his mystical experience, the subsequent instability of his personality, and the glorification of ennui—all seem to carry the story beyond the borders of romance. Two works of fiction that might be classified as "portraits" recall Walter Pater's "The Child in the House" and the concluding scenes of his *Marius the Epicurean*: Symons's "The Childhood of Lucy Newcome" (no. 8:51–61) and Ernest Dowson's "The Dying of Francis Donne" (no. 4:66–74), respectively. These works differ from the realistic short stories in the magazine by being developed, not by dramatic techniques, but by description that sustains a consistent, quiet tone, whatever the action may be, and, especially in "The Dying of Francis Donne," by a concentration on the impressions and ideas that constitute the inner life. Considering this wealth of short fiction, as well as nine other stories published in the *Savoy*, Beardsley's "Under the Hill" (no. 1:151–63; no. 2:174–87) seems not a tone-setter, but an isolated *tour de force*. In the expurgated form printed in the *Savoy*, this work is not a story, but several Beardsley scenes drawn in words, striking in their originality and decorative in function.

The second most outstanding prose genre in the *Savoy* is literary criticism. It consists mainly of three types: commentary on nineteenth-century French writers by English writers who knew them personally; Havelock Ellis's lengthy and instructive essays on Zola, Nietzsche, and Hardy's *Jude the Obscure*, the subjects having been selected because their matter was pivotal and controversial, not for their aesthetic characteristics; and Symons's essays in criticism, the best of which is "Walter Pater: Some Characteristics" (no. 8:33–41), a well-informed, sensitive, disinterested, comprehensive interpretation of Pater unsurpassed even today. The art criticism in the *Savoy* gets off to an admirable start in the first number with Joseph Pennell's "A Golden Decade in English Art [the 1860s]" (pp. 112–24), but there is no recurring form for art criticism in later issues to match Symons's "Literary Causerie." The criticism after the first issue consists of Yeats's sympathetic three-part essay on William Blake and his illustrations to *The Divine Comedy* (no. 1:25–41; no. 3:41–57; no. 5:31–36). As to miscellaneous essays, the most noteworthy are five descriptive sketches by Symons, his translation of Verlaine's "My Visit to London" (no. 2:119–35), and two essays that border on social criticism: G.B. Shaw's "On Going to Church" (no. 1:13–28) and Max Beerbohm's "A Good Prince" (no. 1:45–47).

The poetry of the *Savoy* is not startling, profound, or technically innovative. Not one of the thirty-six original poems would have to be selected for an anthology of outstanding nineteenth-century poetry. The most memorable poem is Beardsley's "The Ballad of a Barber" (no. 3:91–93)—memorable not because the barber, who had never had a "preference for either sex," is smitten by the young daughter of the king while coiffing her hair, but because the barber is as dedicated an artist as any painter or sculptor. He is so indignant because this passion for the girl interferes with his art that he kills her. Another memorable poem, "The Song of the Women," by Ford Madox Hueffer (no. 4:85–86), seems a refinement on Thomas Hood's protest lyrics of the 1840s. The finest lyric is Beardsley's translation of Catullus' "Carmen CI—Hail and Farewell." Wendell V. Harris has explained, in "Innocent Decadence: The Poetry of *The Savoy*," that the only decadent poems are the seventeen written by Dowson and Symons, and that these are decadent only in their melancholy, disillusion, and despair. He states that "one finds little of that morbid imagination, or that thirst for sensation for its own sake, or that jaundiced cynicism, which are so often imputed to decadent art."[3]

The art content of the *Savoy* is less eclectic than the literary content. Apparently, no effort was made to represent the finest painting of the age from the various schools. Half of the ninety-six art works are Beardsley's and several of the others are pen-and-ink drawings in imitation of his style, some by Fred Hyland, William T. Horton, and A. Kay Womrath. Thus, if one turns through the issues without reading, Beardsley seems to be the guiding genius of the magazine. Pennell's street scenes, Beerbohm's caricatures, *The Bacchantes*, after a watercolor by Caresme, the festive neoclassical drawings of Charles Conder, and Phil May's satirical drawing, "Holiday Joys," harmonize with Beardsley's highly sophisticated art. Blake's six illustrations from Dante's *Divine Comedy* blend well with the pervasive religious atmosphere of the literary content of the magazine and with the indifference to science that marks it. Only Charles Haslewood Shannon's four lithographs suggest the poignant human problems treated in many of the stories.

One comes away from the *Savoy* feeling that the fiction in the magazine deserves more attention than it has received and that students who have never studied Zola, Verlaine, Nietzsche, or Pater could not find better introductions to them than those in its pages. And one is impressed by Beardsley's originality, Symons's versatility, and Smithers's dedication to aesthetic ventures.

Notes

1. Stanley Weintraub, " 'The Beardsley': An Introduction," in *"The Savoy": Nineties Experiment* (University Park, Pa., 1966), p. xx.

2. Roger Lhombreaud, *Another Symons: A Critical Biography* (London, 1963), p. 316, n.26.

3. Wendell V. Harris, "Innocent Decadence: The Poetry of *The Savoy*," *Publications of the Modern Language Association of America* 77 (1962):632.

Information Sources

BIBLIOGRAPHY

Casford, E. Lenore. *The Magazines of the 1890's*. University of Oregon Publication, Language and Literature Series, no. 1. Eugene, 1929.

Clark, Kenneth. *The Best of Beardsley*. New York, 1978.

Ferguson, S. C. "Formal Developments in the English Short Story, 1880–1910." Ph.D. dissertation, Stanford University, 1967.

Garbaty, Thomas J. "The French Coterie of *The Savoy*, 1896." *Publications of the Modern Language Association of America* 75 (1960):609–15.

———. "*The Savoy*, 1896: A Re-edition of Representative Prose and Verse, with a Critical Introduction and Biographical and Critical Notes." Ph.D. dissertation, University of Pennsylvania, 1957.

Goldfarb, Russell M. "Late Victorian Decadence." *Journal of Aesthetics and Art Criticism* 20 (1962):369–73.

Harris, Wendell V. "Innocent Decadence: The Poetry of *The Savoy*." *Publications of the Modern Language Association of America* 77 (1962):629–36.

McLean, W. I. "*The Savoy* (1896): Its Genesis and Its Significance as an Organ of the Celtic Revival." Ph.D. dissertation, University of Hull, 1970–1971.

Weintraub, Stanley, ed. "*The Savoy*": *Nineties Experiment*. University Park, Pa., 1966.

INDEXES

Each volume indexed.

REPRINT EDITIONS

Thomas J. Garbaty, "*The Savoy*, 1896: A Re-edition of Representative Prose and Verse, with a Critical Introduction and Biographical and Critical Notes," Ph.D. dissertation, University of Pennsylvania, 1957. Sanley Weintraub, ed., "*The Savoy*": *Nineties Experiment*, University Park, Pa., 1966.

Microform: AMS Press, New York. Early British Periodicals (UMI), reel 29.

LOCATION SOURCES

American

Widely available.

British

Widely available.

Publication History

MAGAZINE TITLE AND TITLE CHANGES

The Savoy: An Illustrated Quarterly, January–April 1896. *The Savoy: An Illustrated Monthly*, July–December 1896.

VOLUME AND ISSUE DATA

Numbers 1–2, January–April 1896; Numbers 3–8, July–December 1896.

FREQUENCY OF PUBLICATION

Quarterly (2 issues, January–April 1896); monthly (6 issues, July–December 1896).

PUBLISHER
Leonard Smithers, Effingham House, Arundel Street, Strand, London.
EDITOR
Arthur Symons.

Billie Andrew Inman

SCOTS OBSERVER, THE

So prevalent is the identification of the *Scots Observer* (later the *National Observer*) with W. E. Henley, its only acknowledged editor, that its ostensible purposes may be overlooked. A prospectus issued shortly before the *Observer*'s 24 November 1888 debut advertised the periodical as a "Sixpenny Weekly Journal for Scotland . . . a Record and a Review of current Politics, Literature, Science, Art, etc." It went on to promise that "while giving due prominence to Imperial and General Affairs, it [would] also deal specially with subjects of National Interest. . . . Politically, *The Scots Observer* will give hearty support to the Constitutional Principles necessary for the maintenance of the unity of the Empire."

The promise was kept. Very much a newspaper with its small tabloid format (above 8 1/2" × 13") of twenty-eight to thirty-two pages, it followed a conservative and generally imperialistic line, while focusing on distinctively Scottish interests. Reviews of literature and music were regular features, and short fiction was occasionally published; yet it is for none of these that the *Observer* is still remembered.

Instead, it is the editorial acumen of Henley that strikes readers almost a century later. He had the courage to sponsor the still young and obscure W. B. Yeats, eighteen of whose poems and several of whose tales were first printed in the *Observer*. Henley had the charisma to attract and to retain Rudyard Kipling, who, although a few months younger than Yeats, could choose his publishers. Over a dozen of Kipling's poems initially appeared in Henley's paper. Furthermore, other significant poets—A. C. Swinburne, Robert Louis Stevenson, Katharine Tynan (Hinkson), Alice Meynell, Edmund Gosse, Kenneth Grahame, and Cosmo Monkhouse—were represented, as were such critics and reviewers as Stéphane Mallarmé (in French), Andrew Lang, William Archer, J. M. Barrie, George Moore, and, again, Alice Meynell and Kenneth Grahame. What makes this list more impressive is that it covers only a half dozen years. (Most prose contributions were unsigned.)

Despite shifts of policy and locale, the format was quite consistent. Each issue contained a nearly equal blend of "leading" and "general" articles, the former being mainly political. Correspondence was encouraged, and in late nineteenth-century fashion readers often used the correspondence columns to conduct extended, sometimes witty, and occasionally acrimonious debate. Although Oscar

Wilde's and Coventry Patmore's letters (not to each other) in the *Observer* are better known, more characteristic was the exchange between R. T. Hamilton-Bruce and R. G. Collingwood, John Ruskin's secretary, on the alleged impropriety of reissuing *Modern Painters*, after a statement in the preface to the 1873 edition had assured purchasers that this thousand-copy edition, because of its deteriorating plates, would be the last.

The Scottish tilt of the *Observer* weakened critical standards. Henley was otherwise too discerning an editor to admit doggerel such as Janet Logie Robertson's "Edinburgh" to the maiden issue: "Thou sittest serene and stately / In a Glamour of the past, / Nor Fearest the Future greatly / Thy charms are those that last!" Scottish authors were not only less subject to dissection, but were even found promising. Reviewing an early J. M. Barrie potboiler, the *Observer* predicted that the author, "if he continues his present rate of progress, [would] ere long take a leading place among the literary men of the present day."

Typically, a poem was published in each issue. Among Stevenson's were "Christmas at Sea" and "The Wanderer." Several of Henley's own poems appeared. These, like all poetry, were signed. Although Yeats contributed Irish tales and columns on the occult, none of his or Kipling's poetry appeared in the *Observer* until 1890, when a slight policy shift occurred. The *Observer* then styled itself "An Imperial Review"; not only was this more appropriate for publishing the work of Kipling that was to become *Barrack-Room Ballads and Other Verses*, but it also emphasized the imperialistic stance of the periodical. That year there appeared "Gunga Din," "Mandalay," "The Young British Soldier," "Screw Guns," "Belts," "The Conundrum of the Workshops," and "Evarre and His Gods." Even Swinburne, whose *Songs Before Sunrise* would have placed him in the opposing camp, sent poetry to the *Observer*, which printed his Dowson-like "Roundel." With such contributions, the weekly was notable to contemporaries for its verse, but it is the then unheralded poetry of Yeats, more than any other factor, that has made the *Observer* memorable.

From April 1890 through August 1894 Yeats submitted poetry to the *Observer*, where first appeared "The Lake Isle of Innisfree," "The White Birds," "The Ballad of Father Gilligan," "The Cap and Bells," and more than a dozen other poems, many of which are now standard anthology pieces. Yeats and Henley were dissimilar in background, age, politics, and temperament—their literary interests could scarcely have been more divergent. Still, Yeats never lost the imprint of Henley's personality, and he revered his truculent editor years after his death:

W. E. Henley was my chief employer. I had become one of that little group of friends who gathered at his house near Bedford Park . . . and were afterwards the staff of his *Scots Observer* and *National Observer*. He alarmed me and impressed me exactly as he did the others who were called Henley's young men, and even today [when I meet] some one among them, showing perhaps the first signs of age, we recognize at once the bond. We have as it were a secret in common: that we have known a man whose power no others can know because it has not found expression in words.[1]

While not as important as Yeats or Kipling, another writer whose emergence is largely attributable to Henley and the *Observer* is Kenneth Grahame. Although his fame rests on *The Wind in the Willows* (1908), his work for Henley often shows the charm, fluency, and power of imagination that reached maturity in his masterpiece. Henley was so impressed by Grahame's essays, beginning with "Of Smoking" in October 1890, that he insisted on his being a regular contributor to the *Observer*. Grahame's recent biographer, Peter Green, suggests that Henley did all he could to persuade Grahame to make literature, not the Bank of England, his vocation.[2] Among Grahame's writings for Henley are such poems as "As You Like It" and "Quis Desiderio" and many of the essays and stories eventually incorporated into *Pagan Papers*, including "The Rural Pan."

Late in 1890 the title became the *National Observer*, as publication was moved to London, although the Edinburgh office was retained. The only visible change in editorial policy was a lessened emphasis on Scottish matters. Despite its name, the *Scots Observer* was never provincial. However, it was not a commercial success. Two thousand was the highest sustained circulation.[3] Undoubtedly, Fitzroy Bell, Henley's major backer, thought that a London address and editorial office would facilitate sales, but in actuality neither circulation nor substance was much affected. True, the series on "Urban Scotland," featuring such cities as Perth, Elgin, and Ayr, was discontinued, and provincial matters (for example, the formation of a Scottish electrical society) figured less prominently among the correspondence, but a northern bent was still encouraged.

If "Urban Scotland" died, "Modern Man" thrived. This was a series of essays, each commenting on the work of a contemporary figure. Among those featured were Benjamin Jowett, Antonin Dvořák, Henry James, Leo Tolstoy, Guissepe Verdi, Emile Zola, T. H. Huxley, Oliver Wendell Holmes, Ernest Renan, Paul Verlaine, Herbert Herkomer, and Björnstjerne Björnson. The *Observer* never prided itself on its editorial tact, but its contempt for democracy and mediocrity, which were related concepts for Henley, was seldom more evident than in this series. Jowett, "The Master of Balliol," is accorded respect verging on reverence, but such is hardly the case with Zola or Herkomer. As to the French novelist's values, "Such are the delusions of democracy," and as to his capabilities, "Mr. Zola, for all his talents and for all his aims, is essentially stupid." But this is lenient treatment compared to that given Herkomer, whom the *Observer* thought a charlatan: "It is Professor Herkomer's peculiar distinction to have failed in more arts than many of his generation. . . . And yet he has never committed a folly which he did not trick out to the public as a veritable triumph." Of course, the entire series was anonymous, but here one suspects the hand of Charles Whibley, perhaps the most stalwart vessel in "Henley's Regatta," who wrote similarly of Herkomer on other occasions.

In March 1894 Henley relinquished the editorship of the *Observer*, and while the review persisted until October 1897, with Henley's departure it perceptibly declined. Not only was Henley's successor anonymous, but the identity of the publisher and place of publication was also omitted, as was an index of signing contributors. The *Observer* was not devoid of interesting features, among them the "Less-Known London" series, in which buildings and institutions such as Somerset House, the Royal Observatory, and the Bank of England were scrutinized. However, the general direction was toward mediocrity, as little fiction or poetry of merit was printed. Yeats's last poem for the *Observer* appeared in the issue for August 1894; and when Stevenson died that December, Katharine Hinkson's elegy appeared in the year's last issue. In its futile search for a new readership, in early 1897 the dying periodical ran a series entitled "Golf Greens Near London."

Without Henley the *National Observer* was no longer viable. It had never been financially successful, but Henley's charisma and editorial brilliance sustained, at least temporarily, an unsound proposition. But a larger factor was more decisive. No 1890s weekly could be as reflective as the magisterial monthlies such as the *Nineteenth Century*,* nor offer the currency or popular interest of the Harmsworths' new journalism, exemplified in the *Daily Mail*, which was launched in May 1896. Nor was the format of the *Observer* compelling. Without photographs or prints, it could appeal only to the especially literate, a small clientele unwilling to accept mediocrity. In March 1896 the *Observer* "amalgamated" with the *British Review*; the price for the consolidated journal was halved to three pence. By the end of July, a typical issue had shrunk to sixteen tabloid pages, and even a reduction in price to two pence was unavailing, as the *Observer* sank into oblivion in October of that year.[4]

Notes

1. W. B. Yeats, *Memoirs: Autobiography—First Draft, Journal* (New York, 1973), pp. 37–38.

2. Peter Green, *Kenneth Grahame* (London, 1959), p. 113.

3. Joseph M. Flora, *William Ernest Henley* (New York, 1970), p. 56.

4. After publication was discontinued with the 7 August issue, the journal was revived as the *National Observer* on 16 October 1897. The reincarnation was brief. No further issues appeared.

Information Sources

BIBLIOGRAPHY

Buckley, Jerome Hamilton. *William Ernest Henley: A Study in the "Counter-Decadence" of the 'Nineties*. 1945. Reprint. New York, 1971.

Flora, Joseph M. *William Ernest Henley*. New York, 1970.

Gross, John. *The Rise and Fall of the Man of Letters: A Study of the Idiosyncratic and the Humane in Modern Literature*. New York, 1969.

Robertson, John Henry [pseud. John Connell]. *W. E. Henley*. London, 1969.

INDEXES

Each volume indexed.

REPRINT EDITIONS

Microform: British Library (Newspaper Library), London. English Literary Periodicals (UMI), reels 603–607.

LOCATION SOURCES

American

Partial runs: Columbia University Library; Harvard University Library; New York Public Library; U. S. Library of Congress; University of Minnesota Library; Yale University Library.

British

Complete run: British Museum.

Partial runs: Edinburgh Public Library; Guildhall Library; Manchester Public Library; National Library of Scotland.

Publication History

MAGAZINE TITLE AND TITLE CHANGES

The Scots Observer, 24 November 1888–15 November 1890; *The National Observer*, 22 November 1890–13 March 1897; *The National Observer and British Review of Politics, Economics, Literature, Science, and Art*, 20 March–22 May 1897; *The British Review and National Observer of Politics, Economics, Literature, Science and Art*, 29 May–7 August 1897; *The National Observer*, 16 October 1897.

VOLUME AND ISSUE DATA

Volumes 1–18, numbers 1–455, 24 November 1888–7 August 1897; new series, vol. 19, no. 456, 16 October 1897.

FREQUENCY OF PUBLICATION

Weekly.

PUBLISHERS

24 November 1888–11 June 1892: John Douglas, 9 Thistle Street, Edinburgh/ 115 Fleet Street, London, E.C. (21 May–11 June 1892). 18 June 1892–13 March 1897: 115 Fleetwood Street, London, E.C./Abbey Buildings, Princess Street, Westminster, London (31 March 1894–13 March 1897). 20 March–7 August 1897: A. C. Hide, 37 & 39 Essex Street, Strand, W.C. London.

EDITORS

None listed, although the editorship of W. E. Henley from the *Observer*'s premiere on 24 November 1888, to 24 March 1894 is undisputed.

Daniel Rutenberg

SHARPE'S LONDON MAGAZINE

Sharpe's London Magazine (1845–1870) was owned by publishers who treated it simply as property, without exercising strong control over its policies or contents. The magazine maintained a generally consistent format—printing serialized novels, short fiction, essays, and brief comments on literature, art, and entertainments—but it frequently changed tone and emphasis as successive editors made it a vehicle for their own tastes.

The magazine began on 1 November 1845 as a three-halfpenny weekly aimed, according to the preface, at the "middle and lower walks of society." With that price and intention, it was competing for the audience that read *Chambers's Edinburgh Journal (Chambers's Journal** [see *RA*]), and tried to woo them by printing woodcuts (*Chambers's* was not illustrated) while emphasizing that, unlike the cheaper illustrated periodicals such as the *London Journal, Sharpe's* was thoroughly suited for the whole family. It was designed for people who did not have a great deal of time for reading; it contained brief essays and tales, articles on antiquarian and historical subjects, and occasional extracts from new books. Although definitely moral, it supported no particular religious platform, and it was aware of urban working people's concerns to the extent of summarizing reports of the public health commissioners and giving advice about joining provident societies.

The formula, however, did not attract the "lower walks" in any significant number. From the beginning most of the sales were in monthly parts; the weekly numbers, which were supposed to appeal to people on more limited budgets, did not pay their way. In January 1848 the magazine became a monthly, at a price of one shilling. In March 1848 it was transferred from T. B. Sharpe to Arthur Hall, and more elegant steel engravings were substituted for the earlier woodcuts.

Meanwhile, Frank Smedley, whose sketches and novels had been featured since May 1846, agreed to become editor in November 1847, although he had to give up the post in February 1849 because of his health. (Smedley suffered from degenerative spinal disease and was confined to a wheelchair.) During Smedley's tenure the magazine gave more space to humor. With his successor, an unidentified editor for volumes 9 and 10 (1849), the magazine featured more essays on social topics—James Acland's "Penal Economy" in March 1849, for example—as well as reviews of books by popular authors like G.P.R. James that filled space cheaply with summaries and long quotations from the books.

In the following year, either because readers had complained or because there was again a new editor, the proportion of fiction diminished and there was a renewed emphasis on brief explanations of scientific principles and similar improving material. The prefaces during 1850 emphasize the magazine's wholesome tone and its "safe and acceptable reading for the Family Circle." Early in 1852 Mrs. S. C. Hall took a hand in the management; her name was added to the magazine in July. During that year there appeared more relatively serious material by and about women—fiction by Mary Howitt, memoirs of lady travelers, Frederika Bremer's "Impressions of England," and a long review-article on Margaret Fuller.

Mrs. Hall left the magazine early in 1853, evidently after a dispute—she refused to complete her novel *Helen Lyndsay*, which she had been serializing. Editors thereafter cannot be positively identified, though continued changes in emphasis make it apparent that successive influences were at work. Prussian-born Bethel Henry Strousberg (who had written *Lawson's Merchant's Magazine* in 1852–1853) is said to have bought *Sharpe's* and edited it for a year in about 1854, which seems quite plausible, since during that year there were several studies of great authors (chiefly Continental) and brief essays on European history.

In 1855 the magazine exhibited its social conscience and awareness of lower-middle-class urban realities. There were many pieces by Eliza Meteyard ("Silverpen"), who typically wrote stories with plots that turned on practical solutions to social problems, and who also provided factual essays on such subjects as "Loans and Loan Offices." One regular feature between 1855 and 1857 was a monthly chess problem. Alfred W. Cole is said to have edited *Sharpe's*; if so, it was probably during this time, for his novel *Lorimer Littlegood* was the featured serial beginning in July 1855.

In 1857 there was a shift to less-improving fiction, including a mildly sensational serial by William Hurton entitled *The Finger of Providence: or, Murder Will Out*. The magazine was evidently once again in the throes of a change in direction. In 1858 it was incorporated with the *Illustrated Magazine* and became primarily a women's magazine. The chess problems vanished. There was much more poetry, a domestic serial, and a number of new regular departments, including a children's page, patterns for crochet and needlework, household hints, fashion notes, and brief notices of concerts and plays.

Even as a women's magazine, however, *Sharpe's London Magazine* continued the shifts in emphasis that reveal either an individual editor's interests or, perhaps, an attempt to discover an identifiable and therefore loyal constituency. Between 1859 and 1863 a regular column, "Passing Events Re-Edited," commented on events that "bear upon the domestic and social condition of our times, especially with reference to women" (n.s. 13:53). It criticized cheapskate advertisements for governesses and promoted telegraphy, engraving, design, medicine, and other occupations for women. The book review column summarized the contents of each new issue of the *English Woman's Journal*. In 1862 and 1863 there were once again more stories by men (largely with titles such as "How I Won My Victoria Cross"), perhaps in the hope of encouraging mothers to buy a family magazine that would also provide reading for their sons.

In 1864 the "Ladies' Page" expanded and the book reviews were increasingly devoted to Amelia B. Edwards, Jean Ingelow, and other women's favorites. In 1866 there was, briefly, renewed interest in social questions, including an article on woman suffrage that conspicuously avoided taking a stand but did suggest that the claims of female householders should at least be listened to without being laughed at (n.s. 29:218). After about 1863, however, the magazine became increasingly lifeless; it depended on women's household features, summaries and quotations from other books and periodicals, and reprints of fiction from American sources.

In its early years, *Sharpe's London Magazine* occupied a specific niche: it was cheaper than half-crown periodicals such as *Bentley's,* Blackwood's** (see

RA), *Fraser's** (see *RA*), more lively than *Chambers's* because of the illustrations and the serialized novels, and yet still respectable enough for family reading, unlike many penny weeklies. After paper prices dropped in the late 1850s *Sharpe's* suddenly shared the field with a great many new shilling monthlies. Most of them were aggressively promoted and edited, printed serials by leading authors, and offered readers much better value for the same price. *Sharpe's* either did not or could not compete on this ground. The only things it had that the others did not were needlework patterns and a children's page. It is perhaps surprising, then, that it survived even until December 1870.

Sharpe's printed its novels in extremely short installments, so that they often ran even longer than the two years that was typical for Victorian serials. It depended on Frank Smedley's fiction for nearly ten years, between 1846 and 1855. All three of his novels—*Frank Fairleigh, Lewis Arundel*, and *Harry Coverdale's Courtship*—first appeared in *Sharpe's*. Alfred W. Cole's *Lorimer Littlegood, Esq.*, subtitled "A Young Gentleman Who Wished to See Society, and Saw It Accordingly," is similar to Smedley's work; both authors took a good-humored look at contemporary high society and reproduced, in great detail, the round of recreations from opera to dinner party to sporting life—for readers who were definitely not a part of that upper class. But the frequent changes in editorship and the evident difficulty in finding a faithful audience kept *Sharpe's* from having a significant influence. Its notices of art exhibits, theater, concerts, and other events were irregular, unsystematic, and uncritical; they were probably often friendly boosts for people the editors knew. The book reviews generally consist of quotation and summary rather than criticism, and are therefore of little interest to scholars. The magazine's evident attempt, however, to discover what would interest lower-middle-class urban subscribers provides data for social historians.

Information Sources

BIBLIOGRAPHY

Bede, Cuthbert [E. Bradley]. *"Sharpe's London Magazine." Notes and Queries*, 5th ser., 11 (1879):330–31.

Boase, George C. *"Sharpe's London Magazine." Notes and Queries*, 5th ser., 11 (1879):293.

Ellis, Stewart M. *Mainly Victorian*. London, 1925.

INDEXES
Each volume indexed; 1846–1870 in *Poole's Index*.

REPRINT EDITIONS
Microform: English Literary Periodicals (UMI), reels 883–891.

LOCATION SOURCES
American
Complete runs: Boston Public Library, Enoch Pratt Library.
Partial runs: Widely available.

British

Complete runs: Bodleian Library; British Museum; Leeds Public Library.
Partial runs: Aberdeen University Library; Birmingham Public Library; Bristol Public Library; Cambridge University Library; Edinburgh Public Library; London University Library; Manchester Public Library; University College of Wales (Aberystwyth) Library.

Publication History

MAGAZINE TITLE AND TITLE CHANGES
Sharpe's London Magazine, a Journal of Entertainment and Instruction, November 1845–February 1849. *Sharpe's London Journal of Entertainment and Instruction for General Reading*, March 1849–June 1852. *Sharpe's London Magazine of Entertainment and Instruction for General Reading*, July 1852–December 1870.

VOLUME AND ISSUE DATA
Volumes 1–15, 1 November 1845–June 1852; new series, volumes 1–37, July 1852–December 1870.

FREQUENCY OF PUBLICATION
Weekly, 1 November 1845–24 December 1847; monthly, January 1848–December 1870 (volume 5–).

PUBLISHERS
Volumes 1–5: T. B. Sharpe, 15 Skinner Street, Snow Hill, London. Volumes 6–new series 37: Arthur Hall and Company (and successors), 25 Paternoster Row, London.

EDITORS
Unidentified, November 1845–October 1847. Frank Smedley, November 1847–February 1849. Unidentified, March 1849–June 1852. Mrs. Samuel Carter Hall, July–December 1852. Frank Smedley (?), January–December 1853. Bethel Henry Strousberg (?), January–December 1854. Unidentified, January 1855–December 1870.

Sally Mitchell

SHILLING MAGAZINE. See DOUGLAS JERROLD'S SHILLING MAGAZINE

SPECTATOR, THE. See RA

STRAND MAGAZINE, THE

On the evening of 13 December 1949, the British Broadcasting Company announced that "*The Strand Magazine*, pioneer of British illustrated magazines, and for many years the most popular of its kind in the world, [was] to cease publication with the March issue next year." With this announcement, many on both sides of the Atlantic lamented the extinction of "a British institution," a pictorial monthly that one nostalgic reader, according to the American *Time* magazine, placed fondly alongside the Bible and *Pilgrim's Progress* as a major source of his youthful reading. The publishers, still bearing the name of the founding editor, George Newnes, had surveyed their domain of some fifty periodicals and had found the *Strand Magazine* a vulnerable victim of rising production costs. Numerous newspapers responded with regret. The London *News Chronicle* echoed the general elegy: "No more will the monthly potpourri of humour, drama and life go out from Southampton Street to the bookstalls of the world." The B.B.C. continued its eulogy with the story of the *Strand*, which "began nearly sixty years ago when Sir George Newnes had an idea for a magazine packed with stories and articles with a picture on every page."[1]

When George Newnes published his first issue of the *Strand Magazine* in January 1891, he did so on the profits of his successful weekly paper *Tit-Bits*, a chatty collection of *Reader's Digest*-type notes from "All of the Most Interesting Books, Periodicals and Newspapers in the World," which he had launched a decade earlier to appeal primarily to the lower-middle-class readership. Thus, in his first issue of the *Strand*, for January 1891, he introduced his purpose:

> The Editor of *The Strand Magazine* respectfully places his first number in the hands of the public. *The Strand Magazine* will be issued regularly in the early part of each month. It will contain stories and articles by the best British writers, and special translations from the first foreign authors. These will be illustrated by eminent artists.
>
> Special new features which have not hitherto found place in Magazine Literature will be introduced from time to time.
>
> It may be said that with the immense number of existing Monthlies there is no necessity for another. It is believed, however, that *The Strand Magazine* will soon occupy a position which will justify its existence.
>
> The past efforts of the Editor in supplying cheap, healthful literature have met with such generous favour from the public, that he ventures to hope that this new enterprise will prove a popular one. He is conscious of many defects in the first issue, but will strive after improvement in the future.
>
> Will those who like this number be so good as to assist, by making its merits, if they are kind enough to think that it has any, known to their friends.

Probably no other middle-class-oriented periodical more closely and consistently lived up to its originally stated purpose than did the *Strand*. As one of its later editors rightly noted, "For more than half a century, it faithfully mirrored their tastes, prejudices, and intellectual limitations. From them it drew a large and loyal readership that was the envy of the publishing world." Even Queen Victoria approved of the publication. In an early issue there appeared a full-page drawing, "The Queen's First Baby," an etching by Her Majesty herself.

The son of a Congregational minister, George Newnes showed far stronger leanings toward business than toward following in his father's clerical footsteps. With a knack for public relations, he knew his intended audience and identified with it. "I am the average man. I don't have to put myself in his place. I am in his place. I know what he wants." Obviously he did. His first issue of the *Strand Magazine*, with its cover design by G. H. Haite and its 112 pages of articles and stories, along with numerous illustrations and advertising pages, sold 300,000 copies at six pence each. Soon it reached a circulation of nearly a half million copies a month—a success story envied by its numerous competitors and imitators. By the turn of the century, the expanding publishing firm of George Newnes, Ltd. added a companion journal, the *Sunday Strand*, a journal of popular religious news designed to "give glimpses of Christian and humane work and workers in all quarters, of missionary romance abroad, and of social enterprise at home." Providing "interesting articles and stories suitable for Sunday reading," the *Sunday Strand* reached more people than Newnes's father dreamed of reaching from his pulpit. For nearly a decade, from 1900 through 1909, it included illustrated articles on clergymen of the day, Bible talks, religious stories and poems, hymns with music, and articles such as "Joseph Chamberlain as a Sunday School Teacher." With the *Sunday Strand*, the son of the Congregational minister proved that a "calling" could be expressed in more ways than one.

If the *Sunday Strand* was more a "mirror" of popular beliefs and attitudes than a challenger of them, it was simply following the spirit of the *Strand Magazine* itself. Indeed, one of the *Strand Magazine*'s later editors, Reginald Pound, aptly entitled his 1966 history of the magazine *Mirror of the Century:"The Strand Magazine" 1891–1950*. Since Pound's is the only significant study of the *Strand* to date, the remaining commentary will be based on his book and on a survey of the magazine itself.

Newnes published his first issue of the *Strand* from his Burleigh Street office off the Strand in London (it nearly became the *Burleigh Street Magazine*) with the able editorial assistance of H. Greenhough Smith, the guiding light of the magazine for forty years, from its beginning until 1930. Later editors included Reeves Shaw (1930–1941), Reginald Pound (1941–1946), and Macdonald Hastings (1946–1950). Although Newnes died in 1910, his name appeared on various publications of his public company which, in 1897, was worth 1 million pounds. In 1959 George Newnes, Ltd. sold for 12 million pounds. At the turn of the century, its most prominent publication was the *Strand Magazine*, with a circulation of about a half million copies a month. An American edition ceased in 1916.

"Information as entertainment" was Newnes's intent. While it was presented as a family magazine, the primary appeal seemed to be to men. Similar to the American illustrated monthlies, *Harpers'* and *Scribners'*, the *Strand* was imitated by such British products as *Pearson's Magazine** and the *London Magazine*. However, neither American nor British imitators approached the *Strand*'s circulation.

The first six issues contained translated stories by Balzac, Pushkin, Dumas, and several others. Among the writers in English were Bret Harte and J. E. Preston Muddock ("Dick Donovan"). Lavishly illustrated features included a regular section, "Portraits of Celebrities at Different Times of Their Lives," a series that appeared over a sixteen-year period, beginning with Lord Tennyson and ending with David Lloyd George. The series, with its numerous photographs and drawings of well-known late Victorians and Edwardians, remains a virtual sourcebook for pictures of these individuals.

Among the better-known artists for the *Strand* were F. Carruthers Gould, Gordon Browne (son of Dickens's illustrator, Hablot K. Browne, or "Phiz"), and Sidney Paget, the creator of the illustrations for the Sherlock Holmes stories by Arthur Conan Doyle. Indeed, later filmings featuring the famous detective chose actors who resembled Paget's artistic rendering, which he modeled after his brother.

Conan Doyle's name appeared in the index to the first volume of the *Strand* next to an article entitled "The Voice of Science." In the second volume he introduced his fictional detective, Sherlock Holmes, in a story, "A Scandal in Bohemia," the first of a highly successful series that included fifty-six stories over thirty-six years, from 1891 to 1927. Doyle was responsible for introducing the practice of publishing short individual stories, rather than the serialized fiction to which Victorian readers had grown accustomed. His experiment proved successful. When he abandoned Sherlock Holmes in 1927, he wrote:

> Sherlock Holmes began his adventures in the very heart of the later Victorian Era, carried them all through the all-too-short reign of Edward, and has managed to hold his own little niche even in these feverish days. Thus it would be true to say that those who first read of him as a young man have lived to see their grown-up children following the same adventures in the same magazine. It is a sterling example of the patience and loyalty of the British public.[2]

In part, Doyle was right in praising the "patience and loyalty" of the *Strand*'s readers. It was also partly Doyle's own loyalty to the magazine and to the readers that helped to make it a British institution.

Doyle, however, was not the only noteworthy contributor to the *Strand*. Others included Rudyard Kipling, Agatha Christie, W. Somerset Maugham, H. G. Wells (whose *War of the Worlds* appeared in condensation in 1920 with illustrations by Johan Briedé), Anthony Hope, O. Henry, Dorothy Sayers, Aldous Huxley, Arnold Bennett, and Graham Greene, among numerous others. Of special note are various contributions of articles and paintings by Winston Churchill. At one point, Churchill was considered as a possible editor to help bring the magazine out of a slump.

Of the *Strand* writers, Reginald Pound comments:

> Those gaily proficient providers of serials and short stories for *The Strand* and other magazines were pedestrian writers in a non-derogatory sense. Their feet were planted squarely on a common ground, where the surface was solid and familiar, where there was no need to look beyond the actual and the obvious. Occasionally, they may have raised their eyes to gaze on the summit of Parnassus. Mostly, they remained content with the surer profits to be earned by toiling on the lower slopes.[3]

Those on the "lower slopes" included such names as P. G. Wodehouse (creator of Jeeves), H. C. McNeele (who as "Sapper" created the character Bulldog Drummond), W. W. Jacobs (creator of Sam Small), Max Pemberton (the English Jules Verne), Jerome K. Jerome (the English Mark Twain), Samuel Crockett, Hugh Walpole, A.E.W. Mason, and Arthur Morrison. Stanley Weyman created stories that Oscar Wilde said were read by his fellow prisoners in Reading Gaol. Women's fiction was contributed by Winifred Graham, E. Nesbit, and a handful of others. Grant Allen helped to popularize science, and Henry Lucy provided a pageant of Parliament in a semi-comical series, "From Behind the Speaker's Chair."

The *Strand* was clearly intended for entertainment. Newnes himself was a lifelong Liberal and, briefly, a member of Parliament, but the magazine itself was not a crusader for social issues and only rarely published mildly controversial pieces. As a mirror of the conventions and curiosities of its intended audience, it succeeded and managed to survive two world wars. Indeed, the rightful celebrations of its twenty-fifth and fiftieth anniversaries were thwarted by the outbreak of these wars. In 1941 the magazine's format was changed to pocket size, like the American *Coronet*. With this new format, it continued as a "British institution" until its final issue in the spring of 1950.

Notes

1. Reginald Pound, *Mirror of the Century: "The Strand Magazine" 1891–1950* (Cranbury, N.J., 1966), pp. 191–92.
2. Ibid., p. 142.
3. Ibid., p. 105.

Information Sources

BIBLIOGRAPHY

Carr, John Dickson. *The Life of Sir Arthur Conan Doyle*. London, 1949.
Doyle, Sir Arthur Conan. *Memories and Adventures*. London, 1924.
Friederichs, Hulda. *The Life of Sir George Newnes*. London, 1911.
Pound, Reginald. *Mirror of the Century: "The Strand Magazine" 1891–1950*. Cranbury, N.J., 1966.

Strand Magazine, Centenary Issue (April 1899). [Contains comments on the magazine's first decade by George Newnes.]

INDEXES
Each volume indexed; in Geraldine Beare, comp., *Index to the "Strand Magazine," 1891–1950*.

REPRINT EDITIONS
Microform: Early British Periodicals (UMI), reels 603–610.

LOCATION SOURCES

American
Complete runs: Buffalo and Erie County Public Library; Iowa State Traveling Library; New York Public Library; University of Michigan Library.
Partial runs: Widely available.

British
Complete run: British Museum.
Partial runs: Widely available.

Publication History

MAGAZINE TITLE AND TITLE CHANGES
The Strand Magazine.

VOLUME AND ISSUE DATA
Volumes 1–118, numbers 1–711, January 1891–March 1950. (American edition with material and arrangement somewhat differently from London edition: volumes 1–51, numbers 1–201, January 1891–February 1916.)

FREQUENCY OF PUBLICATION
Monthly.

PUBLISHER
George Newnes, Ltd., London.

EDITORS
George Newnes with H. Greenhough Smith. (After its beginning in 1891, Newnes himself gradually left editorial matters up to Smith. Newnes died in 1910.) H. Greenhough Smith, 1891–1930. Reeves Shaw, 1930–1941. R. J. Minney, briefly, in 1941. Reginald Pound, 1941–1946. Macdonald Hastings, 1946–1950. (The American edition was edited by James Walter Smith.)

Jerold J. Savory

SYMPOSIUM, THE. See CAMBRIDGE UNIVERSITY
MAGAZINE, THE

T

TAIT'S EDINBURGH MAGAZINE. See RA

TEMPLE BAR

The 1860 prospectus for *Temple Bar: A London Magazine for Town and Country Readers* announced:

> We shall have a domestic romance of English life and manners—and of love: for what is life without love, by "an eminent hand." An experienced reviewer will take the most popular book of decision, and give us a fair and honest description of its contents and its merits. A poet will sound his lyre, and the social essayist, the biographer, the philosopher, the traveler, and the pleasant talker on the engrossing topic of the day, shall each find his allotted space. As for politics, there will not be any, unless there should be aught political in the dominant tone of our journal, which, from headline to imprint, will strive to inculcate thoroughly English sentiments: respect for authority, attachment to the church, and loyalty to the Queen.[1]

So wrote George Augustus Sala, *Temple Bar*'s first editor and an important figure in nineteenth-century periodicals. He was a reporter for the *Daily Telegraph*, had worked on *Household Words** under Dickens, and had contributed articles to *Cornhill Magazine,** *Belgravia,** and others. Besides editing *Temple Bar*, he also wrote two novels and a travel series for it. It was also Sala who chose not only the purple cover for the periodical but its motto, spuriously attributed to Dr. Johnson, " 'Sir', said Dr. Johnson, 'Let us take a walk down Fleet Street.' "[2]

A monthly shilling magazine, *Temple Bar* was first published in December 1860 by John Maxwell, a prosperous publisher of numerous periodicals, who, without a doubt, wished to imitate the popular *Cornhill Magazine*. This latest adventure, as the prospectus revealed, was to be a fairly lively magazine, filled with general articles and directed toward the comfortable upper middle class, one fit for Mudie's lending libraries. It succeeded. Its stories, poetry, and essays were always a "clear and forceful expression of upper middle class Victorianism." The audience was "the resolute householders who had lately begun to acquire wealth and education and servants, who read Tennyson and Dickens and thought much of the state of their souls (gravely, to be sure, without Wesleyan enthusiasm), and who considered the royal family quite the finest example of blended romance, duty, strength, intellect, and pragmatical spirituality that had ever blessed the civilized world."[3]

From its beginning until close to its demise in 1906, its format varied little from that introduced by Sala. Each issue contained two serial novels, which ran for twelve to fourteen months, a handful of short stories, usually three poems, and "six or so miscellaneous articles dealing with political, social, religious, literary, historical, or geographical curiosa, frequently intermixed with moral essays."[4]

The subjects of these miscellaneous articles range from reviews of popular books to discussion of serious subjects such as the treatment of lunatics to the duties of the inspectors of the Poor Law workhouses. Thus, in content and tone, *Temple Bar* aligns itself with a series of other entertaining and popular periodicals of the time: *Belgravia*, another, later Maxwell product, *Argosy*, and the *St. James Magazine*, to name a few. By subscription accounts, *Temple Bar* was successful. At its beginning, circulation was about 30,000, dropping off to 11,000 by 1866 and stabilizing at about 13,000 in 1868.[5]

Sala was assisted by subeditor Edmund Yates, who became editor himself in 1863, when Sala left the magazine to work more extensively with the *Daily Telegraph*. Sala, however, had secured from Maxwell the proprietorship of *Temple Bar* sometime after December 1862 and maintained it until January 1866.[6] Yates, a contributor to *Bentley's Miscellany*,* the *Leader*,* and *All the Year Round*,* had previously edited for Maxwell a gossip paper, *Town Talk*. Other regular assistants were Robert Buchanan, Blanchard Jerrold, John Oxenford, and T. H. Sotheby. Although most of the contributors during Sala's editorship are relatively unknown, a few names stand out: Anthony Trollope, who declined the editorship of *Temple Bar* in August 1861[7]; Mrs. Henry Wood, of *East Lynne* fame; Alfred Austin, the Poet Laureate; and Mary Elizabeth Braddon, equally famous for *Lady Audrey's Secret* and later editor of Maxwell's *Belgravia*. She published her famous *Aurora Floyd* and four other novels in *Temple Bar*. Yates himself wrote one novel for the periodical in 1864, *Broken to Harness: A Story of English Domestic Life*.

In January 1866 Richard Bentley, the founder of *Bentley's Miscellany* and the publisher (Richard Bentley and Son) of over 127 volumes of novels, purchased

Temple Bar from Sala for 2,750 pounds.[8] He appointed his son, George, editor in October or November 1867 when Yates, who had assumed the editorship of *Tinsley's Magazine** in July 1869, departed. George edited *Temple Bar* until his death in 1895. Under his direction the magazine prospered, and in 1879 George Bentley "declared the *Temple Bar* was one of his three most valuable literary properties."[9] During the Bentley years the quality of the periodical improved as he attracted more talent and popular contributors. First, in 1868 he purchased *Bentley's Miscellany*, which had been taken over by William Harrison Ainsworth in 1839, and combined it with *Temple Bar*. Not only did Bentley eliminate another magazine from the field, but he opened the pages of *Temple Bar* to all of the better-known writers who had contributed to *Bentley's Miscellany*.

New contributors were Wilkie Collins, Bret Harte, Sheridan Le Fanu, Marie Corelli, Charles Reade, Robert Louis Stevenson, George Gissing, Henry Kingsley, his brother George Henry Kingsley, A. Conan Doyle, Rhoda Broughton, Edmund Gosse, and Thomas Hood. In addition, stories by Balzac, Chekhov, Daudet, Tolstoy, Turgenev, and Hans Christian Andersen were translated for the English reader. Trollope and Mrs. Henry Wood continued to submit their manuscripts. George Bentley himself frequently wrote articles for the periodical, often commenting on stories by French writers. *Temple Bar* was the vehicle for the first publication of Trollope's *The American Senator* and Collins's *The New Magdalen*, and it published in 1874 under Collins's name a play, *The Frozen Deep*, that he and Dickens had written.

Second, and equally important, was Bentley's knowledge of what his middle-class readers wanted. Although the Victorian period was troubled by Darwinism, industrialism, liberalism, and a myriad of other "isms" in this age of transition, the pages of *Temple Bar* were never filled with persuasive declarations of these new allegiances. Bentley's intent was, instead, "appreciative literary essays not too searching or subtle for his audience. Biographical thesis which tended towards anecdotal travels such as designed to be interesting as well as informative [sic]."[10] Current topics, religious, scientific, or literary, were discussed, but only superficially. These essays accompanied entertaining stories and novels by some of the most popular writers of the period.

With the death of George Bentley in 1895, *Temple Bar* declined in popularity. Although A. Conan Doyle and George Gissing still contributed, and Tolstoy, Balzac, and Daudet were still being translated, most of the novels being serialized were by inferior novelists, among them Egerton Castle, Frances Mary Peard, Constance Smith, J. W. van der Poorten Schwartz—names relatively unknown to scholars of the nineteenth-century novel. Sales in 1896 fell to 8,000.[11] Bentley's son, Richard, became editor in June 1895 and remained until 1898, when Bentley and Son, including the journal, was sold to Macmillan and Company, which struggled with *Temple Bar* until it ceased publication in 1906.

Like so many of the Victorian periodicals, *Temple Bar* seemingly was unable to adapt itself to the twentieth century and the Edwardian Age. Life itself had become faster and more complex and the "time had fled when *Temple Bar* was suited to an honored place on the solid mahogany table in the center of a solid middle-class *parlor*.''[12]

Notes

1. *Bookseller*, 27 October 1860, p. 614.

2. *"Temple Bar,"* in *The Wellesley Index to Victorian Periodicals, 1824–1900*, ed. Walter Houghton (Toronto, 1979) 3:386.

3. Vincent C. De Baum, *"Temple Bar*: Index of Victorian Middle-Class Thought,'' *Journal of the Library of Rutgers University* 14 (1955):16, 10.

4. Ibid., p. 10.

5. *Wellesley Index*, p. 387; Alvar Ellegård, "The Readership of the Press in Mid-Victorian Britain,'' *Victorian Periodicals Newsletter*, no. 13 (September 1971): 19–20. For a discussion of *Temple Bar*'s profit see Royal A. Gettmann, *A Victorian Publisher* (Cambridge, England, 1960), pp. 147–48.

6. *Wellesley Index*, 3:390, n.20.

7. Maxwell offered Trollope 1,000 pounds a year with the understanding that he would "undertake to supply a novel and fill the position that Mr. Sala now occupies." Ibid., 3:387–88.

8. Ibid., 3:390, n. 21.

9. Gettmann, p. 148.

10. Ibid., p. 26.

11. Ibid., p. 149.

12. De Baum, p. 9.

Information Sources

BIBLIOGRAPHY

De Baum, Vincent C. *"The Story of Temple Bar*: A Table of Insights into the Victorian Middle Class." Ph.D. dissertation, Rutgers University, 1958.

———. *"Temple Bar*: Index of Victorian Middle-Class Thought." *Journal of the Library of Rutgers University* 14 (1955):6–16.

Gettmann, Royal. *A Victorian Publisher: A Study of The Bentley Papers*. Cambridge, England, 1960.

Houghton, Walter, ed. *The Wellesley Index to Victorian Periodicals, 1824–1900*. Vol. 3. Toronto, 1979.

Morgan, Charles. *The House of Macmillan (1843–1943)*. London, 1944.

Sala, George Augustus. *The Life and Adventures of George Augustus Sala Written by Himself*. 2 vols. London, 1895.

Straus, Ralph. *Sala: The Portrait of an Eminent Victorian*. London, 1942.

Yates, Edmund. *Recollections and Experiences*. 2 vols. London, 1884.

INDEXES

Volumes 1–99, list of titles, in volume 100; volume 49 lists contents for 1877, volume 55 for 1879, volume 73 for 1855, volume 79 for 1886. 1861–1881 in *Poole's Index*. 1860–1900 in *Wellesley Index* 3.

REPRINT EDITIONS

Microform: Datamics Inc., New York. Early British Periodicals (UMI), reels 244–285. Library of Congress Photoduplication Service, Washington D.C.

LOCATION SOURCES

American

Widely available.

British

Complete runs: Aberdeen University Library; Birmingham Public Library; Bodleian Library; British Museum; Cambridge University Library; Newcastle-upon-Tyne Library.

Partial runs: Widely available.

Publication History

MAGAZINE TITLE AND TITLE CHANGES

Temple Bar, A London Magazine for Town and Country Readers, 1860–1881, 1899–1901. *Temple Bar, (with which is incorporated "Bentley's Miscellany")*, 1882–1898. *Temple Bar, A Monthly Magazine for Town and Country Readers*, 1902–1906. *Temple Bar*, July–December, 1906.

VOLUME AND ISSUE DATA

Volumes 1–132, December 1860–December 1905; new series, volumes 1–2, January–December 1906.

FREQUENCY OF PUBLICATION

Monthly.

PUBLISHERS

1860–1862: John Maxwell, London. 1863–1866: George Augustus Sala, London/Willmer and Rogers, New York. 1866–1898: Richard Bentley, 8 New Burlington Street, London/Willmer and Rogers, New York. (In January 1882 "Paris: Galignani" was added to title page; volume 99 [1893] drops "New York" and "Paris" from title page.) 1898–1906: Macmillan and Company, Limited, St. Martins Street, W.C. London/Macmillan Company, New York.

EDITORS

George Augustus Sala, December 1860–November 1863. Edmund Yates, December 1863–September/October 1867. George Bentley, October/November 1867–May 1895. Richard Bentley II, June(?) 1895–August 1898(?). Gertrude Townshend Mayer, September 1898(?)–December 1900(?).

William H. Scheuerle

THRUSH

In December 1909 a new seventy-six-page, one-shilling London monthly called *Thrush* introduced itself with the observation that "the prevailing spirit of apathy with regard to poetry is no justification for its entire neglect by the enlightened few." There followed twenty-two poems and four substantial articles, including one by Ford Madox Hueffer on "Modern Poetry."

There is little indication that the new *Thrush* saw itself as a reincarnation of T. Mullett Ellis's slight *Thrush* of eight years before, although some of the same poets appear in both. For most contributors to the early *Thrush* (1901–1902), poetry would seem to have been a sideline. For example, Dr. Harry Roberts dealt elsewhere with gardens, health, and religious philosophy; Horace Wyndham published social anecdotes; Keble Howard (John Keble Bell) wrote fiction and comedies; Hilda P[hoebe] Hudson, whose sonnet won first prize in a Newnham College prize competition, later published on mathematical subjects. Many, however, were more fully committed to literature and the arts. Lady Margaret Sackville had already published the first of her many books of verse. Miss Laurence Alma-Tadema, daughter of the painter Sir Lawrence Alma-Tadema, was a poet, playwright, and translator of Maeterlinck. Charles Hamilton Aïdé, art patron and friend of Frederick (Lord) Leighton, was the author of at least two dozen novels, three plays, and three volumes of verse. But Ellis's *Thrush* cannot claim to have made much impact on the literary world. Its approach was democratic rather than coterie, and the editor revealed a genuine humanist concern as he pleaded for more encouragement of the arts.

Although the editor of the later *Thrush* is never named between its grayish cream covers, he was Noël Wills, whose later *Collected Prose and Verse* includes the following:

> Deeply you've read—beyond the title-page
> (With lexicon to see if *"Thrush"* referred
> To some obscure disease or common bird).
> Scanning with care, until you know by rote
> The wisdom of the introductory note,—
> . . . .
> Impetuous youth! how hard a task was mine
> To find a verse containing one good line—
> (Yes, volume one, of others but the herald,
> Was innocent of help from Walter Jerrold.)
> It died, *The Thrush*, though scribblers seemed to need it,
> Died, just because the public wouldn't read it.[1]

Frederick Noël Hamilton Wills was the grandson of the second Henry Overton Wills (the first, by marrying a tobacco merchant's daughter, had begun the dynasty that enriched his descendants) and the son of Sir Frederick Wills, created baronet in 1897. Noël's brother, Sir Gilbert Wills, was chairman of the Imperial Tobacco Company of Great Britain and Ireland, a large combine formed in 1901. This third generation of Bristol philanthropists continued the family tradition of astuteness in business and patronage of education and the arts. Noël Wills, who died at forty, remembered for his "high idealism" as a lover of England and English life and sport, left over 5 million pounds; he was chairman of Food Products Ltd., as well as of the new district fishery board.[2] He founded Rendcome College in Cirencester, Oxfordshire, for children of all ranks of life; he wrote and painted. His wife, Margery Hamilton Wills, gathered and had privately printed after his death a number of pieces, including eleven reproductions of his watercolor drawings and sketches, a children's story, and some speeches and poems. Among the latter, the wryly amusing lines on the *Thrush* quoted above appear to have been dedicated to his brother Gil.

The modest editor found a strong spokesman in Ford Madox Hueffer, who is both denunciatory—"Most of the verse that is written today deals in a derivative manner with medieval emotion. . . . The greater number of our poets are either provincial or snobbish" (1, no. 1:50)—and hopeful: "Modern poetry is a thing not very sturdy, but extraordinarily tenacious of life. We have not got any great poet, but we have an extraordinary amount of lyrical ability. And this, I think, is a very healthy sign. . . . We are approaching, in fact, once more to a state such as that which produced ballads and folk-songs, those productions of the utterly obscure and of the utterly forgotten" (pp. 46, 47).

Frank Swinnerton's "Henry James: An Appreciation," Sidney C. Roberts's "In Defence of Parody," and T. H. Truly on "Reputation," along with a few short unsigned reviews, make a rather interesting prose component of volume 1, number 1 (December 1909) of Wills's *Thrush*. The familiar poets included are A. T. Quiller-Couch (spelled out in the table of contents, though the poems are signed "Q"), John Drinkwater, A. C. Benson, Alfred Perceval Graves, T. Mullett Ellis, and Norman Gale; the last four had contributed to the old *Thrush*.

Thrush for January 1910, the second of six numbers, carried nineteen poems and four articles. In a feature called "Our Library Table," the *Athenaeum** (see *RA*) gave it brief but appreciative notice: "We trust the public interest in new poetry and poets will be sufficient to give adequate support to this praiseworthy venture."[3] The reviewer quoted with approval a stanza from a "luridly effective ballad" by John Endellion, in which the rising sun is compared to a hunting dog summoned "from repose," its rays sniffing the ground. Also singled out for mention was Laurence Housman's "The Book-seller (B.C. 530)"—"an adaptation of the legend of the Sibyl to modern problems." T. H. Lee's "Son of Agamemnon," a one-act tragedy, was commended for "distinct promise in blank verse and dramatic sense alike." Of the prose, "An Imaginary Book of Verse," actually a review of an anonymous new poet's volume entitled *The Horizon*, was described as "a pleasantly suggestive essay in poetical criticism." The last, signed "C.R.S.," was the only article the *Athenaeum* referred to in any detail. The three merely named were "John Ford," by H. F. Brett-Smith, "Stevenson's Portrayal of Women," by W. Douglas Gray, and "The Development of William Butler Yeats," by Francis Bickley, whose 1910 pronouncement it is easy, three-quarters of a century later, to call premature—"Mr. Yeats's immortality will, perhaps, be like Herrick's: not so gay, but as delicately poised on a few songs" (1, no. 2:151).

Number 3, for February 1910, includes in its front matter the contents of numbers 1 and 2, and quotes favorable "opinions of the press"—the Manchester *Guardian*, *Westminster Gazette*, *Literary World*, and *Daily Chronicle*, and, of course, the *Athenaeum*. There are poems by Alfred Noyes, Norman Gale, Lady Margaret Sackville, and Francis Brett Young, who also has an article, "The Dead Village: A Study in Depopulation." C. A. Bennett's "The Jelly-fish: A

Theme with Variations" parodies Swinburne's alliterative excesses, Tennyson's *In Memoriam* meter, and Shakespeare's masterful line, "Sans head, sans arms, sans legs, sans everything." Alfred Perceval Graves translated a Welsh contemporary of Chaucer, Dafydd ab Gwilym. A prefatory note by H. Idris Bell spoke of the characteristic Welsh lettering device, *cynghanedd*, which was by the fourteenth century "a fully developed system" and of the "canon of 24 'strict metres' . . . chief among them the *cywydd*, in which nearly all Dafydd's poems are written" and which Graves imitated in his translation (1, no. 3:171). To poem and note, the *Athenaeum* of 26 March 1910 understandably found that "exceptional literary interest attaches."[4] The *Athenaeum* did not much like the parodies, which, "though metrically blameless, lack the humour and subtlety that go to the essence of sound parody." It had reservations about Edwin Stanley James's blank verse "Pilate" as a "praiseworthy attempt . . . though defective in appreciation of the rhythmical expedients whereby monotony is avoided," while "G. M. Hort's ballad, 'Fellow Sinners' shows vigour and picturesqueness tempered by obscurity." The same page of the *Athenaeum* praised but did not elaborate on Walter Raleigh's "suggestive study of 'Silence' in its relation to poetry" and W. T. Colyer's "sensible 'Reflections on Modern Journalism.' " Presumably, the *Athenaeum* would have been exempt from Colyer's censure: "The business instinct triumphed, and the unique opportunity of making journalism the greatest of educational influences once lost, there arose a race who found it easy and lucrative to exploit the ignorance and even the vices of the proletariat" (1, no. 3:228). Book reviews were mostly unsigned, but Rowland Strong dealt appreciatively with Mme. Alphonse Daudet's *Souvenirs autour d'un groupe littéraire*. All in all, as the unfailing *Athenaeum* acknowledged, "The issue fully maintains the high standard of interest set by its predecessors."

The March number of *Thrush* carried on the tradition with a poem by Katharine Tynan; a prose sketch, "The End of a Day," by Edward Thomas; an article on the Lombard poet Ada Nigri, by Dora McChesney; a story, "Our Crescent," by Richard Whiteing; reviews by Frank Swinnerton and Walter Jerrold, and a particularly perceptive unsigned one of the "almost aggressively original" *Exultations* of Ezra Pound: "Everyone who takes any interest in poetry should certainly study the volume. . . . We should like to find more outward beauty, and yet there is something very difficult to define or express—which tempts one to read more than once. . . . He has great skill in the use of many unfamiliar metres; he respects his art, and has not the fatal gift of fluency, which so often tempts to insincerity" (1, no. 4:312–13).

The April 1910 number launching volume 2 advertised "The Poetry Recital Society" under the presidency of Lady Margaret Sackville, designed "to bring together the lovers of poetry with a view . . . [ultimately] to assist in bringing about 'a poetic renaissance' " and more concretely "to establish lectureships and publish a journal" (2, no. 1:i). Volunteers were sought for "this important literary and ethical movement." Thirty-three poems filled a little over half of this eighty-page number. The prose pieces were: "The White Road," a reflective allegory by F. C. Brunton; a descriptive-historical account of "Modern French Poetry" by Catherine M. Verschoyle, who called *vers libre* "a new form, not . . . an escape from form" (p. 62) and quoted Gustave Kahn, its chief theoretician in the late 1880s in France; "Bunyan for Busy Men" by H. G. Wells, about "a little pamphlet from Messrs. Hiram Cates & Company entitled 'The Rapid Pilgrim's Progress' " (p. 52). Photos of scenes en route (according to Wells) included "the Hygienic Slime Bath (formerly the Slough of Despond), with its adjacent ticket office . . . a charming adaptation of the Temple of Vesta at Tivoli [traveling Englishmen's noses might recall the sulphur baths of Acque Albule five miles west of Tivoli and its fountained gardens]. . . . The ticket does not cover actual admission to the Celestial City at present" since "modern man does not so much seek a destination as experience" (pp. 52–54).

There was no indication in the May 1910 number that it was to be the last *Thrush* published, although it incidentally provided the nearest thing to an index by listing the contents of the preceding five issues as well as its own. It had twenty-seven poems, a substantial review-article by H. F. Brett-Smith of George Saintsbury's *History of English Prosody* (quarreling a bit with Saintsbury's classical preconceptions and ignoring of Anglo-Saxon), and an article on "The Poetry of Mr. Wilfrid W. Gibson," whom W. G. Blaikee Murdoch believed as good as Yeats, but simpler! "The Romance of Sir Hugh" was in part modernized and summarized by Michael West, and two forthcoming volumes of socialist plays were noticed.

With no behind-the-scenes information on the editorial workings of *Thrush* and no reason to think it foundered for lack of funds, we are left to take Wills's words (in the poem quoted from his collected writings) at face value: publication ceased for want of a public. But it was a worthwhile venture that captured a moment in the history of twentieth-century poetry and poetics.

Notes

1. Frederick Noël Hamilton Wills, *Collected Prose and Verse* (London, 1931), pp. 31–32; edited and printed by his widow, Margery Hamilton Wills, "for private circulation." Walter Copeland Jerrold (1865–1929), grandson of Douglas Jerrold of *Punch** and theater fame, had, shortly before Noël Wills's editing venture, brought out a *Book of Living Poets* (London, 1907), many of whom also contributed to *Thrush* old and new.

2. He served in World War I, commissioned (May 1914) as a second lieutenant in the Royal North Devon Hussars.

3. *Athenaeum*, no. 4294 (12 February 1910):186.

4. Ibid., no. 4300 (26 March 1910):367.

Information Sources

BIBLIOGRAPHY

Athenaeum, no. 4294 (12 February 1910):186; no. 4300 (26 March 1910):367.
Dictionary of National Biography. S.v. "Wills, Frederick Noël Hamilton."
Times (London), 20 October 1927, p. 16e; 17 March 1938, p. 15f.
Wills, Frederick Noël Hamilton. *Collected Prose and Verse*. Edited by Margery Hamilton Wills. Privately printed. London, 1931.

INDEXES
:   Tables of contents for all numbers in volume 2, number 2, May 1910.
REPRINT EDITIONS
:   None.
LOCATION SOURCES
:   *American*
:   Widely available.
:   *British*
:   Complete runs: Bodleian Library; British Museum; Cambridge University Library; Leeds Public Library; Trinity College Library, Dublin; Union Society Library. Partial runs: King's College Library; Manchester Public Library.

Publication History

MAGAZINE TITLE AND TITLE CHANGES
:   *Thrush.*
VOLUME AND ISSUE DATA
:   Volume 1, numbers 1–4, December 1909, January, February, and March 1910; volume 2, numbers 1–2, April and May 1910.
FREQUENCY OF PUBLICATION
:   Monthly.
PUBLISHER
:   Chapman and Hall, 11 Henrietta Street, Covent Garden, London WC.
EDITOR
:   Frederick Noël Hamilton Wills.

Mary Anthony Weinig

TINSLEY'S MAGAZINE

When William Tinsley brought out the first issue of *Tinsley's Magazine* in August 1867, the future boded fair for the new monthly. With Edmund Yates as editor during the first two years, and with many good wishes, *Tinsley's Magazine* offered interesting fare on timely subjects. It published articles treating such controversial subjects as the relationship of John Brown and Queen Victoria, the peccadilloes and excellences of Pre-Raphaelite poets, and the Channel Islands locale. The beauty and quasi-supernatural folklore elements intrigued *Tinsley's* writers as they would later captivate Ella D'Arcy, Sheila Kaye-Smith, and Elizabeth Goudge. Despite the goodwill, the venture achieved no great results, although Tinsley later boasted, "I kept my literary child alive for over a quarter of a century."[1] The actual duration, from August 1867 through January 1892 (with publication suspended from June 1887 through January 1888), makes these remarks suspect, as others among Tinsley's memories have proved to be. Yates left the magazine in 1869, but his stamp in the first numbers is strong.

Serial novels were the mainstay of the periodical; Yates's *The Rock Ahead*, among the first in the magazine, typifies the sensational fiction popular in these years. The quick-paced tale of poisoning, thwarted love, concealed identity, suicide, and money interests, with the triumph—at last—of justice and the surviving good characters, sets a model for much to come, in terms of the fiction that appeared during the duration of *Tinsley's Magazine*. By the 1880s and 1890s, a newer realism had supplanted sensationalism, but *Tinsley's Magazine* reveals little awareness of this trend in fiction. During Yates's editorial stint, *Tinsley's Magazine* carried Mrs. Henry Wood's *George Canterbury's Will* and Mrs. J. H. (Charlotte E.) Riddell's *Austin Friars*, two better-known titles by these novelists, who were then often in the public eye. Once Tinsley himself assumed the editor's chair, Thomas Hardy was the only prominent Victorian novelist to provide a novel. Hardy's *A Pair of Blue Eyes*, serialized from August 1872 to July 1873, does not hold a high place in the Hardy canon. Other *Tinsley's* regulars, such as B. L. Farjeon, Justin McCarthy, and James Grant, are little remembered. Often four novels ran simultaneously, and such a plethora of less than first rate fiction undoubtedly accounts for the tiredness apparent in Tinsley's contents during its late years. That debility probably combined with financial mismanagement to end the enterprise.

From the 1870s onward, there appeared some good ghost stories, as well as other types of mysteries and detective tales. One deserving mention as derivative from Wilkie Collins's *The Moonstone* and Charles Dickens's *The Mystery of Edwin Drood* is "The Yellow Boudoir" (1874), although its oriental intrigue, involving opium and violence, is undercut by stilted dialogue. "Lady Farquhar's Old Lady: A True Ghost Story" (1873) is also significant in blending the actual with the supernatural. The narrator emphasizes how many true ghost stories go untold through the fear of those involved.

Tinsley's Magazine also regularly featured verse, literary criticism, and essays on topics from religion and social issues to folklore and music. *Tinsley's* will not be remembered for the quality of its verse. From Walt Whitman's "A Carol of Harvest, for 1867," in volume 1, the quality drops to William Bell Scott's "Eve" (1871), to verses, later, by Susan K. Phillips, William Tirebuck, and Henry S. Leigh. Nonfictional prose divides fairly evenly into essays treating general, timely topics, on the one hand, and, on the other, those centering on literary history or criticism. The series by "Aunt Anastatia" discussed pretty prayer books, modern novels, heroes, Christmas, and themes about polite society. These essays resemble a prose equivalent to *vers de société* so much admired during the time of Austin Dobson and others, and in fact an essay in the issue for December 1874 praises such verse.

Other types of essays present subjects of weightier concern. "Disinfectants," in volume 9, indicates concern with sanitation problems in the British Isles. "Musical Recollections of the Last Half Century" appeared serially, offering critical appreciations of nineteenth-century composers and their music, especially Wagner. The periodical's attitude toward women reveals an unyielding aspect about *Tinsley's* that may, finally, have diminished the number of its subscribers. Condescension is the keynote in matters regarding women, and essays such as

"Old Maids" and "The British Matron," from the 1860s and 1870s, show no objectivity toward the fair sex—a fit term for expressing the dominant Victorian view of woman and her place. The latter essay, however, lets readers know that "angels in the houses" sometimes manifest considerable severity. If essays like these do not reveal much sound thought, they nevertheless give insight into general attitudes of the day, and into the Victorian period in general. Global interest was another popular topic and knew few bounds in the pages of *Tinsley's Magazine*. In an era of lofty imperialism, the Irish neighbors and the Jamaican Maroons—their mores and their lands—were fair game for an enterprising magazine.

Tinsley's was given to general morbidity in its literary imagination. Not only did sensationalized fiction continue to appear after its heyday had passed, but the literary essays are freighted with themes of high-pitched tension and violence. Although essays on George Eliot and Matthew Arnold, hostilely attacking his verse drama *Merope*, do not give much sympathy to violence, other literary critiques do. A long examination of Alfred Tennyson's *Lucretius* is interesting because, of all his many writings, only this one, so fraught with eroticism and violent emotion, receives extended notice. Essays written by Harry Buxton-Forman on the verse of William Morris, Algernon C. Swinburne, William Bell Scott, and Dante Gabriel Rossetti turn increasingly to themes of eroticism, cruelty, pain, and horror. The criticism of Rossetti and Scott presents perceptive comments about trends in contemporaneous ballad poetry. Rossetti's "Sister Helen" is twice cited as the greatest literary ballad of the age.

In keeping with this bias toward the "fleshly" variety of poetry, a note of interest in less savory themes and types elsewhere is detectable in the literary critiques. "Decline of British Pantomime" is about the supposed decline in drama because of sensationalism. The author dismisses this view as nonsense, recalling Matthew Gregory Lewis's *Castle Spectre*, dating from long years past, as compelling if sensational. Similar remarks are made about the "national institution" of Punch and Judy, concluding that it is, after all, not so wonderful. Sensation in literature provides the subject for a later, fine essay by A. H. Wall, in January 1882, titled simply "Literary Gossip." The novels of William Harrison Ainsworth are particulary commended in this essay, with notable attention to that famous crime novel, *Rookwood* (1834). The source for the novel is Charles Macfarlane's *Lives of Banditti*, a text proffered as the single great predecessor of the later crime novel. With the abundance of crime fiction in *Tinsley's Magazine*, it is no wonder that pages were given to acclaiming the early forebears of this genre. For example, Thomas Hardy is mentioned as the author of *Desperate Remedies*—his first novel, and one of lurid proportions—in order to make him appear a sensationalist.

A different variety of literary criticism appears in essays like "The 'Fleshly School' Scandal," dating from 1872, which readily defended the verse of Dante Gabriel Rossetti against the hostile charges of Robert Buchanan. In his anonymous critique of *The House of Life*, he wrenches passages out of context to make them seem more erotic than they are. One wonders whether Buchanan supported Rossetti's cause or wished to strike firmly for greater freedom of written expression. Another essay in 1872, "On the Forms of Publishing Fiction," heartily supports the popular three-volume format for long tales; the British public liked both the three-volume novel and the circulating libraries that maintained it. With William Tinsley's own eye ever alert to commercial possibilities for enriching his publishing company, the thinking presented in this essay would naturally receive a receptive hearing in the pages of his magazine. But the implications in this essay are more far-reaching, as histories of the circulating library demonstrate.[2]

The individual essays selected for comment here represent the best of *Tinsley's*. One can wander through many pages of the magazine without deriving satisfaction from either the theme or the form of its contents. *Tinsley's Magazine* was the production of an uncertain publishing firm, and that shakiness is reflected in its selections. Ironically, Tinsley's company published more significant novels (among them Mary Elizabeth Braddon's *Lady Audley's Secret* and Thomas Hardy's *Desperate Remedies*) in hardcover than within the pages of its magazine. Furthermore, although Tinsley published the thrillers of Joseph Sheridan Le Fanu, he never secured one of his tales for *Tinsley's Magazine*. One could reasonably conclude that, after the passing of the sensational novel and the outcries occasioned by Pre-Raphaelite verse, Tinsley fumbled in attracting current talent and in heeding popular literary trends. The closing years of the magazine give us none of the freshness evident in publications of the first four or five.

Notes

1. William Tinsley, *Random Recollections of an Old Publisher* (London, 1900), 1:316.
2. See Guinevere Griest, *Mudie's Circulating Library and the Victorian Novel* (London, 1970).

Information Sources

BIBLIOGRAPHY
Dictionary of National Biography. S.v. "Tinsley, William."
Downey, Edmund. *Twenty Years Ago: A Book of Anecdotes Illustrating Literary Life in London*. London, 1905.
Edwards, Henry Sutherland. *Personal Recollections*. London, 1900.
Edwards, P. D. *Edmund Yates*. St. Lucia (Australia), 1980.
Longford, Elizabeth. *Queen Victoria: Born to Succeed*. New York, 1965.
Tinsley, William. *Random Recollections of an Old Publisher*. London, 1900.
Yates, Edmund. *Fifty Years of London Life: Memoirs of a Man of the World*. New York, 1884, 1885.
INDEXES
Each volume indexed; 1868–1881 in *Poole's Index*.
REPRINT EDITIONS
Microform: English Literary Periodicals (UMI), reels 787–795.

LOCATION SOURCES

American

Complete runs: Chicago Public Library; Enoch Pratt Library; New York Public Library; Public Library of Cincinnati and Hamilton County.

Partial runs: Widely available.

British

Complete runs: Bodleian Library; British Museum.

Partial runs: Bristol Public Library; Cambridge University Library; Cardiff Public Library; Dundee Public Library; Trinity College Library.

Publication History

MAGAZINE TITLE AND TITLE CHANGES

Tinsley's Magazine, August 1867–January 1892. *The Novel Review: with which is incorporated "Tinsley's Magazine,"* February–December 1892.

VOLUME AND ISSUE DATA

Volumes 1–42, numbers 1–254, August 1867–May 1889; new series, volumes 43–48, numbers 1–34, June 1889–March 1892; third series, volume 1, numbers 1–7, April–December 1892. (Publication suspended June 1887–January 1888.)

FREQUENCY OF PUBLICATION

Monthly.

PUBLISHER

William Tinsley, London.

EDITORS

Edmund Yates, 1867–1869. William Tinsley, 1869–1892.

Benjamin F. Fisher IV

TO-DAY

A single title, *To-Day*, connects the histories of three quite separate British periodicals in the late nineteenth and early twentieth centuries. *To-Day* was the name of an illustrated weekly paper established by Jerome K. Jerome in the 1890s and continued until 1905, when it was incorporated in *London Opinion*. The title was revived briefly when Holbrook Jackson, editor of *T. P.'s Weekly*, renamed his magazine *To-Day* in 1916 for a final series of numbers. Then, in 1917, Jackson founded a new monthly literary magazine which, once more, he entitled *To-Day* and which he edited throughout the seven years of its independent existence. It was issued monthly from March 1917 through August 1920; quarterly, in September, December, March, and June, from September 1920 to September 1923; and monthly again through December 1923. In February 1924 Holbroook Jackson's *To-Day* was absorbed by the recently founded monthly magazine, *Life and Letters** (see *MA*).

The "old" *To-Day*, as Holbrook Jackson called it, was founded by Jerome K. Jerome in 1893.[1] Jerome was already editor, with Robert Barr, of the monthly *Idler.** *"The Idler* was not enough for me,"* Jerome wrote in his autobiography.

"I had the plan in mind of a new weekly paper that should be a combination of magazine and journal."[2] It was essentially a literary periodical in the style of the clique journalism of the 1890s. The first number was issued on 11 November 1893. Jerome was editor, assisted by Barry Pain; both contributed regularly to its columns. Many of the outside contributors were established authors—Rudyard Kipling, R. L. Stevenson, Bret Harte, and Richard Le Gallienne, for example—and some, like George Gissing, were not yet well known; Aubrey Beardsley and Phil May were among the illustrators. From the beginning, it appears to have been an unusually successful venture. Then, in the financial columns for 12 May 1894, the city editor somewhat gratuitously attacked a company promoter named Samson Fox, who sued for libel and won a verdict in May 1897. Jerome was forced to sell the paper to pay the disastrous costs of the defense. Pain succeeded him as editor in October 1897. Eventually, in 1905, *To-Day* was absorbed by *London Opinion*. "But it had, from the beginning, been a one-man paper," wrote Jerome, "and after I went out, it gradually died."[3]

Like Jerome, Thomas Power O'Connor was well known in turn-of-the-century journalism. He was the founder of the *Star*, the *Sun*, *M.A.P.*, and *T. P.'s Weekly*, which his biographer characterized as "the most durable, if not the most brilliant" of his periodicals.[4] *T. P.'s Weekly* was a popular literary journal, priced at one penny and designed, in the words of its prospectus, "to bring to many thousands a love of letters." The first number was issued on 14 November 1902. The second number quoted congratulatory endorsements by George Meredith, William Michael Rossetti, Katharine Tynan, and H. G. Wells, among many others. The roster of contributors was impressive, including George Bernard Shaw, Arnold Bennett, H. G. Wells, G. K. Chesterton, and Joseph Conrad. O'Connor was nominally the editor, as well as the proprietor, but from the beginning the editorial management of the paper was in fact in the hands of Wilfred Whitten. Whitten was "acting editor" and contributor, customarily over the pseudonymous signature by which he became well known, "John o' London." Assistant editors included, at various times, J.A.T. Lloyd, C. Kennet Burrow, and Reginald Buckley; and Walter Grierson was business manager.[5] In 1911 Whitten was succeeded by Holbrook Jackson as acting editor, then, from 4 July 1914, as editor.

In April 1916 Jackson announced a forthcoming change in title from *T. P.'s Weekly* to *To-Day*. The general character of the journal was unchanged. Its contributors continued to include "widely known writers." The contents were advertised as:

Books, Drama, Music, Picture-Plays, Poetry, Men and Women in politics, science and society. High-class Fiction. The best short story weekly. Modes for both sexes. Cartoons by the world's best artists. The Chestnut Tree for after-dinner stories. Exposure of Shams, attacks on abuses. Virility without vulgarity. Jest, humour, fun and wisdom.

The new name, *To-Day*, was adopted for the issue of 6 May 1916, and under this title the paper continued to appear weekly until 6 January 1917, when it abruptly ceased.

In March 1917 Holbrook Jackson inaugurated what he called "a new series" of *To-Day* but which was in fact a completely new magazine unrelated to either *T. P.'s Weekly* or Jerome's *To-Day*. "The idea embodied in this journal is an old one," Jackson wrote in the first number, that of a review of the "life and letters" of the day: "The stoppage of the weekly review of *To-Day* provided me with the opportunity of realizing a long-deferred wish, and the beginning of that realization is now before the reader." Holbrook Jackson was proprietor, publisher, and editor. He also contributed, in addition to his editorials, occasional articles and a regular column, which he called "End Papers" and signed with the pseudonym "Bernard Lintot." Two selections of his essays in *To-Day* were reprinted, one under his own name as *Occasions*, and another, under "Bernard Lintot," entitled *End Papers*.[6] The contents of *To-Day* were somewhat institutionalized in the *To-Day* Literary Circle, an informal biweekly gathering of readers, and, in its last two years, in subscription anniversary dinners.

Francis Meynell characterized Jackson as "the complete amateur, a self-made Horace Walpole."[7] Holbrook Jackson's *To-Day* was a highly personal journal. If the format of the pocket-size magazine anticipated Jackson's later interest in typography and design, his editorial policies represented, as Jackson himself later expressed it, "the point of view, the likes and sometimes dislikes, of one man," and his editorial decisions were consistent with the critical opinions he expressed. As the editor of *To-Day*, Holbrook Jackson was extending the role of literary historian he had assumed in 1913 as the author of *The Eighteen-Nineties*. The pages of *To-Day* record Jackson's perception of contemporary literature between 1917 and 1923. His was, in the main, a conservative view. For example, the issue for January 1918 included an essay on Gerard Manley Hopkins writen by Eric Brett Young, in which Hopkins was presented blandly as "the most neglected of all the Victorian poets." Again, as late as May 1917, Jackson himself characterized William Butler Yeats as a minor Victorian poet and "the outstanding figure" of the Irish national literary movement, in an essay which he called "Men of To-day and Tomorrow: Mr. William Butler Yeats." The number opened with a frontispiece reproducing John Singer Sargent's drawing of Yeats and included Yeats's essay, "Instead of a Theatre," later used as a prefatory note to *At the Hawk's Well*. *At the Hawk's Well* was printed in its entirety in the number for June 1917. Jackson's editorial in the May number referred to *"Noh," or Accomplishment: A Study in the Classical Stage of Japan*, by Ernest Fenellosa and Ezra Pound, but he called *At the Hawk's Well* a "novelty," which "supplanted" Yeats's more characteristic "taste for the theatre," referring, again, to the Yeats of the 1890s and the turn of the century.

Of contemporary writers, the group now remembered as the Georgian poets received consistent attention in the pages of *To-Day*, especially in the early years. John Drinkwater, John Masefield, W. H. Davies, Walter De la Mare,

Gordon Bottomley, and Ralph Hodgson, among others represented in Edward Marsh's collections of *Georgian Poetry*, were also frequent contributors to *To-Day*. The issue for June 1917 opened with a drawing of Masefield and included an essay on his poetry by Eugene Mason; that for November 1917 included a drawing of Drinkwater and an illustrated article on his plays by Mason. Jackson called *Georgian Poetry 1918–1919* "the most authentic anthology of contemporary English poetry of the moderate school." The volumes of *Georgian Poetry 1920–1922* received qualified approval from their anonymous reviewer in March 1923. "The quality is maintained," he wrote, "but the freshness has departed—which means that E.M. has more or less completed his work....The series was at one time representative of the younger school of bards—it is no longer so; indeed it is a misnomer to refer to writers like Drinkwater, Davies, Walter De la Mare, Monro, Lawrence and Squire as 'contemporary poets of the younger generation.' " In the previous December, Jackson, too, had criticized the anthology. "Mr. Marsh in his *Georgian Poets*," he wrote, "has done for the era of our George what Dodsley did for the first three of Thackeray's Georges, but with a keener sense of selection—so keen, indeed, as to be exclusive to unfairness." The editor of *Life and Letters*, announcing the incorporation of *To-Day* in his journal in 1924, still enumerated, as the most notable members of the group of contributors whom Holbrook Jackson had assembled, W. H. Davies, Ralph Hodgson, and Richard Aldington; but Jackson also opened the pages of *To-Day* to less "moderate" contemporaries, including occasional attention to some of the writers who have come to be regarded as the major innovators of those years, Ezra Pound, T. S. Eliot, and James Joyce, for example.

Ezra Pound was the first writer to whom Holbrook Jackson called attention as a representative of a "more modern school" than the Georgians. Jackson used the phrase in introducing three poems by Pound under the general title, "Impressions of François-Marie Arouet [de Voltaire]," which he published in *To-Day* for July 1917. In an unrelated article, "End Papers," in the same issue, Jackson commented on Pound's edition of selected letters of John Butler Yeats. Jackson introduced Pound's poems in a rather long editorial. "For the benefit of readers unacquainted with poetic groups and the personalia of our living poets," Jackson wrote, "it may be recalled that Mr. Pound is an American resident in London, and a leader of the Imagiste group of poets in this country. His most recent volume, 'Lustra' will be reviewed in the August issue." *Lustra, Quia Pauper Amavi*, and *Umbra* all received favorable notices on their publication in *To-Day*. The issues for April and May 1918 carried two articles by Pound on Chinese poetry, and "A Note on Ezra Pound" by T. S. Eliot appeared in the issue for September 1918.[8]

By 1917 Pound was writing to Jackson about his own work and, apparently, about that of James Joyce and T. S. Eliot. Jackson's library contained a copy of Eliot's *Ezra Pound, His Metric and Poetry*, which was anonymously published in 1917, together with a notation, entered in Jackson's hand, that Pound revealed the authorship to him in 1922.[9] (The authorship had in fact been made public some time before 1922.[10]) It may have been Richard Aldington, however, who called Jackson's attention to Eliot's literary criticism. Aldington reviewed *The Sacred Wood* in *To-Day* for September 1921. " 'The Sacred Wood,' " he wrote, "is the most stimulating, the most intelligent, and the most original contribution to our critical literature during the last decade." Commenting, with approval, on Aldington's review, the author of *The Eighteen-Nineties* called *The Sacred Wood* "a stone flung at decadence." In the magazine, Aldington's review was followed by a page of quotations from the essays in *The Sacred Wood*—"a selection of axioms from Mr. Eliot's welcome book," Jackson explained. In November 1923, two months after *The Waste Land* was published in England, Jackson mentioned the poem incidentally in the course of his review of George Saintsbury's collected essays: "I should like to see Mr. Saintsbury apply his excellent theory to, say, James Joyce's *Ulysses*, T. S. Eliot's *The Waste Land*, and Bernard Shaw's *Heartbreak House*, to name but three not, as things go, very wild modern pieces—but it would then be necessary to come back in a hundred years to see whether he was right!"

Joyce was featured prominently in the quarterly number of *To-Day* for June 1921, just after the Egoist Press had reissued *A Portrait of the Artist as a Young Man*.[11] A portrait of Joyce opened the number, and Jackson's editorial column began, "The Frontispiece this quarter is a portrait of Mr. James Joyce, the one living novelist who may be said to have extended the boundaries of the English novel." Jackson continued with a fullness of detail that suggests that Pound or Aldington may have influenced his account of the author: "His first long narrative, *A Portrait of the Artist as a Young Man*, was instantly recognized as an original work of supreme importance, and the appearance of his new novel, *Ulysses*, in the pages of *The Little Review*, the most original of all American literary journals, has created something like a sensation . . . among those who care for what is distinguished in literature." There followed a detailed account of Joyce's difficulties with censorship in America, and of the forthcoming publication of *Ulysses* in Paris by Sylvia Beach's Shakespeare and Company, and, subsequently, in England by the Egoist Press. Jackson concluded by promising that "in a later number of *To-Day* further reference will be made to the work of Mr. Joyce." A year later, in June 1922, Jackson wrote a review-article entitled "Ulysses à la Joyce." He found the novel "like a country without roads" but "with all its faults . . . the biggest event in the history of the English novel since *Jude*." A photograph of Joyce in Paris once more provided a frontispiece for the number of *To-Day*.

In February 1924 *To-Day* was amalgamated with the monthly magazine *Life and Letters*, which had been founded in November 1923. The editor of *Life and Letters* announced the merger, remarking that the title of *To-Day* had long been well known, since the days of Jerome's literary magazine. Holbrook Jackson, in a graceful valedictory, recalled his own assumption of the title and added that by coincidence his statement of policy in 1917 had "anticipated the title with which To-Day is now merged. 'My aim,' I said, 'was, and is, the promotion of a small and companionable review of life and letters.' '' *Life and Letters Incorporating "To-Day"* continued until August 1924, when publication ended.

Notes

1. For consistency, the spelling *To-Day* is used for all three periodicals, except when the title occurs within a direct quotation.

2. Jerome K. Jerome, *My Life and Times* (London, 1926), p. 176.

3. Ibid., p. 186.

4. Hamilton Fyfe, *T. P. O'Connor* (London, 1934), p. 193.

5. Frank Whitaker, Introduction to *The Joy of London and Other Essays by John o' London* [Wilfred Whitten], ed. Whitaker (London, 1943), pp. xiv–xv.

6. Holbrook Jackson, *Occasions: A Volume of Essays on such Diverse Themes as Laughter and Cathedrals, Town and Profanity, Gardens and Bibliomania, Etc.* (London, 1922); Bernard Lintot, *End Papers: Adventures among Ideas and Personalities* (London, 1923).

7. "An Appreciation," preface to *The Holbrook Jackson Library: A Memorial Catalogue.* Elkin Mathews Catalogue 119 (1951).

8. See Donald Gallup, *A Bibliography of Ezra Pound* (London, 1963), C346, C356; Gallup, *A Bibliography of T. S. Eliot* (London, 1952), C68.

9. *Holbrook Jackson Library*, items 948, 581.

10. Gallup, *Bibliography of T. S. Eliot*, A2. See Gallup, *T. S. Eliot and Ezra Pound: Collaborators in Letters* (New Haven, 1970), especially p. 9.

11. John J. Slocum and Herbert Cahoon, *A Bibliography of James Joyce* (New Haven, 1953), A13, n.

Information Sources

BIBLIOGRAPHY

Brophy, John. Preface to *Twenty Unpublished Letters of Holbrook Jackson to Joseph Ishell with an appreciation by John Brophy.* Berkeley Heights, N.J., 1933.

Meynell, Francis. "An Appreciation." In *The Holbrook Jackson Library: A Memorial Catalogue.* Elkin Mathews Catalogue 119 (1951).

INDEXES

Each volume of new series (1917–1923) indexed.

REPRINT EDITIONS

Microform: *T. P.'s Weekly*, Library of Congress.

LOCATION SOURCES

American

Complete runs: Cleveland Public Library; Columbia University Library; Harvard University Library; Princeton University Library; University of Kansas Library.

Partial runs: Buffalo and Erie County Public Library; Hamilton College Library; John B. Stetson University Library; Lehigh University Library; New York Public Library; University of Minnesota Library; Yale University Library.

British

Complete runs: Birmingham Public Library; Brotherton Library; London University Library.

Partial runs: Bodleian Library; British Museum; Cambridge University Library; Manchester Public Library; Norwich Public Library.

Publication History

MAGAZINE TITLE AND TITLE CHANGES

To-Day, 11 November 1893–19 July 1905; incorporated into London Opinion. T. P.'s Weekly, 14 November 1902–29 April 1916; renamed To-Day, 6 May 1916–6 January 1917. To-Day, "new series," March 1917–December 1923; incorporated into Life and Letters.

VOLUME AND ISSUE DATA

To-Day: volumes 1–47, November 1893–19 July 1905. T. P.'s Weekly: volumes 1–27, 14 November 1902–29 April 1916. To-Day: 6 May 1916–6 January 1917. To-Day, "new series": volumes 1–10, numbers 1–58, March 1917–December 1923.

FREQUENCY OF PUBLICATION

To-Day: weekly. T. P.'s and To-Day: weekly. To-Day: monthly, volumes 1–7, numbers 1–42, March 1917–August 1920; quarterly, volumes 8–9, numbers 43–54, September 1920–June 1923; monthly, volume 10, numbers 55–58, September–December 1923.

PUBLISHERS

To-Day: Jerome K. Jerome, 1893–1897. T.P.'s Weekly/To-Day: Thomas Power O'Connor, 1902–January 1917. To-Day (new magazine): Holbrook Jackson, March 1917–1923.

EDITORS

To-Day: Jerome K. Jerome, 1893–1897. Barry Pain, 1897–1905. T. P.'s Weekly/To-Day: Wilfred Whitten, 1902–1911. Holbrook Jackson, 1911–January 1917. To-Day (new magazine): Holbrook Jackson, March 1917–December 1923.

Charlotte C. Watkins

T. P.'S WEEKLY. See TO-DAY

TRIPOD, THE

The "Foreword" of the first issue of *The Tripod: A Magazine of Art, Literature, and Music*, published by students at Cambridge University, states that the universities should "guide the thought of the country." The magazine, the unidentified editor goes on, would aid this effort by providing the leaders of today and tomorrow with an opportunity for "expressing their ideas and their dreams, while distinctly coupling them with the university's" (no. 1:1). The introductory note also makes clear that no particular attitude was to be adopted by the publication, that is, none of the movements in art, literature, or music was to be espoused. Nonetheless, many issues carried essays on futurism, including, in the first number, "Le Futurisme Pictural," by the movement's founder, F. T. Marinetti. Following Marinetti's example, the other articles on futurism were written in French. Most issues, though, avoided the dogmatic manifesto-like qualities of the futurism pieces and were creative or informative, such as "Précis of a Lecture on Chamber Music," by W. W. Cobbett; "Miracles and Moralities:

Their Origin and Development," by Elwyn Wilks; and a series on the Shakespeare festivals beginning at this time at Stratford, by H. Caldwell Cook. Original fiction and poetry were also featured in each number. A review section examined not only books and other publications, but dramatic and musical performances as well.

While much of the content was supplied by students, some came from established figures. Lord Dunsany, Edward John Moreton Plunkett, contributed "Two Tales." Dunsany was a well-known short story writer (*The Gods of Pegana*), dramatist (*The Glittering Gate* and *The Gods of the Mountain*), and lecturer. He was associated with the Irish literary revival and wrote stories and plays often dealing with imaginary countries and fantastic religions. Another established writer whose work appeared in the *Tripod* was Frederick Herbert Trench, a poet, (*Deirdre Wed and Other Poems*), dramatist (*Napoleon*), and artistic director of the Haymarket Theatre. His "Ballad of the Rock of Cloud" was published in the *Tripod*.

The magazine was skillfully edited and produced and provides an accurate if brief view of some contemporary attitudes toward art, literature, and music at the beginning of the twentieth century.

Information Sources

INDEXES
    None.
REPRINT EDITIONS
    None.
LOCATION SOURCES
    American
        None.
    British
        Complete runs: British Library; Cambridge University Library; Edinburgh University Library.

Publication History

MAGAZINE TITLE AND TITLE CHANGES
    The Tripod: A Magazine of Art, Literature, and Music.
VOLUME AND ISSUE DATA
    Numbers 1–6, April 1912–February 1913.
FREQUENCY OF PUBLICATION
    Monthly during university terms.
PUBLISHERS
    W. Heffer and Sons, Ltd., Cambridge.
EDITORS
    None identified.

James W. Parins

TRUTH

Truth made its initial appearance on 4 January 1877 as a six-penny weekly. Its owner-editor, Henry Du Pre Labouchere, promised to "deal with the current topics of the day in as kindly a spirit as the name of the journal permits'' (p. 6). From the start *Truth* was distinguished by the chatty and irreverent style that typified the new "society journalism" of the 1870s.[1] In company with Thomas Gibson Bowes's *Vanity Fair** and Edmund Yates's *World*, Labouchere initially offered readers of *Truth* a weekly diet of clever gossip about the aristocratic and fashionable, witty reviews of current entertainments, exposés of financial scandal, and serious political commentary. Labouchere's decision to season the frivolous gossip characteristic of society journalism with a strong dash of political satire and financial advice proved a wise one. Within ten years circulation rose from 10,000 to 30,000 copies per week, and advertising rates ran 50 percent higher than those of any comparable journal.[2] Judgments about its quality varied, but *Truth* continued to thrive long after most of its rivals in the field of society journalism had disappeared.

The success of *Truth* confounded many knowledgeable journalists of the 1870s who viewed the new weekly somewhat skeptically as the latest toy of an eccentric dilettante who had already sampled a score of careers. Henry Du Pre Labouchere, heir to a banking fortune, had spent most of his forty-five years following his fancies. Having left Cambridge under a cloud without taking his degree, he had embarked on a colorful life of travel spanning three continents. Tired of globetrotting, he entered the diplomatic service and served as attaché in such cities as Constantinople, Munich, St. Petersburg, and Washington, D.C. Discovering that diplomacy bored him, Labouchere eventually returned to London, where he quickly acquired a reputation as a shrewd financier and as a fashionable man-about-town. In 1867 he bought an interest in a London theater and for several years managed the Queen's Theatre Company, which numbered in its ranks Ellen Terry, Henry Irving, and Charles Wyndham. Financial losses, however, compelled him to sell the theater and to embark on yet another career. In 1868 he joined a syndicate which purchased the *Daily News*, and soon after he began life as a part-time journalist. Though he appeared to be a dabbler whose personal fortune insulated him against serious commitment, Labouchere possessed catholic interests, a keen mind, and an amazing range of personal experience that uniquely qualified him for journalism.[3] The letters that he dispatched to the *Daily News* from the besieged city of Paris during the final months of the Franco-Prussian War brought him personal and professional fame. In 1874 he joined the staff of Edmund Yates's *World* as financial editor, regularly contributing a "city" column and often appearing in court to defend himself against libel suits brought by irate stockbrokers and jobbers.[4]

Having learned the trade in his seven years of apprenticeship, Labouchere was ready in 1876 to finance and edit his own weekly. When Yates suggested that the newborn *Truth* was but another Laboucherean venture that would die young, Labby (as he was universally known) replied that his weekly would be "another and a better *World*," utilizing the same formula and competing for the same readers.[5]

As if determined to confound the skeptics, Labouchere for the next three years poured all of his prodigious energies into *Truth*, single-handedly writing dramatic criticism, financial analyses, political editorials, and random essays on a variety of topics ranging from religion to travel. Fortunately he found a competent, experienced business manager, Horace Voules, to perform the routine work that he scorned, thus freeing himself for the more creative task of composing weekly copy.[6] During these years the characteristic Laboucherean style emerged, an idiosyncratic blend of lively satire, colorful personal reminiscence, and calculated outrage, which set the tone of the journal for years to come. The format that Labouchere initially established for *Truth* proved equally durable, surviving virtually unchanged for decades, although the page content of each issue more than doubled during that time.

The first five or six pages of each issue of *Truth* were reserved for a collection of brief social notes detailing the comings and goings of various celebrities under the title "Entre Nous." The "paragraph age" had been launched by Yates of the *World*, who recognized early on that the public of the 1870s, with its avid interest in the doings of its "betters," preferred clever gossip to the solemn dullness and reticence of older publications.[7] Labouchere refined Yates's technique by coupling straightforward social notes with an inexhaustible flow of provocative asides, sly innuendoes, and deliberately shocking observations. Frequently Labouchere's venomous thrusts drew blood, as he pursued a variety of targets ranging from the owner of the *Daily Telegraph* to the chief justice of England. Indeed, from the outset *Truth* found itself involved in constant litigation, and while Labouchere was probably sincere in his campaigns against hypocrisy and fraud, he understood too that the publicity resulting from his spectacular courtroom confrontations did much to stimulate *Truth*'s circulation.

Politically the weekly reflected the radicalism of its owner and his commitment to the Gladstonian formula of peace, retrenchment, and reform. From the start Labouchere was not reluctant to endorse unpopular positions. He labeled the Berlin Treaty of 1878 as a "disastrous shame," at a time when most of the public was rapturously hailing Disraeli as the architect of "peace with honor" (7 November 1878, p. 536). Long before the issue of home rule for Ireland had been allowed to shatter Liberal unity, *Truth* urged that the Irish be permitted "to manage their own local affairs" (20 February 1879, p. 217). With the tide of imperial expansion running high, it took considerable courage for Labouchere to advocate the cause of nonwhite Asians and Africans. *Truth* consistently, however, championed the rights of Zulus, Afghans, and Hindus, inquiring pointedly on one occasion: "Are we to insist upon being masters of the entire world?" (18 March 1880, p. 365).

For three years Labouchere poured vitriolic contempt on what he termed "this ... 'Rule Britannia' nonsense," and upon the jingoes who espoused it (20 February 1879, p. 215). Political commentary, however, was but a small part of his total contribution to the journal. Under the title "Mammon" he wrote a weekly analysis of stock offerings, bond issues, and financial developments.

Simultaneously, he offered investment advice to readers and warnings against fraudulent charities and sham promoters. Well into the next century *Truth* carried a "Cautionary List" of suspect charities and an investigative tradition that survived intact from the first years of its existence.

But the most enduring of Labouchere's accomplishments was the weekly column of theatrical criticism that appeared under the "Scrutator" *nom*. For the student of drama there is, perhaps, no better guide to the London stage in the late Victorian Age. "He 'did' the dramatic criticism," wrote a later editor of *Truth*, "and he never did anything better."[8] This appraisal has been validated by recent scholarship and may be independently confirmed by a brief survey of the "Scrutator" columns that Labouchere supplied to *Truth*, not only during the journal's early years, but intermittently after his election to the House of Commons in 1880 as well.[9] He brought to dramatic criticism insights based on personal experience as a stage manager and intimate associations with actors and writers. Though he once confessed to a weakness for melodrama, in point of fact his taste in plays and acting styles was entirely catholic. The ability to detect sham that inspired his campaigns against charity frauds and stock speculators permeated his dramatic criticism as well. He was an admirer of the great talents of the day—Irving, Terry, Booth, Bernhardt, Modjeska—but he remained always a discriminating judge of each performance. Thus he might praise Irving's Shylock even as he disparaged his Hamlet:

> The error of critics is that if once an actor or actress has played a part well, they imagine that any part must be played equally well, and this error is shared by audiences.... When once a name has been made, the owner of the name may play what he likes. Critics and audiences humbly and reverentially applaud. I admire not only in many of its details but as a whole Mr. Irving's impersonation of Shylock, because it realises my notion of that Venetian Hebrew; but this is no reason why I should go into ecstasies over his Hamlet, which to my mind is utterly at variance with any reasonable conception of the part, and mainly owed its success to its monstrous peculiarities. [1 January 1880, p. 13]

Similarly with Ellen Terry: "As Olivia Miss Terry was excellent because her mannerisms lent themselves to the character, whereas they are utterly at variance with the idea of Portia." Nor was "Scrutator" loath to offer advice to even the most celebrated of performers, such as Edwin Booth: "Comedy is the forte of Mr. Booth, not tragedy. He can laugh better than he howls. His Iago, Richelieu and Bertuccio show this as opposed to his Hamlet, Othello, and Shylock. He is an excellent actor but best when not severely strained" (17 March 1881, p. 396).

Labouchere's "Scrutator" columns were frequently unconventional, often filled with lengthy reminiscences of a personal nature and colorful digressions. But Labouchere was also capable of dealing directly and honestly with a number of controversial questions ranging from stage censorship to the desirability of establishing a tax-endowed national theater (3 June 1880, p. 711). His critical judgments were occasionally flawed; for example, he dismissed *The Pirates of Penzance* as "wearisome" and "monotonous" and predicted that it would quickly disappear from the repertory (8 April 1880, p. 461). As drama critic he reached too often for a glittery phrase and sometimes ridiculed performances as a means of displaying his wit. "It is because she can writhe, and flop, and sigh, and squirm," he wrote of Bernhardt's Fedora, "that she finds favour with a society apt to flop, writhe, sigh, and squirm" (12 July 1883, p. 47). But he brought to dramatic criticism an insider's knowledgeability based on prolonged personal association with the theatrical world, and he utilized a vivid and witty style of expression that was virtually unknown in critical circles before the advent of George Bernard Shaw.[10]

After Labouchere's election to Commons in 1880, Clement Scott, drama critic of the *Daily Telegraph*, was engaged by Voules to fill in occasionally. Scott was but one of a number of deputy "Labbies" employed early in the 1880s to write the columns formerly handled by *Truth*'s owner-editor. A capable staff was assembled by Voules in the eighties, each member an expert in his field, whether finance, horseracing, fashion, or eavesdropping on royalty. The public mistakenly continued to assume, however, that Labouchere was responsible for everything appearing in *Truth*, long after his literary energies had begun to slacken and the major focus of his interest had shifted to his parliamentary career. That the journal retained its characteristic tone and form was entirely attributable to Voules, who edited copy so scrupulously that a uniformity of style was steadfastly maintained. Each anonymous contributor utilized the characteristic Laboucherean locutions and mastered the distinctive turns of phrase so well that there appeared little discernible shift in either editorial policy or prose style from decade to decade.[11]

Moreover, a number of regular contributors remained with the journal for unusual lengths of time. There was, for example, A. A. Dowty, an obscure civil servant, whose satirical verses on topical themes appeared under the title "The Barrel Organ" for twenty-nine years. Dowty's choice of subject ranged widely; one week it might be politics (Disraeli's failure in the election of 1880), another, the contemporary social scene (a destitute woman's trial for the manslaughter of her illegitimate child). The tone was usually one of studied irony; and while the verses are entirely devoid of literary quality, they remain of interest to the social historian who seeks to explore those issues that enlisted the sympathy of progressive elements in late nineteenth-century society. Dowty was also the author of a lengthy year's end review in satiric verse, which became a staple of *Truth*'s Christmas issue. R. M. Freeman succeeded Dowty as *Truth*'s resident poet in 1906 and continued to supply the reader with a weekly diet of topical verse, some of it faintly satiric, much of it merely bathetic.

Another of *Truth*'s longtime literary contributors was George Sidney Paternoster, who, along with Richard Ashe King ("Desmond O'Brien"), handled book reviews. Notices tended to be somewhat abbreviated and consequently superficial, occasionally marred by a labored straining after Laboucherean verbal effects. Moreover, just as Labouchere fancied himself a gadfly born to sting the conscience of the political elite of the day, so too did *Truth*'s critics seem to delight in assailing those whose artistic reputations were well established. Often, however, they succeeded merely in drawing attention to their own limitations as critics. George Meredith, for example, was dismissed on one occasion as "a man of genius who ought to have been a great novelist, and who is somehow not a whit more unpopular than he deserves. . . . After twenty pages of him . . . your eyes ache, your brain whirls, you are bewildered with glare and glitter . . . and you catch yourself hankering after a little good, sound, stupid literature for a change" (20 January 1881, p. 95). Swinburne fared no better: "Mr. Swinburne has learned and forgotten nothing. . . . There is nothing in his verses to touch the human heart, and nothing to affect or impress the human mind" (17 February 1881, p. 230).

The journal's art and music critics were likewise afflicted by a compulsion to deflate established reputations; and a deliberately iconoclastic approach often led them to savage prominent artists of the day—Holman Hunt, Burne-Jones, Rossetti—mainly, one suspects, for the joy of displaying verbal cleverness and without regard to the actual merits or defects of the work in question. One of *Truth*'s art critics of the early nineties, George Bernard Shaw, left the staff precipitously after a series of collisions with Voules. One might conjecture that Shaw, who had for three years contributed reviews of museum shows and exhibition openings, was comfortable neither with the stylistic control maintained by Voules nor with the degree of aesthetic conformity expected of staff writers (5 January 1927, p. 12).

Fiction appeared weekly in *Truth*, but, like the poetry, it was either lightweight or purely topical. In 1877 Grenville Murray contributed the first of a series of "Queer Stories," which quickly became one of *Truth*'s most popular features, and which remained so well into the post–World War I era. The stories originally bore a close relationship to actual events and living characters. It was, indeed, commonly believed that one particularly outrageous composition had enraged the queen and cost Labouchere a cabinet seat in 1892.[12] Eventually, in the hands of Murray's successors, the stories lost their sting. Apparently written to a formula, the "Queer Stories" became entirely innocuous. One contributor in the early nineties, H. G. Wells, published his first short story in *Truth*; unable to comply with Voules's particularities, however, he declined further association with the journal (5 January 1927, p. 12).

For those readers who hungered for news of society, there was for many years "Marmaduke" (C. E. Jermingham), as well as "Madge of *Truth*" (Mrs. Humphrey). Each regaled the public with a steady gush of amusing anecdotes and gossip, ranging from Princess Beatrix's low-necked dresses to recipes for the *canetons en surprise* and *macedoines des fruits* being served at fashionable parties. In 1910 "Mrs. A.'s Diary" was introduced. Interestingly, at a time when votes for women was the major issue of the day, *Truth*, hewing fast to

Labouchere's unshakable prejudice against female enfranchisement, chose to add yet another "girls' gossip" columnist to its staff. The "diary," purportedly the work of a fashionable lady-about-town, was written with considerable verve and wit (2 March 1910, p. 528). With its numerous descriptions of gallery shows and theater openings, it is also an excellent guide to the aesthetic tastes and opinions of the cultivated middle class of London. But its appearance in 1910 was clearly a gesture aimed squarely at the "suffragettes," "Amazons," and "Girl-Bachelors" whom *Truth*, despite its traditional championship of unpopular causes, never tired of ridiculing.

Ironically, one of *Truth*'s most enduring features, the weekly "Letter from Paris," which appeared in every issue from 1877 to 1915, was the work of Emily Crawford, who has been called "the most talented of all women journalists." Mrs. Crawford was equally at home in the Elysée Palace and the *Comédie Française*. Moreover, she expressed herself in the style that typified the best of *Truth*'s contributors: ironic humor, acerbic analysis, and amusing send-ups of the pompous and inflated. She was especially interested in the arts, and her reviews of theater, opera, and dance constitute a veritable cultural history of Paris between 1877 and 1914. She was on familiar terms with Victor Hugo and Dumas *fils*; she heard Patti sing Traviata and applauded Bernhardt as Dona Sol; and she coupled her reviews with lively asides and perceptive observations about the contemporary state of French culture. Her weekly letter might deal with anything from an extended analysis of *Madame Bovary*—"In spite of himself Flaubert was a moralist . . ." —to archly amusing fashion commentary: "Tight lacing spoils the complexion, reddens the nose, and what is worse, checks cerebration. Ideas cannot flow freely when the waist is squeezed. Women who are good writers wear stays as little as they can help" (20 May 1880, p. 652; 2 February 1881, p. 149).

Mrs. Crawford was among those faithful stalwarts who remained with *Truth* throughout an extended career. Many others, however, came and went, their identities often difficult to ascertain. Libel suits were sufficiently commonplace that Labouchere and Voules devised elaborate stratagems to keep the names of writers secret. So successful were they that R. A. Bennett, who succeeded to the editorship of *Truth* in 1909, was unable to identify many early contributors. It is known, however, that Mrs. Lynn Linton contributed a number of satirical essays in *Truth*'s first years, and articles from the prolific pen of George Augustus Sala appeared with great frequency from 1877 to 1889. Sala, a close friend of Labouchere, had won fame both as a political essayist and as a special correspondent for the *Daily Telegraph*. He lived on the fringe of intrigue, both foreign and domestic, and he regularly titillated *Truth*'s readers with an insider's view of contemporary events.[13] Charles Bradlaugh, whose cause the journal championed vigorously in 1880, also contributed several anonymous essays between 1889 and 1891.

After 1880 Labouchere was too preoccupied with his political career to interfere significantly in Voules's editing of the journal. Occasionally, however, he intruded himself in a sensational way.[14] When he was denied a cabinet post in 1892, Labouchere's intemperate attacks on the royal family sent *Truth*'s circulation soaring. In 1899 Labouchere was among a handful of radicals who opposed government policy in South Africa. His pro-Boer position was a lonely one, and *Truth*, one of the few publications in Britain to oppose the war from its start, shared in the unpopularity of the owner. Despite emotional pleas from Voules, Labouchere stood fast on the war issue, although circulation between 1899 and 1901 plummeted (5 January 1927, p. 9). In 1902 Voules, who had held the formal title of editor since 1897, became involved in an embarrassing financial scrape. Although forced to relinquish the title, he remained in *de facto* control of the journal until his death in 1909. R. A. Bennett, Voules's longtime assistant, thereupon succeeded to the title of editor, which had remained vacant for seven years. Bennett persuaded Labouchere to convert his sole proprietorship into a joint stock company and to give the staff an opportunity to buy shares.[15] Labouchere, although living in retirement in Italy, continued to write frequently for *Truth* until his death in 1912, contributing a number of sharply etched analyses of European politics under his old "Scrutator" sobriquet.

Under Bennett's guidance the journal maintained its circulation and celebrated its fiftieth jubilee in 1927. Interestingly, its format remained virtually unchanged in fifty years. "Scrutator," "Mrs. A.'s Diary," "Mammon," "Entre Nous," and "Queer Stories" continued to appear, though "Notes from New York" in the 1920s regularly supplemented the traditional "Letter from Paris."

No one in 1877 would have dared to forecast the astonishing longevity that Labouchere's "hobby horse" ultimately attained. Ralph Nevill wrote in *The World of Fashion*: "Of all the Society Weeklies which were popular at the end of the last century *Truth* now alone survives and what is more, flourishes, remaining as bright and lively as it was when it had to keep pace with a number of cleverly written rivals, all of which have passed away" (5 January 1927, p. 1). Many of *Truth*'s competitors disappeared when daily papers and illustrated weeklies began to embrace the "new journalism" by incorporating lively material and human interest features calculated to appeal to the tastes of a growing number of readers at the turn of the century.[16] *Truth* survived because it had successfully transcended its status as "society print" in the 1880s, by creating a role distinctively its own. When J. H. McCarthy in 1904 hailed its "chivalrous defense of the oppressed, the unpopular, the unjustly judged," he was perhaps validating Labouchere's often expressed view that "so long as there are grievances, the newspaper will be a radical agent."[17] Through the eighties and nineties the society element in *Truth* tended to shrink, while the political and cultural content of the journal expanded. For frivolous readers there remained "Girls' Gossip," "Mrs. A.'s Diary," and "Entre Nous," but the substantial political, financial, and cultural coverage attracted a serious and well-informed readership as well. There is little of enduring literary merit to note in either the poetry or the short fiction published by *Truth* over the years. But the student of history—whether political, social, or cultural—will discover in the numerous columns devoted to art, theater, books, fashion, and contemporary affairs a valuable guide to the vagaries of popular taste, as well as a continuous record of the intellectual and aesthetic life of late Victorian and Edwardian London.

Notes

1. Donald Gray, "Early Victorian Scandalous Journalism," in *The Victorian Periodical Press*, ed. J. Shattuck and M. Wolff (Toronto, 1982), p. 345.

2. R. J. Hind, *Henry Labouchere and the Empire 1880–1905* (London, 1972), p. 3.

3. A. L. Thorald, *The Life of Henry Labouchere* (New York, 1913), pp. 38–73, 95–118; Hesketh Pearson, *Labby: The Life of Henry Labouchere* (London, 1936), pp. 25–69 passim.

4. Pearson, pp. 107–22. Henry Du Pre Labouchere, *Diary of the Besieged Resident in Paris* (London, 1871). For his relationship with the *Daily News*, see Stephen Koss, *The Rise and Fall of the Political Press in Britain* (Chapel Hill, N.C., 1981), pp. 268–69, 281–83.

5. Thorald, pp. 110–11. See also R. A. Bennett, "Mr. Labouchere as a Journalist," in Pearson, p. 492.

6. Pearson, pp. 493–95.

7. E. L. Hancock, "Labouchere and London *Truth*," *Bookman* 18 (1903):407.

8. Thorald, p. 496.

9. See, for example, E. J. West, "An Unappreciated Victorian Dramatic Critic: Henry Labouchere," *Quarterly Journal of Speech* 29 (1943):321–28.

10. West, p. 328.

11. Koss, p. 192.

12. Hind, p. 11. For Labouchere's attitude toward royalty, see Pearson, pp. 249–271.

13. For Sala's relationship with Labouchere, see Ralph Strauss, *Sala* (London, 1942), pp. 255–58, 261–63.

14. For Labouchere and *Truth*'s role in unmasking the Pigott forgeries, see Pearson, pp. 207–10.

15. Thorald, pp. 509–12.

16. On the "new journalism" see Koss, pp. 343–49.

17. Cited in Alan J. Lee, *The Origins of the Popular Press in England 1855–1914* (London, 1976), p. 191. See also Hind, p. 3.

Information Sources

BIBLIOGRAPHY

"Fifty years in *Truth* Office: A Jubilee Retrospect." *Truth*, 5 January 1927, pp. 5–13.
Hancock, E. L. "Labouchere and London *Truth*." *Bookman* 18 (1903):407–9.
Hind, R. J. *Henry Labouchere and the Empire 1880–1905*. London, 1972.
Pearson, Hesketh. *Labby: The Life of Henry Labouchere*. London, 1936.
Thorald, A. L. *The Life of Henry Labouchere*. New York, 1913.
West, E. J. "An Unappreciated Victorian Dramatic Critic: Henry Labouchere." *Quarterly Journal of Speech* 29 (1943):321–28.

INDEXES

Each volume indexed.

REPRINT EDITIONS

Microform: British Library (Newspaper Library), Colindale Avenue, London NW9 5HE: 1877–1899, 58 reels.

LOCATION SOURCES

American

Widely available.

British

Complete run: British Museum.

Partial runs: Birmingham Public Library; Bodleian Library; Cambridge University Library; Dundee Public Library; Liverpool Public Library; Manchester Public Library; Trinity College Library, Dublin.

Publication History

MAGAZINE TITLE AND TITLE CHANGES

Truth.

VOLUME AND ISSUE DATA

Volumes 1–157, numbers 1–4240, January 1877–December 1957.

FREQUENCY OF PUBLICATION

Weekly.

PUBLISHERS

Henry Du Pre Labouchere, Truth Publishing Company Limited, Staples Publications Limited, Cartaret Street, Westminster, London SW1.

EDITORS

Henry Du Pre Labouchere, 1877–1897. Horace St. Clair Voules, 1897–1902. Robert Augustus Bennett, 1909–1929. Thomas Colsey, 1929–1938. Collin Brooks, 1940–1953. Vincent Evans, 1953–1955. George Scott, 1955–1957.

Claire Hirshfield

___ U ___

UNIVERSAL REVIEW, THE

Harry Quilter's launching of the *Universal Review* in May 1888 elicited much enthusiasm, including a full-page notice in the London *Times*. Nevertheless, the *Universal* followed the paths of many other magazines during the last years of the nineteenth century: insufficient financing caused its collapse just two and a half years later; the final issue appeared in December 1890. This periodical, however, reveals the late Victorian age; Quilter's editorial eye looked backward and forward, and the contents of his magazine make it a paradigm of English literature and visual arts in transition from Victorian to modern times. Established names and less seasoned figures alike received space and objective, or near-objective, consideration from this editor.

Quilter was an ardent devotee of the Pre-Raphaelites. Thus his inclusion of George Moore, Laurence Housman, Walter Crane—artistic descendants of the earlier figures, who themselves received ample dues in the *Universal*—should not be astonishing. Others, like William Archer or Grant Allen, espoused other cultural innovations. Exemplars of known, established reputations were Wilkie Collins, Henry James, Eliza Lynn Linton, Thomas Hardy, William E. Gladstone, and Charles Dilke.

Quilter had attempted a history of the Pre-Raphaelites, information coming from William Holman-Hunt (himself the unsuccessful projector of such a book), Thomas Woolner, and Ford Madox Brown. Ultimately, and consequently, the *Universal* betrayed a distinct note of Pre-Raphaelite allegiance. Illustrations especially strengthened ties between the *Universal* and those notorious painters of an earlier day. Graphics by Dante G. Rossetti, John E. Millais, Edward Burne-Jones, and Frederick Sandys graced its pages, as did those by latter-day Pre-Raphaelites, Charles Fairfax Murray, Walter Crane, and Laurence Housman.

George Meredith's tantalizing long poem, *Jump to Glory Jane*, was not only published in the *Universal*; it reappeared in book form with an introduction by Quilter and illustrations by Laurence Housman. Complementing this poem is James Mavor's essay, "The New Crusade," a consideration of the Salvation Army and its founder, General William Booth. Along with Meredith's poem, Algernon C. Swinburne's "Aeolus" and William E. Henley's "In Passing" comprise the poetic high-water mark of the *Universal*. Other verse, like Frederick W. Rolfe's "Sestina in Honour of Lytle Seynt Hew" and Bliss Carman's "Corydon: An Elegy"—this last occasioned by the death of Matthew Arnold—reveal demarcations between "poetry" and "verse," into which latter category they most assuredly fall. Verse seemed generally doomed from the start of the magazine, with Lewis Morris's "Proem," in the first issue, setting a tone of sentimental gush, in the names of "Art" and "Learning," that pervaded most of the verse thereafter. Such a blemish may in part account for the early demise of the *Universal*.

Prose indeed affords the staple of interest for readers of yesterday and today. Its quality is much higher than that of the verse. Like the illustrations, which begin with Pre-Raphaelitism and move to types characterizing the 1890s, the fiction and the nonfiction prose highlight transitional elements in the *Universal*. The journal regularly ran essays treating political issues that were popular periodical fare during the heyday of Victorian imperialism. The older polemics on political economy, from such great Victorians as Thomas Carlyle, John Ruskin, and Matthew Arnold, are mirrored by those of Charles Dilke, William E. Gladstone, and the editor himself. To write about political, social, and religious issues with flare was deemed no mean accomplishment by those—and they were many—who admired the prose essay as an art form. The scene in France, Anglo-Indian relations, and African questions are just a few subjects that appear in such columns. New trends were represented by Samuel Butler's "Deadlock in Darwinism," a two-part treatise. Butler's ideas on evolution betrayed his personal quirks. Likewise, George Fleming's "On a Certain Deficiency in Women" (their incapacity for rational, abstract thought) and Eliza Lynn Linton's "The Philosophy of Marriage" (implying that strict British divorce laws safeguarded women from their own irritable nerves) are set at variance with Grant Allen's "The Girl of the Future" (warmly advocating education and emancipation for improving the feminine lot). Appropriately, Allen's essay appeared in 1890, on the threshold of a decade notorious for women in and out of literature, and of his own novel, *The Woman Who Did*—which brought resoundingly to the fore the nature of woman in the relations of the sexes.

Leo Tolstoy's "Marriage, Morality, and Christianity" sends messages akin to those in his fiction. Other items in the *Universal* attend to Russian themes, and reveal another growing occupation in many British literary circles, a desire for broad acquaintance with foreign masters, one of the pillars in the new school of realistic writing in England and America. Two stories that coalesce with such literary theory are Henry James's "The Lesson of the Master" and Thomas Hardy's "A Tragedy of Two Ambitions."

The high point of the *Universal* is its literary essays. Robert Buchanan, familiar since his onslaught upon Rossetti and Swinburne a decade earlier, deprecates, but simultaneously alerts us to, the increasing reputations of Henry James, Robert Louis Stevenson, George Moore, and William Archer, not to mention a host of foreign writers. In line with his attack on the "Fleshly School" in British verse, Buchanan lambasts *Art pour Art* as "trivialities of invention and temperamental want of creative insight." True, too, to his habitual promotion of his own status among men of letters, he cites that old attack on the Rossetti-Swinburne circle as the foundation for vilification of himself among hostile critics. Essays like his offer cross-lights upon shifting literary perspectives toward the close of the nineteenth century.

An essay by Colin Rae-Brown provides information about Thomas De Quincey's work for *Tait's Edinburgh Magazine** (see *RA*) earlier in the century, and thus furnishes bibliographical data on that Romantic writer. The most significant literary critique in the *Universal* is Quilter's *In Memoriam Amici*, a stout defense and appreciation of Wilkie Collins's fiction. Quilter lists Collins's seminal works, designating *No Name* as the best and complimenting the effective supernaturalism in *Armadale*. In Quilter's emphasis on Collins's "unequalled dramatic instinct" in his fiction, Collins's own previous "Story-Teller's Reminiscences" receives a creditable pendant.

Overall, the *Universal* merits revaluation as a valuable, representative, if short-lived, periodical of its era. Its transitional nature, mingling old and new, gives it a deserved spot in the assessment of contemporaneous journalism. Its attention to simmering cultural currents in general, not the least important of which are remarks about Victorian dramas, makes it a mine of information. Negligible when it comes to verse, the exemplification in the *Universal* of the shift from the fiction of Wilkie Collins toward the fantasy writing of the nineties is also noteworthy. An example is the Pan character in Laurence Housman's "The Green Gaffer," a tale linking the mythic figure of Pan from previous nineteenth-century writing with modifications in that myth late in the century. Although an editorial note might disclaim concurrence in theories set forth by Grant Allen's essay, "The Girl of the Future," the *Universal* in its entirety conveys an objectivity toward writers and artists of its day that is seldom matched by any other monthly magazine during the nineteenth century, save perhaps the *Yellow Book** in its first four or five volumes.

Information Sources

BIBLIOGRAPHY

Earle, Mrs. C. W. *Memoirs and Memories*. London, 1911.
Quilter, Harry. *Opinions*. London, 1909.
————— *Preferences in Art, Life, and Literature*. London, 1892.

INDEXES
    Each volume indexed.
REPRINT EDITIONS
    BUCOP lists 2d ed., n.d.
    Microform: Early British Periodicals (UMI), reels 316–318.
LOCATION SOURCES
American
    Widely available.
British
    Complete runs: Bodleian Library; British Museum; Edinburgh University Library;
    Saint Andrews University Library.

Publication History

MAGAZINE TITLE AND TITLE CHANGES
    The Universal Review.
VOLUME AND ISSUE DATA
    Volumes 1–8, May 1888–December 1890.
FREQUENCY OF PUBLICATION
    Quarterly.
PUBLISHER
    Swann Sonnenschein & Co., London.
EDITOR
    Harry Quilter.

Benjamin F. Fisher IV

____ V ____

VANITY FAIR

On 7 November 1868 London was introduced to the debut edition of *Vanity Fair: A Weekly Show of Political, Social, and Literary Wares*, England's first successful society journal, which treated its readers to weekly displays of wit, wisdom, and celebrity caricatures for nearly a half-century of uninterrupted publication. The first issue stated, "In this Show it is proposed to display the vanities of the week, without ignoring or disguising the fact that they are vanities, but keeping always in mind that in the buying and selling of them there is to be made a profit of truth." Continuing his statement of purpose, the founding editor, Thomas Gibson Bowles, assured his readers that "no solemn praises" would be sung. Persons and events would "be spread out upon their own merits, ticketed with plain words." Thus, he concluded, "Those who think that the Truth is to be found in the Show will probably buy it; those who do not, will pass on their way to another, and both will be equally right."

Under various sobriquets, Bowles wrote most of the material during his ownership of *Vanity Fair* from 1868 to 1889, and the tone and format he set were maintained, with only minor changes, until the twentieth century. Later editors included Oliver A. Fry (1889–1904) and Frank Harris (1907–1911). The latter turned the magazine into a commercial enterprise without the stress on political and social creeds that characterized its Victorian years. In January 1914 *Vanity Fair* merged with a woman's magazine, *Hearth and Home*, with nothing remaining of its original format save its name in the shared title. The twentieth-century American *Vanity Fair* was an entirely different publication.

Until very recently in the mid-twentieth century, almost no studies of *Vanity Fair* had been published, save for a 1915 autobiography, *Forty Years of "Spy,"* by Sir Leslie Ward. Ward was the best known of the magazine's artists, and signed his sobriquet "Spy" to well over half of the more than 2,000 chromolithograph celebrity "cartoons" and caricature portraits in the *Vanity Fair* collection. Indeed, until Leonard E. Naylor's 1965 publication of *The Irrepressible Victorian: The Story of Thomas Gibson Bowles*, general knowledge of the magazine was virtually limited to the popularity of its so-called Spy prints, and the artistic contributions of Ward, Carlo Pellegrini ("Ape"), Max Beerbohm, and others. These remained collectors' items long after the magazine itself had been nearly forgotten. Nonetheless, while *Vanity Fair*'s success stemmed largely from these drawings, the letterpress itself provided Victorian and Edwardian readers with some of the most urbane and witty writing in British journalism.

Thomas Gibson Bowles was born the illegitimate son of Susan Bowles and Thomas Milner Gibson, an influential politician and avid yachtsman. He was taken into the Gibson household, provided with an education, and brought up by Gibson's wife, Arethusa, a remarkably broad-minded woman whose salons were frequented by unusual combinations of aristocrats and bohemians ranging from authors and artists to newspapermen and politicians. Also, through her activities, Bowles became involved in amateur acting and play production with a group of bright young men with whom he moved through social circles of fast living, sports, and the civil service. By his mid-twenties, Bowles was ready to leave his eight-year civil service clerical job at Somerset House to set out on a career that was to include both journalism and politics. Given the influence of his home, the strong friendships he had made among English socialites, and a few years of experience writing for the *Morning Post*, a society journal called the *Owl*, and a satirical magazine, the *Tomahawk*, Bowles was prepared in 1868 to borrow 200 pounds to launch his own society journal.

Vanity Fair's stated purpose worked its way into a wide variety of contents within its usual eight to twelve folio pages, including advertisements. Its bill of fare included social and political columns; book and play reviews; serialized novels; sports and music reports; word games (such as doublets and double acrostics); humor; travel accounts; and features on legal, church, and financial matters, of interest primarily to Londoners. Although the magazine's political bias (pro-Tory and anti-Liberal) is quite obvious in early issues, no one was really beyond Bowles's satirical rebukes when he felt such assaults were well deserved. Consequently, Bowles and his magazine were not without enemies and actions for libel. The fact that he lost only one very minor case was undoubtedly due to his ten-year employment of the legal counsel of Arthur Hepburn Hastie.

Vanity Fair's first issue sold only 619 copies, and the second issue a mere 408, but by the beginning of March 1869 sales were well above 2,500. Almost certainly the sudden popularity began with the "lucky" thirteenth issue on 30 January 1869, which contained, as Bowles previously had announced, a pictorial ware of "an entirely novel character"—a full-page colored caricature of Benjamin Disraeli signed by "Singe," the Italian artist Carlo Pellegrini, who, after his second contribution, a marvelous caricature of Gladstone in the following issue, was to sign his familiar "Ape" on hundreds of cartoons for the next fifteen years.

Although the caricatures were clearly the main cause for *Vanity Fair*'s success, Bowles's repeated defense of his artists' sometimes unflattering drawings gave rise to some of his most insightful commentary on the social function of caricature satire. For example, in response to a *Daily News* charge that the cartoons were too grotesque to be amusing, Bowles wrote:

> There are grim faces made more grim, grotesque figures made more grotesque, and dull people made duller by the genius of our talented collaborator "Ape," but there is nothing that has been treated with a set purpose to make it something that it was not already originally in a lesser degree. . . . Here comes in the caricaturist, and tells us how and from what. With his readier wit he seizes the essential point, and exaggerates it till there is no fear that the dullest intellect will henceforth lose sight of it.[1]

In addition to his writing in the magazine itself, Bowles also wrote a series of prefaces to several yearly bound volumes of the prints. In these, he develops his concept of verbal and visual satire as "the unheroic representation of heroes." One of the regular features bearing Bowles's "Jehu, Junior" sobriquet was the letterpress biographical sketch accompanying each cartoon. Bowles's sharp and often irreverent wit is obvious during his editorship. From the 1890s on, however, this element of satire of national and international events gradually faded, and the later focus is more on the royal family, English upper-class "vanities" (such as listings of parties, balls, court appointments, engagements, and marriage announcements), fashions, resorts, and advertisements featuring food, homes, and other "essentials" for the "good life."

During his editorship, Bowles maintained complete control, working only with invited contributors rather than with a staff. Much of the material he wrote himself under "Jehu Junior," "Blanc Bec," "Auditor," "Choker," and "Pantagruel." Unlike the *Punch** staff, which developed writers and content through the famous "Mahogany Table" weekly discussions, Bowles called his own shots from his St. James Street office. According to Eileen Harris,

> His selection of men and women, protected by anonymity, included Lord Ronald Gower, younger brother of the Duke of Sutherland, an MP, artist and writer; Henry Pottinger Stephens, a former Paris correspondent for *The Times*; Wilmott Dixon, a *bon vivant*, as much in demand for his sporting articles as for his company; John Baker Hopkins, a prolific journalist and novelist; Charles Edward Jerningham, a man-about-town who became widely known as "Marmaduke", the society chronicler for *Truth*[*]; William Wilde, brother of Oscar; Grenville Murray; Charles Waring; Fred Burnaby and his wife Audrey (later Mrs. Le Blond); Lady Florence Dixie, a courageous war correspondent and explorer; Lady Elizabeth Desart.[2]

Working most closely with Bowles during the magazine's first two decades were artists Carlo Pellegrini and Leslie Ward, and the pioneering chromolithography firm of Vincent Brooks, Day and Son, the most regularly employed firm throughout *Vanity Fair*'s history. Pellegrini, a Neapolitan fashion leader and *bon vivant* of the Prince of Wales's set, was the presiding draughtsman, capable of sketching his "victims" from memory after observing them for mental impressions. While later artists, including Ward and Max Beerbohm, acknowledged their debts to the master caricaturist, they seldom matched the expert touch of Pellegrini, the "Ape" of *Vanity Fair*.

Certainly the credit for the drawings', and the magazine's, long-range survival belongs to Leslie Ward, whose "Spy" signature became synonymous with *Vanity Fair* for four decades. Politicians, artists, writers, sportsmen, judges, clergymen, scientists, soldiers, professors, performers, the famous and the infamous, the truly great and the eminent nonentity—all survive in likeable images, captured by "Spy's" prolific pen for the *Vanity Fair* gallery.[3] In some instances, the *Vanity Fair* caricature, portrait, or semi-portrait may be the only available likeness of a certain personality of that day. In the early days of *Vanity Fair*, people viewed caricature as something entirely new, and viewed it in the right spirit, according to Ward, but later they grew particular. "I fancy that I have been of service to a good many tailors in my time," said Ward. "For many of the notables I have cartooned seemed altogether unaware of their habilatory shortcomings til they were confronted by them in my drawings." Sometimes a *Vanity Fair* caricature may capture the personality of subject even better than could a camera or a portrait painter. Victorian photographers and portrait painters tended to pose their subjects for formal renderings. The *Vanity Fair* artists captured what we now might call the "candid camera" impressions of characteristic personality traits.

In addition to Pellegrini and Ward, the magazine employed an international cast of several dozen talented artists, including the French James Tissot and Théobold Chartran, the Belgian François-Pierre Verheyden, the Germans Goedecker and de Grimm, the Italians Adriano Cecioni and Prosperi, the American Thomas Nast, and numerous other English contributors, including (Sir) Francis (Carruthers) Gould, Louise Jopling, Henry Marks, Harry Furniss, (Sir) Bernard Partridge, Walter Sickert, and Max Beerbohm. Beerbohm, an admirer of Pellegrini's style, provided several caricatures during the later years when many of the drawings, including Ward's, tended to move away from caricature toward a frequently flattering portraiture.

This later evolution of the drawings parallels the development of the magazine itself. The earlier cutting edges of Bowles's clever journalism and Pellegrini's comparable visual satire were considerably dulled as the magazine moved into the twentieth century. The reason for this change is well stated by one of *Vanity Fair*'s recent historians: "The English Smart Set had changed too. They were now menaced at home by transformations in the social structure and from abroad by the ominous sounds of war. Because *Vanity Fair* was the Smart Set's gazette, it stands to reason that when the Smart Set began to be affected by social and political developments, its most representative voice in journalism was likewise influenced."[4]

In *Forty Years of "Spy,"* Sir Leslie Ward concludes that "when the history of the Victorian Era comes to be written in true perspective, the most faithful mirror and record of representative men and the spirit of their times will be sought and found in *Vanity Fair.*" A century is probably a good distance from which to attempt such a "true perspective," and there is some reason to believe that Ward was right in his judgment about *Vanity Fair*'s providing the truest mirror of the spirit of the times in which he lived and painted. If, as one historian has claimed, history is the essence of innumerable biographies, *Vanity Fair* can provide us with a stimulating pictorial history of the latter half of the nineteenth century and the first two decades of the twentieth.

Notes

1. Quoted by Leonard E. Naylor in *The Irrepressible Victorian: The Story of Thomas Gibson Bowles* (London, 1965), p. 22.

2. Eileen Harris, "Introduction," *"Vanity Fair": An Exhibition of Original Cartoons* (London, 1976), p. 6.

3. Samples of the cartoons have been reproduced in both color and black-and-white in Jerold J. Savory, *The "Vanity Fair" Gallery: A Collector's Guide to the Caricatures* (New York, 1979). Others, nearly all by "Spy," are reproduced in Leslie Ward's *Forty Years of "Spy"* (1915; rpt. Detroit, 1969).

4. Roy T. Matthews, *"Vanity Fair*: The Smart Set's Gazette." An unpublished paper. Professor Matthews is preparing a history of *Vanity Fair* magazine.

Information Sources

BIBLIOGRAPHY

Harris, Eileen. "Carlo Pellegrini: Man and 'Ape.' " *Apollo Magazine*, January 1976.
———, "Introduction." *"Vanity Fair": An Exhibition of Original Cartoons*. London, 1976.
Jones, Claude E. "*Vanity Fair* Portraits, 1868–1881: A Selected Check List." *Bulletin of Bibliography* 23, no. 7 (1962):159–62.
Mann, Ruth J. " 'The Unheroic Representation of Heroes,' A 'Historical Vignette' on Several of *Vanity Fair*'s Medical Personalities." *Mayo Clinic Proceedings* 46 (1971):197–99.
Manvell, Brian. "Cartoons of Theatrical Interest Appearing in *Vanity Fair.*" *Theatre Notebook* 19 (1965):126–33.
Matthews, Roy. "Spy." *British History Illustrated* 3 (1976):50–57.
Maunsell, H. R. "*Vanity Fair* Cartoons." *Notes and Queries* 66 (21 April 1934):284.
Moxon, Robert K. Three short articles in the *New England Journal of Medicine* on medical personalities Richard Owen (5 July 1962), Sir Henry Thompson (1 November 1962), and Erasmus Wilson (1 April 1976).
Naylor, Leonard E. *The Irrepressible Victorian: The Story of Thomas Gibson Bowles*. London, 1965.

Ormond, Richard. *"Vanity Fair": An Exhibition of Original Cartoons*. Catalogue of a National Portrait Gallery exhibition. London, 1976.

Robinson, B. Fletcher. "Chronicles in Cartoon: A Record of Our Times." *Windsor Magazine* 23 (1905–1906):35–51, 261–76, 383–98, 489–506, 611–30, 733–52; 24 (1906):35–52, 157–78, 279–96, 401–20, 539–60; 25 (1906–1907):83–100, 261–78, 367–86.

Savory, Jerold J. "Collecting *Vanity Fair* Caricatures." *Antiques Journal* 33, no. 3 (1978):12–15.

―――. [Short Notes on Individual Prints:] *Arnoldian* 4 (1977):2; *Notes and Queries*, n.s. 25 (1978):206–8; *Studies in Browning* 5 (1977):71–74; and *Oceans* 10, no. 6 (1977):70.

―――. *The "Vanity Fair" Gallery: A Collector's Guide to the Caricatures*. New York, 1979.

―――. *The "Vanity Fair" Lithographs: An Illustrated Checklist*. New York, 1978.

―――. "Well Known 'Vanities.' " *American History Illustrated* 12, no. 9 (1978):42–46.

Schooling, J. Holt. "A Glance at *Vanity Fair*." *Strand Magazine* 22 (1901):193–200. Illustrated magazines, like *Vanity Fair*'s contemporaries, the *Strand** and the *Sketch*, did frequent pieces on *Vanity Fair*'s artists and editors. The *Sketch*, for example, published articles on Harold Wright, or "Stuff Gownsman" (5 April 1893), Leslie Ward (10 January 1894), Oliver Fry (6 March 1895), and another on Ward (28 October 1903).

Ward, Mrs. E. M. *Memories of Ninety Years*. 2d ed. New York, 1925.

Ward, Leslie. *Forty Years of "Spy."* 1915. Reprint. Detroit, 1969.

INDEXES
None.

REPRINT EDITIONS
Microform: Datamics Inc., New York.

LOCATION SOURCES
American

Complete run: Boston Athenaeum.

Partial runs: Widely available.

British

Partial runs: Widely available.

Publication History

MAGAZINE TITLE AND TITLE CHANGES
Vanity Fair: A Weekly Show of Political, Social, and Literary Wares, 1868–1913. (Merged with *Hearth and Home* and renamed *Vanity Fair and Hearth and Home*, 1914–June 1928.)

VOLUME AND ISSUE DATA
Volumes 1–107, 7 November 1868–June 1928.

FREQUENCY OF PUBLICATION
Weekly.

PUBLISHERS
1868–1889: Thomas Gibson Bowles, St. James Street, London. 1889–1904: Arthur Evans, London. 1904–1913: Harmsworth.

EDITORS

Thomas Gibson Bowles, 1868–1889. A. G. Witherby, 1889–1900. Oliver A. Fry, 1890–1904. B. Fletcher Robinson, 1904–1907. Frank Harris, 1907–1911. T. R. Allinson, 1911–1913.

Jerold J. Savory

VICTORIA MAGAZINE, THE

In 1858 a group of women who congregated around Bessie Rayner Parkes at 19 Langham Place launched the *English Woman's Journal*, a periodical in which the women's movement in Great Britain found its voice. One of the first who came to London to volunteer her services was Emily Faithfull, who left her father's rectory, Headley, near Epsom, when she was twenty-three. In the late 1850s Miss Faithfull worked closely and quietly with Miss Parkes in the editing of the *Journal*. By 1860 she presented a paper at the Glasgow meeting of the National Association for the Promotion of Social Science, in which she expounded Bessie Parkes's dream of establishing a press specifically for the purpose of employing women. Emily Faithfull henceforth devoted her energies to the founding of the Victoria Press and to the publication of the *Victoria Magazine.*[1] With the Victoria Press Miss Faithfull hoped to provide for women's technical advancement, and with the *Victoria Magazine* she attempted to foster women's literary aspirations.[2]

The first issue, for May 1863, contained some extravagantly laudatory lines:

> Free Queen and Empress of the Free, Victoria!
> Guileless of heart and frank of mien, Victoria!
> Once happy wife of noble mate, Victoria!
> Yet, widowed Monarch, left alone, Victoria!
> Royal Mother! happy in the Son—Victoria!
> Bid the last cloud of mourning flee, Victoria![3]

[1:1–2]

Besides displaying her own literary aspirations in this first number, Emily Faithfull also published a poem ([To] L.E.L. "Whose heart was breaking for a little love") by Christina Rossetti, as well as the first three chapters of a novel (*Lindisfarne Close*) by Thomas Adolphus Trollope, Anthony's elder brother. Subsequent issues included works by George Macdonald, Adelaide Procter, Richard Holt Hutton, Nassau W. Senior, and F. D. Maurice. The magazine had definite literary pretensions.

The chief value of the *Victoria Magazine* lies in its chronicling of events in the history of the women's movement. Emily Faithfull herself was involved in the celebrated Codrington divorce case, which began in 1864, and her monthly magazine became an outspoken defender of the wife's rights in the Marriage

Property Act.[4] The position of female convicts, the plight of the London poor (especially their lack of suitable dwellings and adequate sanitation), the situation of sempstresses deprived of their living by the advent of the sewing machine, the destitution of unwanted governesses—these were some of the evils the *Victoria Magazine* would not allow its readers to forget. Neither would it allow important victories of "the Cause" to remain unsung. The steady progress of women's achievement in the London and Cambridge university examinations; the victories of Elizabeth Blackwell and Elizabeth Garrett in overcoming male hostility in the medical profession; even the trivial invention of the "extension grate" by a forgotten Miss Cobb (not Frances Power Cobbe) were all duly heralded.

When John Stuart Mill introduced his petition for the franchise to be extended to women on 12 June 1866, the *Victoria Magazine* began a vigorous discussion of the issue in the August edition, opening with an article entitled "Conflicting Opinions on the Franchise for Women." Both the *Saturday Review** and the *Spectator** (see *RA*) were against the petition, and the *Victoria Magazine* published Frances Power Cobbe's spirited reply (3:288–89). It also published Barbara Bodichon's paper on "The Extension of Suffrage to Women" in the November 1866 issue, as well as Emily Faithfull's own attack on the *Saturday Review* in the July 1868 number (3:47–64; 11:193–201).

The *Victoria Magazine* assumes even greater importance if one considers that the *English Woman's Journal*, which began the crusade for women's rights in March 1858, lasted a bare six years. It was superseded by the *Alexandra Magazine*, which ran from May 1864 until August 1865, a little over a year. For sheer longevity the *Victoria Magazine* merits serious consideration. Emily Faithfull guided the journal from May 1863 until June 1880, a seventeen-year period covering the important early events in the emancipation of women.

One of the most popular sections of the *Victoria Magazine* was entitled "Social Science." Here would appear all matters related to social health and welfare: new bills introduced to the House of Commons and new societies formed for the public good, for example, the Working Men's Club and Institute Union, the National Colonial Emigration Society, and the "Ladies Sanitary Association." Later, sections entitled "Miscellanea" and "Correspondence" were added. The first of these would contain summaries of important articles published in other magazines that had a direct bearing on women's issues. The "Correspondence" feature provided a forum where women could air their views in public. This led to a further item, the "Victoria Discussion Society"; in these sections the best history of the women's movement in Great Britain may be found. As in other journals, the "Literature of the Month" was examined, but even here the books selected related chiefly to women's concerns.

Emily Faithfull was a capable synthesizer and a writer of remarkable force. She was indignant in condemning unfit employments for women. "Society," she writes, "swallows the camel and objects to the gnat. . . . It seems to be taken for granted that women's physical strength may be drawn upon *ad libitum* so long as we carefully avoid giving them the least encouragement to exert their minds" (2:69). And again: "To us it seems as unreasonable to keep the million of single women in idleness because they have not husbands and children to minister to, as it would be to keep the millions of men in similar idleness because they have not wives and children to provide for" (2:71). Accordingly, the *Victoria Magazine* investigated and reported on every new employment found suitable for women: librarian, telegraph operator, clerk, cigarmaker, boxmaker, hairdresser, and so on. Any work that showed women to advantage—no matter how insignificant—was reported. In the November 1876 issue a new feature, "Women and Work—a Guide to Employment for Women," tried to assist women in their search for economic independence. The journal was surprisingly modern in advocating the integration of the sexes in education and the importance of physical education for girls. It was modern, too, in resorting to advertisements to stave off financial problems.

The *Victoria Magazine* might well be termed a one-woman operation. Because of her growing reputation as a speaker, Emily Faithfull seemed to pay more attention to the lecture circuit than she did to her magazine. As the 1870s advanced there was growing evidence of disintegration, and a sad degree of indelicate self-aggrandizement on the part of Miss Faithfull, who seems to have published every good word ever said or written about herself. The stories that formed a staple feature of the magazine became increasingly sentimental—even sensational. But a worse fault was the low quality of the printing. For example, there are two sixth chapters in "Stella's Repentance" in the issue for October 1869, incorrect pagination in August 1871, and even incomplete articles in the April 1877 issue. But faulty as the *Victoria Magazine* may have been, it is significant as a literary document of social history, giving ample coverage to twenty years of intense agitation for women's emancipation in Great Britain.

Notes

1. For previous research on Emily Faithfull, see William E. Fredeman, "Emily Faithfull and the Victoria Press: An Experiment in Sociological Bibliography," *Library* 29 (1974):139–64; James S. Stone, "More Light on Emily Faithfull and the Victoria Press," *Library* 33 (1978):63–67.

2. See "Emily Faithfull on the Victoria Press," *English Woman's Journal* 6, no. 32 (October 1860):122–23, and "Women Compositors," *English Woman's Journal* 8, no. 43 (September 1861):38.

3. That Miss Faithfull flattered the queen is obvious from the first page of the *Victoria Magazine*. In June 1862 Miss Faithfull was appointed "Printer and Publisher in Ordinary to her Majesty" by Royal Warrant. In 1886 she received 100 pounds from the queen.

4. For Faithfull's involvement in the Codrington divorce case, see the London *Times* for 2 March 1864, p. 11; 20 April 1864, p. 11; 29 April 1864, p. 13; 18 July 1864, p. 11; 27 July 1864, p. 11; 29 July 1864, p. 10. See also "Faithfull v. Grant," *Victoria Magazine* 11 (September 1869):385–400.

Information Sources

BIBLIOGRAPHY

Fredeman, William E. "Emily Faithfull and the Victoria Press: An Experiment in Sociological Bibliography." *Library* 29 (1974):139–64.

Stone, James S. "More Light on Emily Faithfull and the Victoria Press." *Library* 33 (1978):63–67.

INDEXES

None.

REPRINT EDITIONS

Microform: Oxford Microform Publications.

LOCATION SOURCES

American

Complete runs: Boston Public Library; Brooklyn Public Library; Chicago Public Library; Public Library of Cincinnati and Hamilton County.

Partial runs: Widely available.

British

Complete run: British Museum.

Partial runs: Bodleian Library; Cambridge University Library; London University Library; National Library of Scotland, Edinburgh.

Publication History

MAGAZINE TITLE AND TITLE CHANGES

The Victoria Magazine.

VOLUME AND ISSUE DATA

Volumes 1–35, numbers 1–206, May 1863–June 1880. Odd-numbered volumes comprise May to October issues. Even-numbered volumes comprise November to April issues.

FREQUENCY OF PUBLICATION

Monthly.

PUBLISHER

The Victoria Press.

EDITOR

Emily Faithfull.

Martha Westwater

W

WALES

The first issue of *Wales*, that for May 1911, carried on its cover a photograph of David Lloyd George; the frontispiece was another photograph of Lloyd George, and the lead article, the first in a continuing series entitled "Representative Welshmen," was devoted to the career and achievements of the then chancellor of the Exchequer. The author of the article and the editor of *Wales*, J. Hugh Edwards, had published in 1908 a biography of Lloyd George, a work whose general tenor may be inferred from its title: *From Village Green to Downing Street*. By 1913, while still editor of *Wales*, Edwards had completed the first volumes of a more ambitious project—*The Life of David Lloyd George* in five volumes, the first volume entitled *A Short History of the Welsh People*.[1] It is not surprising to find that in this first issue of *Wales*, Edwards suggests that Lloyd George "may be well described as the modern incarnation of the last and the greatest of the native princes of Wales," one whose leadership "has served to reveal to the English people the reality and value of Welsh nationality" (no. 1:1).

Educated at Aberystwyth and later returned as a Liberal member of Parliament from Mid-Glamorgan from 1910 to 1922, Edwards had previously edited *Young Wales* (1895–1903). For this new magazine, he solicited "articles dealing with various aspects of Welsh life and of interest to Welshmen." The first issue carried the subtitle "A National Magazine" and announced itself as the "First number of a New Magazine for Wales." The cover of the second issue, that for June 1911, announced a "Great New Magazine for Welshmen All the World Over," and by January 1912, it was simply "*The* National Magazine for the Welsh People."

From the first issue onwards, the magazine included a variety of articles ranging from political, economic, and historical aspects of Welsh life to cultural and literary interests, past and present. There were several continuing series, such as the one on "Representative Welshmen" that presented Lloyd George. Later issues added to the series laudatory articles on the Right Honorable Sir Samuel Evans, Sir Isombard Owen, Professor John Rhys, Owen Morgan Edwards, Sir Edward Anywl, and other Welshmen of note. Other series articles were grouped under such headings as "Cambria's Heroes," "What the World Owes to Welshmen," "As Others See Us" (interviews), "Forgotten Welshmen," "Great Poets of Wales," "Counties of Wales," and "National Institutions of Wales." Edwards himself wrote a monthly feature for each issue, "The Month in Wales," a review of meetings, celebrations, and other events.

During its three years and four months of monthly publication, *Wales* could count among its contributors many eminent Welshmen of the period. The Reverend H. Elvet Lewis, well-known orator and man of letters, wrote the first article in the "Great Poets of Wales" series and other essays thereafter. Another well-known Nonconformist preacher and advocate of social reform, Gwilym Davies, wrote on "The Welsh Tramp," among other topics. There were political articles by such leading Liberal M.P.s as Ellis James Griffith, E. T. John, and W. Llewelyn Williams, a frequent contributor. In addition, the historian J. E. Lloyd and the poets W. J. Gruffeydd and T. Huws Davies (the latter to become editor of *Welsh Outlook*) contributed essays. Not all contributors were Welsh, Nonconformist, and Liberal. Sir Harry Reichel, who wrote one of the "Representative Welshmen" pieces, was an Ulster Tory; he was also, however, first principal of the University College of North Wales. Ormesby-Gore, then a twenty-nine-year-old Tory M.P., wrote "A Secretaryship for Wales" for the issue of June 1914. And Lord Justice Vaughan Williams, of Welsh family, but described in a recent history of Wales as "a prickly Anglican,"[2] wrote a not uncritical essay on "The Celtic Character" in the issue for January 1913. With unacknowledged debts to Matthew Arnold and perhaps to Gibbon, Vaughan Williams announced that the Celtic character is different from the Teutonic and summed up some of the differences in the following passage: "The Celts cannot be said to be orderly or practical, they are addicted to theory and are dreamers of the past.... The Teutons are emphatically industrious, plodding, orderly, practical, and never sacrifice the present or the future to sentiment or dreams of the past" (no. 21:3).

The average issue of *Wales* ran to about sixty pages (including advertisements), and only a few articles exceeded five pages. Many of the shorter pieces were literary. The magazine published poems and occasional short stories, always in English; some of these were contemporary, the short stories typically set in rural or working-class industrial Wales. Others were new English translations of older Welsh literature. In articles like those in the "Great Poets of Wales" series, some material was presented only in translation, but often both the Welsh and its English translation were given.

While many articles and essays were thoughtful and well written, the quality nevertheless varied in individual issues. Although many of the shorter literary and historical articles were informative, others were mere appreciations offering little of memorable value. Only a few really bad pieces appeared. One notable example, by G. Arbour Stephens, asked the question "Do women play their proper part in the national life of Wales?"—with emphasis on what is "proper"— and answered it negatively in a narrowly prejudiced, poorly written, and ill-organized fashion (no. 10:54). The same issue for January 1912, however, introduced an entertaining series by Shôn Dafydd, identified by the editor as M.P. for the University of Wales; "Among the Welsh Members," which appeared in several subsequent issues, reported in a chatty, anecdotal way on the deportment and characteristics of various Welsh M.P.s, with the occasional accompaniment of cartoon drawings.

Generally, then, *Wales* presented an attractive variety of articles and features designed to appeal to Welsh interests. The advertisements indicated that the intended audience was not limited to Wales itself. Perhaps the majority of advertisements were for generally distributed products such as Coleman's Mustard (always on the front cover), Pears soap, and various tobaccos, chocolates, and coffees. Some were from Scottish firms, others from both Welsh and English resorts, and some from London merchants.

Though calling itself the national magazine, *Wales* was published in and distributed from London; in this way, it illustrates the outlook of many Welsh politicians of the time. The movement for political separatism or home rule for Wales had lost its momentum; increasingly, especially with the entrance of Lloyd George into national government, many Welshmen felt that the British Liberal party, rather than a separatist government, offered greater advantages for Wales. W. Llewelyn Williams had addressed the problem in the first issue of *Wales*; in an article entitled "The Welsh Claim for Disestablishment," he pointed out that in desiring the "freedom of Wales from the yoke of the alien Establishment," Welshmen would have to realize that they could not have both Disestablishment *and* Lloyd George in the cabinet (no. 1:9). That first issue, with its cover photograph, frontispiece, and lead article concentrating on Lloyd George, made clear the political sentiments of *Wales*'s editor. In this issue, as in subsequent ones, the cultural nationalism that had seen such resurgence in the 1880s and 1890s was to be emphasized and encouraged; separatism was not.

Notes

1. J. Hugh Edwards, *The Life of David Lloyd George* (London, 1913–1924). Volume 5, a supplement entitled *David Lloyd George: War Minister*, was written by J. Saxon Mills.

2. Kenneth O. Morgan, *Rebirth of a Nation: Wales 1880–1980* (New York, 1981), p. 136.

Information Sources

BIBLIOGRAPHY

Edwards, J. Hugh. *The Life of David Lloyd George with a Short History of the Welsh People*. Introduction by the Right Honorable Sir David Brynmor Jones. 2 vols. London, 1913.

Morgan, Kenneth O. *Rebirth of a Nation: Wales 1880–1890*. New York, 1981.

INDEXES
    Each volume indexed.
REPRINT EDITIONS
    None.
LOCATION SOURCES
    American
        None.
    British
        Complete runs: Birmingham University Library ; Bodleian Library; British Museum; National Central Library; Swansea Public Library; Trinity College Library, Dublin.
        Partial runs: Birmingham Public Library; University College of Wales Library, Aberystwyth; University of South Wales Library, Cardiff.

Publication History

MAGAZINE TITLE AND TITLE CHANGES
    Wales.
VOLUME AND ISSUE DATA
    Volumes 1–6, numbers 1–40, May 1911–August 1914.
FREQUENCY OF PUBLICATION
    Monthly.
PUBLISHERS
    May–December 1911: The Principality Publishing Co., Ltd., 190, St. Stephen's House, Westminster. January 1912–April 1913: F. Chalmers Dixon, 17-21 Tavistock St., Covent Garden. May 1913–August 1914: Cassell and Company, Ltd., London.
EDITOR
    J. Hugh Edwards.

Marylyn J. Parins

WATT'S LITERARY GUIDE. See LITERARY GUIDE

WESTMINSTER AND FOREIGN QUARTERLY REVIEW, THE.
See WESTMINSTER REVIEW, THE (RA)

WINDSOR MAGAZINE

In May 1898, in the forty-first issue of the *Windsor Magazine*, the editor described the aim of the monthly:

The whole contents of *The Windsor Magazine* are planned every month with the idea of providing as widely varied and thoroughly interesting stories and articles as can be obtained. Our aim is to cover the field of all interests and recreations, and to introduce the prominent personalities in the world of science, sport, exploration, literature and the arts. We have always tried to give first rate short stories by eminent authors, and have had the satisfaction of obtaining the highest reputation in this department. [7:665]

The *Windsor* brought to the public works by Marie Corelli, Max Pemberton, Sabine Baring-Gould, Grant Allen, Hall Caine, Rider Haggard, Bret Harte, William Dean Howells, Jack London, and Rudyard Kipling. However, more typical of the authors published in *Windsor* was Eden Phillpotts, whose "Tower of the Wild Hunter" appeared in an early issue. It was written in cockney for local color and offered the appropriate moral: Do not try to explain too much in this world, or else you will probably find yourself explained out of heaven in the next. *Windsor* was written to entertain.

The successful serialization of Guy Newell Boothby's best-known novel, *A Bid for Fortune*, led him to project these mysterious adventures of hero, heroine, and villain through many volumes. But the popularity was also due in part to the author's deference to the modesty of members of the audience; at one point he interrupted his narrative to comment discretely:

"Over the next five minutes, gentle reader, we will draw a curtain with your kind permission. If you have ever met your sweetheart after an absence of several months you will readily understand why.
When we became rational again...." [2:36]

The work of prospective writers was puffed, and forthcoming works were labeled "a thrilling story," "a strong love interest," or "a stirring narrative of love and adventure in olden times" providing "unique opportunities for making his story realistic and sensational." At the end of an 1895 article about Hall Caine—the tireless advocate for abolishing the three-volume novel—which included illustrations of him, his wife, his house, a specimen page of his manuscript, and "A Type for 'Kate' of 'The Manxman,'" appeared a note to the effect that arrangements had been made for Hall Caine's new novel to appear in *Windsor* alone.

Popular fiction was often accompanied by illustrations with additional colored frontispieces, sketches, and photographs. Literary contents shared space with such features as "How Celebrities Are Photographed" and "The Houses of Celebrated People" or a series on "Suburban London." Instant familiarity was the appeal of such articles as "Rising Stars," concerning members of Parliament and major authors; a lengthy series on art, "The See-Saw of Time," showing the oldest and youngest of monarchs, composers, and so on; and "Familiar Features of London Music." Some articles seemed to accompany the photographs, such as "Portraits of Queen Victoria's Eminent Subjects" (June 1897), which presented brief vignettes about minor authors and only one journalist, Frederick Greenwood.

The visual emphasis of the magazine was frequently related to readers' enthusiasm for royalty. "A Water Colour Drawing by Her Gracious Majesty the Queen when Princess Victoria" graced a page. Pictorial studies of Queen Victoria's great-grandchildren, the queen's tutors, the queen's visits to France and Belgium, and "At Sea with the German Emperor" proved popular.

The *Windsor* bore the subtitle *An Illustrated Monthly for Men and Women*, and its articles spanned the interests of both sexes. Pictorial articles that were meant to appeal to women included "The Art Treasures of the Provinces," "Clothes and Character," "Colours in Dress," "Children of the Times," "The Children's Orchestra," "The Romance of the Foundling Hospital," "The Evolution of Christmas Annuals," "The Dangers of Tea Drinking," and "Are Pretty Women Unpopular?" which insisted that plain women attract more interesting people than pretty women unless they have other virtues. For the men, there appeared numerous articles on sports: fishing, golf, hunting, association football, ski-running, baseball, and especially cricket, including a full page of cricketers' autographs. Historical, legal, political, and military articles were equally common, including "Winning the Victoria Cross" by Kipling, which opened the June 1897 issue. In this same issue appeared Prince Ranjit Sinhji's Message to British Boys: "Keep yourself in good condition at all times. Cultivate patience and perseverance; both qualities are necessary for doing things which are well worth the trouble. Do not be despondent at your failures and be modest in the hour of your success. Wishing you all good luck" (6:526).

Windsor sought to please a middle-class audience through an appearance of association with royalty via articles, photos, and the very name of the magazine and the drawing of Windsor Castle on the cover. Readers' interests were decidedly not scholarly; they preferred anecdotal and visual presentation of the famous and the current. Readers wanted to feel comfortable with the assurance that certain features could be counted on. For example, Anthony Hope's "Fly on the Wheel," a kind of Roundabout Paper, was for a time located before either the traditional last page of jokes or a concluding serial. Exciting romance and adventure stories were usually brief or composed of a series of short stories, but the Christmas issues in the late 1890s provided a complete novel. These issues included religious pictures, not always of the Nativity, with emphasis on the art if there was an accompanying article. Despite reader predelictions for bland, safe material that avoided such topics as religion, the magazine sought to maintain a distinct identity even to the extent that when *Pearson's Magazine*,* a competitor, developed a similar feature, *Windsor*, with its more middle-class pretensions, ceased its series of the famous talking about their favorite novels or their houses. Yet there was definite overlap, with "The Emperor of Trusts: J. Pierpont Morgan and His Career" appearing well after *Pearson's* article on American millionaires, and with Kipling's *Stalky and Company* being divided between the two periodicals.

Favoring the patriotic and nationalistic without jingoistic excess, including only a few articles on self-development, no evidence of decadence or other unwholesome fads, or any interest in the scholarly, the basic values of Britain's national heritage were encouraged but not really preached. This was a family magazine designed to entertain.

Information Sources

BIBLIOGRAPHY
Smith, Johnson. "Magazines of the Nineties." *Chambers's Journal*, 8th ser., 1 (1945):8–10.
Tye, J. R. *Periodicals of the Nineties*. Oxford, 1974.
INDEXES
    None.
REPRINT EDITIONS
    Microform: Early British Periodicals (UMI), reels 624–627.
LOCATION SOURCES
    American
    Partial runs: Widely available.
    British
    Complete runs: Bodleian Library; British Museum; Cambridge University Library; National Library of Scotland.
    Partial runs: Birmingham University Library; Dundee Public Library; Manchester Public Library.

Publication History

MAGAZINE TITLE AND TITLE CHANGES
    The Windsor Magazine: An Illustrated Monthly for Men and Women.
VOLUME AND ISSUE DATA
    Volumes 1–90, January 1895–September 1939.
FREQUENCY OF PUBLICATION
    Monthly.
PUBLISHERS
    June 1895–December 1899: Ward, Lock & Bowden/William Clowes & Sons, London. January 1900–September 1939: Ward, Lock & Bowden Ltd., London.
EDITORS
    D. Williamson, 1895–1898. A. Hutchinson, 1898–?

Barbara Quinn Schmidt

WOMAN'S WORLD, THE

In November 1886 the House of Cassell published the first number of *Lady's World*, a shilling monthly "Magazine of Fashion and Society." Sir Thomas Wemyss Reid, general manager of the House of Cassell, who conceived and designed the *Lady's World*, hoped it would appeal to women of "the highest class'' and inform them of the "Doings of Society at Home and Abroad.'' The twelve issues published under Reid's management had as their purpose to provide "a mirror of English society at the present day in its most attractive aspects'' and to describe "ladies of position, with a pictorial account of their homes and surroundings.''[1] From November 1886 through October 1887 the *Lady's World* published occasional fiction, although most of the articles, nearly all of which were unsigned, were concerned with travel, pastimes for women, society gossip, fashion, needlework, and dramatic and musical notes.

In April 1887 Reid invited Oscar Wilde to join the House of Cassell and to serve as editor for the magazine.[2] In addition to having lectured on dress reform during his American tour in 1881–1882, and during his United Kingdom tour in 1883–1885, from October 1884 through February 1885 Wilde had written sympathetic reviews of Ouida's novels and the letters of George Sand, and continued to write several articles on dress for the *Pall Mall Gazette*.[3] In his letter of acceptance, Wilde referred to the subject of dress as one that he had constantly lectured on before institutes and societies of various kinds. "But it seems to me,'' he continued, "the field of *mundus muliebris*, the field of mere millinery and trimmings, is to some extent already occupied by such papers as the *Queen* and *The Lady's Pictorial* and that we should take a wider range, as well as a high standpoint, and deal not merely with what women wear, but with what they think, and what they feel.''[4] Reid undoubtedly thought Wilde was suitably qualified because of his interest in these and other matters related to women.

The first issue of the magazine under Wilde's editorship appeared in November 1887. On the suggestion of Mrs. G. L. Craik, Wilde pointed out to the directors of the House of Cassell that the name of the magazine had "a certain taint of vulgarity about it'' and was inapplicable "to a magazine that aims at being the organ of women of intellect, culture, and position.''[5] The title was changed to the *Woman's World*, which ran under Wilde's editorship through August 1889. Cassell continued to publish the magazine, under the same title, until October 1890, probably under the editorship of Arthur Fish, who had assisted Wilde.[6]

Wilde had made it clear from the time of his acceptance of the editorship that he hoped the magazine "should be made the recognized organ for the expression of women's opinions on all subjects of literature, art, and modern life, and yet it should be a magazine that men could read with pleasure, and consider it a privilege to contribute to.''[7] Apart from his own extensive "Literary Notes,'' among the men who did contribute were Arthur Symons, Walter Crane, Oscar Browning, and Stephen Coleridge. But the articles were chiefly by women, most of whom were prominent in late Victorian literary circles and some of whom continue to command our attention. Articles were signed, unlike those that were published in the *Lady's World*. Under Wilde's editorship, the first two volumes contained poetry and fiction, as well as articles that dealt with literary, cultural, and political issues pertaining to women. Nearly all of the women who contributed to the *Woman's World*, with whom Wilde readily aligned himself, were of some variety of feminist persuasion: Amy Levy, Olive Schreiner, Lady Wilde, "Violet Fane," G. L. Craik, Marie Corelli, Mona Caird, Millicent Fawcett, Janet Hogarth, Jane Harrison, and Beatrice Crane were among them. Wilde's own literary criticism was in the form of paragraphs written, as earlier he had suggested to Reid they should be, "not from the standpoint of the scholar or the pedant, but from the standpoint of what is pleasant to read: if a book is dull let us say nothing about it, if it is bright let us review it."[8] Under the name of "The Editor," his "Literary Notes" consisted largely, although not exclusively, of reviews of books by women, or were concerned with the lives and literary activities of women.

By April 1889 Wilde had plans to leave the House of Cassell in August of that year, and after June 1889 he offered no further contributions.[9] He continued to hope that the magazine would be the "first woman's paper in England" although other matters diverted his attention. Nonetheless, the remaining issues conformed to his plan to "let dress have the end of the magazine; literature, art, travel and social studies the beginning."[10] Wilde himself no longer contributed literary notes and quietly withdrew from the magazine until the *Woman's World* itself was brought quietly to an end in the autumn of 1890.

In contrast to the *English Women's Review*, which was concerned chiefly with political and economic issues, and to the *Lady's Pictorial*, which was concerned chiefly with fashion, the *Woman's World* marked a singular departure from more narrowly conceived women's magazines. Under Wilde's editorship it exemplified and helped to shape the varied concerns and opinions of women at the turn of the century.

Notes

1. H. Montgomery Hyde, *Oscar Wilde: A Biography* (New York, 1975), p. 108; see also Simon Nowell-Smith, *The House of Cassell* (London, 1958), pp. 147–48.

2. Hyde, p. 108.

3. Stuart Mason, *A Bibliography of Oscar Wilde* (London, 1967), pp. 127–30.

4. Oscar Wilde, *The Letters of Oscar Wilde*, ed. Rupert Hart-Davis (London, 1962), p. 194.

5. *Letters*, p. 203; Mrs. Craik, born Dinah Mullock, was the author of the best-selling novel *John Halifax Gentleman*, which was first published serially in the *Woman's World*. See Hyde, pp. 109–10.

6. Nowell-Smith, p. 151; Hyde, p. 115.

7. *Letters*, p. 195; Nowell-Smith, pp. 148–52, 253–59.

8. *Letters*, p. 195.

9. Ibid., p. 242.

10. Ibid., p. 196.

Information Sources

BIBLIOGRAPHY

Hyde, H. Montgomery. *Oscar Wilde, A Biography*. New York, 1975.
Mason, Stuart. *A Bibliography of Oscar Wilde*. London, 1967.
Nowell-Smith, Simon. *The House of Cassell*. London, 1958.

Pearson, Hesketh. *Oscar Wilde, His Life and Wit*. New York, 1946.
Wilde, Oscar. *The Letters of Oscar Wilde*. Edited by Rupert Hart-Davis. London, 1962.
INDEXES
   List of contents at beginning of each bound volume.
REPRINT EDITIONS
   Volume 1, 1898.
LOCATION SOURCES
American
   Complete runs: Boston Public Library; Harvard University Library; Henry E.
   Huntington Library; Iowa State Traveling Library; University of Illinois Library;
   University of Minnesota Library.
   Partial runs: Carnegie Library of Pittsburgh; New York Public Library; Trinity
   College, Watkinson Library; U. S. Library of Congress; University of Michigan
   Library; Western Reserve Historical Society; Yale University Library.
British
   Complete runs: Bodleian Library; British Museum; National Library of Scotland;
   Victoria and Albert Museum Library.
   Partial run: Birmingham Public Library.

Publication History

MAGAZINE TITLE AND TITLE CHANGES
   The Lady's World. A Magazine of Fashion and Society, November 1886–October
   1887. *The Woman's World*, November 1887–October 1890.
VOLUME AND ISSUE DATA
   Volumes 1–12, November 1886–October 1887 (*The Lady's World*). Volumes 1–
   3, November 1887–October 1890 (*The Woman's World*).
FREQUENCY OF PUBLICATION
   Monthly.
PUBLISHER
   Cassell & Co. Ltd., London.
EDITORS
   Anonymous (no name indicated on title page, but probably Sir Wemyss Reid),
   volume 1, numbers 1–15, November 1886–March 1887. Oscar Wilde, volume 1,
   numbers 6–12–volume 2, numbers 1–10, April 1887–August 1889. Anonymous
   (no name indicated on title page, but probably Arthur Fish), volume 2, numbers
   11–12–volume 3, numbers 1–12, September 1889–October 1890.

                                                        Sandra F. Siegel

Y

YELLOW BOOK, THE

The seed of what became the *Yellow Book* was sown during a conversation in early 1894 between Henry Harland, an American-born literary man in his early thirties, and Aubrey Beardsley, an artist in his early twenties who had already attracted attention with his disturbing illustrations for the English edition of Oscar Wilde's exotic *Salomé*. They decided that the appropriate publisher for the high-quality illustrated quarterly they had in mind would be John Lane, whose firm at the sign of the Bodley Head in Vigo Street had become a leading publisher of the emerging writers of the 1890s. Lane agreed to publish the new journal, and some key decisions were soon made: Harland would be the literary editor; Beardsley the art editor; Henry James would be asked to contribute; Oscar Wilde, whose notoriety was increasing, would not be.

The *Yellow Book* was to be a new kind of journal. Each volume would be book length (around three-hundred pages), expensively produced, and printed in hardcover. To quote from the March 1894 "Announcement," the aim was "to provide an Illustrated Magazine which shall be beautiful as a piece of bookmaking, modern and distinguished in its letter-press and its pictures, and withal popular in the better sense of the word. It is felt that such a Magazine, at present, is conspicious by its absence." Contributors would be given a "freer hand" than was permitted by other periodicals. The *Yellow Book* "will be charming, it will be daring, it will be distinguished." And while the journal will seek always "to preserve a delicate, decorous, and reticent mien and conduct, it will at the same time have the courage of its modernness, and not tremble at the frown of Mrs. Grundy."[1]

Modernity and freedom from conventional restrictions would be visually emphasized on the cover by Beardsley's illustrations and by the bright yellow on which they were printed. This color was à la mode, associated with the *livres jaunes* from France—naturalist novels or works like Huysmans's *A Rebours*, "the yellow book" taken up at one point by the title character in Wilde's 1891 novel, *The Picture of Dorian Gray*: "It was the strangest book that he had ever read. It seemed to him that in exquisite raiment ... the sins of the world were passing in dumb show before him. . . . It was a poisonous book. The heavy odour of the incense seemed to cling about its pages and to trouble the brain."[2]

The first volume appeared in April 1894. Like the next three volumes, the issue provoked intemperate reactions. The *Times* called it "a combination of English randiness with French lubricity"; the *Westminster Gazette* asked for "an Act of Parliament to make this kind of thing illegal."[3] From the viewpoint of the late twentieth century it is as difficult to see what the initial fuss was about as it is to understand why the *Yellow Book* has been considered the quintessence of the decadence, aestheticism, and *fin de siècle* temperament of the 1890s.[4] An examination of the contents of the periodical's first issue, rather, corroborates Frank Kermode's observation that what seems most striking about the *Yellow Book* "is the staidness of what lay behind that decadent cover."[5]

One of the volume's nine illustrators was Sir Frederick Leighton, president of the Royal Academy and pillar of the art establishment; one of the verse contributions was by A. C. Benson, a schoolmaster at Eton. Henry James's "The Death of the Lion," a tale of the literary life, took up most of the journal's first fifty pages, and other prose contributions were by such eminently respectable figures as George Saintsbury, Edmund Gosse, and Arthur Waugh, who was represented by a spirited defense of "Reticence in Literature." It is true that Arthur Symons's poem "Stella Maris" described (albeit obliquely) the speaker's encounter with a prostitute, "the Juliet of a night" (1:129); that in his *jeu d'esprit*, "A Defence of Cosmetics" (1:65), the young Max Beerbohm argued that a new epoch of artifice was beginning ("The Victorian era comes to its end and the day of sancta simplicitas is quite ended"); and that the close of Ella D'Arcy's love story was demoralizing. But the only real exception to the description of the first issue as "a remarkably innocuous production. . . .the general tone is pale, mild and refined"[6] is Beardsley's illustrations. Among them is "L'Education Sentimentale," "one of his most perfect drawings," as Kenneth Clark has noted, in which a repellent older prostitute "is adding to the corruption, already manifest, of the young woman, who receives her advice with complacent foreknowledge."[7]

Beardsley's illustrations were among the high points of the next three issues, in which also appeared work by an appreciable number of female contributors, and of such figures of the 1890s as Symons, Beerbohm, Lionel Johnson, Ernest Dowson, John Davidson, William Watson, Richard Le Gallienne, and Theodore Wratislaw. But Beardsley's association with the journal ceased abruptly between the appearance of its fourth and fifth issues, a critical time in the brief history of the *Yellow Book*. The editors and the publisher had been careful to dissociate the *Yellow Book* from the reputation of Oscar Wilde. But when arrested after the failure of his libel action against the Marquis of Queensberry, Wilde was carrying a French novel, the yellow cover of which was mistaken for the periodical. A mob attacked the Bodley Head offices on Vigo Street and some contributors threatened to sever connection with the journal unless Beardsley (linked in the public mind with Wilde) was dismissed. Beardsley was not only dismissed; his illustrations for the journal's fifth issue, then in press, were removed at the eleventh hour. Mrs. Grundy had frowned, and the *Yellow Book* had not only trembled; as a contemporary observer remarked, it had "turned gray in a single night."[8]

Nine more issues were produced before the periodical ceased publication in April 1897, by which time it had ceased to pay dividends to the publishers. During its last two years the journal became more completely what it had always been: not an avant garde publication, but an expensive (five shillings an issue) literary and artistic quarterly for the carriage trade. A better example of the distinctive literary mood of the 1890s would be the *Savoy,** which began in January 1896 as a reaction to the graying of the *Yellow Book* and which during its eight months of existence was edited by Arthur Symons and featured Beardsley's drawings.

During its life span, the *Yellow Book* published the work of 106 artists and 138 writers. The latter included, in addition to those already mentioned, Maurice Baring (who contributed an early appreciation of Anatole France), Evelyn Sharp, Baron Corvo, George Gissing, H. G. Wells, Kenneth Grahame, John Buchan, Evelyn Nesbit, and (in its last issue) W. B. Yeats. But many of the contributions, particularly after the fifth volume, were by undistinguished writers in Harland's circle. The *Yellow Book* could be used to substantiate Frank Kermode's observation that the 1890s "were not a good time for literature, though great things were to grow out of them."[9] One might similarly say that the verse published in its pages recalls Yeats's observation about the poets of the 1890s: "The only thing certain about us is that we are too many."[10]

Its dual interest in art and literature marked the *Yellow Book* as a descendant of the *Germ** (1850), the Pre-Raphaelites' short-lived journal. Of the periodicals written exclusively for those interested in the arts, the *Yellow Book* was among the first to attempt to reach a comparatively large audience. It was an influence on the founding of the *Savoy* and on periodicals like the *Dome.** But perhaps its chief influence was symbolic: when Wyndham Lewis's *Blast** (see *MA*) was begun just before World War I its purpose was described as comprehending the "artistic movement" of its decade just as the *Yellow Book* had done of the 1890s. And in 1935, when John Lehmann began his *New Writing** (see *MA*), he called it the "*Yellow Book* of the thirties."[11]

Notes

1. Quoted in Katherine Lyon Mix, *A Study in Yellow: "The Yellow Book" and Its Contributors* (Lawrence, Kans., 1960), pp. 77–78.

2. Oscar Wilde, *Plays, Prose Writing and Poems* (London, 1930), p. 173.

3. Mix, p. 88.

4. See Stanley Weintraub, ed., *"The Yellow Book": Quintessence of the Nineties* (Garden City, N.Y., 1964).

5. Frank Kermode, "Mislabeled Decadent" (review of Weintraub, ed., *The Yellow Book*"), *New York Times Book Review*, 25 October 1964, p. 22.

6. David Cecil, *Max: A Biography* (Boston, 1965), p. 98.

7. Kenneth Clark, ed., *The Best of Aubrey Beardsley* (New York, 1979), p. 106.

8. Quoted in Mix, p. 147.

9. Kermode, p. 26.

10. *The Trembling of the Veil*, in *The Autobiography of W.B. Yeats* (Garden City, N.Y., 1958), p. 115.

11. Cited in Mix, p. 280.

Information Sources

BIBLIOGRAPHY

Farmer, Albert J. *Le Mouvement esthétique et "décadent" en Angleterre (1873–1900)*. Paris, 1931.

Mix, Katherine Lyon. *A Study in Yellow: "The Yellow Book" and Its Contributors*. Lawrence, Kans., 1960.

Weintraub, Stanley, ed. *"The Yellow Book": Quintessence of the Nineties*. Garden City, N.Y., 1964.

INDEXES

None.

REPRINT EDITIONS

AMS Press, New York. Arno Press, New York, 1968. *The Yellow Book*, ed. Stanley Weintraub, New York, 1964.

Microform: AMS Press, New York. English Literary Periodicals (UMI), reels 894–895.

LOCATION SOURCES

American

Widely available.

British

Widely available.

Publication History

MAGAZINE TITLE AND TITLE CHANGES

The Yellow Book. An Illustrated Quarterly, April 1894–April 1897.

VOLUME AND ISSUE DATA

Volumes 1–13, April 1894–April 1897.

FREQUENCY OF PUBLICATION

Quarterly.

PUBLISHERS

Volumes 1–2, April–July 1894: Elkin Mathew & John Lane, London/Copeland & Day, Boston. Volumes 3–10, October 1894–July 1896: John Lane, The Bodley Head, Vigo Street, London/Copeland & Day, Boston. Volumes 11–13, July 1896–April 1897: John Lane, The Bodley Head, London/New York.

EDITOR

Henry Harland. Aubrey Beardsley was art editor for volumes 1–4.

Kerry McSweeney

Titles Included in
The Augustan Age and the
Age of Johnson,
1698–1788

Aberdeen Magazine, Literary Chronicle and Review, The, 1788–91
Adventurer, The, 1752–54
Analytical Review, The, 1788–99
Babler, The, 1763–67
Bee, The, 1759
Bristol and Bath Magazine, The, 1782–83˙
British Champion, The, 1742–43. See *Champion, The*
British Magazine, The, 1746–51
British Magazine, The, 1760–67
Busy Body, The, 1759
Censor, The, 1715–17
Champion (or Evening Advertiser), The, 1739–43
Common Sense: or, the Englishman's Journal, 1737–43
Connoisseur, The, 1754–56
Country Journal; or the Craftsman, The, 1727–50. See *Craftsman, The*
Court and City Magazine, The, 1763. See *Court Magazine, The*
Court, City, and Country Magazine, The, 1764–65. See *Court Magazine, The*
Court Magazine, The, 1761–65
Court Miscellany, The, 1765–71
Covent Garden Journal, The, 1752
Craftsman, The, 1726–50
Critical Review (or Annals of Literature), The, 1756–1817
Critick, The, 1718
Delights for the Ingenious, 1711
Drury Lane Journal, The, 1752. See *Have At You All*
Edinburgh Magazine, or Literary Amusement, The, 1779–82. See *Weekly Magazine, The*
Edinburgh Magazine, or Literary Miscellany, The, 1785–1803
Edinburgh Magazine and Review, The, 1773–76

Parentheses indicate that the additional title appeared only during part of the run of the magazine.

Edinburgh Weekly Magazine, The, 1783–84, See *Weekly Magazine, The*

Englishman, The, 1713–15

English Review (or An Abstract etc.) *(of Literature, Science*, etc.*), The*, 1784–96

European Magazine, The, 1782–1826

Examiner (or Remarks upon Papers etc.*), The*, 1710–14

Female Spectator, The, 1744–46

Free-Holder, The, 1715–16

Freethinker, The, 1718–21

General Magazine and Impartial Review, The, 1787–92

Gentleman's Magazine (or Monthly Intelligencer) (and Historical Chronicle) (and His-torical Review), The, 1731–1907

Gray's Inn Journal, The, 1752–54

Grub-Street Journal, The, 1730–37

Guardian, The, 1713

Have At You All, 1752

Hibernian Magazine, The, 1771–1811

History of the Works of the Learned, The, 1737–43

Idler, The, 1758–60

Imperial Magazine, The, 1760–62

Intelligencer, The, 1728–29

Jacobite's Journal, The, 1747–48

Ladies Magazine, or, the Universal Entertainer, The, 1749–53

Lady's Magazine, The, 1770–1819

Literary and Antigallican Magazine, The, 1756–58. See *Literary Magazine, The*

Literary Journal, A, 1744-49

Literary Journal or a continuation of the Memoirs of Literature, A, 1730–31

Literary Magazine; or the History of the Works of the Learned, The, 1736–37. See *History of the Works of the Learned, The*

Literary Magazine; or, Universal Review, The, 1756–58

London Magazine, The, 1732–85

London Magazine, The, 1791. See *New London Magazine, The*

London Review of English and Foreign Literature, The, 1775–80

London Spy, The, 1698–1700

Lounger, The, 1785–87

Lounger's Miscellany, The, 1788–89

Memoirs for the Curious, 1709. See *Monthly Miscellany, The*

Memoirs of Literature, 1710–17

Midwife, The, 1750–52/53

Monthly Miscellany: or, Memoirs for the Curious, The, 1707–9

Monthly Review (or Literary Journal) (or New Literary Journal), The, 1749–1844

Muses Mercury, The, 1707–8

Museum, The, 1746–47

New Lady's Magazine, The, 1786–97

New London Magazine, The, 1785–97

New Novelist's Magazine, The, 1786–88

New Review, A, 1783–86

Northern Gazette, Literary Chronicle, and Review, The, 1707. See *Aberdeen Magazine, The*

Novelist's Magazine, The, 1780–89

Olla Podrida, The, 1787–88
Oxford Magazine, 1768–76
Payne's Universal Chronicle, or Weekly Gazette, 1758. See *Idler, The*
Plain Dealer, The, 1724–25
Present State of the Republick of Letters, The, 1728–36
Prompter, The, 1734–36
Rambler, The, 1750–52
Reformer, The, 1748
Review (of the Affairs of France) (of the State of the English Nation), 1704–13
St. James's Magazine (or Literary Chronicle) (or the Literary Transactions of Europe), The, 1762–64
Scots Magazine (Containing a General View etc.) *(or General Repository* etc.) *(and Edinburgh Literary Miscellany), The*, 1739–1817
Sentimental Magazine, The, 1773–77
Spectator, The, 1711–15
Student, The, 1750–51
Tatler, The, 1709–11
Templar, and Literary Gazette, The, 1773
Town and Country Magazine, The, 1769–95
True Patriot, The, 1745–46
Universal Chronical, 1758–60. See *Idler, The*
Universal Magazine (of Knowledge and Pleasure) (or Miscellany of Historical etc.), *The*, 1747–1815
Universal Museum (or Gentlemen's and Ladies' Polite Magazine) (and Complete Magazine of Knowledge and Pleasure), The, 1762–72
Universal Spectator and Weekly Journal, The, 1728–46
Universal Visiter, and Memorialist, The, 1756
Walker's Hibernian Magazine, 1786–1811. See *Hibernian Magazine, The*
Weekly Magazine, or Edinburgh Amusement, The, 1768–84
Weekly Review of the Affairs of France, A, 1704. See *Review*
Westminster Magazine, The, 1773–85
Wit's Magazine, The, 1784–85
World, The, 1753–56

Titles Included in
The Romantic Age,
1789–1836

Album, The, 1822–25

Annals of the Fine Arts, 1816–20

Anti-Jacobin Review (and True Churchmen's Magazine) (and Protestant Advocate), The, 1797–1821

Athenaeum and (London) Literary Chronicle, The, 1828–1921

Augustan Review, The, 1815–16

Beau Monde, Le, 1806–10

Bee, The, 1790–94

Belle Assemblée, La, 1806–37

Blackwood's Edinburgh Magazine, 1817–1980. See also *MA*

British and Foreign Review, The, 1835–44

British Critic, The, 1793–1843

British Lady's Magazine, The, 1815–19

British Magazine, The, 1830

British Review and London Critical Journal, The, 1811–25

Cabinet, The, 1807–9

Cabinet Magazine, or Literary Olio, The, 1796–97

Cambrian (and Caledonian) Quarterly Magazine (and Celtic Repertory), The, 1829–33

Chambers's Edinburgh Journal, 1832–53. See *Chambers's Journal*

Chambers's Journal, 1832–1956

Champion (and Sunday Review etc.*), The,* 1813–22

Companion, The, 1828

Country Literary Chronicle, 1820–24. See *Literary Chronicle and Weekly Review, The*

Court Magazine and Belle Assemblée, The, 1832–37. See *Belle Assemblée, La*

Director, The, 1807

Drakard's Paper, 1813. See *Champion, The*

Dublin Literary Gazette, The, 1830–31

Dublin Review, The, 1836–1969

Parentheses indicate that the additional title appeared only during part of the run of the magazine.

Dublin University Magazine, The, 1833–77
Eclectic Review, The, 1805–68
Edinburgh Magazine and Literary Miscellany, The, 1817–26
Edinburgh Monthly Magazine, The, 1817. See *Blackwood's Edinburgh Magazine*
Edinburgh Monthly Review, The, 1819–23
Edinburgh Review, The, 1802–1929
Englishman's Magazine, The, 1831
Examiner (and London Review), The, 1808–81
Foreign Quarterly Review, The, 1827–46
Fraser's Literary Chronicle, 1835–36
Fraser's Magazine for Town and Country, 1830–82
Gossip, The, 1821
Honeycomb, 1820
Imperial Magazine, The, 1819–34
Imperial Review, The, 1804–5
Indicator, The, 1819–21
Inquirer, or Literary Miscellany, The, 1814–15
Investigator (or Quarterly Magazine), The, 1820-24
Investigator, The, 1822. See *Champion, The*
John Bull, 1820–92
Journal of the Royal Institution of Great Britain, The, 1830–31. See *Quarterly Journal of Science, Literature, and the Arts, The*
Knight's Quarterly Magazine, 1823–25
Leigh Hunt's (London) Journal 1834–51
Liberal, The, 1822–23
Literary and Statistical Magazine for Scotland, The, 1817–22
Literary Chronicle and Weekly Review, The, 1819–28
Literary Examiner, The, 1823
Literary Gazette, The, 1817–63
Literary Gossip, The, 1821–22. See *Gossip, The*
Literary Guardian, The, 1831–32
Literary Journal, The, 1803–6
Literary Journal and General Miscellany, The, 1818–19
Literary Magnet, The, 1824–28
Literary Museum, The, 1822–24
Literary Panorama, The, 1806–19
Literary Sketch-Book, The, 1823–24
Literary Speculum, The, 1821–23
Loiterer, The, 1789–90
London and Westminster Review, The, 1836–40. See *Westminster Review, The*
London Magazine, The, 1791. See *New London Magazine, The (AAAJ)*
London Magazine, The, 1820–29
London Museum, The, 1822–23. See *Literary Museum, The*
London Quarterly Review, The, 1834–83. See *Quarterly Review, The*
London Review, The, 1809
London Review, The, 1835–36. See *Westminster Review, The*
McKay's New British Lady's Magazine, 1817–19. See *British Lady's Magazine, The*
Metropolitan Magazine, The, 1831–50

Titles Included in
The Victorian and
Edwardian Age,
1837–1913

Academy, The, 1869–1916
Academy and Literature, The, 1902, 1910, 1914. See *Academy, The*
Ainsworth's Magazine, 1842–54
All the Year Round, 1859–95
Anglo Saxon Review, 1899–1901
Arrow, The, 1906–9
Art and Poetry, 1850. See *Germ, The*
Author, The, 1890–
Belgravia, 1866–99
Bentley's Miscellany, 1837–68
Blue Review, The, 1913
Bookman, The, 1891–1934
Bookseller, The, 1858–
British Review and National Observer, The, 1897. See *Scots Observer, The*
Cambridge Review, The, 1879–
Cambridge University Magazine, The, 1839–43
Century Guild Hobby Horse, The, 1884–92. See *Hobby Horse, The*
Chambers's Journal, 1832–1956. See *Chambers's Journal (RA)*
Chambers's Journal of Popular Literature, Science and the Arts, 1854–57. See *Chambers's Journal (RA)*
Chambers's London Journal, 1841–43
Chapbook, The, 1913–14; 1919–25
Christian Teacher, The, 1835–44. See *Prospective Review, The*
Contemporary Review, The, 1866–. See also *MA*
Cornhill Magazine, The, 1860–1975. See also *MA*
Cosmopolis, 1896–98
Court Magazine and Monthly Critic, 1838–47
Critic, The, 1843–63

Parentheses indicate that the additional title appeared only during part of the run of the magazine.

Critic: (The London Literary Journal), The, 1850–58. See *Critic, The*
Critic; (A) Weekly Journal of Literature, Art, Science, and the Drama, The, 1858–59.
  See *Critic, The*
Critic of Books [etc.], *The*, 1848–50. See *Critic, The*
Critic of Literature, Art, Science, and the Drama, The, 1843–44. See *Critic, The*
Dana, 1904–5
Dickensian, The, 1905–
Dome, The, 1897–1900
Douglas Jerrold's Shilling Magazine, 1845–48
English Association Bulletin, 1907–35. See *English (MA)*
English Review, The, 1908–37
Examiner and London Review, The, 1869–70. See *Examiner, The* (1808) (RA)
Fortnightly (Review), The, 1865–1954. See also *MA*
Fun, 1861–1901
Germ, The, 1850
Golden Hynde, The, 1913–14
Good Words, 1860–1911
Granta, The, 1889–
Green Sheaf, The, 1903–4
Hobby Horse, The, 1884–94
Hood's Magazine, 1884–49
Household Words, 1850–59
Idler, The, 1892–1911
Lady's World, The, 1886–87. See *Woman's World, The*
Leader, The, 1850–60
Leader and Saturday Analyst, The, 1860. See *Leader, The*
Leigh Hunt's Journal, 1850–51. See *Leigh Hunt's (London) Journal (RA)*
Library, The, 1889–
Literary Guide (and Rationalist Review), 1885–
Literature, 1897–1902
London and Edinburgh Weekly Review, 1865–66. See *Weekly Review*
London Quarterly and Holborn Review, The, 1853–1968
London Review, The, 1850. See *Mirror of Literature . . . , The (RA)*
Longman's Magazine, 1882–1905
Macmillan's Magazine, 1859–1907
Mirror Monthly Magazine, The, 1847–49. See *Mirror of Literature . . . , The (RA)*
Month, The, 1864–
Monthly Chapbook, The, 1919. See *Chapbook, The*
Monthly Chronicle, The, 1838–41
Monthly Review, The, 1900–1907
National Observer, 1890–97. See *Scots Observer, The*
National Review, 1855–64
National Review, 1883–1960
New Age, The, 1894–1938
New Freewoman, 1913. See *Egoist, The (MA)*
New Quarterly Review, 1852–62
New Review, The, 1889–97
New Statesman (and Nation), 1913–
Nineteenth Century, The, 1877–1900

North British Review, The, 1844–71
Notes and Queries, 1849–1981
Novel Review, The, 1892. See *Tinsley's Magazine*
Once a Week, 1859–80
Open Window, 1910–11
Oxford and Cambridge Magazine, The, 1856
Pageant, The, 1896–97
Pall Mall Magazine, 1893–1914
Pearson's Magazine, 1896–1939
Poetical Gazette, 1909–12. See *Poetry Review, The*
Poetry and Drama, 1913-14. See *Chapbook, The*
Poetry Review, The, 1909–
Prospective Review, The, 1845–55
Punch, 1841–
Quiver, The, 1861–1926
Rambler, The, 1848–62
Reader, The, 1863–67
Review of Reviews, The, 1890–1953
Rhythm, 1911–13
St. Martin's Review (in-the-Field Monthly) (Messenger), 1890–
Saint Paul's (Magazine), 1867–74
Samhain, 1901–8
Saturday Analyst and Leader, The, 1860. See *Leader, The*
Saturday Review, The, 1855–1938
Savoy, The, 1896
Scots Observer, The, 1888–97
Sharpe's London Magazine, 1845–70
Shilling Magazine, 1845–48. See *Douglas Jerrold's Shilling Magazine*
Strand Magazine, The, 1891–1950
Symposium, The, 1839–41. See *Cambridge University Magazine, The*
Temple Bar, 1860–1906
Thrush, 1901–2; 1909–10
Tinsley's Magazine, 1867–92
To-Day, 1893–1905; 1916–23
T.P.'s Weekly, 1902–16. See *To-Day*
Tripod, The, 1912–13
Truth, 1877–1957
Universal Review, The, 1888–90
Vanity Fair, 1868–1928
Victoria Magazine, The, 1863–80
Wales, 1911–14
Watt's Literary Guide, 1887–94. See *Literary Guide*
Westminster and Foreign Quarterly Review, The, 1846–51. See *Westminster Review, The (RA)*
Windsor Magazine, 1895–1939
Woman's World, The, 1886–90
Yellow Book, The, 1894–97

Titles Included in
The Modern Age,
1914–1984

Adam. International Review, 1929–
Adelphi, The, 1923–
Agenda, 1959–
Akros. Poetry Magazine, 1965–83
Anglo-Welsh Review, 1949–
Arena. A Literary Magazine, 1949–52
Art & Letters: An Illustrated Quarterly, 1917–20
Athenaeum, 1921–31. See *Nation and Athenaeum*
Aylesford Review, 1955–
Bell: A Survey of Irish Life, The, 1940–54
Bermondsey Book, The, 1923–30
Black Art, 1962–64
Blackfriars: A Monthly Review, 1913–
Blackwood's Edinburgh Magazine (April 1817)–December 1980
Blast. A Review of the Great English Vortex, 1914–15
British Museum Quarterly, 1926–
British Museum Yearbook, 1976–. See *British Museum Quarterly*
Calendar, The. A Quarterly Review, 1926–27. See *Calendar of Modern Letters, The*
Calendar (of Modern Letters), The, 1925–27
Cambridge Journal, The, 1947–54
Catholic Review, The, 1913–18. See *Blackfriars*
Colonnade: A Journal of Literature and the Arts, 1953–56. See *Adam. International Review*
Contemporary Poetry & Prose, 1936–37
Contemporary Review, The (1866)–
Cornhill Magazine (1860)–1975
Coterie, 1919–27
Criterion, The. A Quarterly Review, 1922–39

Parentheses around a date indicate inclusion in early volume. Parentheses around part of a title indicate that the wording appeared only during part of the run of the magazine.

Critical Quarterly, The, 1959–
Decachord; a Magazine for Students & Lovers of Poetry, The, 1924–46
Dock Leaves, 1949–57. See *Anglo-Welsh Review*
Drama, 1919–
Dublin Magazine; a Quarterly Review of Literature, Science, and Art, The, 1923–58
Egoist, The, 1914–19
Encore. The Voice of Vital Theatre, 1954–65
Encounter, 1953–
Enemy, a Review of Art and Literature, The, 1927–29
English, 1936–
English Association Bulletin, 1907–35. See *English*
Enquiry, 1948–50
European Quarterly. A Review of Modern Literature, Art and Life, 1934–35
Experiment, 1928–31
Folios of New Writing, 1940–41. See *New Writing*
Fortnightly (Review), The (1865)–1954
Gambit. (An) International (Theatre Review), 1963–
Gangrel; Literature, Poetry, Music, Philosophy, 1945–46
Golden Hind, a Quarterly Magazine of Art and Literature, The, 1922–24
Horizon, A Review of Literature and Art, 1940–49
Humanist, 1956–71. See *Literary Guide* (VEA)
Interim Drama, 1945–46. See *Drama*
Kingdom Come. The Magazine of War-Time Oxford, 1939–43
Left Review, The, 1934–38
Life and Letters (Today) (and The London Mercury and Bookman), 1928–50
Life of the Spirit, The, 1944–. See *Blackfriars*
Lilliput. The Pocket Magazine for Everyone, 1937–60
Lines. New Poetry, Scotland, 1952–53. See *Lines (Review)*
Lines (Review), 1952–
Listener, The, 1929–
London Aphrodite, The, 1928–29
London (Gallery) Bulletin, 1938–40
London Magazine, a Monthly Review of Literature, The, 1954–61
London Mercury, The, 1919–39
London Mercury and Bookman, The, 1939–50. See *Life and Letters (Today)*
Longman's Miscellany. A Collection of Poetry, Short Stories, etc., 1945–
Lovat Dickson's Magazine, 1933–35
Mandrake. A Miscellany of Prose and Verse, 1945–
Mint, The. A Miscellany of Literature, Art and Criticism, 1946–48
Monthly Criterion, The, 1927–28. See *Criterion, The. A Quarterly Review*
Nation and (the) Athenaeum, The, 1921–31
National and English Review, The, 1950–60. See *National Review* (1883) (VEA)
New Adelphi, The, 1927–30. See *Adelphi, The*
New Blackfriars, 1964–. See *Blackfriars*
New Coterie, A Quarterly of Literature and Art, 1925–27. See *Coterie*
New Criterion, The, 1926–27. See *Criterion, The. A Quarterly Review*
New Departures, 1959–
New English Weekly (and the New Age), The, 1932–49
New Humanist, The, 1972–. See *Literary Guide* (VEA)

Time and Tide (John O'London's) (Business World) (Business Guide), 1920–79
Townsman. A Quarterly Review, 1938–44
Trace, A Chronicle of Living Literature, 1952–70
Transatlantic Review, The, 1924
Twentieth Century, 1951–. See *Nineteenth Century and After, The*
Twentieth Century Verse, 1937–39
Universities' Poetry, 1958–63
VE-(VJ-)Time Drama, 1945. See *Drama*
Voices: In Poetry and Prose, 1919–21
Wales, 1937
War-time Drama, 1939–45. See *Drama*
Wave. New Poetry, 1970
Wheels, 1916–21
Wind and The Rain, The, 1941–51
Windmill, 1944–48
Winter Owl, The, 1923. See *Owl, The*
Workshop (New Poetry), 1967–81
World Review of Reviews, 1936–53. See *Review of Reviews, The* (VEA)
Writer's Workshop, 1967. See *Workshop*
Writing Today, 1957–
X. A Quarterly Review, 1959–62

A Chronology of Social and Literary Events and British Literary Magazines, 1837–1913

BRITISH LITERARY PERIODICALS	YEAR	SOCIAL & LITERARY EVENTS
	1837	
Richard Bentley begins his *Miscellany*; Dickens is the first editor (–1839).		William IV, last Hanoverian, dies; Victoria becomes queen (–1901).
		Swinburne, Mary Elizabeth Braddon are born.
		Thomas Carlyle publishes *The French Revolution*.
		Samuel Morse invents the telegraph.
	1839	
W.M.W. Call edits the *Cambridge University Magazine* and frequently contributes.		First Opium War (–1842) breaks out between Britain and China.
		John Galt, W. M. Praed die; Walter Pater is born.
		Moritz Jacobi invents electrotyping for relief printing.
	1840	
Bentley's Miscellany publishes "The Fall of the House of Usher" anonymously.		Queen Victoria marries Prince Albert.
		Botanical Gardens at Kew open.

BRITISH LITERARY PERIODICALS	YEAR	SOCIAL & LITERARY EVENTS
	(1840)	
Dickens publishes *The Old Curiosity Shop* in *Master Humphry's Clock*. George Henry Lewes begins to publish a nineteen-year span of critical essays in the *Westminster Review*.		Penny postage is developed in Britain. Beau Brummel, Fanny Burney die; Thomas Hardy and John Addington Symonds are born.
	1841	
Punch begins its historic run as the prototypical humor magazine. *Chambers's London Journal* is established to appeal to readers of popular fiction.		Sir Robert Peel becomes prime minister. Edward VII is born. Britain assumes sovereignty over Hong Kong.
	1842	
Popular novelist William Harrison Ainsworth and illustrator George Cruikshank begin *Ainsworth's*, one of the most popular illustrated Victorian magazines.		Riots and strikes break out over industrial Northern England.
	1843	
Four hundred ministers leave the Church of England to found the "Free Kirk" and the next year the *North British Review*, an organ "liberal in politics" (unlike the *Quarterly Review*) and "Christian in tone" (unlike the *Edinburgh Review*). Thomas Hood leaves the *New Monthly* in a dispute over editorial control and begins *Hood's Magazine*.		Dickens publishes *Martin Chuzzlewit* and *A Christmas Carol*. Ruskin begins *Modern Painters* (−1860). Wordsworth is made Poet Laureate. Henry James is born; Robert Southey dies.

BRITISH LITERARY PERIODICALS	YEAR	SOCIAL & LITERARY EVENTS
	1845	
Sharpe's London Magazine, established as a rival to Chambers's London Journal, features woodcuts and popular fiction by Frank Smedley and Alfred Cole.		Revolt against British rule in New Zealand.
		First cable spans the English Channel.
The Unitarian Christian Teacher becomes the Prospective Review to "prevent the cause of liberal theology from slipping into the rut of any Unitarian or any other sect" and includes more literary reviews.		First photographic portraits are made.
	1846	
W. J. Thoms begins a column on folklore in the Athenaeum and encourages readers to contribute; its popularity leads to Notes and Queries three years later.		Evangelical Alliance is formed in London.
The Mirror is transformed under Percy St. John from a miscellany of reprints to a magazine of original popular features.		
	1847	
		Charlotte Brontë publishes Jane Eyre, Emily Brontë Wuthering Heights, Tennyson The Princess, and Thackeray the first parts of Vanity Fair.
	1848	
		The Pre-Raphaelite Brotherhood is formed to overthrow the conventions of the Royal Academy; members include William M. and Dante G. Rossetti, William Holman Hunt, John Everett Millais, Frederic George Stephens.

BRITISH LITERARY PERIODICALS	*YEAR*	*SOCIAL & LITERARY EVENTS*
	1849	

Thornton Hunt begins the *Leader* as an organ for radicalism. George H. Lewes, as literary editor, makes "realism" a valid concept in literary criticism.

Dickens publishes the first parts of *David Copperfield*, Arnold *The Strayed Reveller*, Ruskin *Seven Lamps of Architecture*.

1850

The Pre-Raphaelite Brotherhood begins the *Germ* with William M. Rossetti as editor. Rossetti also becomes art critic for the *Critic*.

Dickens begins *Household Words*.

A. C. Fraser assumes the editorship of the *North British Review* and tries to attract major literary figures, but loses to the better-paying *Quarterly* and *Edinburgh Reviews*.

Leigh Hunt begins his one-man *London Journal* in imitation of *Chambers's* but "with a character a little more southern and literary" and an appeal to readers "of all classes." In the first issue he recommends Tennyson for the laureateship.

Robert Louis Stevenson is born; Wordsworth dies; *The Prelude* is published posthumously.

Tennyson becomes Poet Laureate, publishes *In Memoriam*.

Elizabeth B. Browning publishes *Sonnets from the Portuguese*.

1851

Tenniel's cartoons appear in *Punch*.

The *Leader* is condemned as "socialist" by the *Edinburgh Review*.

Ruskin publishes *The Stones of Venice*, Melville *Moby Dick*.

BRITISH LITERARY PERIODICALS	YEAR	SOCIAL & LITERARY EVENTS
	1852	

George Eliot becomes subeditor of the *Westminster Review*, the first woman to hold such a position on an English review, and advances Lewes's work to establish realism as a criterion for literary evaluation.

The *New Quarterly Review* tries to revive the eighteenth-century methods of the *Critical* and *Monthly* reviews.

Thackeray publishes *Henry Esmond*, Dickens *Bleak House*, Charlotte Brontë *Villette*.

Second Burmese War begins.

Duke of Wellington dies.

| | 1853 | |

In the *Leader* Lewes challenges the "realism" of *Bleak House*; Dickens's response becomes a major essay in the history of realism in England.

Thackeray publishes *English Humorists*, Arnold *The Scholar Gypsy*, Elizabeth Gaskell *Ruth* and *Cranford*.

| | 1854 | |

Dickens serializes *Hard Times* in *Household Words*; circulation reaches 100,000, submissions 900.

The Crimean War begins.

British Civil Service Commission is established.

| | 1855 | |

A.J.B. Beresford Hope begins the *Saturday Review* as "the mouth-piece of the middle and moderate opinion of thoughtful and educated society."

The Newspaper Stamp Act is repealed; the number of daily newspapers increases.

Browning publishes *Men and Women*, Kingsley *Westward Ho*, Tennyson *Maud*, Thackeray *The Newcomers*, Trollope *The Warden*.

| | 1856 | |

Dickens lures William Henry Wills from *Chambers's Edinburgh Journal* to be assistant editor of *Household Words*.

George Bernard Shaw, Oscar Wilde are born.

BRITISH LITERARY PERIODICALS	YEAR	SOCIAL & LITERARY EVENTS
	(1856)	

William Morris's new "Brotherhood" (to replace the Pre-Raphaelites) begins the *Oxford and Cambridge* in the tradition of the *Germ*; the magazine ends when the staff becomes more interested in helping Rossetti paint decorative murals in the Oxford Union.

1857

George Eliot's first "creative" work, "Scenes from a Clerical Life," appears in *Blackwood's*.

The Irish Republican Brotherhood (Fenians) is founded in New York.

Dickens publishes *Little Dorrit*, Trollope *Barchester Towers*.

1859

Dickens buys out *Household Words* and transforms it into *All the Year Round*. After a quarrel with Dickens, his publisher Bradbury and Evans begins *Once a Week* as a rival to *All the Year Round*; Samuel Lucas, literary editor of the *Times*, is appointed editor.

After sixteen years of speculation and planning, *Macmillan's Magazine* becomes the first of the shilling monthlies.

Quarterly Review's long treatment by William Gladstone of *Idylls of the King* is hailed by Tennyson as the best ever published.

Arthur Conan Doyle, Alfred Housman, Francis Thompson are born.

Darwin publishes *On the Origin of Species*, Dickens *A Tale of Two Cities*, Eliot *Adam Bede*, Meredith *The Ordeal of Richard Feverel*, Tennyson *Idylls of the King*, Thackeray *The Virginian*.

Lord Palmerston becomes prime minister.

Jerome K. Jerome is born; Leigh Hunt and Thomas De Quincey die.

1860

Good Words, exemplary of Victorian religious sentiment, is founded.

Eliot publishes *The Mill on the Floss*. Thackeray begins the *Roundabout Papers* (–1863).

BRITISH LITERARY PERIODICALS	YEAR	SOCIAL & LITERARY EVENTS
	(1860)	

The *Cornhill Magazine* begins with Thackeray as editor; the first issue features installments of two novels by Thackeray and one by Trollope.

Boucicault's first play is presented.

Treaty of Peking is signed.

Anton Chekhov, J. M. Barrie are born.

George Augustus Sala begins *Temple Bar* in imitation of the *Cornhill*.

Catholic Times begins publication.

1861

Meredith Townsend and Richard Hutton take over the *Spectator* and establish its tone until 1897 of "educated mid-Victorian critical opinion."

Dickens publishes *Great Expectations*, Eliot *Silas Marner*, Reade *The Cloister and the Hearth*.

1863

The *Reader* appears, recalling the *Athenaeum*, *Critical*, and *Monthly*, and publishes discussions of science and religion.

George Eliot publishes *Romola*, John Stuart Mill *Utilitarianism*.

Edward, Prince of Wales, marries Princess Alexandra.

1864

The *Month* is established as a Catholic counterpart of Thackeray's *Cornhill*.

An essay by Charles Kingsley provokes an exchange of letters with Newman that leads to *Apologia pro Vita Sua*.

1865

Henry James Coleridge assumes editorship of the *Month*.

Rudyard Kipling, W. B. Yeats are born.

George H. Lewes edits the new *Fortnightly*, publishes T. H. Huxley, Meredith, John S. Mill, and Trollope, and adds a renowned group of foreign correspondents.

Arnold publishes *Essays in Criticism*, Carroll *Alice's Adventures in Wonderland*, Dickens *Our Mutual Friend*.

BRITISH LITERARY PERIODICALS	YEAR	SOCIAL & LITERARY EVENTS
	1866	

John Morley castigates Swinburne in the *Saturday Review*; his review is frequently attributed as the cause of the poet's decline.

Trollope contributes parts of the first of his five novels to appear in *Blackwood's*.

Arnold publishes *Thyrsis* in *Macmillan's*.

The *Contemporary Review* begins as an organ for the Metaphysical Society; Arnold will use the review as a forum to answer his critics.

Swinburne publishes *Poems and Ballads*.

Larousse begins publication of the *Grand dictionnaire*.

H. G. Wells, Roger Fry are born; Thomas Love Peacock dies.

London Stock Exchange collapses.

| | 1867 | |

Trollope publishes *The Last Chronicle of Barset* and leaves the editorial board of the *Fortnightly* to become editor of the new *St. Paul's*.

William Tinsley begins *Tinsley's Magazine*, noted for its crime fiction, and serializes Collins's *Moonstone* and Dickens's *Mysteries of Edwin Drood*.

Arnold Bennett, John Galsworthy are born.

Fenians attack in Ireland and Manchester.

The second Parliamentary Reform Act passes.

| | 1868 | |

Vanity Fair, the "smart set's gazette," satirizes upper-class fashions and vanities. Carlo Pellegrini and Leslie Ward provide color caricatures for which the magazine soon becomes famous.

First, Benjamin Disraeli, next, William Gladstone become prime minister.

Robert Browning publishes *The Ring and the Book*, Wilkie Collins *The Moonstone*.

Early Impressionist paintings are exhibited in Paris and London.

BRITISH LITERARY PERIODICALS	*YEAR*	*SOCIAL & LITERARY EVENTS*
	(1868)	

Bentley's Miscellany merges with *Temple Bar* and begins to publish Bret Harte, Wilkie Collins, Arthur Conan Doyle, and Trollope, and translations of Chekhov, Turgenev, Balzac, and Tolstoy.

1869

The *Academy*, founded by Charles Appleton to appeal to the university-educated, is a forerunner of the *Times Literary Supplement* and reaches a new level of academic criticism. Arnold reviews Senancour's *Obermann* in the first issue.

Debtors' prisons are abolished.

Arnold publishes *Culture and Anarchy*, Mill *The Subjection of Women*, Trollope *Phineas Finn*.

1871

Leslie Stephen begins an eleven-year stint editing the *Cornhill*, attracting Hardy's *Far from the Madding Crowd* and James's *Daisy Miller* and *Washington Square*.

Darwin publishes *The Descent of Man*, Carroll *Through the Looking Glass*.

United States and Britain sign the Treaty of Washington.

Bank holidays are inaugurated.

1872

Frederick Waddy begins to contribute to *Once a Week* his cartoons of famous literary figures, among them Tennyson, Browning, and Arnold.

Max Beerbohm, Bertrand Russell are born.

Samuel Butler publishes *Erewhon*, Eliot *Middlemarch*.

1877

John Knowles, editor of the *Contemporary Review* and secretary of the Metaphysical Society, begins the *Nineteenth Century*; society members Tennyson, Huxley, and Gladstone frequently appear.

Victoria becomes Empress of India.

Edison invents the phonograph.

Third Impressionist Exhibition is held in Paris.

BRITISH LITERARY PERIODICALS	YEAR	SOCIAL & LITERARY EVENTS
	(1877)	

Arnold begins to contribute to the *Quarterly Review*.

Hardy's *Return of the Native* is serialized in *Belgravia*.

| | 1879 | |

Arthur Conan Doyle's first story, "The Mystery of Sassassa Valley," appears in *Chambers's Edinburgh Journal*.

Browning publishes the first series of *Dramatic Idylls*, Meredith *The Egoist*.

| | 1882 | |

The *Nineteenth Century* enters the fray over the Channel Tunnel, publishing a protest signed by (among others) Browning, Huxley, Morris, Newman, and Tennyson.

The Fabian Society is formed.

Virginia Woolf and James Joyce are born; Anthony Trollope, D. G. Rossetti, and Charles Darwin die.

British occupy Cairo.

| | 1883 | |

The *National Review* begins its long run (–1960) as a Tory periodical.

| | 1884 | |

The Century Guild of Artists, formed in 1882 and influenced by the work of Morris, begins the *Hobby Horse*, publishing Ernest Dowson and Paul Verlaine.

Oxford English Dictionary begins publication.

First London underground railway opens.

| | 1885 | |

Mowbray Morris edits *Macmillan's* and the magazine becomes more literary, publishing James, Hardy, and Kipling.

D. H. Lawrence is born.

Richard Burton begins the *Arabian Nights*, Gilbert and Sullivan publish *The Mikado*, Pater *Marius the Epicurean*, Ruskin *Praeterita*.

BRITISH LITERARY PERIODICALS	*YEAR*	*SOCIAL & LITERARY EVENTS*
	1887	
Oscar Wilde edits Cassell's *Lady's World*, changing the title to *Woman's World* and featuring Olive Schreiner, Jane Harrison, and other feminists.		Golden Jubilee of Queen Victoria. Arthur Conan Doyle publishes the first Sherlock Holmes story, "A Study in Scarlet."
	1888	
William Ernest Henley edits the new *Scots Observer*, which promises to "give hearty support to the ... unity of the Empire." Pre-Raphaelite devotée Harry Quilter begins the *Universal Review*, which publishes Hardy, Meredith, Tolstoy, Swinburne, and Wilkie Collins.		Kipling publishes *Plain Tales from the Hills*, Wilde *The Happy Prince and Other Tales*.
	1890	
The *Scots Observer* moves to London and becomes the *National Observer*. Yeats publishes the first of eighteen poems there, joining frequent contributors Kipling, Swinburne, Stevenson, and Kenneth Grahame. W. T. Stead establishes the *Review of Reviews* as a comprehensive digest of the most important periodicals, and disseminates his view of the British people as "one of God's chosen agents for the improvement of mankind."		Robert Bridges publishes the *Shorter Poems*, Wilde *The Picture of Dorian Gray*, J. G. Frazer *The Golden Bough*. First films are screened commercially in New York. First English electrical power station opens.
	1891	
George Newnes's new *Strand*, a cheap periodical financed by Leary advertising revenues, refuses to serialize and creates a large demand for short stories.		The "little theater" movement begins. J. M. Barrie publishes *The Little Minister*, Gissing *New Grub Street*, Hardy *Tess of the d'Urbervilles*, Kipling *The Light That Failed*.

BRITISH LITERARY PERIODICALS	YEAR	SOCIAL & LITERARY EVENTS
	1892	
Jerome K. Jerome begins the *Idler*, to which Doyle contributes stories later collected in *Round the Red Lamp*. Contemporary writers respond to such features as "Why Do I Write?" and "My First Book."		Tennyson dies. Kipling publishes *Barrack-Room Ballads*, Wilde *Lady Windermere's Fan*. Gladstone becomes prime minister.
	1893	
Pall Mall Magazine begins its virtual "Who's Who" of major literary contributors: Belloc, Chesterton, Conrad, Ford Madox Ford, Hardy, Huxley, Jack London, Masefield, Meredith, William Rossetti, Shaw, Stevenson, Symons, Wells, and Wodehouse.		The Independent Labor Party is formed. Pinero publishes *The Second Mrs. Tanqueray*, Shaw *Mrs. Warren's Profession*. Irish home rule is defeated a second time in Parliament.
	1894	
Henry Harland and Aubrey Beardsley collaborate on the *Yellow Book*, the quintessence of the *fin de siècle*; Frank Harris edits the *Saturday Review*, attracting Beerbohm, Shaw, and Wells.		Aldous Huxley, J. B. Priestley are born. George Moore publishes *Esther Waters*, Shaw *Arms and the Man*, Yeats *The Land of Heart's Desire*.
	1895	
Beardsley is fired from the *Yellow Book* because of the public's association of him with Wilde, arrested that year. The *Savoy* begins as a rival of the *Yellow Book*, with Arthur Symons as editor, Beardsley as prominent artist. The first issue, containing Yeats's "Rosa Alchemica," is recalled because Beardsley's cover shows male genitalia.		Conrad publishes *Almayer's Folly*, Wells *The Time Machine*, Wilde *The Importance of Being Earnest*, Yeats *Poems*, Marx *Das Kapital 3*. George VI (–1952) is born. The South Africa Company (Zambezi) becomes Rhodesia. Oscar Wilde loses his libel suit against the Marquis of Queensberry.

BRITISH LITERARY PERIODICALS	YEAR	SOCIAL & LITERARY EVENTS
	(1895)	

William Ernest Henley takes over the moribund *New Review*, purchased by his friend William Heinemann and others. Works by his friends, the "Henley Regatta," appear: Gladstone, Stephen Crane, Conrad.

1896

Cartoonist Phil May joins *Punch*.

Hardy publishes *Jude the Obscure*, Housman *A Shropshire Lad*.

The first of two annual *Pageants* appears in hardboards with color reproductions, limited to 150 copies; contributors include Beerbohm, Swinburne, Lionel Johnson, Verlaine, and Yeats.

National Portrait Gallery opens in Westminster.

Royal Victorian Order is founded.

The *National Observer*, in decline, merges with the *British Review*, and ends ten months later.

1897

H. D. Traill edits the new *Literature*, a critical weekly and model for the *Times Literary Supplement*, which appears six days after the cessation of *Literature* in 1902.

Queen Victoria's Diamond Jubilee.

Conrad publishes *The Nigger of the Narcissus*, Kipling *Captains Courageous*, Wells *The Invisible Man*.

1899

Yeats's essays on theater and his poems appear in the *Dome*.

Irish Literary Theatre is founded in Dublin.

Lady Churchill begins the *Anglo-Saxon Review* as a *salon*-in-print for its subscribers—royalty and wealthy commoners—and publishes James, Gissing, and Stephen Crane.

Boer War begins.

Kipling publishes *Stalky and Co.*, Ibsen *When We Dead Awaken*.

Lorca, Noel Coward are born.

BRITISH LITERARY PERIODICALS	YEAR	SOCIAL & LITERARY EVENTS
	1900	
John Muir and Henry Newbolt establish the liberal *Monthly Review* as a twentieth-century *Spectator*.		Boxer Rebellion begins. Oscar Wilde, Stephen Crane, and Nietzsche die.
London *Daily Express* begins publication.		Conrad publishes *Lord Jim*, Freud *The Interpretation of Dreams*.
	1901	
Yeats edits *Samhain*, the journal of the Irish National Theatre Society, and publishes his plays and those of Synge, Lady Gregory, and Douglas Hyde.		Queen Victoria dies, is succeeded by Edward VII (–1910). McKinley is assassinated. Boer War intensifies, Boxer Rebellion ends.
	1902	
Wilfred Whitten (later famous as "John O'London") edits *T. P.'s Weekly*.		Boer War ends. King Edward VII establishes the Order of Merit.
Times Literary Supplement begins.		John Steinbeck is born; Samuel Butler dies. Arnold Bennett publishes *Anna of the Five Towns*, Kipling the *Just-So Stories*.
	1903	
The superbly printed *Green Sheaf* devotes itself to reporting "experiences beyond reality"; Yeats's "Dreams of the World's End" appears in the second number.		The "Entente Cordiale" is established. Henry James publishes *The Ambassadors*, Shaw *Man and Superman*; Butler's *The Way of All Flesh* appears posthumously. The first motor taxis appear in London streets. Emmeline Pankhurst establishes the National Women's Social and Political Union.

BRITISH LITERARY PERIODICALS	YEAR	SOCIAL & LITERARY EVENTS
	1904	

John Eglinton (William Magee) begins *Dana* to promote Irish literature, rejects an early version of Joyce's *Portrait*.

Hardy's *The Dynasts*, Synge's *Riders to the Sea*, Conrad's *Nostromo* appear.

Graham Greene, Christopher Isherwood, and Salvador Dali are born.

Abbey Theatre is founded.

| | 1907 | |

Synge's *Playboy of the Western World* is defended in the *Arrow*, which Yeats edits as director of the Abbey Theatre.

The Theosophical Art Circle publishes *Orpheus*; editor A. E. attracts many Continental authors.

Kipling receives the Nobel Prize for literature.

W. H. Auden is born.

Lumière develops color photography.

| | 1908 | |

Ford Madox Ford begins a short but brilliant editorship of the *English Review*, and publishes Hardy, James, Conrad, Bennett, Wyndham Lewis, Masefield, and D. H. Lawrence; the first issue begins the serialization of Wells's *Tono-Bungay*.

London *Times* is purchased by Lord Northcliffe.

H. H. Asquith becomes prime minister.

Gertrude Stein publishes *Three Lives*, Forster *A Room with a View*, Bennett *The Old Wives' Tale*.

Henry Ford produces the first model-T's.

| | 1910 | |

Open Window provides one of the first outlets for the Georgian school of poets.

Edward VII dies, is succeeded by George V (–1936).

Stravinsky's *Firebird* is first performed in Paris.

Tolstoy, William James die.

BRITISH LITERARY PERIODICALS	*YEAR*	*SOCIAL & LITERARY EVENTS*
	1911	

J. M. Murry and John Fergusson establish the sophisticated *Rhythm* as the *Yellow Book* of modernism.

Winston Churchill appointed First Lord of the Admiralty.

National health insurance begins.

D. H. Lawrence's first novel, *The White Peacock*, appears, as do Rupert Brooke's *Poems* and Pound's "Canzoni."

| | 1913 | |

Harold Monro leaves the *Poetry Review* to begin *Poetry and Drama*, creating a wider audience for D. H. Lawrence, Frost, De la Mare, Pound, and Hardy.

Sidney and Beatrice Webb found the *New Statesman*.

The *Blue Review* succeeds *Rhythm*; Edward March supports the magazine as a voice for Georgianism, which D. H. Lawrence critiques.

D. H. Lawrence publishes *Sons and Lovers*, Mann *Death in Venice*, Proust *Swann's Way*.

Suffragettes demonstrate in London; Mrs. Pankhurst is sentenced for inciting to riot; first woman magistrate is sworn in.

Armory Show is held in New York.

Nineteenth-Century Foreign Reviews

Particularly in the 1820s, 1830s, and 1840s a number of reviews were founded that concerned themselves principally or exclusively with foreign literatures. Most were short-lived; many are difficult to find today. In addition to these, some general reviews published more or less regular features on foreign literature or foreign life and thought; others showed as great an interest without establishing separate departments for the articles. If less attention seems to be given to foreign literature in the latter part of the century, the reason may be that the proselytizing of the earlier years was no longer necessary.

The following lists omit periodicals whose concern is colonial but not non-British; specialized periodicals (professional journals such as the *British and Foreign Medical Journal*; journals of a society or cause, such as *Polonia* or the *British and Foreign Temperance Herald*); periodicals published in a foreign language, often by refugees; and periodicals expressly for prospective tourists and emigrants.

Periodicals Devoted Exclusively or Primarily to Foreign Literature or to Foreign Life and Thought

The British and Foreign Review; or, European Quarterly Review* (see *RA*). Vols. 1–18, 1835–1844. Contributors included Lord Brougham, David Urquhart, Henry Reeve, W. B. Donne, Joseph Mazzini, Antonio Panizzi, W. M. Thackeray, Antonio Gallenga, Sarah Austin, Baden Powell, and George Henry Lewes. See *Wellesley Index to Victorian Periodicals*, vol. 3, for contents and identification of authorship.

Cochrane's Foreign Quarterly Review. Nos. 1–2, March–July 1835. Editor: John George Cochrane. Publisher: Whittaker & Co. Contributors included Henry Reeve, Sarah Austin, and Thomas Wright. A breakaway from the *Foreign Quarterly Review** (see *RA* and below), which Cochrane had edited.

The Critical Figaro of Paris and London: Containing Everything Relative to Literature, Fine Arts, Music, the Drama, Fashions and Utilities, in the Two Great Cities; Interspersed with Squibs on Passing Events. Nos. 1–3, 21 January–4 February 1832. Weekly. Published by Benjamin Steill.

The European Journal of the Progress of Society, Literature, the Arts and Sciences. The British Library has only the first issue, 2 November 1839; but that copy carries the ms. notation, "Several numbers published." Contains reviews of English and foreign books, translations, foreign correspondence, and news of London theaters. The *Tercentenary Handlist of English and Welsh Newspapers, Magazines and Reviews* (1920) and *The Waterloo Directory of Victorian Periodicals* (1976) both list "The European, &c. No. 1. 1839" and "European. No. 1–8. Nov. 2–Dec. 21, 1839." Presumably both entries refer to this journal. Neither the *Handlist* nor *Waterloo* lists a *European Journal* at any date.

The European Review; or, Mind and its Productions, in Britain, France, Italy, Germany, &c. Nos. 1–6, June–October 1824 and January 1826. Alexander Walker the "General Literary Director of the Work"; Mr. Scott the English editor, Mr. Varaigne the French editor, Sign. Villa the Italian editor, and Herr de Prati the German editor (though his name is crossed out in the Cambridge University Library copy). It was to appear simultaneously in London, Paris, Stuttgart, and Florence. Some articles printed in a foreign language, translated into English at the bottom of the page. "Original Papers" as well as reviews. The intention was that most articles would be signed, and some actually were. Contributors included Ugo Foscolo.

The Foreign and Colonial Quarterly Review, continued as *The New Quarterly Review, or Home, Foreign, and Colonial Journal*. Vols. 1–9, 1844–1847. Editor: James William Worthington. Publisher: Whittaker. Worthington wished to promote Conservative and Church of England interests. Contributors included W. E. Gladstone (then at the Board of Trade), A. Gallenga, J. A. Heraud, R. H. Horne, G. H. Lewes, and Thomas Adolphus Trollope. Founded in opposition to the *Foreign Quarterly Review*, which Worthington had previously edited.

Foreign Literary Gazette. Nos. 1–13, 6 January–31 March 1830. Weekly. Editors: William Jerdan, Capt. William John Williams, and Henry William Smith. Many Continental contributors (articles translated into English). For an account, see William Jerdan, *Autobiography* (1853), 4:273–79.

Foreign Monthly Review, and Continental Literary Journal. Nos. 1–6, May–October 1839. Editor: Frederic Shoberl. Publisher: D. Nutt. Wished "to supply its readers with abstracts of such books as seem deserving of their attention and not with disquisitions, having little or no connexion with the subject of them." Most reviews are of German books, a few of French books, and fewer still of Italian books; sometimes reviews are of German translations from other languages. Only foreign publications are reviewed. Contributors included Thomas Wright and J. O. Halliwell.

The Foreign Quarterly Review (see *RA*). Vols. 1–37, 1827–1846. For contents and identification of authorship, see *Wellesley Index to Victorian Periodicals*, vol. 2.

The Foreign Review, and Continental Miscellany. Vols. 1–5, 1828–1830. Quarterly. Editor: William Fraser. Publisher: Black, Young, and Young. Founded as a rival to the *Foreign Quarterly Review* by William Fraser, who had tried to act as assistant editor to the earlier review; combined with the *Foreign Quarterly* in 1830, with the understanding that Fraser would be dropped. Contributors included Thomas Carlyle, Antonio Panizzi, and Robert Southey. Much information about the review can be found in *The Collected Letters of Thomas and Jane Welsh Carlyle*, ed. Charles Richard Sanders et al., vols. 4–5.

The Foreign Weekly Review. Nos. 1–5, 11 May–8 June 1839.

The German Museum. Vols. 1–3, 1800–1802. Monthly. Reviews, biographical sketches, and translations. A wide range of subjects is covered, with particular attention to pedagogy and drama. "The declared aim of the Museum is diffusion of useful knowledge and the light of reason" (3:376).

The Magazine of Foreign Literature. Vol. 1, March–October 1823. Monthly. "Comprehending an Analysis of Celebrated Modern Productions of France, Germany, Italy, Spain, Portugal, Russia, and America. With Copious Extracts, translated into English." Almost all comment is laudatory. Monthly "memoirs" (Chateaubriand, Goethe, Wieland, Mme. de Genlis, Monti, de Jouy, Herder, Mme. de Staël).

The New Quarterly Review, 1844–1847. Continuation of the *Foreign and Colonial Quarterly Review* (see above).

The New Quarterly Review, and Digest of Current Literature, British, American, French, and German. Vols. 1–11 (41 issues), 1852–1862. Publishers: Hookham and Sons (vols. 1–2), Bosworth and Harrison (vols. 5–6). The title is an accurate description of the contents.

The Universal Review; or, Chronicle of the Literature of All Nations. Vols. 1–2, 1824–1825. Editor: George Croly. Publisher: Whittaker.

Periodicals with Titles Indicating Concern with Foreign Literature, Life, and Thought (contents have not been verified)

The Anglo-French Stage Chronicle, continued as the *Anglo-French Chronicle*. Nos. 1–3, June–July 1899.

The Anglo-Russian Literary Society, Proceedings of. Nos. 1–89, 1893–1920.

Bell's Weekly Magazine. Journal of English and Foreign Literature, Science, and the Fine Arts. Nos. 1–17, 18 January–10 May 1834. Publisher: John Percival. Contributors included Douglas Jerrold and Leigh Hunt. It claimed circulation of 10,300. No copies have been found in the United States; the British Library's copy was destroyed in World War II.

The Continental Review. Vols. 1–3, 3 March 1858–30 April 1859. Weekly.

The European Magazine. 4 April 1884–9 January 1885.

The Illustrated Literature of All Nations. Nos. 1–22, 1851–1852.

The Mirror. A Weekly Reflex of the World's Literature. Vols. 1–4, 1872–1874.

The New Century Review. A Monthly International Journal of Literature, &c. Nos. 1–8, 1897–1900.

The Parlour Magazine of the Literature of All Nations. Nos. 1–2, 1851.

The Parthenon; a Weekly Journal of English and Foreign Literature. Vols. 1–4, 26 October 1836–15 February 1840.

The Rover, or Spirit of Domestic and Foreign Literature, Passing and Past. Nos. 1–33, 14 September 1833–26 April 1834. Weekly. Publisher: Benjamin Steill.

Studies in European Literature. 1889–1930. Oxford.

The Translator. Original Translations from Various Languages Ancient and Modern. Nos. 1–3, 1825.

The Universal Medley, Containing Selections from the Best English Authors, Translations from the Most Esteemed Italian and French Writers and a Considerable Portion of Original Matter. Nos. 1–3, 12 January–1 March 1824. Monthly.

Some General Periodicals with Special Features Devoted to Foreign Literature

Blackwood's Edinburgh Magazine* (see *RA*). 1817-1980. In the late 1810s and throughout the 1820s such series appeared as "Horae Germanicae," "Horae Hispanicae," "Horae Italicae," "Gallery of the German Prose Classics," and "Sketches of Italy and the Italians." In the early 1870s and again in the late 1870s there were two long series on "French Home Life." Interest in the Continent flagged in 1827–1828 and in the latter part of the century. Contributors included Thomas De Quincey, R. P. Gillies, J. G. Lockhart, and Frederick Hardman. For contents and identifications of contributors, see A. L. Strout, *A Bibliography of Articles in "Blackwood's Magazine," 1817–1825* (Lubbock, Tex., 1959) and *Wellesley Index to Victorian Periodicals*, vol. 1.

Contemporary Review.* 1866–. Monthly. Main interests include theology, philosophy, social and political questions, education, art and music; some literary criticism. Much attention is given to the Continent. "Contemporary Life and Thought"—in Germany, in France, in Italy, in Russia—appears irregularly. See Profile in this volume, and for contents and identification of contributors see *Wellesley Index to Victorian Periodicals*, vol. 1.

The Critic.* 1843–1863. Title varies: *The Critic of Art, Literature, Science and the Drama*, vol. 1 (1843–1844); *The Critic; Journal of British and Foreign Literature and the Arts*, n.s. vol. 1 (1844). Fortnightly. Publisher: Mr. Crockford. In 1851 it added features on "Foreign Literature," "Gleanings from Foreign Literature," foreign correspondence, etc.

The London Magazine* (see *RA*). 1820-1829. Features in the first series (1820–1824) included "Gleanings from the Foreign Journals"; "Early French Poets" and "Early Italian Poets" (both by H. F. Cary); "Spanish Romances" (by John Bowring); and "Sketch of Foreign Literature"; as well as many articles on Continental and American literatures. It also frequently printed translations. Other contributors to the first series included Thomas De Quincey, Thomas Carlyle, and C. A. Elton (on modern French poets). The new series (1825–1828) included "Letters from Paris" and other contributions by Stendhal, as well as contributions from Sarah Austin, Ugo Foscolo, and Antonio Panizzi. Henry Southern, the editor, wrote frequently on foreign literature. While the third series (1828–1829) printed somewhat fewer articles on foreign literature, it introduced two new features, "Characters of Contemporary Foreign Authors and Statesmen" (by F. DeGeorge) and "The Foreign Portfolio," observations by anonymous foreign literary figures. See Frank P. Riga and Claude A. Prance, *Index to "The London Magazine"* (N.Y., 1978), for contents and identification of authorship; they also index books reviewed, by author and by title.

The Monthly Review* (see *AAAJ*). 1749-1844. Early nineteenth-century numbers contained "Foreign Appendices."

The New Monthly Magazine* (see *RA*). 1814–1884. Of interest here are only those volumes edited by Thomas Campbell and Cyrus Redding, 1821–1830. Proprietor and publisher: Henry Colburn. Much on Spanish, Italian, German, and French literature. Features included "Specimens of German Genius" (Sarah Austin), "Sketches of Parisian Society, Politics, and Literature" (Stendhal), "Letters from Spain" (Joseph Blanco White), "Italian Poets" (Ugo Foscolo). See *Wellesley Index to Victorian Periodicals*, vol. 3, for contents and identification of authorship.

The Scottish Review. Vols. 1–36, 1882–1900. Editor: William M. Metcalfe. Publisher: Alexander Gardner Paisley. Proprietors: Alexander Gardner (1882–1886); J. P. Crichton-Stuart, third Marquess of Bute (1886–1900). Quarterly. All issues contain "Summaries of foreign reviews." For contents and authorship other than the summaries, see *Wellesley Index to Victorian Periodicals*, vol. 2.

The Westminster Review* (see *RA*). 1824–1914. After the merger with the *Foreign Quarterly Review* in 1846, the title page read *The Westminster and Foreign Quarterly Review* through vol. 127 (January 1887). Vols. 46–56 (1846–1851) print separate sections on "Foreign Literature"; vols. 57–60 (1852–1853) drop this heading and in its place feature "Contemporary Literature of America," "Contemporary Literature of Germany," and "Contemporary Literature of France." After 1854 no regular features are devoted to foreign literature. At most periods, however, the *Westminster* reviewed a number of foreign books or literatures. Henry Southern and John Bowring were coeditors, 1824–1828; T. P. Thompson and Bowring, 1829–1836. J. S. Mill edited the *London Review* (1835–1836) and the merged *London and Westminster Review*, 1836–1840. W. E. Hickson edited what was again the *Westminster Review* from 1840 to 1851; and John Chapman or his widow edited it from that point through the end of the century. For full publishing history, contents, and identification of authorship see *Wellesley Index to Victorian Periodicals*, vol. 3.

A Few General Periodicals That Consistently Gave Considerable Attention to Foreign Literature

*The Athenaeum** (see *RA*). 1828–1921. See Leslie A. Marchand, *"The Athenaeum."* *A Mirror of Victorian Culture* (Chapel Hill, N.C., 1941), pp. 215-221, for a brief discussion of their early reviewing of foreign literature.

*Fraser's Magazine for Town and Country** (see *RA*). 1830–1882. Emphasis on foreign literature varies. At its start it inherited several contributors from the defunct *Foreign Review*. For contents and attribution of authorship see *Wellesley Index to Victorian Periodicals*, vol. 2.

*The National Review.** Vols. 1–19, 1855–1864. Quarterly. Editor: Walter Bagehot. Frequent articles on current European literature and affairs and on earlier literature. See *Wellesley Index to Victorian Periodicals*, vol. 3.

New Quarterly Magazine. 1873–1880. Editors: O.J.F. Crawfurd (1873–1878); Francis Hueffer (1878); C. Kegan Paul (1879–1880). See *Wellesley Index to Victorian Periodicals*, vol. 2.

Periodicals Concerned Mainly with the Teaching or Learning of Foreign Languages

The Anglo-German Translator. Vols. 1–2, 1895–1896.

Every Englishman's French Journal. Nos. 1–12, 1884–1885. Continued as *Everyone His Own French Professor.* Nos. 1–35, 1885–1886.

Foreign Languages Made Easy. A Practical Periodical for Practical People. Vols. 1–2, 1894–1896. Collective title of vol. 1: *The Royal Road to Foreign Languages.*

The Franco-English Review. 1896. Monthly. Publisher: F. L. Ballin. Circulated among students and teachers "in Franco-England."

French and German Echoes. Nos. 1–21, 1892–1894. Monthly. Publisher: Blackie & Sons., Ltd. French and German readings. Supplement to *Hughes's French and German Journal* (see below).

The French Companion. Vols. 1–5, 1871–1874. Glasgow.

The French Companion. 1874. Monthly. Publisher: Hachette and Co. A journal of French literature.

The French Professor. 1888. Weekly.

The German Magazine; A Quarterly Journal in the German Language, for English Readers. Nos. 1–7, 1862–1863. Editors: J. and J. McEwen.

Hughes's French and German Journal. Vols. 1–3, no. 4, 1888–1890. Editor: J. J. Beuzemaker. Continued as the *Modern Language Monthly*. Vol. 3, no. 5–vol. 5, 1891–1893.

Hugo's French Journal. 1896–1932.

Languages. A Journal for Linguists, Philologers, &c. Vols. 1–3, 1893–1895. Weekly. Editors: H. Harrison and others. Publisher: H. Harrison.

The Linguist. Vols. 1–2, 1825–1826. Weekly?

The Linguist. Vols. 1–2, 1866.

The Linguist. 1878. Monthly. Educational study of languages.

The Linguist and Educational Review. Vols. 1–2, 1874–1876.

The Linguist's Magazine. A Monthly Review Comprising Five Languages. 1886. Editor: F. Broemel.

The London Polyglot. 1870s.

The Modern Language Teachers' Guide. Vols. 1–2, 1896. Cambridge. Continued as the *Modern Language Quarterly*. Vol. 1, 1897. Continued as the *Modern Quarterly of Language and Literature*. Vols. 1–7, 1898–1904. Editor: H. F. Heath. Continued as the *Modern Language Review*.

The Polyglot Magazine; or, Literary Repository and Self-Instructor. Vols. 1–3, 1836–1838.

The Polyglot Register. No. 1, May 1862.

Selected Series of French Literature. Nos. 1–5, 1853. Editor: J. Lowe.

Eileen M. Curran

Victorian Comic Journals

The early nineteenth-century literary magazine and the journal of political satire prepared the way for the Victorian comic journal. When *Punch** appeared in 1841, its readers had already been exposed not only to the tactics of the political satirist in the *Anti-Jacobin Review** (see *RA*), John Bull* (see *RA*), the *Age*, or *Figaro in London*, but also to social and literary satire and non-satirical humor in *Blackwood's,* *Fraser's Magazine,** the *New Monthly** (for all, see *RA*), or *Bentley's Miscellany.** Comic magazines followed the lead of the literary monthly in printing humorous poems, tales, and sketches. The comic journal may also have been as indebted to the literary magazine as to the political journal for its favorite techniques of imitation, parody, and travesty. However, the literary magazine's most significant contribution to comic journalism was the humorous serial. Douglas Jerrold, who wrote serials for the *New Monthly* in the late 1830s, and William Thackeray, who contributed serials to *Fraser's*, created similar humorous papers as staff writers for *Punch* in the 1840s. Thereafter, the humorous serial became an essential feature of the successful comic journal.

A unique synthesis of the literary magazine and the journal of political satire, *Punch* became the prototype of the Victorian comic journal. The better comic magazines imitated *Punch* in offering a balanced diet of political, social, and literary satire and non-satirical humor in a variety of shapes. Although *Punch*'s influence on comic journalism was pervasive, rival comic weeklies resemble the "London Charivari" more closely than comic monthlies, which are generally less political and less satirical. After 1870, with the exception of *Punch, Fun,** and a few other journals of satire and humor, there is less literature in the comic magazine. By the end of the century, two essentially non-literary variations on the comic journal became popular—the society or gossip magazine, in which reporting replaced creativity, and the pictorial comic paper (the "comics"), in which cartoons displaced words.

A List of Comic Journals

The following list includes periodicals that I have not examined but that have been identified as comic magazines by Marion Spielmann, Francis Cowley Burnand, or Donald Gray. Donald Gray's index of comic periodicals is much more comprehensive than mine and includes many more provincial publications, seriocomic magazines, and illustrated comic papers. In tracing developments in nineteenth-century comic journalism, both Spielmann and Burnand reflect their own allegiance to *Punch* and may not always be reliable. Nonetheless, I have turned to their accounts to supplement information about editors and contributors compiled from biographies and memoirs.

A number of magazines on the list are identified as products of "Figaro-mania," the term Gilbert Abbott à Beckett applied to an epidemic of imitations of *Figaro in London* in 1832 and 1833. This proliferation of penny comic weeklies also coincided with the relaxation in enforcement of the stamp tax laws.

The Age. 15 May 1825–1 Oct. 1843. Weekly. Owner and editor: Charles Molloy Westmacott (1827–1838); Captain Polhill, a co-owner after 1833; other writers: Thomas Littleton Holt, William Maginn. This Tory journal of political satire was notorious for its scandalous gossip, but it was a forerunner of the comic journal nonetheless.

The Almanack of the Month. A Review of Everything and Everybody. January–December 1846. Published at the *Punch* office. Editor: Gilbert Abbott à Beckett; other writers: Shirley Brooks, William Blanchard Jerrold, Percival Leigh, Mark Lemon, Horace Mayhew, Angus Bethune Reach, and W. H. Wills. The *Almanack*, written by *Punch* people, closely resembles its parent weekly, and its satire, like *Punch*'s, is frequently political.

Ariel. See *Puck*.

The Arrow. 2 August–7 December 1864. Biweekly. Publisher: John Camden Hotten. Editor: Henry S. Leigh; other writers: Mortimer Collins, Alfred Thompson. The *Arrow*'s strongest features are poetic parodies and imitations, nonsense poems, and vers de société.

Asmodeus, or Asmodeus in London. See *The Devil in London*.

The Ass; or Weekly Beast of Burden. 1 April–15 July 1826. Weekly. Editor: Robert Mudie(?). This short-lived magazine, which was judged to be dirty and disreputable by Alaric Watts and William Jerdan, offers a balance of political, social, and literary satire.

Banter. 2 September 1867–6 January 1868. Weekly. Editor and leading contributor: George Augustus Sala; other writers: Augustus Mayhew. In addition to the usual comic journal features, the magazine published serialized novels by Sala (*The Bargraves*) and Mayhew (*Mrs. Letts's Diary*).

Black and White. An Organ Playing Two Tunes. 1871. Weekly. Coeditors: Arthur à Beckett and Hamilton Hume. A journal of political satire and commentary offering opposing Liberal (à Beckett) and Conservative (Hume) points of view. [Spielmann/Gray]

Blarney. Ulster's Only Comic Journal. Belfast. 6 March–9 October 1886. Weekly. [Gray]

The Butterfly. March 1899–February 1900. Seriocomic monthly (revival of the 1893 *Butterfly*). Publisher: Grant Richards. Writers: Leonard Raven-Hill, Joseph Pennell, Max Beerbohm (artist). [Gray]

The Butterfly. A Humorous and Artistic Magazine. May 1893–February 1894. Serio-comic monthly. Editors: Leonard Raven-Hill and Arnold Golsworthy; other writers: L. Godfrey Turner. [Gray]

The Censor, a Weekly Journal of Satire. 23 May–7 November 1868. Editor: J. Hain Friswell. [Spielmann/Gray]

Chat. 1847–1849. Owners: Frederick Marriott, then George Augustus Sala and Richard Radcliffe Pond, and, finally, E. L. Blanchard and Mr. Hodge (1849). Editors: Thomas Littleton Holt, then Sala (and then Blanchard?). No copies of the magazine have been found.

The Comic Magazine. 1832–1834. Monthly. Editor: Gilbert Abbott à Beckett ("Bertie Vyse"); other writers: Augustus Walter Arnold, Thomas Dibdin, Isabel Hill, Henry Mayhew ("Ralph Rigamarole"), W. T. Moncrieff, Richard Brinsley Peake, John Poole, and Louisa Henrietta Sheridan. À Beckett's magazine imitates Thomas Hood's *Comic Annual* and Louisa Sheridan's *Comic Offering* in printing social satire and non-satirical humor in tales, poems, and sketches. The monthly's humor is of a very low order, however.

The Comic News. 18 July 1863–14 May 1864. Weekly. Editors: H. J. Byron (then Charles Collins?); other writers: E. L. Blanchard, Sidney Blanchard, William Brough, W. S. Gilbert, Tom Hood, T. S. Jerrold, Charles Matthews, Cosmo Monkhouse, Walter Parke, W. J. Prowse, T. W. Robertson, George Rose ("Arthur Sketchley"), E. A. Sothern, J. Ashby Sterry, Alfred Thompson, Walter Thornbury. Written largely by members of the *Fun* staff, Byron's magazine is inferior to *Fun* and revives several of the worst features of earlier comic journalism—puns, misspellings, and cockneyisms.

Comic Times. 11 August 1855–5 January 1856. Weekly. Owner: Herbert Ingram. Editor: Edmund Yates; other writers: E. L. Blanchard, John Bridgeman, Robert Brough, William Brough, Charles L. Dodgson ("Lewis Carroll"), Edward Draper, Henry Sutherland Edwards, William P. Hale, John Oxenford, G. A. Sala, Frank I. Scudamore, Frank Smedley, Albert Smith, Godfrey Turner. Only one copy of the magazine has been preserved. (See James Ellis, "*The Comic Times*," *Victorian Periodicals Newsletter*, no. 12 (1971):14–15).

The Dart and Midland Figaro (title varies). Birmingham. 28 October 1876–1 September 1911. Seriocomic. [Spielmann/Gray]

The Devil in London (29 February–14 April 1832), *Asmodeus or the Devil in London* (21 April–18 August 1832), then *Asmodeus in London* (until 10 November 1832); collected numbers issued as the *Devil's Memorandum Book for 1833*. Weekly. Absorbed by the *Wag* (1833?). The magazine was started by Henry Mayhew and was the most successful follower of *Figaro in London*. The quality of the humor actually improves and becomes less scandalous after the first title change.

The Devil's Walk. Edited by a Member of Parliament. 17 February 1832–? 1832. Weekly. "Figaro-mania."

Diogenes. 1 January 1853–11 August 1855. Weekly. Editor: Robert Kemp Philp; other writers: E. L. Blanchard, John Bridgeman, Robert Brough, William Brough, Henry Sutherland Edwards, William P. Hale, Watts Phillips, Frank Talfourd. According to F. C. Burnand, *Diogenes* was the "first direct and unblushingly avowed imitation of *Punch*." The magazine is an energetic spokesman for the poor and oppressed, and political satire is its strongest feature.

The English Figaro. 21 January 1832–? 1832. Weekly. "Figaro-mania."

Figaro in Birmingham. 1832. "Figaro-mania." [Gray]

Figaro in Chesterfield. 21 July–29 December 1832. Weekly. "Figaro-mania." [Gray]

Figaro in Liverpool. 1833. "Figaro-mania." [Gray]

Figaro in London. 10 December 1831–31 December 1838. Weekly. Editors: Gilbert Abbott à Beckett (1831–1834, 1837–1838) and Henry Mayhew (1835–1836); circulation reached 70,000. *Figaro in London* is the most influential forerunner of the Victorian comic journal, but it is primarily a journal of political satire and lacks the scope, balance, and variety of *Punch*.

Figaro in London. 28 February–23 May 1857. Writer: H. G. Brooks. The magazine represents itself as a new series "by all the original writers and contributors."

Figaro in Sheffield. 1832–1838. "Figaro-mania." [Gray]

Figaro in Wales. Bangor (1835–1836), then the *Philo-Figaro* (February 1836). [Gray]

Fiz. 14 December 1878–8 March 1879. Weekly. [Gray]

The Fly. With Which Is Incorporated the "Wonder" and "Novelty." 28 October 1837– 26 December 1840. A poorly written seriocomic weekly.

The Free Lance. A Journal of Humour and Criticism. Manchester. 22 December 1866– 28 December 1878. Weekly. Editor and leading writer: Edwin Simpson.

Fun.* 21 September 1861–1901. Weekly. Owners: Charles M'Lean (1861–1864), Edward Wylam (1865–1870), Dalziel brothers (1870–1893). Editors: H. J. Byron (1861– 13 May 1865), Tom Hood (20 May 1865–November 1874), Henry Sampson (5 December 1874–1878), Charles Dalziel (1878–1893); contributors: Thomas Archer, E. C. Barnes, Ambrose Bierce, E. L. Blanchard, Sidney Blanchard, John C. Brough, William Brough, F. C. Burnand, Henry Saville Clarke, T.H.S. Escott, W. S. Gilbert, Andrew Halliday, T. S. Jerrold, Henry S. Leigh, William Jeffrey Prowse, C. W. Quin, Mayne Reid, T. W. Robertson, George Rose ("Arthur Sketchley"), G. A. Sala, Clement Scott, George R. Sims, J. Ashby Sterry, W. B. Tegetmeier, Walter Thornbury, Godfrey Turner. *Fun*, which is remembered now for the publication of Gilbert's "Bab Ballads," was *Punch*'s most successful rival and surpassed *Punch* in its commentary on literature, fine arts, and the theater.

Funny Folks. A Weekly Budget of Funny Pictures, Funny Notes, Funny Jokes, Funny Stories. 12 December 1874–28 April 1894. Weekly. Publisher: James Henderson. Editor and part-owner: William Kingston Sawyer (1880–1882). Circulation reached 60,000 a week in 1876. As Donald Gray points out, *Funny Folks* marks a shift from the comic journal to the illustrated comic paper.

George Cruikshank's Magazine. January–February 1854. Monthly. Editor: Frank Smedley ("Frank Farleigh"); other writers: Edward Bradley ("Cuthbert Bede"), Alfred W. Cole, Horace Mayhew, Edmund Yates.

George Cruikshank's Omnibus. May 1841–January 1842. Monthly. Editor: Laman Blanchard; other writers: H. G. Adams, Edward Howard, Captain Marryat, W. M. Thackeray, Charles H. Walker. Cruikshank claimed that the idea for *Punch* was taken from his *Omnibus.*

George Cruikshank's Table-Book. January–December 1845. Monthly. Published at the *Punch* office and printed by Bradbury & Evans; leading members of the *Punch* staff were contributors: Percival Leigh ("Paul Prendergast"), Mark Lemon, Horace Mayhew, John Oxenford ("Balzac d'Anois"), and W. M. Thackeray ("Michael Angelo Titmarsh"); Angus B. Reach and Shirley Brooks, who also wrote for the *Table-Book*, had not yet joined *Punch*. The *Table-Book* features comic tales, essays, and sketches, and its satire focuses on social issues.

Giovanni in London. 18 February–24 March 1832. "Figaro-mania."

The Girl of the Period Miscellany. March–November 1869. Seriocomic monthly. Editor: Augustus Mayhew; other writers: J. Ashby Sterry.

The Gownsman. See *The Snob.*

The Great Gun. 16 November 1844–28 June 1845. Weekly. Founded by E. Landells. Editors: F.W.N. ("Alphabet") Bayley (three weeks), then Charles Lewis Gruneisen; other writers: Albert Smith, W. H. Maxwell. *The Great Gun* was the first comic weekly with enough literary and artistic talent to compete with *Punch*. Satire directed at Dickens's works, particularly *The Chimes*, is the magazine's most interesting feature.

The Grumbler. 1870. Weekly. Editor: John Swain(?). [Spielmann/Gray]

The Hornsey Hornet (6 March 1866–1 June 1867), then *The Hornet* (15 June 1867–11 February 1880). Bimonthly until 1873 and then weekly. Seriocomic. Founder and editor: Henry S. Sampson; other writers: Thomas Archer, Frederick Claude Broughton, Joseph Hatton (later editor?), Bernard Shaw.

The Idler. A Magazine of Fiction, Belles Lettres, News, and Comedy. January–June 1856. Seriocomic monthly. Editor: Edward Wilberforce (Spielmann claims James Hannay was editor); other writers: William Allingham, Wiltshire Austin, E. Forster Blanchard, Shirley Brooks, Mortimer Collins, Henry Sutherland Edwards, James Hannay, J. Cordy Jeaffreson, T. E. Kebbel, H. W. Sotheby, G. W. Thornbury.

The Illustrated Comic News. 1 June–21 September 1867. Weekly. [Gray]

The Jester. 23 February–16 March 1889. Weekly. [Gray/Gifford]

Joe Miller the Younger. 3 May–6 December 1845. Weekly. Editor: Richard Brinsley Knowles; other writers: Albert Smith. Purchased in December 1845 by T. P. Healey (owner and editor of the *Medical Times*), who changed the name to *Mephistopheles, or the English Scaramouch* (13 December 1845–28 March 1846); Knowles remained editor, Albert Smith evidently continued as a writer, and E. L. Blanchard became a contributor. The magazine directs satirical gibes at Dickens and prints a burlesque of *The Cricket on the Hearth*.

John Bull* (see *RA*). 17 December 1820–19 July 1892. Weekly. Owners: William Shackell, the printer, and Theodore Hook. Editors: Henry Fox Cooper (nominal editor), Theodore Hook (actual editor), Samuel Carter Hall (subeditor in the 1830s); other writers: John Wilson Croker, Richard Harris Barham ("Thomas Ingoldsby"), Thomas Haynes Bayly, James Hook ("Fitz Harding"), William Maginn, Samuel Rogers; circulation reached 12,000 in the twelfth week. This Tory political paper was established to support king and constitution and to attack Queen Caroline and the Whigs.

Judy. 1843. Editor: Leman Rede.

Judy; or, the London Serio-Comic Journal. 1 May 1867–23 Oct. 1907. Weekly. Owner and publisher: Dalziel brothers. Editor: Charles H. Ross; other writers: E. L. Blanchard, Sydney Gosse, Walter Parke, Sydney Montagu Samuel, Charles Stonhouse(?). *Judy* was conservative, and the leading reformers of the day—Bradlaugh, Bright, and Mill—were the favorite satirical butts. After its first two volumes, which are well written, more and more space is taken up by cartoons.

Junius. 1873. Seriocomic weekly. Editor: Gilbert Arthur à Beckett; other writers: Arthur William à Beckett, G. W. Godfrey. Continued as *The Torch* (26 November 1873–28 January 1874); editor: Joseph Hatton.

The Knight Errant. An Independent Journal of Irish Wit and Humour. Dublin. 1870–1874. Weekly. [Gray]

Lika Joko. An Illustrated Weekly Conducted by Harry Furniss. October 1894–April 1895. Monthly, then weekly. Other writers: E. V. Lucas, C. L. Graves.

The Literary Test. A Liberal, Moral, and Independent Weekly Review. 1832. "Figaro-mania."

The Liverpool Lantern. A Critical and Humorous Journal. 12 October 1878–2 December 1882. Weekly. [Gray]

The Liverpool Lion (10 April–25 December 1847), then as *The Lion, or, Lancashire Charivari* (1 January–12 February 1848). Founder and editor: Robert Barnabas Brough; other writers: William Brough.

The London Figaro. A Political, Literary, and Satirical Journal. 17 May 1870–31 December 1898. Daily until 18 March 1871, then a seriocomic weekly. Owner and editor: James Mortimer; other writers: William Archer, Ernest Bendall, Percy Betts, Edward Bradley ("Cuthbert Bede"), Aglen Dowty ("O.P.Q. Philander Smiff"), John Baker Hopkins, Frank Marshall, Edwin J. Milliken, Clement Scott. Augustin Filon attributes the "emancipation" of Victorian drama criticism to this "gallant and witty little journal" under Mortimer's editorship.

The London Policeman. 1833. Weekly. "Figaro-mania." [Spielmann/Burnand/Gray]

The Look-Out. Sheffield. 1882–1883. Weekly. [Gray]

MacPunch, or, the Scottish Charivari. Edinburgh. August 1868–March 1869. [Gray]

The Man in the Moon. January 1847–June 1849. Monthly. Owner: Herbert Ingram. Editors: Angus B. Reach and Albert Smith (vols. 1–2), Reach (vols. 3–5); other writers: Shirley Brooks, Stirling Coyne, Alfred Henry Forrester ("Alfred Crowquill"), James Hannay, Charles L. Kenney, Augustus Mayhew, John Oxenford, G. A. Sala (as artist). A new, inferior weekly series was edited by Robert Brough, who was assisted by his brother William (7 July 1849–11 August 1849?). The *Man in the Moon* was the best written and most successful of *Punch's* rivals in the 1840s. The monthly is distinguished by a large volume of literary satire and by frequent use of burlesque and parody.

The Mask. A Humorous and Fantastic Review of the Month. February–December 1868. Monthly. Editors and writers: Alfred Thompson and Leopold Lewis. Like the *Man in the Moon*, the *Mask* is well written and essentially apolitical; the subjects of its humor and satire are art, literature, and the theater.

The Mask. A Satirical Review of the Week in Caricatures. 10 May–27 August 1879. Weekly. Editor and writer: Alfred Thompson. An unsuccessful attempt to revive the *Mask* as a weekly.

Mephistopheles; or, the English Scaramouch. See *Joe Miller the Younger.*

The Meteor. May–July 1845. A poorly written seriocomic monthly. Editor: John Leslie Buckstone; other writers: Charles Westerton.

Mirth. A Miscellany of Wit and Humour. November 1877–October 1878. Monthly. Owner and publisher: Tinsley brothers. Editor: H. J. Byron; other writers: James Albery, William Archer, E. L. Blanchard, C. S. Cheltnam, Dillon Croker. Henry Sutherland Edwards, W. S. Gilbert, Sidney Grundy, Thomas Anstey Guthrie ("F. Anstey"), John Hollingshead, Evelyn Jerrold, Henry S. Leigh, James Robinson Planché, Robert Reece, Clement Scott, J. Ashby Sterry, Godfrey Turner.

Mrs. Brown's Budget. 1 August 1870–11 January 1871. Editor and leading writer: Rev. George Rose ("Arthur Sketchley").

The Month. A View of Passing Subjects and Manners, Home and Foreign, Social and General. July–December 1851. Monthly. Printers: Bradbury & Evans. Editor: Albert Smith; other writers: E. L. Blanchard, Edward Bradley ("Cuthbert Bede"), Henry Silver. As Albert Smith promised in the first number, the *Month* refrains from "opposing anything or anybody," and its satire and humor are "chiefly social."

Moonshine. July 1879–August 1902. Weekly. Editors: Charles Harrison, then Arthur Clements (after 1893); other writers: Henry S. Leigh, J. G. Lumsden, Ogden Palmer, William Taylor. According to Donald Gray, *Moonshine* "began in *Punch* mode," but by the 1890s was "given a little more to straight political comment and theatrical reviews."

The New Figaro. 17 March–31 March 1832. Weekly. "Figaro-mania." [Spielmann/Gray]

The Odd Fellow. 5 January 1839–10 December 1842. Seriocomic weekly. Publisher: Henry Hetherington. Editors: James Cooke (1839–1841), W. J. Linton (1841–1842); other writers: Thomas Moore?

The Original. A Weekly Miscellany of Humour, Literature, and the Fine Arts. 3 March– 28 July 1832. Seriocomic weekly. Editors: William John Thoms ("W.J.T."), H. P. Grattan ("Fusbos").

The Owl. Birmingham. 30 January 1879–1 September 1911. Weekly. [Gray]

The Owl. A Wednesday Journal of Politics and Society. 20 April 1864–28 July 1869. Weekly journal of political satire. Owner: Sir Algernon Borthwick. Cofounders: Laurence Oliphant and Edward Montagu Stuart Wharncliff. Editor: Evelyn Ashley; other writers: Thomas Gibson Bowles, Philip Currie, Charles Freemantle, Frank Marshall, Rivers Wilson. A successful, cleverly written political journal, having more in common with the turn-of-the-century *Anti-Jacobin* than with *Punch* or *Fun*.

Pasquin. 1850. Weekly. An attempt to revive the 1847 *Pasquin*?

Pasquin. A Satirical, Political, Critical, Theatrical, Whimsical, and Quizzical Chronicle. 14 August–2 October 1847. Weekly. Editors and leading contributors: Henry Sutherland Edwards and James Hannay; other writers: Joseph Crowe? Dickens, Jerrold of *Punch*, and Smith and Reach of the *Man in the Moon* are the favorite satirical targets of this short-lived comic weekly.

Pat. Dublin. 1879–3 March 1883. Weekly. [Spielmann/Gray]

Paul Pry. 18 February–12 August 1826. Journal of political satire.

Paul Pry. 1830. Journal of political satire. Publisher, printer, and editor: Frederick Fox Cooper.

The Penny Punch. A Chip of the Old Block. 1849. Weekly. Published, edited, and largely written by Thomas Frost.

The Penny Satirist. 22 April 1837–25 April 1846. Weekly journal of political satire. Editor: Bernard Gregory; other writers: J. E. "Shepherd" Smith.

The Period. An Illustrated Satirical and Critical Review of What Is Going On. 30 October 1869–18 February 1871. Seriocomic weekly. Alfred Thompson provided illustrations and was probably a literary contributor. This cleverly written magazine is at its best in its poetic parodies and imitations.

The Phonographic Punch. October 1888–September 1891. Editor: J. H. Ford. [Gray]

The Phonographic Punch. A Monthly Illustrated Comic Shorthand Magazine. Birmingham. November 1884–May 1886. [Gray]

Pick-Me-Up. 6 October 1888–2 January 1909. Seriocomic weekly. Editor: Angelo J. Lewis.

The Porcupine. A Journal of Current Events—Social, Political, and Satirical. Liverpool. 6 October 1860–27 March 1915. Weekly. Editor and proprietor: Hugh Shimmin (1860–1871), then Charles Millward(?); other writers: Thomas Cope, T. W. Robertson, Gustave Louis Maurice Strauss.

Puck (12 January 1889–28 June 1890), then as *Ariel, or the London Puck* (5 July 1890–6 February 1892). Weekly. Editor: Israel Zangwill.

Puck. A Journalette of Fun. 6 May–November 1844. Weekly, then biweekly (absorbed by the *Great Gun*, November 1844?). Publisher: Chatto. Editor: Albert Smith; other writers: E. L. Blanchard, Tom Taylor, Watts Phillips (as an artist).

Punch and Judy. 9 October 1869–8 October 1870. Weekly. Owner: Lord Kilmorey (Lord Newry); other writers: V. C. Malins?

Y Punch Cymraeg. Holyhead. 1858–1864. [Spielmann/Gray]

Punch, or, the London Charivari. 17 July 1841–. Weekly.

Punch in Cambridge. 1832. [Gray]

Punch in London. 14 January–4 May 1832. Weekly. Editor (early numbers): Douglas Jerrold. The first of many imitations of *Figaro in London.*

Punchinello. 4 March 1854–17 February 1855. Weekly. Publisher and editor: Peter Morrison; other writers: Thomas Littleton Holt, George Augustus Sala, Gustave Louis Maurice Strauss.

Punchinello! or, Sharps, Flats, and Naturals. A Family Gazette of Fun, Fashion, Literature, and the Drama. 21 January–23 March 1832. Weekly. "Figaro-mania."

The Puppet Show (18 March 1848–14 July 1849), then the *New Puppet-Show* (until 25 August 1849). Weekly. Owner and publisher: Vizetelly brothers. Editor: John Bridgeman; other writers: E. L. Blanchard, Robert Brough, Henry Sutherland Edwards, James Hannay (a cofounder), Charles Mackay, William North, Henry Vizetelly (Henry Vizetelly claims that Shirley Brooks and Angus B. Reach were also contributors). The weekly devotes too much space to satirical gibes at rival comic magazines. The most interesting feature is "Showman and Friend," a series of satirical dialogues in rhyming couplets in imitation of Alexander Pope.

Quiz. A Comical, Satirical, Quizzical . . . Magazine. July–August 1858. Monthly. [Gray]

Quiz. A Comic Political Miscellany. 1869. Weekly. [Spielmann/Gray]

Quiz. The Satirist. 25 June–16 August 1879. Weekly. Publisher: Adolphus Rosenberg. [Spielmann/Gray]

The Quizzical Gazette and Merry Companion (27 August 1831–27 November 1831), then as the *Quizzical Gazette, or Moral and Satirical Reflector* (3 December–17 December 1831). Seriocomic weekly. Editor: John ("Jack" or "Mad") Mitford.

The Razor, or the London Humorist and Satirist. 1868. Weekly. [Spielmann/Gray]

The Reformer, or, the Schoolmaster Abroad. 1832. Weekly. "Figaro-mania."

Round About. 13 May–30 December 1882. Seriocomic weekly. [Gray]

Sam Weller, a Journal of Wit and Humour. 1837.

The Satirist, or Monthly Meteor* (see *RA*). October 1807–August 1814. Journal of political satire. Founder and part-owner: George Manners. Editors: George Manners (until 1812), William Jerdan (1812–1814); other writers: Lancelot Sharpe.

The Satirist, or the Censor of the Times. 10 April 1831–15 December 1849. A weekly journal of political satire and scandal, universally condemned for its scurrility. Editor: Bernard Gregory; other writers: Hewson Clarke, Tom Moore(?).

The Schoolmaster at Home. 9 June–14 July 1832. Weekly. "Figaro-mania."

The Scorpion. A Regular Stinger. 13 October–10 November 1877. Weekly.

The Scourge, or, Monthly Expositor of Imposture and Folly* (see *RA*) (January 1811–April 1814), then the *Scourge and Satirist, or, Literary, Theatrical and Miscellaneous Magazine* (May 1814–December 1816). A journal of political, social, and literary satire and scandal. Owner: Mr. Earle. Editor: John ("Jack" or "Mad") Mitford; other writers: Hewson Clarke, John Gwilliam.

The Serio-Comic Magazine. Conducted by I. Z. Ximenes (1868); then the *Iris. A Serio-Comic Magazine* (1868–1869). Monthly. [Gray]

The Shorthand Star. October 1888–August 1891. A seriocomic phonographic monthly. Editor: Edward J. Nankivell.

The Snob. A Literary and Scientific Journal, NOT "Conducted by Members of the University" (1829); then as *The Gownsman. A Literary and Scientific Journal, Now Conducted by Members of the University* (1829–1830). Writer: W. M. Thackeray. Thackeray made his debut as a humorist and satirist as a contributor to the two Cambridge University magazines. The bad puns, the frequent poems and jokes about smoking and drinking, and the town-gown sketches become tiresome, but there are several good burlesques and parodies in these undergraduate magazines.

The Squib. A Granulation of Wit, Satire, and Amusement. 28 May–17 December 1842. Weekly. Owner, publisher, and printer: Joseph Last. Editor: Henry Willoughby Grattan Plunkett ("Henry Plunkett Grattan") or Gilbert Abbott à Beckett. This weekly resembles *Punch*, and Gilbert Abbott à Beckett and other *Punch* writers were contributors.

The Squib. A Satire on Passing Events in Lancashire. Manchester. 28 July 1832–20 April 1833. [Gray]

Swansea Boy. South Wales Critic and Humorist. Swansea. 1878–1881. Weekly. [Gray]

T. Dibdin's Penny Trumpet. 20 October 1832–? 1832. Seriocomic weekly. Owners: Gilbert Abbott à Beckett and Thomas Littleton Holt. Editor: Gilbert Abbott à Beckett. Thomas Dibdin's writing is featured.

Toby. An Illustrated Satirical Journal for London. 27 March 1886–12 October 1889. Weekly. [Gray]

Toby, the London Comic Critic. 1867–1868. Weekly. Editor: Percy Cruikshank. [Spielmann/Gray]

The Tomahawk. A Saturday Journal of Satire. 11 May 1867–27 August 1870. A weekly which achieved a circulation of 50,000. Editor: Arthur William à Beckett; other writers: Gilbert Arthur à Beckett, Alfred Austin, Thomas Gibson Bowles, Frederick C. Clay, R.H.S. Escott, Frank Marshall, Alfred Thompson. Liberal in its politics, the *Tomahawk* is well written and successfully combines features of both *Punch* and the *Owl*.

The Torch. See *Junius.*

The Town. A Journal of Original Essays, Characteristic of the Manners, Social, Domestic, and Superficial, of London and the Londoners. 3 June 1837–26 January 1842. Publisher: Mr. Forrester. Printer and part owner: Joseph William Last. Editor: Renton Nicholson; other writers: E. L. Blanchard, J. G. Canning, William Maginn, Henry Pellott. A journal of social and political scandal and innuendo.

Town Talk. 8 May 1858–14 November 1859. Seriocomic weekly. Founder: John Maxwell. Editor: Edmund Yates; other writers: Andrew Halliday, John Hollingshead, Watts Phillips. Although the magazine investigates social problems of the day, sometimes seriously and sometimes satirically, the typical issue is given over largely to "talk" or gossip on a wide range of subjects.

The Train. A First-Class Magazine. January 1856–June 1858. A seriocomic monthly funded initially with the pooled contributions of the staff of the *Comic Times* after its collapse. Editor: Edmund Yates; other writers: Thomas Archer, E. L. Blanchard, John Bridgeman, Robert and William Brough, Lewis Carroll, Maurice Davis, Edward Draper, Henry Sutherland Edwards, J. Hain Friswell, Andrew Halliday, William P. Hale, John Hollingshead, John Oxenford, G. A. Sala, J. Palgrave Simpson, Frank Smedley, Moy Thomas, Godfrey Turner.

The Wag. 1833. Monthly? Spielmann attributes its editorship to Gilbert Abbott à Beckett.

The Wag. 23 September 1837–? 1837. Weekly. Editor: Gilbert Abbott à Beckett?

The Wasp. A Literary Satire. 30 September–16 December 1826. Weekly. Editor: Robert Mudie?

The Weekly Show-Up, or Practical, Satirical, and General Humorist. 1832. "Figaro-mania."

The Whig Dresser. 5 January 1833–? 1833. Monthly. A Tory magazine of political satire with a format similar to *Figaro in London*.

Will-o'-the-Wisp. 12 September 1868–3 September 1870. Seriocomic weekly. Editor: Hamilton Hume. During its first eight or nine months, the *Will-o'-the-Wisp* is well written, focuses on politics, and resembles the *Owl*. During April 1869 the magazine begins to look like *Judy* in its decline and prints less satire and more humorous serials and cartoons.

Yorick. A Journal of Wit, Humour, and Satire. 1 December 1876–1877. Weekly? Founder: Richard Dowling. This magazine is supposed to have taken the *Tomahawk* for its model.

The Yorkshireman. Bradford. January 1875–27 May 1899. Weekly. [Gray]

Zoz. Dublin. 8 July 1876–11 October 1879. Weekly. [Gray]

Zozimus. Dublin. 18 May 1870–31 August 1872. Weekly. Editor and leading contributor: Richard Dowling.

A Selected Bibliography of Sources

À Beckett, Arthur William. *The à Becketts of "Punch."* London, 1903.

Blanchard, Edward Leman. *The Life and Adventures of Edward Leman Blanchard*. Edited by Clement Scott and Cecil Howard. 2 vols. London, 1891.

Burnand, Francis Cowley. "Mr. Punch: His Predecessors and Contemporaries." *Pall Mall Magazine* 29 (1903):95–105, 255–65, 390–97.

Ellis, James. "*The Comic Times.*" *Victorian Periodicals Newsletter*, no. 12 (1971):14–15.

Ellis, Ted R., III. "The Dramatist and the Comic Journal in England, 1830–1870." *Victorian Periodicals Newsletter*, no. 14 (1971):29–31.

Gifford, Denis. *Victorian Comics*. London, 1976.

Gray, Donald J. "A List of Comic Periodicals Published in Great Britain, 1800–1900, with a Prefatory Essay." *Victorian Periodicals Newsletter*, no. 15 (1972):2–39.

[Hannay, James]. "English Political Satires." *Quarterly Review* 101 (1857):394–441.

James, Louis. *Fiction for the Working Man, 1830–1850*. London, 1963.

Jerdan, William. *The Autobiography of William Jerdan*. 2 vols. London, 1852.

Lauterbach, Edward S. "*Fun* and Its Contributors: The Literary History of a Victorian Humor Magazine." Ph.D. dissertation, University of Illinois, Urbana, 1961.

Price, R.G.G. *A History of "Punch."* London, 1957.

Sala, George Augustus. *The Life and Adventures of George Augustus Sala*. 2 vols. New York, 1895.

Scott, Clement. "The Foundations of *Fun*." *Sketch*, 20 September 1898, p. 412.

Spielmann, Marion H. *The History of "Punch."* New York, 1895.

———. "The Rivals of *Punch*." *National Review* 25 (1895):654–66.

[Thackeray, William Makepeace]. "Half-a-Crown's Worth of Cheap Knowledge." *Fraser's Magazine* 17 (1838):279–90.

Thorington, James Monroe. *Mont Blanc Sideshow: The Life and Times of Albert Smith*. Philadelphia, 1943.

Vizetelly, Henry. *Glances Back Through Seventy Years*. 2 vols. London, 1893.

Worth, George J. *James Hannay: His Life and Works*. Lawrence, Kans., 1964.

Yates, Edmund. *Edmund Yates: His Recollections and Experiences*. 2 vols. London, 1884.

Ted R. Ellis III

Nineteenth-Century Religious Magazines with Literary Contents

Arminian Magazine. 1778–1797; then *Methodist Magazine*, 1798–1821; then *Wesleyan Methodist Magazine*, 1822–1926; then *Methodist Magazine*, 1927–. Monthly. Methodist (Wesleyan). Editors: John Wesley, 1778–1791; George Story, 1791–1803; Joseph Benson, 1804–1821; Jabez Bunting, 1822–1824; T. Jackson, 1824–?; G. Cubitt; W. L. Thornton; W. H. Rule. Contains poetry; reviews after 1821.

Atlantis. 1858–1860, 1862–1863, 1870. Semiannual to 1860, later annual. Roman Catholic (Catholic University of Ireland). Editors: J. H. Newman, 1858; W. K. Sullivan, 1858–1863; P. le P. Renouf, 1859–1863; Bartholomew Woodlock, 1870. Scholarly, half literary and half scientific.

Baptist Magazine. 1809–1904. Monthly. Baptist (particular). Editor: Thomas Smith, 1809–? Contains short reviews. Absorbed *New Baptist Miscellany* 1833, which superseded *New Baptist Magazine* 1827.

British Critic* (see *RA*). 1793–1843. Monthly; quarterly from 1825. Anglican (High Church 1814, Tractarian 1838). Editors: Robert Nares, 1793–1813; (H. H. Norris, director, 1814–1838); A. M. Campbell, 1824–1833; J. S. Boone, 1834–1837; S. R. Maitland, 1838; J. H. Newman, 1836–1837, 1838–1841; Thomas Mozley, 1841–1843. 10–20 percent literary. Merged with *Quarterly Theological Review* (1824–1827). Replaced by *English Review*, 1844–1853.

British Quarterly Review. 1845–1886. Quarterly. Nonconformist (moderate, chiefly Congregationalist). Editors: Robert Vaughan, 1845–1865; Henry Allon, 1866–1886; H. R. Reynolds, 1866–1874. 15–20 percent literary; section of short reviews. Contributors include G. H. Lewes, David Masson, Coventry Patmore, and Herbert Spencer.

British Weekly. 1886–. Weekly. Nonconformist. Editor: William Robertson Nicoll, 1886–1923. Some literary criticism. Nicoll also edited *Expositor*, 1875–1925, monthly, for the ministry.

Christian Ambassador. 1863–1878; then *Primitive Methodist Quarterly Review*, 1879–1909; then *Holborn Review*, 1910–1932. Quarterly. Primitive Methodist. Editors: C. C. M'Kechnie, 1863–1878(?); John Watson; H. B. Kendall, 1910–1932. Essays. Merged with *London Quarterly Review* 1932.

Christian Observer. 1802–1877. Monthly. Anglican (evangelical). Editors: Josiah Pratt, 1802; Zachary Macaulay, 1802–1816; S. C. Wilks; J. W. Cunningham. Some literary criticism, poetry. Contributors include T. B. Macaulay and J. H. Newman. Best of the evangelical periodicals.

Christian Reformer. 1815–1863. Monthly. Unitarian. Editors: Robert Aspland, 1815–1844; R. B. Aspland, 1844–1863. Less literary than other Unitarian magazines; expanded 1834 to replace *Monthly Repository*. Succeeded by *Theological Review* 1864.

Christian Remembrancer. 1819–1868. Monthly; quarterly from 1844. Anglican (High Church). Editors: Frederick Iremonger, 1819–?; William Scott, 1841–?. Contributors include R. W. Church. Some literary content.

Christian Teacher. 1835–1844. Monthly. Unitarian. Editors: J. R. Beard, 1835–1838; J. H. Thom, 1838–1844. Contributors include Harriet and James Martineau. Occasioned by the lapse of *Monthly Repository*. Continued by *Prospective Review** 1845.

Church Quarterly Review. 1875–. Quarterly. Anglican. Editor: A. R. Ashwell, 1876–1879. 10–15 percent literary; short notices.

Church Review. 1861–1902. Monthly; weekly from 1862. Anglican (High Church: English Church Union). Widened 1862 to general topics.

Contemporary Review.* 1866–. Monthly. Nonsectarian, but religious until 1882. Editors: Henry Alford, 1866–1870; J. T. Knowles, 1870–1877; Alexander Strahan, 1877–1882; Percy Bunting, 1882–? 10–15 percent literary; short notices 1868–1870, 1877–? Contributors include F. Max Müller, T. H. Huxley, Walter Bagehot, Herbert Spencer, John Ruskin, Fitzjames Stephen, R. H. Hutton, Matthew Arnold, Alfred Austin, and W. H. Mallock.

Dublin Review* (see *RA*). 1836–1969. Quarterly. Roman Catholic (official from 1850). Editors: M. J. Quinn, 1836; M. A. Tierney, 1836; James Smith, 1837; H. R. Bagshawe (directed by Nicholas Wiseman and C. W. Russell), 1837–1863; W. G. Ward, 1863–1878; J. C. Hedley, 1879–1884; Herbert Vaughan, 1885–1891; James Moyes, 1892–? 20 percent literary, short notices.

Eclectic Review* (see *RA*). 1805–1868. Monthly. Nonconformist. Editors: Samuel Greathead, 1805; Daniel Parken; Theophilus Williams, 1812–1814; Josiah Conder, 1814–1836; Thomas Price, 1837–1855; W. H. Stowell, 1851–1855; J. E. Ryland, 1855–1856; E. P. Hood, 1861–1868. Literary reviews.

English Churchman. 1843–1864; then *Churchman*, 1864–1868; then *English Churchman*, 1868–. Weekly. Anglican (High Church). Some literary content.

Evangelical Magazine. 1793–1904. Monthly. Evangelical, primarily Nonconformist. Editors: John Eyre, 1793–1802; George Burder, 1802–? Some literary articles, poetry.

Friend. 1843–. Monthly; weekly from 1892. Quaker. Some literary content. (Not to be confused with Coleridge's *Friend*, 1809–1810.) Absorbed *British Friend*, founded 1843, in 1913.

Friends' Quarterly Examiner. 1867–. Quarterly. Quaker. Editor: W. C. Westlake. A magazine rather than a review; some literary articles.

*Good Words.** 1860–1911. Weekly. Evangelical (Church of Scotland). Editor: Norman Macleod, 1860–1872. Popular, with serialized novels. Contributors include Charles Kingsley and Anthony Trollope.

Guardian. 1846–. Weekly. Anglican (High Church). Editors: Frederick Rogers, Montague Bernard, Thomas Haddan, R. W. Church, James Mozley. Extensive and able literary section.

Home and Foreign Review. 1862–1864. Quarterly. Roman Catholic (liberal). Editor: Sir John Acton. 10–15 percent literary articles; many short notices, 20 percent literary. Scholarly. Succeeded *Rambler.**

Inquirer. 1842–. Weekly. Unitarian. Editors: R. H. Hutton, Walter Bagehot, 1851–1853. Contributors include James Martineau. Less exclusively religious than most religious newspapers.

Journal of Sacred Literature. 1848–1868. Quarterly. Nonsectarian, orthodox. Editors: John Kitto, 1848–1854; Henry Burgess, 1854–1862; B. H. Cooper, 1861–1868. Scholarly, specialized reviewing of "religious, theological and philosophical literature."

London Christian Instructor, or Congregational Magazine, 1818–1824; then *Congregational Magazine*, 1835–1845; then *Biblical Review and Congregational Magazine*, 1846–1850. Monthly. Congregationalist. Essays and reviews; less literary than *Eclectic Review*.

*London Quarterly Review.** 1853–1968 (styled *London Review* 1858–1862). Quarterly. Methodist. 10–15 percent literary; short reviews. Absorbed *Holborn Review* (formerly *Christian Ambassador*) 1932.

Modern Review. 1880–1884. Quarterly. Unitarian (open). Editors: R. A. Armstrong, 1880–1881; R. C. Jones, 1882–1884. 10 percent literary, short reviews.

*Month.** 1864–. Monthly. Roman Catholic (from 1865, Society of Jesus). Editors: Fanny M. Taylor, 1864–1865; H. J. Coleridge, 1865–1881; R. F. Clarke, 1882–1894; John Gerard, 1894–1897, 1901–1912; S. F. Smith, 1897–1901. 10–15 percent literary; short reviews, plus "Literary Record" from 1882; novels and poetry in earlier volumes. Increasingly philosophical and historical.

Monthly Repository. 1806–1838. Monthly. Unitarian (less religious from 1832, secular by 1836). Editor: Robert Aspland, 1802–1826; W. J. Fox, 1828–1836; R. H. Horne, 1836–1837; Leigh Hunt, 1837–1838. Literary reviews (more from 1829), some poetry, translations, some fiction from 1832. Contributors include H. Crabb Robinson, Harriet Martineau, J. S. Mill, James Martineau, and Robert Browning. Succeeded *Universal Theological Magazine* (1802–1805), successor of *Universalist's Miscellany* (1796–1802), both edited by William Vidler.

National Review.* 1855–1864. Quarterly. Unitarian (general liberal Christian from 1862). Editors: Walter Bagehot, 1855–1864; R. H. Hutton, 1855–1862; C. H. Pearson, 1862–1863. 30 percent literary. Contributors include James Martineau, Francis Newman, Coventry Patmore, Mark Pattison, Herbert Spencer, Fitzjames Stephen, J. A. Froude, and Matthew Arnold. Succeeded *Prospective Review* and *Christian Teacher*. (Not to be confused with the *National Review*,* 1883–1960.)

North British Review.* 1844–1871. Quarterly. Free Church of Scotland; from 1869, Roman Catholic (liberal). Editors: David Welsh, 1844–1845; E. F. Maitland, 1845–1846; William Hanna, 1847–1850; A. C. Fraser, 1850–1857; John Duns, 1857–1860; W. G. Blaikie, 1860–1863; David Douglas, 1863–1869; T. F. Wetherell, 1869–1871. 20 percent literary; extensive short reviews from 1869. Contributors include Lord Acton.

Patriot. 1832–1866; then *English Independent*, 1867–1879. Weekly. Congregationalist. Editor: Josiah Conder, 1832–1855. Some general literature, well reviewed. Absorbed *British Banner* (1848–1858). Merged with *Nonconformist* (1841–1890, not literary) 1880.

Prospective Review.* 1845–1855. Quarterly. Unitarian. Editors: James Martineau, J. J. Tayler, J. H. Thom, 1845–1855; Charles Wicksteed, 1845–1854; W. C. Roscoe, 1852–1855; R. H. Hutton, 1853–1855. 20 percent literary; occasional short notices. Contributors include Walter Bagehot, Francis Newman. Succeeded *Christian Teacher*; succeeded by *National Review*.

Rambler.* 1848–1862. Weekly; from September 1848 monthly; from May 1859 bimonthly. Roman Catholic (liberal). Editors: J. M. Capes, 1848–1852, 1854–1857; J. S. Northcote, 1852–1857; Richard Simpson, 1858–1859; J. H. Newman, 1859; Sir John Acton, 1859–1862. 15 percent literary articles; short notices, expanded 1858; serializ·d novels to 1857; some poetry. Succeeded by *Home and Foreign Review*.

Spectator* (see *RA*). 1828–. Weekly. From 1861 to 1897, Broad Church Anglican. Editor: R. H. Hutton, 1861–1897. Distinguished literary reviewing.

Theological Review. 1864–1879. Bimonthly; from 1866, quarterly. Unitarian (increasingly open). Editor: Charles Beard. 5–10 percent literary; short notices. Succeeded *Christian Reformer*, 1815–1863.

Josef L. Altholz

Index

Contributors

JOSEF L. ALTHOLZ, Professor of History at the University of Minnesota, is the author of *The Liberal Catholic Movement in England* (1962) and past president of the Research Society for Victorian Periodicals.

WILLIAM BAKER is Senior Lecturer in English at the West Midlands College of Higher Education (Walsall, England). He has contributed to *Victorian Studies, Nineteenth Century Fiction,* and *English Studies,* and edits the *George Eliot-George Henry Lewes Newsletter.*

J. O. BAYLEN is Regents' Professor of History Emeritus at Georgia State University and coeditor of the four-volume *Biographical Dictionary of Modern British Radicals, 1770–1940* (1978).

ED BLOCK, JR.'s essays on Victorian subjects appear in the *Victorian Periodicals Review, Victorian Studies,* and the *Journal of the History of Ideas.*

DARWIN F. BOSTICK, Associate Professor of History at Old Dominion University, has published several articles in the *Victorian Periodicals Review.*

JOHN F. BYRNE teaches at Illinois Benedictine College and is Associate Editor of the *Review of Contemporary Fiction.*

FRANKLIN E. COURT has published two books on Pater—*Pater and His Early Critics* and *Walter Pater: An Annotated Bibliography of Writings About Him* (1980)—and numerous articles on Victorian and transitional literature in such journals as *Victorian Newsletter, ELH, English Literature in Transition, Victorians Institute Journal, Papers on Language and Literature* and *Modern Fiction Studies.*

EILEEN M. CURRAN, Professor at Colby College, is an Associate Editor for the *Wellesley Index to Victorian Periodicals* and author of several reviews in *Victorian Periodicals Review.*

CORNELIUS P. DARCY is Professor at Western Maryland College.

BARBARA J. DUNLAP is on the library staff at City College of the City University of New York.

TED ELLIS teaches English at East Carolina University and has written on comic journals in *Victorian Periodicals Review* (1971, 1982).

BENJAMIN FRANKLIN FISHER IV is Associate Professor of English and Editor of the *University of Mississippi Studies in English*.

RICHARD D. FULTON is Coeditor of the *North American Union List of Victorian Serials*.

JOHN R. GRIFFIN has written about the *Quarterly Review* in *Review of English Studies* and the *Edinburgh Review* in the *Intellectual Milieu of Lord Macaulay*.

MARY HEATH is Senior Editor of the *Massachusetts Review*.

CLAIRE HIRSHFIELD is Professor of History at the Pennsylvania State University, Ogontz Campus, and author of articles on late Victorian political journalism in the *Victorian Periodicals Review* and *Cahiers Victoriens et Edouardiens*.

ROBERT STAHR HOSMON is the Assistant for Cultural Affairs in the Florida Department of State.

BILLIE ANDREW INMAN, Professor of English at the University of Arizona, has written about Walter Pater in essays in *Papers on Language and Literature* and *Prose Studies*.

CHRISTOPHER KENT is a Director of the Research Society for Victorian Periodicals and author of *Brains and Numbers, Elitism, Comtism and Democracy in Victorian England* (1978).

MISSY DEHN KUBITSCHEK is Assistant Professor at the University of Nebraska at Omaha.

CATHARINE WEAVER McCUE is Assistant Professor at Framingham State College.

KERRY McSWEENEY, Professor at Queen's University (Kingston, Ontario), is the author of *Tennyson and Swinburne as Romantic Naturalists* (1981) and *Four Contemporary Novelists: Angus Wilson, Brian Moore, John Fowles, V. S. Naipaul* (1983) and editor of Eliot's *Middlemarch* (1984).

PATRICIA MARKS is the author of *The Smiling Muse: Victoriana in the Comic Press* and *Index to Drama and Literary Reviews, 1880-1900*.

NANCY AYCOCK METZ teaches at the Virginia Polytechnic Institute and State University.

SALLY MITCHELL, Assistant Professor of English at Temple University, is the author of *Dinah Mulock Craik* (1983) and *The Fallen Angel: Chastity, Class and Women's Reading, 1835–1880* (1981). She is a member of the board of directors of the Research Society for Victorian Periodicals.

HANS OSTROM, who teaches English at the University of Puget Sound, has written *Leigh Hunt: A Reference Guide* (1984) and is currently studying the verse satire that appeared in British periodicals during the Romantic period.

JAMES W. PARINS, Professor at the University of Arkansas at Little Rock, is coauthor of A *Biobibliography of Native American Writers, 1772–1924* (1981) and a volume in Greenwood Press Historical Guides to the World's Periodicals and Newspapers series: *American Indian and Alaska Native Newspapers and Periodicals, 1826–1924* (1984).

MARYLYN J. PARINS teaches at the University of Arkansas at Little Rock and is writing a book on Arthurian romance criticism in the nineteenth century.

KERRY POWELL is the author of four recent essays on *Dorian Gray* in the *Victorian Newsletter, Philological Quarterly, Papers on Language and Literature,* and *English Language Notes.*

CLAUDE A. PRANCE has studied magazines extensively in his *Index to the London Magazine* (1978), *Peppercorn Papers* (1965), *The Laughing Philosopher* (1976), and *Companion to Charles Lamb* (1983).

RONALD PRIMEAU is Coeditor of the *Great Lakes Review: A Journal of Midwest Culture.*

DANIEL RUTENBERG is Professor at the University of South Florida and has published widely on late Victorian periodicals.

CAROL DE SAINT VICTOR, Associate Professor of English at the University of Iowa, has published essays on *The Spirit of the Age*, Dickens's early fiction, and the American feminist and scholar, Anne Allinson.

JEROLD J. SAVORY is Professor and Vice President for Administration at Columbia College and author of *The Smiling Muse: Victoriana in the Comic Press* (1984) (coauthored with Patricia Marks), *The Vanity Fair Gallery* (1979), and *The Vanity Fair Lithographs* (1978).

WILLIAM H. SCHEUERLE is Professor of English and Dean of Undergraduate Studies at the University of South Florida. He is coordinator for the *DNB* Periodicals Project and on the board of the Research Society for Victorian Periodicals.

BARBARA QUINN SCHMIDT teaches at Southern Illinois University at Edwardsville. She recently published a study of the *Cornhill Magazine* in *Innovators and Preachers: The Role of the Editor in Victorian Britain.*

SANDRA SIEGEL teaches English at Cornell University.

CHARLES L. P. SILET, Associate Professor of English at Iowa State University, has prepared *Transition: An Author Index* (1980) and *"The American Caravan*: An Author Index."

DICKIE A. SPURGEON, Professor of English at Southern Illinois University at Edwardsville, is editor of *Tudor Translations of the Colloquies of Erasmus* (1972) and *Three Tudor Dialogues* (1978).

JANE W. STEDMAN, Professor of English at Roosevelt University, has published articles and reviews in *Twentieth Century Crime and Mystery Writers, Modern Philology, Dickensian, College English, Bulletin of the New York Public Library, Education Theatre Journal, Gilbert and Sullivan Journal, Opera News, Journal of Popular Culture, Journal of American Culture*, and *Theatre Notebook*.

J. DON VANN is coauthor with Rosemary T. VanArsdel of *Victorian Periodicals: A Guide to Research* (1978) and is the former bibliographer and compiler of annual bibliography for the *Victorian Periodicals Newsletter*.

CYNTHIA WAGUESPACK is a graduate student at Emory University.

ROGER P. WALLINS is Assistant Dean of the Graduate School and Associate Professor of English at the University of Idaho. He is an Idaho contributor to the *Union List of Victorian Serials* (1984).

CHARLOTTE C. WATKINS is Professor Emeritus of English at Howard University. Her articles on eighteenth-century literature and Victorian studies have appeared in the *Victorian Periodicals Review*.

MARY ANTHONY WEINIG, SHCJ, is author of *Coventry Patmore* (1981) and *Verbal Pattern in Four Quartets* (1982).

MARK A. WEINSTEIN, who teaches English at the University of Nevada at Las Vegas, is the author of *William Edmondstoune Aytoun and the Spasmodic Controversy* (1968) and *"Tait's* on the Cheap and Dear Periodicals," *Victorian Periodicals Newsletter* (1981).

MARTHA WESTWATER is the author of *The Wilson Sisters: A Biographical Study of Upper Middle-Class Victorian Life* (1983). Her essay on Emily Faithfull appears in the Oxford microform publication of the *Victoria Magazine*, 1980.

BRUCE A. WHITE teaches at Gallaudet College and has contributed essays to *Modern Age* and the *Victorian Periodicals Review*.

KEITH WILSON, Associate Professor of English at the University of Ottawa, has published on Victorian and modern British literature in *Victorian Poetry, Etudes Anglaises, English Literature in Transition, Ariel, English Studies in Canada* and *Colby Library Quarterly*.

About the Editor

ALVIN SULLIVAN is Professor of English at Southern Illinois University, Edwardsville, and Editor of *Papers on Language and Literature*. A specialist in modern British literature and literary criticism, he has written *D. H. Lawrence and The Dial*; *The Dial—Two Author Indexes*; and articles for *Journal of Modern Literature*, *Explicator*, *D. H. Lawrence Review*, *Modern Fiction Studies*, and *Studies in English Literature*.